T0025105

Langenscheidt Universal Dictionary

Korean

Korean – English
English – Korean

Langenscheidt

Compiled by LEXUS with Dr Michael Finch, Kim Jin
Heui 김 진희, Jiyoung Nam 남 지영, Okjoo Lee 이 옥주,
Dr Judith Cherry, MBE

Contents

1. Auflage 2022 (1,02 - 2022)
© PONS GmbH, Stöckachstraße 11, 70190 Stuttgart 2022
All Rights Reserved.

www.langenscheidt.com

Print: Druckerei C. H. Beck, Nördlingen
Printed in Germany

ISBN 978-3-12-514461-3

Preface

This Korean Dictionary focuses on modern usage in English and Korean.

The two sides of the book, the Korean-English dictionary and the English-Korean dictionary, are different in structure and purpose. The Korean-English is a decoding dictionary, designed to enable the native speaker of English to understand Korean. The English-Korean is designed for productive usage, for self-expression in Korean.

A system of signposting helps the user find the correct translation.

Grammar labels (*n, adj, v/t*) are given when it is necessary to identify *which* use or uses of an English word are being translated.

Indicators in *italics* (typical objects of verbs, synonyms of nouns etc) and subject area labels are given to clarify *which* sense or area of usage of a headword is being translated.

In the Korean-English dictionary the Korean headwords are alphabetically ordered according to their romanized pronunciation.

White lozenges (◊) are used in the Korean-English dictionary to separate out different English grammatical categories, when all of these correspond to one single Korean word.

The pronunciation of Korean

The romanization of Korean in this dictionary is written in a form of the McCune-Reischauer standard, specially modified so as to more accurately represent spoken Korean. Where this romanization and the official Korean government system differ, the ROK official version is given in parentheses.

Vowels

아	a	c*a*t; or as in f*a*ther when at the end of a word or before a vowel or diphthong
어	ŏ (eo)	British pronunciation of n*o*t
오	o	*o*we
우	u	d*o*
으	ŭ (eu)	h*ea*ven
이	i	t*i*n; or as in s*ee* when at the end of a word or before a vowel or diphthong
애	ae	b*ea*t (but no r sound)
에	e	*e*delweiss
야	ya	*ya*m; or as in *ya*rd when at the end of a word or before a vowel or h
여	yŏ (yeo)	*Yo*rk (but no r sound)
요	yo	*yo*del
유	yu	*you*
얘	yae	*yea*h
예	ye	*Ya*le
와	wa	*wa*h-wah pedal
왜	wae	*whe*re
외	oe	*wa*y (but sometimes shorter as in *whe*n)
워	wŏ (wo)	*wa*sh
웨	we	*wa*y
위	wi	w*i*nd; or as in *wea*n when at the end of a word or before a vowel or diphthong
의	ŭi (ui)	uh-ee but colloquially as in Y*a*le

Consonants

	initial		medial	final
ㄱ	k (g)	between *k* and *g*	g	k
ㄴ	n	standard *n* sound	n	n
ㄷ	t (d)	between *t* and *d*	d	t
ㄹ	l	between *r* and *l*	r	l
ㅁ	m	standard *m* sound	m	m
ㅂ	p (b)	between *p* and *b*	b	p
ㅅ	s/sh (s)	*s*, *sh* before some vowels	s/sh (s)	t
ㅇ	silent	unpronounced	ng	ng
ㅈ	ch (j)	between *ch* and *j*	j	t
ㅊ	ch' (ch)	*ch* with aspiration*	ch' (ch)	t
ㅋ	k' (k)	*k* with aspiration	k' (k)	k
ㅌ	t' (t)	*t* with aspiration	t' (t)	t
ㅍ	p' (p)	*p* with aspiration	p' (p)	p
ㅎ	h	standard *h*	h	

* These aspirated consonants are uttered with a puff of air.

Double Consonants

These are pronounced with more force than their single equivalents:

ㄲ	kk	book *k*eeper	ㅆ	ss	those *s*ongs
ㄸ	tt	hi*t t*en	ㅉ	tch (jj)	tha*t j*udge
ㅃ	pp	to*p p*eople			

Notes

Double vowels are each given their full value.
g is always as in *g*ive not as in *g*in.
s is always as in loo*s*e not as in lo*s*e.
There is no stress in Korean, so give equal weight to all syllables.
The romanization system used in this dictionary reflects the fact that certain combinations of Korean consonants or vowels create sounds that are not indicated by the Korean script. So, for example, 독립 (**tok-lip**) is romanized as it is actually pronounced, **tongnip** and 맞다 (**mat-ta**) as **mat-tta**.

Abbreviations

adj	adjective	MIL	military
adv	adverb	MUS	music
ANAT	anatomy	*n*	noun
AUTO	motoring	NAUT	nautical
BIOL	biology	*pej*	pejorative
BOT	botany	PHOT	photography
Br	British English	POL	politics
COMM	commerce, business	*prep*	preposition
COMPUT	computers, IT term	*pron*	pronoun
conj	conjunction	®	registered trademark
ELEC	electricity,	RADIO	radio
	electronics	RAIL	railroad
fig	figurative	REL	religion
FIN	financial	sb	somebody
form	formal usage	SCHOOL	education
GRAM	grammar	SPORTS	sports
H	humble, showing	sth	something
	humility to the	TEL	telecommunications
	listener	THEAT	theater
infml	familiar, colloquial	TV	television
JUR	law	*v/i*	intransitive verb
MATH	mathematics	*v/t*	transitive verb
MED	medicine	→	see

Korean – English

A

abŏji 아버지 father
ach'im 아침 morning
ach'ŏm 아첨 flattery
ach'ŏmhada 아첨하다 flatter
adamhan 아담한 compact
adongbok 아동복 children's clothes
adŭl 아들 son
aeguk-kka 애국가 national anthem
aegukctcha 애국자 patriot
aehoga 애호가 fan; connoisseur
aehohada 애호하다 be fond of
aein 애인 boyfriend; girlfriend
aejŏng 애정 affection
aekch'e 액체 liquid
aemaemohohan 애매모호한 ambiguous
aemu 애무 caress
aengmusae 앵무새 parrot
aessŭda 애쓰다 make an effort
aet'age parada 애타게 바라다 long for
aewandongmul 애완동물 pet (animal)
agasshi 아가씨 ma'am; miss

agi 아기 baby
agŏ 악어 alligator; crocodile
agŭi 악의 ill will; malice
ahop 아홉 nine
ahŭn 아흔 ninety
ai 아이 child
aishyop'inghada 아이쇼핑하다 go window-shopping
...ajida …아지다 become ..., get ...
ajik 아직 yet
ajiktto 아직도 still
ajirang-i 아지랑이 haze
ajŏsshi 아저씨 uncle (not actually related)
aju 아주 very; completely
ajumma 아줌마 aunt (not actually related)
ajumŏni 아주머니 polite form of ajumma
ak 악 evil; vice
akch'wi 악취 stench
akdan 악단 band
akkaptta 아깝다 be regrettable
akkida 아끼다 stint on; hold dear
ak-kki 악기 (musical) instrument

akkyŏ ssŭda

akkyŏ ssŭda 아껴 쓰다 use sparingly

akppo 악보 sheet music

akssu 악수 handshake

akssuhada 악수하다 shake hands

akttang 악당 villain

ak'ada 악하다 be evil

ak'wadoeda 악화되다 deteriorate

al 알 egg

alda 알다 know; understand

alk'o-ol 알코올 alcohol

allak'an 안락한 comfortable

allida 알리다 inform

allim 알림 announcement

allyak 알약 tablet

allyŏjida 알려지다 become known

allyŏjin 알려진 noted

allyŏjuda 알려주다 inform

almajŭn 알맞은 fitting

almat-tta 알맞다 be fitting

almomŭi 알몸의 nude

am 암 cancer

ama(do) 아마 (도) perhaps; probably

amgihada 암기하다 memorize

amho 암호 password

amhŭk 암흑 darkness

amk'ae 암캐 bitch *(dog)*

amk'ŏt 암컷 female

amnyŏgŭl kahada 압력을 가하다 pressure, force

amnyŏk 압력 pressure

amnyuhada 압류하다 impound

amsal 암살 assassination

amsarhada 암살하다 assassinate

amshi 암시 pointer; hint

amshihada 암시하다 imply; point to; indicate

amso 암소 cow

amt'ak 암탉 hen

amu 아무 any; none; anyone; so-and-so

amudo 아무도 nobody

amu ...do 아무 …도 any ...at all

amugae 아무개 so-and-so; any person

amu kŏt 아무 것 nothing

amuri 아무리 no matter how...

amurŏk'e 아무렇게 in whatever way

amurŏk'ena hanŭn 아무렇게나 하는 offhand

amurŏn 아무런 any

amu ttae 아무 때 any time

amut'ŭn 아무튼 anyway

an 안 inside

an... 안… not

anae 안내 wife

anaewŏn 안내원 tour operator

anbu 안부 (kind) regards

andwaetkkunyo! 안됐군요! what a pity!

...ane(sŏ) …안에 (서) in

an-gae 안개 fog
angma 악마 devil
angmong 악몽 nightmare
an-gwa ŭisa 안과 의사
  ophthalmologist
an-gyŏng 안경 glasses
anida 아니다 be not
anin 아닌 no
anio 아니오 no
anjŏn 안전 safety
anjŏngdoeda 안정되다
  stabilize
anjŏnhada 안전하다 be
  safe; be secure
anjŏnhage 안전하게 safely
anjŏnhan 안전한 safe
anmahada 안마하다
  massage
annae 안내 guidance
annaehada 안내하다 guide
annaeja 안내자 guide;
  usher
annyŏng 안녕 hi; so long
annyŏnghaseyo
  안녕하세요 good morning;
  good afternoon; good evening
annyŏnghi
  chumushipssshiyo 안녕히
  주무십시요 good night
annyŏnghi chumusyŏssŏyo
  안녕히 주무셨어요 good
  morning (on waking up)
annyŏnghi kaseyo 안녕히
  가세요 goodbye (to person
  leaving)
annyŏnghi kyeseyo안녕히
  계세요 goodbye (to person
  staying)
anppang 안방 master
  bedroom
ansaek 안색 complexion
anshikch'ŏ 안식처 haven
anshim 안심 peace of mind
anshimhada 안심하다
  feel safe
anshimhanŭn 안심하는
  secure
anshimshik'ida 안심시키다
  reassure
antchoguro 안쪽으로
  inward
antchok 안쪽 inside
antta 안다 hug
antta 앉다 sit down; settle
ant'a 않다 be not; do not
anŭi 안의 internal
anŭk'an 아늑한 cozy
anŭro 안으로 inside ◊ into
ap 앞 front
appa 아빠 dad
appak'ada 압박하다 oppress
appubun 앞부분 opening,
  beginning
ap sŏn 앞 선 advanced
apssŏ kada 앞서 가다 lead
aptchang sŏda 앞장 서다
  lead on
...aptchoge(sŏ) ...
  앞쪽에 (서) in front of
aptchogŭi 앞쪽의 front
apttohada 압도하다
  dominate; overwhelm

apttohanŭn

apttohanŭn 압도하는 devastating

apttwiro 앞뒤로 to and fro

ap'ahada 아파하다 be in pain

ap'at'ŭ 아파트 apartment

ap'at'ŭ tanji 아파트 단지 apartment block

ap'e(sŏ) 앞에 (서) in front

ap'ŭda 아프다 hurt

ap'ŭm 아픔 pain

ap'ŭn 아픈 sick; painful

ap'ŭro 앞으로 forward; onward

araboda 알아보다 check; check out; identify

arabol su innŭn 알아볼 수 있는 recognizable

arach'aeda 알아채다 notice; sense; spot

arach'arida 알아차리다 perceive; interpret

arae 아래 the lower part ◊ under

araech'ŭng-ŭi 아래층의 downstairs

...araee(sŏ) …아래에 (서) below; lower than

araetchogŭro 아래쪽으로 down

araet saram 아랫 사람 subordinate

aranaeda 알아내다 identify

ara tŭt-tta 알아 듣다 hear

arŭmdaptta 아름답다 be beautiful

arŭmdaun 아름다운 beautiful

aryak 알약 pill

ausŏng 아우성 outcry

...aya handa …아야 한다 have to

...ayaman hada …아야만 하다 must

CH

cha 자 ruler

chabaek 자백 confession

chabaek'ada 자백하다 confess

chabaltchŏgin 자발적인 voluntary

chabamŏktta 잡아먹다 prey on; absorb

chaba ppoptta 잡아 뽑다 pull up *plant*

chaba tanggida 잡아 당기다 pull; tug

chaba t'ada 잡아 타다 catch *bus etc*

chabi 자비 mercy

chabiroun 자비로운 merciful

chabon 자본 capital

chabon-ga 자본가 capitalist

chabonjuŭi 자본주의

capitalism

chabushim 자부심 self-esteem

chach'wi 자취 trace

chach'wi-rŭl kamch'uda 자취를 감추다 disappear

chada 자다 sleep; drop (of wind)

chadong 자동 automatic

chadongch'a 자동차 automobile

chadongch'a suriso 자동차 수리소 garage (for repairs)

chadonghwahada 자동화하다 automate

chadong p'anmaegi 자동 판매기 vending machine

chadong-ŭngdapkki 자동응답기 answerphone

chadong-ŭro 자동으로 automatically

chadu 자두 plum

chae 재 ash

chaebaech'ihada 재배치하다 relocate

chaebaeyŏrhada 재배열하다 rearrange

chaebal 재발 relapse

chaebangsong 재방송 rerun

chaebarhada 재발하다 recur

chaebŏl 재벌 conglomerate

chaebongsa 재봉사 tailor

chaebongt'ŭl 재봉틀 sewing machine

chaech'aegi 재채기 sneeze

chaech'i 재치 tact; wit

chaech'i innŭn 재치 있는 tactful; witty

chaech'i ŏmnŭn 재치 없는 tactless

chaech'ok'ada 재촉하다 hurry up

chaedan 재단 organization

chaegae 재개 renewal

chaegaebarhada 재개발하다 redevelop

chaegaehada 재개하다 resume

chaegaejanghada 재개장하다 reopen

chaegŏmt'ohada 재검토하다 review

chaegŏrae 재거래 repeat business

chaehae 재해 disaster

chaehae chiyŏk 재해 지역 disaster area

Chaehŏnjŏl 재헌절 Constitution Day

chaehoe 재회 reunion

chaehoehada 재회하다 reunite

chaehonhada 재혼하다 remarry

chaemi kyop'o 재미 교포 Korean resident in the USA

chaejalgŏrida 재잘거리다 yap

chaejŏng 재정 finance ◊ financial

chaejŏngnihada
재정리하다 readjust;
reschedule; rearrange
chaejurŭl purida 재주를
부리다 juggle; deal with
chaemi 재미 fun
chaemiinnŭn 재미있는
amusing; interesting
chaemiro 재미로 for fun
chaemok 재목 lumber
Chaemujanggwan
재무장관 Treasury Secretary
chaemul 재물 worldly goods
chaengban 쟁반 tray
chaenŭng 재능 talent
chaenŭng-innŭn 재능있는
talented
chaeppalli 재빨리 quickly
chaepparŭn 재빠른 quick;
nimble
chaep'an 재판 judgment
JUR; reprint
chaep'anhada 재판하다 try
JUR; reprint
chaep'ojanghada
재포장하다 resurface
chaep'yŏnsŏng 재편성
reorganization
chaep'yŏnsŏnghada
재편성하다 reorganize
chaeryo 재료 material
chaesaeng 재생 playback;
reproduction
chaesaeng iyong 재생
이용 recycling
chaesaeng iyonghada 재생

이용하다 recycle
chaesan 재산 assets
chaesayonghada
재사용하다 reuse
chaesayong-i kanŭnghan
재사용이 가능한 reusable
chaeshihap'ada
재시합하다 replay
chaesuŏpkkun! 재수없군!
hard luck!
chaettŏri 재떨이 ashtray
chaet'ujahada 재투자하다
reinvest
chagae changshik 자개
장식 mother-of-pearl inlay
chagajida 작아지다 grow
smaller
chagal 자갈 gravel; pebble;
gravestone
chagi 자기 china (pottery);
darling; magnetism ◊ magnetic
chagi chashin 자기 자신
oneself
chagi maŭmdaero hada have
자기 마음대로 하다 have
one's (own) way
chagi pang-ŏ 자기 방어
self-defense
chagi ponwiŭi 자기 본위의
self-centered
chagi suyang 자기 수양
self-discipline
chagiya! 자기야! darling!
chagŏptchang 작업장
workshop
chagŭk 자극 incentive

chagŭk'ada 자극하다
  stimulate; spur on; arouse
chagŭk'anŭn 자극하는
  provocative; pungent
chagŭktchŏgin 자극적인
  electric *atmosphere*;
  stimulating; sharp *taste*
chagŭm 자금 fund
chagŭn 작은 small
chaguk 자국 mark; one's
  own country
chagung 자궁 uterus
chagungnada 자궁나다
  become stained
chagyŏgi innŭn 자격이
  있는 eligible
chagyŏgŭl chuda 자격을
  주다 qualify
chagyŏgŭl ŏt-tta 자격을
  얻다 qualify
chagyŏk 자격 qualification
chagyŏktchŭng 자격증
  certificate
chagyŏktchŭng-i innŭn
  자격증이 있는 qualified
chagyong 작용 action;
  function
chainhada 자인하다 admit
chajangga 자장가 lullaby
chajehada 자제하다 control
  oneself
chajehanŭn 자제하는
  lowkey
chajinhaesŏ hada 자진해서
  하다 volunteer
chajŏng 자정 midnight

chajŏn-gŏ 자전거 bicycle
chajonshim 자존심 self-
  respect
chaju 자주 often
chaju onŭn 자주 오는
  frequent
chak-kka 작가 writer
chak-kkok-kka 작곡가
  composer
chak-kkok'ada 작곡하다
  compose
chakppyŏl insa 작별 인사
  parting greeting
chakp'um 작품 work
  (literary etc)
chakssŏnghada 작성하다
  draw up
chaktchŏnghada 작정하다
  determine
chaktchŏng-ida 작정이다
  intend
chaktta 작다 be small
chakttonghada 작동하다
  function; engage
chal 잘 well
chal allyŏjin 잘 알려진
  well-known
chal anŭn 잘 아는 familiar
chal cha 잘 자 *infml* good
  night
chal hada 잘 하다 do well
chal igŭn 잘 익은 well-
  done *food*
chal ijŏbŏrinŭn 잘
  잊어버리는 forgetful
chal it-tta 잘 있다 be well

chaljalmot

chaljalmot 잘잘못 right and wrong

challaborida 잘라버리다 slash

challanaeda 잘라내다 cut off

challan ch'ŏk'anŭn 잘난 척하는 pretentious

challanŭn ppang 잘라놓은 빵 sliced bread

chal mandŭrŏjin 잘 만들어진 well-made

chalmot 잘못 error; wrong ◊ wrongly; badly

chalmot kŏllin chŏnhwa 잘못 걸린 전화 wrong number

chalmot match'uda 잘못 맞추다 mismatch

chalmot-ttoeda 잘못되다 go wrong

chalmot-ttoen 잘못된 wrong; unfortunate

chal nan ch'ehanŭn 잘 난 체하는 smug

chal padadŭrida 잘 받아들이다 be receptive to

chal saenggin 잘 생긴 good-looking

chal sagwida 잘 사귀다 cultivate *person*

chal salp'yŏboda 잘 살펴보다 examine

chal tadŭmŏjin 잘 다듬어진 accomplished

chal toeda 잘 되다 turn

out well

chal towajunŭn 잘 도와주는 supportive

cham 잠 sleep

chaman 자만 conceit

chamanhanŭn 자만하는 conceited

chamanshim 자만심 vanity

chamdŭlda 잠들다 fall asleep

chamgŭda 잠그다 fasten; lock; turn off *faucet*

chami kkaeda 잠이 깨다 wake (up)

chamjaehada 잠재하다 lurk

chamjaejŏgin 잠재적인 potential

chamjaejŏguro 잠재적으로 potentially

chamjarie tŭlda 잠자리에 들다 go to bed

chamkkan 잠깐 a while

chamkkanmanyo 잠깐만요 just a moment

cham mot irunŭn 잠 못 이루는 sleepless

chamot 잠옷 pajamas; nightdress

chamshidong-an 잠시동안 briefly

chamshi hu 잠시 후 a little later

chamshi mŏmurŭda 잠시 머무르다 stop over

chamshi tong-an 잠시

동안 for a moment
chamsuhada 잠수하다
submerge; go diving
chamsuham 잠수함
submarine
chamulssoe 자물쇠 bolt;
lock
chamyŏngjong shigye
자명종 시계 alarm clock
chan 잔 cup; glass
chanch'itssang 잔칫상
banquet
chandi 잔디 lawn; turf
chandibat 잔디밭 lawn
chandon 잔돈 change
chang 장 chief; sheet *(of
paper)*; chapter; scene *(in
theater)*; exposure *(on film)*;
copy; ice rink ◊ *countword for
paper and thin flat objects*
chang-ae 장애 problem;
disorder MED; hindrance;
burden
chang-aemul 장애물
stumbling-block; hurdle SPORTS
chang-ak'ada 장악하다
take over
changbi 장비 equipment
changboda 장보다 do one's
shopping
changbu 장부 accounts
book; (real) man
changch'i 장치 apparatus;
system
changgap 장갑 glove
changgi 장기 Korean chess

changgijŏgin 장기적인
long-range
changgiŭi 장기의 long-term
changgŏriŭi 장거리의 long-
distance
changgo 장고 hourglass
drum
changgun 장군 general MIL;
checkmate
changgwan 장관 minister;
spectacle
changgyo 장교 officer MIL
changhak-kkŭm 장학금
scholarship
changhwa 장화 boot
chang-in ŏrŭn 장인 어른
father-in-law
changjo 장조 major MUS
changma 장마 the rains
changmach'ŏl 장마철 rainy
season
changmi 장미 rose
changmun 작문 composition
changmyŏn 장면 scene
changnaeŭi hŭimang
장래의 희망 expectations
changnan 장난 prank
changnanch'ida 장난치다
fool around
changnankkam 장난감 toy
changnankkurŏgi
장난꾸러기 little rascal
Changno Kyohoe 장로
교회 Presbyterian Church
changnong 장롱 chest
changnyeshik 장례식 funeral

changnyŏn ŏnjen-ga 작년 언젠가 sometime last year

chang-ŏ 장어 eel

chan-go 잔고 balance

changp'yŏn yŏnghwa 장편 영화 feature movie

changsahada 장사하다 do business

changshik 장식 decoration

changshik-kka 장식가 painter

changso 장소 place

changsshikp'um 장식품 ornament

changsshik'ada 장식하다 decorate

changtchŏm 장점 merit

chang-ŭisa 장의사 mortician

chaninhada 잔인하다 be cruel

chaninhage 잔인하게 brutally

chansorihada 잔소리하다 nag

chanttŭk mŏktta 잔뜩 먹다 eat one's fill

chaoesŏn 자외선 ultraviolet rays

chapch'o 잡초 weed

chap-ppi 잡비 incidental expenses

chaptchi 잡지 magazine

chaptta 잡다 catch; hold

chapttam 잡담 chat

chap'an-gi 자판기 vending

machine

chap'yetchŭng-ŭi 자폐증의 autistic

charada 자라다 grow

charanada 자라나다 grow up

charang 자랑 pride

charanghada 자랑하다 boast

charangsŭrŏptta 자랑스럽다 be proud

charangsŭrŏun 자랑스러운 proud

charhada 잘하다 be good at

chari 자리 seat; floor mat

charijaptta 자리잡다 settle down

charŏ kada 자러 가다 go to bed

charŭda 자르다 carve; cut

charyo 자료 materials; data

chasal 자살 suicide

chasarhada 자살하다 commit suicide

chase 자세 posture

chasehada 자세하다 be detailed

chasehage 자세하게 in detail

chashin 자신 self-confidence

chashin innŭn 자신 있는 self-confident

chasŏk 자석 magnet

chasŏn 자선 charity

chasŏn tanch'e 자선 단체 charity (organization)

chasŏnŭi 자선의 charitable

chason 자손 descendant

chattchip 찻집 tearoom

chattchujŏnja 찻주전자
teapot

chat'aek kŭnmu 자택 근무
work from home

chaŭishigi kanghan
자의식이 강한 self-
conscious

chawŏn 자원 resource

chawŏnja 자원자
volunteer

chayŏn 자연 nature

chayŏn kwahaktcha 자연
과학자 natural scientist

chayŏn shikp'um 자연
식품 whole food

chayŏnsŭrŏpke
자연스럽게 naturally

chayŏntchŏgin 자연적인
natural *death*

chayu 자유 freedom

chayujuŭiŭi 자유주의의
liberal

chayuro 자유로 at liberty

chayurowajin 자유로와진
liberated

chayuŭi 자유의 free

che 제 my

chean 제안 approach;
suggestion

cheanhada 제안하다
suggest; offer

chebal 제발 please

chebi 제비 swallow

chebikkot 제비꽃 violet

chebi ppopkki 제비 뽑기
raffle

chebirŭl ppoptta 제비를
뽑다 draw

chebok 제복 uniform

chech'uran 제출안
submission

chech'urhada 제출하다
submit

chedaero 제대로 properly

chedan 제단 altar

chegiral 제기랄 damn!

chegŏ 제거 elimination

chegŏhada 제거하다
eliminate

chegong 제공 offer

chegonghada 제공하다
provide

chegugŭi 제국의 imperial

cheguk 제국 empire

chegwajŏm 제과점
confectioner's

chehan 제한 restriction;
qualification

chehandoen 제한된
confined *space*; limited

chehan-guyŏk 제한구역
restricted area

chehanhada 제한하다
restrict; qualify

chehan shigan 제한 시간
time limit

cheil 제일 best

cheil choahanŭn 제일
좋아하는 favorite

cheja 제자 disciple

chejak 제작 production

chejaktcha 제작자 producer

chejak'ada 제작하다 produce

chejarie tollyŏnot'a 제자리에 돌려놓다 put back

chejŏngshinŭl ilt'a 제정신을 잃다 go insane; be beside oneself

chejohada 제조하다 manufacture

chemok 제목 title

chemul 제물 sacrifice

chenjang! 젠장! damn it!

cheŏhada 제어하다 bring under control

cheoehada 제외하다 rule out

cheoeshik'ida 제외시키다 leave out

chep'um 제품 product; goods

chesa 제사 ancestral rite

cheshigane 제시간에 on time

cheshihada 제시 하다 put in *request*

chet'ŭgi 제트기 jet

cheŭi 제의 proposition

chewang chŏlgae 제왕 절개 Cesarean section

cheyagŭi 제약의 pharmaceutical

cheyak 제약 pharmaceuticals

chiap 지압 acupressure

massage

chibae 지배 control

chibaehada 지배하다 control

chibaein 지배인 manager

chibaejŏgin 지배적인 domineering

chibang 지방 region; province; fat ◊ regional

chibang chach'i 지방 자치 local government

chibang-i manŭn 지방이 많은 fatty

chibang saram 지방 사람 local (inhabitant)

chibang t'ŭkssanmul 지방 특산물 local produce

chiban il 집안 일 housework

chibe 집에 at home

chibŏmnŭn 집없는 homeless

chibŏ nŏt'a 집어 넣다 get in; store; fit in

chibŏ tŭlda 집어 들다 pick up

chibul 지불 payment

chibung 지붕 roof

chiburhada 지불하다 pay up

chich'ehada 지체하다 delay

chich'ida 지치다 tire

chich'ige hada 지치게 하다 tire out

chich'ige hanŭn 지치게 하는 tiring

chich'in 지친 tired out

chich'ul 지출 expenditure

chida 지다 lose; go down *(of sun)*; be out *(of sun, flower)*

chidae 지대 zone

chido 지도 map; leadership

chidoch'aek 지도책 atlas

chidoja 지도자 leader

chidok'ada 지독하다 be vicious

chidok'age 지독하게 terribly

chidoryŏk 지도력 leadership skills

chigak 지각 awareness

chigak'ada 지각하다 be delayed

chigap 지갑 pocketbook

chigŏbtchŏgin 직업적인 professional

chigŏp 직업 job

chigŏp annaeso 직업 안내소 employment agency

chigŏpssang-ŭi 직업상의 vocational

chigo it-tta 지고 있다 be behind

chigŭjaegühyŏng 지그재그형 zigzag

chigŭlgŏrida 지글거리다 sizzle

chigŭm 지금 now

chigŭmbut'ŏ 지금부터 from now on

chigŭmkkaji 지금까지 ever; yet

chigŭmtchŭm 지금쯤 by now

chigŭmŭn 지금은 at the moment

chigŭp'ada 지급하다 issue

chigu 지구 earth; globe

chigubon 지구본 globe

chigwŏn 직원 attendant; staff

chigyŏng 지경 boundary; verge

chigyŏwŏhada 지겨워하다 loathe

chiha 지하 underground

chihach'ŏl 지하철 subway

chihach'ŭng 지하층 basement

chihado 지하도 underpass

chihashil 지하실 basement

chihwihada 지휘하다 conduct MUS

chihwija 지휘자 conductor

chihye 지혜 wisdom

chijida 지지다 fry

chijihada 지지하다 support; confirm

chijin 지진 earthquake

chijŏbunhada 지저분하다 be messy

chijŏgwida 저저귀다 twitter

chijŏk'ada 지적하다 point out

chijŏm 지점 branch

chijŏnghada 지정하다 designate

chik-kkaguro 직각으로 at right-angles to

chikssagak'yŏng 직사각형 rectangle

chiktchang-e it-tta 직장에 있다 be at work

chiktchŏp 직접 directly

chiktchŏptchogin 직접적인 direct

chiktchŏptchoguro 직접적으로 firsthand

chik'aeng-ŭi 직행의 nonstop

chik'aeng-ŭro 직행으로 nonstop

chik'ang 직황 direct flight

chik'ida 지키다 defend; keep *promise*

chik'yŏboda 지켜보다 watch; look after

chilbyŏng 질병 disease

chilgin 질긴 stout; tough

chiljil kkŭlda 질질 끌다 drag on

chillida 질리다 be fed up with

chillin 질린 fed up

chillo 진로 path

chillyobi 진료비 fee

chillyo kwajŏng 진료 과정 course of treatment

chillyoso 진료소 clinic

chilmun 질문 question

chilmunhada 질문하다 question

chilmunsŏ 질문서 questionnaire

chiltchu 질주 sprint

chiltchuhada 질주하다 race; gallop

chilt'u 질투 jealousy

chilt'uhada 질투하다 be jealous

chilt'uhanŭn 질투하는 jealous

chin 진 gin; resin

chinach'ida 지나치다 overdo

chinach'ige 지나치게 excessively

chinach'ige sŏlch'inŭn 지나치게 설치는 hyperactive

chinach'in 지나친 excessive

chinaeda 지내다 celebrate; get along

chinagada 지나가다 pass; get on

chinan myŏch'il 지난 며칠 the past few days

chinan pŏne 지난 번에 last time

chinasŏ 지나서 beyond; past

chinbo 진보 advance

chinbohada 진보하다 progress

chinbojŏgin 진보적인 progressive

chinch'arhada 진찰하다 examine

chinch'ul 진출 penetration

chinch'urhada 진출하다 penetrate

chinch'wijŏgin 진취적인 enterprising

chindansŏ 진단서 medical certificate

chindoga nagada 진도가

나가다 progress
chindong 진동 vibration
chindonghada 진동하다 vibrate
ching 징 gong
chingmul 직물 textile
chingmyŏnhada 직면하다 face
chin-gong ch'ŏngsogi 진공 청소기 vacuum cleaner
chinhaeng 진행 progress
chinhaengdoeda 진행되다 proceed
chinhaenghada 진행하다 advance; front tv
chinhaenghanŭn 진행하는 progressive
chinhan 진한 dark; deep *color*; strong *tea etc*
chinhŭk 진흙 clay; mud
chinhwa 진화 evolution
chinhwahada 진화하다 evolve
chinigo tanida 지니고 다니다 carry around
chinimno 진입로 access road
chinjihage 진지하게 earnestly
chinjihan 진지한 earnest
chinjŏng 진정 lull
chinjŏngdoeda 진정되다 quieten down
chinjŏngshik'ida 진정시키다 control; pacify; keep down *costs*
chinjŏngŭro 진정으로

seriously
chinju 진주 pearl
chinshil 진실 truth
chinshillo 진실로 truly
chinshimŭi 진심의 whole-hearted
chinshimŭro 진심으로 sincerely
chinshirhada 진실하다 be truthful
chinsul 진술 statement
chintcha 진짜 the real thing ◇ genuine
chint'ang surŭl mashida 진탕 술을 마시다 go on a bender
chint'ongje 진통제 painkiller
chint'onik 진토닉 gin and tonic
chinŭng 지능 intelligence
chinyŏl 진열 display
chinyŏltchang 진열장 display cabinet
chinyŏlttae 진열대 stall
chinyŏrhada 진열하다 display
chiŏnaen iyagi 지어낸 이야기 story
chiok 지옥 hell
chip 집 home; house; collection *(writings)*; straw
chipch'ak'ada 집착하다 cling to
chipkkwŏnhanŭn 집권하는 in power

chipp'iltcha 집필자 author

chipsaram 집사람 wife

chiptchung 집중 concentration

chiptchunghada 집중하다 concentrate

chiptchungjŏgin 집중적인 intensive

chiptchungshik'ida 집중시키다 concentrate

chiptchuso 집주소 home address

chipttan 집단 group

chipttanjŏgin 집단적인 collective

chipttŭri 집들이 housewarming

chip'ŏrŭl chamgŭda 지퍼를 잠그다 zip up

chip'oe 집회 congregation REL

chip'yŏngsŏn 지평선 horizon

chirado 지라도 even though

chiri 지리 geography

chiroe 지뢰 mine

chiroepat 지뢰밭 minefield

chirŭmkkil 지름길 short cut

chiruhada 지루하다 be tedious

chiruhaejida 지루해지다 be bored

chiruhan 지루한 boring

chisang 지상 the ground ◇ ground; earthly

chishigi innŭn 지식이 있는 knowledgeable

chishigin 지식인 intellectual

chishihada 지시하다 instruct

chishik 지식 knowledge

chisŏng 지성 intellect

chisŏng-in 지성인 intellectual

chisok 지속 persistence

chisok'ada 지속하다 persist; sustain

chitchŏgin 지적인 intellectual

chitchŏguro 지적으로 mentally

chit-tta 짖다 bark

chit'aenghada 지탱하다 support

chit'ŭn 질은 thick

chiuda 지우다 erase

chiugae 지우개 eraser

chiwi 지위 status

chiwŏn 지원 application; backup

chiwŏnhada 지원하다 apply for

chiwŏnsŏ 지원서 application form

chiyŏk 지역 area; region; district; quarter

chŏ 저 H I; me; mine; that

chŏ araee 저 아래에 down there

chŏbŏ nŏt'a 접어 넣다 tuck in

chŏch'uk ŭnhaeng 저축 은행 savings bank

chŏch'uk'ada 저축하다
save

chŏdang 저당 mortgage

chŏgiap 저기압 low pressure

chŏgi araetchoge 저기
아래쪽에 down there

chŏgŏdo 적어도 at least

chŏgŏt 저것 that one

chŏgori 저고리 short jacket

chŏgŭmhada 저금하다
save

chŏgŭn 적은 small; slight; a
small number of

chŏgŭnghada 적응하다
adapt

chŏgŭngnyŏgi innŭn
적응력이 있는 adaptable

chŏgyongdoeda 적용되다
apply (to)

chŏgyonghada 적용하다
apply

chŏhang 저항 resistance

chŏhanghada 저항하다
resist

chŏjak-kkwŏn 저작권
copyright

chŏjang 저장 store

chŏjanghada 저장하다
store; preserve; save COMPUT

chŏjangshikp'um 저장식품
preserves

chŏjibang-ŭi 저지방의
low-fat

chŏjŏllo 저절로 by itself

chŏjŭn 젖은 soggy

chŏju 저주 curse

chŏk 적 enemy

chŏk-kkŭktchŏgin
적극적인 positive

chŏksshida 적시다 soak

Chŏksshiptcha 적십자
Red Cross

chŏktcha 적자 deficit

chŏktchaga nada 적자가
나다 in the red

chŏktchŏrhan 적절한
appropriate

chŏktta 적다 take notes

chŏkttanghada 적당하다 be
suitable; be adequate

chŏkttanghage 적당하게
moderately

chŏkttanghan 적당한
adequate; moderate; decent;
suitable

chŏkttanghi hada 적당히
하다 moderate

chŏk'alloriŭi 저칼로리의
low-calorie

chŏk'ap'ada 적합하다 be
suited for

chŏk'ap'age 적합하게
properly

chŏk'ap'an 적합한 morally
fit

chŏl 절 clause; passage; verse;
obeisance; Buddhist temple

chŏlbyŏk 절벽 cliff

chŏlch'a 절차 procedure

chŏlgyohada 절교하다 drop

chŏllŭmbariŭi 절름발이의
lame

chŏllyak

chŏllyak 전략 strategy
chŏllyaktchŏgin 전략적인 strategic
chŏlmang 절망 despair
chŏlmanghada 절망하다 despair
chŏlmangjŏgin 절망적인 desperate
chŏlmtta 젊다 be young
chŏlmŭn 젊은 young
chŏlmŭni 젊은이 youth
chŏlsshirhan 절실한 pressing
chŏltchŏng 절정 climax; height
chŏlttae 절대 absolutely
chŏlttaejŏgin 절대적인 absolute
chŏm 점 dot; spot; mole
chŏmch'ajŏgin 점차적인 gradual
chŏmch'ajŏguro 점차적으로 gradually
chŏmgŏm 점검 inspection
chŏmgŏmhada 점검하다 check; vet
chŏmjaeng-i 점쟁이 fortune-teller
chŏmjanŭn 점잖은 gentle
chŏmjŏm 점점 by degrees
chŏmnŭn 접는 folding
chŏmnyŏng 점령 capture; occupation
chŏmnyŏnghada 점령하다 capture; occupy
chŏmshim 점심 lunch

chŏmsŏn 점선 dotted line
chŏmsŏngga 점성가 astrologer
chŏmsŏngsul 점성술 astrology; horoscope
chŏmsu 점수 point
chŏmwŏn 점원 assistant; clerk
chŏmyŏnghan 저명한 distinguished
chŏn 전 pancake (Korean)
chŏn(ŭi) 전 (의) preceding; front; former ◊ before; ago
chŏnap 전압 voltage
chŏnbanjŏgin 전반적인 overall
chŏnbŏnŭi 전번의 last
chŏnbok 전복 overthrow
chŏnbu 전부 in all; altogether
chŏnbuŭi 전부의 complete
chŏnch'e 전체 whole
chŏnch'ejŏgin 전체적인 general
chŏnch'ejŏguro 전체적으로 throughout
chŏnch'eŭi 전체의 entire
chŏndangp'o 전당포 pawnshop
chŏndarhada 전달하다 communicate; deliver
chŏndŭnggat 전등갓 lampshade
...chŏne ···전에 before
chŏn-gaehada 전개하다 develop
chŏng-aek 정액 semen

chŏngbandaeŭi 정반대의 diametrically opposed

chŏngbidoeda 정비되다 be in good order

chŏngbo 정보 information

chŏngboga manŭn 정보가 많은 informative

chŏngbo chŏngbok conquest

chŏngbo kisul 정보 기술 IT

chŏngboktcha 정복자 conqueror

chŏngbo kwahak 정보 과학 information science

chŏngbok'ada 정복하다 conquer

chŏngbu 정부 government; mistress

chŏngch'aek 정책 policy

chŏngch'ak'ada 정착하다 settle

chŏngch'i 정치 politics

chŏngch'iga 정치가 politician

chŏngch'ijŏgin 정치적인 political

chŏngdang 정당 party

chŏngdanghage 정당하게 justifiably

chŏngdanghan 정당한 legitimate

chŏngdanghwahada 정당화하다 justify

chŏngdo 정도 degree

chŏngdondoen 정돈된 tidy

chŏngdonhada 정돈하다 clear up

chŏnggage 정각에 on time

chŏnggi iptchangkkwŏn 정기 입장권 season ticket

chŏnggijŏgŭro 정기적으로 periodically

chŏnggi kudok'ada 정기 구독하다 subscribe to

chŏnggi sŭngch'akkwŏn 정기 승차권 season ticket

chŏnggŏjang 정거장 depot RAIL

chŏnghada 정하다 set

chŏnghwahada 정화하다 purify

chŏnghwak 정확 precision

chŏnghwak'ada 정확하다 be right

chŏnghwak'age 정확하게 precisely

chŏnghwak'an 정확한 accurate; definite

chŏnghwak'i 정확히 exactly; punctually

chŏn-gi 전기 electricity; biography

chŏn-gi kisa 전기 기사 electrician

chŏn-gi papssot 전기 밥솥 (electric) rice cooker

chŏn-gisŏn 전기선 power line

chŏn-giŭi 전기의 electric

chŏngja 정자 sperm

chŏngje 정제 tablet

chŏngjehada 정제하다 refine

chŏngjeso 정제소 refinery
chŏngjik 정직 honesty
chŏngjik'ada 정직하다 be on the level
chŏngjik'an 정직한 honest
chŏngjishik'ida 정지시키다 suspend
chŏngjŏn 정전 power cut
chŏngjunghage 정중하게 respectfully
chŏngjunghan 정중한 courteous
chŏngkkwŏn 정권 regime
chŏngmaek 정맥 vein
chŏngmal 정말 truth; fact ◊ really; very
chŏngmallo 정말로 actually; really
chŏngmil chosahada 정밀 조사하다 investigate in detail
chŏngmun 정문 front entrance
chŏngmyŏn 정면 façade
chŏngmyŏnch'ungdorŭi 정면충돌의 head-on
chŏngnyŏltchŏgin 정열적인 passionate
chŏngnyŏn 정년 retirement age
chŏngnyujang 정류장 (bus) depot; (bus) shelter; (bus) stop
chŏngnyuktchŏm 정육점 butcher's
chŏng-o 정오 midday
chŏn-gonghada 전공하다 major in
chŏngsa 정사 love affair
chŏngsang 정상 norm; summit ◊ normal
chŏngsanghwahada 정상화하다 normalize
chŏngsang-ŭro 정상으로 normally
chŏngshigŭi 정식의 proper
chŏngshik 정식 set meal
chŏngshin 정신 mind; spirit ◊ mental
chŏngshin chang-aega innŭn 정신 장애가 있는 mentally handicapped
chŏngshin ch'arige hada 정신 차리게 하다 bring around
chŏngshini mŏnghan 정신이 멍한 dazed
chŏngshini nagada 정신이 나가다 be out of one's mind
chŏngshinkkwaŭi 정신과의 psychiatric
chŏngshin pagyaktcha 정신박약자 imbecile
chŏngshinppyŏng 정신병 mental illness
chŏngshinppyŏng-wŏn 정신병원 mental hospital
chŏngt'ong 정통 familiarity
chŏngt'onghada 정통하다 know; master
chŏng-ŭi 정의 justice; definition
chŏng-ŭirŭl naerida 정의를

내리다 define
chŏn-gu 전구 light bulb
chŏng-wŏn 정원 garden
chŏng-wŏnsa 정원사
gardener
chŏn-gyŏng 전경 foreground
chŏnhada 전하다 pass on
chŏnhanŭn mal 전하는 말
message
chŏnhwa 전화 telephone;
phone call
chŏnhwabŏnhobu
전화번호부 phone book
chŏnhwa kŏlda 전화 걸다
phone
chŏnhwan 전환 change;
conversion
chŏnhwa pŏnho 전화 번호
telephone number
chŏnhwarŭl hada 전화를
하다 make a telephone call
chŏnhyang 전향 convert
chŏnhyangshik'ida
전향시키다 convert *person*
chŏnhyŏ 전혀 completely
chŏnhyŏng 전형 stereotype
chŏnhyŏngjŏgin 전형적인
typical
chŏnja 전자 the former;
electron ◊ electronic
chŏnjaeng 전쟁 war
chŏnja orak 전자 오락
electronic game
chŏnjarenji 전자렌지
microwave
chŏnji 전지 battery

chŏnjin 전진 advance
chŏnjinhada 전진하다
advance
chŏnjip 전집 collected works
chŏnkkwa 전과 criminal
record
chŏnmang-i chŏun chijŏm
전망이 좋은 지점 vantage
point
chŏnmun 전문 specialty
chŏnmun-ga 전문가 expert
chŏnmunjŏgin 전문적인
professional
chŏnmunŭi 전문의 technical
chŏnmunŭro hada
전문으로 하다 specialize
(in)
chŏnnyŏm 전념 dedication
chŏnnyŏmhada 전념하다
dedicate oneself to; keep one's
mind on
chŏnnyŏmhanŭn 전념하는
single-minded
chŏnsanhwahada
전산화하다 computerize
chŏnsegŭm 전세금 deposit
for an apartment lease
chŏnsegyeŭi 전세계의
global
chŏnse not'a 전세 놓다
lease an apartment on a deposit
basis
chŏnshi 전시 display;
wartime
chŏnshihada 전시하다
exhibit

chŏnshinju

28

chŏnshinju 전신주 utility pole

chŏnshin mach'wi 전신 마취 general anesthetic

chŏnsŏl 전설 legend

chŏnsŏljŏgin 전설적인 legendary

chŏnsŏn 전선 front MIL, *(of weather)*; cord; cable

chŏnsonghada 전송하다 export COMPUT

chŏnsongnyŏguro hada 전속력으로 하다 flat out

chŏnt'ong 전통 tradition

chŏnt'ongjŏgin 전통적인 traditional

chŏnt'u 전투 battle

chŏnŭi 전의 former

chŏnya 전야 eve

chŏnyŏk 전역 evening; all parts

chŏnyŏk shiksa 저녁 식사 supper

chŏnyŏm 전염 transmission

chŏnyŏmdoenŭn 전염되는 contagious

chŏnyŏmshik'ida 전염시키다 transmit *disease*

chŏnyŏmssŏng-ŭi 전염성의 infectious

chŏnyul 전율 thrill

chŏŏgada 저어가다 row

chŏpch'aktche 접착제 adhesive

chŏpch'ak'ada 접착하다 stick

chŏpch'ok 접촉 contact; touch

chŏpch'ok'ada 접촉하다 contact; touch

chŏpkkŭn 접근 access

chŏpkkŭnhada 접근하다 access

chŏpssi 접시 plate

chŏpssoksshik'ida 접속시키다 connect

chŏpssok'ada 접속하다 interface; connect with; go on-line to

chŏpssuwŏn 접수원 receptionist

chŏptta 접다 fold

chŏp'ae it-tta 접혀 있다 border

chŏp'ida 접히다 fold up

chŏp'yŏnŭro 저편으로 beyond

chŏrida 절이다 marinate; pickle

chŏrim 저림 pins and needles

chŏrŏn! 저런! good heavens!

chŏryak 절약 saving

chŏryak'ada 절약하다 economize

chŏryak'anŭn 절약하는 economical

chŏsok'an 저속한 vulgar

chŏsŭng 저승 underworld

chŏtkkarak 젓가락 chopsticks

chŏtkkasŭm 젖가슴 breast

chŏt-tta 젖다 get wet

chojik'ada

chŏt-tta 젓다 paddle
chŏũi 저의 H my
chŏũm poepkkessŭmnida
처음 뵙겠습니다 how
do you do (formal, on first
meeting)
chŏũmũi 저음의 deep; bass
chŏul 저울 scales
chŏ wie 저 위에 over there
cho 조 trillion; millet; article;
dynasty; tune
choahada 좋아하다 like
choajida 좋아지다 improve
choayo 좋아요 OK
chobŭn 좁은 narrow
chobŭn kil 좁은 길 lane
chobumo 조부모
grandparents
choch'ado 조차도 even
choch'i 조치 measure
choch'wirŭl ch'wihada
조취를 취하다 take action
choe 죄 sin
choech'aek-kkam 죄책감
guilt
choein 죄인 sinner
choeoehada 제외하다
rule out
choesonghamnida
죄송합니다 excuse me
choesu 죄수 prisoner
chogak 조각 bit; sculpture
chogak-kka 조각가 sculptor
chogak naeda 조각 내다
shred
chogakp'um 조각품

sculpture
chogangnada 조각나다
splinter
choging 조깅 jog; jogging
choginghada 조깅하다 jog
chogŭm 조금 a little ◊ any
◊ some; slightly
chogŭmahan 조그마한 tiny
chogŭmdo 조금도 (not) at
all
chogŭmsshik 조금씩 little
by little
chogŭmũi 조금의 a few
chohang 조항 article;
provision
chohap 조합 association;
union
chohoe 조회 reference
chohoehada 조회하다
refer to
chohwa 조화 harmony;
reconciliation
chohwadoen 조화된
harmonious
chohwashik'ida
조화시키다 harmonize;
reconcile
choida 조이다 tie
chojak'ada 조작하다
manufacture; fix; manipulate
chojik 조직 organization;
system; organ ANAT; tissue
chojiktchŏgin 조직적인
systematic
chojik'ada 조직하다
organize

chojŏnghada 조정하다 set

chojŏrhada 조절하다 tune up

chojong 조종 operation; aviation

chojonghada 조종하다 operate; steer; pilot

chojonghanŭn 조종하는 manipulative

chojongsa 조종사 pilot

chokkŏn 조건 condition

chokkŏnbuŭi 조건부의 conditional

chokppo 족보 genealogy book

choktchipkke 족집게 tweezers

chok'a 조카 nephew

chok'attal 조카딸 niece

cholda 졸다 doze

chollamaeda 졸라매다 fasten tightly

chollida 졸리다 be sleepy

chollin 졸린 sleepy

choltchak 졸작 trash

chom 좀 some; something

chomajomahage hanŭn 조마조마하게 하는 nerve-racking

choman-gan 조만간 sooner or later

chomirhada 조밀하다 be dense

chomiryo 조미료 seasoning

chommŏktta 좀먹다 erode

chomyŏng 조명 lighting

chomyŏnghada 조명하다 illuminate

chong 종 species; bell

chong-ari 종아리 calf

chongdalssae 종달새 lark

chonggyo 종교 religion

chonggyojŏgin 종교적인 religious

chonghap pohŏm 종합 보험 comprehensive insurance

chong-i 종이 paper

chong-i mukkŭm 종이 묶음 pad

chong-i ullida 종이 울리다 chime

chongnyohada 종료하다 log off; shut down

chongnyu 종류 kind

chongsahada 종사하다 practice

chongtchŏm 종점 terminus

chon-gyŏng 존경 respect

chon-gyŏnghada 존경하다 respect

chonjae 존재 existence

chonjaehada 존재하다 exist

chonjunghada 존중하다 respect

choŏn 조언 advice; hint

choŏnhada 조언하다 advise

choptta 좁다 be narrow

choribŏp 조리법 recipe

chorip 조립 assembly

chorip'ada 조립하다 assemble

chorŏp 졸업 graduation

chorŏp'ada 졸업하다 graduate

chorong 조롱 taunt

chorŭda 조르다 press for; pester

choryu 조류 current; tide; birds

chosa 조사 investigation; survey

chosahada 조사하다 survey

chosang 조상 ancestor; ancestry

chosang sungbae 조상 숭배 ancestral worship

choshim 조심 caution

choshimhada 조심하다 take care

choshimsŭrŏpke 조심스럽게 carefully

choshimsŭrŏun 조심스러운 cautious

Chosŏn Minjujuŭi Inmin Konghwaguk 조선 민주주의 인민 공화국 Democratic People's Republic of Korea, DPRK

chosu 조수 assistant; tide

chot'a 좋다 be good

choŭn 좋은 good

choyonghada 조용하다 be quiet

choyonghage 조용하게 quietly

choyonghan 조용한 quiet

choyonghi! 조용히! hush!

choyurhada 조율하다 tune

chŭk 즉 namely

chŭk-kkaktchŏgin 즉각적인 prompt; instant

chŭksshi(ro) 즉시 (로) immediately

chŭksshiŭi 즉시의 immediate

chŭkssŏk shikp'um 즉석 식품 fast food

chŭlgida 즐기다 enjoy

chŭlgŏpke hada 즐겁게 하다 entertain

chŭlgŏptta 즐겁다 be delightful

chŭlgŏun 즐거운 enjoyable

chŭlgŏun Sŏngt'ani toegirŭl paramnida! 즐거운 성탄이 되기를 바랍니다! Merry Christmas!

chŭngbarhada 증발하다 evaporate

chŭngga 증가 increase

chŭnggahada 증가하다 increase

chŭnggahanŭn 증가하는 increasing

chŭnggŏ 증거 evidence

chŭnggŏrŭl taeda 증거를 대다 substantiate

chŭng-in 증인 witness

chŭng-insŏk 증인석 witness stand

chŭngjŏnghada 증정하다 present

chŭngjobu

chŭngjobu 증조부 great-grandfather

chŭngjomo 증조모 great-grandmother

chŭngkkwŏn kŏraeso 증권 거래소 stock exchange

chŭngkkwŏn shijang 증권 시장 stock market

chŭngmyŏnghada 증명하다 prove

chŭngmyŏngsŏ 증명서 certificate; ID

chŭng-ŏn 증언 evidence

chŭng-ŏnhada 증언하다 give evidence

chŭng-o 증오 hatred

chŭngson 증손 great-grandchild

chu 주 note; province, state; week; Lord

chubang 주방 kitchen

chubu 주부 housewife

chuch'a 주차 parking

chuch'a changso 주차 장소 parking place

chuch'agŭmji 주차금지 no parking

chuch'ahada 주차하다 park

chuch'a yogŭmgi 주차 요금기 parking meter

chuch'iŭi 주치의 family doctor

chuda 주다 give; assign; allow

chudang 주당 weekly rate

chudo 주도 initiative

chudoen 주된 main

chudohada 주도하다 lead the way

chudojŏgin 주도적인 leading

chudung-i 주둥이 muzzle; spout

chugan 주간 weekly

chugida 죽이다 kill; deaden

chugijŏgin 주기적인 periodic

chugŏganŭn 죽어가는 dying

chugŏŭi 주거의 residential

chugŭn 죽은 dead

chugŭnkkae 주근깨 freckle

chugŭp 주급 weekly payment

chugwanjŏgin 주관적인 subjective

chugyo 주교 bishop

chuhaeng 주행 drive

Chuhan Migun 주한 미군 American Military Forces in Korea

chuhongsaek 주홍색 scarlet

chuin 주인 host; landlord; owner; mistress

chuip 주입 injection; transfusion

chuip'ada 주입하다 infuse; indoctrinate; pump

chujang 주장 argument; assertion; allegation; team captain

chujangdoen 주장된

alleged
chujanghada 주장하다 assert
chuje 주제 motif; topic
chujega 주제가 theme song
chujŏhanŭn 주저하는 tentative
chujŏnja 주전자 kettle; jug; teapot; coffee pot
chuju 주주 shareholder
chujung-e 주중에 midweek
Chu Kidomun 주 기도문 Lord's Prayer
chuktta 죽다 die
chul 줄 column; file; strap; string
chulda 줄다 decrease
chulgi 줄기 stem; trunk; wisp
chulgot 줄곧 all the time
chulja 줄자 tape measure
chullŏmkkihada 줄넘기하다 skip
chulmunŭi 줄무늬 stripe
chul sŏda 줄 서다 line up
chumal 주말 weekend
chumŏk 주먹 fist
chumŏktchil 주먹질 punch
chumŏni 주머니 pouch; pocket
chumok 주목 attention
chumok'ada 주목하다 pay attention
chumok'ae chushipsshio 주목해 주십시오 your attention please
chumok'al manhan 주목할

chumanhan 만한 remarkable; notable
chumun 주문 order; magic spell
chumunhada 주문하다 order
chunbi 준비 preparation
chunbidoen 준비된 ready
chunbihada 준비하다 arrange; prepare
chunbihaesŏ 준비해서 in preparation for
chung 중 Buddhist monk; middle ◊ among ◊ while
chung-ang 중앙 center ◊ central
chungbokdoeda 중복되다 overlap
chungdaehada 중대하다 be important
chungdaehan 중대한 significant; great; grave
chungdan 중단 disruption
chungdanhada 중단하다 interrupt; pause
chungdan ŏmnŭn 중단 없는 non-stop
chungdo-e 중도에 midway
chungdogida 중독이다 be addicted to
chungdok 중독 addiction
chungdoktcha 중독자 addict
Chungdong 중동 Middle East
chungdŭng kyoyuk 중등 교육 secondary education
chunggae 중개 mediation

chunggaehada 중개하다
mediate

chunggaeŏp 중개업 agency

chunggane 중간에 halfway

chunggan irŭm 중간 이름
middle name

chunggan k'ŭgi 중간 크기
medium size

chungganŭi 중간의 middle;
medium; intermediate

chunggoŭi 중고의
secondhand

Chunggug-ŏ 중국어
Chinese (language)

Chungguk saram 중국
사람 Chinese (person)

chunggyehada 중계하다
relay

chunggyein 중계인 contact

chunghwanjasil 중환자실
intensive care (unit)

chung-ida 중이다 be in the
middle of

chungji 중지 cessation

chungjihada 중지하다
discontinue

chungjishik'ida 중지시키다
break up

chungmae kyŏrhon 중매
결혼 arranged marriage

chungnip 중립 neutrality

chungnip wich'i 중립 위치
neutral

chungnyŏn 중년 middle age
◇ middle-aged

chungnyohada 중요하다 be

important

chungnyohan 중요한
important

chungnyosŏng 중요성
importance

chung-ŏlgŏrida 중얼거리다
mutter

chungsanch'ŭng 중산층
middle classes

chungshimga 중심가 main
street

chungshimjŏk 중심적
central

chungshimŭi 중심의 central

chungshimŭl tuda 중심을
두다 center on

chungt'ae 중태 serious
condition MED

chungt'ae-esŏ pŏsŏnan
중태에서 벗어난 out of
danger MED

chungt'oeja 중퇴자 dropout

chun-gyŏlssŭng 준결승
semifinal

chung-yohada 중요하다 be
important

chung-yohan 중요한
important

Chunim 주님 Lord (Jesus)

chunjun-gyŏlssŭng
준준결승 quarter-final

chuŏ 주어 subject GRAM

churida 줄이다 reduce; turn
down *volume, heating*; cut
down; cut short; shorten

churŏdŭlda 줄어들다 go

down; shrink
churo 주로 mainly
churŭm 주름 pleat; crease;
wrinkle
chusa 주사 injection
chusahada 주사하다 inject
chusawi 주사위 dice
chushik 주식 stocks
chushik shijang 주식 시장
stock market
chuso 주소 address
chusorok 주소록 address
book
chut'aek 주택 housing
chuŭi 주의 attention;
warning; notice
chuŭigip'ŭn 주의깊은
watchful
chuŭihada 주의하다 pay
attention
chuŭirŭl kiurida 주의를
기울이다 pay attention

chuwi 주위 perimeter
◊ around
chuwiŭi 주위의 surrounding
chuwŏ moŭda 주워 모으다
gather up
chuwŏ ollida 주워 올리다
pick up
chuyohan 주요한 main
chuyuso 주유소 gas station
chwach'ŭgŭi 좌측의 port;
left-hand
chwadamhoe 좌담회 talk
show
chwaigŭi 좌익의 left-wing
chwaik 좌익 left wing
chwajŏl 좌절 setback;
discouragement
chwajŏrhada 좌절하다
collapse; get discouraged
chwayak 좌약 suppository
chwi 쥐 mouse; rat
chyusŭ 쥬스 juice

CH'

ch'a 차 vehicle; car; tea
ch'abŏrida 차버리다 ditch
ch'abunhan 차분한 placid
ch'abyŏl 차별 discrimination
ch'abyŏrhada 차별하다
differentiate between;
discriminate against
ch'ach'a 차차 by degrees
ch'ach'uk 차축 axle
ch'ada 차다 be packed; be

satisfied; expire; kick; reject
ch'adanhada 차단하다
exclude
ch'ae 채 bat ◊ countword for
buildings
ch'aegim 책임 responsibility
ch'aegimja 책임자 person
in charge
ch'aegurhada 채굴하다
mine for

ch'aegwŏnja 채권자
creditor

ch'aek 책 book

ch'aekkwŏn 채권 bond

ch'aeksang 책상 desk

ch'aenŏl 채널 channel

ch'aet'aek 채택 selection;
adoption

ch'aeuda 채우다 complete;
do up, fasten; fill; chill

ch'aewŏ nŏt'a 채워 넣다
stuff

ch'agaptta 차갑다 be cold

ch'agi 차기 kick

ch'agwandan 차관단
consortium

ch'agyonghada 착용하다
put on; wear

ch'ai 차이 difference

ch'ajaboda 찾아보다 look;
look up; look out for

ch'ajagada 찾아가다 visit

ch'aja tanida 찾아 다니다
search

ch'akch'wihada 착취하다
exploit

ch'ak-kkak 착각 delusion

ch'ak-kkak'ada 착각하다
mistake

**ch'aksshirhan saenghwarŭl
hada** 착실한 생활을 하다
go straight

ch'akssuhada 착수하다
commence

ch'aktchap'an 착잡한
complex

ch'alssak ttaerim 찰싹
때림 blow

ch'amara! 참아라! patience!

ch'amch'i 참치 tuna

ch'amga 참가 participation

ch'amgahada 참가하다
participate

ch'amgasik'ida 참가시키다 enter

ch'amgohada 참고하다
consult

ch'amgyŏnhada 참견하다
poke one's nose into

ch'amho 참호 trench

ch'amp'aeshik'ida
참패시키다 thrash SPORTS

ch'amsŏk 참석 attendance

ch'amsŏnhada 참선하다
meditate (Buddhism)

ch'amŭlssŏng innŭn 참을성
있는 patient

ch'amŭlssŏng ŏmnŭn
참을성 없는 impatient

ch'amŭl su ŏmnŭn 참을 수
없는 intolerable

ch'amŭro 참으로 vitally

ch'anban yangnon 찬반
양론 the pros and cons

ch'angbaek'an 창백한 pale

ch'angjaktcha 창작자
author

ch'angjo 창조 creation

ch'angjoja 창조자 creator

ch'angmun 창문 window

ch'angnyuk changch'i 착륙
장치 undercarriage

ch'angnyukshik'ida
착륙시키다 land

ch'angshija 창시자
originator

ch'angsŏltcha 창설자
founder

ch'angt'ŏk 창턱 windowsill

ch'annip 찻잎 tea leaf

ch'ansa 찬사 compliment

ch'ansahanŭn 찬사하는
complimentary

ch'ansŏnghada 찬성하다
approve (of)

ch'ansongga 찬송가 hymn

ch'antchang 찬장 cupboard
(in kitchen); sideboard

ch'a pongji 차 봉지 teabag

ch'ap'okttŭng 차폭등
sidelight

ch'aryang kyŏninso 차량
견인소 pound (for cars)

ch'aryang tŭngnok pŏnho
등록 번호 license plate
number

ch'arye 차례 turn

ch'aryŏ ipta 차려 입다
dress up

ch'aryŏnaeda 차려내다
serve up

ch'a sech'ŏk 차 세척 car
wash

ch'asŏn 차선 (traffic) lane

ch'atkki himdŭn 찾기 힘든
elusive

ch'attchŏmja 차점자
runner-up

ch'ayongja 차용자 tenant

ch'e 체 sieve; pretense

ch'ege 체계 system

ch'egejŏguro 체계적으로
systematically

ch'egyŏk 체격 physique

ch'ehada 체하다 pretend

ch'ejil 체질 constitution

ch'ejobok 제조복 leotard

ch'ejung midarŭi 체중
미달의 underweight

ch'ello 첼로 cello

ch'emyŏnŭl ch'arinŭn
체면을 차리는 image-
conscious

ch'emyŏnŭl ilt'a 체면을
잃다 lose face

ch'eŏ lip'ŭt'ŭ 체어 리프트
chair lift

ch'ep'o 체포 arrest

ch'ero ch'ida 체로 치다 sift

ch'eryŏginnŭn 체력있는
athletic

ch'esŭp'an 체스판 chessboard

ch'eyuk 체육 gymnastics

ch'eyuk kyosa 체육 교사
gymnast

ch'ia 치아 teeth ◊ dental

ch'ia kŏmsa 치아 검사
dental checkup

ch'igwan 치관 crown

ch'ikkwa 치과 dental clinic

ch'ik'yŏ ollagan 치켜
올라간 slanting

ch'il 칠 seven; paint; varnish;
laquer

ch'ilp'an 칠판 blackboard

ch'ilsship 칠십 seventy

ch'im 침 saliva;
acupuncture

ch'ima 치마 skirt

ch'imbŏm 침범 invasion;
intrusion

ch'imch'ak 침착 composure;
poise

ch'imch'ak'ada 침착하다
keep one's cool

ch'imch'ak'am 침착함
presence of mind

ch'imch'ehan 침체한
stagnant

ch'imdaeppo 침대보
bedcover

ch'imhaehada 침해하다
encroach on *rights*

ch'imip 침입 invasion; raid

ch'imiptcha 침입자 invader;
intruder

ch'imjŏnmul 침전물
sediment

ch'immugŭl chik'ida 침묵을
지키다 stay silent

ch'immukshik'ida
침묵시키다 silence

ch'imnyak 침략 invasion

ch'imshik'ada 침식하다
erode

ch'imshil 침실 bedroom

ch'imsul 침술 acupuncture

ch'imt'u 침투 penetration

ch'imŭl hŭllida 침을 흘리다
dribble

ch'imŭl paet-tta 침을
뱉다 spit

ch'imurhae it-tta 침울해
있다 be gloomy

ch'imurhage nŭkkida
침울하게 느끼다 feel low

ch'imyŏngsang-ŭi 치명상의
fatally injured

ch'inaehanŭn 친애하는
dear

ch'inch'ŏgi toenŭn 친척이
되는 related

ch'inch'ŏk 친척 relative

ch'ingch'an 칭찬 praise

ch'ingch'anhada 칭찬하다
praise

ch'ingho 칭호 form of
address

ch'ing-ŏlgŏrida 칭얼거리다
whine

ch'ingsong 칭송 praise

ch'ingsonghada 칭송하다
praise

ch'in-gŭnhan 친근한
familiar

ch'in-guga toeda 친구가
되다 make friends

ch'in-gyo moim 친교 모임
get-together

ch'inhada 친하다 be close

ch'injŏl 친절 kindness

ch'injŏrhada 친절하다
be kind

ch'injŏrhan 친절한 kind

ch'insuk'am 친숙함
intimacy

ch'irhŭk 칠흑 pitch black

ch'irŭda 치르다 pay; take exam; undergo; hold event

ch'irwŏl 칠월 July

ch'iryo chŏnmun-ga 치료 전문가 therapist

ch'iryohada 치료하다 treat; cure

ch'iryoŭi 치료의 therapeutic

ch'isŏk 치석 plaque

ch'isot-tta 치솟다 shoot up

ch'issu 치수 size; measurements

ch'issurŭl chaeda 치수를 재다 measure

ch'itssol 칫솔 toothbrush

ch'it'ong 치통 toothache

ch'iuda 치우다 brush; clear; remove; put away

ch'iyŏrhan 치열한 cut-throat

ch'iyok 치욕 a disgrace

ch'iyokssŭrŏpkke 치욕스럽게 shamefully

ch'ŏbanghada 처방하다 prescribe

ch'ŏbangjŏn 처방전 prescription

ch'ŏbŏl 처벌 punishment

ch'ŏbŏrhada 처벌하다 punish

ch'ŏbun 처분 disposal

ch'ŏhada 처하다 run into

ch'ŏhyŏng 처형 sister-in-law (wife's elder sister)

ch'ŏje 처제 sister-in-law (wife's younger sister)

ch'ŏjida 처지다 hang down

ch'ŏk 척 countword for boats

ch'ŏktto 척도 yardstick

ch'ŏk'ada 척하다 pretend

ch'ŏlssŏk ttaerida 철썩 때리다 whack

ch'ŏlssu 철수 withdrawal

ch'ŏlssusik'ida 철수시키다 withdraw

ch'ŏltcha 철자 spelling

ch'ŏltcha hwagin togu 철자 확인 도구 spellchecker

ch'ŏltchŏhage 철저하게 thoroughly

ch'ŏltchŏhi chosahada 철저히 조사하다 look through

ch'ŏma 처마 eaves

ch'ŏmbusŏ 첨부서 covering letter

ch'ŏmgaje 첨가제 (food) additive

ch'ŏn 천 cloth; thousand

ch'ŏndung 천둥 thunder

ch'ŏngbaji 청바지 jeans

ch'ŏngch'un-gi 청춘기 youth (age)

ch'ŏngch'wihada 청취하다 tune in to

ch'ŏnggak chang-ae 청각 장애 deafness

ch'ŏnggangsaeng 청강생 auditor

ch'ŏnggu 청구 claim

ch'ŏngguhada 청구하다 charge; claim

ch'ŏnggyodo 청교도 puritan
ch'ŏnghada 청하다 request
ch'ŏnghon 청혼 proposal
ch'ŏngja 청자 celadon ware
ch'ŏngjin-gi 청진기
stethoscope
ch'ŏngjinhada 청진하다
sound
ch'ŏngnoksaek 청록색
turquoise
ch'ŏngnyŏk 청력 hearing
ch'ŏngsajin 청사진 blueprint
ch'ŏngsanhada 청산하다
go into liquidation; settle;
write off
ch'ŏngsobu 청소부 cleaner
ch'ŏngsokkwa 청소과
sanitation department
ch'ŏngsonyŏn pihaeng
청소년 비행 youthful
misdemeanors
ch'ŏnan 천국 heaven
ch'ŏnhan 천한 menial
ch'ŏnjae 천재 genius
ch'ŏnjaejibyŏn 전재지변
catastrophe
ch'ŏnjinhan 천진한
childlike; disarming
Ch'ŏnjugyo shinja 천주교
신자 Catholic
ch'ŏnmagŭl ch'ida 천막을
치다 camp
ch'ŏnmak 천막 tent
ch'ŏnmaneyo 천만에요
you're welcome
ch'ŏnmunhaktcha

천문학자 astronomer
ch'ŏnmunhaktchŏgin
천문학적인 astronomical
ch'ŏn pŏnŭi 천 번의
thousandth
ch'ŏnshik 천식 asthma
ch'ŏnyŏn kassŭ 천연 가스
natural gas
ch'ŏrhada 철하다 file
ch'ŏrhaktcha 철학자
philosopher
ch'ŏrhoehada 철회하다
pull out; dispense with
ch'ŏrihada 처리하다 deal
with; process
ch'ŏrŏm 처럼 like
ch'ŏt 첫 first
ch'ŏshinhada 처신하다
conduct oneself
ch'ŏt-tchaero 첫째로 in the
first place
ch'ŏtwŏlgŭp 첫 월급
starting salary
ch'ŏŭm 처음 start
ch'ŏŭmenŭn 처음에는
at first
ch'ŏŭmŭi 처음의 first
ch'ŏŭmŭro 처음으로 first
ch'o 초 candle; excerpt;
second; draft; vinegar;
beginning ◊ ultra-
ch'och'im 초침 second hand
ch'odae 초대 invitation
ch'odaehada 초대하다 invite
ch'odŭnghak-kkyo kyosa
초등학교 교사 elementary

teacher

ch'oech'ŏmdanŭi 최첨단의 state-of-the-art

ch'oech'oŭi 최초의 original; initial

ch'oedae 최대 maximum

ch'oego suwi 최고 수위 high water

ch'oegowiŭi 최고위의 supreme

ch'oegŭn 최근 newly

ch'oegŭne 최근에 recently

ch'oejŏk 최적 optimum

ch'oejŏ saenghwal sujun 최저 생활 수준 subsistence level

ch'oejong 최종 the last; the end ◊ final

ch'oemyŏnsul 최면술 hypnosis

ch'oerugasŭ 최루가스 tear gas

ch'oesang-ŭi 최상의 best

ch'oeshin chŏngborŭl chuda 최신 정보를 주다 update

ch'oeshinŭi 최신의 latest

ch'oeshin yuhaeng-ŭi 최신 유행의 trendy

ch'oesŏnŭl tahada 최선을 다하다 do one's best

ch'oeso 최소 minimum

ch'oesohwahada 최소화하다 minimize

ch'oesoryang 최소량 least

ch'oesoŭi 최소의 minimal

ch'ogangdaeguk 초강대국 superpower

ch'ogi 초기 infancy

ch'ogiŭi 초기의 early

ch'ogosok yŏlch'a 초고속 열차 bullet train

ch'ogwahada 초과하다 exceed; overrun *time*

ch'ogwahanŭn 초과하는 in excess of

ch'ogwa suhamul 초과 수하물 excess baggage

ch'oinjŏgin 초인적인 enormous

ch'oinjong 초인종 doorbell

ch'ojŏnyŏge 초저녁에 at nightfall

ch'ojohaehada 초조해하다 panic, flap

ch'ojohan 초조한 edgy

ch'okssu 촉수 tentacle

ch'oktchin 촉진 boost

ch'oktchinje 촉진제 catalyst

ch'ok'ŭ 초크 choke

ch'ong 총 gun

ch'ong-aek 총액 total amount of money

ch'ong-al 총알 bullet

ch'ongch'ong kŏrŭmŭro kada 총총 걸음으로 가다 trot

ch'onggi hyudaeja 총기 휴대자 gunman

ch'onggye 총계 total; sum

ch'ongmyŏngham 총명함 intelligence

ch'ongsang 총상 gunshot
wound

ch'ongsarhada 총살하다
shoot dead

ch'on-gŭk 촌극 sketch THEAT

ch'onsŭrŏpkke hwaryŏhan
촌스럽게 화려한 gaudy

ch'oraehada 초래하다
bring about

ch'orahan 초라한 humble

ch'osohyŏng 초소형
miniature

ch'ossŭngttal 초승달 new
moon

ch'otchŏm 초점 focus

ch'ot-ttae 촛대 candlestick

ch'oŭmp'a 초음파
ultrasound

ch'owŏltchŏgin 초월적인
transcendental

ch'oyŏnhan 초연한 remote

ch'ŭktchŏng 측정
measurement

ch'ŭktchŏngppŏp 측정법
system of measurement

ch'ŭng 층 layer; floor; deck

ch'ŭnggyech'am 층계참
landing

ch'ubang 추방 exile

ch'ubun 추분 fall equinox

ch'uch'ŏn 추천
recommendation

ch'uch'ŏnhada 추천하다
recommend

ch'uch'ŏntchang 추천장
testimonial

ch'uch'ŭk 추측 guess

ch'udohada 추도하다
mourn

ch'uga-aek 추가액
supplement FIN

ch'uganp'an 추간판 slipped
disc

ch'ugaro 추가로 in addition

ch'uga yogŭm 추가 요금
extra charge

ch'ugu 추구 search; pursuit

ch'uguhada 추구하다
pursue; seek

**ch'uhu t'ongjiga issŭl
ttaekkaji** 추후 통지가
있을 때까지 until further
notice

ch'ujap'an 추잡한 lewd

ch'ujinhada 추진하다 drive;
go ahead with; set things in
motion

ch'ujŏk 추적 pursuit

ch'ujŏktcha 추적자 pursuer

ch'ujŏk'ada 추적하다
pursue; trace

ch'ujŏngdoeda 추정되다
be presumed

ch'ukch'uk'age hada
축축하게 하다 dampen

ch'uk-kka 축가
congratulatory song

ch'uk-kku 축구 soccer

ch'uk-kku sŏnsu 축구 선수
soccer player

ch'uk-kkugong 축구공
football

ch'ukppok'ada 축복하다
bless

ch'uksohada 축소하다
cut back

ch'uktche 축제 festival

ch'uktcheŭi 축제의 festive

ch'uk'a 축하 congratulations

ch'uk'a haengsa 축하 행사
festivities

ch'uk'ayŏn 축하연
celebration

ch'ulbal shigan 출발 시간
departure time

ch'ulbaltchŏm 출발점
starting point; threshold

ch'ulbarhada 출발하다
depart

ch'ulgŭnhada 출근하다 go
to work

ch'ullabwŏn 출납원 cashier

ch'ullyŏk 출력 output

ch'ulp'an 출판 publication

ch'ulp'andoeda 출판되다
be published

ch'ulp'anŏptcha 출판업자
publisher (person)

ch'ulp'ansa 출판사
publisher (company)

ch'ulssaeng chŏnŭi 출생
전의 prenatal

ch'ulssaengguk 출생국
native country

ch'ulssaeng-ŭi 출생의
native

ch'ulsshihada 출시하다
appear; release

ch'ulsshin sŏngbun 출신
성분 background

ch'ulssŏk 출석 attendance

ch'ultchang 출장 business
trip

ch'ulttongshik'ida
출동시키다 call out

ch'ulttu 출두 court
appearance

ch'ulttuhada 출두하다
appear (in court); report

ch'um 춤 dance

ch'unbun 춘분 spring
equinox

ch'ungbunhada 충분하다
be sufficient

ch'ungbunhage 충분하게
sufficiently

ch'ungbunhan yang 충분한
양 enough

ch'ungbunhi 충분히 enough

ch'ungch'i 충치 cavity

ch'ungch'iga saenggida
충치가 생기다 tooth
decay

ch'ungdol 충돌 collision;
conflict

ch'ungdolshik'ida
충돌시키다 crash

ch'ungdongjŏgin 충동적인
impulsive

ch'ungdong kumae 충동
구매 impulse buy

ch'ungdongtchŏguro
충동적으로 on the spur of
the moment

ch'ungdorhada 충돌하다
crash; collide with; clash

ch'unggo 중고 advice;
warning

ch'unggyŏgŭl pat-tta
충격을 받다 be shocked

ch'unggyŏk 충격 shock

ch'unghyŏldoen 충혈된
bloodshot

ch'ungmanhada 충만하다
be full

ch'ungnongtchŭng 축농증
sinusitis

ch'ungshimŭro 충심으로
heartily

ch'ungshirhada 충실하다
be loyal

ch'ungsŏngshim 충성심
sense of loyalty

ch'ungsuyŏm 충수염
appendicitis

ch'up'a 주파 leer

ch'urak 추락 crash

ch'urhanghada 출항하다
sail

ch'urhyŏn 출현 appearance

ch'urhyŏrhada 출혈하다
bleed

ch'urimul 주리물 whodunnit

ch'urip 출입 access

ch'urip kŭmji 출입 금지
off limits

ch'urip'ang kŭmji 출입항

금지 embargo

ch'uron 추론 deduction

ch'uronhada 추론하다
deduce

ch'uryŏnaeda 추려내다
remove

ch'uryŏnjin 출연진 cast
(of play)

ch'ushin 추신 PS

Ch'usŏk 추석 Harvest
Festival

ch'usu 추수 harvest

Ch'usu Kamsajŏl 추수
감사절 Thanksgiving (Day)

ch'uun 추운 cold

ch'uwi 추위 cold

ch'uwŏrhada 추월하다
pass AUTO

ch'waryŏng 촬영
photography

ch'waryŏng kisa 촬영 기사
cameraman

ch'widŭk'ada 취득하다
take

ch'wigŭp 취급 treatment

ch'wigŭp chuŭi 취급 주의
handle with care!

ch'wihada 취하다 get drunk

ch'wihan 취한 drunk

ch'wijung-ŭi 취중의
drunken

ch'wimi 취미 hobby

ch'wiso 취소 cancellation

D

...dago hani ···다고 하니 that

...dani ···다니 that

...dörado ···더라도 even though

...do ···도 as well

...do öptta ···도 없다 without any ... at all

...dorok ···도록 so that; till; as ... as possible

E

...e ···에 in; at; on; for

...eda(ga) ···에다 (가) at; in; on

...ege ···에게 to *(a person)*

Eijǔ 에이즈 Aids

Eijǔ yangsöng panǔng 에이즈 양성 반응 HIV-

positive

enamel kajuk 에나멜 가죽 patent leather

enǒji 에너지 energy, power

ent'ǒ k'i 엔터 키 enter key

...esǒ ···에서 in; at; on; from

G

...ga ···가 *subject particle* → **...ka** ···가

...get... ···겠··· shall

...gi wihae ···기 위해 in order to

...go ···고 and

H

habǔihada 합의하다 agree

hada 하다 ◇ do; make; play; put on ◇ *(makes nouns into verbs)*: **saranghada** 사랑하다 love ◇ **...ge hada**

···게 하다 make; let

hadan 하단 lower part

hae 해 harm

haebang 해방 liberation

haeboda 해보다 try

haebyŏn 해변 beach
haech'ehada 해체하다 break up; take down
haech'ida 해치다 harm
haech'iuda 해치우다 finish off *task*; kill
haech'o 해초 seaweed
haedanghada 해당하다 correspond to
haedap 해답 answer
haego 해고 dismissal
haegohada 해고하다 lay off
haegol 해골 skeleton; skull
haegoshik'ida 해고시키다 dismiss
haegüi 핵의 nuclear
haegun 해군 navy
haegyŏl 해결 solution
haegyŏrhada 해결하다 solve
haejil muryŏp 해질 무렵 sunset
haek 핵 nucleus ◊ nuclear
haeksshim 핵심 core
haeksshimjŏgin 핵심적인 essential
haemyŏnghada 해명하다 explain
haenaeda 해내다 beat; succeed; accomplish
haenagada 해나가다 carry on
haendŭl 핸들 (steering) wheel
haendŭp'on 핸드폰 cell phone
haeng 행 bound for

haengbok 행복 happiness
haengbok'ada 행복하다 be happy
haengbok'an 행복한 happy
haengdong 행동 act; behavior
haengdonghada 행동하다 behave
haengjinhada 행진하다 march
haengjŏng 행정 administration
haengjŏng samu 행정 사무 civil service
haengju 행주 dishcloth
haengsa 행사 event
haeng-un 행운 good fortune
haeoe 해외 abroad
haeoe kyop'o 해외 교포 overseas Koreans
haep'ari 해파리 jellyfish
haeroun 해로운 harmful
haesam 해삼 sea slug
haesanmul 해산물 seafood
haesŏk 해석 interpretation
haesŏk'ada 해석하다 interpret
haesŏltcha 해설자 commentator
haetppit 햇빛 sunshine
haetppyŏch'e t'aeuda 햇볕에 태우다 get a suntan
haetppyŏt'e(sŏ) 햇볕에(서) in the sun
haeyang 해양 ocean
hagang 하강 descent

haganghada 하강하다
descend

hagŭp 하급 low class

hagwi 학위 degree

hagwŏn 학원 institute

hak-kki 학기 semester

hak-kkŭp 학급 class

hak-kkwa 학과 department

hak-kkyo 학교 school

hak-kkyo sŏnsaengnim
학교 선생님 schoolteacher

hakppi 학비 tuition fee

hakssaeng 학생 student

hakssal 학살 slaughter

hakssŭp 학습 learning

haktcha 학자 scholar

haktchang 학장 dean

hakttae 학대 abuse

hakttaehada 학대하다 abuse

halkkamalkka
saenggak'ada 할까말까
생각하다 think about doing

hal marŭl irŭn 할 말을
잃은 be compelled to ...

halmŏni 할머니 grandmother

hal su ŏpsshi ... 할 수
없이 ··· be compelled to ...

hamburo taruda 함부로
다루다 mishandle

hamjŏng 함정 pitfall; trap

hamkke 함께 with ◊ together

hamkke hada 함께 하다
share *feelings*

hamnihwahada 합리화하다
rationalize

hamnijŏgin 합리적인
rational

han 한 limit; *...nŭn han* ···는
한 so long as

hana 하나 one

hanaga toen 하나가 된
united

hanasshik 하나씩 one
by one

hanbŏn 한번 once

hanbok 한복 Korean costume

hanch'ang ttaeida 한창
때이다 be in one's prime

hando 한도 limit

handoga ŏmnŭn 한도가
없는 open-ended

...handokkajinŭn
···한도까지는 to such an
extent that

hangahan ttaee 한가한
때에 in an idle moment

hang-ari 항아리 storage jar

han-gaunde 한가운데
center

hangbok 항복 surrender

hangbok'ada 항복하다
surrender

hanggonggi 항공기 aircraft

hanggongp'yŏn pŏnho
항공편 번호 flight number

hanggongp'yŏnŭro
항공편으로 by air

hanggongsa 항공사 airline

hanggong-up'yŏn 항공우편
airmail

hanggu 항구 port

hanghae 항해 voyage

hanghaehada 항해하다
navigate

han-gil 한길 mainroad

hangmok 항목 item

hangmun 학문 scholarship

hangnyŏn 학년 academic
year

hangsang 항상 always

hangso 항소 appeal JUR

hang-ŭi 항의 protest

hang-ŭihada 항의하다
protest

han-gŭl 한글 Korean script

Han-gugŏ 한국어 Korean
(language)

Han-guk 한국 (South) Korea
◊ (South) Korean

Han-guk-kkye 한국계
Korean descent

Han-guk saram 한국 사람
(South) Korean

Han-gukssan 한국산 made
in Korea

han-gye 한계 limitation

hangyŏul 한겨울 midwinter

hanjŏngdoen 한정된
restricted

hanjŏnghada 한정하다
limit

hankkŏbone 한꺼번에
at once

han kyŏure 한 겨울에 in
the depths of winter

**hanp'yŏnŭronŭn ...,
tarŭn hanp'yŏnŭronŭn**
한편으로는…, 다른

한편으로는 on the one hand
..., on the other hand

hanshimhan 한심한 pitiful

hansum 한숨 sigh

hansum chada 한숨 자다
take a nap

hansum chit-tta 한숨
짓다 sigh

hantcha 한자 Chinese
character

hanttae(e) 한때 (에) once

hant'ŏk naeda 한턱 내다
treat

hanŭisa 한의사 Chinese
herbal medicine practitioner

hanŭiwŏn 한의원 Chinese
medicine clinic

hanŭl 하늘 sky

Hanŭnim 하느님 God

hanyak 한약 Chinese herbal
medicine

hapch'ang 합창 chorus

hapkkye 합계 total

hapkkyehada 합계하다
add up

hapkkyŏk'ada 합격하다
pass examination

hapttanghada 합당하다 be
appropriate

hap'um 하품 yawn

hap'umhada 하품하다
yawn

harabŏji 할아버지
grandfather

harak 하락 fall

harak'ada 하락하다 fall

harin 할인 discount
harinhada 할인하다 discount
harinkka(gyŏk) 할인가 (격) bargain price
harin p'anmae 할인 판매 sale
haru 하루 day
haru chong-il 하루 종일 all day
haru kŏnnŏ 하루 건너 every other day
haruppamŭl chinaeda 하룻밤을 지내다 stay overnight
hasugin 하숙인 lodger
hasuk 하숙 board and lodging
hasuk'ada 하숙하다 board with
hawi 하위 low rank
hayan 하얀 white
hayat'a 하얗다 be white
hayŏt'ŭn 하여튼 anyhow
hech'yŏnagada 헤쳐나가다 wriggle out of
hemaeda 헤매다 stray
heŏjida 헤어지다 part
him 힘 energy; power
himdŭlda 힘들다 be difficult
himdŭn 힘든 difficult
himŏmnŭn 힘없는 weak
himssen 힘센 strong
hŏbihada 허비하다 waste
hŏga 허가 permission
hŏgahada 허가하다 permit

hŏgatchŭng 허가증 license
hŏlda 헐다 demolish
hŏlgŏpkke 헐겁게 loosely
hŏlgŏun 헐거운 loose
hŏlttŏk-kkŏrida 헐떡거리다 gasp
hŏmdam 험담 gossip
hŏmulda 허물다 pull down
hŏmurŏjin 허물어진 dilapidated
hŏnbyŏng 헌병 MP, military police
hŏnggŏp(tchogak) 헝겊 (조각) patch
hŏnshin 헌신 devotion; donation
hŏnshinjŏgida 헌신적이다 be devoted to
hŏnshinjŏgin 헌신적인 devoted
hŏp'ung 허풍 tall story
hŏp'ung-ŭl ttŏlda 허풍을 떨다 exaggerate
hŏrak 허락 permission
hŏrak'ada 허락하다 allow
hŏri 허리 waist
hŏritti 허리띠 belt
hŏrŭmhan 허름한 run-down
hŏshigŏmnŭn 허식없는 unpretentious
hŏshik 허식 affectation
hŏshimt'anhoehada 허심탄회하다 be open-minded
hŏsuabi 허수아비 scarecrow
hŏtchŏm 허점 blind spot

hŏtkkallida

hŏtkkallida 헛갈리다
mix up

hŏtkkich'imhada
헛기침하다 clear one's
throat

hŏtssorihada 헛소리하다
rave

hŏtsugo 헛수고 vain effort

hŏt-ttidida 헛디디다
stumble

hŏt-ttoege 헛되게 in vain

hŏt-ttoen 헛된 vain

hŏyak 허약 infirmity

hŏyak'ada 허약하다 be frail

hŏyak'an 허약한 delicate

hŏyŏngsim 허영심 vanity

hobak 호박 pumpkin; amber

hoe 회 round; raw fish

hoebi 회비 fee

hoebok 회복 recovery

hoebok'ada 회복하다
rebuild; recover

hoegye 회계 accounts

hoegyesa 회계사 accountant

hoegye tamdangja 회계
담당자 treasurer

hoehwa 회화 conversation;
picture

hoejin 회진 round

hoejŏn 회전 revolution

hoejŏnhada 회전하다 rotate

hoejŏnshik'ida 회전시키다
spin

hoengdan 횡단 crossing

hoengdan podo 횡단 보도
crosswalk

hoengnyŏng 횡령
embezzlement

hoengp'oŭrŭl purinŭn 횡포를
부리는 dictatorial

hoengsŏlsusŏl 횡설수설
gibberish

hoe-oribaram 회오리바람
whirlwind

hoep'i 회피 evasion

hoep'ihada 회피하다 evade

hoesa 회사 company

hoesaek 회색 gray

hoesang 회상 reminiscence

hoesanghada 회상하다
recollect

hoeŭi 회의 meeting

hoeŭijŏgin 회의적인
skeptical

hoeŭishil 회의실 conference
room

hoewŏn 회원 member;
membership

hoewŏntchŭng 회원증
membership card

hogami kanŭn 호감이 가는
likable

hogishim 호기심 curiosity

hogishim manŭn 호기심
많은 inquisitive

hogŭn 혹은 or

hohŭp 호흡 breathing

hohŭp kollan 호흡 곤란
breathlessness

hohwaroptta 호화롭다 be
luxurious

hohwaroun 호화로운 de

luxe

hojŏk 호적 census registration; census register

hojŏn 호전 improvement

hojŏnjŏgin 호전적인 belligerent

hojŏnshik'ida 호전시키다 turn around

Hoju 호주 Australia
◊ Australian

hojumŏni 호주머니 pocket

hok 혹 lump; hump

hoksshi 혹시 sometimes; perhaps

hokttok'an 혹독한 brutal

hollan 혼란 confusion

hollanhada 혼란하다 be confused

hollanshik'ida 혼란시키다 confuse

hollansŭröun 혼란스러운 topsy-turvy

hollo 홀로 by itself

hollye 혼례 marriage

holssu 홀수 odd number

holtchuk'an 홀쭉한 sunken

holttak ppajida 홀딱 빠지다 dote on

homil ppang 호밀 빵 rye bread

hom kyŏnggi 홈 경기 home game

hondonghada 혼동하다 confuse

hongbo 홍보 public relations

hongch'a 홍차 black tea

honghap 홍합 mussel

hong-igin-gan 홍익인간 devotion to the welfare of mankind

hongnyŏk 홍역 measles

hongsu 홍수 flood

honhammul 혼합물 mixture

honhap 혼합 blend; hybrid; solution

honhap'ada 혼합하다 blend

honja 혼자 alone

honjap 혼잡 congestion

honjasŏ 혼자서 by oneself

honjŏn(ŭi) 혼전 (의) premarital

honsu sangt'ae 혼수 상태 coma; trance

hop 홉 hop BOT

horanggashinamu 호랑가시나무 holly

horang-i 호랑이 tiger

hosohada 호소하다 appeal for; complain of

hosŭ 호스 hose

hosu 호수 lake

hot'el 호텔 hotel

hot'el chong-ŏbwŏn 호텔 종업원 maid

hoŭi 호의 favor; goodwill

hoŭijŏgin 호의적인 favorable

hŭbip 흡입 suction

hŭbip'ada 흡입하다 inhale

hŭbyŏn 흡연 smoking

hŭbyŏnja 흡연자 smoker

hŭgin 흑인 black (person)

hŭibak'an

hŭibak'an 희박한 thin; sparse

hŭida 희다 be white

hŭimang 희망 hope

hŭimang-e ch'an 희망에 찬 hopeful

hŭimanghada 희망하다 hope

hŭimihaejida 희미해지다 fade

hŭimihan 희미한 faint

hŭisaeng 희생 sacrifice; death toll; victim

hŭisaenghada 희생하다 sacrifice

hŭisaengja 희생자 victim

hŭk 흙 earth

hŭlkkŭt poda 흘끗 보다 catch sight of

hŭllida 흘리다 shed; spill

hŭmjabŭlde ŏmnŭn 흠잡을데 없는 faultless

hŭmjaptta 흠잡다 find fault with

hŭmppŏk chŏjŭn 흠뻑 젖은 soaking wet

hŭndŭlda 흔들다 shake; swing; wave; undermine

hŭndŭlgŏrinŭn 흔들거리는 shaky

hŭngbun 흥분 excitement

hŭngbunhada 흥분하다 get excited

hŭngbunshik'inŭn 흥분시키는 exciting

hŭngjŏnghada 흥정하다 bargain

hŭngmijinjinhan 흥미진진한 very interesting

hŭngmirŭl kajida 흥미를 가지다 take an interest in

hŭnhaji anŭn 흔하지 않은 uncommon

hŭnŭkkim 흐느낌 sob

hŭpssuhada 흡수하다 absorb

hŭpssussŏng-ŭi 흡수성의 absorbent

hŭrida 흐리다 be cloudy

hŭrin 흐린 overcast

hŭrit'an 흐릿한 dim; fuzzy; glazed

hŭrŭda 흐르다 flow; stream

hŭrŭnŭn 흐르는 flowing; runny

hŭryŏjida 흐려지다 mist over

hŭryŏjin 흐려진 misty

hŭt'ŏjida 흩어지다 disperse

hŭt'ŏjin 흩어진 scattered

huban 후반 second half

hubida 후비다 dig up

huboja 후보자 candidate

hubul 후불 deferred payment

huch'u 후추 pepper

hue 후에 after

huhoe 후회 repentance

huhoehada 후회하다 regret; repent

huhoesŭrŏpkkedo 후회스럽게도 regretfully

hujin 후진 reverse (gear)

hujinhada 후진하다 reverse
hullyŏn 훈련 training
hullyŏnhada 훈련하다 train
hullyunghada 훌륭하다
be great
hullyunghage 훌륭하게
wonderfully
hullyunghan 훌륭한 brilliant
hultchŏk-kkŏrida
훌쩍거리다 sniffling
hult'ŏboda 훑어보다 skim
through; look over *person*
humch'ida 훔치다 steal
hunjehada 훈제하다 smoke
ham etc
hushik 후식 dessert
hut'oe 후퇴 setback; retreat
huwŏn 후원 sponsorship
huwŏnja 후원자 sponsor
hwanada 화나다 get angry
hwa 화 anger
hwabun 화분 pollen;
flowerpot
hwabyŏng 화병 vase;
hypochondria
hwach'anghada 화창하다
be bright
hwadan 화단 flowerbed
hwaetppul 횃불 torch *(with
flame)*
hwaga 화가 painter
hwaga nada 화가 나다
get angry
hwaga nan 화가 난 angry
hwagin 확인 inspection;
confirmation; identification

hwaginhada 확인하다
check; confirm; identify; query
hwahae 화해 reconciliation
hwahaehada 화해하다 be
reconciled
hwahak 화학 chemistry
hwahak chep'um 화학
제품 chemical
hwajae 화재 fire
hwajae kyŏngbogi 화재
경보기 fire alarm
hwajang 화장 cremation;
make-up; beauty care
hwajanghada 화장하다
cremate; put on make-up
hwajangji 화장지 tissue;
toilet paper
hwajangp'um 화장품 make-
up; cosmetics
hwajangshil 화장실 restroom
hwaje 화제 topic
hwajerŭl pakkuda 화제를
바꾸다 change the subject
hwaksshin 확신 certainty
hwaksshinhada 확신하다
be positive
hwaksshinhanŭn 확신하는
certain
hwaksshirhada 확실하다
be certain
hwaksshirhan 확실한
definite
hwaksshirhi 확실히
definitely
hwaktae 확대 zoom in
hwaktchang 확장 expansion

hwaktchanghada

hwaktchanghada 확장하다
expand; diversify

hwaktchŏngdoeda
확정되다 be finalized

hwaktchŭng 확증
confirmation

hwaktchŭnghada 확증하다
confirm

hwakttaehada 확대하다
enlarge; escalate

hwal 활 bow MUS

hwalbarhada 활발하다
be lively

hwalgi 활기 vigor

hwalgi ch'an 활기 찬 lively

hwaltchak p'in 활짝 핀 in
full bloom

hwaltchak ut-tta 활짝 웃다
smile broadly

hwalttongga 활동가 activist

hwalttongjŏgin 활동적인
active

hwamyŏn 화면 screen

hwanada 화나다 be
annoyed; get annoyed

hwanaege hada 화내게
하다 anger

hwanan 화난 exasperated

hwanbul 환불 refund

hwanburhada 환불하다
refund

hwandae 환대 hospitality

hwandaehanŭn 환대하는
hospitable

hwan-gap 환갑 sixtieth
birthday

hwanggŭmshiganttae
황금시간대 prime time

hwanggŭp'i 황급히 in
double-quick time

hwanghorhan 황홀한
ecstatic

hwan-gi changch'i 환기
장치 ventilator; ventilation

hwangso 황소 bull

hwan-gyŏng 환경
environment

hwan-gyŏngboho 환경보호
environmental protection

hwan-gyŏng-oyŏm
환경오염 environmental
pollution

hwanhada 환하다 be bright;
be open

hwanhage 환하게 brightly

hwanhan 환한 bright

hwanho 환호 cheer;
jubilation

hwanhohada 환호하다
cheer

hwanhŭi 환희 delight

hwanja 환자 patient

hwanjŏnhada 환전하다
exchange

hwannyul 환율 exchange rate

hwansaeng 환생
reincarnation

hwansang 환상 fantasy

hwansangjŏgin 환상적인
fantastic

hwanyŏng 환영 welcome;
vision; illusion

hwanyŏnghada 환영하다
welcome

hwap'urihada 화풀이하다
take it out on

hwarŭl ch'amtta 화를 참다
keep one's temper

hwarŭl naeda 화를 내다
lose one's temper

hwaryŏhada 화려하다 be
sumptuous

hwaryŏham 화려함 splendor

hwaryonghada 활용하다
utilize

hwasal 화살 arrow

hwasan 화산 volcano

hwasang 화상 burn *(injury)*

hwayoil 화요일 Tuesday

hwesonhada 훼손하다
mutilate; defame

hwibaryu 휘발유 gasoline

hwida 휘다 bend

hwijŏt-tta 휘젓다 stir; whisk

hwin 휜 bent

hwip'aram 휘파람 whistle

hwŏnhada 훤하다 be broad;
be well versed in

hwŏnhi t'ŭin 훤히 트인
open and bright

hyang 향 incense

hyanggi 향기 scent; bouquet

hyangginanŭn 향기나는
fragrant

hyanghada 향하다 face

hyanghayŏ 향하여 toward

hyangsang 향상
improvement

hyangsangdoeda 향상되다
get better

hyangsangshik'ida
향상시키다 improve

hyangsu 향수 perfume;
nostalgia

hyangsuppyŏng-ŭl alt'a
향수병을 앓다 be homesick

hyesŏng 혜성 comet

hyŏ 혀 tongue

hyŏksshin 혁신 innovation

hyŏksshinjŏgin 혁신적인
innovative

hyŏlgwan 혈관 blood vessel

hyŏlssaegi anjohŭn 혈색이
안좋은 sickly

hyŏlt'ong 혈통 lineage

hyŏmnyŏk kwan-gye 협력
관계 partnership

hyŏmnyŏktchŏgin 협력적인
cooperative

hyŏmnyŏk 협력 cooperation

hyŏmnyŏk'ada 협력하다
cooperate

hyŏmo 혐오 disgust

hyŏmohada 혐오하다 detest

hyŏmosŭrŏun 혐오스러운
disgusting

hyŏnak-kki 현악기 stringed
instrument

Hyŏnch'ung-il 현충일
Memorial Day

hyŏndae 현대 modern times
◇ modern

hyŏndaehwa 현대화
modernization

hyŏndaehwahada

hyŏndaehwahada
현대화하다 modernize

hyŏndaejŏgin 현대적인
modern

hyŏng 형 (man's) elder
brother

hyŏnshiljŏgin 현실적인
realistic

hyŏngbu 형부 brother-in-
law (woman's elder sister's
husband)

hyŏnggwang-ŭi 형광의
fluorescent

hyŏn-gitchŭng 현기증
giddiness; vertigo

hyŏngje chamae 형제 자매
brothers and sisters

hyŏngmyŏng 혁명
revolution

hyŏngmyŏngjŏgin 혁명적인
revolutionary

hyŏngp'yŏnŏmnŭn
형편없는 wretched

hyŏngp'yŏnŏpsshi
형편없이 dreadfully

hyŏngsa 형사 detective;
criminal case

hyŏngsang 형상 figure

hyŏngshik 형식 format;
formality

hyŏngshiktchŏgin 형식적인
formal

hyŏngshiktchŏgŭro
형식적으로 formally

hyŏngsu 형수 sister-in-law
(elder brother's wife)

hyŏn-gŭm 현금 cash

hyŏn-gŭm inch'ulgi 현금
인출기 ATM

hyŏn-gŭmŭro naeda
현금으로 내다 pay cash

hyŏnjae 현재 the present

hyŏnjaerŏnŭn 현재로는 at
the moment

hyŏnjaeŭi 현재의 current

hyŏnjang 현장 scene

hyŏnji shigan 현지 시간
local time

hyŏnmigyŏng 현미경
microscope

hyŏnmyŏnghada 현명하다
be wise

hyŏnmyŏng-hage 현명하게
wisely

hyŏnmyŏnghan 현명한
clever; wise; advisable

hyŏnsang 현상 phenomenon;
development

hyŏnsanghada 현상하다
develop film

hyŏnshil 현실 reality

hyŏnshiltchŏgin 현실적인
realistic

hyŏnshiltchŏgŭro
현실적으로 in practice

hyŏnshiltchuŭija
현실주의자 realist

hyŏp-ppak 협박 threat

hyŏp-ppak'ada 협박하다
intimidate

hyŏpssang 협상 negotiation

hyŏpssanghada 협상하다

negotiate

hyŏpttong 협동 cooperation

hyŏpttong chohap 협동 조합 cooperative COMM

hyŏpttonghada 협동하다 pull together

hyŏraek kŏmsa 혈액 검사 blood test

hyŏraek'yŏng 혈액형 blood group

hyŏrap 혈압 blood pressure

hyo 효 filial piety

hyokkwajŏgin 효과적인 effective

hyoryŏgi innŭn 효력이 있는 effective

hyoyul 효율 efficiency

hyoyulchŏgin 효율적인 efficient

hyudaeyong-(ŭi) 휴대용 (의) portable

hyuga 휴가 vacation; leave

hyugeso 휴게소 service area

hyuil 휴일 holiday

hyuji 휴지 toilet paper; waste paper

hyujit'ong 휴지통 waste basket

hyujŏn 휴전 cease-fire

hyunghada 흉하다 be hideous; be unlucky

hyunghan 흉한 ugly

hyungnae 흉내 impersonation

hyungnaenaeda 흉내내다 mimic

hyungt'ŏ 흉터 scar

hyushik 휴식 rest

hyushikch'ŏ 휴식처 resting place

hyuyangji 휴양지 resort

I

...i ···이 *(subject particle)*

i 이 two ◊ tooth; louse; profit; interest FIN; reason; person ◊ this

ibalssa 이발사 barber

ibŏboda 입어보다 try on

ibŭl tamulda 입을 다물다 clam up

ibul 이불 coverlet

ibwŏnhada 입원하다 go into hospital

ibwŏn hwanja 입원 환자 in-patient

ibyang 입양 adoption

ibyanghada 입양하다 adopt

ibyŏl 이별 farewell

ich'ie matkke 이치에 맞게 reasonably

ich'ŭng ch'imdae 이층 침대 bunk beds

ida 이다 be

idong 이동 transfer; mobility

idong chŏnhwa 이동 전화
cell phone
idonghada 이동하다 travel
around; change direction
igida 이기다 win; mix
igijŏgin 이기적인 selfish
igŏt 이것 this ◊ this one
igŭn 익은 ripe
iguktchŏgin 이국적인
exotic
igyŏn 이견 different opinion
igyŏnaeda 이겨내다
overcome
iha 이하 less than; below; the
following
ihae 이해 understanding
ihaehada 이해하다
understand
ihaeryŏk 이해력
comprehension
ihaeshik'ida 이해시키다
make understand
ihangnyŏn 이학년
sophomore
ihon 이혼 divorce
ihonhada 이혼하다 get
divorced
ihuro 이후로 since
iigi ŏmnŭn 이익이 없는
unprofitable
iigi toeda 이익이 되다
benefit
iik 이익 profit
iinyong pang 이인용 방
double room
ija 이자 interest

ijayul 이자율 interest rate
ije 이제 now
ijiltchŏgin 이질적인 alien
ijŏbŏrida 잊어버리다 forget;
lose
ijŏne 이전에 before
ijŏngp'yo 이정표 milestone
ijŏnhada 이전하다 relocate
ijul su ŏmnŭn 잊을 수 없는
unforgettable
iju 이주 emigration;
immigration
ijuhada 이주하다 migrate;
immigrate
ijuja 이주자 immigrant
ijungch'ang 이중창 duo
ijung in-gyŏkja 이중
인격자 two-faced person
ijungju 이중주 duet
ijungt'ŏk 이중턱 double chin
ijung-ŭi 이중의 dual
ijung yuri 이중 유리 double
glazing
ikki 이끼 moss
ikkŭlda 이끌다 lead; steer
ikkŭlgo kada 이끌고 가다
lead up to
ikssahada 익사하다 be
drowned
ikssuk'aejida 익숙해지다
get used to
ikssuk'aji anŭn 익숙하지
않은 unfamiliar
iktta 익다 get used to; get
cooked; ripen
ik'ida 익히다 familiarize;

cook

il 일 one; affair; business; job; pursuit; work; things

ilbangjŏgin 일방적인 one-sided

ilbang t'onghaengno 일방 통행로 one-way street

ilbanhwa 일반화 generalization

ilbanhwahada 일반화하다 generalize

ilbanjŏgin 일반적인 general

ilbanjŏguro 일반적으로 generally

ilbŏlle 일벌레 workaholic

ilbo 일보 a step

Ilbon 일본 Japan ◊ Japanese

Ilbonŏ 일본어 Japanese (language)

ilbubun 일부분 one part

ilburŏ 일부러 deliberately

ilbu saramdŭl 일부 사람들 some people

ilch'i 일치 agreement; match

ilch'ihada 일치하다 agree

ilch'ihanŭn 일치하는 matching

ilch'ŭng 일층 first floor

ilch'ul 일출 sunrise

ilgan shinmun 일간 신문 daily paper

ilgi 일기 diary

ilgi yebo 일기 예보 weather forecast

ilgop 일곱 seven

ilgwa 일과 routine

ilgwansŏng 일관성 consistency

ilgwansŏng innŭn 일관성 있는 consistent

iljiksŏnŭro 일직선으로 in a straight line

illanssŏng ssangdung-i 일란성 쌍둥이 identical twins

illyŏk 인력 manpower

illyŏne 일년에 in a year

illyŏne han pŏnŭi 일년에 한 번의 annual

illyu 인류 humanity

ilmol 일몰 sunset

ilmyŏn 일면 front page

ilsangjŏgin 일상적인 everyday

ilssang 일상 everyday

ilssangjŏgin 일상적인 routine

ilssangjŏguro 일상적으로 routinely

ilsshibul 일시불 lump sum

ilsshijŏgin 일시적인 temporary

ilsshijŏguro 일시적으로 temporarily

ilsson 일손 worker

...iltchido morŭnda … 일지도 모른다 might be

iltchik 일찍 early

iltchŏne 일전에 the other day

iltchŏng 일정 schedule

iltchŏnghada 일정하다 be regular

iltchŏnghan 일정한 particular; regular

iltta 읽다 read

ilttŭngshil 일등실 first class cabin / compartment

ilt'a 잃다 lose

ima 이마 forehead

imdae 임대 lease

imdae chadongch'a 임대 자동차 rental car

imdaehada 임대하다 lease

imdaeryo 임대료 rent

imeil 이메일 e-mail

imeil chuso 이메일 주소 e-mail address

imi 이미 already

imin 이민 emigrant

iminhada 이민하다 emigrate

immasŭl tashida 입맛을 다시다 lick one's lips

immu 임무 task; duty

immyŏng 임명 appointment

immyŏnghada 임명하다 appoint

imnyŏkshik'ida 입력시키다 enter COMPUT

imnyŏk'ada 입력하다 key in

imo 이모 aunt (mother's sister)

imobu 이모부 uncle (mother's sister's husband)

imshijŏgin 임시적인 temporary

imshinhada 임신하다 conceive; be pregnant

imun 이문 margin

...inae-e ···이내에 within

inbun 인분 feces; portion

inch'ul 인출 withdrawal

inch'urhada 인출하다 withdraw

indo 인도 sidewalk; surrender; India ◊ Indian

indohada 인도하다 lead; extradite

Indoin 인도인 Indian

in-gan 인간 human (being)

in-ganjŏgin 인간적인 humane

in-ganssŏng 인간성 humanity

ingkko 잉꼬 budgerigar

in-gong 인공 man-made

in-gongjŏgin 인공적인 artificial

in-gong-wisŏng 인공위성 satellite

in-gu 인구 population

inhaesŏ: kŭgŏsŭ(ro) inhaesŏ 그것으로 인해서 so

inhwa 인화 print

inhyŏng 인형 doll

...inji ···인지 if; whether

injil 인질 hostage

injŏng 인정 acknowledgment

injŏnghada 인정하다 admit; approve of

injŏng-innŭn 인정있는 humane

injong 인종 race

injong ch'abyŏltchuŭija 인종 차별주의자 racist

inkki 인기 popularity
inkkiinnŭn 인기있는 popular
inkki-it-tta 인기있다 be popular
inmom 잇몸 gum *(in mouth)*
inmul 인물 character
inp'yŏnŭro 인편으로 by hand
insa 인사 greeting
insaek'ada 인색하다 be miserly
insaek'an 인색한 stingy
insaeng 인생 life
insahada 인사하다 greet
insam 인삼 ginseng
insang 인상 raise; image; impression
insangjŏgin 인상적인 impressive
inshik 인식 awareness
inshim chot'a 인심 좋다 be generous
inshim choŭn 인심 좋은 good-hearted
insu 인수 takeover; factor
insuhada 인수하다 take over
inswae 인쇄 print
inswaehada 인쇄하다 printout
int'ŏbyu 인터뷰 interview
int'ŏbyuhada 인터뷰하다 interview
int'ŏbyuhanŭn saram 인터뷰하는 사람 interviewer

inyong 인용 quotation
inyonghada 인용하다 quote
inyongmun 인용문 quote *(from author)*
...iŏsŏ ···이어서 next to
...ioe-e ···이외에 except for
ip 잎 leaf
ip 입 mouth
ipch'ullyŏk'ada 입출력하다 access
ipkkimŭl pulda 입김을 불다 blow
ipku 입구 entrance
ipkkuk 입국 arrivals *(at airport)*; entry *(to country)*
ipkkuk hŏga 입국 허가 admission *(to country)*
ipkkukpija 입국비자 entry visa
i ppajin chaguk 이 빠진 자국 chip *(in cup etc)*
ipssahada 입사하다 join
ipssanghan 입상한 prizewinning
ipssŏk 입석 standing room
ipssul 입술 lip
iptchang 입장 entrance; stance; situation
iptchang kŭmji 입장 금지 no admittance
iptchangnyo 입장료 entrance fee
iptchŭng 입증 verification
iptchŭnghada 입증하다 prove
iptta 입다 wear; put on

ip'akkŭm 입학금 fee

ip'ak wŏnsŏ 입학 원서 application form

ip'ubo 입후보 candidacy

iraero 이래로 since

irhada 일하다 work

irhoe 일회 once

irhoeyong 일회용 disposable

irhŭn 일흔 seventy

irŏbŏrin 잃어버린 missing

irŏktchŏrŏk 이럭저럭 somehow or other

irŏk'e 이렇게 this way

irŏn 이런 like this

irŏna antta 일어나 앉다 sit up

irŏnada 일어나다 happen; get up

irŏsŏda 일어서다 stand (up)

iron 이론 theory

ironsang-ŭro 이론상으로 in theory

irŭda 이르다 come to; carry (of sound); range

irŭk'ida 일으키다 cause; cast *doubt*

irŭm 이름 name; first name

irŭmp'yo 이름표 nametag

irŭn 이른 early

irŭn 잃은 lost

irwŏl 일월 January

irwŏnida 일원이다 belong to

iryŏkssŏ 이력서 résumé

iryoil 일요일 Sunday

iryongp'um 일용품 daily necessity

iryuk 이륙 takeoff

iryuk'ada 이륙하다 take off

iryu (ŭi) 이류 (의) second-rate; inferior

isa 이사 director; move

isahada 이사하다 move house

isahŭl 이사흘 couple of days

isang 이상 not less than ◊ ideal ◊ strangeness

isanghada 이상하다 strange

isanghage 이상하게 strangely

isangjŏgin 이상적인 ideal

isaoda 이사오다 move in

ishik susul 이식 수술 transplant

ishik'ada 이식하다 transplant

iship 이십 twenty

isŏng 이성 opposite sex; reason

issŭl su ŏmnŭn 있을 수 없는 unacceptable

issushigae 이쑤시개 toothpick

isŭl 이슬 dew

isŭlbi 이슬비 drizzle

itchŏm 이점 advantage; plus

Itchoguro 이쪽으로 this way

itta 잇다 join; inherit; preserve

it-tta 있다 be; exist; be located; have

it-tta 잊다 forget
it-ttarün 잇따른 successive
it'al 이탈 departure
it'ülmada 이틀마다 every
  other day
iut 이웃 neighbor

iwŏl 이월 February
iyagi 이야기 story
iyagihada 이야기하다 tell
iyong 이용 use
iyonghada 이용하다 use
iyu 이유 reason

J

-ja -자 *suffix used for
persons*

...ja maja …자 마자 as
  soon as

K

...ka …가 *subject particle*
kabal 가발 wig
kabang 가방 bag
kabyŏpkke 가볍게 lightly
kabyŏpta 가볍다 be light
kabyŏun 가벼운 light
kach'i 가치 value
kach'i 같이 together; with
kach'i anün 같지 않은
  unlike
kach'i chada 같이 자다
  sleep with; have sex with
kach'iga orüda 가치가
  오르다 rise in value
kach'iga ttŏröjida 가치가
  떨어지다 fall in value
kach'iŏmnün 가치없는
  worthless
kach'i oda 같이 오다 come
  along

kach'uk 가축 livestock
kada 가다 go; come
kadük ch'ada 가득 차다
  fill up *(of place)* ◊ full up
kadük ch'aeuda 가득
  채우다 fill up
kaduda 가두다 lock in
kae 개 dog ◊ *general
  countword*
kaebal 개발 development
kaebaldosangguk
  개발도상국 developing
  country
kaebangdoen 개방된 open
kaebarhada 개발하다
  develop
kaebyŏltchŏgüro
  개별적으로 individually
kaech'arhada 개찰하다
  punch *ticket*

Kaech'ŏnjŏl 개천절
National Foundation Day

kaeda 개다 clear up; fold

kaegae 개개 individually

kaegaeŭi 개개의 individual

kaegulgaegul ulda
개굴개굴 울다 croak

kaeguri 개구리 frog

kaehoeshik 개회식 opening
ceremony

kaehyŏk 개혁 reform

kaehyŏk'ada 개혁하다
reform

kaein 개인 individual

kaein hwagin pŏnho 개인
확인 번호 PIN

kaeinjuŭi 개인주의
individualism

kaein kyosŭp 개인 교습
(private) tuition

kaeintchŏgin 개인적인
personal

kaejip 개집 kennel

kaejo 개조 conversion;
renovation

kaejohada 개조하다
convert; renovate

kaekkwanjŏgin 객관적인
objective

kaemi 개미 ant

kaengshin 갱신 renewal

kaengshinhada 갱신하다
renew

kaeŏp'ada 개업하다 set up
(in business)

kaeshi 개시 initiation

kaeshihada 개시하다
initiate

Kaeshin-gyo 개신교
Protestantism

kaeul 개울 stream

kage 가게 store

kage chuin 가게 주인
storekeeper

kagonghada 가공하다
process food, raw materials

kagonghaji anŭn 가공하지
않은 raw sugar, iron

kagu 가구 furniture

kagyebu 가계부
housekeeping book

kagyŏgi orŭda 가격이
오르다 increase in value

kagyŏgi pissan 가격이
비싼 expensive

kagyŏk 가격 cost; price

kaip'ada 가입하다 join

kajang 가장 most ◊ wage
earner; masquerade

kajanghada 가장하다
pretend

kajangjari 가장자리 edge

kaji 가지 branch; twig;
eggplant

kajida 가지다 have; hold

kajigakssaegŭi 가지각색의
miscellaneous

kajigakssaek 가지각색
assortment

kajigo it-tta 가지고 있다
have got

kajigo kada 가지고 가다

take
kajigo nolda 가지고 놀다
toy with
kajirŏ kada 가지러 가다
collect
kajirŏ oda 가지러 오다
collect
kajŏng 가정 assumption;
home
kajŏng kyoyuk 가정 교육
home education
kajŏnghada 가정하다
assume
kajŏngjŏgin 가정적인
homeloving
kajŏnjep'um 가전제품
(household) appliance
kajok 가족 family
kajok kyehoek 가족 계획
family planning
kajoktchŏgin 가족적인
paternalistic
kajuk 가죽 hide; leather
kajyŏoda 가져오다 bring;
get; earn
kak 각 each; angle
kakkai 가까이 near ◊ about
kakkaie 가까이에 at hand
◊ near
kakkaie(sŏ) 가까이에 (서)
locally
kakkapkke 가깝게 close
kakkaptta 가깝다 be close
kakkasŭro 가까스로 barely
kakkaun 가까운 close
kak-kkak 각각 each

kakkŭm 가끔 sometimes
kaktcha 각자 each other
kalbi 갈비 spare ribs
kalbitchim 갈비찜 steamed
(beef) ribs
kalbi t'ang 갈비탕 beef
rib soup
kalda 갈다 replace; sharpen;
plow
kalga mŏktta 갈아 먹다
nibble
kalgyŏ ssŭda 갈겨 쓰다
scribble
kallyak 간략 brevity
kallyakhada 간략하다 be
brief
kalmaegi 갈매기 seagull
kalmang 갈망 longing
kalmanghada 갈망하다
long for
kalp'i 갈피 sense
kalsaek 갈색 brown
kalssurok tŏ 갈수록 더
increasingly
kaltchŭng 갈증 thirst
kama 가마 kiln
kamang 가망 chance
kamang-innŭn 가망있는
hopeful
kamang ŏmnŭn 가망 없는
hopeless
kamangsŏng 가망성
probability
kamanhi 가만히 still
kamchwŏjin 감춰진 hidden
kamch'ok 감촉 feeling; touch

kamch'uda 감추다 conceal

kamdanghada 감당하다 control

kamdok 감독 director *(of movie)*; direction *(of movie)*

kamdoktcha 감독자 supervisor

kamdok'ada 감독하다 direct *movie*; supervise

kamdongjŏgin 감동적인 emotional

kamdongshik'ida 감동시키다 move

kamgagŏmnŭn 감각없는 numb

kamgak 감각 sensation; sense *(sight, smell etc)*

kamgaktchŏgin 감각적인 sensuous

kamgi 감기 cold *(illness)*

kamgie kŏllida 감기에 걸리다 catch a cold

kamgyŏk'ada 감격하다 be thrilled

kamgyŏk'age hanŭn 감격하게 하는 thrilling

kamhi 감히 daringly

kamhihada 감히 하다 dare

kamja 감자 potato

kamja ch'ip 감자 칩 potato chip

kamjŏng 감정 emotion; valuation

kamjŏngjŏgin 감정적인 emotional

kammyŏng 감명 deep impression

kammyŏng chuda 감명 주다 make an impression

kamok 감옥 prison

kamsahada 감사하다 thank; audit

kamsahagedo 감사하게도 thankfully

kamsahanŭn 감사하는 thankful

kamsang 감상 sentimentality

kamsangjŏgin 감상적인 sentimental

kamshihada 감시하다 watch; picket

kamso 감소 decrease

kamsohada 감소하다 decrease

kamsok'ada 감속하다 slow down

kamtta 감다 wind up *clock*; close

kamt'an 감탄 admiration

kamt'anhada 감탄하다 admire

kamum 가뭄 drought

kamyŏm 감염 infection

kamyŏmdoeda 감염되다 become infected

kamyŏmdoen 감염된 infected

kamyŏn 가면 mask

ka-myŏng 가명 pseudonym

kan 간 liver *(food)*

kanan 가난 poverty

kananhada 가난하다 be poor

kananhan 가난한 poor

kanch'ŏnghada 간청하다 implore

kanch'ŏp 간첩 secret agent

kang 강 river

kang-aji 강아지 puppy

kangbak kwannyŏme sarojap'in 강박 관념에 사로잡힌 obsessive

kangbyŏn 강변 riverside

kangdo 강도 intensity; burglar; burglary

kangdojil 강도질 robbery

kangdojirhada 강도질하다 burglarize

kanggan 강간 rape

kangganbŏm 강간범 rapist

kangganhada 강간하다 rape

kanghada 강하다 be strong

kanghaejida 강해지다 strengthen; harden (of attitude); intensify

kanghage 강하게 strongly

kanghan 강한 strong

kangje 강제 force

kangjejŏgin 강제적인 forced

kangjero 강제로 by force

kangjo 강조 emphasis

kangjohada 강조하다 emphasize

kangnyŏk'ada 강력하다 be powerful

kangnyŏk'age 강력하게 violently

kangnyŏk'an 강력한 strong

kangp'an 강판 grater

kangp'ung 강풍 gale

kangsa 강사 instructor

kangse 강세 strength; emphasis

kangtchŏm 강점 strong point

kangt'a 강타 blow

kangt'ahada 강타하다 smash

kangt'al 강탈 extortion

kangt'arhada 강탈하다 rob

kang-ŭi 강의 lecture

kang-ŭihada 강의하다 lecture

kang-ŭishil 강의실 lecture hall

kan-gyŏk 간격 space

kan-gyŏrhage 간결하게 briefly

kan-gyŏrhan 간결한 brief

kangyohada 강요하다 force; urge

kanho 간호 (nursing) care

kanhosa 간호사 nurse

kanjang 간장 soy sauce; liver ANAT

kanjilppyŏng hwanja 간질병 환자 epileptic

kanjirŏp'ida 간지럽히다 tickle

kanjŏptchŏgin 간접적인 indirect

kanjŏptchŏguro 간접적으로 indirectly

kanjŏrhada 간절하다 be earnest

kanjŏrhan 간절한 eager

kanjŏrhi 간절히 eagerly

kanp'an 간판 signboard; cover organization

kansahae poinŭn 간사해 보이는 shifty-looking

kansahan 간사한 deceitful

kanshik 간식 snack

kanshinhi 간신히 barely

kansŏndoro 간선도로 arterial road

kansŏp 간섭 interference

kansŏp'ada 간섭하다 interfere

kanttanhada 간단하다 be simple

kanttanhage 간단하게 simply

kanttanhan 간단한 simple

kanttanhi 간단히 simply

kant'ong 간통 adultery

kanŭlda 가늘다 be thin

kanŭn 가는 thin; fine

kanŭnghada 가능하다 be possible

kanŭnghan 가능한 possible

kanŭngssŏng 가능성 possibility

kanŭn kire: ...*ro kanŭn kire* ...로 가는 길에 on the way

kanyalp'ŭn 가냘픈 slender

kap 갑 pack (*of cigarettes*)

kap 값 price

kap pissan 값 비싼 expensive

kapsshi ssan 값이 싼 inexpensive

kaptchagi 갑자기 suddenly

kaptchakssŭrŏn 갑작스런 sudden

kaptta 갚다 repay

kara-anjŭn 가라앉은 subdued

karaantta 가라앉다 subside; sink

karaiptta 가라입다 change *clothes*

karat'ada 갈아타다 change *train etc*

karik'ida 가리키다 indicate

karodŭng 가로등 streetlight

karŭch'ida 가르치다 teach

karu 가루 powder

karyŏnaeda 가려내다 sort out

karyŏptta 가렵다 itch

kashi 가시 thorn; spine; splinter; fish bone

kasok 가속 acceleration

kasok'ada 가속하다 accelerate

kasŭ 가스 gas (*for cooking*)

kasŭm 가슴 chest

kasŭpkki 가습기 humidifier

kasu 가수 singer

kat 갓 traditional horsehair hat

katcha 가짜 fake

katch'i 같이 like; together with

kigwan

kat-tta 같다 be like; be equal
kat'a poida 같아 보이다
seem like
kat'ŭn 같은 such as ◊ same;
equal
kaŭl 가을 fall
kaunde 가운데 middle
◊ among
kawi 가위 scissors
kayagŭm 가야금 Kaya zither
ke 게 crab
kedaga 게다가 moreover
kegŏlssŭrŏpke
게걸스럽게 ravenously
kegŏlssŭrŏpta 게걸스럽다
be ravenous
kegŏlssŭrŏun 게걸스러운
ravenous
keim 게임 game (in tennis)
keshi 게시 notice
keshihada 게시하다 put up
a notice
keship'an 게시판 bulletin
board
...ket ···겠··· shall
keŭrŭda 게으르다 be lazy
keŭrŭmbaeng-i 게으름뱅이
layabout
keŭrŭn 게으른 lazy
ki 기 era; flag; energy
kiban 기반 basis
kibonjŏgin 기본적인 basic
kibonjŏgŭro 기본적으로
basically
kibu 기부 contribution
kibuhada 기부하다

contribute
kibun 기분 mood
kibunjoŭn 기분좋은
agreeable
kich'a 기차 train
kich'ayŏk 기차역 railroad
station
kich'e 기체 gas (oxygen etc)
kich'im 기침 cough
kich'imhada 기침하다
cough
kich'im yak 기침 약 cough
medicine
kich'o 기초 basis; foundations
◊ basic
kich'o chagŏp 기초 작업
groundwork
kich'ohada 기초하다 be
based on
kich'ojŏgin 기초적인 basic
kida 기다 crawl
kidae 기대 expectation
kidaeda 기대다 rely on; lean;
balance; recline
kidaedoenŭn 기대되는
prospective
kidaehada 기대하다 expect
kidarida 기다리다 wait (for)
kido 기도 prayer
kidohada 기도하다 pray
Kidok-kkyo shinja 기독교
신자 Christian (person)
kidung 기둥 pillar
kigan 기간 period
kigwan 기관 institution;
machinery (governmental)

kigwanch'ong 기관총 machine gun

kigye 기계 machine ◊ mechanical

kigyehwahada 기계화하다 mechanize

kigyejŏgin 기계적인 mechanical

kigyejŏguro 기계적으로 mechanically

kiho 기호 symbol; choice

kihoe 기회 opportunity

kihonja 기혼자 married person

kihu 기후 climate

kiip'ada 기입하다 fill in

kija 기자 reporter

kijahoegyŏn 기자회견 press conference

kijinmaektchinhan 기진맥진한 dog-tired

kijŏgwi 기저귀 diaper

kijŏk 기적 miracle

kijŏktchŏgin 기적적인 miraculous

kijŏrhada 기절하다 faint

kijŭng 기증 donation

kijŭnghada 기증하다 donate

kijun 기준 standard

kikkŏi 기꺼이 gladly

kikkwŏn 기권 abstention

kikkwŏnhada 기권하다 abstain

kil 길 route; road; path

kilda 길다 be long

kilge 길게 at length

kilge pomyŏn 길게 보면 in the long run

kilka 길가 roadside

kim 김 steam; laver

kimch'i 김치 kimchee *(spicy pickled cabbage)*

kimppap 김밥 rice rolled in edible seaweed

kin 긴 long

kin-gŭp 긴급 urgency

kinjang 긴장 tension

kinjangdoeda 긴장되다 be tense

kinjangdoen 긴장된 tense

kinjanghan 긴장한 tense

kinjang-ŭl p'ulda 긴장을 풀다 relax

kin somaeŭi 긴 소매의 long-sleeved

kinyŏm 기념 commemoration ◊ memorial

kinyŏmbi 기념비 monument

kinyŏmhada 기념하다 commemorate

kinyŏmil 기념일 (wedding) anniversary

kiŏk 기억 memory

kiŏk'ada 기억하다 remember; store COMPUT

kiŏngnyŏk 기억 memory

kippke 깊게 deeply

kippŏhada 기뻐하다 be delighted

kippŏhanŭn 기뻐하는 delighted

kiptta 깊다 be deep

kippŭda 기쁘다 be glad
kippŭge 기쁘게 happily
kippŭn 기쁜 pleased
kip'i 깊이 depth ◊ deeply
kip'ŏgada 깊어가다 advance
kip'ŭn 깊은 deep
kiri 길이 length
kirin 기린 giraffe
kirogŭl kkaenŭn 기록을 깨는 record-breaking
kirok 기록 memo; archives; writing (script); record
kirŭda 기르다 keep; grow; breed
kirŭm 기름 oil
kirŭmch'irŭl hada 기름칠을 하다 oil
kirŭmkki manŭn 기름기 많은 oily
kisa 기사 article (in paper); engineer; (machine) operator
kisang yebo 기상 예보 weather forecast
kisŏngbok 기성복 ready-to-wear clothes
kiso 기소 prosecution
kisohada 기소하다 prosecute
kisuk hak-kkyo 기숙 학교 boarding school
kisukssa 기숙사 dormitory
kisulchŏgin 기술적인 technical
kisulchŏgŭro 기술적으로 technically
kit 깃 collar

kitppal 깃발 flag
kit'a 기타 the rest; and so on; guitar
kit'adŭngdŭng 기타 등등 and so on
kiulda 기울다 slant; swing
kiulgi 기울기 slope
kiuni nada 기운이 나다 cheer up
kiurida 기울이다 devote; tilt
kiyŏ 기여 contribution
kiyŏhada 기여하다 contribute (to discussion)
kkadaroptta 까다롭다 be difficult; be strict; be picky
kkadaroun 까다로운 fussy; tricky
kkaeda 깨다 break record; rouse
kkaedarŭm 깨달음 enlightenment
kkaedat-tta 깨닫다 realize
kkaejida 깨지다 break
kkaejin 깨진 broken
kkaekkŭshi 깨끗이 completely
kkaekkŭt'ada 깨끗하다 be clean; be pure; be chaste
kkaekkŭt'an 깨끗한 clean; pure; neat
kkaeŏinnŭn 깨어있는 awake
kkaeŏjigi shiun 깨어지기 쉬운 breakable
kkaettŭrida 깨뜨리다 break; break off; terminate

kkaeuda

kkaeuda 깨우다 wake

kkaji 까지 until; by; to; up to

kkaktta 깎다 cut; trim; shave; sharpen; peel; haggle

kkakttugi 깍두기 *spicy, pickled white radish*

kkamtchak nollada 깜짝 놀라다 be astonished

kkamtchak 깜짝

kkangmarŭn 깡마른 skinny

kkangp'ae 깡패 gangster

kkangt'ong 깡통 can

kkich'ida 끼치다 cause

kkilkkil ut-tta 낄낄 웃다 giggle

kkiwŏ nŏt'a 끼워 넣다 insert

kkŏjida 꺼지다 go out *(of candle)*; collapse; vanish

kkŏjin 꺼진 dead *battery*

kkŏktta 꺾다 destroy; break off; pluck; dash

kkŏm 껌 chewing gum

kkŏnaeda 꺼내다 take out

kkŏptchil 껍질 shell; peel

kkŏrida 꺼리다 shun

kkŏrimch'ik'ada 꺼림칙 하다 be uncomfortable about

kkobak 꼬박 whole

kkoch'i p'ida 꽃이 피다 flower

kkoda 꼬다 twist

kkoe 꾀 strategem

kkojiptta 꼬집다 pinch

kkok 꼭 surely; firmly; exactly

kkoktchi 꼭지 stem; faucet; nipple; handle

kkokttaegi 꼭대기 top

kkoma 꼬마 urchin

kkomtchak'ada 꼼짝하다 budge

kkongch'o 꽁초 stub

kkonnip 꽃잎 petal

kkori 꼬리 tail

kkorip'yo 꼬리표 label

kkot 꽃 flower

kkotppyŏng 꽃병 vase

kkot-tta 꽂다 attach; pin

kkot-ttabal 꽃다발 bouquet

kkŭda 끄다 blow out; switch off; be off; stall

kkŭdŏmnŭn 끝없는 endless

kkŭlda 끌다 pull; move slowly; attract; prolong; appeal to

kkŭllida 끌리다 trail; be dragged; be attracted to

kkŭlt'a 끓다 boil

kkŭmtchik'ada 끔찍하다 be hideous

kkŭmtchik'an 끔찍한 hideous

kkŭn 끈 band *(material)*; lace *(for shoe)*; tie; string; strap

kkŭn-gi 끈기 perseverance

kkŭnimŏpsshi kyesok'aesŏ 끊임없이 계속해서 endlessly

kkŭnjilgin 끈질긴 dogged; high-powered; nagging *pain*

kkŭnnada 끝나다 end; result in

kkŭnnaeda 끝내다 finish

kkŭnŏjida 끊어지다 break;

blow *fuse*; break off with; be interrupted; run out
kkŭnŏjin 끊어진 dead *(phone)*
kkŭnt'a 끊다 give up; disconnect; hang up TEL
kkŭrida 끓이다 boil
kkŭrŏ nŏmch'ida 끓어 넘치다 boil over
kkŭrŏ ollida 끓어 올리다 boost; push up; connect
kkŭt 끝 end *(of street)*; edge; point; nozzle ◊ exit COMPUT
kkŭt'ŭro 끝으로 in conclusion
kkubŏk-kkubŏk cholda 꾸벅꾸벅 졸다 doze off
kkubulkkuburhan 꾸불꾸불한 winding *road*
kkujit-tta 꾸짖다 scold
kkujunhada 꾸준하다 be persistent
kkujunhan 꾸준한 unrelenting
kkul 꿀 honey
kkum 꿈 dream
kkumgat'ŭn 꿈같은 dreamlike
kkumin iyagi 꾸민 이야기 fiction
kkumkkuda 꿈꾸다 dream
kkumuldaenŭn 꾸물대는 slow
kkumulgŏrida 꾸물거리다 dawdle
kkurŏmi 꾸러미 bundle

kkwae 꽤 quite
kkwaenggwari 꽹과리 small gong *(made of brass)*
kkwak 꽉 hard; fast; full; compact
kkwak chwida 꽉 쥐다 clasp
kkwak ch'ada 꽉 차다 be jam-packed
kkwak ch'an 꽉 찬 completely full
kkwemaeda 꿰매다 sew; stitch; darn
kkyŏantta 껴안다 clasp
kŏaegŭi sanggŭm 거액의 상금 jackpot
kŏbe chillida 겁에 질리다 be terrified
kŏbe chillin 겁에 질린 panic-stricken
kŏbi manŭn 겁이 많은 easily frightened
kŏbuhada 거부하다 veto; reject
kŏbuk 거북 turtle; tortoise
kŏbuk'aehada 거북해하다 feel awkward
kŏbuk'an 거북한 awkward
kŏch'ida 걷히다 lift *(of fog)*
kŏch'ilda 거칠다 be rough
kŏch'in 거친 rough
kŏch'yŏsŏ 거쳐서 via
kŏdaehada 거대하다 be enormous
kŏdaehan 거대한 enormous
kŏji 거지 beggar

kŏjinmal 거짓말 lie

kŏjinmaljaengi 거짓말쟁이 liar

kŏjinmarhada 거짓말하다 lie

kŏjit 거짓 pretense

kŏjŏrhada 거절하다 deny; reject; refuse

kŏjuhada 거주하다 inhabit; reside

kŏjuja 거주자 inhabitant; resident

kŏkkuro 거꾸로 upside down; back to front

kŏkkuro hada 거꾸로 하다 reverse

kŏkkuro toen 거꾸로 된 inverse *order*; reverse

kŏktchŏng 걱정 worry

kŏktchŏnghada 걱정하다 worry; be worried

kŏktchŏnghanŭn 걱정하는 anxious

kŏktchŏngsŭrŏn 걱정스런 worried

kŏlda 걸다 hang; stake; be on *(of brake)*

kŏlle 걸레 cloth; tramp *(woman)*

kŏllejirhada 걸레질하다 mop; swab; wipe

kŏltchuk'age hada 걸쭉하게 하다 thicken

kŏltchuk'an 걸쭉한 thick

kŏm 검 sword

kŏman 거만 arrogance

kŏmanhada 거만하다 be arrogant

kŏmanhan 거만한 arrogant

kŏmda 검다 be black; be dark

kŏmi 거미 spider

kŏmjŏngsaek 검정색 black

kŏmmanŭn 겁많은 timid

kŏmmŏkta 겁먹다 be afraid

kŏmmunso 검문소 checkpoint

kŏmnada 겁나다 be frightened (of)

kŏmnage hanŭn 겁나게 하는 terrifying

kŏmnanŭn 겁나는 frightening

kŏmsa 검사 examination *(of patient)*; prosecutor ◇ exploratory

kŏmsaek'ada 검색하다 navigate

kŏmt'ohada 검토하다 check; consider

kŏmŭn 검은 black

kŏmyŏrhada 검열하다 censor

kŏnbae 건배! cheers!

kŏnbaehada 건배하다 toast

kŏnbangjida 건방지다 be impertinent

kŏnbangjin 건방진 insolent

kŏnch'uk 건축 building

kŏnch'ungmul 건축물 structure

kŏn-gang 건강 health

kŏn-ganghada 건강하다

be healthy

kŏn-ganghan 건강한
healthy

kŏn-gang sangt'ae 건강
상태 state of health

kŏnjŏnhan 건전한
wholesome

kŏnjogi 건조기 drier; dry
season

kŏnjohada 건조하다 be dry

kŏnjohan 건조한 dry

kŏnnejuda 건네주다 hand
over

kŏnnŏda 건너다 cross

kŏnnŏ p'yŏn 건너 편 on the
other side of

kŏnnŏsŏ 건너서 across

kŏnp'odo 건포도 raisin

kŏptchaeng-i 겁쟁이 coward

kŏptchuda 겁주다 frighten

kŏp'um 거품 bubble; foam

kŏrae 거래 deal; business

kŏraehada 거래하다 deal
with; bank with

kŏri 거리 distance; street

kŏri 걸이 rack

kŏrŏdanida 걸어다니다
walk around

kŏrŏsŏ 걸어서 on foot

kŏrŭda 거르다 filter

kŏrŭm 걸음 step

kŏshida: ...*I kŏshida* ... ㄹ
것이다 will

kŏshiktchŭng 거식증
anorexia

kŏshil 거실 living room

kŏsŭllŏ ollagada 거슬러
올라가다 go back

kŏt 것 thing

kŏt-tta 걷다 walk

kŏt'ŭronŭn 겉으로는
outwardly

kŏŭi 거의 almost

kŏul 거울 mirror

...ko …고 and

koa 고아 orphan

koap 고압 high voltage;
high pressure ◊ high-voltage;
high-pressure

koap kkassŭ 고압 가스
propellant

koawŏn 고아원 orphanage

kobaek 고백 confession

kobaek'ada 고백하다
confess

kobal 고발 accusation

kobarhada 고발하다 accuse

koch'ida 고치다 correct;
repair

koch'ŭng piltting 고층 빌딩
high-rise building

koch'u 고추 chili pepper

koch'ugaru 고추가루 chili
(pepper) powder

koch'ujang 고추장 chili
pepper paste

kodae 고대 antiquity
◊ ancient

kodok 고독 solitude

kodok'ada 고독하다 be
solitary

kodok'an 고독한 solitary

kodŭn 곧은 straight

kodŭrŭm 고드름 icicle

koemul 괴물 monster

koengjanghada 굉장하다 be awesome

koengjanghage 굉장하게 extremely

koengjanghan 굉장한 awesome

koengjanghi 굉장히 tremendously

koerop'ida 괴롭히다 torment

koetcha 괴짜 crank

kogaek 고객 customer

kogaerŭl kkŭdögida 고개를 끄덕이다 nod one's head

kogi 고기 meat

kogŭp 고급 high-class

koguk 고국 home; native country

kogwihan 고귀한 noble

kohae 고해 confession

kohaehada 고해하다 confess

koham 고함 roar

koham chirŭda 고함 지르다 yell

kohwan 고환 testicle

kohyang 고향 home(town)

kohyŏrap 고혈압 hypertension

koin 고인 the deceased

koindol 고인돌 dolmen

kojajiljaeng-i 고자질쟁이 telltale

kojajirhada 고자질하다 tell tales

kojang 고장 breakdown; crash (of computer)

kojang-i nada 고장이 나다 break down; crash COMPUT

kojangnan 고장난 out of order

kojip 고집 obstinacy

kojip'ada 고집하다 be stubborn; adhere to

kojishik'an 고지식한 conservative

kojŏn 고전 classic

kojŏngdoeda 고정되다 be fixed

kojŏngdoen 고정된 fixed

kojŏnghada 고정하다 fix

kojŏngshik'ida 고정시키다 fix; attach; stabilize; strap in

kokka toro 고가 도로 overpass

kolch'itkkŏri 골칫거리 bother

kolch'o 골초 heavy smoker

kolk'ip'ŏ 골키퍼 goalkeeper

kollan 곤란 hardship; embarrassment

kollanhada 곤란하다 be arduous; be awkward

kolmok 골목 alley

kolmok-kkil 골목길 side street

kolp'ŭ 골프 golf

koltchagi 골짜기 valley

koltchitkkŏri 골칫거리

nuisance

kolttongp'um 골동품 antique

kom 곰 bear *(animal)*

komak 고막 eardrum

komapkkedo 고맙게도 thankfully

komaptta 고맙다 thank

komin 고민 distress

komindoenŭn 고민되는 vexed

kominhada 고민하다 worry

komo 고모 aunt *(own, sister of father)*; consult

komobu 고모부 uncle *(own, father's sister's husband)*

komp'ang-i p'in 고팡이 핀 moldy

komtta 곪다 go septic

komu 고무 rubber

komun 고문 adviser; torture

komunhada 고문하다 torture

konch'ung 곤충 insect

kongbaek 공백 blank; empty space; gap

kongbu 공부 study

kongbuhada 공부하다 study

kongch'aek 공책 notebook

kongch'ŏga 공처가 henpecked husband

kongdong 공동 cooperation ◊ joint

kongdongch'e 공동체 community

konggaehada 공개하다 unveil *plans*

konggaejŏgin 공개적인 public

konggaejŏguro 공개적으로 publicly

konggal 공갈 blackmail

konggal ch'ida 공갈 치다 blackmail

konggan 공간 space

konggi 공기 air; (rice) bowl

konggo 공고 notice

konggohada 공고하다 notify

konggong 공공 notice

konggŭp 공급 supply

konggŭp'ada 공급하다 supply

konggun 공군 air force

konggyŏk 공격 offensive

konggyŏktchŏgin 공격적인 aggressive

konggyŏk'ada 공격하다 attack

konghang 공항 airport

konghŏn 공헌 contribution

konghŏnhada 공헌하다 contribute *(with time)*

Kongja 공자 Confucius

kongjang 공장 factory

kongjŏnghada 공정하다 be fair

kongjŏnghage 공정하게 fairly

kongjŏnghan 공정한 fair

kongjŭng 공증 notarization

kongjung 공중 public; air; midair

kongjung chŏnhwa 공중 전화 pay phone

kongmuwŏn 공무원 civil servant

kongno 공로 credit

kongnyŏnhada 공연하다 perform; co-star; be futile

kongnyong 공룡 dinosaur

kongp'o 공포 horror

kongp'o yŏnghwa 공포 영화 horror movie

kongp'yŏnghan 공평한 detached

kongsa 공사 construction; public and private affairs; minister

kongsajang 공사장 building site

Kongsandang 공산당 Communist Party

kongsang kwahak sosŏl 공상 과학 소설 science fiction

kongshik 공식 formula; formality ◊ formal

kongshiktchŏgin 공식적인 ceremonial

kongshiktchŏguro 공식적으로 officially

kongsŏk 공석 vacancy

kongsonhada 공손하다 be polite

kongsonhage 공손하게 politely

kongsonhan 공손한 polite

kongtcharo 공짜로 for free

kongtchŏgin 공적인 official

kongtchŏguro 공적으로 formally

kongt'eip'ŭ 공테이프 blank tape

kongt'ong 공통 common

kongt'ong-ŭro 공통으로 in common

kong-wŏn 공원 park

kong-yŏn 공연 performance

kong-yŏnhada 공연하다 perform

kopssem 곱셈 multiplication

kopssülgŏrinŭn 곱슬거리는 curly

koptta 곱다 be fine; be fair; be pretty; be gentle

kop'ada 곱하다 multiply

kora ttŏrŏjida 끓아 떨어지다 crash out

korae 고래 whale

koripsshik'ida 고립시키다 isolate

koripttoen 고립된 lonely

korŭda 고르다 choose

korŭge 고르게 evenly

koryŏ 고려 consideration

koryŏhada 고려하다 allow for; consider

kosaeng 고생 hardship; toil

kosaenghada 고생하다 suffer

kosang 고상 elegance

kosanghan 고상한 elegant

kosokttoro 고속도로 expressway

kosok yŏlch'a 고속 열차 high-speed train

kot 곧 soon

kot 곳 joint; place; patch

kotppparo 곧바로 straight; straight away

kot-tchang 곧장 straight; directly

kot'ong 고통 suffering

kot'ongsŭrŏun 고통스러운 painful

koun 고운 fine

koyak'ada 고약하다 be foul; be bad

koyak'an 고약한 ugly; vicious; foul; bad

koyang-i 고양이 cat

koyo 고요 peace; silence

koyohada 고요하다 be calm

koyohan 고요한 calm

koyongdoen 고용된 in the pay of

koyonghada 고용하다 employ

koyong-in 고용인 employee; servant

koyongju 고용주 employer

kŭ 그 the ◊ he

kŭbakke 그밖에 everyone else

kŭ chik'ue 그 직후에 whereupon

kŭ chŏne paro 그 전에 바로 shortly before that

kŭ chŏngdo 그 정도 thereabouts

kŭ chŏngdo-ŭi 그 정도의 such a ◊ to that extent

kŭ chŏnjue 그 전주에 the week before

kŭ chŏnnal 그 전날 the day before

kŭ chŏnnare 그 전날에 the day before

kŭch'ida 그치다 stop

kŭgŏsŭn 그것은 it

kŭ hue 그 후에 subsequently

kŭ ihue 그 이후에 after that

kŭjŏkke 그저께 the day before yesterday

kŭjŏ kŭrŏn 그저 그런 so so

kŭk 극 pole

kŭ kose 그 곳에 there

kŭkppok'ada 극복하다 overcome

kŭktchang 극장 theater

kŭktchŏgin 극적인 dramatic

kŭlsshi 글씨 handwriting

kŭltcha 글자 letter; character

kŭltcha kŭdaero 글자 그대로 literally

kŭm 금 gold; fracture

kŭmaek 금액 amount

kŭmanduda 그만두다 stop; drop; drop out

kŭmbang 금방 immediately

kŭmbung-ŏ 금붕어 goldfish

kŭmhada 금하다 forbid

kŭmi kada 금이 가다 crack; split up

kŭmi kan

kŭmi kan 금이 간 cracked
kŭmji 금지 ban
kŭmjidoen 금지된 forbidden
kŭmjihada 금지하다 forbid
kŭmnyoil 금요일 Friday
kŭmshik 금식 fast *(no eating)*
kŭmul 그물 net
kŭmyŏn 금연 no smoking
kŭnbon 근본 origin
kŭnbonjŏgin 근본적인 basic
kŭnbonjŏguro 근본적으로 radically
kŭnch'ŏ 근처 vicinity
kŭne 그네 swing
kŭngjŏngjŏgin 긍정적인 positive
kŭn-gyo 근교 suburbs ◊ suburban
kŭnmuhada 근무하다 serve
kŭnmu shigan 근무 시간 work hours
kŭnsahan 근사한 gorgeous
kŭnshianŭi 근시안의 shortsighted
kŭnŭl 그늘 shade
kŭnŭljin 그늘진 shady
kŭnŭn 그는 he
kŭnyang 그냥 as it is; just
kŭnyŏ 그녀 she
kŭnyuk 근육 muscle ◊ muscular
kŭpssangssŭng 급상승 sudden increase
kŭpssangssŭnghada 급상승하다 increase

kŭp'ada 급하다 be urgent; be impatient; be sudden
kŭp'aeng 급행 express; haste
kŭp'an 급한 urgent; hasty
kŭraedo 그래도 nevertheless
kŭraesŏ 그래서 and; so that; that's why
kŭraeyaman hada 그래야만 하다 must do
kŭraeyo 그래요 really; yes
kŭri 그리 so ◊ there
kŭrida 그리다 draw; paint
kŭrigo 그리고 and
kŭrigo nasŏ 그리고 나서 then
kŭrim 그림 picture
kŭrimgwa kat'ŭn 그림과 같은 picturesque
kŭrimja 그림자 shadow
kŭrimŭl kŭrida 그림을 그리다 draw
kŭrimyŏpssŏ 그림엽서 (picture) postcard
kŭriwŏhada 그리워하다 miss
kŭrŏch'i anŭmyŏn 그렇지 않으면 otherwise
kŭrŏch'iman 그렇지만 but
kŭrŏgil paramnida 그러길 바랍니다 I hope so
kŭrŏktchŏrŏk hada 그럭저럭 하다 get by
kŭrŏk'e 그렇게 such; so
kŭrŏlttŭt'an 그럴듯한 probable
kŭrŏmedo pulguhago

그럼에도 불구하고 nevertheless

kŭrŏmŭro 그러므로 therefore

kŭrŏmyŏnsŏdo 그러면서도 at the same time

kŭrŏn 그런 such

kŭrŏna 그러나 but

kŭrŏnde 그런데 but

kŭrŏt'a 그렇다 be that way; be true

kŭrŏt'a hadŏrado 그렇다 하더라도 even so

kŭrŏt'amyŏn 그렇다면 then; if so

kŭrŏt'ŏrado 그렇더라도 though

kŭrŭl ssŭda 글을 쓰다 write

kŭrŭt 그릇 dish ◊ countword for cooked rice

kŭrŭttoen 그릇된 false

kŭ saie 그 사이에 meanwhile

kŭ tangshienŭn 그 당시에는 in those days

kŭ taŭmnal 그 다음날 the next day

kŭ ttae 그 때 at that time

kŭ ttaenŭn 그 때에는 by then

kŭŭi 그의 his

kŭ yŏja 그 여자 she

ku 구 nine; sphere; district

kuburida 구부리다 bend

kuburigi shwiun 구부리기 쉬운 flexible

kuburŏjin 구부러진 crooked

kubyŏl 구별 distinction

kubyŏlhada 구별하다 differentiate

kuch'urhada 구출하다 extricate

kudŏgi 구더기 maggot

kudu 구두 shoe

kudusoe 구두쇠 miser

kudu susŏntchip 구두 수선집 shoe repairer

kugida 구기다 crease

kugimsal 구김살 crease

Kugŏ 국어 Korean language

kugŏrhada 구걸하다 beg

kugŭpch'a 구급차 ambulance

kugyŏjida 구겨지다 crease; ruffle

kugyŏng 구경 sightseeing; aperture; caliber

kugyŏnghada 구경하다 see; watch; see the sights

kugyŏngkkun 구경꾼 onlooker

kuhada 구하다 rescue

kujo 구조 set-up; structure; rescue; salvation

kujo chŏjŏng 구조 조정 structural alteration

kujohada 구조하다 rescue

kujowŏn 구조원 lifeguard

kyejwa 구좌 account

kyejwa pŏnho 구좌 번호 account number

kuk 국 soup

kuk kŭrŭt

kuk kŭrŭt 국 그릇 soup bowl

kukki 국기 (national) flag

kuk-kka 국가 nation; national anthem

kuk-kkyŏng 국경 border

kukkun 국군 armed forces

kukssu 국수 noodles

kuktcha 국자 ladle

kuktche 국제 international

kuktchejŏgin 국제적인 international

kuktchŏk 국적 nationality

kuk'wa 국화 chrysanthemum

kul 굴 oyster; tunnel; burrow

kulgok 굴곡 bend

kulttuk 굴뚝 chimney; funnel

kumae 구매 purchase

kumaehada 구매하다 purchase

kumjurida 굶주리다 starve

kumŏng 구멍 hole; pit; puncture

kumŏng ttult'a 구멍 뚫다 puncture; punch a hole in

kun 군 army; county; Mr; Lord

kunch'im hŭllida 군침 흘리다 drool

kunggŭmhada 궁금하다 wonder

kunghada 궁하다 be in want

kungji 궁지 predicament

kungmin 국민 citizen

kungmul 국물 broth

kungnip kong-wŏn 국립

공원 national park

kun-goguma 군고구마 baked sweet potato

kunin 군인 soldier; serviceman

kunjung 군중 crowd

kunsal 군살 flab

kuptta 굽다 bake; roast; broil

kurŭm 구름 cloud

Kusegun 구세군 Salvation Army

kushik 구식 old-fashioned

kuship 구십 ninety

kusŏk 구석 corner

kusŏnghada 구성하다 constitute

kusok'ada 구속하다 restrict; intern

kusŭl 구슬 beads

kut 굿 shaman exorcism

kut'a 구타 beating

kut'ahada 구타하다 beat up

kut'o 구토 vomit

kuun 구운 baked

kuwŏl 구월 September

kuwŏn 구원 salvation

kuwŏnhada 구원하다 redeem

Kuyak Sŏngsŏ 구약 성서 Old Testament

kwa 과 department; faculty; lesson ◊ with ◊ and

kwabansu 과반수 majority

kwabu 과부 widow

kwaench'ant'a 괜찮다 be alright

kwaench'anŭn 괜찮은
acceptable

kwagŏ 과거 past

kwagŏe 과거에 in the past

kwahak 과학 science

kwahaktcha 과학자 scientist

kwail 과일 fruit

kwail chyussŭ 과일 쥬스
fruit juice

kwajang 과장 exaggeration;
department manager

kwajangdoen 과장된
exaggerated

kwajanghada 과장하다
exaggerate

kwajaryu 과자류
confectionery

kwaje 과제 project

kwajŏng 과정 process

kwak 곽 carton; holder; tub

kwalli 관리 management;
administration; mandarin

kwalliin 관리인 manager;
administrator; caretaker

kwallyŏn 관련 connection

kwallyŏndoeda 관련되다
be connected with; be relevant

kwallyŏndoen 관련된
related; relevant

kwamok 과목 subject

kwan 관 casket; pipe; tube;
crown; mansion

kwanch'al 관찰 observation

kwanch'arhada 관찰하다
observe

kwandaehada 관대하다 be

generous

kwandaehan 관대한
generous; broadminded

-kwang -광 fan; craze

kwan-gaek 관객 spectator

Kwangboktchŏl 광복절
Liberation Day

kwangch'ŏnsu 광천수
mineral water

kwanggo 광고
advertisement; advertising

kwanggohada 광고하다
advertise

kwanggyŏng 광경 spectacle

kwangjang 광장 plaza

kwangsan 광산 mine

kwangshinja 광신자 fanatic

kwangshinjŏgin 광신적인
fanatical

kwan-gwang 관광 sightseeing

kwan-gwang annaeso 관광
안내소 tourist (information)
office

kwan-gwanggaek 관광객
tourist

kwan-gwanghada 관광하다
tour; go sightseeing

kwan-gwang yŏhaeng 관광
여행 sightseeing tour

kwan-gye 관계 relationship

kwan-gyedoeda 관계되다
get involved with

kwan-gyedoenŭn 관계되는
concerned

kwan-gyehada 관계하다
involve; get mixed up with

kwan-gyeŏmnŭn 관계없는 unrelated

kwanhada 관하다 be related to

kwanhae tŭt-tta 관해 듣다 hear about

kwanjung 관중 audience

kwanjungsŏk 관중석 auditorium

kwanshim 관심 interest

kwanshimi innŭn 관심이 있는 interested

kwanshimŭl kajida 관심을 가지다 care about

kwansŭp 관습 custom

kwansŭptchŏgin 관습적인 customary

kwantchŏm 관점 point of view

kwarho 괄호 parenthesis

kwaro 과로 overwork

kwarohada 과로하다 overwork

kwashi 과시 demonstration

kwashihada 과시하다 show off

kwashihanŭn 과시하는 ostentatious

kwasok 과속 speeding

kwasok pŏlgŭm 과속 벌금 speeding fine

kwasok'ada 과속하다 speed

kwasuwŏn 과수원 orchard

kwi 귀 ear

kwich'ant'a 귀찮다 be a nuisance

kwiga 귀가 homecoming

kwigahada 귀가하다 return home

kwigori 귀고리 earring

kwijunghada 귀중하다 be precious

kwijunghan 귀중한 precious

kwimŏgŭn 귀먹은 deaf

kwishin 귀신 ghost

kwitturami 귀뚜라미 cricket (insect)

kwiyŏptta 귀엽다 be cute

kwiyŏun 귀여운 cute

kwŏlli 권리 right

kwŏn 권 bloc ◊ countword for books

kwŏnch'ong 권총 pistol

kwŏnhada 권하다 offer

kwŏnt'u shihap 권투 시합 boxing match

kwŏnt'u sŏnsu 권투 선수 boxer

kwŏnwi 권위 authority

kwŏnwiinnŭn 권위있는 authoritative

-kye: *chaejŭgye* 재즈계 jazz scene; *yŏngŭk-kkye* 연극계 the world of the theater

kye 계 loan club

kyebu 계부 stepfather

kyedan 계단 stair

kyegŭp 계급 class; stripe

kyegŭp chojik 계급 조직 hierarchy

kyehoek 계획 plan; project; strategy

kyehoektchŏgin 계획적인
premeditated

kyehoek'ada 계획하다 plan

kyejibae 계집애 little girl;
babe

kyejŏl 계절 season

kyemo 계모 stepmother

kyeran 계란 egg

kyesan 계산 calculation

kyesanhada 계산하다
calculate

kyesanjŏgin 계산적인
calculating

kyesansŏ 계산서 bill

kyesok ... it-tta 계속 ...
있다 remain

kyesok salda 계속 살다
live on

kyesoktchŏgin 계속적인
continual

kyesokttoeda 계속되다
continue

kyesokttoenŭn 계속되는
continuous

kyesok'ada 계속하다
continue; pursue

kyesok'aesŏ 계속해서 in
succession; perpetually

kyesŭng 계승 succession

kyesŭnghada 계승하다
succeed (to the throne)

kyeyak 계약 contract

kyeyak-kkŭm 계약금 down
payment

kyeyaktcha 계약자
contractor

kyŏdŭrang-i 겨드랑이
armpit

kyŏja 겨자 mustard

kyŏktta 겪다 experience

kyŏlbaek 결백 innocence

kyŏlbaek'an 결백한
innocent

kyŏlgŭn 결근 absence

kyŏlgŭnhan 결근한 absent

kyŏlguk 결국 finally

kyŏlkkwa 결과 result

kyŏlk'o 결코 surely

kyŏllon 결론 conclusion;
decision

kyŏllonŭl naerida 결론을
내리다 conclude

kyŏlsshim 결심
determination

kyŏlsshimhada 결심하다
decide

kyŏlssŏk 결석 absence

kyŏlssŏk'ada 결석하다
be absent

kyŏlssŏk'an 결석한 absent

kyŏlssŭngjŏn 결승전 finals

kyŏltchŏm 결점
shortcoming

kyŏltchŏm innŭn 결점 있는
faulty

kyŏltchŏng 결정 decision

kyŏltchŏnghada 결정하다
decide

kyŏltchŏngjŏgin 결정적인
conclusive

kyŏmson 겸손 humility

kyŏmsonhada 겸손하다
be humble

kyŏmsonhan 겸손한
modest; humble

kyŏndida 견디다 endure;
resist

kyŏndil su innŭn 견딜 수
있는 bearable

...kyŏng …경 about

kyŏngbiwŏn 경비원 security
guard

kyŏngbogi 경보기 alarm

kyŏngch'al 경찰 police

kyŏngch'also 경찰서 police
station

kyŏngch'i 경치 landscape;
view

kyŏnggi 경기 game; meet;
fight; play; business; things;
times

kyŏnggo 경고 warning

kyŏnggohada 경고하다 warn

kyŏnggwa 경과 passage

kyŏnggwahada 경과하다
elapse

kyŏnggye 경계 boundary

kyŏnggyehada 경계하다
look out for

kyŏnghŏm 경험 experience

kyŏnghŏminnŭn 경험있는
experienced

kyŏnghohada 경호하다
escort

kyŏngjaeng 경쟁 contest

kyŏngjaenghada 경쟁하다
compete

kyŏngjaengja 경쟁자
competitor

kyŏngjaengjŏgin 경쟁적인
competitive

kyŏngje 경제 economy

kyŏngjejŏgin 경제적인
economical

kyŏngjejŏguro 경제적으로
economically

kyŏngjeŭi 경제의 economic

kyŏngju 경주 race

kyŏngjuhada 경주하다 race

kyŏngmae 경매 auction

kyŏngmaehada 경매하다
auction

kyŏngmyŏl 경멸 contempt

kyŏngmyŏrhada 경멸하다
despise

kyŏngmyŏrhanŭn 경멸하는
derogatory

kyŏngnye 경례 salute; bow

kyŏngnyehada 경례하다
salute; bow

kyŏngnyŏ 격려 boost

kyŏngnyŏhada 격려하다
encourage

kyŏngnyŏng 경영
management

kyŏngnyŏnghada 경영하다
manage *big company*

kyŏngnyŏrhada 격렬하다
be violent

kyŏngnyŏrhage 격렬하게
violently

kyŏngnyŏrhan 격렬한

drastic *change*; turbulent

kyŏngŭirŭl p'yohada 경의를 표하다 show respect to

kyŏn-gwa 견과 nut

kyŏnhae 견해 opinion

kyŏninhada 견인하다 tow away

kyŏnjŏk 견적 estimate

kyŏnjŏk'ada 견적하다 quote

kyŏnyang 겨냥 aim

kyŏnyanghada 겨냥하다 aim (at); measure

kyŏrhap 결합 combination

kyŏrhap'ada 결합하다 combine

kyŏrhon 결혼 marriage

kyŏrhon kinyŏmil 결혼 기념일 wedding anniversary

kyŏrhon panji 결혼 반지 wedding ring

kyŏrhon saenghwal 결혼 생활 married life

kyŏrhonhada 결혼하다 get married

kyŏrhonhan 결혼한 married

kyŏrhonshik 결혼식 wedding

kyŏruda 겨루다 play; fight

kyŏt'e(sŏ) 곁에 (서) beside

kyŏu 겨우 barely

kyŏul 겨울 winter

kyobok 교복 uniform

kyoch'a 교차 intersection

kyoch'ahada 교차하다 intersect

kyoch'ajŏm 교차점 junction

kyodae 교대 shift; turn

kyodaehada 교대하다 relieve

kyodoso 교도소 penitentiary

kyohoe 교회 church

kyohun 교훈 moral; school motto

kyohwan 교환 exchange

kyohwang 교황 pope

kyohwanhada 교환하다 exchange

kyojang 교장 (school) principal

kyoje 교제 contact

kyojehada 교제하다 associate with

kyojŏng 교정 manipulation

kyojŏnghada 교정하다 manipulate

kyokkwa kwajŏng 교과 과정 course; curriculum

kyokkwasŏ 교과서 textbook

kyomyohada 교묘하다 be crafty

kyomyohan 교묘한 be sneaky

kyo-oe 교외 suburb

kyosa 교사 teacher; academic

kyoshil 교실 classroom

kyosu 교수 professor

kyot'ong 교통 traffic

kyot'ong honjap 교통 혼잡 traffic congestion

kyot'ong shinho 교통 신호 traffic sign

kyoyuk 교육 education

kyoyukpadŭn 교육받은 educated

Kyoyukppu 교육부
  Department of Education

kyoyuktchŏgin 교육적인
  educational

kyoyuk'ada 교육하다
  educate

kyuch'ik 규칙 rule

kyuch'iktchŏgin 규칙적인
  regular

kyujŏng 규정 stipulation

kyujŏnghada 규정하다
  stipulate

kyunhyŏng 균형 balance

kyunhyŏng chap'in 균형
잡힌 balanced

k'al 칼 knife

k'allal 칼날 blade

k'altchip 칼집 sheath

k'an 칸 compartment; panel;
section

k'ap'e 카페 café

k'i 키 height; key; helm

k'iga k'ŭn 키가 큰 tall

k'ilk'il ut-tta 킬킬 웃다
chuckle

k'ŏjida 커지다 grow

k'ŏmp'yut'ŏ 컴퓨터
computer

k'ŏmp'yut'ŏ keim 컴퓨터
게임 computer game

**k'ŏmp'yut'ŏro
t'ongjedoenŭn** 컴퓨터로
통제되는 computer-
controlled

k'ŏndishyŏn 컨디션
condition

k'ŏnyŏng 커녕 to say
nothing of

k'ŏp 컵 cup; glass

k'ŏp'i 커피 coffee

k'o 코 nose; trunk; stitch

k'okkiri 코끼리 elephant

k'o kolda 코 골다 snore

k'ong 콩 bean; soy bean

k'ongp'at 콩팥 soy and red
beans; kidney ANAT

k'onmul 콧물 mucus

k'onnoraerro purŭda
콧노래로 부르다 hum

k'op'i 코피 nosebleed; copy

k'otkkumŏng 콧구멍
nostril

k'ŭda 크다 be big

k'ŭge 크게 large ◊ very;
greatly; loudly

k'ŭgi 크기 size

k'ŭllik'ada 클릭하다 click
on

k'ŭn 큰 big

k'ŭn ton 큰 돈 big money

k'unghanŭn sori 쿵하는
소리 thud

k'ung'ung kŏt-tta 쿵쿵
걷다 tramp

k'waehwalhada 쾌활하다
be lively

k'waejŏk'an 쾌적한
delightful

k'walk'wal hŭllŏnaoda 콸콸
흘러나오다 gush out

k'wang! 꽝! bang!

k'wang pudich'ida 꽝

부딪히다 bang
k'wang tach'ida 쾅 닫히다
be slammed shut
k'wang tat-tta 쾅 닫다
slam shut
k'yŏda 켜다 switch on
k'yŏlle 켤레 pair ◊ *countword for shoes, socks*

L

...l ...ㄹ *future particle*
ladio 라디오 radio
ladio pangsongguk 라디오
방송국 radio station
lago hanŭn kŏsŭn 라고
하는 것은 so-called
lait'ŏ 라이터 lighter
lakk'ŭllol 락큰롤
rock'n'roll
lak'et 라켓 racket
launji 라운지 lounge
leida yŏngsang 레이더
영상 blip
leijyŏ 레이저 laser
leisŭ 레이스 lace
lemon 레몬 lemon
lenjŭ 렌즈 lens

lep'ot'ŭ 레포트 essay
lesŭlling 레슬링 wrestling
lidŭm 리듬 rhythm
lihŏsŏl 리허설 practice;
rehearsal
lihŏsŏrhada 리허설하다
rehearse
ling 링 ring
lipssŭt'ik 립스틱 lipstick
lisait'ŭl 리사이틀 recital
lŏning shyŏch'ŭ 러닝 셔츠
undershirt
logo 로고 logo
lolppang 롤빵 (bread) roll
lomaent'ik'ada 로맨틱하다
be romantic
loshyŏn 로션 lotion

M

mabi 마비 paralysis
mabŏbe kŏllin 마법에 걸린
spellbound
mabŏbŭi 마법의 occult
mabŏp 마법 the occult
mach'al 마찰 friction
mach'i ...ch'ŏrŏm 마치

...처럼 as though
mach'ida 마치다 end
mach'im 마침 just
mach'imnae 마침내 finally
mach'imp'yo 마침표 period
mach'wije 마취제 anesthetic
madi 마디 joint; word; phrase

mae-

mae- 매 each
maeda 매다 knot
maedalda 매달다 suspend
maedallida 매달리다 cling to
maedalmada 매달마다 monthly
maedŭp 매듭 knot; tassel
maehok 매혹 charm
maehoktchŏgin 매혹적인 charming
maehokttoeda 매혹되다 be fascinated by
maehok'ada 매혹하다 charm
maeil 매일 every day
maeil pame 매일 밤에 nightly
maejŏnghan 매정한 heartless
maeju 매주 every week
maejumada 매주마다 weekly
maekppak 맥박 pulse
maektchu 맥주 beer
maemaeshijang 매매시장 market
maen araetchok 맨 아래쪽 bottom
maenbarida 맨발이다 be barefoot
maeng-in 맹인 the blind
maengsehada 맹세하다 swear
maenwiŭi 맨위의 top
maenyŏn 매년 yearly

maeptta 맵다 be spicy
maep'yoso 매표소 ticket office
maeryŏginnŭn 매력있는 attractive
maeryŏk 매력 attraction
maeryŏktchŏgin 매력적인 charming
maeu 매우 tremendously
maeun 매운 spicy
maeunt'ang 매운탕 spicy fish soup
maewŏl 매월 every month
magae 마개 plug
magaerŭl ppoptta 마개를 뽑다 uncork
magamil 마감일 deadline
magi 막이 screen
mahŭn 마흔 forty
maik'ŭ 마이크 microphone
majayo! 맞아요! that's right!
maji 맏이 the eldest
majihada 맞이하다 meet with
majijak-kkŏrida 만지작거리다 fiddle with
majimagŭro 마지막으로 finally, lastly
maji mot'ae 마지 못해 reluctantly
majuhada 마주하다 confront
majungnagada 마중나가다 meet
majung naoda 마중 나오다 pick up

mak 막 membrane; slick; curtain; act

mak haryŏgo hada 막 하려고 하다 be about to

mak-kkŏlli 막걸리 rice wine

maktta 막다 block; prevent

makttaegi 막대기 stick

makttarŭn kil 막다른 길 cul-de-sac

mak'ida 막히다 clog up

mak'im 막힘 congestion

mal 말 horse; piece *(in game)*; end; word

malbŏl 말벌 wasp

malda 말다 stop

maldaekkuhada 말대꾸하다 answer back

maldat'umhada 말다툼하다 argue

maldo andoenda! 말도 안된다! out of the question!

maldo andoenŭn sori 말도 안 되는 소리 nonsense

malgajida 맑아지다 brighten up

malgŭn 맑은 clear

malgwallyang-i 말괄량이 tomboy

malktta 맑다 be clear; be honest

mallida 말리다 dry; dissuade; break up *fight*

mallin 말린 dried *fruit etc*

malssŏng 말썽 trouble

malssŏngkkun 말썽꾼 troublemaker

malttuk 말뚝 stake

malt'u 말투 way of speaking

mamurihada 마무리하다 finalize

man 만 bay; gulf; ten thousand ◊ after ◊ only

manbarhada 만발하다 come into full bloom

manch'an 만찬 dinner

manch'wihan 만취한 drunken

mandŭlda 만들다 make

mandu 만두 stuffed dumpling

mang-aji 망아지 foal

mangboda 망보다 keep watch

mangch'i 망치 hammer

mangch'ida 망치다 destroy

mangch'ijirhada 망치질하다 hammer

mangch'yŏnot'a 망쳐놓다 spoil

manggattŭrida 망가뜨리다 ruin

manghada 망하다 fail

man-gi 만기 termination

man-gidoeda 만기되다 expire

mangshinshik'ida 망신시키다 shame

mangsŏrida 망설이다 hesitate

mangsŏrim 망설임 hesitation

manhada 만하다 be worth

manhwa 만화 cartoon

manhwa ch'aek

manhwa ch'aek 만화 책
comic book

mani 많이 a lot; much

manjang-ilch'ihada
만장일치하다 be unanimous
on

manjang-ilch'iro
만장일치로 unanimously

manjida 만지다 touch

manjijak-kkŏrida
만지작거리다 meddle with

manjok 만족 satisfaction

manjokssŭrŏun 만족스러운
satisfactory

manjok'ada 만족하다 be
satisfied

manjok'an 만족한
satisfactory

manjok'anŭn 만족하는
content

mank'ŭm 만큼 as

mannada 만나다 meet

mannaeda 맛내다 flavor

mannam 만남 meeting

mannŭn 맞는 correct

manse! 만세! hurray!

mant'a 많다 be many

manŭl 마늘 garlic

manŭn 많은 many; much;
heavy

manura 마누라 wife

manyak 만약 ⋯myŏn 만약 ⋯면
if; on condition that

marhada 말하다 talk; speak;
say; tell

mari 마리 countword for

animals

mari manŭn 말이 많은
talkative

marŭda 마르다 dry; waste
away; run out (of money)

marŭl kkŏnaeda 말을
꺼내다 bring up

marŭl tŭt-tchi annŭn 말을
듣지 않는 disobedient

marŭn 마른 dry; thin

marutppadak 마룻바닥
floor

maryŏnhada 마련하다
provide

mashida 마시다 drink

mashinnŭn 맛있는 delicious

masul 마술 magic

masuljŏgin 마술적인
magical

masulssa 마술사 magician

mat 맛 taste

match'uda 맞추다 adjust; fit
together; be appropriate

matkkida 맡기다 entrust

matpakkuda 맛바꾸다
exchange

matppoda 맛보다 taste

mattanghage 마땅하게
justly

mattanghan 마땅한 due

mat-tchi ant'a 맞지 않다
be alien to

mat-tta 맞다 be right; fit;
take on job; suit; match; strike;
hit; meet; be exposed to; be
struck by; get

maŭl 마을 village

maŭm 마음 heart; mind; spirit

maŭme tŭlda 마음에 들다 be to sb's liking

maŭmi chobŭn 마음이 좁은 narrow-minded

maŭmi nŏlbŭn 마음이 넓은 broad-minded

maŭmŭl chŏnghada 마음을 정하다 make up one's mind

maŭmŭl pakkuda 마음을 바꾸다 change one's mind

mausŭ 마우스 mouse COMPUT

mayak 마약 drug

mayak p'anmaeja 마약 판매자 drug dealer

meari 메아리 echo

melppang 멜빵 suspenders

melppang paji 멜빵 바지 dungarees

memo 메모 note; memo

menyu 메뉴 menu also COMPUT

mesŭkkŏun 메스꺼운 repulsive

meuda 메우다 fill in

mianhamnida 미안합니다 form (I'm) sorry

mich'ida 미치다 go mad; be crazy; reach; happen; match

mich'igwang-i 미치광이 lunatic

mich'in 미친 insane

mich'in tŭshi 미친 듯이 madly

mich'yŏgada 미쳐가다 become insane

midaji mun 미닫이 문 sliding door

midŭm 믿음 belief

migak 미각 taste; palate

Migugin 미국인 American

mihaenghada 미행하다 follow

mijigŭnhan 미지근한 lukewarm

mikkŭrŏjida 미끄러지다 slip

mikkŭrŏmt'ŭl 미끄럼틀 slide

mikkŭrŏptta 미끄럽다 be slippery

mikkŭrŏun 미끄러운 slippery

mikssŏgi 믹서기 blender

milbong 밀봉 seal

milbonghada 밀봉하다 seal

milda 밀다 push

milgam 밀감 tangerine

milkkaru 밀가루 flour

milkkaru panjuk 밀가루 반죽 dough

millyŏ it-tta 밀려있다 be behind with

milmul 밀물 incoming tide

milmurida 밀물이다 the tide is out

milssu 밀수 smuggling

milssuhada 밀수하다 smuggle

miltchip 밀짚 straw

miman 미만 under

minbak 민박 vacation home

minbang-wi 민방위 civil
defense

min-gamhada 민감하다 be
sensitive

min-ganin 민간인 civilian

min-ganŭi 민간의 civil

mingk'ŭ k'ot'ŭ 밍크 코트
mink (coat)

minjogŭi 민족의 ethnic

Minjudang 민주당
Democratic Party of the USA

minjujuŭi 민주주의
democracy

minsok ch'um 민속 춤
folk dance

minsok ŭmak 민속 음악
folk music

minyo 민요 folk song

mirae 미래 future

miri 미리 beforehand

miri naeda 미리 내다
advance

miro 미로 maze

misa 미사 REL mass

Mishik ch'uk-kku 미식
축구 (American) football

mishin 미신 superstition

misŏngnyŏnja 미성년자
minor (child)

misŏngnyŏnŭi 미성년의
underage

miso 미소 smile

misojit-tta 미소짓다 smile
(at)

misulgwan 미술관 art
gallery

mit 밑 base

mitppadak 밑바닥 bottom

mit-tta 믿다 believe

mit'e 밑에 underneath

mit'ing 미팅 meeting; blind
date

mium 미움 hate

miwŏhada 미워하다 hate

miyongsa 미용사 beautician;
hairdresser

miyongshil 미용실 beauty
parlor

mŏdŏmnŭn 멋없는 tasteless

mŏgi 먹이 prey

mŏgida 먹이다 feed

mŏgŏ ch'iuda 먹어 치우다
eat up

mŏgŭjan 머그잔 mug

mŏgŭl su innŭn 먹을 수
있는 edible

mŏktta 먹다 eat

mŏlda 멀다 be distant; be
unskilled

mŏlli 멀리 far ◊ remotely

mŏlli ttŏrŏjin 멀리 떨어진
far away

mŏmch'uda 멈추다 stop;
stall; seize up

mŏmurŭda 머무르다 stay

mŏn 먼 distant

mŏngch'ŏng-i 멍청이 idiot

mŏngdŭlda 멍들다 bruise

mŏnghan 멍한 vacant

mŏngmŏng-i 멍멍이 doggie

mŏnjirŭl t'ŏlda 먼지를 털다 dust

mŏnjŏ 먼저 first

mŏnjŏtppŏnŭi 먼젓번의 past

mŏn kose(sŏ) 먼 곳에 (서) in the distance

mŏri 머리 head; hair; brains

mŏri kamtta 머리 감다 shampoo

mŏrik'arak 머리카락 hair

mŏrip'in 머리핀 hairpin

mŏrirŭl charŭda 머리를 자르다 have a haircut

mŏritkkisa 머릿기사 headline

mŏshinnŭn 멋있는 stylish; good-looking

mŏtchida 멋지다 be stylish

mŏtchige 멋지게 impeccably

mŏtchin 멋진 stylish

mobang 모방 imitation

mobanghada 모방하다 imitate

mobil 모빌 cell phone

mobŏmjŏgin 모범적인 exemplary

modakppul 모닥불 camp fire

model 모델 model

moderŭl hada 모델을 하다 model *clothes*

modok 모독 violation

modok'ada 모독하다 violate; blaspheme

modŭn 모든 all; whole; every

modu 모두 everyone

mogi 모기 mosquito

mogihyang 모기향 mosquito coil

mogijang 모기장 mosquito net

mogi marŭda 목이 마르다 be thirsty

mogi t'ada 목이 타다 be parched

mogugŏ 모국어 mother tongue

moguk 모국 native country

mogyoil 목요일 Thursday

mogyok 목욕 bath

mogyok'ang 목욕탕 public bathhouse

mogyok'ada 목욕하다 have a bath

mohŏm 모험 adventure

mohŏmjŏk 모험적 adventurous

mohŏmŭl hada 모험을 하다 venture

moida 모이다 meet

moim 모임 gathering

moja 모자 hat

mojarada 모자라다 be short of; be stupid

mojaranŭn 모자라는 scarce

mojop'um 모조품 imitation

mojori 모조리 without exception

mok 목 neck; throat

mok 몫 share

mok-kkŏri 목걸이 necklace
mok-kkŏrijul 목걸이줄 chain *(jewelry)*
mok-kkyŏktcha 목격자 (eye)witness
mok-kkyŏk'ada 목격하다 witness
mokkumŏng 목구멍 throat
mokp'yo 목표 objective
mokp'yoro hada 목표로 하다 target
mokssa 목사 priest
moksshwin 목쉰 hoarse
mokssori 목소리 voice
moktchŏk 목적 objective
moktchŏktchi 목적지 destination
mokttori 목도리 scarf
molda 몰다 drive
mollae 몰래 secretly
molttuhan 몰두한 preoccupied
mom 몸 body
mome kkok mannŭn 몸에 꼭 맞는 skin-tight
momi pulp'yŏnhan 몸이 불편한 unwell
mommae 몸매 figure
momttung-i 몸뚱이 trunk
momyŏnhada 모면하다 escape
monaegi 모내기 rice planting
mongmarŭda 목마르다 be thirsty
mongmarŭn 목마른 thirsty

mongnok 목록 list
mongsangga 몽상가 (day)dreamer
mongsanghada 몽상하다 (day)dream
mopsshi 몹시 terribly
morae 모래 sand
moranaeda 몰아내다 repel
more 모레 the day after tomorrow
morŭda 모르다 not know; not appreciate; ignore
morŭnŭn 모르는 unknown; ignorant
moshida 모시다 serve; accompany
mosŏng 모성 motherhood
mossaenggida 못생기다 be ugly
mosun 모순 contradiction
mosundoen 모순된 contradictory
mot 못 nail; peg
mot... 못… cannot
mot salge kulda 못 살게 굴다 bully
motssaenggin 못생긴 plain
mot-ttoen 못된 nasty
mot'ung-i 모퉁이 turning
moŭda 모으다 collect; save
moŭn 모은 collected
moyang 모양 appearance; shape
moyŏ it-tta 모여 있다 be gathered together
moyok 모욕 insult

moyok'ada 모욕하다 insult

mu... mu… non…

mu 무 radish

mubunbyŏl 무분별 indiscretion

mubunbyŏrhan 무분별한 indiscreet

much'ŏk 무척 extremely

mudae 무대 stage

mudang 무당 shaman (female)

mudin 무딘 blunt

mudŏm 무덤 grave

mudŏmdŏmhan 무덤덤한 impervious to

mugamgak'an 무감각한 callous; numb

muge 무게 weight

mugi 무기 weapon

mugŏptta 무겁다 be heavy; be important

mugŏun 무거운 heavy

mugonghaeŭi 무공해의 nonpolluting

Mugunghwa 무궁화 Rose of Sharon

mugwanshim 무관심 indifference

mugwanshimhan 무관심한 indifferent

muhan 무한 infinity

muhanhan 무한한 infinite

muhanŭi 무한의 boundless

muhyoyorohada 무효로 하다 annul

muhyoŭi 무효의 invalid

mujabihan 무자비한 merciless

mujanghan 무장한 armed

mujang kangdo 무장 강도 armed robbery; gunman

mujangshik'ida 무장시키다 arm

muji 무지 ignorance

mujigae 무지개 rainbow

mujilssŏ 무질서 lawlessness; disorder

mujilssŏhan 무질서한 disorganized

mujŏn-gi 무전기 walkie-talkie

mujokkŏnŭi 무조건의 unconditional

mujut'aektcha 무주택자 the homeless

mukke hada 묵게 하다 give accommodation

muk-kke hada 묽게 하다 dilute

mukkŏ not'a 묶어 놓다 tie down

mukkŭm 묶음 bundle; bunch

mukssang 묵상 meditation

mukssanghada 묵상하다 meditate

muktta 묶다 tie

mul 물 water

mulch'e 물체 object

mulda 물다 bite

mulgŏn 물건 stuff

mulgŭn 묽은 thin

mulkkae 물개 seal

mulkkam

mulkkam 물감 paint

mulkkirŭl ppaeda 물기를 빼다 drain

mulkkogi 물고기 fish

mulkkyŏl 물결 ripple; stream

mulli ch'iryo 물리 치료 physiotherapy

mullŏnada 물러나다 back away

mullon 물론 of course

mulloniji 물론이지 no problem

mullyŏjuda 물려주다 hand down; make over

mulmangch'o 물망초 forget-me-not

mulmul kyohwan 물물 교환 barter

mulppurigae 물뿌리개 watering can

multchip 물집 blister

multchirul 물질의 material

mulyak 물약 medicine

mumyŏng-ŭi 무명의 anonymous

mun 문 door

munbanggujŏm 문방구점 stationer's

mungch'i 뭉치 bundle

mungch'ida 뭉치다 unite

munhak 문학 literature

munhwa 문화 culture

munhwajŏgin 문화적인 cultural

munjang 문장 sentence

munje 문제 problem; trouble; question

munje haegyŏl 문제 해결 problem solving

munjeŏpsshi 문제없이 without any problems

munjirŭda 문지르다 rub

munmyŏng 문명 civilization

munŏjida 무너지다 collapse

munŏttŭrida 무너뜨리다 flatten

munppŏp 문법 grammar

munppŏpssang-ŭi 문법상의 grammatical

munshin 문신 tattoo

munsŏ 문서 document

muntcha 문자 character

muntchibang 문지방 doorstep

munŭi 문의 inquiry

munŭi 무늬 pattern

munŭihada 문의하다 inquire

munŭi innŭn 무늬 있는 patterned

munŭng 무능 inability

munŭnghada 무능하다 be incompetent

munŭngnyŏk'an 무능력한 incompetent

muŏshidŭn 무엇이든 whatever

muŏt 무엇 something; anything; what

muŏttpodado 무엇보다도 above all

muri 무리 group; strain

murihada 무리하다 be
unreasonable

murihanŭn 무리하는
compulsive

murihan yogu 무리한 요구
excessive demand

murirŭl hada 무리를 하다
strain; injure

muri tŭlda 물이 들다 dye;
be stained; become infected

murŏboda 물어보다
question

murŏttŭtda 물어뜯다
bite off

murŭikkta 무르익다 ripen

murŭmp'yo 물음표 question
mark

murŭp 무릎 knee; lap

murŭp kkult'a 무릎 꿇다
kneel

murye 무례 rudeness

muryehada 무례하다 be
rude

muryehan 무례한 rude

muryo iptchang 무료 입장
admission free

muryoro 무료로 free of
charge

muryoŭi 무료의 free

musahada 무사하다 be
in safety

musahan 무사한 unharmed

musahi 무사히 safely

mushi 무시 disregard

mushihada 무시하다
ignore; dismiss

mushimushihan
무시무시한 dreadful

musŏnghan 무성한
overgrown

musŏnŭi musŏn 무선의 wireless

musŏptta 무섭다 be
frightening

musŏwŏhada 무서워하다
be afraid of

Musok Shinang 무속 신앙
Shamanism

musŭn 무슨 any; some; what
kind of ◊ what

musŭngbu 무승부 dead heat

musul 무술 martial arts

mut-tta 묻다 ask

muttukttuk'an 무뚝뚝한
surly

muŭimi 무의미 nonsense

muŭimihan 무의미한
meaningless

mu-ŭishik 무의식 the
subconscious

muŭishiktchŏgin
무의식적인 unconscious

muyŏk 무역 trade

muyŏk pangnamhoe 무역
박람회 trade show

muyŏn hwibaryu 무연
휘발유 unleaded gasoline

muyong 무용 dancing

mwŏrago? 뭐라고? what?

mwŏragoyo? 뭐라고요?
excuse me?

myŏlch'i 멸치 anchovies

myŏltchong 멸종 extinction

myŏltchongdoen

myŏltchongdoen 멸종된
extinct

myŏltchongshik'ida
멸종시키다 exterminate

myŏn 면 cotton; aspect;
township

myŏndo 면도 shave

myŏndohada 면도하다 shave

myŏndonal 면도날 razor
blade

myŏngbaek'ada 명백하다
be clear

myŏngbaek'age 명백하게
obviously

myŏngbaek'i 명백히
explicitly

myŏngham 명함 business
card

myŏnghwak'age hada
명확하게 하다 clarify

myŏnghwak'an 명확한
definite

myŏnghwak'i 명확히
explicitly

myŏngjak 명작 masterpiece

myŏngnanghada 명랑하다
be bright

myŏngnyŏng 명령 order

myŏngnyŏnghada 명령하다
command

myŏngnyŏngjŏgin 명령적인
dictatorial

myŏngsang 명상 meditation

myŏngsanghada 명상하다
meditate

myŏngsŏk'an 명석한 clear

myŏng-ye 명예 honor

myŏnhŏ pat-tta 면허 받다
be licensed

myŏnhŏtchŭng 면허증
license

myŏnhoe shigan 면회 시간
visiting hours

myŏnje 면제 immunity

myŏnjedoeda 면제되다 be
exempt from

myŏnjedoen 면제된 exempt

myŏnjŏk 면적 area

myŏnjŏp 면접 interview

myŏnjŏpkkwan 면접관
interviewer

myŏnjŏp'ada 면접하다
interview

myŏnmyŏch'ŭi 몇몇의
several

myŏnsejŏm 면세점 duty-
free shop

myŏnseŭi 면세의 duty-free

-myŏnsŏ 면서 while

myŏnŭri 며느리 daughter-
in-law

myŏnyŏgŭi 면역의 immune

myŏt 몇 how many; how much

myŏt kae 몇 개 several

myŏt pŏnina kyesok 몇
번이나 계속 time and again

myŏt shiimnikka? 몇
시입니까? what's the time?

myoji 묘지 cemetery

myosa 묘사 description

myosahada 묘사하다
describe

N

na 나 I ◊ me ◊ mine
nabang 나방 moth
nabi 나비 butterfly
nabi nekt'ai 나비 넥타이
bow tie
na chashin 나 자신 myself
nach'ehwa 나체화 nude
(painting)
nach'imban 나침반 compass
nach'uda 낮추다 turn down;
belittle
nada 나다 it's me ◊ flare up
nae 내 my
naebaet-tta 내뱉다 spit out
naebŏrida 내버리다 throw
out
naebŏryŏduda 내버려두다
leave alone
naebu 내부 inside
naeda 내다 provide; serve;
spare; give off; pay
naedaboda 내다보다 look
out (of)
naegi 내기 bet
naeil 내일 tomorrow
nae kŏt 내 것 mine
naembi 냄비 saucepan
naemsae 냄새 smell; scent
naemsaega nada 냄새가
나다 smell
naemsae nanŭn 냄새 나는
smelly

naenae 내내 all the time
naengbang 냉방 air-
conditioning
naengdong 냉동 freezing
naengdongshil 냉동실
freezer
naengjanggo 냉장고
fridge
naengjŏnghada 냉정하다
be cool
naengjŏnghan 냉정한
dispassionate; hardheaded
naengmyŏn 냉면 chilled
noodles
naenot'a 내놓다 set out
naerida 내리다 get out;
disembark; come down (of
rain); lower; unload; bring in
(verdict); percolate
naeri tŏpch'ida 내리
덮치다 swoop
naeryŏ chuda 내려 주다 let
off (from car)
naeryŏgada 내려가다 go
down
naeryŏoda 내려오다 come
down
naesŏngjŏgin 내성적인
introspective
naeŭi 내의 underwear
naeyong 내용 content(s)
nagada 나가다 go out

nagage hada 나가게 하다
let out

nagwŏn 낙원 paradise

nai 나이 age

nai chigŭt'an 나이 지긋한
elderly

nai kapssŭl hae! 나이 값을
해! grow up!

naje 낮에 by day

najŭn 낮은 low

najung-e 나중에 later

**najung-e tashi
chŏnhwahada** 나중에
다시 전화하다 call back

nakch'ŏnjŏgin 낙천적인
optimistic

nakch'ŏnjuŭi 낙천주의
optimism

nakkda 낚다 fish; lure

nakssshi 낚시 fishing

naksshihada 낚시하다 fish

nakssŏ 낙서 graffiti

nakt'ae 낙태 abortion

nakt'aehada 낙태하다 have
an abortion

nak'asan 낙하산 parachute

nal 날 day; edge; blade

nalda 날다 fly

nalgae 날개 wing

nalgŭn 낡은 old; outmoded

nalkkŏsŭl 날것을 raw

nalktta 낡다 be old; be old-
fashioned

nalk'aroptta 날카롭다 be
sharp; be incisive

nalk'aroun 날카로운 sharp;
incisive

nallibŏpssŏk ttŏlda
난리법석 떨다 make a fuss

nallida 날리다 spend

nalsshi 날씨 weather

nalsshinhada 날씬하다
be slim

nalsshinhan 날씬한 slim

naltcha 날짜 date

naltchaga chinan 날짜가
지난 out of date

nambuŭi 남부의 southern

namdongsaeng 남동생
(younger) brother

namdongtchok 남동쪽
southeast

namgida 남기다 leave

Namgŭk-kkwŏn 남극권
Antarctic

namgyŏjida 남겨지다
remain

Namhan 남한 South Korea
◊ South Korean

namja 남자 man

namja ch'in-gu 남자 친구
boyfriend

namja paeu 남자 배우
actor

nam mollae saltchak 남
몰래 살짝 on the sly

nam morŭge 남 모르게
behind the scenes

namnŭn shigan 남는 시간
spare time

namnuhan 남루한 ragged

namŏji 나머지 the rest

namp'yŏn 남편 husband
namsaek 남색 navy blue
namsŏngjŏgin 남성적인 masculine
namtchok 남쪽 south
namtta 남다 be left
namŭn kŏt 남은 것 left-overs
namu 나무 tree; wood
namuga ugŏjin 나무가 우거진 wooded
namkkun 나무꾼 woodcutter
namurada 나무라다 reprimand
namyong 남용 abuse
nanari 날날이 day by day
nanbang 난방 heating
nan-gan 난간 handrail
nangbi 낭비 waste
nangbiga shimhan 낭비가 심한 wasteful
nangbihada 낭비하다 waste
nanjangp'an 난장판 madhouse
nanmin 난민 refugee
nanp'ok'age 난폭하게 violently
nanp'ok unjŏnja 난폭 운전자 road hog
nanp'ok'an 난폭한 rough
nanuda 나누다 divide
nanuŏ chuda 나누어 주다 hand out
nanutssem 나눗셈 division
naoda 나오다 come out;

add up to
napch'i 납치 kidnapping
napch'ibŏm 납치범 kidnapper
napch'ihada 납치하다 kidnap
nappajida 나빠지다 deteriorate
nap-ppuhada 납부하다 pay
nappŭda 나쁘다 be bad
nappŭge 나쁘게 badly
nappŭn 나쁜 bad
nap'al 나팔 brass trumpet
nara 나라 nation
naragada 날아가다 fly away
naranhi 나란히 side by side
narŭda 나르다 carry
narutppae 나룻배 ferry
nasŏda 나서다 appear
nat 낮 daylight
natch'uda 낮추다 lower; keep down
natch'un 낮춘 subdued
natch'uŏ poda 낮추어 보다 look down on
natssŏn saram 낯선 사람 stranger
nattcham 낮잠 nap
nattchamŭl chada 낮잠을 자다 have a nap
nat-tta 낫다 heal
nat-tta 낮다 be low
nat'a 낳다 give birth to; lay; spawn
nat'anada 나타나다 appear; manifest itself; haunt

naŭi 나의 my
ne pŏn 네 번 four times
net 넷 four
nŏ 너 *infml* you
nŏgŭrŏun 너그러운 decent
nŏlbŭn 넓은 wide
nŏlke 넓게 widely
nŏlptta 넓다 be wide
nŏlp'ida 넓히다 broaden;
dilate
nŏmch'ida 넘치다 exceed;
overflow
nŏmgida 넘기다 turn
nŏmgyŏjuda 넘겨주다
hand over
nŏmŏ 넘어 past *(in time)*
nŏmŏjida 넘어지다 fall
(over)
nŏmŏsŏ 넘어서 beyond
nŏmu 너무 too; too much
nŏmu honjap'an 너무
혼잡한 overcrowded
nŏmu mani 너무 많이 too
much
nŏmu pissan 너무 비싼 too
expensive
nŏngnŏk'an 넉넉한 plentiful
nŏptchŏkttari 넓적다리
thigh
nŏt'a 넣다 put in
noa tuda 놓아 두다 put
noch'ida 놓치다 miss; lose
one's hold on; pass up
noch'ul 노출 exposure
nodong 노동 labor
nodong chohap 노동 조합
labor union
nodongja 노동자 laborer
noemul 뇌물 bribe
noemul susu 뇌물 수수
bribery
nogida 녹이다 melt;
dissolve; defrost
nogi sŭn 녹이 슨 rusty
nogoltchŏguro 노골적으로
pointblank
nogonhan 노곤한 lethargic
nogŭmhada 녹음하다 tape
nogŭn 녹은 molten
nokch'a 녹차 green tea
nokssaegŭi 녹색의 green
nokssŭlda 녹슬다 rust
noktta 녹다 thaw; melt
nok'ŭhada 노크하다 knock
nok'wahada 녹화하다
record
nolda 놀다 play
nolgo chinaeda 놀고
지내다 loaf around
nolgo innŭn 놓고 있는 idle
nollada 놀라다 be surprised
nollapk'e 놀랍게 suprisingly
nollaun 놀라운 wonderful
nolli 논리 logic
nollida 놀리다 tease
nollijŏgin 논리적인 logical
nonbat 논밭 rice fields and
dry fields
nong-ak 농악 farmer's music
nongbu 농부 farmer
nongdam 농담 joke
nongdamhada 농담하다

joke

nongdamŭro 농담으로 jokingly

nonggu 농구 basketball

nongjang 농장 farm

nongsa 농사 agriculture

nonhada 논하다 argue

nonjaeng 논쟁 controversy

nonjaenghada 논쟁하다 debate

nonjaengjŏgin 논쟁적인 provocative

nonp'yŏnghada 논평하다 review

nonŭi 논의 discussion

nonŭihada 논의하다 discuss

nopkke 높게 high

noptta 높다 be high

nop'i 높이 height; altitude

nop'ida 높이다 increase; elevate

norae 노래 song

noraehada 노래하다 sing

noran 노란 yellow

nori 놀이 play ◊ game

norit'ŏ 놀이터 playground

norŭnja 노른자 yolk

noryŏk 노력 effort

noryŏk'ada 노력하다 try

not'a 놓다 put; put down

noŭl 노을 twilight

nŭjŏjinda 늦어진다 it's getting late

nŭjŭn 늦은 late

nŭkkida 느끼다 feel

nŭkkim 느낌 sense

nŭl 늘 always

nŭlda 늘다 expand; mount up

nŭlgŭn 늙은 old

nŭlktta 늙다 grow old

nŭllida 늘리다 extend; raise; lengthen; let out

nŭlsshihan 늘씬한 trim

nŭnggŭlmajŭn usŭm 능글맞은 웃음 smirk

nŭngnyŏk 능력 ability

nŭngnyŏk innŭn 능력 있는 capable

nŭngsuk 능숙 proficiency

nŭngsuk'ada 능숙하다 be skilled

nŭngsuk'an 능숙한 skillful

...nŭn kŏt …는 것 *(creates a noun form)* …ing

nŭp 늪 swamp

nŭrida 느리다 be slow; be loose

nŭrige hada 느리게 하다 slow down

nŭrin 느린 slow

nŭrŏjida 늘어지다 stretch

nŭrŏjin 늘어진 flabby

nŭrŏnada 늘어나다 stretch

nŭryŏjida 느려지다 slow down

nŭsŭnhan 느슨한 loose

nŭttcham chada 늦잠 자다 sleep late

nŭt-tta 늦다 be late

nuch'ul 누출 escape

nuch'uldoeda 누출되다 escape

nugŭrŏjida 누그러지다
ease off
nugu 누구 who
nugudo 누구도 anybody;
nobody
nuguna 누구나 everybody
nugun-ga 누군가 somebody;
anybody
nuguŭi 누구의 whose
nun 눈 eye; snow
nunbushida 눈부시다 be
dazzling
nunbushige pinnada
눈부시게 빛나다 glare
nunbushin 눈부신 dazzling
nunch'ich'aeda 눈치채다
observe
nune ttŭida 눈에 띄다
stand out
nune ttŭige 눈에 띄게
visibly
nune ttŭinŭn 눈에 띄는
visible

nuni naerida 눈이 내리다
snow
nuni onŭn 눈이 오는 snowy
nun kkamtchak'al saie 눈
깜짝할 사이에 in a flash
nunkkŏp'ul 눈꺼풀 eyelid
nun mŏn 눈 먼 blind
nunmul 눈물 tear
nunmul ŏrin 눈물 어린
tearful
nunmurŭl hŭllida 눈물을
흘리다 be in tears
nunsat'ae 눈사태 avalanche
nunsong-i 눈송이
snowflake
nunssŏp 눈썹 eyebrow
nunttongja 눈동자 pupil
nuptta 눕다 lie down
nurŭda 누르다 push; click
nyŏn 년 year; woman *pej*
nyusŭ 뉴스 news
nyusŭ podo 뉴스 보도
news report

Ŏ

Ŏbŏinal 어버이날 Parents'
Day
ŏbu 어부 fisherman
-ŏch'i -어치 worth
ŏdi 어디 where
ŏdidŭnji 어디든지
everywhere
ŏdin-ga-e 어딘가에
somewhere

ŏditch'ŭme(sŏ)
어디쯤е (서) whereabouts
ŏduptta 어둡다 be dark; be in
the dark; be weak
ŏduun 어두운 dark
ŏduwŏjida 어두워지다
get dark
ŏgaptchŏgin 억압적인
repressive

ŏgap'ada 억압하다 repress

ŏhwi 어휘 vocabulary

ŏje 어제 yesterday

ŏjetppam 어젯밤 last night

...ŏjida ...어 지다 become ...

ŏjiрŏptta 어지럽다 feel faint; be chaotic

ŏjirŏun 어지러운 giddy; messy

ŏjirŭda 어지르다 mess up

ŏkkae 어깨 shoulder

ŏkssen 억센 strong

ŏkssen sanai 억센 사나이 tough guy

ŏkssugat'ŭn 억수같은 torrential

ŏlda 얼다 freeze

ŏlgul 얼굴 face

ŏlgurŭl pulk'ida 얼굴을 붉히다 blush

ŏllida 얼리다 freeze

ŏlluk 얼룩 mark; smear

ŏlma 얼마 how much; how long; how many; how far

ŏlmana ...? 얼마나 ...? how much...?

ŏlmana chaju? 얼마나 자주? how often?

ŏlmana chŏne? 얼마나 전에? how long ago?

ŏlmana mani? 얼마나 많이? how many?

ŏmaŏmahan 어마어마한 huge

ŏmch'ŏngnada 엄청나다 be preposterous

ŏmch'ŏngnage 엄청나게 extraordinarily

ŏmch'ŏngnan 엄청난 extraordinary

ŏmhage tasŭrida 엄하게 다스리다 crack down on

ŏmhan 엄한 grim; strict

ŏmkkyŏk 엄격 severity

ŏmkkyŏk'ada 엄격하다 be strict

ŏmkkyŏk'age 엄격하게 strictly

ŏmkkyŏk'an 엄격한 strict

ŏmma 엄마 mom

ŏmmu 업무 business

ŏmŏni 어머니 mother

ŏmp'o 엄포 bluff; deception

ŏmp'orŭl not'a 엄포를 놓다 bluff

ŏndŏk 언덕 hill

ŏngdŏng-i 엉덩이 buttocks

ŏngk'ida 엉키다 get tangled up

ŏngmang 엉망 mess

ŏngmang-ŭro mandŭlda 엉망으로 만들다 wreck

ŏngnullin 억눌린 repressed

ŏngt'ŏri 엉터리 broken *Korean etc*

ŏnje 언제 when

ŏnjekkajina 언제까지나 forever

ŏnjena 언제나 always

ŏnjen-ga 언젠가 someday

ŏnŏ 언어 language

ŏnŭ 어느 what; which

ŏnŭ han tchogŭi 어느 한
쪽의 either

ŏnŭ kŏt 어느 것 which

ŏnŭ kot 어느 곳 anywhere

ŏnŭ nal 어느날 one day

ŏnŭ tchogina 어느 쪽이나
either

ŏpssaeda 없애다 get rid of

…ŏpsshi …없이 without

ŏpssŏjida 없어지다
disappear

ŏpchirŭda 엎지르다 spill

ŏpchŏk 업적 achievement

ŏptta 없다 there is no; not
have

ŏrimdo ŏpssŏ! 어림도
없어! no way!

Ŏrininal 어린이날 Children's
Day

ŏrisŏgŭn 어리석은 foolish

ŏrisŏktta 어리석다 be foolish

ŏrŭm 얼음 ice

ŏrŭn 어른 adult

ŏrŭn 얼은 frozen

ŏrŭnsŭrŏun 어른스러운
grown-up

ŏryŏmp'ut'an 어렴풋한
vague

ŏryŏpkke 어렵게 with
difficulty

ŏryŏptta 어렵다 be difficult

ŏryŏun 어려운 difficult

ŏsŭllŏnggŏrida
어슬렁거리다 hang about;
saunter

ŏtchaet-ttŭn 어쨋든 anyhow

ŏtchŏl su ŏpssŏyo 어쩔 수
없어요 it can't be helped

ŏtchŏnji 어쩐지 somehow

ŏtkkallida 엇갈리다 miss
(not meet)

ŏttaeyo 어때요 how; how
about

ŏttŏk'e 어떻게 how

ŏttŏk'edŭnji 어떻게든지
somehow

ŏttŏn 어떤 any; some; which;
what; particular

ŏttŏn kŏt 어떤 것 something

ŏt-tta 얻다 get; earn

ŏullida 어울리다 go with;
match

…ŏya handa …어야 한다
have to

…ŏyaman hada …어 야만
하다 have (got) to

O

o 오 five; oh!

oda 오다 come

odumak 오두막 hut

oe 외 outside; except

oeadŭl 외아들 only son

oebusaram 외부사람
outsider

oech'ida 외치다 cry

oedongttal 외동딸 only daughter

oegugin 외국인 foreigner

oegyo 외교 diplomacy
◊ diplomatic

oegyogwan 외교관 diplomat

oehalmöni 외할머니 maternal grandmother

oeharaböji 외할아버지 maternal grandfather

oehwa 외화 foreign currency

oemu 외무 foreign affairs
◊ foreign

oemyönhada 외면하다 turn away

oensonjabi 왼손잡이 left-handed

oentchoguro 왼쪽으로 to the left

oentchok 왼쪽 left

oeroptta 외롭다 be lonely

oeroun 외로운 lonely

oesamch'on 외삼촌 uncle (mother's brother)

oesang 외상 credit FIN

oeshik'ada 외식하다 eat out

oesungmo 외숙모 aunt (mother's brother's wife)

oettan 외딴 isolated

oeuda 외우다 memorize

ogap'ada 억압하다 supress

ohae 오해 misunderstanding

ohaehada 오해하다 misunderstand

ohiryö 오히려 rather

ohu 오후 afternoon

oi 오이 cucumber

ojik 오직 only

ojing-ö 오징어 squid

ojön 오전 morning

ojon 오존 ozone

ojum nuda 오줌 누다 urinate

okssusu 옥수수 maize

olbaruda 올바르다 be straight; be upright

olbaruge 올바르게 correctly

olbarün 올바른 right

olk'e 올케 sister-in-law (woman's brother's wife)

ollaoda 올라오다 come up

olt'a 옳다 be right ◊ OK

omgida 옮기다 move; carry

omgyök'ada 옮겨타다 transfer

onch'ön 온천 spa

ondo 온도 temperature

ondol 온돌 heated floor

onsunhan 온순한 gentle

onül 오늘 today

onül pam 오늘 밤 tonight

oppa 오빠 brother (woman's elder)

orae 오래 a long while

oraedoen 오래된 old

orak 오락 entertainment

oraksshisöl 오락시설 amenities

ori 오리 duck

orüda 오르다 climb; increase

orün 옳은 correct

orŭnp'yŏne

orŭnp'yŏne 오른편에 on the right-hand side

orŭntchoguro 오른쪽으로 to the right

orŭntchok 오른쪽 right

oryŏnaeda 오려내다 cut out

oship 오십 fifty

osŭl iptta 옷을 입다 dress

ot 옷 clothes

otkkŏri 옷걸이 clothes hanger

owŏl 오월 May

oyŏm 오염 pollution

oyŏmshik'ida 오염시키다 pollute

P

pa 바 way; thing; crossbar

pabo 바보 idiot

pabosŭrŏun 바보스러운 idiotic

pada 바다 sea; ocean

padadŭrida 받아들이다 assimilate; accept; keep down

padajŏktta 받아적다 write down

padassŭgi 받아쓰기 dictation

pae 배 stomach; embryo; ship; pear

paeban 배반 betrayal

paebanhada 배반하다 betray

paebanhanŭn 배반하는 treacherous

paebanja 배반자 traitor

paeburŭda 배부르다 full up

paech'i 배치 layout; batch

paech'ihada 배치하다 arrange

paech'u 배추 Chinese cabbage

paedal 배달 delivery

paedarhada 배달하다 deliver

paegin 백인 white *(person)*

paegŏp 백업 backup

paegop'ŭda 배고프다 be hungry

paegop'ŭn 배고픈 hungry

paegu 배구 volleyball

paegyŏng 배경 background

paegyŏng ŭmak 배경 음악 soundtrack

paek 백 hundred; white; back; bag

paek-kkŭm 백금 platinum

paekkop 배꼽 navel

paek'wajŏm 백화점 department store

paemŏlmi 배멀미 seasickness

paemŏlmihada 배멀미하다 get seasick

paenang 배낭 rucksack

paenang yŏhaengja 배낭
여행자 backpacker

paengman 백만 million

paengman changja 백만
장자 millionaire

paesang 배상 compensation

paesanghada 배상하다
compensate

paet'al 배탈 upset stomach

paet'alnada 배탈나다 have
an upset stomach

paeuda 배우다 learn

paeuja 배우자 spouse

paeunghada 배웅하다
see off

pagaji ssŭiuda 바가지
씌우다 overcharge

pairŏsŭ 바이러스 virus
COMPUT

paji 바지 pants

pakk 밖 outside

...pakke ...밖에 outside (of)

pakkuda 바꾸다 change;
swap; vary; move on

pakkwida 바뀌다 change;
vary

pakkwŏt'ada 바꿔타다
transfer

pakssa 박사 PhD

pakssŭ 박스 carton; booth

pakssurŭl ch'ida 박수를
치다 clap

paktcha 박자 beat

pak'ae 박해 persecution

pak'aehada 박해하다
persecute

pak'wi 바퀴 wheel; lap

pak'wi pŏlle 바퀴 벌레
cockroach

pal 발 foot; paw

palgabŏsŭn 발가벗은 naked

palgajida 밝아지다 brighten
up

palgyŏn 발견 discovery

palgyŏnhada 발견하다
discover

palkkarak 발가락 toe

palkke hada 밝게 하다
light up

palkkŏrŭm 발걸음 tread

palktta 밝다 be bright; be keen;
be expert; be cheerful; dawn

palk'ida 밝히다 reveal;
express

palk'yŏnaeda 밝혀내다
find out

palmae 발매 launch; release;
sale

palmaehada 발매하다
launch; release; bring out

palmok 발목 ankle

palmyŏnghada 발명하다
invent

palp'an 발판 scaffolding;
stepping stone

palp'yo 발표 release;
presentation

palssaeng 발생 happening

palssahada 발사하다
launch

palssonghada 발송하다
dispatch

palssong-in 발송인 sender

paltchaguk 발자국 footprint

paltchŏn 발전 development

paltchŏnhada 발전하다 develop

paltta 밟다 tread (on)

palt'op 발톱 toenail; claw

pam 밤 night; chestnut

pamsae 밤새 overnight

pan 반 half

panbaji 반바지 shorts

panbak 반박 retort

panbak'ada 반박하다 contradict; protest; retort

panbok'ada 반복하다 repeat

panch'an 반찬 side dish

panch'anggo 반창고 adhesive tape; Band-Aid®

panch'ik 반칙 foul

pandae 반대 opposite; objection

pandaedoeda 반대되다 run counter to

pandaehada 반대하다 object (to); oppose

pandaero 반대로 on the other hand

pandŭshi 반드시 necessarily

pang 방 room

pangbŏp 방법 method

pangbuje 방부제 preservative

panggŭm 방금 just now

panggwi kkwida 방귀 뀌다 fart

panghae 방해 obstacle; setback

panghaehada 방해하다 disturb; hinder; jam

panghaemul 방해물 obstruction; deterrent

panghyang 방향 direction(s)

pangmang-i 방망이 bat

pangmulgwan 박물관 museum

pangmun 방문 door; visit

pangmunhada 방문하다 visit

pangnanghada 방랑하다 wander

pangnangja 방랑자 drifter

pang-ŏ 방어 defense

pang-ŏhada 방어하다 defend

pang-ŏjŏgin 방어적인 defensive

pangsasŏn 방사선 radiation

pangshik 방식 manner; system; method; form

pangsong 방송 broadcast(ing)

pangsongguk 방송국 station RADIO, TV

pangsonghada 방송하다 broadcast

pangsong-in 방송인 broadcaster

pangsudoenŭn 방수되는 waterproof

pang-ŭm 방음 soundproofing ◊ soundproof

pang-ul 방울 drip

pang-yŏnghada 방영하다
televise

panhal manhan 반할 만한
adorable

panhang 반항 defiance

panhanghada 반항하다
defy

panhangjŏgin 반항적인
defiant

panhwan 반환 return

panji 반지 ring

panju 반주 accompaniment

panjurŭl hada 반주를 하다
accompany MUS

pannŭn chŭksshiro 받는
즉시로 by return (of mail)

panp'arŭl 반팔의 short-
sleeved

pansonghada 반송하다
send back

pantchagida 반짝이다
twinkle

pantchak 반짝 glint

pantchak-kkŏrinŭn
반짝거리는 shiny

panŭi 반의 half

panŭjil 바느질 needlework

panŭjirhada 바느질하다
sew

panŭng 반응 reaction

panŭnghada 반응하다
respond

panŭnghanŭn 반응하는
responsive

pap 밥 rice

pap kŭrŭt 밥 그릇 rice bowl

pappŭda 바쁘다 be busy

pappŭn 바쁜 busy

parada 바라다 hope (for);
wish (for)

paraedajuda 바래다주다
escort

paraen 바랜 faded

param 바람 desire; wind

paramjik'an 바람직한
desirable

param mach'ida 바람
맞히다 stand up (on date)

param punŭn 바람 부는
windy

paramŭl p'iuda 바람을
피우다 have an affair

parhaeng 발행 publication

parhaenghada 발행하다
print

parhyohada 발효하다
ferment

paro 바로 properly; directly;
straight; just; exactly

parŭda 바르다 be straight; be
right; stick; spread

parŭge hada 바르게 하다
straighten out

parŭm 발음 pronunciation

parŭmhada 발음하다
pronounce

parŭn 바른 proper; orderly;
honest

pat 밭 (dry) field

patattkka 바닷가 seaside

patch'imttae 받침대

pattchul 밧줄 rope
pat-tta 받다 receive; undergo; sustain
pawi 바위 rock
peda 베다 cut
pegae 베개 pillow
pekkyŏ ssŭda 베껴 쓰다 copy
peŏnaeda 베어내다 cut off
peranda 베란다 balcony; veranda
pesŭt'ŭsellŏ 베스트셀러 best-seller
pi 비 rain
pibimppap 비빔밥 rice with meat and vegetables
pich'amhada 비참하다 be miserable
pich'ida 비치다 flash
pich'inŭn 비치는 see-through
pich'uda 비추다 shine; reflect
pidan 비단 silk
pidio 비디오 video
pidŭm 비듬 dandruff
pidulgi 비둘기 dove; pigeon
piga oda 비가 오다 rain
pigida 비기다 tie
pigŏp 비겁 cowardice
pigŏp'an 비겁한 cowardly
pigongshiktchŏgŭro 비공식적으로 unofficially
pigŭk 비극 tragedy
pigŭktchŏgin 비극적인 tragic
pigwanjŏgin 비관적인 pessimistic
pigyohada 비교하다 compare
pigyojŏgin 비교적인 relative
pigyojŏgŭro 비교적으로 comparatively
pihaenggi 비행기 airplane
pija 비자 visa
pijŭnisŭ k'ŭllaesŭ 비즈니스 클래스 business class
pikkonŭn 비꼬는 ironic
pik'ida 비키다 get out of the way
pilda 빌다 beg; pray; wish
pillida 빌리다 borrow; lend
pillin 빌린 on loan
pillyŏjuda 빌려주다 lend; rent out
pimil 비밀 secret
pimil pŏnho 비밀 번호 PIN
pimirŭi 비밀의 secret
pimyŏng 비명 screech
pimyŏngŭl chirŭda 비명을 지르다 screech
pin 빈 empty
pinan 비난 blame; accusation; reproach
pinanhada 비난하다 accuse; blame
pinanhanŭn 비난하는 reproachful
pindungbindung chinaeda 빈둥빈둥 지내다 be lazy
pingbing tollida 빙빙 돌리다 twirl
pin-got 빈 곳 gap

pinhyŏltchŭng 빈혈증 anemia

pinil pongji 비닐 봉지 plastic bag

pinjŏngdaeda 빈정대다 criticize

pinjŏngdaenŭn 빈정대는 sarcastic

pinollijŏgin 비논리적인 illogical

pint'ŏlt'ŏri 빈털터리 down-and-out

pinŭl 비늘 scale (on fish)

pinu 비누 soap

pip'anjŏgin 비판적인 critical

pip'anjŏguro 비판적으로 critically

pip'yŏng 비평 criticism

pip'yŏnghada 비평하다 criticize

pirŏmŏgŭl 빌어먹을! blast!

pirok 비록 … l / ŭltchirado 비록 … ㄹ / 을지라도 although

piryo 비료 fertilizer

pisang 비상 emergency

pisanggu 비상구 emergency exit

pisŏ 비서 secretary

pisŏk 비석 tombstone

pissada 비싸다 be expensive

pissan 비싼 expensive

pisŭt'ada 비슷하다 be similar

pisŭt'an 비슷한 similar

pisugi 비수기 low season

pit 빗 comb

pit 빚 debt

pit 빛 light

pitcharu 빗자루 broom

pitchida 빚지다 owe

pitchirhada 빗질하다 brush

pitppang-ul 빗방울 raindrop

pit'amin 비타민 vitamin

pit'ŭ 비트 bit COMPUT

piuda 비우다 empty; vacate

piunnŭn 비웃는 derisive

piut-tta 비웃다 laugh at

piyong 비용 expense

pŏdunggŏrida 버둥거리다 squirm

pŏl 벌 bee; pack; suit; pair; set; punishment ◊ countword for clothes

pŏlda 벌다 earn

pŏlgŭm 벌금 fine

pŏlle 벌레 bug

pŏllida 벌리다 open

pŏlssŏ 벌써 already

pŏltŏk 벌떡 suddenly

pŏmin 범인 culprit

pŏmjoe 범죄 crime; guilt ◊ criminal

pŏmjoeja 범죄자 criminal

pŏmnyul 법률 legislation

pŏmurida 버무리다 toss

pŏmwi 범위 extent

pŏn 번 time; number; duty

pŏnch'ang 번창 prosperity

pŏnch'anghada 번창하다 prosper

pŏnch'anghanŭn 번창하는 prosperous

pŏn-gae 번개 lightning

pŏn-gaetppul 번갯불 bolt
of lightning

pŏng-ŏri 벙어리 mute

pŏnho 번호 number

pŏnhwahan 번화한 bustling

pŏnnamu 벚나무 cherry tree

pŏnshik 번식 breeding

pŏnshik'ada 번식하다
breed

pŏnyŏk 번역 translation

pŏnyŏkka 번역가 translator

pŏnyŏk'ada 번역하다
translate

pŏnyŏnghada 번영하다
flourish

pŏp 법 law; method

pŏptchŏgin 법적인 legal

pŏptchŏng 법정 court

pŏrida 버리다 throw away

pŏrigo ttŏnada 버리고
떠나다 abandon

pŏrŭt 버릇 habit

pŏrŭt ŏmnŭn 버릇 없는
spoilt *(child)*

pŏryŏduda 버려두다
abandon

pŏryŏjin 버려진 neglected

pŏsŏnada 벗어나다 break
away; elude; outgrow

pŏsŏt 버섯 mushroom

pŏsŭ 버스 bus

pŏsŭ chŏngnyujang 버스
정류장 bus stop

pŏtkkida 벗기다 remove;
strip; undress; unveil; shell

pŏt-tta 벗다 remove

pŏt'ida 버티다 resist

pŏt'ŏ 버터 butter

poan 보안 security

pobok 보복 revenge

poboktchŏgin 보복적인
vindictive

pobok'ada 보복하다 take
one's revenge

poch'ŏnggi 보청기 hearing
aid

poch'ung 보충 compensation

poch'unghada 보충하다
supplement

poda 보다 look (at); see;
watch ◊ than

podo 보도 report

podohada 보도하다 report

pogienŭn 보기에는
seemingly

pogiwanŭn tarŭn 보기와는
다른 deceptive

pogo 보고 report

pogohada 보고하다 report

Pogŭm 복음 the Word REL

pogwan 보관 storage

pogwan changso 보관
장소 storage space

pogwanhada 보관하다 store

pogyongppŏp 복용법
directions *(for medicine)*

pohaenggi 보행기 walker
(for baby)

pohaengja 보행자
pedestrian

pohamhada 포함하다

include

pohŏm 보험 insurance

pohŏme tŭlda 보험에 들다
insure

poho 보호 protection

pohohada 보호하다 protect

poho kuyŏk 보호 구역
(wild animal) sanctuary

poida 보이다 be able to see;
be visible; show; seem

poinŭn 보이는 visible

pojal kŏt ŏmnŭn 보잘 것
없는 worthless

pojang 보장 guarantee

pojanghada 보장하다
guarantee

pojogae 보조개 dimple

pojogŭm 보조금 grant

pojon 보존 preservation

pojonhada 보존하다
preserve

pojŭng 보증 guarantee

pojŭnghada 보증하다
guarantee

pojŭng kigan 보증 기간
guarantee period

pok-kku 복구 restoration

pok-kkuhada 복구하다
restore

pokssa 복사 copy

pokssahada 복사하다
photocopy

pokssŭp'ada 복습하다
review

pokssuhada 복수하다
retaliate

pokssung-a 복숭아 peach

poktchap'ada 복잡하다 be
complicated

poktchiksshik'ida
복직시키다 reinstate

poktchi kuk-kka 복지 국가
welfare state

poktta 볶다 stir-fry

poktto 복도 corridor

pokt'ong 복통 stomach-ache

pollae 본래 originally

polling 볼링 bowling

pollinghada 볼링하다 bowl

pollingjang 볼링장 bowling
alley

polp'en 볼펜 ballpoint (pen)

pom 봄 look; spring

pomch'ŏl 봄철 springtime

pomul 보물 treasure

ponaeda 보내다 pass;
spend; send

ponbu 본부 headquarters

ponggoch'a 봉고차 van

ponggŭmnal 봉급날 payday

ponggŭp 봉급 pay check

ponghada 봉하다 seal *letter*

pongji 봉지 packet; seal

pongsahada 봉사하다 serve

pongt'u 봉투 envelope

ponin 본인 oneself; himself;
herself

ponjiltchŏgin 본질적인
fundamental; substantial

ponjiltchŏgŭro 본질적으로
fundamentally

ponnŭng 본능 instinct

ponnŭngjŏgin 본능적인
instinctive

ponsa 본사 head office

porami innŭn 보람이 있는
worthwhile

pori 보리 barley

porich'a 보리차 roasted
barley tea

porŭmttal 보름달 full moon

Posal 보살 Bodhisattva

posalp'ida 보살피다 look
after

posang 보상 reward;
compensation

posanghada 보상하다
compensate for

poshint'ang 보신탕 dog
meat soup

posŏk 보석 bail; jewel

posŭlbi 보슬비 drizzle

posu 보수 pay; reward;
conservativeness
◊ conservative

posuhada 보수하다
renovate; repair

posujŏgin 보수적인
conservative

pot'ong 보통 ordinary
◊ usually

pot'ongsŏk 보통석 economy
class

pot'ong-ŭi 보통의 normal

pot'ong-ŭro 보통으로
normally

pot'ong yegŭm 보통 예금
savings account

poyŏjida 보여지다 appear;
be visible

poyŏjuda 보여주다 show

poyugwŏn 보육원
kindergarten

ppaeat-tta 빼앗다 take
by force

ppaeda 빼다 drain off; omit;
subtract

ppaedalmŭn mosŭp 빼닮은
모습 image

ppaenaeda 빼내다 take out;
eject; drain

ppaengsoni unjŏnsu
뺑소니 운전수 hit-and-run
driver

ppajida 빠지다 drain away;
sink in; fall in; fall out; pull
out; be hooked on; miss

ppajyŏ nagada 빠져
나가다 slip out; ebb away

ppalda 빨다 wash; suck

ppalgan 빨간 red

ppalgat'a 빨갛다 be red

ppallae 빨래 washing

ppalli 빨리 quickly

ppalli hada 빨리 하다
speed up

ppang 빵 bread

ppangjip 빵집 bakery

ppanhi ch'yŏdaboda 빤히
쳐다보다 stare (at)

pparŭda 빠르다 be fast

pparŭge 빠르게 quickly

pparŭn 빠른 fast

ppattŭrida 빠뜨리다 omit

ppŏnppŏnhada 뻔뻔하다
be impudent

ppŏnppŏnhan 뻔뻔한
impudent

ppŏnppŏnsŭrŏun
뻔뻔스러운 shameless

ppŏtppŏt'aejida 뻣뻣해지다
stiffen

ppoppo 뽀뽀 kiss

ppoppohada 뽀뽀하다 kiss

ppun 뿐 nothing but

ppuri 뿌리 root

ppurida 뿌리다 scatter;
sprinkle; spray

ppuri kip'ŭn 뿌리 깊은
deep-rooted

ppurut'unghada
뿌루퉁하다 pout

ppyam 뺨 cheek

ppyŏ 뼈 bone

pu 부 copy (of book);
ministry; wealth

pŭraujŏ 브라우저 browser
COMPUT

pŭreik'ŭrŭl kŏlda
브레이크를 걸다 brake

pubu 부부 couple

pubun 부분 part; portion

pubuntchŏgŭro 부분적으로
partially

puch'aejirhada 부채질하다
fan oneself

puch'ida 붙이다 attach;
pin up

puch'ŏ 부처 Buddha;
department

puch'u 부추 leek

puch'ugida 부추기다
encourage

pudam 부담 burden

pudamhada 부담하다 bear
costs etc

pudanghada 부당하다 be
unjust

pudanghage 부당하게
wrongly

pudanghan 부당한 wrongful

pudodŏk 부도덕 immorality

pudodŏk'an 부도덕한
immoral

pudŭrŏpkke 부드럽게
softly

pudŭrŏptta 부드럽다 be soft

pudŭrŏun 부드러운 soft

pudu 부두 dock

pudut-kka 부둣가 quayside

pugyosu 부교수 associate
professor

puhwal 부활 resurrection

Puhwaltchŏl 부활절 Easter

puhwarhada 부활하다
revive

puinhada 부인하다
contradict; deny

puja 부자 sage; father and
son; rich man

pujagyong 부작용 side
effect

pujang 부장 managing
director; assistant director

pujayŏnsŭrŏun
부자연스러운 unnatural

pujirŏnhan 부지런한
diligent

pujŏkttanghada 부적당하다
be unsuitable

pujŏkttanghan 부적당한
unsuitable; inadequate

pujŏng 부정 denial; injustice;
infidelity

pujŏnghan 부정한
dishonest; unfaithful

pujŏngjik 부정직 dishonesty

pujŏngjik'an 부정직한
dishonest

pujok 부족 shortage; tribe

pujok'ada 부족하다 be
lacking

puk 북 drum; north

Puk-kkyŏng 북경 Beijing

pukkkurŏptta 부끄럽다 be
ashamed; be shy

pukkkurŏun 부끄러운
shameful

Puk'an 북한 North Korea
◊ North Korean

pul 불 fire; dollar; Buddha;
France ◊ French

pul- 불- not; un-; in-; non-

pulch'ansŏng 불찬성
disapproval

pulch'ansŏnghada
불찬성하다 disapprove of

pulch'injŏrhada 불친절하다
be unkind

pulch'injŏrhan 불친절한
unkind

pulch'ippyŏng-ŭi 불치병의

terminally ill

pulch'ungssil 불충실
disloyalty

pulch'ungsshirhan
불충실한 disloyal

pulda 불다 blow; inflate

pulganŭng 불가능
impossibility

pulganŭnghada 불가능하다
be impossible

pulganŭnghan 불가능한
impossible

pulgap'ihada 불가피하다
be unavoidable

pulgogi 불고기 barbecued
beef

pulgongjŏnghan 불공정한
unfair

pulgongp'yŏnghada
불공평하다 be unfair

pulguhago 불구하고 in
spite of

pulgyŏnggi 불경기 recession

Pulgyo 불교 Buddhism
◊ Buddhist

pulgyuch'iktchŏgin
불규칙적인 irregular

pulkkil 불길 flames

pulkkot 불꽃 flame; spark

pulk'wae 불쾌 displeasure

pulk'waehada 불쾌하다
repel

pulk'waehan 불쾌한
unpleasant; offensive, rotten;
sick

pulli 분리 separation

pullihada 분리하다 separate; unfix

pullihada 불리하다 be prejudicial to

pullihan 불리한 disadvantageous

pulluk'ada 불룩하다 bulge

pullyangbae 불량배 hooligan

pullyu 분류 classification

pullyuhada 분류하다 classify

pullyunŭi kwangye 불륜의 관계 (love) affair

pulman 불만 discontent

pulmanida 불만이다 be unhappy with

pulmyŏnghwak'an 불명확한 uncertain

pulpŏp 불법 illegality ◊ illegal

pulp'iryohan 불필요한 unnecessary

pulp'yŏn 불편 inconvenience

pulp'yŏng 불평 complaint

pulp'yŏnghada 불평하다 complain (about)

pulp'yŏnhada 불편하다 be uncomfortable; be inconvenient

pulp'yŏnhan 불편한 uncomfortable; inconvenient

pulssanghada 불쌍하다 be piteous

pulssanghan 불쌍한 piteous

pulssanghi yŏgida 불쌍히 여기다 take pity on

pulshin 불신 mistrust

pulshinhada 불신하다 mistrust

pulssuk nat'anada 불쑥 나타나다 pop up

pulsunhan 불순한 impure

pumbida 붐비다 be crowded

pumbinŭn 붐비는 crowded

pumo 부모 parent

pun 분 face powder; minute; flowerpot; anger; person *(respectful)* ◊ countword for people (respectful)

punbae 분배 distribution

punbaehada 분배하다 share

punbyŏl innŭn 분별 있는 prudent

pun-gae 분개 resentment; outrage

pun-gaehada 분개하다 resent

pun-gaehan 분개한 resentful; indignant

punggoe 붕괴 collapse

punggoedoeda 붕괴되다 disintegrate; crash

Pungmi 북미 North America ◊ North American

punhaehada 분해하다 dismantle

punhongsaek 분홍색 pink

punjaeng chiyŏk 분쟁 지역 hot spot

punman 분만 delivery; labor

punmanhada 분만하다 give birth to

punmyŏnghada 분명하다 be obvious

punmyŏnghage 분명하게 clearly

punmyŏnghan 분명한 clear

punmyŏnghi 분명히 clearly

punp'il 분필 chalk

punsŏk 분석 analysis

punsŏk'ada 분석하다 analyze

punsu 분수 fraction; fountain

punwigi 분위기 atmosphere; mood

punyŏl 분열 division

punyŏrhada 분열하다 be divided

puŏk 부엌 kitchen

puŏ orŭn 부어 오른 swollen

pup'ae 부패 decay

pup'aehada 부패하다 decay

pup'aehan 부패한 rotten; corrupt

pup'ullida 부풀리다 inflate; expand

pup'um 부품 (spare) part

puran 불안 alarm

puranhada 불안하다 be uneasy

puranhan 불안한 insecure

purhaeng 불행 unhappiness; misfortune

purhaenghada 불행하다 be unhappy; be unlucky

puraenghan 불행한 unfortunate; unhappy

purhaenghi 불행히 unfortunately

purhwaksshirhada 불확실하다 be doubtful

purhwaksshirhan 불확실한 uncertain

purŏjida 부러지다 break

purŏjin 부러진 broken

purŏun 부러운 enviable

purŏwŏhada 부러워하다 be envious of

purŏwŏhanŭn 부러워하는 envious

purŭda 부르다 call

purŭl puch'ida 불을 붙이다 set on fire

pusangja 부상자 injured; wounded

pusŏjida 부서지다 break; shatter

pusŏjin 부서진 broken

pusŭrŏgi 부스러기 crumb

pusŭrŏjida 부스러지다 crumble

pusuda 부수다 break; force

puttchaptta 붙잡다 hold *prisoner etc*

put-tta 붙다 stick

put'ak'ada 부탁하다 ask (for); arrange for

...put'ŏ ...kkaji ···부터 ···까지 from ... to

puyang 부양 support

puyanghada 부양하다
support

puyang kajok 부양 가족
dependents

puyuhada 부유하다 be rich

puyuhan 부유한 rich

pyŏk 벽 wall

pyŏl 별 star ◊ different;
unusual

pyŏllada 별나다 be strange

pyŏllan 별난 eccentric

pyŏllo 별로 nothing much

pyŏlloyeyo 별로예요 not
really

pyŏlmyŏng 별명 nickname

pyŏnanhada 편안하다 feel
at ease

pyŏnbi 변비 constipation

pyŏnbie kŏllin 변비에 걸린
constipated

pyŏndŏk 변덕 freak; whim

pyŏndŏkssŭrŏpta
변덕스럽다 be fickle

pyŏndŏkssŭrŏun
변덕스러운 temperamental

pyŏnduri 변두리 outskirts

pyŏng 병 bottle; illness

pyŏngdŭlda 병들다 fall ill

pyŏng-e kŏllida 병에
걸리다 catch an illness

pyŏngttagae 병따개 bottle-
opener

pyŏng-wŏn 병원 hospital

pyŏn-gyŏng 변경 alteration

pyŏn-gyŏnghada 변경하다
be deflected from

pyŏnhada 변하다 change

pyŏnhagi shwiun 변하기
쉬운 unsettled

pyŏnhohada 변호하다
defend

pyŏnhosa 변호사 attorney

pyŏnhwa 변화 change

pyŏnhwahada 변화하다
change

pyŏnhwashik'ida
변화시키다 change

pyŏnjang 변장 disguise

pyŏnjanghada 변장하다
wear a disguise

pyŏnmyŏng 변명 excuse

pyŏruk 벼룩 flea

P'

p'a 파 scallion; faction; par
(in golf)

p'ada 파다 dig; mine

p'ado 파도 wave

p'aebaeshik'ida 패배시키다
defeat

p'aeja 패자 loser

p'aek'iji kwangwang
패키지 관광 package tour

p'aekssŭ 팩스 fax

p'aengch'ang 팽창
expansion

p'aengch'anghada

p'aengch'anghada 팽창하다 expand

p'aenŏlt'i kuyŏk 패널티 구역 penalty area

p'agoe 파괴 destruction; ruin

p'agoehada 파괴하다 destroy; ruin

p'ahech'ida 파헤치다 dig up

p'al 팔 arm; eight

p'alda 팔다 sell

p'alkkumch'i 팔꿈치 elbow

p'allida 팔리다 fetch price

p'alsship 팔십 eighty

p'altchi 팔찌 bracelet

p'ama hada 파마 하다 perm

p'amut-tta 파묻다 bury

p'an 판 sheet (of glass, metal); tray; board; edition

p'andan 판단 judgment

p'andanhada 판단하다 judge

p'an-gyŏl 판결 sentence

p'an-gyŏrhada 판결하다 judge

p'anmae 판매 sale; selling

p'anmaehada 판매하다 sell

p'anmae kagyŏk 판매 가격 asking price

p'ansa 판사 judge

p'ansori 판소리 epic songs

p'aŏp 파업 strike

p'aŏptcha 파업자 striker

p'aran 파란 blue

p'aranmanjanghan 파란만장한 checkered

p'arat'a 파랗다 be blue

p'ari 파리 fly (insect)

p'arwŏl 파월 August

p'asan 파산 bankruptcy

p'asanhada 파산하다 go bankrupt; be ruined

p'ason 파손 breakage

p'at'i 파티 party

p'at'ibok 파티복 party dress

p'enp'al ch'in-gu 펜팔 친구 pen pal

p'ibu 피부 skin

p'ida 피다 open; unroll; blossom

p'igonhada 피곤하다 be tired

p'igonhan 피곤한 tired

p'ihada 피하다 avoid; ward off; shelter

p'ihae 피해 damage

p'ihaerŭl ip'ida 피해를 입히다 damage

p'ihal su ŏmnŭn 피할 수 없는 inevitable

p'iim 피임 contraception

p'iimhada 피임하다 use contraception

p'iimyak 피임약 the pill

p'illŭm 필름 film

p'ilssajŏgin 필사적인 desperate

p'ilssujŏgin 필수적인 essential

p'ilssup'um 필수품
necessity
p'imang 피망 pimento
p'inanch'ŏ 피난처 refuge
p'inanhada 피난하다 take
refuge
p'inggye 핑계 excuse
p'iri 피리 Korean oboe
p'iryo 필요 need
p'iryohada 필요하다 want;
need
p'iryohan 필요한 necessary
p'iryossŏng 필요성
necessity
p'iuda 피우다 burn; smoke;
give off *smell*; play *trick*
p'ŏdakkŏrida
퍼덕거리다 flutter
p'ŏjida 퍼지다 spread
p'ŏllŏgida 펄럭이다 flap;
flutter; wave
p'ŏltchŏk ttwida 펄쩍 뛰다
jump
p'ŏngk'ŭ 펑크 blow-out
p'ŏttŭrida 퍼뜨리다 spread;
circulate
p'odae 포대 bag; sack
p'odaegi 포대기 baby quilt
(for carrying baby on back)
p'odo 포도 grape
p'odoju 포도주 wine
p'odongp'odonghan
포동포동한 plump
p'odowŏn 포도원 vineyard
p'ogihada 포기하다 give up
p'ogŭmhada 폭음하다

drink too much
p'ogu 폭우 downpour
p'ogyŏk 포격 gunfire
p'ogyŏk'ada 포격하다 shell
p'ohamhada 포함하다
include
p'ohamhan 포함한 inclusive
p'ojang 포장 packaging
p'ojanghada 포장하다
pack; giftwrap
p'ojangji 포장지 wrapping
paper
p'ok 폭 width
p'okppal 폭발 explosion
p'okpparhada 폭발하다
explode; erupt
p'okp'o 폭포 waterfall
p'okp'ung 폭풍 storm
p'okp'ung-u 폭풍우
rainstorm
p'oksshik 폭식 gluttony
p'oksshik'ada 폭식하다 eat
too much
p'okssorŭl t'ŏttŭrida 폭소를
터뜨리다 burst out laughing
p'okttong 폭동 riot
p'okt'an 폭탄 bomb
p'ok'aeng 폭행 assault
p'ok'aenghada 폭행하다
assault
p'ong-nŏlbŭn 폭넓은 wide
p'ongno 폭로 revelation
p'ongnohada 폭로하다
expose
p'ongnyŏk 폭력 force;
outrage

p'ongnyŏktchŏgin
폭력적인 violent

p'o-ong 포옹 cuddle; hug

p'o-onghada 포옹하다 hug

p'oro 포로 captive

p'oshik'ada 포식하다
overeat

p'owihada 포위하다
surround

p'owi konggyŏk'ada 포위
공격하다 lay siege to

p'ŭllŏgŭrŭl kkot-tta
플러그를 꽂다 plug in

p'ŭllŏgŭrŭl ppoptta
플러그를 뽑다 unplug

p'ŭrogŭraem 프로그램
program

p'uda 푸다 scoop

p'uk chamdŭlda 푹 잠들다
be (fast) asleep

p'ukssinhan 푹신한 soft

p'ul 풀 glue; grass

p'ulda 풀다 undo; unpack;
solve; release brake

p'ullin 풀린 frayed

p'ullo puch'ida 풀로
붙이다 glue

p'umjil 품질 quality

p'umjil kwalli 품질 관리
quality control

p'umkkyŏk 품격 grace

p'umwi innŭn 품위 있는
gracious

p'ungbu 풍부 abundance

p'ungbuhada 풍부하다 be
abundant

p'ungbuhan 풍부한
abundant ◊ a wealth of

p'ungch'a 풍차 windmill

p'unggyŏng 풍경 scenery

p'unggyŏnghwa 풍경화
landscape (painting)

p'ungja 풍자 satire

p'ungjajŏgin 풍자적인
satirical

p'ungmunŭro 풍문으로 by
hearsay

p'ungnyoropke hada
풍요롭게 하다 enrich

p'ungsŏn 풍선 balloon

p'ungsŏnkkŏm 풍선껌
bubble gum

p'ung-yo 풍요 plenty

p'ung-yoroun sahoe
풍요로운 사회 affluent
society

p'urŏjuda 풀어주다 untie

p'urŏ poda 풀어 보다
unwrap

p'ye 폐 lung

p'yeam 폐암 lung cancer

p'yegihada 폐기하다
discard

p'yegimul 폐기물 waste

p'yegishik'ida 폐기시키다
scrap

p'yegyŏnggi 폐경기
menopause

p'yehoeshik 폐회식 closing
ceremony

p'yejihada 폐지하다 abolish

p'yejŏm 폐점 closure

p'yejŏmhada 폐점하다
close down

p'yŏp'ada 폐업하다 close
down

p'yŏda 펴다 unfold; smooth
out

p'yŏlli 편리 convenience

p'yŏllihada 편리하다 be
convenient

p'yŏllihan 편리한 convenient

p'yŏn 편 side; means;
tendency; editing; volume;
part

p'yŏnanhada 편안하다 be
comfortable

p'yŏnanhan 편안한
comfortable

p'yŏndo sŭngch'akkwŏn
편도 승차권 one-way ticket

p'yŏndut'ong 편두통
migraine

p'yŏnbŏmhan 평범한
commonplace

p'yŏngdŭng 평등 equality

p'yŏnggyun 평균 average

p'yŏnggyunnaeda 평균내다
average out

p'yŏnghaeng 평행 parallel
(line)

p'yŏnghaenghanŭn
평행하는 parallel

p'yŏnghwa 평화 peace

p'yŏnghwaropkke 평화롭게
peacefully

p'yŏnghwaroptta 평화롭다
be peaceful

p'yŏnghwaroun 평화로운
peaceful

p'yŏng-il 평일 weekday

p'yŏngkka 평가 evaluation

p'yŏngkkahada 평가하다
assess

p'yŏngnon 평론 write-up

p'yŏngnon-ga 평론가
reviewer

P'yŏngnyang 평양
Pyongyang

p'yŏn-gok 편곡 arrangement
MUS

p'yŏn-gok'ada 편곡하다
arrange MUS

p'yŏng-on 평온 calm

p'yŏng-onhada 평온하다
be tranquil

p'yŏng-onhan 평온한
serene

p'yŏngp'an 평판
reputation

p'yŏngp'ani choŭn 평판이
좋은 reputable

p'yŏngp'yŏnghada
평평하다 be even

p'yŏngp'yŏnghan 평평한
flat

p'yŏngsaeng 평생 lifetime

p'yŏngsangbok 평상복
casual wear

p'yŏngsangshich'ŏrŏm
평상시처럼 as usual

p'yŏn-gyŏn 편견 bias

p'yŏn-gyŏnŭl kajin 편견을
가진 biased

p'yŏnhan 편한 be
  comfortable

p'yŏnhi shwida 편히 쉬다
  relax

p'yŏnji 편지 letter

p'yŏnjihada 편지하다 mail

p'yŏnjip 편집 editing
  ◊ editorial

p'yŏnjiptcha 편집자 editor

p'yŏnjip'ada 편집하다 edit;
  compile

p'yŏnjirŭl ssŭda 편지를
  쓰다 write a letter

p'yŏnŭl tŭlda 편을 들다
  take sides

p'yo 표 table (of figures);
  ticket

p'yobaek 표백 bleach

p'yobaek'ada 표백하다
  bleach

p'yohyŏn 표현 expression

p'yohyŏnhada 표현하다
  express

p'yoji 표지 cover (of book)

p'yojŏk 표적 target

p'yojŏng 표정 appearance

p'yojŏng-i p'ungbuhan
  표정이 풍부한 expressive

p'yojun 표준 standard

p'yojun midarŭi 표준
  미달의 substandard

p'yomyŏn 표면 surface

p'yomyŏnjŏgin 표면적인
  superficial

p'yoshi 표시 indication;
  token

p'yoshihada 표시하다
  display; stand for; mark up

R

...rago ...라고 that...

...ranŭn ...라는 that

...ro ...로 by; because of;
  of; into; in; with; to;
  toward

...robut'ŏ ...로부터 from

...rosŏ ...로서 as

...rŭl ...를 object particle

...ryŏgo hada ...려고 하다
  intend to

S

sa 사 four

sabang 사방 all directions

sabok 사복 plain clothes

sabon 사본 copy; transcript

sabunŭi il 사분의 일 quarter

sach'i 사치 extravagance

sach'isŭrŏptta 사치스럽다
  be extravagant

sach'isŭrŏun 사치스러운
  extravagant
sach'on 사촌 cousin
sach'un-gi 사춘기 puberty
sada 사다 buy
sadari 사다리 ladder
sae 새 bird ◊ new
saebyŏk 새벽 dawn
saech'igihada 새치기하다
  cut in line
saeda 새다 leak
saegida 새기다 carve; engrave
saegin색인 index
Saehae 새해 New Year
saejang 새장 bird cage
saekkaman 새까만 jet-black
saekki 새끼 young animal;
  kid; brat
saekki koyang-i 새끼
  고양이 kitten
saek-kkal 색깔 color
saek-kkal innŭn 색깔 있는
  tinted
saek'omdalk'omhan
  새콤달콤한 sweet and sour
saem 샘 spring (water); envy
saengbangsong 생방송
  live broadcast
saenggagi kip'ŭn 생각이
  깊은 thoughtful
saenggak 생각 thought
saenggak'ada 생각하다
  think
saenggang 생강 ginger
saenggangch'a 생강차
  ginger tea

saenggi 생기 liveliness
saenggida 생기다 occur;
  come into existence
saenggiga nada 생기가
  나다 perk up
saenggiinnŭn 생기있는
  lively
saenggye 생계 living
saenghwal 생활 life
saenghwalbi 생활비 living
  expenses
saenghwal pangsshik 생활
  방식 way of life
saenghwal sujun 생활 수준
  standard of living
saeng-il 생일 birthday
saengjonhada 생존하다
  exist; survive
saengjonja 생존자 survivor
saeng k'ŭrim 생 크림
  whipped cream
saengmaektchu 생맥주
  draft (beer)
saengmaeng 색맹 color-
  blindness ◊ color-blind
saengmyŏng 생명 life
saengmyŏng pohŏm 생명
  보험 life insurance
saengni 생리 menstruation;
  period
saengnihada 생리하다
  menstruate
saengnyak'ada 생략하다
  omit
saengnyŏnwŏril 생년월일
  date of birth

saengsaenghada 생생하다
be vivid

saengsaenghan 생생한
vivid

saengsan 생산 production

saengsanhada 생산하다
produce

saengshikki 생식기 genitals

saengsŏn 생선 fish

saengsu 생수 mineral water

saeppalgan kŏjinmal
새빨간 거짓말 downright
lie

saeroptta 새롭다 be new

saeroun 새로운 new

sae tanjanghada 새
단장하다 redecorate

saeu 새우 shrimp

sagak'yŏng 사각형 square

sagi 사기 swindle; morale
◇ fraudulent

sagi ch'ida 사기 치다 cheat

sagikkun 사기꾼 con man

sago 사고 accident; thought

sagwa 사과 apology; apple

sagwahada 사과하다
apologize

sagwida 사귀다 get
acquainted

sagyojŏgin 사교적인
sociable

sahaktcha 사학자 historian

sahoe 사회 society ◇ social

sahoehak 사회학 sociology

sahoeja 사회자 chairperson;
MC

sahoejuŭi 사회주의
socialism

sahoejuŭijŏgin
사회주의적인 socialist

sahyŏng sŏn-gorŭl pat-tta
사형 선고를 받다 be
sentenced to death

sai 사이 interval; relationship

sai-e 사이 between

saiga chot'a 사이가 좋다
be friendly with

saiga t'ŭrŏjida 사이가
틀어지다 fall out

saijok'e chinaeda 사이좋게
지내다 get along

saja 사자 lion

sajang 사장 boss

sajik 사직 resignation

sajik'ada 사직하다 resign

sajin 사진 photograph

sajinaelbŏm 사진앨범
photo album

sajinsa 사진사 photographer

sajin tchiktta 사진 찍다
photograph

sajŏn 사전 dictionary

sak-kkam 삭감 cut

sak-kkamhada 삭감하다
reduce

sakkŏn 사건 incident

saktche 삭제 deletion

saktchehada 삭제하다
delete

sal 살 flesh; years of age;
arrow; spoke (of wheel)

salda 살다 live

salgŭmŏni 살그머니 stealthily

salgŭmsalgŭm kŏt-tta 살금살금 걷다 creep

salgyundoen 살균된 sterile

salk'ogi 살고기 lean meat

sallim kyŏngbiwŏn 산림 경비원 forest ranger

sal ppaeda 살 빼다 slim

salp'yŏboda 살펴보다 look into; check on; examine

salsal 살살 softly

sal su innŭn 살 수 있는 inhabitable

sal su ŏmnŭn 살 수 없는 uninhabitable

saltchak 살짝 furtively; easily; lightly

saltchak sŭch'ida 살짝 스치다 touch lightly

saltchida 살찌다 get fatter

sam 삼 three

samak 사막 desert

samang 사망 death

samangnyul 사망률 death rate

sambunŭi il 삼분의 일 one third

samch'on 삼촌 uncle

samgak 삼각 triangle
◊ triangular

samgak'yŏng 삼각형 triangle

samgyet'ang 삼계탕 chicken boiled with ginseng

samgyŏpssal kui 삼겹살

구이 barbecued belly of pork

Samiltchŏl 삼일절 March First Memorial Day

samjungju 삼중주 trio

samnyu 삼류 third class

samohada 사모하다 adore

samonim 사모님 Madam (respectful)

Samp'alssŏn 삼팔선 38th Parallel

samship 삼십 thirty

samtta 삶다 boil

samul 사물 thing

samushil 사무실 office

samwŏl 삼월 March

samyŏng 사명 mission

san 산 mountain; acid

sanagin 산악인 mountaineer

sanaptta 사납다 be fierce; be unlucky

sanaun 사나운 fierce

sanbuinkkwa 산부인과 maternity hospital

sanch'aek 산책 ramble

sanch'aek'ada 산책하다 go for a walk

sandaejŏgŭro 상대적으로 relatively

sandŏmi 산더미 mound

sandŭlpparam 산들바람 breeze

sang 상 prize; icon; statue; table; mourning

sang-a 상아 ivory

sangbandoen 상반된 opposite

sangch'ŏ 상처 wound; sore; bruise

sangch'ŏ ibŭn 상처 입은 wounded

sangch'ŏnan 상처난 emotionally painful

sangch'ŏ patkki shwiun 상처 받기 쉬운 vulnerable

sangch'ŏrŭl chuda 상처를 주다 bruise; hurt

sangch'ŏrŭl pat-tta 상처를 받다 get hurt

sangch'u 상추 lettuce

sangdae 상대 opponent; companion

sangdaejŏgin 상대적인 relative

sangdam 상담 consultancy; advice

sangdambi 상담비 (consultancy) fee

sangdamhada 상담하다 counsel

sangdanghada 상당하다 appropriate; be considerable; be reasonable; be equivalent

sangdanghage 상당하게 substantially

sangdanghi 상당히 quite ... **sang-e** 상에 on

sangga 상가 mall

sanggihada 상기하다 recall; relive

sanggishikida 상기시키다 remind

sanggŭm 상금 winnings

sanggŭp 상급 senior rank; advanced level ◊ senior

sanggwanŏmnŭn 상관없는 irrelevant

sanggwanŏptta 상관없다 be irrelevant; not mind

sanghada 상하다 go bad; be injured; be emaciated

sanghan 상한 sour

sanghoganŭi 상호간의 mutual

sanghwang 상황 situation

sang-in 상인 merchant

san-gisŭlk 산기슭 foot of a mountain

sangja 상자 box

sangjing 상징 symbol

sangjinghada 상징하다 symbolize

sangjingjŏgin 상징적인 symbolic

sangjŏm 상점 store

sangk'waehada 상쾌하다 feel fresh

sangk'waehan 상쾌한 refreshing

sangmak'ada 삭막하다 be bleak

sangmak'an 삭막한 stark

sangnyŏnghada 상영하다 show *movie*

sangnyu 상류 upper reaches; upper classes ◊ upper-class

sangnyu sahoe 상류 사회 high society

sangŏ 상어 shark

sang-ŏp 상업 commerce
◊ commercial

sang-ŏpssang-ŭi 상업상의
commercial

sangp'um 상품 goods

sangp'umhwahada
상품화하다 commercialize

sangp'umkkwŏn 상품권
token

sangp'yo 상표 brand

sangsa 상사 boss

sangsang 상상 imagination

sangsanghada 상상하다
imagine

sangsangnyŏgi
p'ungbuhan 상상력이
풍부한 imaginative

sangsehada 상세하다 be
detailed

sangsehage 상세하게
minutely

sangsehan 상세한 detailed

sangshik 상식 sense

sangshil 상실 loss

sangshirhada 상실하다
forfeit

sangsogin 상속인 heir

sangsok 상속 inheritance

sangsok'ada 상속하다
inherit

sangsŭng 상승 rise ◊ rising

sangsŭnghada 상승하다
rise

sangsŭrŏptta 상스럽다
be crude

sangsŭrŏun 상스러운 vulgar

sangsudo 상수도
waterworks

sangt'ae 상태 state;
circumstances

sanjŏk 산적 bandit; kabob

sanmaek 산맥 (mountain)
range

sanmanhada 산만하다 be
loose; be vague

sanmanhage 산만하게
loosely

sanmanhan 산만한 loose;
vague

sannamul 산나물 wild greens

sanŏp 산업 industry
◊ industrial

sanŏp'wahada 산업화하다
industrialize

sansanjogak naeda
산산조각 내다 smash to
pieces

sansat'ae 산사태 landslide

sanshin 산신 mountain spirit

sanso 산소 oxygen; ancestral
grave

santtŏmi 산더미 heap

santtŭngsŏng-i 산둥성이
ridge

sant'okki 산토끼 hare

sanyang 사냥 hunting

sanyanghada 사냥하다
hunt

sanyangkkun 사냥꾼 hunter

saŏp 사업 business

saŏpkka 사업가
businessman

sap 삽 shovel; scoop; spade

sapsshigane 삽시간에 in an instant

sap'wa 삽화 illustration

sap'warŭl kŭrida 삽화를 그리다 illustrate

saragada 살아가다 keep on living

sara innŭn 살아 있는 live

sarait-tta 살아있다 be alive

sarajida 사라지다 disappear

saram 사람 person
◊ countword for people

saramdaun 사람다운 humane

sarami salji annŭn 사람이 살지 않는 uninhabited

saranada 살아나다 revive; survive

sara nagada 살아 나가다 carry on living

saranamtta 살아남다 survive

sarang 사랑 love

sarang-e ppajida 사랑에 빠지다 fall in love (with)

saranghada 사랑하다 love

saranghanŭn 사랑하는 beloved

sarang-ni 사랑니 wisdom tooth

sarangsŭrŏun 사랑스러운 lovable

sarhae 살해 killing

sarhaehada 살해하다 kill

sari 사리 coil; self-interest;

Buddhist saint's relic; reason

sarin 살인 murder

sarinbŏm 살인범 homicide; murderer

sarinhada 살인하다 murder

sarojaptta 사로잡다 capture

sarŭl enŭndŭshi 살을 에는듯이 bitterly cold

saryŏ kip'ŭn 사려 깊은 thoughtful

saryo 사료 fodder

sasaeng-a 사생아 illegitimate child

sasaenghwal 사생활 privacy

sasang 사상 ideology; death and injury ◊ in history

sasangja 사상자 casualty

sashil 사실 fact

sashilssang 사실상 in fact; in effect

sashilssang-ŭi 사실상의 actual; virtual

sashiltchuŭi 사실주의 realism

saship 사십 forty

sashirŭn 사실은 in fact

sasŏham 사서함 PO Box

sasŏl 사설 editorial

sasohada 사소하다 be trivial

sasohan 사소한 trivial

sasŭm 사슴 deer

satchŏgin 사적인 private

Sat'an 사탄 Satan

sat'ang 사탕 candy

sat'ang susu 사탕 수수

sugar cane

sat'uri 사투리 dialect

saundŭ k'adŭ 사운드 카드
sound card

sawi 사위 son-in-law

sawŏl 사월 April

sawŏn 사원 temple REL

sayanghada 사양하다
decline with thanks

sayong 사용 use

sayonghada 사용하다 use;
exercise *restraint*; work

sayongja 사용자 user

sayong sŏlmyŏngsŏ 사용
설명서 instruction manual

sebal chajŏn-gŏ 세발 자전거
자전거 tricycle

sech'ashik'ida 세차시키다
get the car washed

seda 세다 count (up)

sedae 세대 generation

sedae ch'ai 세대 차이
generation gap

sege ch'ida 세게 치다
punch; push

segi 세기 century

segŭm 세금 tax

segwanwŏn 세관원 customs
officer

segye 세계 world

segyehwa 세계화
globalization

segyejŏgin 세계적인
worldwide

segyejŏgŭro 세계적으로
worldwide

segye kyŏngje 세계 경제
global economy

segye onnanhwa 세계
온난화 global warming

segye taejŏn 세계 대전
world war

segyun 세균 germ

seil chung-ida 세일 중이다
be on sale (*reduced prices*)

sem 셈 count; intention

semŭro ch'ida 셈으로 치다
count

semyŏndae 세면대

semyŏn-gi 세면기
washbasin

semyŏnjang 세면장
bathroom

senoe 세뇌 brainwashing

senoehada 세뇌하다
brainwash

se pŏntchae 세 번째 third

sep'o 세포 cell

serye 세례 baptism

seryehada 세례하다 baptize

seryŏk 세력 power; influence

seryŏndoen 세련된 cultured

sesang 세상 world

seshim 세심 carefulness

seshimhan 세심한
meticulous

sesogŭi 세속의 secular

sesoktchŏgin 세속적인
worldly

se ssangdung-i 세 쌍둥이
triplets

set 셋 three

set'ak-kki 세탁기 washing machine

set'aksso 세탁소 laundry; dry cleaner

set'ak'ada 세탁하다 launder

set'inghada 세팅하다 set up

seuda 세우다 build; erect; establish; turn up *collar*; stop *person in street*

shi 시 poetry; poem; city; o'clock

shiabŏji 시아버지 father-in-law *(husband's father)*

shibi 십이 twelve

shibiwŏl 십이월 December

shibo 십오 fifteen

shibobun 십오분 fifteen minutes

shich'a 시차 time-lag

shich'al 시찰 inspection

shich'arhada 시찰하다 inspect

shich'e 시체 corpse

shich'ŏng 시청 city hall

shich'ŏnghada 시청하다 view

shich'ŏngja 시청자 audience; viewer

shich'o 시초 beginning

shida 시다 be sour

shidae 시대 era

shidallida 시달리다 be harassed

shidallin 시달린 harassed

shido 시도 attempt

shidohada 시도하다 try

shidongdoeda 시동되다 start

shigaktchŏgin 시각적인 visual

shigaktchŏguro 시각적으로 visually

shigan 시간 time; hour

shigan chŏryak 시간 절약 timesaving

shiganjero 시간제로 part-time

shigan mada 시간 마다 every hour

shigan ŏmsu 시간 엄수 punctuality

shiganp'yo 시간표 schedule

shiganŭl chik'inŭn 시간을 지키는 prompt

shiganŭl hŏbihada 시간을 허비하다 dawdle

shiganŭl match'uŏ 시간을 맞추어 in time

shigi 시기 period

shigi yoppŏp 식이 요법 diet *(as cure)*

shigol 시골 countryside

shigolkkil 시골길 country lane

shigoltchip 시골집 cottage

shigŭmch'i 시금치 spinach

shigye 시계 clock; watch

shigye panghyang-ŭro tora 시계 방향으로 돌아 clockwise

shigyogŭl todunŭn 식욕을 돋우는 appetizing

shigyok 식욕 appetite

shihan p'okt'an 시한 폭탄
time bomb

shihap 시합 tournament;
game; bout *(in boxing)*

shihŏm 시험 exam

shihŏmgwan 시험관
examiner; test tube

shihŏmhada 시험하다
examine

shiin 시인 confession; poet

shiinhada 시인하다 admit

shijak 시작 beginning

shijakdoeda 시작되다
begin; break out

shijak'ada 시작하다 begin;
institute; take up; log on

shijang 시장 market;
marketplace; mayor

shijangboda 시장보다
sell; buy

shijŏl 시절 season; time

shik 식 event; ceremony;
eclipse

shikch'o 식초 vinegar

shikkŭrŏptta 시끄럽다
be loud

shikkŭrŏun 시끄러운 noisy

shikp'umjŏm 식품점
grocery (store)

shikssa 식사 meal

shikssahada 식사하다
dine

shikssa shigan 식사 시간
mealtime

shikssŏng 식성 taste

shiktchungdok 식중독 food
poisoning

shiktta 식다 cool down

shikttan 식단 menu

shikttang 식당 restaurant;
dining room

shikttanp'yo 식단표 menu

shikt'ak 식탁 dining table

shik'ida 식히다 cool down

shil 실 thread

shillae(sŏ) 실내에(서)
indoors

shillang 신랑 bridegroom

shilloe 신뢰 trust

shilloehada 신뢰하다 trust

shilloehanŭn 신뢰하는
trusting

shilloessŏng 신뢰성
trustworthiness

shillye 실례 illustration;
impoliteness

shillyehamnida 실례합니다
excuse me

shilmang 실망
disappointment

shilmanghada 실망하다
disappoint

shilmanghan 실망한
disappointed

shilmangsŭrŏun
실망스러운 disappointing

shilmari 실마리 clue

shilp'ae 실패 failure;
breakdown; reel

shilp'aehada 실패하다 fail;
break down; lose out; be out

shilp'aehan 실패한
unsuccessful

shilp'aero kkŭnnada 실패로
끝나다 end in failure

shilsshidoeda 실시되다
come into effect

shilsshihada 실시하다
carry out

shilsu 실수 mistake

shilssuhada 실수하다 make
a mistake

shilssuro 실수로 by mistake

shilche 실제 truth; fact;
practice ◊ practical

shiltchejŏgin 실제적인
practical

shiltcheŭi 실제의 actual

shiltchik'ada 실직하다 lose
one's job; be unemployed

shiltchik'an 실직한
unemployed

shiltchŏm 실점 lost points

shiltchong 실종
disappearance

shiltchŭng nada 싫증 나다
be tired of

shiltta 싣다 load

shilt'ohada 실토하다
confess

shim 심 pith

shimburŭm 심부름 errand

shimgak'ada 심각하다 be
serious

shimgak'an 심각한 serious

shimhada 심하다 be awful

shimhage 심하게 seriously

shimhan 심한 bad

shimin 시민 citizen

shiminkkwŏn 시민권
citizenship

shimjang 심장 heart

shimjang ishik 심장 이식
heart transplant

shimjang mabi 심장 마비
heart attack

shimmun 심문 interrogation

shimmunhada 심문하다
interrogate

shimnanhan 심란한
distracted

shimni 심리 hearing JUR

shimnijŏgin 심리적인
psychological

shimnijŏguro 심리적으로
psychologically

shimp'an 심판 referee

shimsahada 심사하다 judge

shimsasuk-kkohan
심사숙고한 thoughtful

shimsa wiwŏn 심사 위원
judge

shimsa wiwŏndan 심사
위원단 jury

shimsulgujŭn 심술궂은
bad-tempered

shimtta 심다 plant

shimuruk'an 시무룩한 glum

shimyuk 십육 sixteen

shin 신 god ◊ our

shinae t'onghwa 시내 통화
local call

shinang 신앙 belief

shinbal 신발 shoe

shinbalkkage 신발가게 shoestore

shinbi 신비 mystery

shinbihada 신비하다 be mysterious

shinbihage 신비하게 mysteriously

shinbihan 신비한 mysterious

shinbu 신부 bride; (Catholic) priest

shinbun 신분 rank

shinbun chüngmyŏngsŏ 신분 증명서 identity card

shinbuntchŭng 신분증 (identity) papers

shinch'am 신참 newcomer

shinch'e chang-ae 신체 장애 physical disability

shinch'e chang-aeja 신체 장애자 the disabled

shinch'ŏng 신청 application

shinch'ŏnghada 신청하다 apply for

shinch'ŏngsŏ 신청서 application form

shigandang 시간당 hourly rate

shinggŭt ut-tta 싱긋 웃다 grin

shingminji 식민지 colony

shingminjiŭi 식민지의 colonial

Shingmogil 식목일 Arbor Day

shingmul 식물 plant
◊ botanical

shin-gohada 신고하다 register; declare; inform; turn in (to police)

shin-gyŏng 신경 creed; nerve

shin-gyŏng-i ssŭida 신경이 쓰이다 bother

shin-gyŏngjiltchŏgin 신경질적인 fussy

shin-gyŏng kwaminŭi 신경 과민의 neurotic

shin-gyŏngtchilnage hada 신경질나게 하다 irritate

Shin-gyodo 신교도 Protestant

shinhak 신학 theology

shinho 신호 signal

shinhodŭng 신호등 traffic light

shinhohada 신호하다 signal

shinhon yŏhaeng 신혼 여행 honeymoon

shinhwa 신화 myth

shinhwaŭi 신화의 mythical

shinip sawŏnŭl ppoptta 신입 사원을 뽑다 recruit

shinipssaeng 신입생 freshman

shinja 신자 believer

shinjang 신장 kidney ANAT

Shinjŏng 신정 New Year

shinjung 신중 prudence

shinjunghada 신중하다 be careful

shinjunghage 신중하게
carefully

shinmun 신문 newspaper

shinnyŏm 신념 conviction

shinsa 신사 gentleman

shinse 신세 debt of gratitude

shinsŏndo 신선도 freshness

shinsŏng 신성 sanctity

shinsŏnghan 신성한 divine

shinsŏnhada 신선하다
be fresh

shinsŏnhan 신선한 fresh

shinssok 신속 rapidity

shinssok'an 신속한 rapid

shintta 신다 put on *shoes*

shinŭmhada 신음하다
groan

shinui 시누이 sister-in-law
(*husband's sister*)

Shinyak Sŏngsŏ 구약 성서
New Testament

shinyong 신용 credit

shinyonginnŭn 신용있는
creditworthy

shinyong k'adŭ 신용 카드
credit card

shinyung 시늉 act

shiŏmŏni 시어머니 mother-
in-law (*wife's*)

shioe pŏsŭ 시외 버스 bus

ship 십 ten

ship nyŏn 십 년 decade

ship ŏk 십억 billion

ship tae 십 대 teens
◇ teenage

shiptchaga 십자가 cross

shiptchungp'algu 십중팔구
in all likelihood

shiptta 싶다 want; seem

shirhaeng 실행 fulfillment;
execution (*of plan*); return
COMPUT

shirhaenghada 실행하다
carry out; fulfill; run *software*

shirhaeng kanŭnghan 실행
가능한 feasible

shirhŏm 실험 experiment

shirhŏmhada 실험하다
experiment

shirhŏmshil 실험실
laboratory

shirhŏmŭi 실험의
experimental

shirhyŏn 실현 realization

shirhyŏndoeda 실현되다
come true

shirŏhada 싫어하다 dislike

shirŏp 실업 unemployment

shirŏptcha 실업자 the
unemployed

shirŭl ppoptta 실을 뽑다
remove stitches

shirŭn 싫은 distasteful

shiryŏk 시력 eyesight

shiryongjŏgin 실용적인
practical

shisa 시사 current affairs;
preview

shishihada 시시하다 be
trivial; be tame (*of joke*); be
stupid

shisŏl 시설 facilities

shiso 시소 seesaw

shisok 시속 speed per hour

shitta 싣다 load (on a ship, truck)

shittchŏgin 시적인 poetic

shiwi 시위 demonstration

shiwihada 시위하다 demonstrate

shiwŏl 시월 October

shiwŏnhada 시원하다 be cool

shwida 쉬다 rest

shwin 쉰 fifty

shwin mokssoriŭi 쉰 목소리의 husky

shwinŭn nal 쉬는 날 day off

shwipkke 쉽게 easily

shwiptta 쉽다 be easy

shwishwihaebŏrida 쉬쉬해버리다 hush up

shwiun 쉬운 easy

shyawŏ 샤워 shower

shyawŏhada 샤워하다 shower

shyo 쇼 show; vaudeville

shyo pijŭnisŭ 쇼 비즈니스 show business

shyop'ingssent'ŏ 쇼핑센터 mall

sik'ye 식혜 malted rice drink

sŏ 서 west

sŏbissŭ chegonghoesa 서비스 제공회사 service provider

sŏbissŭhada 서비스하다

service machine, car

sŏbŏ 서버 server COMPUT

sŏch'ihada 서치하다 search COMPUT

sŏda 서다 stand; stop

sŏdullŏ! 서둘러! hurry up!

sŏdullŏ ttŏnada 서둘러 떠나다 dash off

sŏdurŭda 서두르다 rush

sŏdurŭn 서두른 hurried

sŏgŭlp'ŭn 서글픈 sad

sŏgyu 석유 petroleum

Sŏhae 서해 West Sea (Yellow Sea)

sŏjae 서재 study (room)

sŏjŏm 서점 bookstore

sŏkkida 섞이다 blend in

sŏk-kkin 섞인 mixed

sŏkkŏ not'a 섞어 놓다 mix up

sŏkkŭn kŏt 섞은 것 mixture

sŏkppang 석방 release

sŏkppanghada 석방하다 release

sŏkssa (hagwi) 석사 (학위) master's (degree)

sŏkssoero kuptta 석쇠로 굽다 grill

sŏktta 섞다 mix

sŏlch'i 설치 installation

sŏlch'ihada 설치하다 install

sŏlgŏji hada 설거지하다 wash the dishes

sŏlgyehada 설계하다 design

sŏlgyesa 설계사 architect

sŏlgyo 설교 sermon

sŏlgyohada 설교하다 preach

Sŏllal 설날 Lunar New Year

sŏlliptcha 설립자 founder

sŏllip'ada 설립하다 establish

sŏlma! 설마! come on! *(disbelief)*

sŏlmyŏng 설명 explanation

sŏlmyŏnghada 설명하다 explain

sŏlmyŏngsŏ 설명서 manual

sŏlssa 설사 diarrhea

sŏltttŭk 설득 persuasion

sŏltttŭk'ada 설득하다 persuade

sŏl't'ang 설탕 sugar

sŏm 섬 island

sŏmttŭk'an 섬뜩한 scary

sŏmyŏng 서명 signature

sŏmyŏnghada 서명하다 sign

sŏmyŏnŭro 서면으로 in writing

sŏn 선 line; gland; (space) module; Zen; goodness

sŏnbak 선박 boat

sŏnbal kwajŏng 선발 과정 selection process

sŏnban 선반 shelf; rack

sŏnbarhada 선발하다 choose

sŏnbul 선불 advance *(money)* ◊ prepaid

sŏnbul yogŭm 선불 요금 advance payment

sŏnburhada 선불하다 put down *deposit*

sŏnburŭi 선불의 prepaid

sŏnch'urhada 선출하다 vote in

sŏndu 선두 lead *(in race)*

sŏndu chuja 선두 주자 forerunner

sŏnduŭi 선두의 leading

sŏng 성 gender; surname; castle; ministry

sŏngch'wi 성취 achievement

sŏngch'wihada 성취하다 accomplish

sŏngdang 성당 cathedral

sŏngga 성가 hymn

sŏnggashige hada 성가시게 하다 annoy

sŏnggashin 성가신 annoying

sŏnggong 성공 success

sŏnggonghada 성공하다 succeed

sŏnggonghan 성공한 prosperous

sŏnggongtchŏgin 성공적인 successful

sŏnggongtchŏgŭro 성공적으로 successfully

sŏnggŭm 성금 donation

sŏnggŭp'ada 성급하다 be impatient

sŏnggŭp'age 성급하게 impatiently

sŏnggŭp'an 성급한 short-tempered

sŏnggwan-gye 성관계
relationship *(sexual)*

sŏnggyŏgi chohŭn 성격이
좋은 good-natured

Sŏnggyŏng 성경 Bible

sŏnggyo 성교 sexual
intercourse

sŏnggyohada 성교하다
have sex

sŏngham 성함 name

sŏnghŭirong 성희롱 sexual
harassment

sŏnghyŏng-oekkwa
성형외과 cosmetic surgery

sŏnghyŏng susul 성형
수술 plastic surgery

sŏng-in 성인 adult *(over 20)*
◊ adult; saint

sŏng-i nada 성이 나다 get
ruffled

sŏngjang 성장 growth

sŏngjanghada 성장하다
grow *(of business)*; dress up

sŏngjiktcha 성직자
clergyman

sŏngjŏgŭl naeda 성적을
내다 grade

sŏngjŏk 성적 grade

sŏngjŏkp'yo 성적표 report
card

sŏngkkal innŭn 성깔 있는
bad-tempered

sŏngkkyŏk 성격 character

sŏng kwan-gyerŭl kajida 성
관계를 가지다 make love

sŏngmi kŭp'an 성미 급한
bad-tempered

sŏngmyŏng 성명
name *(on form)*

sŏngnada 성나다 be angry

sŏngnan 성난 angry

sŏngnŭng 성능 capacity

sŏngnyang 성냥 matches

sŏngnyangkkap 성냥갑
box of matches

Sŏngnyŏng 성령 Holy Spirit

sŏn-gŏ 선거 election

sŏn-gŏil 선거일 election day

sŏn-gŏ undong 선거 운동
election campaign

sŏngsaenghwal 성생활
sex life

sŏngshil 성실 sincerity

sŏngshirhada 성실하다
be sincere

sŏngshirhan 성실한 sincere

sŏngsŏ-ŭi 성서의 biblical

sŏngsŭrŏptta 성스럽다
be holy

sŏngsŭrŏun 성스러운 holy

sŏngsuk'ada 성숙하다 be
mature; reach maturity

sŏngsuk'an 성숙한 mature

sŏngtchŏk maeryŏgi innŭn
성적 매력이 있는 sexually
attractive

Sŏngt'anjŏl 성탄절
Christmas

sŏn-gŏhada 선거하다 elect

sŏn-gŭm 선금 cash in
advance

sŏn-guja 선구자 pioneer

sŏn-gujŏgin 선구적인 pioneering

sŏn-gyŏnjimyŏng 선견지명 foresight

sŏn-gyosa 선교사 missionary

sŏnho 선호 preference

sŏnhohada 선호하다 prefer

sŏninjang 선인장 cactus

sŏnipkkyŏn 선입견 prejudice

sŏnjam 선잠 doze

sŏnjang 선장 captain

sŏnjin-guk 선진국 advanced country

sŏnjŏn 선전 publicity

sŏnjŏnhada 선전하다 publicize

sŏnjŏn hwalttong 선전 활동 propaganda

sŏnmul 선물 gift

sŏnmyŏngdo 선명도 resolution

sŏnmyŏnghada 선명하다 be vivid

sŏnmyŏnghan 선명한 vivid

sŏnnyul 선율 melody

sŏnŏn 선언 declaration

sŏnŏnhada 선언하다 proclaim

sŏnp'unggi 선풍기 fan

sŏnsaeng 선생 teacher

sŏnshil 선실 cabin

sŏnsŏhada 서서하다 swear

sŏnsu 선수 athlete; player

sŏnsuch'ida 선수치다 outwit

sŏnsugwŏn 선수권 championship (title)

sŏnt'aegŭi 선택의 optional

sŏnt'aegŭi pŏmwi 선택의 범위 choice

sŏnt'aek 선택 choice

sŏnt'aek'ada 선택하다 choose

sŏnŭl kŭt-tta 선을 긋다 mark out

sŏnŭrhaejida 서늘해지다 cool down

sŏnwŏn 선원 seaman

sŏpsshi 섭씨 centigrade

sŏp'ung 서풍 west wind

sŏrap 서랍 drawer

sŏraptchang 서랍장 chest of drawers

sŏri 서리 frost

sŏriga naerinŭn 서리가 내리는 frosty

sŏro 서로 one another

sŏro mannŭn 서로 맞는 compatible

sŏron 서론 introduction

sŏrŭn 서른 thirty

sŏryu 서류 document

sŏryuch'ŏl 서류철 file

sŏryu kabang 서류 가방 briefcase

sŏsŏhi kkŭltta 서서히 끓다 simmer

sŏsŏngdaeda 서성대다 prowl

sŏtchogŭi 서쪽의 western

sŏtchok 서쪽 west

sŏt'urŭda 서투르다 be bad at

sŏt'urŭn 서투른 poor

Sŏul 서울 Seoul

Sŏyang 서양 the West
◇ Western

sŏyanghwadoen 서양화된 westernized

Sŏyang saram 서양 사람 Westerner

sŏye 서예 calligraphy

sobangch'a 소방차 fire truck

sobangsŏ 소방서 fire department

sobi 소비 consumption

sobihada 소비하다 consume

sobija 소비자 consumer

sobyŏn 소변 urine

sobyŏnŭl poda 소변을 보다 urinate

sodok'ada 소독하다 disinfect

sodong 소동 disturbance

sodongnyak 소독약 disinfectant

soe 쇠 iron

soegogi 쇠고기 beef

soesasŭl 쇠사슬 chain

soet'oe 쇠퇴 decay

soet'oehada 쇠퇴하다 decay

soet'oehanŭn 쇠퇴하는 decaying

sogae 소개 introduction

sogaehada 소개하다 introduce

sogak'ae pŏrida 태워버리다 burn down

sogam 소감 opinion

...soge ...소에 in

sogida 속이다 deceive

sogimsu 속임수 trick

sogimsurŭl ssŭda 속임수를 쓰다 cheat

sogŏ 속어 slang

sogogi kukppap 소고기 국밥 beef soup with rice

sogot 속옷 underwear

sogŭm 소금 salt

sohwa 소화 digestion

sohwagi 소화기 fire extinguisher

sohwahada 소화하다 digest; extinguish

sohwa pullyang 소화 불량 indigestion

sohyŏng 소형 small size

sohyŏngch'a 소형차 compact (car)

sohyŏng pŏsŭ 소형 버스 minibus

sojil 소질 talent; temperament

sojip'ada 소집하다 convene

sojip'um 소지품 belongings

soju 소주 soju (a distilled liquor)

sojunghi hada 소중히 하다 cherish

sojunghi yŏgida 소중히 여기다 value

sok 속 core; filling

sokch'ima 속치마 underskirt

sok-kkan shinmun 석간 신문 evening paper

sok-kki shwiun 속기 쉬운 gullible

sokppo 속보 news flash

sokssagida 속삭이다 whisper

sokssagim 속삭임 whisper

sokssanghada 속상하다 be upsetting

sokssanghan 속상한 upsetting

sokttam 속담 proverb

sokto 속도 speed

sokto chèhan 속도 제한 speed limit

sokto naeda 속도 내다 speed up

sol 솔 brush

soljirhada 솔질하다 brush

solssŏnhada 솔선하다 lead the way

soltchik'ada 솔직하다 be frank

soltchik'age 솔직하게 bluntly

soltchik'i 솔직히 frankly

somae 소매 sleeve

somaech'igi 소매치기 shoplifter; pickpocket

somaega ŏmnŭn 소매가 없는 sleeveless

somsshi 솜씨 workmanship

somsshi innŭn 솜씨 있는 workmanlike

somun 소문 rumor

somyŏl 소멸 disappearance; demise

somyŏrhada 소멸하다 die out

son 손 hand

sonagi 소나기 shower (rain)

sonamu 소나무 pine (tree)

sonaraet saram 손아랫 사람 junior

sonaraeŭi 손아래의 junior

song-aji 송아지 calf

songbyŏrhoe 송별회 leaving party

songgŭmhada 송금하다 transfer

song-i 송이 cluster
◇ countword for flowers, bunches of grapes

songmaŭmŭl t'ŏnot'a 속마음을 터놓다 open up (of person)

songnunssŏp 속눈썹 eyelash

song-ŏ 송어 trout

songp'yŏn 송편 rice cake steamed with pine needles

sonhae 손해 harm; loss

sonja 손자 grandson

sonjabi 손잡이 handle; knob; stem (of glass)

sonjirhada 손질하다 trim; groom; touch up

sonkkaragŭro karik'ida 손가락으로 가리키다

point (to)
sonkkarak 손가락 finger
sonmok 손목 wrist
sonmok shigye 손목 시계 wrist watch
sonnim 손님 guest
sonnyŏ 손녀 granddaughter
sonppadak 손바닥 palm (of hand)
sonsang 손상 damage
sonsangshik'ida 손상시키다 damage
sonsangshik'inŭn 손상시키는 damaging
sonshil 손실 loss
sonshiri k'ŭn 손실이 큰 costly
sonsugŏn 손수건 handkerchief
sonsu mandŭlgi 손수 만들기 DIY
sont'op 손톱 fingernail
sont'opkkak-kki 손톱깎이 nail clippers
sonŭl hŭndŭlda 손을 흔들다 wave (to)
sonŭl taeda 손을 대다 touch; feel up (sexually)
sonŭro 손으로 by hand
sonŭro hanŭn 손으로 하는 manual
sonŭro ssŭn 손으로 쓴 handwritten
sonwiŭi 손위의 senior
sonyŏ 소녀 girl
sonyŏn 소년 boy

so-oegam 소외감 sense of alienation
sop'a 소파 sofa
sop'o 소포 parcel
sop'ung 소풍 picnic
soran 소란 uproar
soranhada 소란하다 be noisy
soranhan 소란한 noisy
soransŭrŏun 소란스러운 tumultuous
sori 소리 sound
sorich'ida 소리치다 shout; scream
sorich'yŏ purŭda 소리쳐 부르다 shout
sorinop'yŏ ut-tta 소리높여 웃다 howl (with laughter)
sori ŏmnŭn 소리 없는 silent
sorirŭl naeŏ 소리를 내어 aloud
sorŭm 소름 gooseflesh
soryang 소량 dab
sosa orŭda 솟아 오르다 soar; lift off
soshik 소식 news
sosŏl 소설 novel
sosŏlga 소설가 novelist
sosong 소송 lawsuit
sosong sakkŏn 소송 사건 court case
sossŭ 소스 sauce; dressing
sosu 소수 decimal
sosu minjok 소수 민족 ethnic minority

sosup'a

sosup'a 소수파 minority

soŭm 소음 sound

sowŏn 소원 wish

sowŏnhada 소원하다 be estranged; petition

sowŏnhan 소원한 distant

soyongŏmnŭn 소용없는 pointless

soyuhada 소유하다 possess

soyuja 소유자 owner

soyukkwŏn 소유권 ownership

soyumul 소유물 possession(s)

soyuyogi kanghan 소유욕이 강한 possessive

ssaollida 쌓아올리다 heap up

ssada 싸다 wrap; pack; cheap; be fast; excrete

ssaguryŏmulgŏn 싸구려물건 cheap goods

ssak 싹 germ; bud

ssal 쌀 rice *(uncooked)*

ssalssarhada 쌀쌀하다 be chilly

ssalssarhan 쌀쌀한 chilly; fresh; icy; standoffish

ssan 싼 cheap; low

ssang 쌍 pair; couple

ssangdung-i 쌍둥이 twins

ssan mulgŏn 싼 물건 cheap goods

ssat'a 쌓다 stack; run up *debts*

ssauda 싸우다 fight

ssaum 싸움 fight

ssaumjirhada 싸움질하다 brawl

ssayŏjida 쌓여지다 accumulate

sseda 세다 be strong; turn gray; count

ssekssihan 섹시한 sexy

ssekssŭ 섹스 sex

ssen 센 strong

sshi 씨 Mr; Ms; seed

sshijok 씨족 clan

sshing chinagada 씽 지나가다 whizz by

sshiptta 씹다 chew

sshirŭm 씨름 (Korean) wrestling

sshirŭmhada 씨름하다 grapple with

sshit-tta 씻다 wash

ssŏbŏrida 써버리다 use up

ssŏgŭn 썩은 rotten

ssŏk-kki shwiun 썩기 쉬운 perishable

ssŏktta 썩다 go bad

ssŏlda 썰다 chop

ssŏlmae 썰매 sled; sleigh

ssŏlmul 썰물 ebb tide

ssoda 쏘다 fire; shoot; sting

ssoda put-tta 쏟아 붓다 pour

ssŭda 쓰다 use; spend; write; put on; be bitter

ssŭdadŭmtta 쓰다듬다 stroke; smooth *hair*

ssŭgi 쓰기 writing; use

ssŭiuda 씌우다 cover; get on; crown *tooth*

ssŭlda 쓸다 sweep

ssŭlmo 쓸모 usefulness

ssŭlmoinnŭn 쓸모있는 useful

ssŭlmoŏmnŭn 쓸모없는 useless; waste

ssŭl su innŭn 쓸 수 있는 usable

ssŭn 쓴 bitter

ssŭrebatkki 쓰레받기 dustpan

ssŭregi 쓰레기 garbage; scum *(people)*

ssŭregi t'ong 쓰레기 통 garbage can

ssŭrŏjida 쓰러지다 fall down

ssukssuk charada 쑥쑥 자라다 shoot up *(of kids)*

ssushida 쑤시다 prod; have a stitch; hurt

ssushyŏ nŏt'a 쑤셔 넣다 jam

sŭk'aenhada 스캔하다 scan

sŭk'ech'ihada 스케치하다 sketch

sŭk'eit'ŭ t'agi 스케이트 타기 skating

sŭk'i t'agi 스키 타기 skiing

sŭlgŭmŏni 슬그머니 stealthily

sŭlp'ŏhada 슬퍼하다 lament

sŭlp'ŭda 슬프다 be sad

sŭlp'ŭge 슬프게 sadly

sŭlp'ŭm 슬픔 sadness; sorrow

sŭlp'ŭn 슬픈 sad

sŭltchŏk kajyŏgada 슬쩍 가져가다 steal

sŭmul 스물 twenty

sŭnggaek 승객 passenger; occupant

sŭnggaeksŏk 승객석 passenger seat

sŭngganggi 승강기 elevator

sŭng-in 승인 approval

sŭng-inhada 승인하다 approve; recognize; grant

sŭngjin 승진 promotion

sŭngjinhada 승진하다 promote

sŭngma 승마 riding; horse

sŭngmahada 승마하다 ride

sŭngmuwŏn 승무원 cabin crew

sŭngni 승리 victory

sŭngnihan 승리한 victorious

sŭngnija 승리자 victor

Sŭpein 스페인 Spain

Sŭpeinŭi 스페인의 Spanish

sŭpkki 습기 humidity; moisture

sŭpkkich'an 습기찬 damp

sŭpkki innŭn 습기 있는 moist

sŭpkkwan 습관 custom

sŭpkkwanjŏgin 습관적인 customary

sŭptchin 습진 eczema

sŭpttŭk'ada

sŭpttŭk'ada 습득하다
acquire

sŭp'aijisŭl hada 스파이짓을
하다 spy

sŭp'an 습한 humid

Sŭp'einŏ 스페인어 Spanish
(language)

sŭp'och'ŭi 스포츠 sport(s)

sŭp'och'ŭin 스포츠인
athlete

sŭp'och'ŭran 스포츠란
sports page

sŭsŭro 스스로 by oneself

sŭt'ŭresŭ 스트레스 stress

sŭt'ŭresŭga shimhan
스트레스가 심한 stressful

sŭt'ŭresŭrŭl shimhage
pannŭn 스트레스를
심하게 받는 stressed out

su 수 number; quantity; move
(chess) ◊ hydro-

su: …*l su it-tta* …ㄹ 수
있다 can; …*l su ŏptta* …ㄹ
수 없다 cannot

subak 수박 water melon

subanhada 수반하다
involve

subi 수비 defense

subisu 수비수 defense player

subunkonggŭp'aek
수분공급팩 moisturizing
face mask

such'aehwa 수채화
watercolor

such'ishim 수치심 shame

such'isŭrŏptta 수치스럽다

be disgraceful

such'isŭrŏun 수치스러운
disgraceful

such'ŏk'an 수척한
emaciated

su ch'ŏnŭi 수 천의
thousands of

such'uk'ada 수축하다
contract

such'ul 수출 export

such'urhada 수출하다
export

such'wiin 수취인 recipient

suda 수다 chatter

sudajaeng-i 수다쟁이
chatterbox

sudasŭrŏun 수다스러운
chatty

suda ttŏlda 수다 떨다
chatter

sudo 수도 capital *(city)*;
metropolis; waterworks

sudong pŭreik'ŭ 수동
브레이크 parking brake

sudu 수두 chicken pox

suganghada 수강하다 take
a course

sugap 수갑 handcuffs

sugida 숙이다 bow

sugŏn 수건 towel; washcloth

sugŏn kŏri 수건 걸이
towel rail

sugo 수고 effort

sugong-ŭi 수공의 handmade

sugong-ye 수공예
handicraft

sugŭrŏdŭlda 수그러들다
die schwer

suhaenghada 수행하다
conduct

suhagŭi 수학의 mathematical

suhak 수학 mathematics

suhaktcha 수학자
mathematician

suhoja 수호자 protector

suhwa 수화 sign language

suhwak 수확 crop

suhwak'ada 수확하다 reap

suhwamul 수화물 baggage

suhyŏl 수혈 blood transfusion

suigi chŏun 수익이 좋은
profitable

suip 수입 import; takings

suip'ada 수입하다 import

sujigŭi 수직의 vertical

sujip 수집 collection

sujipkka 수집가 collector

sujip'ada 수집하다 collect

sujŏ 수저 spoon and
chopsticks

sujŏng 수정 amendment;
crystal

sujŏnghada 수정하다
amend

sujŏngshik'ida 수정시키다
fertilize

sujubŏhada 수줍어하다
be shy

sujubŏhanŭn 수줍어하는
shy

sujun 수준 level

suk-kko 숙고 consideration

suk-kkohada 숙고하다
deliberate

sukssŏng 숙성 ripeness

sukssŏnghan 숙성한 ripe;
mellow

suktche 숙제 homework

suk'ŏsŭi 수컷의 male

sul 술 liquor; fringe; tassel

sul chanch'i 술 잔치
drinking party

sul ch'wihan 술 취한 drunk

sulgorae 술고래 heavy
drinker

sullye 순례 pilgrimage

sullyeja 순례자 pilgrim

sultchip 술집 bar

sum 숨 breath

sumanŭn 수많은 a large
number of

sumbakkoktchil 숨바꼭질
hide-and-seek

sumch'an 숨찬 breathless

sumgida 숨기다 hide;
hold back

sumgimŏmnŭn 숨김없는
frank

sumgimŏpsshi 숨김없이
frankly

sumgyŏjin 숨겨진 hidden

sumshwida 숨쉬다 breathe

sumtta 숨다 hide

sumyŏn 수면 surface

sumyŏng 수명 life (of
machine)

sumyŏnje 수면제 sleeping
pill

sun

sun 순 pure *gold*; complete ◇ ten days; ten years

sunch'al 순찰 patrol

sunch'algwan 순찰관 patrolman

sunch'arhada 순찰하다 patrol

sun-gan 순간 moment

sun-ganŭi 순간의 momentary

sungbae 숭배 worship

sungbaehada 숭배하다 worship

sungmo 숙모 aunt (*father's younger brother's wife*)

sungnyŏ 숙녀 lady

sungnyŏndoen 숙련된 skilled

sun-gyŏrŭl ilt'a 순결을 잃다 lose one's virginity

sun-gyoja 순교자 martyr

sunhada 순하다 be gentle

sunhan 순한 mild

sunhwan 순환 cycle; circulation

suniik 순이익 net profit

sunjinhada 순진하다 be innocent

sunjinhan 순진한 innocent

sunjong 순종 obedience

sunjonghada 순종하다 obey

sunjonghanŭn 순종하는 obedient

sunjongjŏgin 순종적인 submissive

sunjoroun 순조로운 smooth

sunot'a 수놓다 embroider

sunshik-kkane 순식간에 in an instant

sunsŏ 순서 sequence; system

sunsŏdaero 순서대로 in sequence

sunsuhan 순수한 pure; natural; neat; net

sunyŏ 수녀 nun

suŏp 수업 lesson

sup 숲 forest; wood

sup'yŏngsŏn 수평선 horizon (*at sea*)

sup'yo 수표 check FIN

surak 수락 form acceptance

surak'ada 수락하다 form accept offer; undertake *task*

sure ch'wihada 술에 취하다 get drunk

surihada 수리하다 repair

suro 수로 waterway

surŭl mashida 술을 마시다 drink *alcohol*

surŭl seda 수를 세다 count

suryut'an 수류탄 grenade

susaek 수색 search

susaek'ada 수색하다 search for

susaek'anŭn 수색하는 searching

susang 수상 premier

susanghada 수상하다 win a prize; be suspicious

susanghan 수상한 suspicious

susangja 수상자 prizewinner
suseshik pyŏn-gi 수세식 변기 water closet
sushin 수신 reception *(for TV etc)*; for the attention of
sushinin pudamŭi chŏnhwa 수신인 부담의 전화 collect call
susŏn 수선 repair
susŏnhada 수선하다 mend
susong 수송 transport
susonghada 수송하다 transport
susuhan 수수한 modest; conservative
susukkekki 수수께끼 puzzle
susul 수술 surgery
susurŭl hada 수술을 하다 operate
susurŭl pat-tta 수술을 받다 have an operation
susuryo 수수료 commission

sut 숱 thickness
sut 숯 charcoal
sutcha 숫자 numeral
sutch'ŏnggak 숫총각 (male) virgin
sutkarak 숟가락 spoon
sut'ak 수탉 cock *(chicken)*
suwŏrhada 수월하다 be easy
suwŏrhan 수월한 easy
suyang pŏdŭl 수양 버들 weeping willow
suyŏhada 수여하다 award
suyŏm 수염 beard; mustache
suyŏng 수영 swimming
suyŏnghada 수영하다 swim
suyŏngjang 수영장 swimming pool
suyoil 수요일 Wednesday
suyong inwŏn 수용 인원 intake *(of people)*
suyongso 수용소 camp

T

ta 다 completely
tabang 다방 café
ta charan 다 자란 full-grown
tach'aeropkke hada 다채롭게 하다 jazz up
tach'aeroun 다채로운 colorful
tach'ida 닫히다 close
tach'ige hada 다치게 하다

하다 hurt
tach'in 닫힌 shut, closed
tadŭmtta 다듬다 polish; trim hair; smooth out
tae 대 great ◊ versus ◊ stem ◊ countword for vehicles, machines, cigarettes
taebubun 대부분 most
taebubunŭn 대부분은 mostly

taebyŏnin 대변인
spokesperson

taech'ero 대체로 on the
whole

taech'u 대추 date *(fruit)*

taedamhada 대담하다 be bold

taedanhage 대단하게
enormously

taedanhan 대단한
enormous; serious ◊ a great
deal of

taedanhi 대단히 extremely

taedap 대답 answer

taedap'ada 대답하다
answer

taedasu 대다수 majority

taedoshi 대도시 metropolis

taedŭnghada 대등하다
equalize

taegae 대개 mainly

taegang 대강 general
features ◊ roughly

taegihada 대기하다 stand
by

taegija myŏngdan 대기자
명단 waiting list

taegi oyŏm 대기 오염
atmospheric pollution

taegishil 대기실 waiting
room

taegŭm 대금 *(large)* flute

taegyumoŭi 대규모의 large
scale

taehae(sŏ) ...e taehae(sŏ)
...에 대해 (서) about

taehagwŏn 대학원 graduate

school

taehak 대학 university

taehakssaeng 대학생
university student

taehan ...e taehan ...의
대한 about

Taehanmin-guk 대한민국
Republic of Korea

taehapsshil 대합실
departure lounge

taehayŏ ...e taehayŏ ...에
대하여 with regard to

taehoe 대회 convention;
contest

taehongsu 대홍수 deluge

taehwa 대화 conversation

taehyŏng 대형 large size

taejŏp 대접 dish; bowl;
beaker

taejŏp'ada 대접하다
entertain; treat

taejohada 대조하다 contrast

taejojŏgin 대조적인
contrasting

taejop'yo 대조표 checklist

taejung 대중 the public
◊ popular

taejunggayo 대중가요 pop

taejung kyot'ong 대중 교통
public transportation

taejungchŏgin 대중적인
popular

taemach'o 대마초 cannabis

Taeman 대만 Taiwan
◊ Taiwanese

taemŏriŭi 대머리의 bald

taemun 대문 gate

taemyŏnhago 대면하고 face to face

taenaje 대낮에 in broad daylight

taenamu 대나무 bamboo

taenggŭranghanŭn sori 댕그랑하는 소리 chink (sound)

taep'ihada 대피하다 evacuate

taep'ishik'ida 대피시키다 evacuate

taep'iso 대피소 shelter

taep'o 대포 artillery

taep'yohada 대표하다 represent

taep'yoja 대표자 representative

taeri 대리 deputy

taerihada 대리하다 represent

taeriin 대리인 substitute

taerip 대립 conflict

taerisŏk 대리석 marble

taeryang 대량 large quantity

taeryang saengsanhada 대량 생산하다 mass-produce

taeryang-ŭro 대량으로 in bulk

taeryuk 대륙 continent

taesa 대사 speech; ambassador

taesagwan 대사관 embassy

taesang 대상 object

taesangp'ojin 대상포진 shingles

taeshikka 대식가 glutton

taeshin 대신 substitute; compensation ◊ instead of

taeshine 대신에 instead (of)

taeshinhada 대신하다 replace; take over; substitute

taesŏnggong 대성공 coup; great success

taesŏnggong-ida 대성공이다 be a success

Taesŏyang 대서양 Atlantic

taet'ongnyŏng 대통령 president

taeu 대우 treatment

taeuhada 대우하다 treat

taeyong 대용 substitution

taeyongp'um 대용품 substitute

taeyuhaeng 대유행 fashionable ◊ craze

tagagada 다가가다 walk up to

tagaoda 다가오다 approach

tagaonŭn 다가오는 forthcoming

tagugŏŭi 다국어의 multilingual

tagwa 다과 tea and cookies

ta hada 다 하다 run out (of time); carry out

tahaenghido 다행히도 luckily

taibing tae 다이빙 대 diving board

taiŏt'ŭhada 다이어트하다
diet; be on a diet

tajaedanŭnghan
다재다능한 versatile

tajŏngdagamhan
다정다감한 warm-hearted

tajŏnghada 다정하다 be
affectionate; be friendly

tajŏnghan 다정한
affectionate

tak 닭 chicken

takkanaeda 닦아내다
wipe off

tak-kkogi 닭고기 chicken
(as food)

taktta 닦다 wipe; clean;
wash; mop up

takttari 닭다리 drumstick
(of poultry)

tal 달 month; moon

talch'angnyuksŏn
달착륙선 lunar module

talda 달다 fit; attach; be sweet

talge hada 달게 하다
sweeten

talgyal 달걀 egg

talgyarhyŏng 달걀형 oval

talk'omhada 달콤하다 be
sweet

tallabut-tta 달라붙다 stick
(to); cling

tallanggŏrida 달랑거리다
dangle

tallida 달리다 hang; depend;
be attached; run short; run;
drive

talligi 달리기 run; running

tallŏ 달러 dollar

tallyŏdŭlda 달려들다 tackle

tallyŏk 달력 calendar

tallyŏnhada 단련하다
build up

tallyŏnshik'ida 단련시키다
exercise

talppit 달빛 moonlight

talp'aeng-i 달팽이 snail

tam 담 wall

tambae 담배 tobacco;
cigarette

tambae kkongch'o 담배
꽁초 cigarette butt

tamdang 담당 charge ◊ in
charge

tamdanghada 담당하다
take charge of

tamgŭda 담그다 immerse

tamnyo 담요 blanket

tamtta 담다 contain

tamtta 닮다 resemble

tamyo 담요 rug

tan 단 column; rung; hit
squad; tuck (in dress) ◊ sweet
◊ countword for firewood,
spinach etc

tanbaektchil 단백질 protein

tanch'e 단체 organization

tanch'u 단추 button

tanch'urŭl ch'aeuda 단추를
채우다 button (up)

tandanhada 단단하다 be
solid; be firm; be tight

tandanhi 단단히 tight

tandanhi choida 단단히 조이다 tighten

tandanhi muktta 단단히 묶다 lash down *(with rope)*

tandogŭi 단독의 single-handed

tang 당 party

-tang -당 per

tangbŏn 당번 rota

tangbun-gan 당분간 for the moment

tangch'ŏmdoen 당첨된 winning

tangch'ŏmja 당첨자 winner

tanggida 당기다 pull

tanggŭn 당근 carrot

tanggu 당구 pool *(game) (like billiards)*

tanggujang 당구장 pool hall

tanghok 당혹 perplexity

tanghok'an 당혹한 perplexed

tanghwang 당황 alarm

tanghwanghada 당황하다 be embarrassed

tanghwanghan 당황한 embarrassed

tan-gigan 단기간 short-term

tan-gijŏgŭro 단기적으로 in the short term

tangjang 당장 right now

tangnagwi 당나귀 donkey

tangyŏnhada 당연하다 be natural

tangyŏnhan 당연한 natural

tangnyŏnhi 당연히 naturally

tangnyoppyŏng 당뇨병 diabetes ◊ diabetic

tan-gol 단골 custom; regular *(person)*

tan-gollo tanida 단골로 다니다 patronize

tangshin 당신 *(polite)* you

tangshinŭi 당신의 *(polite)* your

tan-gye 단계 stage

tang-yŏnhae! 당연해! no wonder!

tang-yŏnhi 당연히 of course

tan hanaŭi 단 하나의 sole

tanji 단지 only ◊ mere ◊ jar; container; housing development

tanjŏnghada 단정하다 determine; be neat; be decent

tanjŏnghan 단정한 tidy; decent

tanjŏnghi hada 단정히 하다 tidy oneself up

tankkwa taehak 단과 대학 college

tannyŏm 단념 resignation

tannyŏmhada 단념하다 relinquish

tannyŏmshik'ida 단념시키다 deter

tanŏ 단어 word

tanp'ungnamu 단풍나무 maple

tanp'yŏn 단편 fragment

tanp'yŏnsosŏl 단편소설 short story

tanp'yŏntchŏgin 단편적인 fragmentary

tansang 단상 platform

tanshigan 단시간 a short time

tanshik 단식 singles *(tennis)*

tansok 단속 crackdown

tansok'ada 단속하다 crack down

tansume 단숨에 at a stretch

tansunhada 단순하다 be simple

tansunhwahada 단순화하다 simplify

tantchŏm 단점 disadvantage

tanwi 단위 unit *(of measurement)*

tap 답 answer

tappssahada 답사하다 travel; explore

taptchang 답장 reply

tapttap'ada 답답하다 be gloomy; be stifling; be anxious

tap'ada 답하다 answer

tarajida 닳아지다 wear (away)

tarakppang 다락방 attic

taramjwi 다람쥐 squirrel

taranada 달아나다 run away

tarappajin 닳아빠진 worn-out

tari 다리 bridge; leg

tarimi 다리미 iron

tarimjirhada 다림질하다 iron

tarŭda 다르다 be different

tarŭge 다르게 differently

tarŭn 다른 different; another; other

tarŭn kŏt 다른 것 another

tarŭn nugun-ga 다른 누군가 someone else

taruda 다루다 handle; manage; treat

tarugi ŏryŏun 다루기 어려운 awkward; not user-friendly

tarugi shwiun 다루기 쉬운 manageable

tashi 다시 again

tashi ch'aeuda 다시 채우다 refill

tashi ch'irhada 다시 칠하다 repaint

tashi hwaginhada 다시 확인하다 doublecheck

tashi nat'anada 다시 나타나다 reappear

tashi padadŭrida 다시 받아들이다 take back

tashi ssŭda 다시 쓰다 rewrite

tasŏt 다섯 five

taso 다소 number; amount; a litte

tasŭrida 다스리다 govern

tasuŭi 다수의 many

tatch'ida 닫히다 shut

tatki 닫기 close COMPUT

tatkki shwiun 닿기 쉬운 easy to reach

tat-tta 닫다 close; fasten;

be closed

tat'a 닿다 reach

tat'uda 다투다 fight

tat'um 다툼 quarrel

taŭm 다음 next

taŭme 다음에 next

taŭmnal 다음날 the day after

tayanghada 다양하다 be diverse

tayanghan 다양한 varied

tayangssŏng 다양성 variety

tayongdoŭi 다용도의 all-purpose

tchaenggŭrŏnghanŭn sori 쨍그렁하는 소리 clink

tchajangmyŏn 짜장면 noodles and black bean sauce

tchajŭngnage hada 짜증나게 하다 irritate

tchajŭngnanŭn 짜증나는 irritating

tchajŭngnanŭn kŏt 짜증나는 것 irritation

tchak 짝 partner

tchakssuŭi 짝수의 even *number*

tchalbŭn 짧은 short

tchalkke charŭda 짧게 자르다 cut shorter

tchalkke hada 짧게 하다 shorten

tchalkke pomyŏn 짧게 보면 in the short run

tchalptta 짧다 be short

tcham 짬 slot *(in schedule)*

tchan 짠 salty

tchida 찌다 steam

tchigŏ mŏktta 찍어 먹다 dip *(food)*

tchigŭrŏttŭrida 찌그러뜨리다 crush

tchijŏjige kananhan 찢어지게 가난한 poverty-stricken

tchijŏjin 찢어진 ragged

tchikkŏgi 찌꺼기 dregs

tchiktchik-kkŏrida 찍찍거리다 squeak

tchimt'ong 찜통 steamer *(for cooking)*

tchinggŭrida 찡그리다 scowl; contort; screw up *eyes*

tchinŭn tŭshi tŏun 찌는 듯이 더운 scorching hot

tchip'urida 찌푸리다 frown

tchip'urin ŏlgul 찌푸린 얼굴 frown

tchirŭda 찌르다 thrust; prick; stab

tchit-tta 찢다 rip

tchit'ŭn 짙은 thick

tchoch'abŏrida 쫓아버리다 chase away

tchoch'anaeda 쫓아내다 expel

tchogaeda 쪼개다 split

tchok 쪽 page; slice

tchotkkyŏnada 쫓겨나다 be expelled

-tchŭm -쯤 approximately

tchuk ppŏt-tta 쭉 뻗다 stretch

teda 데다 get burnt
teit'ŏ ch'ŏri 데이터 처리 data processing
teit'ŏ peisŭ 데이터 베이스 database
teit'ŏ poho 데이터 보호 data protection
teit'ŭ hada 데이트하다 date
temo 데모 demo
temohada 데모하다 demonstrate
temo haengjin 데모 행진 demo
temoja 데모자 demonstrator
terigo nagada 데리고 나가다 take out *(lunch etc)*
terirŏ kada 데리러 가다 call for *(a person)*
terirŏ oda 데리러 오다 come for *(a person)*
teryŏdajuda 데려다주다 take back *(a person)*
teryŏgada 데려가다 lead
teryŏoda 데려오다 bring *(a person)*
teuda 데우다 heat up
teun 데운 heated
tidimttol 디딤돌 stepping stone
tijain 디자인 design
tijainhada 디자인하다 design
tijainŏ 디자이너 designer
tijel 디젤 diesel
tisŭk'o 디스코 disco
tŏ 더 more

tŏbinghada 더빙하다 dub
tŏch'e kŏllida 덫에 걸리다 be trapped
tŏdŏl ttŏlda 덜덜 떨다 tremble
tŏdŭmtta 더듬다 stumble over *words*
tŏhada 더하다 add
tŏhayŏ 더하여 plus
tŏ isang 더 이상 any more
tŏk 덕 virtue
...tŏkppune ...덕분에 thanks to
tŏl 덜 less
tŏlda 덜다 ease
tŏldŏl ttŏllida 덜덜 떨리다 chatter *(of teeth)*
tŏl ik'in 덜 익힌 underdone
tŏlk'ŏk-kkŏrida 덜컥거리다 rattle
tŏm 덤 bonus
tŏ manŭn 더 많은 more
tŏmbyŏdŭlda 덤벼들다 attack
tŏmi 더미 pile
tŏ mŏlli 더 멀리 farther
tŏ naajida 더 나아지다 be better
tŏ nappajida 더 나빠지다 worsen
tŏ nappŭn 더 나쁜 worse
tŏ natkke 더 낮게 better
tŏng-ŏri 덩어리 lump; loaf
tŏnjida 던지다 throw
tŏnjigi 던지기 throw
tŏpch'ida 덮치다 pounce;

swoop on

tŏpkkae 덮개 cover

tŏpssuruk'an 덥수룩한 shaggy

tŏptta 덥다 be hot; be warm

tŏptta 덮다 cover

tŏrŏptta 더럽다 be dirty; be sordid

tŏrŏp'ida 더럽히다 dirty; smear *character*

tŏt 덫 trap

tŏtppuch'ida 덧붙이다 add

tŏtssem 덧셈 addition

tŏuk 더욱 more

tŏugi 더욱이 moreover

tŏun 더운 hot; warm

...to ...도 too

to 도 province, do; degree

tobaehada 도배하다 paper *walls*

tobak 도박 gambling

tobak'ada 도박하다 gamble

tobo yŏhaeng 도보 여행 walking tour

toboyŏhaengja 도보여행자 hiker

toch'ak 도착 arrival

toch'ak'ada 도착하다 arrive

toch'ak'anŭn 도착하는 incoming

toch'ŏnghada 도청하다 bug

todarhada 도달하다 arrive at

todŏkssŏng 도덕성 morality

todŏktchŏgin 도덕적인

moral

toduk 도둑 thief

toduktchil 도둑질 theft

toduktchirhada 도둑질하다 steal

toech'at-tta 되찾다 recover

toeda 되다 become

toedollyŏjuda 되돌려주다 give back

toedollyŏnot'a 되돌려놓다 put back

toedoragada 되돌아가다 go back

toedoraoda 되돌아오다 come back

toejŏra! 뒈저라 ! go to hell!

toenjang 된장 fermented soya paste

toeŏ it-tta 되어 있다 be scheduled

toep'uridoenŭn 되풀이되는 repetitive

toep'urihada 되풀이하다 repeat

Togil 독일 Germany

◇ German

Togirin 독일인 German

togu 도구 tool

toip 도입 introduction; injection; input

toip'ada 도입하다 introduce; inject, contribute; input

tojagi 도자기 ceramics

tojang 도장 paintwork; seal

tojang tchiktta 도장 찍다 stamp

tojŏhi 도저히 at all

tojŏn 도전 challenge

tojŏnhada 도전하다 challenge

tojung-e 도중에 on the way

tok 독 poison; pot; dock

tokch'ang 독창 solo

tokch'angjŏgin 독창적인 clever

tokch'oktchang 독촉장 reminder COMM

tok-kkam 독감 flu

tokssarhada 독살하다 poison

toksshinja 독신자 single (person)

toksső 독서 reading

toksső chang-aeja 독서 장애자 dyslexic

tokssőga 독서가 reader

tokssŏnjŏgin 독선적인 dogmatic

tokssuri 독수리 eagle; vulture

toktchaeja 독재자 dictator

toktchaejŏgin 독재적인 dictatorial

toktchŏm 독점 monopoly

toktchŏmhada 독점하다 monopolize

toktchŏmjŏgin 독점적인 exclusive

toktchu 독주 solo

toktchuja 독주자 soloist

tokt'ŭk'ada 독특하다 be unique

tokt'ŭk'an 독특한 unique

tok'ada 독하다 be poisonous; be strong (of drink); be spiteful; be firm

tol 돌 stone

tol 돌 first birthday

tolboda 돌보다 look after

tolbwajuda 돌봐주다 look after

tolch'ul 돌출 bulge

tolch'urhada 돌출하다 jut out

tolda 돌다 turn; circulate

tolkkorae 돌고래 dolphin

tollida 돌리다 turn; pass around; deal; direct

tollyŏbat-tta 돌려받다 get back

tollyŏjuda 돌려주다 give back; pass on costs

tollyŏnot'a 돌려놓다 put back

tollyŏ ponaeda 돌려 보내다 send back

tolp'ari 돌팔이 itinerant tradesman ◊ quack

tomabaem 도마뱀 lizard

tomae 도매 wholesale

tomang 도망 escape

tomangch'ida 도망치다 escape

ton 돈 money

tonan kyŏngbogi 도난 경보기 burglar alarm

tong 동 sub-district, dong

...tong-an …동안 during

◊ while

tongbanhada 동반하다 accompany

tongbanja 동반자 escort

tongbong 동봉 inclosure
◊ inclosed

tongbonghada 동봉하다 attach

tongbuk 동북 north-east

tongdŭnghada 동등하다 be equal

tongdŭnghage 동등하게 equally

tongdŭnghan 동등한 equal

tonggamhada 동감하다 empathize with

tonggisaeng 동기생 contemporary

tonggŏhada 동거하다 cohabit

tonggŭrami 동그라미 circle

tonggul 동굴 cave

Tonggyŏng 동경 Tokyo

Tonghae 동해 East Sea, Sea of Japan

tonghwa 동화 fairy tale

tong-irhan 동일한 identical

tongjak 동작 motion

tongjŏn 동전 coin

tongjŏng 동정 pity; virginity; collar

tongjŏnghada 동정하다 pity

tongjŏnghanŭn 동정하는 sympathetic

tongjŏngshim 동정심 sympathy

tongmu 동무 friend; comrade

tongmul 동물 animal

tongmurwŏn 동물원 zoo

tongnip 독립 independence
◊ independent

Tongnip Kinyŏmil 독립 기념일 Independence Day

tongniptchŏgin 독립적인 independent

tongniptchŏgŭro 독립적으로 independently

tongnip'ada 독립하다 break away

Tongnyang 동양 East Asia
◊ East Asian

Tongnyang saram 동양 사람 East Asian

tongnyo 동료 companion; colleague

tongnyo 동요 nursery rhyme; turbulence

tong-ŏp 동업 partnership

tongsa 동사 verb

tongsamuso 동사무소 sub-district office

tongshi 동시 the same time
◊ simultaneous ◊ nursery rhyme

tongshie 동시에 at the same time

tongsŏ 동서 sister-in-law (husband's younger / elder brother's wife)

tongsŏng-aeja 동성애자 homosexual

tongtchŏm 동점 draw

tongtchŏmi toeda 동점이 되다 draw

tongtchok 동쪽 east

tong-ŭi 동의 agreement

tong-ŭihada 동의하다 agree (with)

tonŭl naeda 돈을 내다 pay

tonŭl pŏlda 돈을 벌다 earn money

toptta 돕다 help

top'yo 도표 diagram

toragada 돌아가다 go back

toraoda 돌아오다 come back

toratanida 돌아다니다 move around

torie mannŭn 도리에 맞는 honorable

torip'ada 돌입하다 fall

toro 도로 roadway

toro chido 도로 지도 road map

toro kongsa 도로 공사 road works

toro p'yojip'an 도로 표지판 roadsign

tosal 도살 slaughter

tosarhada 도살하다 slaughter

toshi 도시 city; town ◊ urban

toshihwa 도시화 urbanization

toshim-ŭi 도심의 down-town

toshirak 도시락 lunch box

tosŏgwan 도서관 library

tot 돛 sail

totppogi 돋보기 magnifying glass

toŭi 도의 (moral) principle

toum 도움 help

toumi toenŭn 도움이 되는 helpful

toye 도예 pottery

toyeji 도예지 pottery (place)

ttabunhan 따분한 boring

ttada 따다 win; pick; pop

ttadollida 따돌리다 ostracize

ttae 때 occasion; grime; -*l ttae* - ㄹ 때 when

ttaega toemyŏn 때가 되면 in due course

ttaekkaji 때까지 until

ttaem 댐 dam

... ttaemune ... 때문에 because ◊ because of; out of

... ttaemunŭro ... 때문으로 because of

ttaerida 때리다 hit

ttaettaero 때때로 sometimes

ttak 딱 punctually; exactly

ttakttak'ada 딱딱하다 be hard

ttakkŭmgŏrida 따끔거리다 sting

ttakkŭmgŏrinŭn 따끔거리는 prickly

ttak tallabut-tta 딱 달라붙다 adhere

ttakchi 딱지 scab

ttakttak-kkŏrida 딱딱거리다 snap

ttakttak'an 딱딱한 hard

ttakttak'an kkŏptchil
딱딱한 껍질 crust

ttak'anŭn sori 딱하는 소리
snap

ttal 딸 daughter

ttalgi 딸기 strawberry

ttalkkuktchil 딸꾹질 hiccup

ttallanggŏrida 딸랑거리다
jingle

ttallangttallang 딸랑딸랑
jingling

ttam 땀 sweat

ttamnae nanŭn 땀내 나는
sweaty

ttamul hŭllida 땀을 흘리다
sweat

ttang 땅 land

ttangk'ong 땅콩 peanut

ttan 딴 another; different;
separate; irrelevant

ttaragada 따라가다 follow

ttarasŏ 따라서 therefore ◊ in
accordance with; along

ttaro 따로 separately ◊ extra

ttarŭda 따르다 abide by;
pour out

ttarŭmyŏn 따르면 according
to

ttattŭt'ada 따뜻하다 be
warm

ttattŭt'age 따뜻하게 warmly

ttattŭt'an 따뜻한 warm

ttaŭn mŏri 땋은 머리 braid

tte 떼 crowd; herd; flock

tti 띠 sash

ttŏdoradanida
떠돌아다니다 wander

ttŏdori 떠돌이 hobo

ttŏdŭlssŏk'an 떠들썩한
boisterous

ttŏk 떡 rice cake

ttŏk-kkuk 떡국 rice cake
soup

ttŏkppok-kki 떡볶기 rice
cake in hot sauce

ttŏlda 떨다 tremble; shiver

ttŏllida 떨리다 tremble

ttŏllinŭn 떨리는 wobbly

ttŏmat-tta 떠맡다 take
charge

ttŏnada 떠나다 go away

ttŏnaganŭn 떠나가는
outgoing

ttŏngmanduguk 떡만두국
rice cake and dumpling soup

ttŏorŭda 떠오르다 occur to;
haunt (of memory); surface

ttŏrŏjida 떨어지다 fall; run
out (of); come off (of handle
etc); strike (of disaster); set
(of sun); deteriorate; be apart;
separate; be left behind; fail
exam; miscarry; get finished;
die; get over illness

ttŏrŏjyŏsŏ 떨어져서 apart

ttŏrŏttŭrida 떨어뜨리다
lower; shed leaves; strip
leaves; throw off

tto 또 also

ttohan 또한 also

tto hana 또 하나 another

ttokkatkkehada 똑같게하다
tie the score

ttok-kkat-tta 똑같다 be
exactly like

ttokpparo 똑바로 straight
(ahead); upright

ttokpparŭge hada 똑바르게
하다 straighten

ttokpparŭn 똑바른 straight

ttokttok'ada 똑똑하다 be
intelligent

ttokttok'an 똑똑한
intelligent

ttong 똥 dung; poop;
excrement

ttonŭn 또는 or

tto tarŭn 또 다른 additional

ttŭgaejil 뜨개질 knitting

ttŭgaejirhada 뜨개질하다
knit

ttŭgŏptta 뜨겁다 be hot

ttŭgŏun 뜨거운 hot

ttŭiŏmttŭiŏm 띄엄띄엄
sparsely; intermittently; slowly

ttŭl 뜰 garden

ttŭn-gurum chapkki 뜬구름
잡기 wild-goose chase

ttŭppakke 뜻밖에
unexpectedly

ttukkŏng 뚜껑 lid; top; flap

ttukttuk ttŏrŏjida 뚝뚝
떨어지다 dribble

ttult'a 뚫다 drill; pierce ears;
unblock

ttungbo 뚱보 fatty

ttungttunghada 뚱뚱하다

be fat

ttungttunghan 뚱뚱한 fat

tturyŏt'ada 뚜렷하다 be
clear

tturyŏt'age 뚜렷하게 clearly

tturyŏt'an 뚜렷한 clear

ttwida 뛰다 pound

ttwiŏdanida 뛰어다니다
jump

ttwiŏdŭlda 뛰어들다 dive;
burst into

ttwiŏnada 뛰어나다 excel

ttwiŏnage 뛰어나게
extremely

ttwiŏnan 뛰어난 excellent

ttwiŏ nŏmtta 뛰어 넘다
jump

ttwiŏ orŭda 뛰어 오르다
jump

tŭk 득 profit

tŭktchŏm 득점 score; goal

tŭktchŏmhada 득점하다
score; touch down

tŭlda 들다 enter; join; catch
cold; contain; accommodate;
get; begin; dye; be pleased;
cost; put up hand; take out
policy; cut; grow older; hold
pen; lift; cite example; eat;
drink

tŭlgo kada 들고 가다 carry

tŭllida 들리다 hear; be
audible; be rumored; be
obsessed by; be lifted up

tŭlŭlda 들르다 drop in

tŭlp'an 들판 field

tültchungnaltchuk'an 들쭉날쭉한 ragged

tümppuk 듬뿍 plenty

tümulda 드물다 be rare

tümulge 드물게 rarely

tümun 드문 rare

tündünhan 든든한 stalwart

tüng 등 back (of book); light

tüngban 등반 climb

tüngbanhada 등반하다 climb

tüngdae 등대 lighthouse

tünggüp 등급 grade

tüngjang 등장 entrance THEAT

tüngjang inmul 등장 인물 characters THEAT

tüngkki up'yŏn 등기 우편 registered letter

tüngnok 등록 enrollment

tüngnok pŏnho 등록 번호 license number

tüngnok'ada 등록하다 register

tüngppul 등불 lamp

tüngsan 등산 mountaineering

tüngsanhwa 등산화 climbing boots

tünŏlbŭn 드넓은 spacious

türaik'üllining set'aksso 드라이클리닝 세탁소 dry-cleaner

türibat-tta 들이받다 knock down

türida 드리다 give

türimashida 들이마시다 suck in; inhale

türishwida 들이쉬다 breathe in

türŏgada 들어가다 enter; let in

türŏ it-tta 들어 있다 be inside

türŏjuda 들어주다 grant wish

türŏ mat-tta 들어 맞다 fit

türŏnuptta 드러눕다 lie down

türŏoda 들어오다 come in

türŏ ollida 들어 올리다 lift; hand; take up carpet etc

türŏsŏda 들어서다 enter

türyŏnot'a 들여놓다 stock up on

türyŏ ponaeda 들여 보내다 send in

tüt-tta 듣다 hear; listen (to)

tu 두 two

tubu 두부 tofu

tudürida 두드리다 beat

tudunhada 두둔하다 cover up for

tugoboda 두고보다 watch

tugo kada 두고 가다 leave behind

tugün-gŏrida 두근거리다 flutter

tuk 둑 dike; weir

tukkŏbi 두꺼비 toad

tukkŏbijip 두꺼비집 fusebox

tukkŏun 두꺼운 thick

tukkŏptta 두껍다 be thick

tu kyŏbŭi 두 겹의 double

tul

tul 둘 two

tulle 둘레 around

tullŏboda 둘러보다 look around

tullŏ ssada 둘러 싸다 enclose

tul ta 둘 다 both

tumesankkol 두메산골 the sticks

tunggŭlda 둥글다 be round

tunggŭn 둥근 round

tungji 둥지 nest

tunhan 둔한 stupid

tunoe 두뇌 brain

tu pae 두 배 double

tu pŏn 두 번 twice

tu pŏntchae 두 번째 second

tup'yoham 투표함 ballot box

turumagi 두루마기 (traditional) long coat

turumari 두루마리 scroll

turyŏpta 두렵다 be fearful

turyŏum 두려움 fear

turyŏwŏhada 두려워하다 be afraid (of)

tut'ong 두통 headache

tuyu 두유 soy milk

twaeji 돼지 hog

twaeji chŏgŭmt'ong 돼지 저금통 piggybank

twaeji chokppal 돼지 족발 pig's trotters

twaejigogi 돼지고기 pork

twaejiuri 돼지우리 pigpen

twi 뒤 back

twibŏmbŏk 뒤범벅 jumble

twich'ŏgida 뒤척이다 stir

twich'uk 뒤축 heel (of shoe)

twidoraboda 뒤돌아보다 look back

twie namgida 뒤에 남기다 leave behind

twie namtta 뒤에 남다 stay behind

twijibŏjida 뒤집어지다 turn over (of vehicle)

twijibŏsŏ 뒤집어서 inside out

twijida 뒤지다 poke around

twijiptta 뒤집다 overturn; capsize; fold; back; demolish argument; turn inside out

twijukppaktchugin 뒤죽박죽인 topsy-turvy

twikkumch'i 뒤꿈치 heel

twinggulda 뒹굴다 roll over

twinmun 뒷문 backdoor

twinmyŏn 뒷면 back

twiŏptta 뒤엎다 overturn

twiro tanggida 뒤로 당기다 draw back

twirŭl paltta 뒤를 밟다 stalk

twisŏk-kkida 뒤섞이다 be mixed up (of figures, papers)

twisŏkkta 뒤섞다 shuffle

twitchot-tta 뒤쫓다 chase

twitkkil 뒷길 back road

twittpatch'imhae chuda 뒷받침해 주다 back up claim

twittchoge(sŏ) 뒷쪽에 (서) behind

twittchumŏni 뒷주머니 hip pocket

twittchogŭro 뒷쪽으로 backward

twittŏrŏjida 뒤떨어지다 lag behind

twittchok 뒷쪽 back

twit-ttŭl 뒷뜰 backyard

T'

t'aak-kki 타악기 percussion instrument

t'abŏrida 타버리다 burn down

t'ada 타다 get in (to car); board; catch bus; mount; ride horse, bike; fly; burn; glow

t'adanghada 타당하다 be just; be valid

t'adanghan 타당한 just; valid

t'adangsŏng 타당성 validity

t'aea 태아 embryo

t'aedo 태도 attitude

T'aeguk 태국 Thailand ◊ Thai

t'aeksshi 택시 taxi

t'aemanhada 태만하다 neglect

t'aeŏnada 태어나다 be born

t'aep'ung 태풍 typhoon

T'aep'yŏng-yang 태평양 Pacific (Ocean)

t'aetchul 탯줄 umbilical cord

t'aeuda 태우다 burn; give a ride

t'aewŏbŏrida 태워버리다 burn out

t'aewŏ chuda 태워 주다 take

t'aeyang 태양 sun

t'aeyang enŏji 태양 에너지 solar energy

t'agonan 타고난 innate; natural

t'agonan chaenŭng 타고난 재능 natural ability

t'ahyŏp 타협 compromise

t'ahyŏp'ada 타협하다 compromise

t'airŭda 타이르다 preach

t'aja ch'ida 타자 치다 type

t'ak-kku 탁구 ping-pong

t'alch'um 탈춤 mask dance

t'alch'urhada 탈출하다 escape; bail out

t'alch'urhan 탈출한 at large

t'alch'wi 탈취 hijack

t'alch'wibŏm 탈취범 hijacker

t'alch'wihada 탈취하다 hijack

t'allak 탈락 elimination

t'allak'ada 탈락하다 be eliminated

t'allo 탄로 exposure

t'allonada 탄로나다 be out (of secret)

t'allyŏginnŭn 탄력있는 elastic

t'alssŏndoeda 탈선되다 be derailed

t'alssudoen 탈수된 dehydrated

t'alssugi 탈수기 spin-dryer

t'altchimyŏn 탈지면 absorbent cotton

t'alt'oehada 탈퇴하다 break away

t'amhŏm 탐험 exploration

t'amhŏmga 탐험가 explorer

t'amji 탐지 detection

t'amjigi 탐지기 detector

t'amjihada 탐지하다 detect

t'amjŏng sosŏl 탐정 소설 detective novel

t'amnanŭn 탐나는 desirable

t'amsaek 탐색 search

t'amsaek'ada 탐색하다 explore; seek

t'an-gwang 탄광 coal mine

t'ansaeng 탄생 birth

t'ansansu 탄산수 soda (water)

t'ansuhwamul 탄수화물 carbohydrate

t'aorŭda 타오르다 blaze

t'ap 탑 pagoda; tower

t'apssŭnggu 탑승구 gate

t'apssŭngkkwŏn 탑승권 boarding card

t'arak 타락 corruption

t'arak'ada 타락하다 degenerate; be corrupt

t'arak'an 타락한 corrupt

t'arok'ada 탈옥하다 break out

t'arŭishil 탈의실 changing room

t'aryŏnghada 탈영하다 desert MIL

t'at 탓 fault; result; effect

t'at'ada 탓하다 blame

t'awŏnhyŏng 타원형 ellipse

t'e 테 frame; hoop

t'eduri 테두리 brim

t'ellebi 텔레비 TV

t'ema 테마 theme

t'enissŭ chang 테니스 장 tennis court

t'enissŭ kong 테니스 공 tennis ball

t'erŏbŏm 테러범 terrorist

t'erŏ chojik 테러 조직 terrorist organization

t'imjang 팀장 team captain

t'ineijŏ 틴에이저 teenager

t'i ŏmnŭn 티 없는 immaculate

t'ŏjida 터지다 burst

t'ŏjin 터진 burst

t'ŏk 턱 chin; jaw; ledge

t'ŏkppaji 턱받이 bib

t'ŏkssuyŏm 턱수염 beard

t'ŏl 털 hair; fur; bristles

t'ŏlssŏk naeryŏnot'a 털썩 내려놓다 slam down

t'ŏmuniŏmnŭn 터무니없는
outrageous

t'ŏng pin tŏng 텅 빈 empty

t'ŏnot'a 터놓다 pour out
woes

t'ŏŏnaeda 털어내다 brush
off dust etc

t'ŏŏronot'a 털어놓다 confide

t'ŏttŭrida 터뜨리다 burst;
give vent to

t'oburo k'yŏda 톱으로 켜다
saw of

t'oebohada 퇴보하다
degenerate

t'oebohanŭn 퇴보하는
backward society

t'oehak 퇴학 expulsion

t'oejanghada 퇴장하다
leave; exit; walk out

t'oejangshik'ida 퇴장시키다
expel from the game

t'oejikkŭm 퇴직금 golden
handshake

t'oep'yejŏgin 퇴폐적인
decadent

t'oetcha 퇴짜 brush-off

t'oewŏn 퇴원 discharge

t'oewŏnshik'ida 퇴원시키다
discharge

t'ogi 토기 earthenware

t'ohada 토하다 vomit

t'okki 토끼 rabbit

t'omak 토막 fragment

t'omakch'ida 토막치다
cut up

t'omnibak'wi 톱니바퀴 cog

t'omok kisa 토목 기사 civil
engineer

t'ong 통 pack; tub; barrel;
t'ong, subdivision of a city
◊ countword for letters or
documents

t'ongch'ihada 통치하다
rule

t'ongch'ija 통치자 ruler
(of state)

t'ongdok'ada 통독하다 read
through

t'onggi 통기 ventilation

t'onggi kumŏng 통기 구멍
vent

t'onggŭnhada 통근하다
commute

t'onggŭnja 통근자
commuter

t'onggŭn yŏlch'a 통근 열차
commuter train

t'onggwashik'ida
통과시키다 carry
proposal

t'onggye 통계 statistics
◊ statistical

t'onggyehak 통계학
statistics

t'onghada 통하다 flow; be
understood; be versed in; go
through; open onto

t'onghaengnyo 통행료 toll

t'onghap'ada 통합하다
integrate

t'onghwa 통화 currency;
telephone call

t'onghwahada 통화하다 get
through TEL

t'ong-il 통일 unification;
reunification

t'ong-irhada 통일하다 unify

t'ongjang 통장 bank book;
head of a *t'ong*

t'ongjehada 통제하다
control

t'ongji 통지 notice (to quit)

t'ongjorim 통조림 can

t'ongmilppang 통밀빵
wholewheat bread

t'ongnamu 통나무 log

t'ongnamu odumaktchip
통나무 오두막집 log cabin

t'ongno 통로 aisle;
passageway

t'ongp'ung 통풍 draft

t'ongp'ung-i chal toenŭn
통풍이 잘 되는 drafty

t'ongsin 통신
(tele)communications

t'ongsin wisŏng 통신
위성 communications
satellite

t'ongsollyŏk 통솔력
leadership

t'ongsorhada 통솔하다 lead

t'ongt'onghan 통통한
chubby

t'ongyŏk 통역 interpretation

t'ongyŏk-kka 통역가
interpreter

t'ongyŏk'ada 통역하다
interpret

t'op 톱 saw

t'op-ppap 톱밥 sawdust

t'oron 토론 discussion

t'oyoil 토요일 Saturday

t'uda 트다 open *bank
account; sprout (of seed)*

t'ŭgihan 특이한 peculiar to

t'ŭgyuŭi 특유의 distinctive

t'ŭkch'urhan 특출한
outstanding

t'ŭk-kkwŏnŭl kajin 특권을
가진 privileged

t'ŭkppyŏl chosadan 특별
조사단 task force

t'ŭkppyŏrhada 특별하다
be special

t'ŭkppyŏrhage 특별하게
especially

t'ŭkppyŏrhan 특별한 special

t'ŭkp'awŏn 특파원 (special)
correspondent

t'ŭkssŏng 특성 characteristic

t'ŭktching 특징 feature

t'ŭktchŏnghada 특정하다
specify

t'ŭktchŏnghan 특정한
particular

t'ŭk'i 특히 especially

t'ŭk'ŏ 특허 patent

t'ŭl 틀 frame; casing; mold

t'ŭlda 틀다 turn on

t'ŭlli 틀니 false teeth

t'ŭllida 틀리다 be / go wrong

t'ŭllige 틀리게 incorrectly

t'ŭllimŏptta 틀림없다
must be

t'ullin 틀린 incorrect

t'üm 틈 space; gap

t'ümsae 틈새 niche

t'ünt'ŭnhan 튼튼한 robust

t'ŭre kkiuda 틀에 끼우다
frame

t'ŭre nŏŏ mandŭlda 틀에
넣어 만들다 mold

t'ŭrim 트림 belch

t'ŭrimhada 트림하다 belch

t'ŭröllin mŏri 틀어올린
머리 bun (in hair)

t'udŏlgŏrida 투덜거리다
grumble

t'ugi 투기 speculation;
jealousy

t'ugihada 투기하다
speculate FIN

t'uja 투자 investment

t'ujaeng 투쟁 fight

t'ujaengtchŏgin 투쟁적인
militant

t'ujahada 투자하다 invest

t'ujaja 투자자 investor

t'umyŏnghan 투명한
transparent

t'ungmyŏngssŭrŏun
퉁명스러운 abrupt

t'uok 투옥 imprisonment

t'uok'ada 투옥하다 imprison

t'up'yo 투표 vote; voting

t'up'yohada 투표하다 vote

t'wida 튀다 bounce; splash

t'wigida 튀기다 splatter;
deep-fry

t'wigim 튀김 deep fried
food

t'winggida 튕기다 twang

t'wiŏ naoda 튀어나오다
bulge

Ŭ

...ŭi ...의 of

ŭibok 의복 garment

ŭibudadŭl 의붓아들 stepson

ŭibut'yŏngje 의붓형제
stepbrother

ŭibyŏng 의병 righteous army

ŭido 의도 intention

ŭidohada 의도하다 intend

ŭidojŏgin 의도적인
intentional

ŭigiyangyang 의기양양
elation

ŭigyŏn 의견 opinion

ŭigyŏn ch'ai 의견 차이
disagreement

ŭihae 의해 by

ŭihak 의학 medicine
◊ medical

ŭihak pakssa 의학 박사
MD

ŭihoe 의회 assembly;
parliament

ŭija 의자 chair

ŭijang 의장 chairman

üiji 의지 will
üijihada 의지하다 rely on
üijiryŏk 의지력 willpower
üijonhada 의존하다 depend
üijonhanŭn 의존하는 dependant
üimi 의미 sense
üimihada 의미하다 signify
üimiinnŭn 의미있는 meaningful
üimu 의무 duty
üimujŏgin 의무적인 compulsory
üimun 의문 query
üinonhada 의논하다 discuss
üiroe 의뢰 commission (job)
üiroein 의뢰인 client
üiryo pohŏm 의료 보험 medical insurance
üiryu 의류 clothing
üisa 의사 doctor
üisa chŏndal 의사 전달 communication
üisang 의상 outfit
üisa p'yoshi 의사 표시 gesture
üishigi innŭn 의식이 있는 conscious
üishigŭl ilt'a 의식을 잃다 lose consciousness
üishik 의식 ceremony; consciousness
üishik sangshil 의식 상실 blackout
üishiktchŏgin 의식적인 conscious

üishim 의심 suspicion
üishimhada 의심하다 doubt
üishimsŭrŏpkke 의심스럽게 doubtfully
üishimsŭrŏptta 의심스럽다 be doubtful (of person)
üishimtchŏgin 의심쩍은 doubtful
üiwŏn 의원 councilor
üiyok 의욕 will
ŭkkaeda 으깨다 mash
...ŭl ...을 object particle; future particle
...(ŭ)lsurok ...(으) ㄹ수록 the more ... the more ...
ŭmak 음악 music
ŭmak-kka 음악가 musician
ŭmaktchŏgin 음악적인 musical person
ŭmban 음반 album
ŭmch'imhan 음침한 bleak
ŭmgye 음계 scale MUS
ŭmjŏl 음절 syllable
ŭmjŏng-i mannŭn 음정이 맞는 in tune
ŭmju 음주 drinking
ŭmjuja 음주자 drinker
ŭmju unjŏn 음주 운전 drink driving
ŭmmi 음미 taste
ŭmmihada 음미하다 taste
ŭmmo 음모 conspiracy; pubic hair
ŭmmohada 음모하다 plot
ŭmmorŭl kkumida 음모를 꾸미다 frame

ŭmnanhada 음란하다 be
  obscene
ŭmnanhan 음란한 obscene
ŭmnyang 음량 volume
ŭmnyang 음양 yin and yang
ŭmnyang chojŏlgi 음량
  조절기 volume control
ŭmnyŏk 음력 lunar calendar
ŭmnyo 음료 drink
ŭmnyosu 음료수 drinking
  water
ŭmshik 음식 food
ŭn 은 silver
ŭnch'ong 은총 blessing
ŭndunja 은둔자 hermit
ŭngdal 응달 shade
ŭngdap 응답 answer
ŭngdap'ada 응답하다
  answer
ŭngŭp ch'iryo 응급 치료
  first aid
ŭnghada 응하다 comply
  (with)
ŭngmoja 응모자 applicant
ŭngmo sŏryu 응모 서류
  entry form
ŭngshi 응시 gaze
ŭngshihada 응시하다
  gaze (at)
ŭngshija 응시자 entrant
ŭn-gŭnhi 은근히 politely;
  secretly
ŭng-wŏnhada 응원하다
  cheer on
ŭnhaeng 은행 bank
ŭnhaeng yungja 은행 융자

bank loan
ŭnhye 은혜 moral
  indebtedness
ŭnmirhi 은밀히 secretly
ŭnŏ 은어 slang
ŭnppich'ŭi 은빛의 silver
ŭnshinch'ŏ 은신처 hideaway
ŭnshinhada 은신하다 be
  in hiding
ŭn togŭmhan 은 도금한
  silver-plated
ŭnt'oe 은퇴 retirement
ŭnt'oehada 은퇴하다 retire
ŭnt'oehan 은퇴한 retired
ŭp 읍 large township
...ŭro ...으로 by; from,
  because of; of; into; in; with;
  to; toward
...ŭrobut'ŏ ...으로부터 from
...ŭrosŏ ...으로서 as
ŭrŭrŏnggŏrida
  으르렁거리다 growl
uahan 우아한 graceful
ubak 우박 hail
ubi 우비 raincoat
uch'ebu 우체부 mailman
uch'eguk 우체국 post office
uch'et'ong 우체통 mailbox
udumŏri 우두머리 leader
ugŏjin 우거진 dense foliage
uhoe 우회 detour
uhoehada 우회하다 bypass
uhoero 우회로 bypass
uik 우익 right wing
ujŏng 우정 friendship
uju 우주 universe

ujuin 우주인 astronaut

ujusŏn 우주선 spaceship

ulbujit-tta 울부짖다 howl

ulda 울다 cry

ullida 울리다 go off *(of alarm)*; blow; ring; honk

ultchŏk'ada 울적하다 be melancholy

ult'ari 울타리 fence; hedge; barrier

ult'ungbult'unghan 울퉁불퉁한 bumpy

umch'urida 움추리다 curl up

umjigida 움직이다 move; operate

umjiginŭn 움직이는 moving

umk'yŏjaptta 움켜잡다 grasp

umul 우물 well

un 운 fortune; rhyme

unban 운반 haulage

unbanhada 운반하다 convey

unbanin 운반인 porter

un chok'e 운 좋게 luckily

un choŭn 운 좋은 lucky

undong 운동 movement; exercise ◊ sporting

undongga 운동가 athlete; campaigner

undonghada 운동하다 exercise; play SPORTS

undonghwa 운동화 sneakers

undongjang 운동장 arena

ungbyŏn-ga 웅변가 speaker

ungdaehan 웅대한 majestic

ungdŏng-i 웅덩이 pool; puddle

ungjanghan 웅장한 grand

ungk'ŭrida 웅크리다 stoop

unha 운하 canal

unhaengdoeda 운행되다 run *(of trains etc)*

unjŏn 운전 driving

unjŏnhada 운전하다 drive

unjŏn hagwŏn 운전 학원 driving school

unjŏnja 운전자 driver

unjŏn myŏnhŏ shihŏm 운전 면허 시험 driving test

unjŏn myŏnhŏtchŭng 운전 면허증 driver's license

unjŏnsa 운전사 driver

unmyŏng 운명 fate

unŏmnŭn 운없는 unlucky

unŏpkke 운없게 unluckily

unyŏng 운영 operations

unyŏnghada 운영하다 manage

up'yŏn 우편 mail ◊ postal

up'yŏnham 우편함 mailbox

up'yŏn pŏnho 우편 번호 zip code

up'yŏn yogŭm 우편 요금 postage

up'yo 우표 stamp

uri 우리 we; us ◊ cage; pen; pound

uri chashin 우리 자신 ourselves

uriŭi 우리의 our; my

urŏnada 우러나다 well up;
soak out

uryŏhada 우려하다 worry

usan 우산 umbrella

usang 우상 idol

usŏn 우선 firstly

usŏnhada 우선하다 take
precedence (over)

usŏnkkwŏni it-tta 우선권이
있다 have priority

usŏnŭn 우선은 first of all

usŭgae sori 우스개 소리
joke

usŭkkwangsŭrŏun
우스꽝스러운 comical

usŭm 웃음 laugh(ter)

usŭngja 우승자 winner

usŭngk'ŏp 우승컵 trophy

usŭngp'ae 우승패 shield

usŭpkkedo 우습게도
funnily enough

usŭptta 우습다 be funny

usŭun 우스운 funny

utchuldaenŭn 우쭐대는
big-headed

utkkida 웃기다 amuse

utkkige 웃기게 comically

uttchuldaeda 우쭐대다
show off pej

ut-tta 웃다 laugh

uul 우울 gloom

uultchŭng 우울증
depression

uurhan 우울한 depressed

uyŏn 우연 chance

uyŏnhada 우연하다 be
accidental

uyŏnhan 우연한 accidental

uyŏnhi 우연히 by chance

uyŏnŭi ilch'i 우연의 일치
coincidence

uyu 우유 milk

uyubudan 우유부단
indecisiveness

uyubyŏng 우유병 bottle
(for baby)

W

...wa ...와 and

wae 왜 why

waegari 왜가리 heron

waegok'ada 왜곡하다
distort

**waenyahamyŏn ...ki
ttaemunida** 왜냐하면 ...기
때문이다 because

wanbyŏk 완벽 perfection

wanbyŏkjuŭija 완벽주의자
perfectionist

wanbyŏk'age 완벽하게
perfectly; soundly beaten

wanbyŏk'an 완벽한 perfect

wanduk'ong 완두콩 pea

wang 왕 king

wan-ganghan 완강한
stubborn

wangbok yŏhaeng

wangbok yŏhaeng 왕복 여행 round trip

wangbok'ada 왕복하다 shuttle

wangguk 왕국 kingdom

wanggwan 왕관 crown

wangja 왕자 prince

wangjo 왕조 dynasty

wangjok 왕족 royalty

wangjwa 왕좌 throne

wan-gohan 완고한 inflexible

wangsŏnghan 왕성한 hearty

wang-wie ollida 왕위에 올리다 crown

wanjep'um 완제품 end product

wanjŏnhada 완전하다 be complete

wanjŏnhage 완전하게 totally

wanjŏnhan 완전한 complete

wanjŏnhi 완전히 purely; completely; outright *win*

wanmanhan 완만한 sluggish

wansŏng 완성 completion

wansŏngdoen 완성된 complete

wansŏnghada 완성하다 complete

wep 웹 the Web

wep sa-it'ŭ 웹 사이트 web site

wi 위 top; superiority; rank; position; stomach ◊ gastric ◊ over

wian 위안 comfort

wianhada 위안하다 comfort

wiban 위반 violation

wibanhada 위반하다 violate

wich'i 위치 position

wich'ihada 위치하다 be located

wich'ŭng-e 위층에 on the floor above

widaehada 위대하다 be great

widaehan 위대한 grand

widok'ada 위독하다 be critically ill

widok'an 위독한 critical

wie 위에 up; above; on top of

wigi 위기 crisis

wigijŏgin 위기적인 critical

wihae 위해 for

wihan 위한 for

wihayŏ 위하여 on behalf of; for the sake of; in favor of

whŏm 위험 danger

whŏmhada 위험하다 be dangerous

whŏmhan 위험한 dangerous

wihyŏp 위협 threat

wihyŏp'ada 위협하다 threaten

wihyŏp'anŭn 위협하는 threatening

wiim 위임 delegation

wiimhada 위임하다 delegate

wijang 위장 disguise; insides

wijanghada 위장하다 disguise; impersonate

wijaryo 위자료 alimony

wijo 위조 forgery

wijohada 위조하다 forge

wijop'um 위조품 forgery

wing-winggŏrida 윙윙거리다 hum

wing-winghanŭn sori 윙윙하는 소리 buzz

wiŏmminnŭn 위엄있는 dignified

wiro 위로 upward
◊ consolation

wirohada 위로하다 console

wiro ollida 위로 올리다 scroll up

wisaeng 위생 hygiene
◊ sanitary

wisaengjŏgin 위생적인 sanitary

wisŏn 위선 hypocrisy

wisŏnja 위선자 hypocrite

wisŏnjŏgin 위선적인 hypocritical

wit'aeroptta 위태롭다 be in jeopardy

wit'aeroun 위태로운 dangerous

wi tchogŭi 위 쪽의 upper

witssaram 윗사람 superior

wiŭi 위의 upper

wiwŏnhoe 위원회 committee

wŏl 월 month; moon

wŏlbu 월부 monthly installment

wŏlganji 월간지 monthly (magazine)

wŏlgŭp 월급 salary

wŏlgŭp pongt'u 월급 봉투 wage packet

wŏlgyŏng 월경 menstruation

wŏlgyŏnghada 월경하다 menstruate

wŏllae 원래 originally

wŏllyo 원료 raw materials

Wŏlnam 월남 Vietnam
◊ Vietnamese

wŏlsshik 월식 lunar eclipse

wŏn 원 circle; won FIN

wŏnbon 원본 original manuscript

wŏnch'ik 원칙 principle

wŏnch'ŏn 원천 source

wŏn-go 원고 claimant; manuscript

wŏnhada 원하다 want

wŏnhan 원한 rancor

wŏnin 원인 cause

wŏnja 원자 atom ◊ atomic

wŏnjaryŏk paltchonso 원자력 발전소 nuclear power station

wŏnjohada 원조하다 assist

wŏnkka 원가 cost price

wŏnmang 원망 resentment

wŏnmanghada 원망하다 resent

wŏnsu 원수 enemy

wŏnmin 원어민 native speaker

wŏnsung-i 원숭이 monkey

wŏnshijŏgin 원시적인 primitive

wŏntchang 원장 ledger

wŏnye 원예 gardening

wŏnso 원소 element

wŏnyu 원유 crude (oil)

wŏryoil 월요일 Monday

X

Xsŏn x선 X-ray

Y

yach'ae 야채 vegetable

yadanbŏpsŏgŭl p'iuda 야단법석을 피우다 play up (of child)

yadang 야당 opposition

yagan hak-kkyo 야간 학교 night school

yagan kŭnmu 야간 근무 night shift

yagu 야구 baseball

yagujang 야구장 ballpark

yagu pangmang-i 야구 방망이 baseball bat

yagu sŏnsu 야구 선수 baseball player

yahan 야한 gaudy; vulgar

yak 약 medicine around

yakkan 약간 a little slightly

yak-kkuk 약국 pharmacy

yakssa 약사 pharmacist

yaksshigŭi 약식의 informal

yakssok 약속 promise; appointment

yakssok changso 약속 장소 meeting place

yakssok'ada 약속하다 promise

yaktcha 약자 weakling; monogram; abbreviation

yaktchŏm 약점 weak point

yakt'arhada 약탈하다 loot

yak'ada 약하다 be weak; have a weakness for; abridge; omit

yak'aejinŭn 약해지는 ailing

yak'an 약한 weak; muted

yak'on 약혼 engagement

yak'onhada 약혼하다 get engaged

yak'onhan 약혼한 engaged

yalbda 얇다 be thin

yalbŭn 얇은 thin

yamang 야망 ambition

yamjŏnhan 얌전한 meek

yang 양 Ms; quantity; sheep;
tripe

yangbaech'u 양배추
cabbage

yangban 양반 aristocrat

yangbo 양보 concession

yangbohada 양보하다 yield

yangbok 양복 suit *(man's)*

yangbumo 양부모 foster
parents

yangch'ijirhada 양치질하다
brush *teeth*

yangch'o 양초 candle

yangdong-i 양동이 bucket

yanggogi 양고기 lamb *(meat)*

yanggwibi 양귀비 poppy

yanghoshil 양호실 infirmary

yangjojang 양조장 brewery

yangmal 양말 sock

yangnowŏn 양로원 nursing
home

yangnyŏm 양념 seasoning

yangnyŏmtchang 양념장
dip

yangnyuk-kkwŏn 양육권
custody

yangnyuk'ada 양육하다
bring up *child*

yangp'a 양파 onion

yangshik 양식 document;
pattern *(in behavior)*; style;
Western-style food; food

◊ Western-style

yangshim 양심 conscience

yangshimjŏgin 양심적인
conscientious

yangshimŭi kach'aek
양심의 가책 qualm; guilty
conscience

yangtchok 양쪽 both; both
sides

yaoe 야외 open air

yaoeesŏ 야외에서 outdoors

yashiminnŭn 야심있는
ambitious

yat-tta 얕다 be shallow; be
superficial; be low

yat'ŭn 얕은 shallow

yayu 야유 jeer

yayuhada 야유하다 jeer

ye 예 example; old times;
ceremony; courtesy; salute;
bow ◊ yes

yebaedang 예배당 chapel

yebang 예방 prevention;
precaution

yebang chŏptchonghada
예방 접종하다 vaccinate

yebanghada 예방하다
ward off

yebang-ŭi 예방의 preventive

yebihada 예비하다
anticipate

yebok 예복 robe *(of priest)*

yegam 예감 premonition;
hunch; idea

yegop'yŏn 예고편 trailer
(of movie)

yegŭm 예금 deposit

yegŭmhada 예금하다 deposit

yejŏn 예전 former times

yejŏne 예전에 way back

yejŏng 예정 schedule

yejŏnghada 예정하다 schedule

yennal 옛날 old days

yŏn 예언 prophecy

yŏnhada 예언하다 foretell

yeoe 예외 exception

yeppŭda 예쁘다 be pretty

yeppŭn 예쁜 pretty

yerihada 예리하다 be sharp

yerŭl tŭlmyŏn 예를 들면 for example

yerŭl tŭrŏ 예를 들어 for instance

yesan 예산 budget

yesang 예상 anticipation; forecast; prospect

yesanghada 예상하다 expect; forecast

yesanhada 예산하다 work out in advance

yesanŭl seuda 예산을 세우다 budget

yeshihada 예시하다 illustrate (with examples)

yeshiktchang 예식장 wedding hall

yesul 예술 art

yesulga 예술가 artist

yesulp'um 예술품 (work of) art

yesultchŏgin 예술적인 artistic

yesun 예순 sixty

Yesu(nim) 예수 (님) Jesus

yeŭi 예의 politeness

yeŭi parŭn 예의 바른 polite

yeyak 예약 reservation

yeyak-kkŭm 예약금 deposit

yeyaktoen 예약된 reserved

yeyak'ada 예약하다 reserve; arrange

yŏbo 여보 honey (to husband or wife)

yŏboge! 여보게! buddy!

yŏboseyo 여보세요 hello TEL

yŏdŏl 여덟 eight

yŏdŭn 여든 eighty

yŏdŭrŭm 여드름 spot (pimple)

yŏga 여가 leisure

yŏga shigan 여가 시간 leisure time

yŏgi 여기 here

yŏgida 여기다 consider

yŏgijŏgi 여기저기 here and there

yŏgwan 여관 guesthouse

yŏhaeng 여행 journey; travel

yŏhaenghada 여행하다 travel

yŏhaeng kabang 여행 가방 travel bag

yŏhaengsa 여행사 travel agency

yŏhaksaeng 여학생 schoolgirl

yŏja 여자 woman

yŏja ch'in-gu 여자 친구
girl friend

yŏja hwajangshil 여자
화장실 ladies' room

...yŏjida ...여지다 become

yŏjŏnhi 여전히 as ever

yŏjong-ŏbwŏn 여종업원
hostess

yŏjuin 여주인 landlady;
mistress

yŏk 역 station; role

yŏk-kkyŏptta 역겹다 be
nauseating; be nauseated; feel
nauseous

yŏk-kkyŏun 역겨운
nauseating

yŏkkwŏn 여권 passport

yŏkssa 역사 history

yŏkssajŏgin 역사적인
historical

yŏksshi 역시 also; still;
after all

yŏkssŏl 역설 paradox

yŏkssŏltchŏgin 역설적인
paradoxical

yŏktto 역도 weightlifting

yŏktto sŏnsu 역도 선수
weightlifter

yŏl 열 ten; row; line; tier; heat;
fever; temperature

yŏlda 열다 open; be off (of
lid); inaugurate; throw party

yŏlgwang 열광 fascination

yŏlgwanghada 열광하다 be
crazy about; go wild

yŏlgwanghan 열광한
delirious

yŏlgwangtchŏgin 열광적인
rapturous

yŏllak 연락 contact

yŏllakch'ŏ 연락처 contact
number

yŏllak'ada 연락하다 contact

yŏllida 열리다 open; take
place

yŏllin 열린 open

yŏllip chut'aek 연립 주택
row house

yŏllyŏrhan 열렬한
enthusiastic

yŏllyo 연료 fuel

yŏlsoe 열쇠 key

yŏlshim 열심 enthusiasm

yŏltchunghada 열중하다 be
enthusiastic about

yŏlttaeŭi 열대의 tropical

yŏlttae urim 열대 우림
tropical rain forest

yŏlttŭng ŭishik 열등 의식
inferiority complex

yŏmmyŏn 옆면 side

yŏmnyŏ 염려 anxiety

yŏmnyŏhada 염려하다 be
anxious

yŏmnyŏhanŭn 염려하는
anxious

yŏmsaek 염색 tint

yŏmsaek'ada 염색하다 dye

yŏmso 염소 goat; chlorine

yŏmtchŭng 염증
inflammation

yŏn

yŏn 연 kite
yŏnae kyŏrhon 연애 결혼 love marriage
yŏnae p'yŏnji 연애 편지 love letter
yŏnan 연안 coast
yŏnbong 연봉 annual salary
yŏnch'ul 연출 direction
yŏnch'ultcha 연출자 director
yŏnch'urhada 연출하다 direct
yŏndae 연대 regiment; chronology; era
yŏng 영 zero
yŏng-anshil 영안실 morgue
yŏnggam 영감 inspiration; old man; husband; sir
yŏnggujŏgin 영구적인 permanent
Yŏngguk 영국 Britain; United Kingdom; England ◊ British; English
yŏnggwang 영광 glory
yŏnggwangsŭrŏun 영광스러운 glorious
yŏngha 10to 영하 10도 10 below zero
yŏngha-ŭi 영하의 subzero
yŏnghon 영혼 soul
yŏnghwa 영화 movie
yŏnghwagwan 영화관 movie theater
yŏnghyang 영향 effect; influence
yŏnghyang chuda 영향 주다 influence

yŏnghyangnyŏk innŭn 영향력 있는 influential
yŏn-gi 연기 action; acting; portrayal; smoke; postponement
yŏn-gidoen 연기된 belated
yŏn-giga nada 연기가 나다 smoke
yŏn-gihada 연기하다 act; portray; delay
yŏn-gija 연기자 act; actor
yŏngnihada 영리하다 be clever
yŏngnihan 영리한 clever
yŏngnyang 영양 nutrition
yŏngnyangbun 영양분 nourishment
yŏngnyang shiltcho 영양 실조 malnutrition
yŏngnyŏk'ada 역력하다 be clear
Yŏng-ŏ 영어 English
yŏn-goja 연고자 relative
yŏngsagwan 영사관 consulate
yŏngsujŭng 영수증 receipt
yŏngt'o 영토 territory ◊ territorial
yŏn-gŭk 연극 theater; play ◊ theatrical
yŏn-gŭm 연금 pension
yŏn-gu 연구 research
yŏn-guhada 연구하다 research
yŏng-ung 영웅 hero

yŏng-ungjŏgin 영웅적인
heroic

yŏn-guso 연구소 research
institute

yŏn-guwŏn 연구원
researcher

yŏn-gwan 연관 link

yŏn-gwanjit-tta 연관짓다
link

yŏngwŏn 영원 eternity

yŏngwŏnhan 영원한 eternal

yŏn-gyŏl 연결 connection

yŏn-gyŏrhada 연결하다
connect

yŏnhada 연하다 be tender

yŏnhan 연한 weak; tender

yŏnhap 연합 union; coalition;
federation

yŏnhapttoen 연합된 united

yŏnjang 연장 extension

yŏnjanghada 연장하다
prolong

yŏnju 연주 rendering

yŏnjuhada 연주하다 play

yŏnjuhoe 연주회 concert

yŏnjuja 연주자 musician

yŏnjung 연중 throughout the
year ◊ annual

yŏnjung-ŭi 연중의 annual

yŏnmot 연못 pond

yŏnnalligi 연날리기 kite
flying

yŏnŏ 연어 salmon

yŏnp'il 연필 pencil

yŏnsang-ŭi 연상의 elder

yŏnse 연세 age

yŏnsŏl 연설 speech

yŏnsŏrhada 연설하다 make
a speech

yŏnsok 연속 series;
succession; sequence

yŏnsoktchŏgin 연속적인
consecutive

yŏnsok tŭrama 연속
드라마 soap (opera)

yŏnssŭp 연습 exercise;
practice

yŏnssŭptchang 연습장
exercise book

yŏnssŭp'ada 연습하다
practice; exercise

yŏnswaejŏm 연쇄점 chain
store

yŏnyak'an 연약한 feeble

yŏnyein 연예인 entertainer

yŏpkkuri 옆구리 side

yŏpssŏ 엽서 (post)card

yŏptchip 옆집 next door

yŏp'e 옆에 next to

yŏri innŭn 열이 있는
feverish

yŏri it-tta 열이 있다 have a
temperature

yŏrŏ 여러 various

yŏrŏbun 여러분 everyone
(polite address)

yŏrŏgaji 여러가지 all
sorts of

yŏrŏ pŏn 여러 번 many
times

yŏrŭm 여름 summer

yŏsa 여사 Mrs (honorific term)

yŏshin 여신 goddess

yŏsŏng 여성 female; women; feminine

yŏsŏng haebang undong 여성 해방 운동 women's lib

yŏsŏngjŏgin 여성적인 feminine

yŏsŏt 여섯 six

yŏttŭt-tta 엿듣다 intercept *message*; eavesdrop

yŏu 여우 fox

yŏwang 여왕 queen

...yŏya handa …여야 한다 have to

...yŏyaman hada …여야만 하다 have (got) to

yŏyuga it-tta 여유가 있다 afford

yŏyuroun 여유로운 free and easy

yoch'ŏng 요청 request

yoch'ŏnghada 요청하다 request

yogŭl hada 욕을 하다 swear (at)

yogŭm 요금 fare; charge

yogŭmp'yo 요금표 price

yogu 요구 demand

yoguhada 요구하다 demand

yojŏng 요정 fairy

yojŭŭm 요즈음 nowadays

yok 욕 verbal abuse

yoksshim 욕심 greed

yoksshim manŭn 욕심 많은 greedy

yokssŏl 욕설 bad language

yoktcho 옥조 bathtub

yok'ada 욕하다 abuse *(verbally)*

yong 용 dragon

yongbyŏnboda 용변보다 relieve oneself

yonggamhada 용감하다 be brave

yonggamhan 용감한 brave

yonggi 용기 container; courage; spirit

yonggi innŭn 용기 있는 courageous

yonggirŭl naeda 용기를 내다 pluck up courage

yongmang 욕망 desire

yongmo 용모 beauty

yongnyang 용량 capacity; memory

yong-ŏ 용어 term

yongsŏ 용서 forgiveness

yongsŏhada 용서하다 forgive

yongsuch'ŏl 용수철 spring

yongtton 용돈 allowance

yoranhada 요란하다 be loud

yori 요리 cooking; dish; food

yorich'aek 요리책 cookbook

yorihada 요리하다 cook

yorisa 요리사 cook

yosul 요술 magic

yosuljaeng-i 요술쟁이 magician

yosurŭl purida 요술을 부리다 juggle

yotchŏm 요점 point *(in argument)*; gist

yot'ŭ 요트 yacht

yot'ŭ kyŏnggi 요트 경기 sailing

yoyak 요약 summary

yoyak'ada 요약하다 summarize

yua 유아 infant

yuagi 유아기 infancy

yubang 유방 breast

yubok'an 유복한 fortunate

yubunam 유부남 married man

yuch'anghada 유창하다 be fluent

yuch'anghan 유창한 fluent

yuch'ihada 유치하다 be childish

yuch'ihan 유치한 childish

yuch'iwŏn 유치원 kindergarten

Yudaein 유대인 Jew ◊ Jewish

yudo 유도 judo

Yuen 유엔 UN

yugam 유감 regret; grudge

yugamsŭrŏpkkedo 유감스럽게도 regrettably

yugamsŭrŏun 유감스러운 regrettable

yugashil 육아실 nursery

Yugio Tongnan 육이오 동란 Korean War

yugoebŏm 유괴범 kidnapper

yugoehada 유괴하다 kidnap

Yugyo 유교 Confucianism

yuhaeng 유행 fashion

yuhaenghanŭn 유행하는 in fashion

yuhaeng-ida 유행이다 be around *(of illness)*

yuhok 유혹 temptation; seduction

yuhok'ada 유혹하다 tempt

yuhwa 유화 oil painting

yuhyohan 유효한 valid

yuhyo mallyoil 유효 만료일 expiration date

yuik'an 유익한 beneficial

yuirhada 유일하다 be unique

yuirhan 유일한 sole; unique

yujep'um 유제품 dairy products

yuji 유지 upkeep; grease

yujihada 유지하다 hold; stay; keep

yujŏk 유적 ruins

yujŏn 유전 inheritance *(characteristics)*; oil field

yujŏndoenŭn 유전되는 hereditary

yujŏnja 유전자 gene

yujŏnjŏgin 유전적인 genetic

yujŏnjŏgŭro 유전적으로 genetically

yuk 육 six

yukch'e 육체 flesh ◊ physical

yukch'ejŏgŭro 육체적으로 physically

yukch'in 육친 blood relative

yuk-kkun 육군 army

yukkwŏnja 유권자 voter; electorate

yukkyo 육교 footbridge

yuksship 육십 sixty

yuktchi 육지 land

yuk'waehada 유쾌하다 be pleasant

yuk'waehan 유쾌한 pleasant

yulmuch'a 율무차 Job's tears tea

yumŏ kamgak 유머 감각 sense of humor

yumo 유모 nanny

yumoch'a 유모차 buggy; baby carriage

yumul 유물 remnant

yumullon 유물론 materialism

yumyŏng 유명 fame

yumyŏnghada 유명하다 be famous (for)

yumyŏnghan 유명한 famous

yun 윤 gloss

yungja 융자 financing

yun-gwagŭl chaptta 윤곽을 잡다 outline

yun naeda 윤 내다 polish

yunyŏm 유념 regard

yunyŏmhada 유념하다 pay heed to

yuri 유리 glass

yurihada 유리하다 be profitable

yurihan 유리한 advantageous

Yurŏp 유럽 Europe ◊ European

yuryŏng 유령 ghost

yuryo toro 유료 도로 turnpike

yusa 유사 similarity; analogy; quicksand

yusahan 유사한 close; comparable

yusan 유산 heritage; estate; miscarriage

yusŏ 유서 will

yut 윷 Four-Stick Game

yut'ong 유통 distribution

yut'onghada 유통하다 distribute

yuwŏl 유월 June

yuwŏnji 유원지 amusement park; recreation ground

yuyongssŏng 유용성 utility

English – Korean

A

a, an ◊ *(no equivalent)*: *a book* ch'aek 책 ◊ *(with countword)* hanaŭi 하나의, han 한; *a cup of coffee* k'ŏp'i han chan 커피 한 잔

abandon *object* pŏryŏduda 버려두다; *person* pŏrigo ttŏnada 버리고 떠나다; *plan* p'ogihada 포기하다

abbreviation yaktcha 약자

ability nŭngnyŏk 능력

able *(skillful)* nŭngnyŏginnŭn 능력있는

abolish p'yejihada 폐지하다

abortion nakt'ae 낙태

about 1 *prep (concerning)* …e kwanhan …에 관한; *what's it ~?* muŏse kwanhan kŏshimnikka? 무엇에 관한 것입니까? **2** *adv (roughly)* yak 약; *be ~ to …* mak …haryŏgo hada 막 …하려고 하다

above 1 *prep* …poda wi …보다 위; *(more)* …poda tŏ …보다 더 **2** *adv* wie 위에

abroad *live* haeoeesŏ 해외에서; *go* haeoero 해외로

abrupt *departure* kaptchakssŭrŏn 갑작스런

absent *adj (from school)* kyŏlssŏk'an 결석한; *(from work)* kyŏlgŭnhan 결근한

absent-minded mŏnghan 멍한

absolutely *(completely)* wanjŏnhi 완전히

absorb *liquid, group* hŭpssuhada 흡수하다

abstain *(from voting)* kikkwŏnhada 기권하다

abstract *adj* ch'usangjŏgin 추상적인

absurd ŏrisŏgŭn 어리석은

abuse *n (insults)* yok 욕; *(of child)* haktae 학대

academic 1 *n* kyosa 교사 **2** *adj* kodŭnggyoyugŭi 고등교육의

academy hagwŏn 학원

accelerate 1 *v/i* ppallajida 빨라지다 **2** *v/t production* kasokshik'ida 가속시키다

accent *(speaking)* akssent'ŭ 악센트

accept *gift* padadŭrida 받아들이다; *conditions* kyŏndida 견디다

acceptance padadŭrim 받아들임

access *(to building)* ch'urip 출입

accident uyŏnhan sakkŏn 우연한 사건; *(crash)* sago 사고; *by ~* uyŏnhi 우연히

accommodations sukppak shisŏl 숙박 시설

accompany tongbanhada 동반하다; MUS panjurŭl hada 반주를 하다

accomplice kongbŏm 공범

accomplish *task* sŏngch'wihada 성취하다

according: *~ to* …e ttarŭmyŏn …에 따르면

◆ **account for** *(explain)* sŏlmyŏnghada 설명하다

accountant hoegyesa 회계사

account number kyejwa pŏnho 구좌 번호

accounts hoegye 회계

accumulate 1 *v/t* moŭda 모으다 **2** *v/i* moida 모이다

accuracy chŏnghwak 정확

accurate chŏnghwak'an 정확한

accusation pinan 비난

accuse pinanhada 비난하다; *be ~d of* JUR …(ŭ)ro kobaldoeda … (으) 로 고발되다

accused: *the ~* JUR p'igo 피고

ace *(cards, tennis)* eisŭ 에이스

ache *v/i* ap'ŭda 아프다

achieve sŏngch'wihada 성취하다

achievement sŏngch'wi 성취; *(thing achieved)* ŏptchŏk 업적

acid *n* san 산

acknowledge injŏnghada 인정하다

acknowledg(e)ment injŏng 인정

acquaintance *(person)* anŭn saram 아는 사람

acquire *skill* sŭpttŭk'ada 습득하다; *property* hoekttŭk'ada 획득하다

acrobat kogyesa 곡예사

across 1 *prep* ~ *(on other side of)* …ŭi majŭn p'yŏne(sŏ) …의 맞은 편에(서) ◊ *(to other side of)* …ŭi majŭn p'yŏnŭro …의 맞은 편으로 **2** *adv (to other side)* kŏnnosŏ 건너서

act 1 *v/i* THEA yŏn-gihada 연기하다; *(pretend)* kajanghada 가장하다; *(take action)* haengdonghada 행동하다; *~ as* …ŭl / rŭl taerihada …을 / 를 대리하다 **2** *n (deed)* haengdong 행동; *(of play)* mak 막; *(in vaudeville)* yŏn-gija 연기자; *(pretense)* shinyung 시늉; *(law)* pŏmnyŏng 법령

acting 1 *n* yŏn-gi 연기 **2** *adj (temporary)* imshiŭi 임시의

action haengwi 행위

active hwalttongjŏgin 활동적인

activity hwalbarhan umjigim 활발한 움직임; *(pastime)* hwalttong 활동

actor namja paeu 남자 배우

actress yŏja paeu 여자 배우

actual *(real)* shiltchel 실제의

acupuncture ch'imsul 침술

acute *pain* kŭkshimhan 극심한

adapt 1 *v/t* chŏk'ap'age hada 적합하게 하다 **2** *v/i* chŏgŭnghada 적응하다

adapter ELEC ŏdaept'ŏ 어댑터

add MATH tŏhada 더하다; *salt etc* puŏ nŏt'a 부어 넣다

addict chungdoktcha 중독자

addiction chungdok 중독

addition MATH tŏtssem 덧셈; *(to list etc)* ch'uga 추가

additional ch'ugaŭi 추가의

additive ch'ŏmgaje 첨가제

address 1 *n* chuso 주소; *form of* ~ ch'ingho 칭호 **2** *v/t letter* chusorŭl ssŭda 주소를 쓰다; *audience* yŏnsŏrhada 연설하다

address book chusorok 주소록

adequate chŏkttanghan 적당한

adhesive *n* chŏpch'aktche 접착제

adjourn *v/i (of court)* hyujŏngdoeda 휴정되다; *(of meeting)* chungdandoeda 중단되다

adjust *v/t match'uda* 맞추다

administration *(of company)* kwalli 관리; *(government)* chŏngbu 정부

administrative haengjŏng-ŭi 행정의

admiration kamt'an 감탄

admire kamt'anhada 감탄하다

admirer ch'anmija 찬미자

admission *(confession)* shiin 시인; ~ *free* muryo iptchang 무료 입장

admit *(allow in)* tŭrŏonŭn kŏsŭl hŏgahada 들어오는 것을 허가하다; *(confess)* shiinhada 시인하다

adolescent *n* sach'un-giŭi namnyŏ 사춘기의 남녀

adopt *child* ibyanghada 입양하다; *plan* ch'aet'aek'hada 채택하다

adult *n* ŏrŭn 어른; *(over 20)* sŏng-in 성인

adultery kant'ong kwan-gye 간통 관계

advance 1 *n (money)* sŏnbul 선불; *(in science etc)* chinbo 진보; MIL chŏnjin 전진; *in* ~ miri 미리

advanced ap sŏn 앞 선; ~ *learner* sanggŭptcha 상급자; ~ *level* sanggŭp 상급

advantage yurihan chŏm 유리한 점

adventure mohŏm 모험

advertise *v/t & v/i* kwanggohada 광고하다

advertisement kwanggo 광고
advice choŏn 조언
advisable hyŏnmyŏnghan 현명한
advise *person* choŏnhada 조언하다; *caution* ch'unggohada 충고하다; ~ *sb to ...* nuguege ...rago choŏnhada 누구에게 ...라고 조언하다
adviser komun 고문
aerobics eŏrobik 에어로빅
affair *(matter)* il 일; *(business)* ŏmmu 업무; *(love)* pullyun 불륜
affect MED palbyŏnghada 발병하다; *(influence)* yŏnghyang-ŭl mich'ida 영향을 미치다
affection aejŏng 애정
affectionate tajŏnghan 다정한
afford yŏyuga it-tta 여유가 있다
afraid: *be ~* turyŏwŏhada 두려워하다; *be ~ of ...* ...ŭl / rŭl musŏwŏhada ...을 / 를 무서워하다
Africa Ap'ŭrik'a 아프리카
African 1 *adj* Ap'ŭrik'aŭi 아프리카의 **2** *n* Ap'ŭrik'a saram 아프리카 사람
after 1 *prep* hue 후에; *(in position)* taŭme 다음에; ~ *all* kyŏlguk 결국; *it's ten ~ two* tushi shippunimnida 두시 십분입니다 **2** *adv*

(afterward) taŭme 다음에, hue 후에; *the day ~* taŭmnal 다음날
afternoon ohu 오후
afterward najung-e 나중에
again tashi 다시
against *(opposed to)* ...e pandaehayŏ ...에 반대하여; *(leaning on)* ...e kidaeŏ ...에 기대어
age *n* nai 나이; *(respectful: of older person)* yŏnse 연세; *(era)* ki 기
agency chunggaeŏp 중개업
agenda iltchŏng 일정
agent taeriin 대리인
aggressive konggyŏktchŏgin 공격적인
agitated tong-yohan 동요한
ago: *3 days ~* samil chŏne 3일 전에; *long ~* orae chŏne 오래 전에
agony kot'ong 고통
agree tong-ŭihada 동의하다
agreement tong-ŭi 동의; *(contract)* kyeyak 계약
agriculture nong-ŏp 농업
ahead: *be ~ of ...* ...ŭi ap'e ...의 앞에
Aids eijŭ 에이즈
aim 1 *n* kyŏnyang 겨냥; *(objective)* moktchŏk 목적 **2** *v/i* kyŏnyanghada 겨냥하다; ~ *to do sth* muŏsŭl hanŭn kŏsŭl mokp'yoro samtta 무엇을 하는 것을 목표로

삼다

air n konggi 공기; **by** ~ travel pihaenggiro 비행기로;
send hanggongp'yŏnŭro 항공편으로

air-conditioned naengbangjung 냉방중

airline hanggongsa 항공사

airplane pihaenggi 비행기

airport konghang 공항

alarm (device) kyŏngbogi 경보기

alarm clock chamyŏngjong shigye 자명종 시계

alcohol alk'o-ol 알코올

alcoholic 1 n alk'o-ol chungdoktcha 알코올 중독자 **2** adj alk'o-olssŏng-ŭi 알코올성의

alert adj kyŏnggyehanŭn 경계하는

alibi allibai 알리바이

alien (foreigner) oegugin 외국인; (from space) oegyein 외계인

alike: be ~ pisŭt'ada 비슷하다

alimony wijaryo 위자료

alive: be ~ sarait-tta 살아있다

all 1 adj modŭn 모든; **the time** hangsang 항상 **2** pron modu 모두; ~ **of us / them** uridŭl / kŭdŭl modu 우리들 / 그들 모두; **that's** ~, **thanks** twaessŭmnida, kamsahamnida 됐습니다, 감사합니다 **3** adv: ~ **at**

once (suddenly) kaptchagi 갑자기; ~ **right** choayo 좋아요; **they're not at** ~ anassŏyo 그들은 전혀 닮지 않았어요; **not at** ~! (please do) chŏnmaneyo! 천만에요!;
two ~ (in score) i tae iro 통tchŏm 이 대 이로 동점

allegation chujang 주장

allergic: be ~ to ...e allerŭgi panŭng-i it-tta ...에 알레르기 반응이 있다

allergy allerŭgi 알레르기

alleviate pain tŏlda 덜다

alliance tongmaeng 동맹

alligator ago 악어

allow hŏrak'ada 허락하다;
money, time chuda 주다

allowance (money) kŭbyŏ 급여; (pocket money) yongtton 용돈

all-wheel drive saryun-gudong 사륜구동

ally n (state) tongmaengguk 동맹국; (person) hyŏmnyŏktcha 협력자

almond amondŭ 아몬드

almost kŏŭi 거의

alone honja 혼자

along 1 prep ...ŭl / rŭl ttarasŏ ...을 / 를 따라서 **2** adv hamkke 함께; **all** ~ (all the time) naenae 내내

aloud sorirŭl naeŏ 소리를 내어

alphabet alp'abet 알파벳

already pŏlssŏ 벌써

alright that's ~ (doesn't matter) kwaench'anayo 괜찮아요; (after thank you) ch'ŏnmaneyo 천만에요; (quite good) choŭndeyo 좋은데요

also ttohan 또한

alter v/t pakkuda 바꾸다

alteration pyŏn-gyŏng 변경; (to clothes) susŏn 수선

alternate 1 v/i kyoch'ehada 교체하다 2 adj pŏn-gara hanŭn 번갈아 하는

alternative 1 n taean 대안 2 adj taeshinhal 대신할

alternatively taeshin 대신

although pirok ...haljirado 비록 …할지라도

altitude haebalgodo 해발고도; (of plane) kodo 고도

altogether (completely) wanjŏnhi 완전히; (in all) chŏnbu 전부

aluminum alluminyum 알루미늄

always hangsang 항상

amateur n amach'uŏ 아마추어

amaze kkamtchak nollage hada 깜짝 놀라게 하다

amazement kkamtchak nollam 깜짝 놀람

amazing (surprising) aju nollaun 아주 놀라운; (very good) aju choŭn 아주 좋은

ambassador taesa 대사

ambiguous aemaemohohan 애매모호한

ambition yamang 야망; (something desired) yashiminnŭn 야심있는

ambitious person, plan yashiminnŭn 야심있는

ambulance kugŭpch'a 구급차

amendment sujŏng 수정

amends make ~ posangŭl hada 보상을 하다

America Miguk 미국

American 1 adj Migugŭi 미국의 2 n Miguk saram 미국 사람

ammunition t'anyak 탄약

amnesty n samyŏn 사면

amongst kaunde 가운데

amount yang 양; (sum of money) kŭmaek 금액

amplifier aemp'ŭ 앰프

amputate chŏlttanhada 절단하다

amuse (make laugh) utkkida 웃기다; (entertain) chŭlgŏpkkehada 즐겁게하다

amusement chaemi 재미; (entertainment) chŭlgŏum 즐거움

amusing chaemiinnŭn 재미있는

analysis punsŏk 분석

analyze punsŏk'ada 분석하다

anarchy mujŏngbu sangt'ae 무정부 상태

anatomy haebuhak 해부학
ancestor chosang 조상
ancient *adj* kodaeŭi 고대의
and ◊ *(joins nouns)* wa / kwa
와 / 과 ◊ *(joins adjectives)* ...
go ...고; *(joins verbs)* ...
...하고; *(starts new sentence)*
kŭrigo 그리고; *(expresses
result)* ...haesŏ ...해서
anemic: be ~ pinhyŏltchŭng-
ida 빈혈증이다
anesthetic mach'wije 마취제
anger *n* noyǒum 노여움
angle *n* kak 각
angry hwaga nan 화가 난;
be ~ with sb nuguege hwaga
nada 누구에게 화가 나다
animal tongmul 동물
animated cartoon manhwa
yŏnghwa 만화 영화
animosity chŭng-o 증오
ankle palmok 발목
annex *n* *(building)* pyŏlgwan
별관
anniversary *(wedding ~)*
kinyŏmil 기념일
announce kongshiktchŏgŭro
allida 공식적으로 알리다
announcement allim 알림;
(official) konggo 공고
announcer TV, RADIO anaunsŏ
아나운서
annoy sŏnggashigehada
성가시게 하다; **be ~ed**
hwanada 화나다
annual *adj* *(once a year)* illyŏne

han pŏnŭi 일년에 한 번의;
(of a year) yŏnjung-ŭi 연중의
anonymous ingmyŏng-ŭi
익명의
another 1 *adj* *(different)* tarŭn
다른; *(additional)* tto hana 또
하나 **2** *pron* *(different one)*
tarŭn kŏt 다른 것; *(additional
one)* tto tarŭn kŏt 또 다른 것;
one ~ sŏro 서로
answer 1 *n* tap 답; *(to
problem)* haedap 해답 **2** *v/t*
tap'ada 답하다
answerphone chadong-
ŭngdapkki 자동응답기
ant kaemi 개미
antenna TV ant'ena 안테나
antibiotic *n* hangsaeng multchil
항생 물질
anticipate *(expect)* yesanghada
예상하다
antidote haedoktche 해독제
antique dealer kolttongp'um
sang-in 골동품 상인
antiseptic *n* sodongnyak
소독약
antivirus program pairŏsŭ
paeksshin p'ŭrogŭraem
바이러스 백신 프로그램
anxiety kŏktchŏng
걱정
anxious kŏktchŏnghanŭn
걱정하는; *(eager)* maeu
paranŭn 매우 바라는
any 1 *adj* ◊ *(no translation)*:
are there ~ glasses? chani
issŏyo? 잔이 있어요?; *(in*

negatives) amu 아무; *there
aren't ~ glasses* amu chando
ŏpssŏyo 아무 잔도 없어요
◊ (*emphatic*) ŏttŏn 어떤
2 *pron* (*thing*) amu kŏt 아무
것; (*person*) nugudo 누구다
anybody nugun-ga 누군가;
(*with negatives*) amudo ...
(+ negative verb) 아무도
... ◊ (*emphatic*) nugurado
누구라도
anyhow ŏtchaet-ttŭn 어쨌든
anyone → *anybody*
anything muŏt 무엇; (*with
negatives*) amu kŏt-tto 아무
것도
anyway → *anyhow*
anywhere ŏdidŭnji 어디든지;
(*with negatives*) amudedo
아무데도
apart ttŏrŏjyŏsŏ 떨어져서;
live ~ kakki ttaro salda 각기
따로 살다
apartment ap'at'ŭ 아파트
apartment block ap'at'ŭ tanji
아파트 단지
apologize sagwahada
사과하다
apology sagwa 사과
apparently pogie 보기에
appeal *n* (*charm*) maeryŏk
매력; (*for funds*) kanch'ŏng
간청; JUR hangso 항소
appear nat'anada 나타나다; *it
~s that* ...in kŏt kat-tta ...인
것 같다

appearance (*arrival*)
ch'urhyŏn 출현 (*look*)
p'yojŏng 표정
appendicitis maengjangnyŏm
맹장염
appetite shigyok 식욕; *fig*
yokku 욕구
applaud *v/t* ... ŭl sŏng-wŏnŭl
ponaeda 성원을 보내다
applause sŏng-wŏn 성원
apple sagwa 사과
appliance kigye 기계;
(*household*) kajŏnjep'um
가전제품
applicant ŭngmoja 응모자
application (*for job, university
etc*) chiwŏn 지원; (*for visa*)
shinch'ŏng 신청
apply 1 *v/t* chŏgyonghada
적용하다; *cream* p'yŏ parŭda
펴 바르다 **2** *v/i* (*of rule*)
chŏgyongdoeda 적용되다
♦ **apply for** *job, university*
chiwŏnhada 지원하다;
passport shinch'ŏnghada
신청하다
appoint (*to position*)
immyŏnghada 임명하다
appointment (*to position*)
immyŏng 임명; (*meeting*)
yaksok 약속
appreciate *v/t* (*value*)
p'yŏngkkahada 평가하다;
(*be grateful for*) kamsahada
감사하다 **2** *v/i* FIN kagyŏgi
orŭda 가격이 오르다

197 arrange

apprehensive puranhan
불안한
apprentice kyŏnsŭpsaeng
견습생
approach 1 n chean 제안;
(offer etc) kyosŏp 교섭; (to
problem) chŏpkkŭn pangbŏp
접근 방법 2 v/t kakkai
tagagada 가까이 다가가다;
problem taruda 다루다
appropriate adj chŏktchŏrhan
적절한
approve 1 v/i ch'ansŏnghada
찬성하다 2 v/t sŭng-inhada
승인하다
approximate adj taeyagŭi
대략의
apricot salgu 살구
April sawŏl 사월
aquarium yuri sujokkwan
유리 수족관
Arab 1 adj Arabŭi 아랍의 2 n
Arabin 아랍인
archeologist kogohaktcha
고고학자
archeology kogohak 고고학
architect sŏlgyesa 설계사
architecture (style)
kŏnch'ungnyangshik
건축양식
archives kirok 기록
area chiyŏk 지역; (of activity)
punya 분야; (square meters
etc) myŏnjŏk 면적
area code TEL chiyŏk pŏnho
지역 번호

argue v/i (quarrel)
maldat'umhada 말다툼하다;
(reason) nonhada 논하다
argument nonjaeng 논쟁;
(reasoning) nolli 논리
arise (of situation, problem)
irŏnada 일어나다
arithmetic sansul 산술
arm n p'al 팔; (of chair)
p'algŏri 팔걸이
armchair allak ŭija 안락 의자
armed forces kukkun 국군
armed robbery mujang
kangdo 무장 강도
arms (weapons) kunbi 군비
army yuk-kkun 육군
aroma hyanggi 향기
around 1 prep (in circle) ...ŭi
chuwi ...의 주위; (roughly)
taeyak ... 대략 ...; (with
time) yak ... tchŭm 약 ... 쯤
2 adv (in the area) kŭnch'ŏe
근처에; (encircling) tullee
둘레에; be ~ (somewhere
near) kŭnch'ŏe it-tta 근처에
있다
arouse feelings pullŏ irŭk'ida
불러 일으키다; (sexually)
chagŭk'ada 자극하다
arrange (put in order)
paeyŏrhada 배열하다;
furniture paech'ihada
배치하다; flowers kajirŏnhi
kkot-tta 가지런히 꽂다;
meeting etc chunbihada
준비하다; time and place

yeyak'ada 예약하다
arrangement *(plan)* kyehoek
계획; *(agreement)* tong-ŭi
동의; *(of furniture)* paech'i
배치; *(of flowers)* kkotkkoji
꽃꽂이
arrest 1 *n* ch'ep'o 체포 2 *v/t*
ch'ep'ohada 체포하다
arrival toch'ak 도착; *~s (at
airport)* ipkkuk 입국
arrive toch'ak'ada 도착하다
arrogance kŏman 거만
arrogant kŏmanhan 거만한
art yesul 예술
artery MED tongmaek 동맥
art gallery misulgwan 미술관
article *n* p'ummok 품목;
(in paper) kisa 기사
artificial in-gongjŏgin
인공적인
artist *(painter)* misulga 미술가
artistic yesulchŏgin 예술적인
as 1 *conj* ~ *(while)* …hal
ttae …할 때 ◊ *(because)*
waenyahamyŏn …(i)ki
ttaemunida 왜냐하면
… (이)기 때문이다 ◊ *(like)*
…ch'ŏrŏm …처럼; ~ *usual*
p'yŏngsoch'ŏrŏm 평소처럼 2 *adv* mank'ŭm
만큼; ~ *high* … …mank'ŭm
nop'ŭn …만큼 높은 3 *prep*
…(ŭ)ro(sŏ) …(으)로 (서);
work ~ a teacher
sŏnsaengnimŭro irhada

선생님으로 일하다
ashamed: be ~ of …ege
pukkŭrŏpkke yŏgida …에게
부끄럽게 여기다
ashore mut'e 뭍에
ashtray chaettŏri 재떨이
Asia Ashia 아시아
Asian *adj* Ashiaŭi 아시아의
2 *n* Ashiain 아시아인
aside ttŏrŏttŭryŏ 떨어뜨려,
~ *from* …ŭl / rŭl cheoehago
…을 / 를 제외하고; *(in
addition to)* …edaga tŏ
…에다가 더
ask 1 *v/t (put question to)* …ege
mut-tta …에게 묻다; *(invite)*
ch'odaehada 초대하다;
question chilmunhada
질문하다; *favor* put'ak'ada
부탁하다; ~ *sb for* nuguege
…ŭl / rŭl put'ak'ada 누구에게
…을 / 를 부탁하다; ~ *sb to
do* nuguege … haedallago hada
누구에게 … 해달라고
하다 2 *v/i* mut-tta 묻다
♦ **ask for** …ŭl / rŭl put'ak'ada
…을 / 를 부탁하다; *person*
…ŭl / rŭl ch'at-tta …을 / 를
찾다
♦ **ask out** teit'ŭ shinch'ŏnghada
데이트 신청하다
asleep: be ~ p'uk chamdŭlda
푹 잠들다; *fall ~* chamdŭlda
잠들다
aspect myŏn 면
aspirin asŭp'irin 아스피린

assassinate amsarhada
암살하다

assault n p'ok'aeng 폭행

assemble 1 v/t parts
chorip'ada 조립하다 2 v/i (of
people) moida 모이다

assembly (of parts) chorip
조립; POL ŭihoe 의회

assertive
tanjŏngtchŏgin 단정적인

assess p'yŏngkkahada
평가하다

asset FIN, fig chasan 자산

assignment (task) immu 임무;
SCHOOL suktche 숙제

assist toptta 돕다

assistant chosu 조수

associate 1 v/t (in one's mind)
yŏnsanghada 연상하다 2 v/i:
~ with kyojehada 교제하다
3 n tongnyo 동료

association tanch'e hyŏp'oe
단체 협회; in ~ with
...wa / kwa hyŏmnyŏk'ayŏ
...와 / 과 협력하여

assume (suppose) kajŏnghada
가정하다

assumption kajŏng 가정

assurance pojŭng 보증;
(confidence) chashin 자신

assure (reassure) pojanghada
보장하다

asthma ch'ŏnshik 천식

astonish: be ~ed kkamtchak
nollada 깜짝 놀라다

astonishing maeu nollaun

매우 놀라운

astonishment kkamtchak
nollam 깜짝 놀람

astrology chŏmsŏngsul
점성술

astronaut ujuin 우주인

astronomical price
ŏmch'ŏngnage nop'ŭn
엄청나게 높은

asylum (political) mangmyŏng
망명

at (with places) ...e(sŏ)
...에 (서); ~ Joe's cho
nechibesŏ(sŏ) 조 네집에(서);
~ 10 dollars 10tallŏro
10달러로; ~ 5 o'clock
5shie 5시에; be good ~ sth
muŏse nŭngsuk'ada 무엇에
능숙하다

atheist mushillonja
무신론자

athlete undongga 운동가

athletics undonggyŏnggi
운동경기

Atlantic n Taesŏyang 대서양

ATM hyŏn-gŭm inch'ulgi 현금
인출기

atmosphere taegi 대기;
(ambiance) punwigi 분위기

atomic wŏnjaŭi 원자의

atrocity hyung-ak 흉악

attach puch'ida 붙이다;
(to letter) tongbonghada
동봉하다

attachment (to email)
ch'ŏmbup'ail 첨부파일

attack 1 *n* konggyŏk 공격
2 *v/t* konggyŏk'ada 공격하다
attempt 1 *n* shido 시도 **2** *v/t* shidohada 시도하다
attend ch'amsŏk'ada 참석하다
attendance ch'amsŏk 참석;
  (at school) ch'ulssŏk 출석
attention chuŭi 주의; *pay ~*
  chuŭihada 주의하다
attitude t'aedo 태도
attorney pyŏnhosa 변호사
attract kkŭlda 끌다
attraction *(also romantic)*
  maeryŏk 매력
attractive maeryŏginnŭn
  매력있는
audible tŭril su innŭn 들을
  수 있는
audience ch'ŏngjung 청중;
  (in theater) kwanjung 관중; *TV*
  shich'ŏngja 시청자
audiovisual shich'ŏnggagŭi
  시청각의
audition *n* odishyŏn 오디션
auditor FIN kamsagwan 감사관
August p'arwŏl 팔월
aunt *(own, paternal)* komo
  고모; *(own, maternal)* imo
  이모; *(somebody else's)*
  ajumma 아줌마
Australia Hoju 호주
Australian 1 *adj* Hojuŭi
  호주의 **2** *n* Hojuin 호주인
authentic chintchaŭi 진짜의
author chakka 작가
authority kwŏnwi 권위;

(permission) hŏga 허가
authorize kwŏnhanŭl chuda
  권한을 주다; *be ~d*
  to ......l / ŭl hŏga pat-tta
  ...ㄹ / 을 허가 받다
auto *n* chadongch'a 자동차
autobiography chasŏjŏn
  자서전
automate chadonghwahada
  자동화하다
automatic chadong-ŭi
  자동의
automatically chadong-ŭro
  자동으로
automobile chadongch'a
  자동차
available *product* ŏdŭl su
  innŭn 얻을 수 있는; *person*
  shiganinnŭn 시간있는
avenue *also fig* kil 길
average 1 *adj* p'yŏnggyunŭi
  평균의; *(ordinary)* pot'ong-ŭi
  보통의 **2** *n* p'yŏnggyun 평균;
  on ~ pot'ong 보통
avoid p'ihada 피하다
awake *adj* kkaeŏinnŭn
  깨어있는
award 1 *n (prize)* sang 상 **2** *v/t*
  suyŏhada 수여하다
aware: *be ~ of sth* muŏsŭl
  alda 무엇을 알다; *become*
  ~ of sth muŏsŭl arach'arida
  무엇을 알아차리다
awareness inshik 인식
away: *be ~ (traveling)*
  ŏptta 없다; *run ~*

tomanggada도망가다; *it's 2 miles ~* 2mail ttŏrŏjyŏt-tta 2마일 떨어져있다

awesome *infml* (terrific) koengjanghan 굉장한

awful shimhan 심한

awkward (clumsy) sŏt'urŭn 서투른; (difficult) himdŭn 힘든; (embarrassing) kŏbuk'an 거북한

ax 1 *n* tokki 도끼 **2** *v/t job etc* tchallida 짤리다

B

baby *n* agi 아기

baby-sitter agirŭl tolbwajunŭn saram 아기를 돌봐주는 사람

bachelor ch'onggak 총각

back 1 *n* (of person) tŭng 등; (of bus, paper) twinmyŏn 뒷면; (of house) twittchok 뒷쪽, SPORTS huwi 후위; *in ~ antchoge*(sŏ) 안쪽에(서); *~ to front* kŏkkuro 거꾸로 **2** *adj* twittchoge innŭn 뒷쪽에 있는; *~ road* twikkil 뒷길 **3** *adv: please stand ~* twie sŏ chushipsshiyo뒤에서 주십시요; *give ~* toedollyŏjuda 되돌려주다; *she'll be ~ tomorrow* kŭnyŏnŭn naeil toraol kŏshimnida 그녀는 내일 돌아올 것입니다 **4** *v/t* (support) huwŏnhada 후원하다; *car* hujinshik'ida 후진시키다

♦ **back down** yangbohada 양보하다

♦ **back up** (support) huwŏnhada 후원하다; *claim* twitppatch'imhae chuda 뒷받침해 주다; *file* paegŏp'ada 백업하다

backdate sogŭp'ayŏ chŏgyongshik'ida 소급하여 적용시키다

backer huwŏnja 후원자

background paegyŏng 배경; (of person) ch'ulshin sŏngbun 출신 성분

backing (support) chiji 지지; MUS panju 반주

backpacker paenang yŏhaengja 배낭 여행자

backward 1 *adj child* twittŏrojin 뒤떨어진; *glance* twittchogŭi 뒷쪽의 **2** *adv* twittchogŭro 뒷쪽으로

bacon peik'ŏn 베이컨

bacteria pakt'eria 박테리아

bad nappŭn 나쁜; *spelling* sŏt'urŭn 서투른; *headache etc* shimhan 심한; (rotten) ssŏgŭn 썩은; *it's not ~*

kwaench'anayo 괜찮아요

badge paeji 배지

badly nappŭge 나쁘게;
(making mistakes) chalmot
잘못; *injured, damaged*
shimhage 심하게

baffle tanghwanghage hada
당황하게 하다

bag kabang 가방; *(purse)*
haendŭbaek 핸드백

baggage suhwamul 수화물

bake v/t kuptta 굽다

bakery ppangjip 빵집

balance 1 *n* kyunhyŏng 균형;
(remainder) chanyŏgŭm
잔여금 *(of bank account)*
chan-go 잔고 2 v/t & v/i
kyunhyŏng chaptta 균형 잡다

balance sheet
taech'adaejop'yo 대차대조표

balcony peranda 베란다;
(in theater) ich'ŭng chwasŏk
이층 좌석

bald taemŏriŭi 대머리의

ball kong 공

ballet palle 발레

balloon *(child's)* p'ungsŏn
풍선; *(for flight)* kigu 기구

ballot *n* t'up'yo 투표

ballpoint (pen) polp'en 볼펜

bamboo taenamu 대나무

bamboo shoots chuksun죽순

ban 1 *n* kŭmji 금지 2 v/t
kŭmjihada 금지하다

banana panana 바나나

band akdan 악단; *(pop)* paendŭ
밴드

bandage *n* pungdae 붕대

Band-Aid® panch'anggo
반창고

bang 1 *n (noise)* k'wang hanŭn
sori 쾅 하는 소리; *(blow)*
k'wang pudich'im 쾅 부딪힘
2 v/t *door* k'wang tat-tta 쾅
닫다; *(hit)* k'wang pudich'ida
쾅 부딪히다

bank¹ *(river)* chebang 제방

bank² FIN ŭnhaeng 은행

bank account ŭnhaeng kujwa
은행 구좌

bankrupt p'asanhan 파산한;
go ~ p'asanhada 파산하다

bank statement chan-go
chohoe 잔고 조회

banner ki 기

banquet yŏnhoe 연회

baptize seryehada 세례하다

bar¹ *(iron)* pitchang 빗장;
(chocolate) makttaegi 막대기;
(for drink) sultchip 술집;
(counter) kyesandae 계산대

bar² v/t kŭmhada 금하다

barbecue 1 *n* pabek'yu
바베큐 2 v/t t'ongtchaero
kuptta 통째로 굽다

barbed wire kashi ch'ŏlssa
가시 철사

barber ibalsa 이발사

bare adj *(naked)* palgabŏsŭn
발가벗은; *room* t'ŏng pin
텅 빈

barefoot: *be ~* maenbarida

맨발이다

barely kanshinhi 간신히

bargain 1 n (deal) yakssok
약속; (good buy) ssan mulgŏn
싼 물건 2 v/i hŭngjŏnghada
흥정하다

bark v/i (of dog) chit-tta 짖다

barracks MIL maksa 막사

barrel (container) t'ong 통

barricade n parik'eidŭ
바리케이드

barrier ult'ari 울타리;
(cultural) chang-ae 장애

base 1 n (bottom) mit 밑;
(center) ponbu 본부; MIL
chaktchŏn kiji 작전 기지
2 v/t: ~ on ...e pat'angŭl tuda
···에 바탕을 두다

baseball (ball) yagugong
야구공; (game) yagu 야구

baseball cap yagu moja
야구 모자

basement chihashil 지하실;
(in store) chihach'ŭng 지하층

basic kŭnbonjŏgin 근본적인;
(rudimentary) kibonjŏgin
기본적인

basically kibonjŏguro
기본적으로

basics: the ~ kich'o 기초

basin semyŏndae 세면대

basis kich'o 기초; (of
argument) kŭn-gŏ 근거

basket paguni 바구니; (in
basketball) pasŭk'et 바스켓

basketball nonggu 농구

bass n MUS peisŭ 베이스

bat¹ (baseball) pangmang-i
방망이

bat² (animal) pakchwi 박쥐

bath mogyok 목욕; have a ~
mogyok'ada 목욕하다

bathrobe mogyok kaun 목욕
가운

bathroom yokshshil 욕실;
(toilet) hwajangshil 화장실

bathtub yoktcho 욕조

battery chŏnji 전지; AUTO
paet'ŏri 배터리

battle n chŏnt'u 전투

be ◊ ida 이다; there is, there
are ...i / ga it-tta ···이 / 가
있다 ◊ (with adjectives): she
is pretty kŭnyŏnŭn yeppŭda
그녀는 예쁘다; ~ careful
choshimhaseyo 조심하세요;
I've never been to Korea
nanŭn Han-guge kabon chŏgi
ŏptta 나는 한국에 가본
적이 없다

beach haebyŏn 해변

beam 1 n (in roof) tŭlppo 들보
2 v/i (smile) hwaltchak ut-tta
활짝 웃다

beansprouts k'ongnamul
콩나물

bear v/t weight chit'aenghada
지탱하다; costs pudamhada
부담하다; (tolerate) kyŏndida
견디다

bearable kyŏndil su innŭn
견딜 수 있는

beard t'ŏkssuyŏm 턱수염

beat 1 n *(of heart)* kodong 고동; *(of music)* paktcha 박자 **2** v/i *(of heart)* kodongch'ida 고동치다 **3** v/t *(in competition)* igida 이기다; *(hit)* ttaerida 때리다

beating ch'imdae 침대; *(of flowers)*

beautiful arŭmdaun 아름다운; *day* mŏtchin 멋진; *weather* hwach'anghan 화창한

beauty arŭmdaum 아름다움

because ttaemune …때문에; **~ of …** ttaemune …때문에

become ◇ *(+ adj)* …haejida …해지다; *the weather became colder* nalsshiga ch'uwŏjyŏt-tta 날씨가 추워졌다 ◇ *(+ noun)* …i ga toeda …이/가 되다

bed ch'imdae 침대; *(of flowers)* hwadan 화단; *(of sea, river)* mitppadak 밑바닥; *go to ~* chamjarie tŭlda 잠자리에 들다

bedroom ch'imshil 침실

bee pŏl 벌

beef n soegogi 쇠고기

beer maektchu 맥주

beetle ttaktchŏngbŏlle 딱정벌레

before 1 prep & conj …chŏne …전에 **2** adv ijŏne 이전에; *the day ~* kŭ chŏnnare 그전날에

beforehand miri 미리

beg v/i kugŏlhada 구걸하다

beggar kŏji 거지

begin 1 v/i shijakttoeda 시작되다 **2** v/t shijak'ada 시작하다

beginner ch'oboja 초보자

beginning shijak 시작; *(origin)* shich'o 시초

behalf: on ~ of … …ŭl / rŭl wihayŏ …을 / 를 위하여

behave v/i haengdonghada 행동하다; **~ (oneself)** yeŭi parŭge haengdonghada 예의 바르게 행동하다

behavior haengdong 행동

behind 1 prep … twittchoge(sŏ) … 뒷쪽에(서); *(in progress, order)* …e twijyŏsŏ …에 뒤져서; *be ~ … (responsible)* …e ch'aegimi it-tta …에 책임이 있다; *(support)* chijihada 지지하다 **2** adv *(at the back)* twie(sŏ) 뒤에(서)

Beijing Puk-kkyŏng 북경

being chonjae 존재; *(creature)* saengmul 생물

belief midŭm 믿음; *(religious)* shinang 신앙

believe mit-tta 믿다

bell chong 종

bellhop pelboi 벨보이

belly *(of person)* pae 배

♦ **belong to …** …ŭi kŏshida …의 것이다; *club* …ŭi irwŏnida

bill

…의 일원이다

belongings sojip'um 소지품

below 1 *prep* … arae(sŏ) …
아래에 (서); *(amount)* …
iharo … 이하로 2 *adv* araet-
tchoge(sŏ) 아랫쪽에 (서);
10 degrees … yŏngha shipto
영하 십도

belt hŏritti 허리띠

bend 1 *n* man-gok 만곡
2 *v/t* kuburida 구부리다
3 *v/i* hwida 휘다; *(of person)*
kuburida 구부리다

♦ **bend down** kuburida
구부리다

beneath 1 *prep* …ŭi araee(sŏ)
…의 아래에 (서); *(in status,
value)* … poda natkke …
보다 낮게 2 *adv* araee(sŏ)
아래에 (서)

beneficial yuik'an 유익한

benefit 1 *n* iik 이익 2 *v/t*
iigi toeda …의 이익이 되다

beside …ŭi kyŏt'e(sŏ) …의
곁에 (서)

besides 1 *adv* kedaga 게다가
2 *prep (apart from)* …
ioe-e … 이외에

best 1 *adj* kajang chŏun 가장
좋은 2 *adv* kajang chal
가장 잘 3 *n: do one's ~*
ch'oesŏnŭl tahada 최선을
다하다; *the ~ (thing)* ch'oego
최고

best before date ch'oego
p'umjil pojŭng kigan 최고

품질 보증 기간

best man *(at wedding)* shillang
tŭllŏri 신랑 들러리

bet 1 *n* naegi 내기 2 *v/i*
naegirŭl kŏlda 내기를 걸다

betray paebanhada 배반하다

better 1 *adj* poda naŭn 보다
나은; *get ~ (health)* pyŏng-i
nat-tta 병이 낫다; *he's
~ (health)* kŭui kŏn-gang-i
choajyŏt-tta 그의 건강이
좋아졌다 2 *adv* tŏ chal 더
잘; *I'd really ~ not* nanŭn
haji annŭn p'yŏni natkkessŏyo
나는 하지 않는 편이
낫겠어요

better-off yubok'an 유복한

between *prep* saie 사이에

beware:
♦ **~ of** …ŭl / rŭl
choshimhada …을 / 를
조심하다

beyond 1 *prep (in time)*
…ŭl / rŭl chinaso …을 / 를
지나서; *(in space)* …ŭl / rŭl
nŏmŏsŏ …을 / 를 넘어서; *(in
degree)* …ŭi pŏmwirŭl nŏmŏsŏ
…의 범위를 넘어서 2 *adv*
chŏp'yŏnŭro 저편으로

bias(s)ed p'yŏn-gyŏnŭl kajin
편견을 가진

Bible Sŏnggyŏng 성경

bicycle *n* chajŏn-gŏ 자전거

bid *n (auction)* ipch'al 입찰

big k'ŭn 큰

bike chajŏn-gŏ 자전거

bill *n (money)* chip'ye 지폐

(for electricity) ch'ŏnggusŏ 청구서; *(in restaurant etc)* kyesansŏ 계산서

billboard kwanggop'an 광고판

billfold chigap 지갑

billion ship ŏk 십억

bind *v/t (tie)* muktta 묶다; *(oblige)* …ŭi ŭimurŭl chiuda …의 의무를 지우다

binoculars ssang-an-gyŏng 쌍안경

biography chŏn-gi 전기

biological saengmurhagŭi 생물학의

biology saengmurhak 생물학

biotechnology saengch'e konghak saengmul 생명 공학

bird sae 새

birth *(of child)* t'ansaeng 탄생; *(labor)* ch'ulssan 출산; *date of ~* saengnyŏnwŏril 생년월일

birth certificate ch'ulssaeng chŭngmyŏngsŏ 출생 증명서

birth control sana chehan 산아 제한

birthday saeng-il 생일; *happy ~!* saeng-il ch'uk'ahamnida! 생일 축하합니다!

biscuit pisŭk'ŏt 비스켓

bit *n (piece)* chogak 조각; *(part)* pubun 부분; *a ~ (a little)* chogŭm 조금; *(a while)* chamkkan 잠깐

bitch amk'ae 암캐; *infml (woman)* nappŭn nyŏn

나쁜 년

bite 1 *n* mum 묾 **2** *v/t & v/i* mulda 물다

bitter *taste* ssŭn 쓴; *person* pit'onghan 비통한

black 1 *adj* kŏmŭn 검은 **2** *(color)* kŏmjŏngsaek 검정색; *(person)* hŭgin 흑인

blackboard ch'ilp'an 칠판

black box pŭllaek pakssŭ 블랙 박스

black eye mŏngdŭn nun 멍든 눈

blackmail *n* konggal 공갈

black market amshijang 암시장

blackout ELEC chŏngjŏn 정전; MED ŭishik sangshil 의식 상실

black tea hongch'a 홍차

blade *(of knife)* k'allal 칼날

blame 1 *n* pinan 비난; *(responsibility)* ch'aegim 책임 **2** *v/t* pinanhada 비난하다

blank 1 *adj page* kongbaegŭi 공백의; *look* mŏnghan 멍한 **2** *n (space)* kongbaek 공백

blanket *n* tamnyo 담요

blast *n* p'okppal 폭발

blatant ppŏnppŏnsŭrŏun 뻔뻔스러운

blaze *n (fire)* hwajae 화재

bleach *v/t* p'yobaek 표백

bleak *countryside* hwangnyanghan 황량한; *future* ŏduun 어두운

bleed v/i ch'urhyŏrhada
출혈하다

blend v/t honhap 혼합

bless ch'ukppok'ada 축복하다

blessing REL ŭnch'ong 은총

blind 1 adj nun mŏn 눈 먼 **2** n:
the ~ maeng-in 맹인

blink v/i kkamppakkŏrida
깜박거리다

blister n multchip 물집

blizzard shimhan nunbora 심한
눈보라

bloc POL kwŏn 권

block 1 n tŏng-ŏri 덩어리;
(in town) kuhoek 구획 **2** v/t
makta 막다

blockage mak'yŏ innŭn kŏt
막혀있는 것

blog kŭllogŭ 블로그

blond adj kŭmbarŭi 금발의

blonde n (woman) kŭmbal mŏri
yŏja 금발 머리 여자

blood p'i 피

blood group hyŏraek'yŏng
혈액형

blood pressure hyŏrap 혈압

blood test hyŏraek kŏmsa
혈액 검사

blood transfusion suhyŏl
수혈

bloom 1 n kkot 꽃 **2** v/i
kkoch'i p'ida 꽃이 피다

blossom 1 n kkot 꽃 **2** v/i
p'ida 피다

blouse pŭllausŭ 블라우스

blow¹ kangt'a 강타; (shock)

ch'unggyŏk 충격

blow² 1 v/t pulda 불다; ~
one's nose k'orŭl p'ulda 코를
풀다 **2** v/i (of wind)
pulda 불다; (of whistle) ullida
울리다; (of fuse) kkŭnŏjida
끊어지다; (of tire) t'ŏjida
터지다

♦ **blow up** v/t building
p'okp'ahada 폭파하다;
balloon pulda 불다; photo
hwakttaehada 확대하다

blow-dry v/t tŭraiŏ mŏrirŭl
mallida 드라이어로 머리를
말리다

blue adj p'aran 파란

blueberry pŭlluberi 블루베리

blue-collar worker yukch'e
nodongja 육체 노동자

blues MUS pŭllusŭ 블루스

bluff n (deception) ŏmp'o
엄포 **2** v/i ŏmp'orŭl not'a
엄포를 놓다

blunt adj mudin 무딘; person
soltch'ik'an 솔직한

blush v/i ŏlgurŭl pulk'ida
얼굴을 붉히다

blusher poryŏnji 볼연지

BO (body odor) amnae 암내

board 1 n p'anja 판자; (for
game) p'an 판; (for notices)
keship'an 게시판; ~ (of
directors) isahoe 이사회;
on ~ (plane) pihaenggi ane
비행기 안에; (train) kich'a
ane 기차 안에; (boat) pae

ane 배 안에 2 v/t airplane etc
t'ada 타다

boarding card
t'apssŭngkkwŏn 탑승권

boarding school kisuk hak-
kkyo 기숙 학교

board meeting isa hoeŭi
이사 회의

boast w/i charanghada
자랑하다

boat pae 배

body mom 몸; (dead) shich'e
시체

bodyguard kyŏnghowŏn
경호원

body odor amnae 암내

boil v/t samtta 삶다; liquid
kkŭrida 끓이다

boiled rice pap 밥

boiled water kkŭrin mul
끓인 물

boiler poillŏ 보일러

bold 1 adj taedamhan 대담한
2 n (print) kulgŭn kŭlsshich'e
굵은 글씨체

bolt 1 n polt'ŭ 볼트; (on door)
chamulssoe 자물쇠 2 v/t
(fix) polt'ŭro choeda 볼트로
죄다; (close) chamulssoero
chamgŭda 자물쇠로 잠그다

bomb 1 n p'okt'an 폭탄 2 v/t
p'okp'ahada 폭파하다

bomber n (airplane) p'okkyŏk-
kki 폭격기; (terrorist)
p'okp'abŏm 폭파범

bond (tie) kkŭn 끈; FIN

bone n ppyŏ 뼈

bonus (money) ponŏsŭ 보너스;
(extra) tŏm 덤

boo 1 n yayuhanŭn sori
야유하는 소리 2 v/t & v/i
yayuhada 야유하다

book 1 n ch'aek 책 2 v/t
(reserve) yeyak'ada 예약하다;
(for crime) pŏlgŭm changbue
ollida 벌금 장부에 올리다

bookcase ch'aektchang 책장

booklet soch'aektcha 소책자

bookseller ch'aek changsa
책 장사

bookstore sŏjŏm 서점

boom n (economic) pum 붐

boost 1 n (sales)
ch'oktchin 촉진 2 v/t
sales ch'oktchinshik'ida
촉진시키다; ego toduda
돋우다

boot n changhwa 장화

booth (at market) chŏmp'o
점포; (in restaurant)
k'anmagihan chwasŏk
칸막이한 좌석; (at
exhibition) kwallamsŏk 관람석

border n (of countries) kuk-
kkyŏng 국경; (edge) kajangjari
가장자리

bore¹ v/t hole ttult'a 뚫다

bore² 1 n (person) ttabunhan
saram 따분한 사람 2 v/t
siltchŭngnage hada 싫증나게
하다

bow tie

bored: *be* ~ chiruhaejida 지루해지다

boredom kwŏnt'ae 권태

boring ttabunhan 따분한

born: *be* ~ t'aeŏnada 태어나다

borrow pilda 빌다

boss sajang 사장

botanical shingmulŭi 식물의

both 1 *adj* yangtchogŭi 양쪽의 2 *pron* tul ta 둘 다 3 *adv*: ~ ... and ... (*with nouns*) ...wa/kwa ..., tul ta ...와/과 ..., tul ta ...ㅘ/과 ..., 둘 다; (*with adjs*) ...go ...ta ...고 ...다

bother kŏlch'itkkŏri 골칫거리; *it's no* ~ pyŏl il animnida 별 일 아닙니다 2 *v/t* (*disturb*) kwich'ank'e hada 귀찮게 하다; *person working* sŏnggashige hada 성가시게 하다 3 *v/i*: *don't* ~! shin-gyŏng ssŭji maseyo! 신경 쓰지 마세요!

bottle *n* pyŏng 병; (*for baby*) uyubyŏng 우유병

bottled water p'anŭn mul 파는 물

bottleneck pyŏngmok 병목

bottle-opener pyŏngttagae 병따개

bottom 1 *adj* maen mittpadagŭi 맨 밑바닥의 2 *n* (*inside*) antchok ppadak 안쪽 바닥; (*underside*) mittpadak 밑바닥; (*of hill*) ŭi kajang araettppubun 가장 아랫부분;

(*of pile*) maen araetchok mittch'ŭng 아래쪽; (*of street*) kkŭt 끝; (*buttocks*) ŏngdŏng-i 엉덩이

♦ **bottom out** padagŭl pŏsŏnada 바닥을 벗어나다

bottom line (*financial*) ch'ongkyŏlssan 총결산; (*real issue*) kajang chungnyohan sahang 가장 중요한 사항

bounce *v/i* (*of ball*) t'wida 튀다; (*on sofa*) ttwiŏdanida 뛰어다니다; (*of check*) pudoga toeŏ toeraoda 부도가 되어 되돌아오다

bouncer kyŏngbiwŏn 경비원

bound: *be* ~ *to* (*sure to*) t'ŭllimŏpssi ...hal kŏshida 틀림없이 ...할 것이다

boundary kyŏnggye 경계

bouquet kkot-ttabal 꽃다발; (*of wine*) hyanggi 향기

bourbon pŏbon wisŭk'i 버본 위스키

bout MED palppyŏng 발병; (*in boxing*) shihap 시합

bow¹ 1 *n* (*as greeting*) chŏl 절 2 *v/i* insahada 인사하다

bow² (*knot*) maedŭp 매듭; MUS, (*weapon*) hwal 활

bowels ch'angja 창자

bowl (*container*) kŭrŭt 그릇; (*rice*) konggi 공기; (*soup*) taejŏp 대접

bowling polling 볼링

bow tie nabi nekt'ai 나비 넥타이

box

box *n* sangja 상자; *(on form)* pin k'an 빈 칸

boxer kwŏnt'u sŏnsu 권투 선수

boxing kwŏnt'u 권투

boxing match kwŏnt'u shihap 권투 시합

box office maep'yoso 매표소

boy sonyŏn 소년; *(son)* adŭl 아들

boycott *n* poik'ot 보이콧

boyfriend namja ch'in-gu 남자 친구

bracelet p'altchi 팔찌

bracket *(support)* kkach'ibal 까치발; *(in text)* kwarho 괄호

brag charanghada 자랑하다

braid *n (in hair)* ttaŭn mŏri 땋은 머리; *(trim)* tan ch'ŏri 단처리

brain tunoe 두뇌

brains *(mind)* chinŭng 지능

brainwashing senoe 세뇌

brake 1 *n* p'ŭreik'ŭ 브레이크 **2** *v/i* p'ŭreik'ŭrŭl kŏlda 브레이크를 걸다

branch *n (of tree)* kaji 가지; *(of bank)* chijŏm 지점

brand *n* sangp'yo 상표

brand name sangp'yomyŏng 상표명

brand-new shinp'umŭi 신품의

brandy p'ŭraendi 브랜디

brassière p'ŭrejiŏ 브레지어

brat *pej* saekki 새끼

brave *adj* yonggamhan 용감한

bravery yonggamham 용감함

breach of contract JUR kyeyak wiban 계약 위반

bread *n* ppang 빵

breadth p'ok 폭

break 1 *n (in bone etc)* kŭm 금; *(rest)* hyushik 휴식; *(in relationship)* hyushik-kki 휴식기기 **2** *v/t device, toy* pusuda 부수다; *stick, leg* purŏttŭrida 부러뜨리다; *glass, egg* kkaettŭrida 깨뜨리다; *rules, promise* wibanhada 위반하다; *record* kkaeda 깨다 **3** *v/i (of device, toy)* pusŏjida 부서지다; *(of glass, egg)* kkaejida 깨지다; *(of stick)* purŏjida 부러지다

♦ **break down 1** *v/i (of vehicle)* kojangnada 고장나다; *(of talks)* shilp'aehada 실패하다; *(in tears)* urŭmŭl t'ŏttŭrida 울음을 터뜨리다 **2** *v/t door* pusugo yŏlda 부수고 열다; *figures* pullyuhada 분류하다

♦ **break even** COMM tŭksshil ŏpkke toeda 득실이 없게 되다

♦ **break up 1** *v/t fight* mallida 말리다 **2** *v/i (of ice)* kkaejida 깨어지다; *(of couple)* heŏjida 헤어지다; *(of band, meeting)* haech'ehada 해체하다

breakdown *(of vehicle)* kojang 고장; *(of talks)* shilp'ae 실패; *(nervous ~)* shin-gyŏng soeyak

신경 쇠약; *(figures)* punsŏk
분석

breakfast *n* ach'im shiksa
아침 식사

break-in ch'imip 침입

breakthrough *(in talks)*
t'agae 타개; *(in science)* k'ŭn
paltchŏn 큰 발전

breakup *(of partnership etc)*
purhwa 불화

breast yubang 유방

breastfeed *v/t* moyurŭl mŏgida
모유를 먹이다

breath sum 숨

breathe sumshwida 숨쉬다

breathtaking summak'il
chŏngdoŭi 숨막힐 정도의

breed 1 *n* p'umjong 품종
2 *v/t* kirŭda 기르다 3 *v/i*
(of animals) pŏnshik'ada
번식하다

breeze sandŭlpparam
산들바람

brew 1 *v/t beer* yangjohada
양조하다 2 *v/i (of storm)* ilda
일다; *(of trouble)* irŏnaryŏgo
hada 일어나려고 하다

bribe 1 *n* noemul 뇌물 2 *v/t*
maesuhada 매수하다

bribery noemul susu 뇌물
수수

brick pyŏkttol 벽돌

bride shinbu 신부

bridegroom shillang 신랑

bridesmaid shinbu tŭllŏri 신부
들러리

bridge *n* tari 다리; *(of ship)*
sŏn-gyo 선교

brief *adj* kan-gyŏrhan 간결한

briefcase sŏryu kabang 서류
가방

briefing pŭrip'ing 브리핑

briefly chamshidong-an
잠시동안; *(in few words)* kan-
gyŏrhage 간결하게

briefs p'aench'ŭ 팬츠

bright *color, future* palgŭn
밝은; *(sunny)* hwach'anghan
화창한; *(intelligent)*
ttokttok'an 똑똑한

brilliant *sunshine* palgŭn 밝은;
(very good) hullyunghan
훌륭한; *(very intelligent)*
much'ŏk ttokttok'an 무척
똑똑한

bring *object* kajyŏoda
가져오다; *person* teryŏoda
데려오다

♦ bring back *(return)*
tollyŏjuda 돌려주다;
(re-introduce) toetollida
되돌리다; *memories*
saenggangnage hada
생각나게 하다

♦ bring down *government*
chŏnbokshik'ida 전복시키다;
plane ssoa ttŏrŏttŭrida 쏘아
떨어뜨리다; *price* naerige
hada 내리게 하다

♦ bring out *sesang-e naenot'a*
세상에 내놓다; *video, CD*
ch'ulsshihada 출시하다; *new*

bring up

product palmaehada 발매하다

♦ **bring up** *child* yangnyuk'ada 양육하다; *subject* marŭl kkŏnaeda 말을 꺼내다; *(vomit)* t'ohada 토하다

Britain Yŏngguk 영국

British 1 *adj* Yŏnggugŭi 영국의 **2** *n: the ~* Yŏngguin 영국인

broad p'ok nŏlbŭn 폭 넓은; *shoulders* ttŏk pŏrŏjin 떡 벌어진; *smile* hwanhan 환한; *(general)* ilbanjŏgin 일반적인

broadcast 1 *n* pangsong 방송 **2** *v/t* pangsonghada 방송하다

broadcasting pangsong 방송

broadminded kwandaehan 관대한

broccoli pŭrok'olli 브로콜리

brochure pŭrŏshyŏ 브로셔

broil *v/t* kuptta 굽다

broiler kumnŭn kigu 굽는 기구; *(chicken)* kuiyong yŏnggye 구이용 영계

broke *infml* muilp'unŭi 무일푼의

broken *adj* pusŏjin 부서진; *window, promise* kkaejin 깨진; *arm* purŏjin 부러진

broken-hearted maŭmŭi sangch'ŏrŭl ibŭn 마음의 상처를 입은

bronchitis kigwanjiyŏm 기관지염

brooch pŭrŏch'i 브로치

broth mulgŭn sup'ŭ 묽은

수프; *(stock)* kungmul 국물

brothel maech'un-gul 매춘굴

brother *(man's elder)* hyŏng 형; *(woman's elder)* oppa 오빠; *(younger)* namdongsaeng 남동생; *~s and sisters* hyŏngje chamae 형제 자매

brother-in-law *(woman's elder sister's husband)* hyŏngbu 형부; *(wife's younger brother)* ch'ŏ-nam 처남; *(man's elder sister's husband)* maehyŏng 매형

brown *adj* kalsaegŭi 갈색의; *(tanned)* haeppyŏch'e t'an 햇볕에 탄

browse *(in store)* kugyŏngman hago tanida 구경만 하고 다니다; *(on web)* yŏllamhada 열람하다

bruise *n* mŏng 멍

brunette kalssaek mŏriŭi yŏja 갈색 머리의 여자

brush 1 *n* sol 솔 **2** *v/t hair, floor* pitchirhada 빗질하다; *teeth* yangch'ijirhada 양치질하다

brutal chaninhan 잔인한

brutality chaninham 잔인함

bubble *n* kŏp'um 거품

bubble gum p'ungsŏnkkŏm 풍선껌

buck *n infml (dollar)* tallŏ 달러

bucket *n* yangdong-i 양동이

buckle¹ *n* pŏk'ŭl 버클

buckle² *v/i (of metal)*

kuburŏjida 구부러지다

Buddha Puch'ŏ 부처

Buddhism Pulgyo 불교

Buddhist 1 *n* pulgyo shinja 불교 신자 **2** *adj* pulgyoŭi 불교의

Buddhist temple sach'al 사찰

buddy *infml* ch'in-gu 친구; *(address)* yŏboge 여보게

budget *n* yesan 예산; *(of family)* saenghwalbi 생활비

buffalo tŭlsoso 들소

bug 1 *n (insect)* pŏlle 벌레; *(virus)* pairŏsŭ 바이러스; *(device)* toch'ŏnggi 도청기; COMPUT pŏgŭ 버그 **2** *v/t infml (annoy)* koerop'ida 괴롭히다

buggy *(for baby)* yumoch'a 유모차

build 1 *n (of person)* ch'egyŏk 체격 **2** *v/t* seuda 세우다

♦**build up 1** *v/t strength* tallyŏnhada 단련하다; *relationship* ssaa ollida 쌓아 올리다 **2** *v/i* ssayŏjida 쌓여지다

builder kŏnch'ugŏptcha 건축업자; *(company)* kŏnch'ugŏp 건축업

building kŏnmul 건물; *(activity)* kŏnch'uk 건축

building site kongsajang 공사장

build-up ssayŏjim 쌓여짐; *(publicity)* sŏnjŏn 선전

built-up area shigaji 시가지

bunk beds

bulb BOT kugŭn 구근; *(light)* chŏn-gu 전구

bulge 1 *n* tolch'ul 돌출 **2** *v/i (of pocket)* pulluk'ada 불룩하다; *(of wall, eyes)* t'wiŏ naoda 튀어 나오다

bulk taebubun 대부분; **in ~** taeryang-ŭro 대량으로

bulky pup'iga k'ŭn 부피가 큰

bulldozer puldoujŏ 불도우저

bullet ch'ong-al 총알

bulletin keshi 게시

bulletin board keship'an 게시판

bullet-proof pangt'anŭi 방탄의

bull's-eye kwanyŏgŭi hanbokp'an 과녁의 한복판

bully 1 *n* kkangp'ae 깡패 **2** *v/t mot salge kulda* 못 살게 굴다

bum *n infml (hobo)* purangja 부랑자; *(worthless person)* mangnani 망나니

bump 1 *n (swelling)* hok 혹; *(in road)* yunggi 융기 **2** *v/t* puditch'ida 부딪히다

bumper *n* AUTO pŏmp'ŏ 범퍼

bunch *(of people)* muri 무리; *(of keys)* mungch'i 뭉치; **a ~ of flowers** kkot hantabal 꽃 한 다발; **a whole ~ of** manŭn 많은

bungle *v/t* sŏt'urŭge mandŭlda 서투르게 만들다

bunk beds ich'ŭng ch'imdae 이층 침대

burden n chim 짐; fig pudam 부담

bureau (furniture) sŏraptchang 서랍장; (office) samuguk 사무국

bureaucracy (red tape) pŏngŏrŏun haengjŏng chŏlch'a 번거러운 행정 절차; (system) kwallyoje 관료제

bureaucrat kwallyo ch't'ang

bureaucratic kwallyojŏgin 관료적인

burger haembŏgŏ 햄버거

burglar kangdo 강도

burglar alarm tonan kyŏngbogi 도난 경보기

burglarize kangdojirhada 강도질하다

burglary kangdo 강도

burial maejang 매장

burn 1 n hwasang 화상 2 v/t t'aeuda 태우다 3 v/i t'ada 타다

♦ **burn down** 1 v/t t'aewŏbŏrida 태워버리다 2 v/i t'abŏrida 타버리다

burp 1 n t'ŭrim 트림 2 v/i t'ŭrimhada 트림하다

burst 1 n (in pipe) p'ayŏl 파열 2 adj tire t'ŏjin 터진 3 v/t balloon t'ŏttŭrida 터뜨리다 4 v/i of balloon, tire t'ŏjida 터지다; ~ out laughing p'oksorŭl t'ŏttŭrida 폭소를 터뜨리다

bury p'amut-tta 파묻다

bus n pŏsŭ 버스; (long distance) shioe pŏsŭ 시외 버스

bush (plant) kwanmok 관목

business (trade) muyŏk 무역; (company) hoesa 회사; (work) il 일; (affair, matter) sakkŏn 사건

business class pijŭnisŭ k'ŭllaesŭ 비즈니스 클래스

business hours ŏmmu shigan 업무 시간

businessman saŏpkka 사업가

business studies kyŏngnyŏnghak 경영학

business trip ch'ultchang 출장

businesswoman yŏsŏng saŏpkka 여성 사업가

bus station pŏsŭ t'ŏminŏl 버스 터미널

bus stop pŏsŭ chŏngnyujang 버스 정류장

bust n (of woman) kasŭm 가슴

busy adj pappŭn 바쁜; street pŏnhwahan 번화한; (making money) pumbinŭn 붐비는; (full of people) puktchŏkttaenŭn 사람들이 북적대는; TEL t'onghwajungin 통화중인

but …hajiman …하지만

butcher ch'ultchukttchom chuin 정육점 주인

butter n pŏt'ŏ 버터

butterfly (insect) nabi 나비

buttocks ŏngdŏngi 엉덩이

button n tanch'u 단추; (on

machine) pŏt'ŭn 버튼; *(badge)*
paeji 배지
buy *v/t* sada 사다
buyer kumaeja 구매자; *(for a
company)* paiŏ 바이어
buzzer pujŏ 부저
by *prep* …e ŭihae
…에 의해 ◊ *(near, next to)*

…yŏp'e …옆에 ◊ *(no later
than)* …kkaji …까지 ◊ *(past)*
…ŭl / rŭl chinasŏ …을 / 를
지나서 ◊ *(mode of transport)*
…(ŭ)ro …(으) 로 ◊ ~
oneself honjasŏ 혼자서
bye(-bye) annyŏng 안녕
by-product pusanmul 부산물

C

cab *(taxi)* t'aekshi 택시; *(of
truck)* unjŏnsŏk 운전석
cabbage yangbaech'u 양배추
cab driver t'aekshi unjŏnsa
택시 운전사
cabin *(of plane, for crew)*
sŭngmuwŏnshil 승무원실;
(for passengers) kaekshil
객실; *(on ship)* sŏnshil 선실
cabin crew sŭngmuwŏn
승무원
cabinet changshiktchang
장식장; POL naegak 내각
cable k'eibŭl 케이블; ~ *(TV)*
yusŏn pangsong 유선 (방송)
cab stand t'aekshi t'anŭn kot
택시 타는 곳
café tabang 다방
caffeine k'ap'ein 카페인
cage *(for bird)* saejang 새장;
(for lion) uri 우리
cake k'eik'ŭ 케이크
calculate sanch'urhae naeda
산출해 내다; *(in math)*

kyesanhada 계산하다
calculation kyesan 계산
calculator kyesan-gi 계산기
calendar tallyŏk 달력
calf *(young cow)* song-aji
송아지
call 1 *n* TEL chŏnhwa 전화;
(shout) oech'im 외침 2 *v/t*
TEL chŏnhwarŭl kŏlda 전화를
걸다; *(summon)* purŭda
부르다; *meeting* sojip'ada
소집하다; *(describe as)*
…rago purŭda …라고
부르다; *(shout)* sorich'yŏ
purŭda 소리쳐 부르다 3 *v/i*
TEL chŏnhwahada 전화하다;
(shout) sorich'yŏ purŭda
소리쳐 부르다; *(visit)*
pangmunhada 방문하다
◆ **call back** *v/t* TEL najung-e
tashi chŏnhwahada 나중에
다시 전화하다; *(visit)*
tashi pangmunhada 다시
방문하다

◆ call for *(goods)* …ŭl / rŭl kajirŏ kada …을 / 를 가지러 가다; *person* …ŭl / rŭl terirŏ kada …을 / 를 데리러 가다; *(demand)* yoguhada 요구하다; *(require)* …i / ga p'iryohada …이 / 가 필요하다
◆ call in *(expert)* pullŏ tŭrida 불러 들이다
◆ call on *(urge)* yoguhada 요구하다; *(visit)* pangmunhada 방문하다
caller TEL chŏnhwa kŏn saram 전화 건 사람; *(visitor)* sonnim 손님
calligraphy sŏye 서예
calm *adj sea* koyohan 고요한; *person* ch'imch'ak'an 침착한
◆ calm down 1 *vt* karaanch'ida 가라앉히다
2 *vi* koyohaejida 고요해지다; *(of person)* ch'imch'ak'aejida 침착해지다
calorie k'allori 칼로리
Cambodia K'ambodia 캄보디아
Cambodian 1 *adj* K'ambodiaŭi 캄보디아의
2 *n (person)* K'ambodia saram 캄보디아 사람
camcorder k'aemk'odŏ 캠코더
camera k'amera 카메라
cameraman ch'waryŏng kisa 촬영 기사

camouflage *n* wijang 위장
camp 1 *n* k'aemp'ŭ 캠프; *(for refugees)* suyongso 수용소
2 *v/i* ch'ŏnmagŭl ch'ida 천막을 치다
campaign *n* undong 운동
camper k'aemp'ŭhanŭn saram 캠핑하는 사람; *(vehicle)* k'aemp'ŭyong t'ŭreillŏ 캠프용 트레일러
campsite yayŏngji 야영지
campus taehak k'aemp'ŏsŭ 대학 캠퍼스
can¹ ◊ *(ability)* …hal su it-tta …할 수 있다; *I ~ do it by tomorrow* naeil kkaji hal su issŏyo 내일까지 할 수 있어요 ◊ *(in negative)* …hal su ŏptta …할 수 없다; *I ~'t see* pol su ŏpssŏyo 볼 수 없어요 ◊ *(permission)* …hayŏdo chot'a …하여도 좋다; *~ I use the phone?* chŏnhwarŭl ssŏdo toemnikka? 전화를 써도 됩니까?; *~ I have a beer?* maektchuga issŏyo? 맥주가 있어요?
can² *n (for drinks etc)* kkangt'ong 깡통
Canada K'aenada 캐나다
Canadian 1 *adj* K'aenadaŭi 캐나다의 **2** *n* K'aenada saram 캐나다 사람
canal *(waterway)* unha 운하
cancel ch'wisohada 취소하다
cancellation ch'wiso 취소

cancer am 암
candid soltchik'an 솔직한
candidacy ip'ubo 입후보
candidate huboja 후보자; (in exam) ŭngshija 응시자
candle yangch'o 양초
candor hŏshim t'anhoe 허심 탄회
candy sat'ang 사탕
canned fruit etc t'ongjorimdoen 통조림된
cannot → **can**[1]
can opener kkangt'ong ttagae 깡통 따개
canteen (in factory) kunae shikttang 구내 식당
canyon kip'ŭn hyŏpkkok 깊은 협곡
cap (hat) k'aep 캡; (of bottle, pen etc) ttukkŏng 뚜껑
capability nŭngnyŏk 능력
capable (efficient) nŭngnyŏk innŭn 능력 있는
capacity (of container, engine) yongnyang 용량
capital n (city) sudo 수도; (letter) taemuntcha 대문자; (money) chabon 자본
capitalism chabonjuŭi 자본주의
capitalist adj chabonjuŭijŏk 자본주의적
capital punishment kŭk'yŏng 극형
capsize v/i twijip'ida 뒤집히다

capsule MED, (in space) k'aepsshyul 캡슐
captain n (of ship) sŏnjang 선장; (of plane) kijang 기장; (of team) t'imjang 팀장
caption n k'aepsshyŏn 캡션
captivate maŭmŭl sarojapta 마음을 사로잡다
captivity kamgŭm 감금
capture v/t person, animal sarojapta 사로잡다; city chŏmnyŏnghada 점령하다
car chadongch'a 자동차; (of train) ch'aryang 차량
carbohydrate t'ansuhwamul 탄수화물
carbon monoxide ilssanhwat'anso 일산화탄소
carbureter, carburetor k'aburet'ŏ 카부레터
card k'adŭ 카드; (post-) yŏpssŏ 엽서; (business ~) myŏngham 명함
cardboard p'anji 판지
cardigan k'adigŏn 카디건
care 1 n (of baby) tolbom 돌봄; (of elderly) posalp'im 보살핌; (of sick) kanho 간호; (medical ~) ch'iryo 치료; (worry) kŏktchŏng 걱정; take ~ choshimhada 조심하다 2 v/i kwanshimŭl kajida 관심을 가지다; I don't ~! sanggwan ŏpssŏ! 상관 없어!
♦ **care about** …e kwanshimŭl kajida …에 관심을 가지다

career (*profession*) kyŏngnyŏk
경력; (*path through life*)
saeng-ae 생애

careful choshimsŏng innŭn
조심성 있는; (*thorough*)
shinjunghan 신중한

careless choshimsŏng ŏmnŭn
조심성 없는

caretaker kwalliin 관리인

cargo sŏnjŏk hwamul 선적
화물

caricature *n* p'ungja manhwa
풍자 만화

caring *adj* chal tolbonŭn 잘
돌보는

carousel (*at airport*)
hoejŏnshik k'onbeiŏ 회전식
콘베이어; (*merry-go-round*)
hoejŏn mongma 회전 목마

carpet k'ap'et 카펫

carrier (*company*) unsong
hoesa 운송 회사; (*of disease*)
pogyunja 보균자

carrot tanggŭn 당근

carry (*in hand*) tŭlgo kada 들고
가다; (*on one's person*) chinigo
tanida 지니고 다니다;
disease omgida 옮기다; (*of
plane, bus etc*) narŭda 나르다

♦ **carry out** *survey*
shilsshihada 실시하다; *order*
shirhaenghada 실행하다

cart chimmach'a 짐마차

cartel k'arŭt'el 카르텔

carton (*storage*) pakssŭ 박스;
(*for eggs*) kwak 곽; (*of milk*

etc) p'aek 팩; (*of cigarettes*)
kap 갑

cartoon (*in paper*) manhwa
만화; (*on TV*) manhwa
yŏnghwa 만화 영화

cartridge (*for gun*)
t'anyakt'ong 탄약통; (*for
toner*) k'at'ŭriji 카트리지

carve *meat* charŭda 자르다;
wood saegida 새기다

car wash ch'a sech'ŏk 차
세척

case¹ *n* (*container*) k'eisŭ
케이스; (*wine*) sangja 상자

case² *n* (*instance*) kyŏng-u
경우; (*argument*) chujang
주장; (*for investigation*)
sakkŏn 사건; MED chŭngsa
병세; JUR sosong sakkŏn
소송 사건; *in ~ ...* manil
...hal kyŏng-urŭl saenggak'ayŏ
만일 ...할 경우를
생각하여; *in any ~* ŏtchaettŭn
어쨌든

cash 1 *n* hyŏn-gŭm 현금 2 *v/t*
check hyŏn-gŭmŭro pakkuda
현금으로 바꾸다

cash desk kyesandae 계산대

cash flow hyŏn-gŭm yuch'urip
현금 유출입

cashier *n* (*in store etc*)
ch'ullabwŏn 출납원

cash register kŭmjŏn
tŭngnok-kki 금전 등록기

casino k'ajino 카지노

casket (*coffin*) kwan 관

Celsius

cassette nogŭm t'eip'ŭ 녹음
테이프
cassette player nogŭmgi
녹음기
cast 1 n (of play) ch'uryŏnjin
출연진 2 v/t doubt irŭk'ida
일으키다
castle sŏng 성
casual (chance) uyŏnhan
우연한; (offhand)
mugwanshimhan 무관심한;
(not formal) p'yŏngsang-ŭi
평상의; (not permanent)
ilsshijŏgin 일시적인
casualty sasangja 사상자
cat koyang-i 고양이
catalog n mongnok 목록
catastrophe ch'ŏnjaejibyŏn
천재지변
catch 1 n chapkki 잡기; (of
fish) nakkŭn kŏt 낚은 것;
(locking device) kori 고리
2 v/t ball, prisoner, fish chapta
잡다; bus chaba t'ada 잡아
타다; (to speak to) ttarajapta
따라잡다; illness …e kŏllida
…에 걸리다
♦ **catch up** v/i ttarajapta
따라잡다
♦ **catch up on** …ŭl / rŭl
poch'unghada …을 / 를
보충하다
catcher (in baseball) k'aech'ŏ
캐처
catching disease
chŏnyŏmsŏng-ŭi 전염성의

category pŏmju 범주
Catholic 1 adj Ch'ŏnjugyoŭi
천주교의 2 n Ch'ŏnjugyo
shinja 천주교 신자
cattle so 소
cauliflower k'ollip'ŭllawŏ
콜리플라워
cause 1 n wŏnin 원인;
(grounds) iyu 이유 2 v/t
irŭk'ida 일으키다
caution n choshim 조심
cautious choshimsŭroun
조심스러운
cave tonggul 동굴
caviar k'aebia 캐비아
cavity ch'ungch'i 충치
CD shidi 시디
cease v/i chungdanhada
중단하다
ceasefire hyujŏn 휴전
ceiling ch'ŏnjang 천장; fig
ch'oego hando 최고 한도
celebrate ch'uk'ahada
축하하다
celebration ch'uk'ayŏn
축하연
celebrity yumyŏng insa 유명
인사
celery sellŏri 셀러리
cell (for prisoner) kambang
감방; BIOL sep'o 세포
cellar chihashil 지하실
cello ch'ello 첼로
cell(ular) phone haendŭp'on
핸드폰
Celsius sŏpsshi 섭씨

cemetery myoji 묘지

censor v/t kŏmyŏrhada 검열하다

censorship kŏmyŏl chedo 검열 제도

cent sent'ŭ 센트

centennial paek chunyŏn 백 주년

center n han-gaunde 한가운데; (place) sent'ŏ 센터; (region) chungshimji 중심지; POL chungdo'a 중도파

central chungshimŭi 중심의; apartment chungshimbue innŭn 중심부에 있는; (main) chuyohan 주요한

central heating chung-ang nanbang 중앙 난방

centralize chiptchung kyŏrŭihada 집중 결의하다

century segi 세기

CEO ch'oego kyŏngyŏngja 최고 경영자

cereal (grain) kongmul 곡물; breakfast ~ shiriŏl 시리얼

ceremony (event) shik 식; (ritual) ŭishik 의식

certain hwaksshinhanŭn 확신하는; (particular) ŏttŏn 어떤

certainly hwaksshirhi 확실히; (of course) mullon 물론

certainty (inevitability) hwaksshin 확신; (inevitability) hwaksshilssŏng 확실성

certificate (qualification) chagyŏktchŭng 자격증; (paper) chŭngmyŏngsŏ 증명서

certify pojŭnghada 보증하다

Cesarean n chewang chŏlgae 제왕 절개

CFC sshiep'ŭsshi 씨에프씨

chain n soesasŭl 쇠사슬; (jewelry) mok-kkŏrijul 목걸이줄; (for bicycle, tire) ch'ein 체인; (of stores) ch'einjŏm 체인점

chain reaction yŏnswae panŭng 연쇄 반응

chair n ŭija 의자

chairman ŭijang 의장

challenge 1 n (task) haebol manhan il 해볼 만한 일; (race) tojŏn 도전 2 v/t (to race) tojŏnhada 도전하다; (call into question) hwan-gishik'ida 환기시키다

champagne shyamp'ein 샴페인

champion n SPORTS ch'aemp'iŏn 챔피언

championship sŏnsugwŏn taehoe 선수권 대회; (title) sŏnsugwŏn 선수권

chance (possibility) kamang 가망; (opportunity) kihoe 기회

change 1 n (to plan) pyŏnhwa 변화; (coins) chandon 잔돈; for a ~ kibun chŏnhwanŭro

기분 전환으로 2 v/t
pakkuda 바꾸다; *world*
pyŏnhwashik'ida 변화시키다;
bankbill pakkuŏ chuda 바꾸어
주다; *(replace)* kalda 갈다;
trains karat'ada 갈아타다;
clothes pakkuŏ iptta 바꾸어
입다 3 v/i pakkuŏjida
바뀌어지다; *(put on different
clothes)* pakkuŏ iptta 바꾸어
입다; *(in travel)* karat'ada 갈
아타다

channel TV, RADIO ch'aenŏl
채널; *(waterway)* suro 수로

chant n norae 노래

chaos taehollan 대혼란

chaotic hollansŭrŏun
혼란스러운

chapter chang 장

character *(nature)* sŏngkkyŏk
성격; *(person)* inmul 인물;
(in book, play) tŭngjang inmul
등장 인물; *(letter)* muntcha
문자

characteristic n t'ŭkssŏng
특성

charbroiled sutppure kuwŏjin
숯불에 구워진

charge 1 n *(fee)* yogŭm
요금; JUR hyŏmŭi 혐의; *be
in* ~ tamdang-ida 담당이다;
take ~ matt'a 맡다 2 v/t *sum* ch'ŏngguhada
청구하다; *(to account)* ap'uro
tarŏnot'a 앞으로 달아놓다;
JUR kobarhada 고발하다;

battery ch'ungjŏnshik'ida
충전시키다

charge account oesang kŏrae
외상 거래

charge card shinyong k'adŭ
신용 카드

charitable *institution* chasŏnŭi
자선의

charity *(organization)* chasŏn
tanch'e 자선 단체

charm 1 n *(quality)* maeryŏk
매력 2 v/t *(delight)*
maehok'ada 매혹하다

charming maehoktchŏgin
매혹적인

chart *(diagram)* top'yo
도표; NAUT haedo 해도; *(for
airplane)* ch'yat'ŭ 챠트

charter v/t chŏnse naeda 전세
내다

chase 1 n ch'ugyŏk 추격 2 v/t
twitchot-tta 뒤쫓다

chat 1 n chapttam 잡담 2 v/i
chapttamhada 잡담하다

chatter v/i *(talk)* suda ttŏlda
수다 떨다; *(of teeth)* tŏldŏl
ttŏllida 덜덜 떨리다

chatterbox sudajaeng-i
수다쟁이

chauffeur n chagayong unjŏnsa
자가용 운전사

chauvinist *(male ~)*
namsŏng uwŏltchuйija 남성
우월주의자

cheap adj ssan 싼; *(mean)*
insaek'an 인색한

cheat 1 *n* sogimsu 속임수
2 *v/t* sogida 속이다 **3** *v/i* (in
exam etc) sogimsurŭl ssŭda
속임수를 쓰다

check¹ 1 *adj* shirt ch'ek'ŭ
munŭiŭi 체크 무늬의 **2** *n*
ch'ek'ŭ munŭi 체크 무늬

check² FIN sup'yo 수표; (in
restaurant) kyesansŏ 계산서

check³ 1 *n* (to verify sth)
hwagin 확인 **2** *v/t* (verify)
hwaginhada 확인하다; (with
~mark) ch'ek'ŭ p'yoshirŭl
hada 체크 표시를 하다;
coat, package pogwanso
matkkida 보관소에 맡기다
3 *v/i* hwaginhae chuda 확인해
주다

◆ **check in** (airport) t'apsŭng
susogŭl hada 탑승 수속을
하다; (hotel) ch'ek'ŭinhada
체크인하다

◆ **check out 1** *v/i* (of hotel)
ch'ek'ŭaut'ada 체크아웃하다
2 *v/t* (look into) chosahada
조사하다

checkbook sup'yoch'aek
수표책

check-in (counter) t'apsŭng
susok k'aunt'ŏ 탑승 수속
카운터

checking account tangjwa
yegŭm kujwa 당좌 예금
구좌

check-in time (hotel) t'usuk
shigan 투숙 시간; (airport)

t'apssŭng susok shigan 탑승
수속 시간

checklist taejop'yo 대조표

checkmark ch'ek'ŭ p'yoshi
체크 표시

checkout kyesandae 계산대

checkpoint MIL kŏmmunso
검문소; (in race)
ch'ek'ŭp'oint'ŭ 체크포인트

checkroom (for coats)
hyudaep'um pogwanso
휴대품 보관소; (for
baggage) suhamul pogwanso
수하물 보관소

checkup MED kŏn-gang
chindan 건강 진단

cheek (of face) ppyam 뺨

cheer 1 *n* hwanho 환호; ~s!
(toast) kŏnbae! 건배! **2** *v/t &*
v/i hwanohada 환호하다

◆ **cheer up 1** *v/i* kiuni nada
기운이 나다; ~! kiun nae!
기운 내! **2** *v/t* kiunŭl naege
hada 기운을 내게 하다

cheerful myŏngnanghan
명랑한

cheerleader ch'iŏridŏ
치어리더

cheese ch'iju 치즈

chef chubangjang 주방장

chemical 1 *adj* hwagŭŭi
화학의 **2** *n* hwahak chep'um
화학 제품

chemist hwahaktcha 화학자

chemistry hwahak 화학

chemotherapy hwahak

yoppŏp 화학 요법

cherry p'otchi 버찌; *(tree)* pŏnnamu 벚나무

cherry blossom pŏtkkot 벚꽃

chess ch'esŭ 체스

chessboard ch'esŭp'an 체스판

chest *(of person)* kasŭm 가슴; *(box)* changnong 장롱

chestnut pam 밤; *(tree)* pamnamu 밤나무

chew *v/t* sshipta 씹다

chewing gum kkŏm 껌

chicken tak 닭; *(food)* takkkogi 닭고기

chicken pox sudu 수두

chief *adj* chuyohan 주요한

chiefly churo 주로

child ai 아이

childhood ŏrinshijŏl 어린시절

childish *pej* ch'ŏihan 유치한

chill *(in air)* han-gi 한기; *(illness)* kamgi 감기

chilly *weather* ssalssarhan 쌀쌀한

chimney kulttuk 굴뚝

chin t'ŏk 턱

China Chungguk 중국

china chagi 자기

Chinese 1 *adj* Chunggugŭi 중국의 **2** *n (language)* Chunggugŏ 중국어; *(person)* Chungguk saram 중국 사람

chip *(fragment)* t'omak 토막; *(damage)* i ppajin chaguk 이 빠진 자국; *(in gambling),*

COMPUT ch'ip 칩; ~s p'ot'eit'o ch'ipssŭ 포테이토 칩스

chiropractor ch'ŏkch'u chiapssa 척추 지압사

chlorine yŏmso 염소

chocolate ch'ok'ollit 초콜릿

choice *n* sŏnt'aek 선택; *(selection)* sŏnt'aegŭi pŏmwi 선택의 범위

choir hapch'angdan 합창단

choke 1 *n* AUTO ch'ok'ŭ 초크 **2** *v/i* mogi maeida 목이 메이다

cholesterol k'ollesŭt'erol 콜레스테롤

choose *v/t & v/i* sŏnt'aek'ada 선택하다

chop 1 *n (meat)* tukkŏpkke charun kogitchŏm 두껍게 자른 고깃점 **2** *v/t wood* p'aeda 패다; *food* ssŏlda 썰다

chopsticks chŏtkkarak 젓가락

chore chiban il 집안 일

choreography anmu 안무

chorus hapch'angdan 합창 *(singers)* hapch'angdan 합창단

christen seryehada 세례하다

Christian 1 *n* Kidok-kyo shinja 기독교 신자 **2** *adj* Kidok-kyoŭi 기독교의

Christmas Sŏngt'anjŏl 성탄절; *at ~* Sŏngt'anjŏre 성탄절에; *Merry ~!* meri K'ŭrisŭmasŭ! 메리 크리스마스!

Christmas card K'ŭrisŭmasŭ k'adŭ 크리스마스 카드
Christmas Day Sŏngt'anjŏl 성탄절
Christmas Eve K'ŭrisŭmasŭ ibŭ 크리스마스 이브
Christmas present K'ŭrisŭmasŭ sŏnmul 크리스마스 선물
Christmas tree K'ŭrisŭmasŭ t'ŭri 크리스마스 트리
chrome k'ŭrom 크롬
chronic mansŏng-ŭi 만성의
chronological yŏndaesunŭi 연대순의
church kyohoe 교회
CIA Miguk chung-ang chŏngbobu 미국 중앙 정보부
cigar yŏsong-yŏn 여송연
cigarette tambae 담배
cinema *(industry)* yŏnghwa sanŏp 영화 산업; *Br (building)* yŏnghwagwan 영화관
cinnamon kyep'i 계피
circle **1** *n* wŏn 원; *(group)* chipttan 집단 **2** *v/i (of plane)* pingbing tolda 빙빙 돌다
circular *adj* tunggŭn 둥근
circulate *v/i memo etc* p'ŏttŭrida 퍼뜨리다
circulation BIOL sunhwan 순환; *(of newspaper)* parhaeng pusu 발행 부수

circumstances sanghwang 상황
circus sŏk'ŏsŭ 서커스
citizen shimin 시민
citizenship shiminkkwŏn 시민권
city toshi 도시
civil yeŭi parŭn 예의 바른; *(not military)* min-ganŭi 민간의
civil engineer t'omok kisa 토목 기사
civilian *n* min-ganin 민간인
civilization munmyŏng 문명
civil servant kongmuwŏn 공무원
civil war naejŏn 내전
claim 1 *n (for damages)* ch'ŏnggu 청구; *(right)* kwŏlli 권리; *(assertion)* chujang 주장 **2** *v/t (ask for as a right)* ch'ŏngguhada 청구하다; *(assert), property* chujanghada 주장하다
clamp *n (fastener)* choemsoe 죔쇠
clandestine pimirŭi 비밀의
clap *v/i (applaud)* pakssurŭl ch'ida 박수를 치다
clarify myŏnghwak'age hada 명확하게 하다
clarity myŏnghwak'am 명확함
clash 1 *n* ch'ungdol 충돌; *(of personalities)* purilch'i 불일치 **2** *v/i* ch'ungdorhada 충돌하다
clasp 1 *n* kŏlsoe 걸쇠 **2** *v/t (in*

hand) kkwak chwida 꽉 쥐다

class n *(lesson)* suŏp 수업;
(students) hak-kkŭp 학급;
(social) kyegŭp 계급;
(category) puryu 부류

classic 1 *adj (typical)*
chŏnhyŏngjŏgin 전형적인;
(definitive) kwŏnwi innŭn 권위
있는 **2** n kojŏn 고전

classical k'ŭllaeshik 클래식

classified *information* kimirŭl
기밀의

classified ad hangmokppyŏl
kwanggo 항목별 광고

classify *(categorize)* pullyuhada
분류하다

classroom kyoshil 교실

clause *(in agreement)* chohang
조항

claustrophobia milsshil
kongp'otchŭng 밀실 공포증

claw n palt'op 발톱

clean 1 *adj* kkaekkŭt'an
깨끗한 **2** *vt* kkaekkŭt'age
hada 깨끗하게 하다; *teeth,*
shoes taktta 닦다; *house, room*
ch'ŏngsohada 청소하다; *car,*
face shitch'ida 씻긴다; *clothes*
ppalda 빨다

cleaning woman
ch'ŏngsohanŭn ajumma
청소하는 아줌마

cleanser k'ŭllenjŏ 클렌저

clear 1 *adj voice, weather,*
water, skin malgŭn 맑은;
(bright) palgŭn 밝은; *vision*

tturyŏt'an 뚜렷한; *(easy to*
understand) punmyŏnghan
분명한; *(obvious)*
myŏngbaek'an 명백한
2 *vt roads* ch'iuda 치우다;
(acquit) mujoero hada 무죄로
하다; *(authorize)* hŏgahada
허가하다 **3** *vi (of mist)* kaeda
개다

♦ **clear up** *vi* chŏngdonhada
정돈하다; *(of weather)* kaeda
개다; *(of illness)* nat-tta 낫다
2 *vt (tidy)* chŏngdonhada
정돈하다

clearance *(authorization)*
hŏga 허가

clearly *(with clarity)* tturyŏt'age
뚜렷하게; *(evidently)*
punmyŏnghi 분명히

clench *teeth* angmulda 악물다;
fist kkwak chwida 꽉 쥐다

clerk *(administrative)*
samugwan 사무관; *(in store)*
chŏmwŏn 점원

clever ttokttok'an 똑똑한;
gadget tokch'angjŏgin
독창적인

client *(of lawyer etc)* ŭiroein
의뢰인; *(customer)* kogaek
고객

climate kihu 기후

climax n chŏltchŏng 절정

climb 1 *(up hill)* tŭngban
등반 **2** *vt oruda* 오르다 **3** *vi*
oruda 오르다; *(in mountains)*
tŭngbanhada 등반하다

climber

climber tŭngsan-ga 등산가

clingfilm p'ojangnyong laep 포장용 랩

clinic chillyoso 진료소

clip¹ 1 *n (fastener)* k'ŭllip 클립 2 *v/t* k'ŭlliburo kojŏngshik'ida 클립으로 고정시키다

clip² 1 *n (extract)* palch'we 발췌 2 *v/t with hair, hedge* kawiro charŭda 가위로 자르다

clipping *(from newspaper etc)* oryŏnaen kŏt 오려낸 것

clock shigye 시계

clockwise shigye panghyang-ŭro tora 시계 방향으로 돌아

close¹ 1 *adj family* kakkaun 가까운; *friend* ch'inhan 친한; *resemblance* yusahan 유사한 2 *adv* kakkapkke 가깝게

close² 1 *v/t* tat-tta 닫다; *eyes* kamtta 감다 2 *v/i* tach'ida 닫히다; *(of eyes)* kamgida 감기다

closed *store* tach'in 닫힌; *eyes* kamgin 감긴

closely *listen* yŏlsshimhi 열심히; *cooperate* ŏmmirhi 엄밀히

closet ot-chang 옷장

closing time *(of store)* p'yejŏm shigan 폐점 시간

clot *(of blood)* p'it-ttŏng-ŏri 핏덩어리

cloth *(fabric)* ch'ŏn 천; *(for kitchen)* haengju 행주; *(for cleaning)* kŏlle 걸레

clothes ot 옷

cloud *n* kurŭm 구름

cloudy hŭrin 흐린

club *n (golf, organization)* k'ŭllŏp 클럽

clue shilmari 실마리

clumsy *person* haengdong-i ŏsusŏnhan 행동이 어수선한

clutch 1 *n* AUTO k'ŭllŏch'i 클러치 2 *v/t* kkwak chaptta 꽉 잡다

coach 1 *n (trainer)* k'och'i 코치 2 *v/t* karŭch'ida 가르치다

coal sŏkt'an 석탄

coalition yŏnhap 연합

coarse kŏch'in 거친

coast *n (golf, organization); at the ~* yŏnane(sŏ) 연안에 (서)

coastal yŏnan 연안의

coastguard yŏnan kyŏngbidae 연안 경비대

coastline haeansŏn 해안선

coat 1 *n* sang-ŭi 상의; *(over-)* oet'u 외투; *(of paint)* tŏtch'il 덧칠 2 *v/t (cover)* ssŭiuda 씌우다

coathanger otkkŏri 옷걸이

coating ssŭium 씌움

coax kusŏllida 구슬리다

cocaine k'ok'ain 코카인

cock *n (chicken)* sut'ak 수탉

cockpit *(of plane)* chojongshil 조종실

cockroach pak'wi pŏlle 바퀴 벌레

coconut k'ok'oyaja yŏlmae 코코야자 열매

code *n* k'odŭ 코드

coeducational namnyŏ konghagŭi 남녀 공학의

coexistence kongjon 공존

coffee k'ŏp'i 커피

coffee break kabyŏun hyushik shigan 가벼운 휴식 시간

coffee maker k'ŏp'i kkurinŭn kigu 커피 끓이는 기구

coffee shop k'ŏp'i shyop 커피 숍

coffin kwan 관

cog t'omnibak'wi 톱니바퀴

coherent chŏnghaptchŏgin 정합적인

coin *n* tongjŏn 동전

coincide tongshie irŏnada 동시에 일어나다

coincidence uyŏnŭi ilch'i 우연의 일치

Coke® k'ok'a k'olla 코카 콜라

cold 1 *adj weather* ch'uun 추운; *water* ch'agaun 차가운; *it's* ~ ch'uptta 춥다 2 *n* ch'uwi 추위; *I have a* ~ kamgi kŏllyŏt-tta 감기 걸렸다

collaborate kongdong-ŭro irhada 공동으로 일하다; *(with enemy)* hyŏmnyŏk'ada 협력하다

collaboration hyŏpttong 협동; *(on book etc)* kongjŏ 공저

collapse munŏjida 무너지다;

(of person) chwajŏrhada 좌절하다

collar kit 깃; *(for dog)* kae mok-kkŏri 개 목걸이

colleague tongnyo 동료

collect 1 *v/t person* terirŏ kada 데리러 가다; *tickets, cleaning etc* kajirŏ kada 가지러 가다; *(as hobby)* sujip'ada 수집하다 2 *adv: call* ~ sushinin pudamŭro chŏnhwahada 수신인 부담으로 전화하다

collection sujip 수집; *(in art)* sojangp'um 소장품; *(in fashion)* shinjakp'um 신작품

collector sujipkka 수집가

college tankkwa taehak 단과 대학

collision ch'ungdol 충돌

colonial *adj* shingminjiŭi 식민지의

colony shingminji 식민지

color *n* saek-kkal 색깔

color-blind saengmaeng-ŭi 색맹의

colorful saekch'aega p'ungbuhan 색채가 풍부한; *fig* tach'aeroun 다채로운

color photograph k'alla sajin 칼라 사진

column *(architectural)* kidung 기둥; *(of text)* tan 단; *(in newspaper)* nan 난

columnist kigoga 기고가

coma honsu sangt'ae 혼수 상태

comb

comb 1 n pit 빗 **2** v/t pit-tta
빗다

combat 1 n chŏnt'u 전투 **2** v/t
ssauda 싸우다

combination kyŏrhap 결합;
(of safe) chamulssoeŭi pŏnho
자물쇠의 번호

combine v/t kyŏrhap'ada
결합하다

come (toward speaker) oda
오다; (toward listener) kada
가다

♦ **come back** toraoda
돌아오다

♦ **come down** v/i naeryŏoda
내려오다; (in price) ttŏrŏjida
떨어지다

♦ **come in** tŭrŏoda 들어오다;
~! tŭrŏoseyo! 들어오세요!

♦ **come off** (of handle etc)
ttŏrŏjida 떨어지다

♦ **come on** (progress)
chinhaengdoeda 진행되다;
~! sŏdullŏ! 서둘러!; (in
disbelief) sŏlma! 설마!

♦ **come out** (of person, sun,
product) naoda 나오다; (of
stain) ppajida 빠지다

comedian k'omidiŏn
코미디언

comedy hŭigŭk 희극

comfort 1 n allak 안락;
(consolation) wian 위안 **2** v/t
wianhada 위안하다

comfortable chair p'yŏnanhan
편안한; house, room allak'an

안락한

comic 1 n (magazine) manhwa
chaptchi 만화 잡지 **2** adj
hŭigŭgŭi 희극의

comma shwimp'yo 쉼표

command 1 n myŏngnyŏng
명령 **2** v/t myŏngnyŏnghada
명령하다

commander saryŏnggwan
사령관

commemorate kinyŏmhada
기념하다

comment 1 n ŏn-gŭp 언급
2 v/i ŏn-gŭp'ada 언급하다

commentary haesŏl 해설

commentator haesŏltcha
해설가

commercial 1 adj sang-ŏbŭi
상업의 **2** n (ad) kwanggo
광고

commission 1 n (payment)
susuryo 수수료; (job) ŭiroe
의뢰; (committee) wiwŏnhoe
위원회 **2** v/t (for a job)
ŭiroehada 의뢰하다

commit crime pŏmhada
범하다; ~ oneself ŏnjirŭl
chuda 언질을 주다

commitment (in professional
relationship) chŏllyŏm 전념;
(in personal relationship)
hŏnshin 헌신; (responsibility)
ch'aegim 책임

committee wiwŏnhoe 위원회

commodity iryongp'um
일용품

common *(not rare)* pot'ong-ŭi
보통의; *(shared)* kongt'ong-ŭi
공통의

common sense sangshik
상식

communicate 1 *v/i* ŭisarŭl
sot'onghada 의사를
소통하다 2 *v/t* chŏndarhada
전달하다

communications t'ongshin
통신

communicative marhagi
choahanŭn 말하기
좋아하는

communism kongsanjuŭi
공산주의

communist 1 *adj*
kongsanjuŭiŭi 공산주의의;
2 *n* Kongsanjuŭija
공산주의자

Communist Party
Kongsandang 공산당

community kongdongch'e
공동체; *(social group)* sahoe
사회

commute *v/i (to work)*
t'onggŭnhada 통근하다

compact disc k'omp'aekt'ŭ
tisŭk'ŭ 콤팩트 디스크

companion tongnyo 동료

company COMM hoesa 회사;
(companionship) tongmuro
sagwigi 동무로 사귀기;
(guests) sonnim 손님

comparatively pigyojŏgŭro
비교적으로

compare *v/t* pigyohada
비교하다

comparison pigyo 비교

compassion tongjŏngshim
동정심

compatible *people* sŏro
mannŭn 서로 맞는; *blood
types* ilch'ihanŭn 일치하는

compel ŏktchiro ...shik'ida
억지로 ...시키다

compensate 1 *v/t (with
money)* paesanghada
배상하다 2 *v/i:* ~ *for* ...
ŭl / rŭl posanghada ...을 / 를
보상하다

compensation *(money)*
paesang 배상; *(reward)*
poch'ung 보충

compete kyŏngjaenghada
경쟁하다; *(take part)*
ch'ultchŏnhada 출전하다

competent *person* nŭngnyŏk
innŭn 능력 있는; *work*
chungbunhan 충분한

competition kyŏngjaeng 경쟁;
(competitors) kyŏngjaengja
경쟁자

competitive kyŏngjaengjŏgin
경쟁적인; *price*
kyŏngjaengnyŏk innŭn 경쟁력
있는

competitor kyŏngjaengja
경쟁자; kyŏngjaeng
sangdae 경쟁 상대

complain *v/i* pulp'yŏnghada
불평하다

complaint

complaint pulp'yŏng 불평;
MED pyŏng 병
complete 1 adj (total)
wanjŏnhan 완전한; (whole)
chŏnbuŭi 전부의; (finished)
wansŏngdoen 완성된 **2** v/t
task wansŏnghada 완성하다
completely wanjŏnhi 완전히
completion wansŏng 완성
complicated poktchap'an
복잡한
compliment n ch'ansa 찬사
complimentary ch'ansahanŭn
찬사하는; (free) muryoŭi
무료의
comply: ~ **with** …e ŭnghada
…에 응하다
component (part) kusŏng yoso
구성 요소; (of machine etc)
pup'um 부품
compose v/t kusŏnghada
구성하다; MUS chak-kkok'ada
작곡하다
composer MUS chak-kkok-kka
작곡가
composure ch'imch'ak 침착
comprise: be ~d of …(ŭ)ro
kusŏngdoeŏ it-tta … (으) 로
구성되어 있다
compromise n t'ahyŏp 타협
compulsory ŭimujŏgin
의무적인
computer k'ŏmp'yut'ŏ
컴퓨터
computer game k'ŏmp'yut'ŏ
keim 컴퓨터 게임

conceal kamch'uda 감추다
conceited chamanhanŭn
자만하는
concentrate v/i
chiptchunghada 집중하다
concentration chiptchung
집중
concept kaenyŏm 개념
concern 1 n (anxiety)
kŏktchŏng 걱정; (care)
yŏmnyŏ 염려; (company)
hoesa 회사 **2** v/t (involve)
…e kwan-gyehada …에
관계하다
concerned (anxious)
kŏktchŏnghanŭn 걱정하는
concert yŏnjuhoe 연주회
concise kan-gyŏrhan 간결한
conclude v/t (deduce)
kyŏllonŭl naerida 결론을
내리다; (end) kkŭnnaeda
끝내다
conclusion (deduction) kyŏllon
결론; (end) kyŏlmal 결말
concrete n k'onk'ŭrit'ŭ
콘크리트
concussion noejint'ang
뇌진탕
condensation ŭngch'uk 응축
condescending kyŏmsonhan
ch'ŏk'anŭn 겸손한 척하는
condition (state) sangt'ae
상태; (of health) kŏn-gang
sangt'ae 건강 상태;
(requirement) chokkŏn 조건;
~s (circumstances) hwan-

gyŏng 환경

conditioner *(for hair)*
k'ondishyŏnŏ 콘디셔너

condolences aedo 애도

condom k'ondom 콘돔

conduct 1 *n (behavior)* haeng-wi 행위 2 *v/t (carry out)*
suhaenghada 수행하다; ELEC
chŏndohada 전도하다; MUS
chihwihada 지휘하다

conductor MUS chihwija
지휘자; *(on train)* ch'ajang
차장

conference hoeŭi 회의

confess *v/t & v/i* kobaek'ada
고백하다; *(to police)*
chabaek'ada 자백하다

confession kobaek 고백; *(to
police)* chabaek 자백; REL
kohae 고해

confidence *(assurance)*
hwaksshin 확신; *(trust)* shilloe
신뢰

confident *(self-assured)*
chashinhanŭn 자신하는;
(convinced) hwaksshinhanŭn
확신하는

confidential kŭkppiŭi 극비의

confirm hwaginhada 확인하다

confirmation hwagin 확인

confiscate apssuhada
압수하다

conflict 1 *n (disagreement)*
taerip 대립; *(clash)*
ch'ungdol 충돌 2 *v/i (clash)*
ch'ungdorhada 충돌하다

conform sunŭnghada
순응하다; *(of product)* ttarŭda
따르다

confront *(face)* majuhada
마주하다; *(tackle)* matssŏda
맞서다

confrontation taegyŏl 대결

confuse *(muddle)*
hollanshik'ida 혼란시키다 ~
... with ... hondonghada
… 혼동하다

confusing hollanshik'inŭn
혼란시키는

confusion hollan 혼란

congestion *(on roads)* honjap
혼잡; MED mak'im 막힘

congratulate ch'uk'ahada
축하하다

congratulations ch'uk'a 축하

congregation REL chip'oe
집회

congress hoeŭi 회의;
Congress (in US) Kuk'oe
국회

congressional kuk'oeŭi
국회의

congressman kuk'oe ŭiwŏn
국회 위원

conjunctivitis kyŏlmangnyŏm
결막염

con man sagikkun 사기꾼

connect yŏn-gyŏrhada
연결하다; *(link)*
kwallyŏnshik'ida
관련시키다; *(to power
supply)* chŏpssoksshik'ida

접속시키다
connecting flight yŏn-gyŏlp'yŏn 연결편
connection (in wiring) chŏpsok 접속; (link) kwallyŏn 관련; (in travel) yŏn-gyŏlp'yŏn 연결편
conquer chŏngbok'ada 정복하다; fear etc kŭkpok'ada 극복하다
conscience yangshim 양심
conscious adj (aware) chigaki innŭn 지각이 있는; MED ŭishigi innŭn 의식이 있는
consciousness chigak 지각; MED ŭishik 의식
consecutive yŏnsoktchŏgin 연속적인
consent 1 n tong-ŭi 동의 2 v/i tong-ŭihada 동의하다
consequence kyŏlkwa 결과
consequently ttarasŏ 따라서
conservative adj posujŏgin 보수적인; clothes susuhan 수수한
consider (regard) yŏgida 여기다; (show regard for) koryŏhada 고려하다
considerable sangdanghan 상당한
considerate tongjŏngshimi manŭn 동정심이 많은
consideration (thought) suk-kko 숙고; (thoughtfulness, concern) koryŏ 고려; take into ~ koryŏhada 고려하다

consignment COMM wit'ak 위탁
♦ **consist of** ...(ŭ)ro irujŏ it-tta ··· (으) 로 이루어져 있다
consistent ilgwansŏng innŭn 일관성 있는
consolation wiro 위로
console v/t wirohada 위로하다
conspicuous tudŭrŏjin 두드러진
conspiracy ŭmmo 음모
constant kyesokttoenŭn 계속되는
constipation pyŏnbi 변비
constitution POL hŏnppŏp 헌법
construction (of building etc) kŏnsŏl 건설; (building etc) kŏnch'ungmul 건축물
construction industry kŏnsŏrŏp 건설업
construction worker kongsajang inbu 공사장 인부
constructive kŏnsŏltchŏgin 건설적인
consul yŏngsa 영사
consulate yŏngsagwan 영사관
consult (seek advice of) ...ŭi ŭigyŏnŭl mut-tta ···의 의견을 묻다
consultancy (company) k'ŏnssŏlt'ŏnt'ŏp 컨설턴트업; (advice) sangdam 상담
consultant k'ŏnssŏlt'ŏnt'ŭ

컨설턴트
consumer sobija 소비자
consumption sobi 소비
contact 1 n (person)
chunggyein 중개인;
(communication) yŏllak 연락;
(physical) chŏpch'ok 접촉
2 v/t yŏllak'ada 연락하다
contact lens k'ont'aekt'ŭrenjŭ
콘택트렌즈
contagious chŏnyŏmdoenŭn
전염되는
contain tamkko it-tta 담고
있다; flood maktta 막다
container yonggi 용기; comm
k'ŏnt'einŏ 컨테이너
contamination oyŏm 오염
contemporary 1 adj
hyŏndaeŭi 현대의 **2** n
tongnyŏnbaeŭi saram
동년배의 사람; (at school)
tonggisaeng 동기생
contempt kyŏngmyŏl 경멸
contender kyŏngjaengja
경쟁자; (against champion)
tojŏnja 도전자
content¹ n naeyong 내용
content² adj manjok'anŭn
만족하는
contentment manjok 만족
contents naeyong 내용
contest¹ n (competition) taehoe
대회; (for power) kyŏngjaeng
경쟁
contest² v/t leadership etc
kyŏruda 겨루다

contestant kyŏngjaengja
경쟁자
context munmaek 문맥; look
at in ~ munmaege match'wŏ
문맥에 맞춰
continent n taeryuk 대륙
continual kyesoktchŏgin
계속적인
continue 1 v/t kyesok'ada
계속하다 **2** v/i kyesokttoeda
계속되다
continuous kkŭnimŏmnŭn
끊임없는
contraception p'iim 피임
contraceptive n p'iim kigu
피임 기구; (pill) p'iimyak
피임약
contract n kyeyak 계약
contractor kyeyaktcha 계약자
contradict statement puinhada
부인하다; person panbak'ada
반박하다
contrary 1 adj pandaeŭi
반대의; ~ to …e panhayŏ
…에 반하여 **2** n: on the ~
pandaero 반대로
contrast 1 n taejo 대조 **2** v/t
taejohada 대조하다
contribute v/t money kibuhada
기부하다
control 1 n (of organization
etc) chibae 지배 **2** v/t (govern)
chibaehada 지배하다;
(restrict) chehanhada
제한하다; (regulate)
t'ongjehada 통제하다

control panel cheŏban 제어반

control tower kwanjet'ap 관제탑

controversial nonjaeng-ŭl irŭk'inŭn 논쟁을 일으키는

convalescence hoebok-kki 회복기

convenience p'yŏlli 편리

convenience store p'yŏnŭijŏm 편의점

convenient p'yŏllihan 편리한

convention (tradition) kwansŭp 관습; (conference) taehoe 대회

conventional chŏnt'ongjŏgin 전통적인

convention center k'ŏnbenshyŏn sent'ŏ 컨벤션 센터

conversation taehwa 대화

conversion chŏnhwan 전환; (of measurement) hwansan 환산

convert 1 n chŏnhyang 전향 2 v/t pyŏnhage hada 변하게 하다; unit of measurement hwansanhada 환산하다; building kaejohada 개조하다; person chŏnhyangshik'ida 전향시키다

convertible n (car) kŏnbŏt'ŏbŭl 컨버터블

convict 1 n kigyŏlssu 기결수 2 v/t LAW yujoerŭl sŏn-gohada 유죄를 선고하다

conviction JUR yujoeŭi p'an-gyŏl 유죄의 판결; (belief) shinnyŏm 신념

convince hwaksshinshik'ida 확신시키다

convincing sŏlttŭngnyŏk innŭn 설득력 있는

cook 1 n yorisa 요리사 2 v/t & v/i yorihada 요리하다

cookbook yorich'aek 요리책

cookie k'uk'i 쿠키

cooking (food) yori 요리

cool 1 adj weather shiwŏnhan 시원한; drink ch'agaun 차가운; (calm) naengjŏnghan 냉정한; (unfriendly) naengdamhan 냉담한; infml (great) kimak'ige kŭnsahan 기막히게 근사한 2 v/i (of food) shiktta 식다; (of tempers) karaantta 가라앉다

cooperate hyŏmnyŏk'ada 협력하다

cooperative n COMM hyŏpttong chohap 협동 조합 2 adj (helpful) hyŏmnyŏktchŏgin 협력적인

coordinate chojŏng chohwashik'ida 조정 조화시키다

coordination (of activities) chojŏng chohwa 조정 조화; (of body) undong shingyŏng 운동 신경

cop infml kyŏngch'al 경찰

cope: ~ with ...ŭl / rŭl ch'ŏrihada …을 / 를

처리하다
copier *(machine)* pokssagi
복사기
copilot pujojongsa 부조종사
copper *n (metal)* kuri 구리
copy 1 *n* mobang 모방;
(photocopy) pokssa 복사;
(of book) pu 부; *(of CD)*
chang 장 2 *v/t* mobanghada
모방하다; *(photocopy)*,
COMPUT pokssahada 복사하다;
(cheating) mollae pekkida
몰래 베끼다
copyright *n* chŏjak-kkwŏn
저작권
cord *(string)* nokkŭn 노끈;
(cable) chŏnsŏn 전선
core 1 *n (of fruit)* sok 속
2 *adj issue* haekssimjŏgin
핵심적인
cork k'orŭk'ŭ magae 코르크
마개; *(material)* k'orŭk'ŭ
코르크
corkscrew p'odoju pyŏng
ttagae 포도주 병 따개
corn oksssusu 옥수수
corner *n* kusŏk 구석; *(of table)*
mot'ung-i 모퉁이; *(of road)*
kilmot'ung-i 길모퉁이; *(in
soccer)* k'onŏk'ik 코너킥; **on
the ~** *(of street)* mot'ung-ie(sŏ)
모퉁이에 (서)
corporal punishment
ch'ehyŏng 체형
corporate COMM pŏbinŭi
법인의

corpse shich'e 시체
corral *n* kach'uk uri 가축 우리
correct 1 *adj* orŭn 옳은 2 *v/t*
koch'ida 고치다
correspondence *(letters)*
p'yŏnji 편지; *(exchange)*
sŏhwan wangnae 서신 왕래
correspondent *(reporter)*
t'ŭkp'awŏn 특파원
corridor pokto 복도
corroborate hwakssshirhage
hada 확실하게 하다
corrosion pushik 부식
corrupt *adj* t'arak'an 타락한;
COMPUT t'ŭllin koshi manŭn
틀린 곳이 많은
corruption t'arak 타락
cosmetics hwajangp'um
화장품
cosmetic surgery sŏnghyŏng-
oekkwa 성형외과
cost 1 *n* kagyŏk 가격; *(price)*
wŏnkka 원가; *fig* hŭisaeng
희생; **~s** piyong 비용 2 *v/t*
money, time tŭlda 들다
cost of living saenghwalbi
생활비
cot *(camp-bed)* kani ch'imdae
간이 침대
cotton 1 *n* myŏn 면 2 *adj*
myŏnŭro mandŭn 면으로
만든
couch *n* sop'a 소파
cough 1 *n* kich'im 기침 2 *v/i*
kich'imhada 기침하다
could: ~ *I have my key?*

yŏlsoerŭl chushigessŏyo? 제 열쇠를 주시겠어요?; ~ *you help me?* chŏl towajushil su issŏyo? 절 도와주실 수 있어요 ?; *you ~ be right* nega majŭl sudo issŏ 네가 맞을 수도 있어

council (*assembly*) hoeŭi 회의; POL ŭihoe 의회

councilor ŭiwŏn 의원

counselor (*adviser*) sangdamnyŏk 상담역; JUR pyŏnhosa 변호사

count 1 *v/i* (*to ten etc*) surŭl seda su를 세다; (*calculate*) kyesanhada 계산하다; (*be important*) kach'iga it-tta 가치가 있다 2 *v/t* (*~ up*) seda 세다; (*include*) ch'ida 치다

♦ **count on** ...ege kidaeda ...에게 기대다

countdown ch'o ilkki 초 읽기

counter (*in café*) k'aunt'ŏ 카운터; (*in game*) san-gaji 산가지

counteract chunghwahada 중화하다

counterfeit *adj* wijohi 위조의

counterpart (*person*) kat'ŭn chiwiŭi saram 같은 지위의 사람

counterproductive yŏk'yokkwaŭi 역효과의

countless sel su ŏmnŭn 셀 수 없는

country nara 나라; (*not town*) shigol 시골

countryside shigol 시골

coup POL k'udet'a 쿠데타

couple (*married*) pubu 부부; (*man & woman*) namnyŏ han ssang 남녀 한 쌍; *just a ~* chogŭm 조금; *a ~ of* (*people*) tusŏnŏsŭi 두서넛의

courage yonggi 용기

courier paedal 배달; (*with tourists*) annaewŏn 안내원

course *n* (*lessons*) kyokkwa kwajŏng 교과 과정; (*of meal, for race*) k'osŭ 코스; (*of ship, plane*) haengno 행로; *of ~* (*certainly*) mullon 물론, (*naturally*) tang-yŏnhi 당연히

court *n* JUR pŏptchŏng 법정; SPORTS k'ot'ŭ 코트

courthouse pŏbwŏn 법원

courtroom pŏptchŏng 법정

cousin sach'on 사촌

cover 1 *n* (*protective*) tŏpkkae 덮개; (*of book, magazine*) p'yoji 표지; (*for bed*) ch'imdaeppo 침대보; (*shelter*) p'inanch'ŏ 피난처 2 *v/t* tŏpta 덮다; (*hide*) sumgida 숨기다; *distance* tapp'ahada 답파하다

♦ **cover up** *v/t* tŏpta 덮다; *fig* kamch'uda 감추다

coverage (*media*) podo 보도

covert pimiriŭi 비밀의

coverup ŭnp'ye 은폐

cow *n* amso 암소

coward kŏptchaeng-i 겁쟁이

cowboy k'auboi 카우보이

cozy anŭk'an 아늑한

crab n ke 게

crack 1 n kallajin kŭm 갈라진 금 2 v/t kŭmgage hada 금가게 하다; nut kkaeda 깨다; code p'ulda 풀다

♦ crack down on …ŭl / rŭl ŏmhage tasŭrida …을 / 를 엄하게 다스리다

cracker (to eat) k'ŭraek'ŏ 크래커

craft (art) kong-ye 공예; (skill) kinŭng 기능

craftsman chang-in 장인

cramped room pijobŭn 비좁은

cramps kŭpkkyŏk'an pokt'ong 급격한 복통

crane (machine) kijunggi 기중기; (bird) hak 학

crash 1 n (noise) k'wang hanŭn sori 쾅 하는 소리; (accident) ch'ungdol 충돌; (plane ~) ch'urak 추락; COMM munŏjim 무너짐; COMPUT kojang 고장 2 v/i (make noise) k'wang hanŭn sorirŭl naeda 쾅 하는 소리를 내다; (of car) ch'ungdorhada 충돌하다; (of plane) ch'urak'ada 추락하다; (of market) punggoehada 붕괴하다; COMPUT kojangnada 고장나다 3 v/t car ch'ungdolshik'ida 충돌시키다

crash helmet anjŏn hwelmet 안전 헬멧

crater (of volcano) punhwagu 분화구

craving kalmang 갈망

crawl v/i (on floor) kida 기다; (move slowly) nŭrinnŭrit kada 느릿느릿 가다

crayon k'ŭreyong 크레용

crazy adj mich'in 미친; be ~ about …e yŏlgwanghada …에 열광하다

cream n (for skin, coffee) k'ŭrim 크림

crease n kugimsal 구김살; (deliberate) churŭm 주름

create v/t ch'angjohada 창조하다

creative ch'angjojŏgin 창조적인

creature tongmul 동물

credible midŭl manhan 믿을 만한; candidate shilloegam kanŭn 신뢰감 가는

credit n FIN oesang oesang 외상; (honor) kongno 공로; (payment) yegŭmaek 예금액

credit card shinyong k'adŭ 신용 카드

creditor ch'aegwŏnja 채권자

creek chagŭn nae 작은 내

creep 1 n pej anikkoun saram 아니꼬운 사람 2 v/i salgŭmsalgŭm kŏt-tta 살금살금 걷다

cremation hwajang 화장

crew n (of ship, plane) sŭngmuwŏn chŏnwŏn 승무원 전원

crime pŏmjoe 범죄

criminal 1 n pŏmjoeja 범죄자 **2** adj pŏmjoeŭi 범죄의; (shameful) yugamsŭrŏn 유감스런

crisis wigi 위기

crisp adj day sangk'waehan 상쾌한; apple p'asapk'asak'an 파삭파사삭한; shirt, bill ppatppat'an 빳빳한

criterion kijun 기준

critic pip'yŏngga 비평가

critical (criticizing) pip'anjŏgin 비판적인; (serious) wigijŏgin 위기적인; moment kyŏltchŏngjŏgin 결정적인; MED widŏk'an 위독한

criticism pip'yŏng 비평

criticize v/t pip'yŏnghada 비평하다

crook n (dishonest) sagikkun 사기꾼

crooked (twisting) kuburŏjin 구부러진; (dishonest) pujŏnghan 부정한

crop 1 n nongjangmul 농작물 **2** v/t (cut) tchalkke charŭda 짧게 자르다

cross 1 adj (angry) sŏngnan 성난 **2** n (X) shiptchaga 십자가; (Christian) shiptchaga 십자가 **3** v/t (go across) kŏnnŏgada 건너가다 **4** v/i (go across)

kŏnnŏgada 건너가다; (of lines) kyoch'ahada 교차하다

♦ **cross out** chiuda 지우다

cross-examine pandae shimmunhada 반대 심문하다

crosswalk hoengdan podo 횡단 보도

crossword kŭltcha match'ugi nori 글자 맞추기 놀이

crouch v/i momŭl kuburida 몸을 구부리다

crowd n kunjung 군중; (at sports event) kwanjung 관중

crowded pumbinŭn 붐비는

crucial kyŏltchŏngjŏgin 결정적인

crude adj (vulgar) sangsŭrŏun 상스러운; (simple) chojap'an 조잡한

cruel chaninhan 잔인한

cruelty chaninham 잔인함

cruise liner sunhangsŏn 순항선

crumb pusŭrŏgi 부스러기

crumble v/i pusŏjida 부서지다; fig munŏjida 무너지다

crusade n fig kaehyŏk undong 개혁 운동

crush v/t pakssarŭl naeda 박살을 내다; (crease) kugida 구기다

crust (on bread) ttakttak'an kkŏptchil 딱딱한 껍질

crutch (for walking) mokttari 목다리

cry *v/i (weep)* ulda 울다

cub saekki 새끼

cube *(shape)* ip-ppangch'e 입방체

cucumber oi 오이

cuddle 1 *n* p'oong 포옹 2 *v/t* kkok kkyŏantta 꼭 껴안다

cue *n (actor, pool)* k'yu 큐

cuff *n (of shirt)* somaetppuri 소맷부리; *(of pants)* pajittan 바지단

culinary yoriŭi 요리의

culmination chŏltchŏng 절정

culprit pŏmin 범인

cult sagyo chipttan 사교 집단

cultivate *land* kyŏngjak'ada 경작하다

cultivated *person* seryŏndoen 세련된

cultural munhwajŏgin 문화적인

culture *n* munhwa 문화

cunning 1 *n* kyohwaham 교활함 2 *adj* kyohwarhan 교활한

cup *n* chan 잔

cupboard ch'antchang 찬장

curator k'yureitŏ 큐레이터

curb 1 *n (of street)* yŏnsŏk 연석 2 *v/t* ŏktchehada 억제하다

cure MED 1 *n* ch'iryo 치료 2 *v/t* ch'iryohada 치료하다

curiosity hogishim 호기심

curious hogishim manŭn 호기심 많은; *(strange)*

isanghan 이상한

currency *(money)* t'onghwa 통화; *foreign ~* oehwa 외화

current 1 *n* hŭrŭm 흐름; *(tidal)* choryu 조류; ELEC chŏllyu 전류 2 *adj (present)* chigŭmŭi 지금의

current affairs shisa 시사

currently chigŭm 지금

curriculum kyokkwa kwajŏng 교과 과정

curse *n (spell)* chŏju 저주

cursor k'ŏsŏ 커서

curtain k'ŏt'ŭn 커튼; THEAT mak 막

curve 1 *n* kokssŏn 곡선 2 *v/i* kuburŏjida 구부러지다

cushion *n* k'ushyŏn 쿠션

custody *(of children)* yangnyuk-kkwŏn 양육권; *in ~* JUR kuryu chung 구류 중

custom *(tradition)* kwansŭp 관습

customer kogaek 고객

customs kwanse 관세

customs officer segwanwŏn 세관원

cut 1 *n (with knife)* pegi 베기; *(injury)* pen sangch'ŏ 상처 2 *v/t (with knife)* peda 베다; *(reduce)* sak-kkamhada 삭감하다; *get one's hair ~* mŏriŭl charŭda 머리를 자르다

♦ **cut back** *(in costs)* ch'ukssohada 축소하다

cut down

◆ **cut down 1** *v/t* peŏ nŏmŏttŭrida 베어 넘어뜨리다 **2** *v/i (in smoking etc)* churida 줄이다
◆ **cut off** *(with knife)* peŏnaeda 베어내다; *(isolate)* koripsshik'ida 고립시키다; TEL kkŭnt'a 끊다
cute *(pretty)* kwiyŏun 귀여운; *(sexually)* maeryŏktchŏgin 매력적인; *(clever)* yŏngnihan 영리한

cutting *adj remark* shillarhan 신랄한
cycle 1 *n (bicycle)* chajŏn-gŏ 자전거 **2** *v/i* chajŏn-gŏro kada 자전거로 가다
cyclist chajŏn-gŏ t'anŭn saram 자전거 타는 사람
cylinder *(in engine)* kit'ong 기통
cynic pikkonŭn saram 비꼬는 사람
cynical naengsojŏgin 냉소적인

D

DA (= district attorney) chibang kŏmsa 지방 검사
dad appa 아빠
daily 1 *n (paper)* shinmun 신문 **2** *adj* maeirŭi 매일의
dairy products yujep'um 유제품
dam *n (for water)* ttaem 댐
damage 1 *n* p'ihae 피해; *(to reputation etc)* sonsang 손상 **2** *v/t* p'ihaerŭl ip'ida 피해를 입히다
damages JUR sonhae paesanggŭm 손해 배상금
damn *infml* **1** *interjection* chegirŏl 제기랄 **2** *adj* pirŏmŭgŭl 빌어먹을
damp *cloth* ch'ukch'uk'an 축축한; *room* sŭpkkich'an 습기찬

dance 1 *n* ch'um 춤; *(event)* taensŭ p'ati 댄스 파티 **2** *v/i* ch'umch'uda 춤추다
dancer ch'umch'unŭn saram 춤추는 사람; *(performer)* muyongga 무용가
dancing muyong 무용
danger wihŏm 위험
dangerous wihŏmhan 위험한
dare *v/i: he didn't ~* kŭnŭn kamhi hal su ŏpssŏssŏyo 그는 감히 할 수 없었어요
daring *adj* taedamhan 대담한
dark 1 *n* ŏdum 어둠 **2** *adj* ŏduun 어두운; *hair, eyes* kŏmusŭrŭmhan 거무스름한; *color* chinhan 진한
darling *~!* chagiya! 자기야!
dash 1 *n (in text)* taeshi 대시 **2** *v/i* tansume tallyŏgada

단숨에 달려가다

data teit'ŏ 데이터

database teit'ŏ peisŭ 데이터 베이스

data protection teit'ŏ poho 데이터 보호

date¹ *(fruit)* taech'u 대추

date² n naltcha 날짜; *(meeting)* teit'ŭ 데이트; *what's the ~ today?* onŭl myoch'irijyo? 오늘 몇일이죠?; *out of ~* naltchaga chinan 날짜가 지난

daughter ttal 딸; *(somebody else's)* ttanim 따님

daughter-in-law myŏnŭri 며느리; *(somebody else's)* myŏnŭrinim 며느님

dawn n saebyŏk 새벽

day nal 날; *by ~* nanari 나날이; *the other ~* iltchŏne 일전에

daylight nat 낮

daytrip tang-ilch'igi yŏhaeng 당일치기 여행

dazed *(by a blow)* chŏngshini mŏnghan 정신이 멍한

dazzle v/t nunbushige hada 눈부시게 하다

dead 1 *adj* chugŭn 죽은; *battery* tarŭn 닳은; *phone* kkŭnŏjin 끊어진; *infml place* hwalgi ŏmnŭn 활기 없는 **2** n: *the ~* koin 고인

dead end *(street)* makttarŭn 막다른

deadline *(day)* magamil 마감일; *(hour)* magamshigan 마감시간

deadlock n kyoch'ak sangt'ae 교착 상태

deaf kwimŏgŭn 귀먹은

deaf-and-dumb nong-aŭi 농아의

deafening kwich'ŏng-i ttŏrŏjil ttŭt'an 귀청이 떨어질 듯한

deal n *(contract)* kyeyak 계약; *(in business)* kŏrae 거래; *a good ~* charhan hŭngjŏng kŏrae 흥정 거래; *a great ~ of* manŭn 많은

dealer COMM sang-in 상인; *(drugs)* mayak tillŏ 마약 딜러

dealings kŏrae 거래

dear *adj* ch'inaehanŭn 친애하는; *Dear Sir* chŏn-gyŏnghanŭn sŏnsaengnimkke 존경하는 선생님께; *Dear Richard* saranghanŭn Rich'adŭ 사랑하는 리차드

death chugŭm 죽음; *~s (fatalities)* samangja 사망자

death penalty sahyŏng 사형

death toll samangjasu 사망자수

debate 1 n nonjaeng 논쟁 **2** v/t nonjaenghada 논쟁하다

debit 1 n chan-goran 잔고란 **2** v/t *account* chan-gorane kiip'ada 잔고란에 기입하다

debris p'ap'yŏn 파편

debt pit 빛

debtor ch'aemuja 채무자

decade ship nyŏn 십 년

decaffeinated k'ap'eini chegŏdoen 카페인이 제거된

decay 1 n pup'ae 부패 **2** v/i pup'aehada 부패하다

deceased: *the ~* chugŭn saram 죽은 사람

deceitful namŭl soginŭn 남을 속이는

deceive sogida 속이다

December shibiwŏl 십이월

decency yeŭi parŭm 예의 바름

decent person nŏgŭrŏun 너그러운; (*reasonable*) sangdanghi choŭn 상당히 좋은

deception sogim 속임

deceptive pogiwanŭn tarŭn 보기와는 다른

decide kyŏltchŏnghada 결정하다; (*settle*) kyŏltchŏng-ŭl naerida 결정을 내리다

decipher p'andok'ada 판독하다

decision kyŏltchŏng 결정

decision-maker ŭisa kyŏltchŏngja 의사 결정자

decisive (*resolute*) tanhohan 단호한; (*crucial*) kyŏltchŏngjŏgin 결정적인

deck (*of ship*) kapp'an 갑판; (*of cards*) han p'ŏl 한 벌

declare kongp'yohada 공표하다; *independence*

sŏnŏnhada 선언하다; (*customs*) shin-gohada 신고하다

decline 1 n kamso 감소 **2** v/t *offer* kŏjŏrhada 거절하다 **3** v/i (*refuse*) kŏjŏrhada 거절하다; (*decrease*) kamsohada 감소하다; (*of health*) ak'wadoeda 악화되다

decode haedok'ada 해독하다

décor changsshik 장식

decorate changsshik'ada 장식하다; *soldier* hunjang-ŭl suyŏhada 훈장을 수여하다

decoy n yuinyŏng 유인용

decrease 1 n kamso 감소 **2** v/t churida 줄이다 **3** v/i chulda 줄다

dedicate *book etc* pach'ida 바치다

dedication (*to cause, work*) chŏnnyŏm 전념

deduce ch'uronhada 추론하다

deduct ppaeda 빼다

deduction (*from salary*) kongje 공제; (*conclusion*) ch'uron 추론

deed n (*act*) haeng-wi 행위; JUR kimyŏng narinhan chŭngsŏ 기명 날인한 증서

deep kip'ŭn 깊은; *voice* chŏŭmŭi 저음의

deep freeze n naengsok naengjanggo 급속 냉동 냉장고

deep-fry tŭmppuk t'wigida
듬뿍 튀기다

deer sasŭm 사슴

deface woegwanŭl
sonsangshik'ida 외관을
손상시키다

defamation pibang 비방

defeat 1 n p'aebae 패배 2 v/t
p'aebaeshik'ida 패배시키다

defect n kyŏlchŏm 결점

defective kyŏltchŏmi innŭn
결점이 있는

defend chik'ida 지키다;
(justify) chŏngdanghwahada
정당화하다; JUR pyŏnhohada
변호하다

defendant p'igoin 피고인

defense n pang-ŏ 방어; MIL,
POL pang-wi 방위; SPORTS subi
수비; JUR p'igoch'ŭk 피고측;
(justification) pyŏllon 변론

defense lawyer p'igoch'ŭk
pyŏnhosa 피고측 변호사

defiance panhang 반항

defiant panhangjŏgin
반항적인

deficit chŏktcha 적자

define chŏng-ŭirŭl naerida
정의를 내리다; objective
ttŭsŭl palk'ida 뜻을 밝히다

definite article chŏnggwansa
정관사

definitely hwaksshirhi 확실히

definition (of word) chŏng-ŭi
정의; (of objective) ttŭsŭl
palk'im 뜻을 밝힘

deformity kihyŏng 기형

defraud sach'wihada
사취하다

defrost v/t food nogida 녹이다;
fridge sŏrirŭl ŏpssaeda 서리를
없애다

defuse bomb shin-gwanŭl
chegŏhada 신관을 제거하다;
situation chinjŏngshik'ida
진정시키다

defy panhanghada 반항하다

degrading ch'emyŏnŭl
sonsangshik'inŭn 체면을
손상시키는

degree (university) hagwi
학위; (of temperature etc)
to 도; (amount) chŏngdo 정도

dehydrated t'alssudoen
탈수된

dejected nakttamhan 낙담한

delay 1 n yŏn-gi 연기 2 v/t
yŏn-gihada 연기하다; (of
plane) yŏnch'ak'ada 연착하다

delegate 1 n taep'yoja 대표자
2 v/t task wiimhada 위임하다

delegation (of task) wiim
위임; (people) taep'yodan
대표단

delete saktchehada 삭제하다

deli shikp'umjŏm 식품점

deliberate 1 adj koŭijŏgin
고의적인 2 v/i suk-kkohada
숙고하다

deliberately ilburŏ 일부러

delicate fabric sŏmsehan
섬세한; problem mimyohan

미묘한; *health* hŏyak'an
허약한
delicious mashinnŭn 맛있는
delight *n* kippŭm 기쁨
delighted kippŏhanŭn
기뻐하는
delightful chŭlgŏun 즐거운;
person yuk'waehan 유쾌한
deliver paedalhada
배달하다; *message*
chŏndarhada 전달하다; *baby*
punmanshik'ida 분만시키다
delivery paedal 배달; *(of baby)*
punman 분만
delusion ch'ak-kkak 착각
de luxe hohwaroun 호화로운
demand 1 *n* yogu 요구; COMM
suyo 수요 **2** *v/t* yoguhada
요구하다
demanding *job* sangdanghan
noryŏgi yogudoenŭn 상당한
노력이 요구되는; *person*
yoguga shimhan 요구가 심한
democracy minjujuŭi
민주주의
democrat minjujuŭija
민주주의자; *Democrat* POL
Minjudang-wŏn 민주당원
democratic minjujuŭiŭi
민주주의의
demolish p'agoehada
파괴하다
demonstrate 1 *v/t*
iptchŭnghada 입증하다;
machine shiryŏnhada
실연하다 **2** *v/i (politically)*

shiwihada 시위하다
demonstration *(display)*
kwashi 과시; *(protest)* shiwi
시위; *(of machine)* shiryŏn
실연
demonstrator *(protester)* shiwi
ch'amgaja 시위 참가자
demoralized kiga kkŏkkin
기가 꺾인
denial *(of accusation)* pujŏng
부정; *(of request)* kŏjŏl 거절
denims ch'ŏngbaji 청바지
denomination FIN aengmyŏn
kŭmaek 액면 금액; REL
chongp'a 종파
dense tchit'ŭn 짙은; *foliage*
ugŏjin 우거진; *crowd*
miltchŭn 밀집한
dent 1 *n* ump'uk p'aein
kot 움푹 패인 곳 **2** *v/t*
ump'uk tŭrŏgage hada 움푹
들어가게 하다
dental ch'iaŭi 치아의; *school*
ch'ikwa 치과
dentist ch'ikkwa ŭisa 치과
의사
dentures ŭich'i 의치
deny *charge, rumor* puinhada
부인하다; *request* kŏjŏrhada
거절하다
deodorant t'alch'wije 탈취제
department *(of company)* pusŏ
부서; *(of university)* hak-kkwa
학과; *(of government)* puch'ŏ
부처; *(of store)* maejang 매장
department store

paek'wajŏm 백화점

departure ch'ulbal 출발

departure lounge taehapsshil 대합실

departure time ch'ulbal shigak 출발 시각

depend ŭijonhada 의존하다; that ~s sanghwang-e ttara tarŭda 상황에 따라 다르다; it ~s on the weather nalsshie tallyŏit-tta 날씨에 달려있다

dependence ŭijon 의존

dependent n puyang kajok 부양 가족

deplorable hant'anhal 한탄할

deport kugoero ch'ubanghada 국외로 추방하다

deposit 1 n (in bank) yegŭm 예금; (on purchase) yeyak-kkŭm 예약금; (for lease of apartment) chŏnsegŭm 전세금 2 v/t money yegŭmhada 예금하다

depressed person uurhan 우울한

depressing uurhagehanŭn 우울하게하는

depression MED ultchŭng 우울증; (economic) pulgyŏnggi 불경기; (weather) chŏgiap 저기압

deprive ppaeat-tta 빼앗다

deprived child puruhan 불우한; area kananhan 가난한

depth kip'i 깊이

deputy taeri 대리

derelict adj pŏryŏjin 버려진

derive v/t ŏt-tta 얻다

derogatory kyŏngmyŏrhanŭn 경멸하는

descend 1 v/t naeryŏgada 내려가다 2 v/i (of plane) haganghada 하강하다; (of road) kyŏngsajida 경사지다

descendant chason 자손

descent (from hill) hasan 하산; (of plane) hagang 하강; (ancestry) kagye 가계

describe myosahada 묘사하다

description myosa 묘사

desert¹ n samak 사막

desert² 1 v/t pŏrida 버리다 2 v/i (of soldier) t'aryŏnghada 탈영하다

deserted injŏgi kkŭn'in 인적이 끊긴

deserter MIL t'aryŏngbyŏng 탈영병

deserve padŭl manhada 받을 만하다

design 1 n tijain 디자인; (for building, car etc) sŏlgyedo 설계도 2 v/t tijainhada 디자인하다; building, car, etc sŏlgyehada 설계하다

designer clothes yumyŏng tijainŏŭi ot 유명 디자이너의 옷

desire n param 바람; (sexual) yongmang 욕망

desk ch'aeksang 책상; *(in hotel)* tesŭk'ŭ 데스크

desktop publishing kŏmp'yut'ŏ ch'ulp'an 컴퓨터 출판

despair n chŏlmang 절망

desperate p'ilssajŏgin 필사적인; *situation* chŏlmangjŏgin 절망적인

despise kyŏngmyŏrhada 경멸하다

despite pulguhago …에도 불구하고

dessert hushik 후식

destination moktchŏktchi 목적지

destiny unmyŏng 운명

destitute pi-gonhan 빈곤한

destroy p'agoehada 파괴하다

destruction p'agoe 파괴

detach tteŏnaeda 떼어내다

detached *(objective)* kongp'yŏnghan 공평한

detail n sebu sahang 세부 사항; *(information)* chasehan naeyong 자세한 내용

detailed sangsehan 상세한

detain chich'eshik'ida 지체시키다; *(as prisoner)* kamgŭmhada 감금하다

detainee ŏngnyuja 억류자

detect arach'aeda 알아채다; *(of device)* t'amjihada 탐지하다

detective hyŏngsa 형사

detention *(prison)* kamgŭm 감금

deter tannyŏmshik'ida 단념시키다

detergent sech'ŏktche 세척제

deteriorate ak'wadoeda 악화되다

determination kyŏlsshim 결심

determined kyŏlsshimhan 결심한; *effort* hwakkohan 확고한

deterrent n panghaemul 방해물

detest hyŏmohada 혐오하다

devaluation FIN p'yŏngkka chŏrha 평가 절하

develop 1 v/t land, *(invent)* kaebarhada 개발하다; *business* paltchŏnshik'ida 발전시키다; *film* hyŏnsanghada 현상하다; *(progress)* palttalshik'ida 발달시키다; *illness* …e kŏllida …에 걸리다 **2** v/i *(grow)* paltchŏnhada 발전하다

developing country kaebaldosangguk 개발도상국

development *(of land)* kaebal 개발; *(of business, country)* sŏngjang 성장; *(event)* nyussŭ 뉴스; *(of film)* hyŏnsang 현상; *(progression)* paltchŏn 발전

device changch'i 장치; *(tool)* togu 도구

devil angma 악마

devise koanhada 고안하다

devote *time, money* pach'ida 바치다; *effort* kiurida 기울이다

devotion *(to person)* hŏnshin 헌신; *(to job)* chŏnnyŏm 전념

devour kegŏlssŭrŏpkke mŏkta 게걸스럽게 먹다

diabetes tangnyoppyŏng 당뇨병

diagonal *adj* taegakssŏnŭi 대각선의

diagram top'yo 도표

dial 1 *n (of clock)* chap'an 자판; *(of meter)* nun-gŭmp'an 눈금판 **2** *v/t number* taiŏrŭl tollida 다이얼을 돌리다

dialect sat'uri 사투리

dialog taehwa 대화

diameter chik-kkyŏng 직경

diamond taiamondŭ 다이아몬드

diaper kijŏgwi 기저귀

diarrhea sŏlssa 설사

diary ilgi 일기

dictator toktchaeja 독재자

dictionary sajŏn 사전

die chuktta 죽다

diet 1 *n* shikttan 식단; *(for weight)* taiŏt'ŭ 다이어트; *(for health)* shigi yoppŏp 식이요법 **2** *v/i (to lose weight)* taiŏt'ŭhada 다이어트하다

differ *(be different)* tarŭda 다르다

difference ch'ai 차이

different tarŭn 다른

difficult himdŭn 힘든

difficulty ŏryŏum 어려움

dig *v/t* p'ada 파다

digest *v/t* sohwahada 소화하다

digestion sohwa 소화

digital tijit'ŏl 디지털

dignified wiŏm innŭn 위엄 있는

dignity chonŏm 존엄

dilapidated hŏmurŏjin 허물어진

dilemma chint'oeyangnan 진퇴양난

dilute *v/t* muk-kke hada 묽게 하다

dim *adj light* ŏdumch'imch'imhan 어둠침침한; *outline* hŭrit'an 흐릿한

dimension ch'isu 치수

diminish *v/i* chulda 줄다

dim sum tchin kogi mandu 찐 고기 만두

dine shikssahada 식사하다

diner *(person)* shikssahanŭn saram 식사하는 사람

dining room shikttang 식당

dinner *(evening)* manch'an 만찬; *(midday)* och'an 오찬

dinner jacket yakssik yahoebok 약식 야회복

dinner party tinŏ p'at'i 디너 파티

dinosaur kongnyong 공룡

dip *n (food)* yangnyŏmtchang

diploma (in road) kyŏngsajin kot 경사진 곳
diploma chŭngsŏ 증서
diplomat oegyogwan 외교관
diplomatic oegyoŭi 외교의; (tactful) suwani choŭn 수완이 좋은
direct 1 adj chiktchŏptchŏgin 직접적인; flight, train chik'aeng-ŭi 직행의; person nogoltchŏgin 노골적인
2 v/t (to place) annaehada 안내하다; movie kamdok'ada 감독하다
direction panghyang 방향; ~s (instructions) annae 안내; (to place) panghyang 방향; (for use) sayonggppŏp 사용법; (for medicine) pogyongppŏp 복용법
director (of company) isa 이사; (of movie) kamdok 감독
directory chuso sŏngmyŏngnok 주소 성명록; TEL chŏnhwa pŏnhobu 전화 번호부
dirt mŏnji 먼지
dirty tŏrŏun 더러운
disabled n: the ~ shinch'e chang-aeja 신체 장애자
disadvantage n tantchŏm 단점
disagree ŭigyŏni tarŭda 의견이 다르다
disagreement ŭigyŏn ch'ai 의견 차이; (argument) maldat'um 말다툼

disappear sarajida 사라지다
disappearance (of thing) somyŏl 소멸; (of person) shiltchong 실종
disappoint shilmangshik'ida 실망시키다
disappointed shilmanghan 실망한
disappointment shilmang 실망
disapproval pulch'ansŏng 불찬성
disapprove pulch'ansŏnghada 불찬성하다
disaster ch'ŏnjaejibyŏn 천재지변
disastrous p'ihaega makssshimhan 피해가 막심한
discharge v/t (from hospital) t'oewŏnshik'ida 퇴원시키다; (from army) chedaeshik'ida 제대시키다
disciple REL cheja 제자
discipline n kyuyul 규율
disc jockey tisŭk'u chak'i 디스크 자키
disclosure (of information) nusŏl 누설
disco tisŭk'o 디스코
disconnect pullishik'ida 분리시키다; supply chungdanshik'ida 중단시키다; phone kkŭnt'a 끊다
discotheque tisŭk'o t'ek 디스코 텍

dismay

discount *n* harin 할인

discourage *(dissuade)*
mot'age hada 못하게 하다;
(dishearten) nakttamshik'ida
낙담시키다

discover palgyŏnhada
발견하다

discovery palgyŏn 발견

discreet shinjunghan 신중한

discrepancy *(in story)* mosun
모순; *(in accounts)* purilch'i
불일치

discretion shinjungham
신중함

discrimination ch'abyŏl 차별

discuss t'oronhada 토론하다

discussion t'oron 토론

disease chilbyŏng 질병

disembark *v/i* naerida 내리다

disgrace *n* pulmyŏng-ye
불명예

disgraceful such'isŭrŏun
수치스러운

disguise *n* wijang 위장;
(costume, make-up) pyŏn-jang
변장

disgust 1 *n* hyŏmo 혐오
2 *v/t* hyŏmogamŭl irŭk'ida
혐오감을 일으키다

disgusting hyŏmosŭrŏun
혐오스러운; *smell* kuyŏktchil
nanŭn 구역질 나는

dish *(part of meal)* yori 요리;
(container) kŭrŭt 그릇; *(for
rice)* konggi 공기; *(for soup)*
taejŏp 대접

dishcloth haengju 행주

disheartened nakttamhan
낙담한

dishonest pujŏngjik'an
부정직한

dishonesty pujŏngjik 부정직

dishonor *n* pulmyŏng-ye
불명예

dishwasher sŏlgŏjihanŭn
saram 설거지하는 사람;
(machine) sŏlgŏji kigye
설거지 기계

dishwashing liquid
chubangyong seje 주방용
세제

disinfectant sodongnyak
소독약

disintegrate hŏmurŏjida
허물어지다; *(of building)*
punggoedoeda 붕괴되다

disk *(shape)* wŏnbanhyŏng
원반형; COMPUT tisŭk'et
디스크

diskette tisŭk'et 디스켓

dislike *v/t* shirŏhada 싫어하다

dislocate t'algushik'ida
탈구시키다

disloyal pulch'ungsshirhan
불충실한

dismal *weather* ŭmsanhan
음산한; *news* ch'imurhan
침울한; *(depressed)* uurhan
우울한

dismantle haech'ehada
해체하다

dismay *n* *(alarm)* tanghwang

dismiss

당황; *(disappointment)*
nakttam 낙담

dismiss *employee*
haegoshik'ida 해고시키다

disobedience pulboktchong
불복종

disobedient marŭl tŭt-tchi
annŭn 말을 듣지 않는

disobey kŏyŏk'ada 거역하다

disorder *(unrest)* hollan 혼란;
MED chang-ae 장애

disorganized mujilssŏhan
무질서한

disoriented panghyang
kamgagŭl irŏbŏrin 방향
감각을 잃어버린

disown ŭijŏrhada 의절하다

dispatch *v/t (send)*
palssonghada 발송하다

dispensary *(in pharmacy)*
chojeshil 조제실

display 1 *n* chŏnshi
전시; *(in store)* chinyŏl
진열; COMPUT tisŭp'ŭllei
디스플레이 **2** *v/t emotion*
p'yoshihada 표시하다; *exhibit*
chŏnshihada 전시하다;
(in store) chinyŏrhada
진열하다; COMPUT hwamyŏne
p'yoshihada 화면에
표시하다

displeasure pulk'wae 불쾌

disposable ssŭgo pŏril su
innŭn 쓰고 버릴 수 있는

disposal ch'ŏbun 처분; *(of
waste)* p'yegi 폐기

dispose: ~ *of* …ŭl / rŭl
ch'ŏbunhada …을 / 를
처분하다

disposition *(nature)* kijil 기질

disproportionate
pulgyunhyŏnghan 불균형한

disprove panjŭnghada
반증하다

dispute 1 *n* nonjaeng 논쟁;
(between states) punjaeng
분쟁; *(industrial)* chaeng-ŭi
쟁의 **2** *v/t (disagree with)*
pallonhada 반론하다

disqualify chagyŏgŭl
pakt'arhada 자격을
박탈하다

disrespectful muryehan
무례한

disrupt *trains* tujŏlshik'ida
두절시키다; *meeting*
chungdanshik'ida 중단시키다

disruptive punyŏlshik'inŭn
분열시키는

dissatisfaction pulman 불만

dissatisfied pulmansŭrŏun
불만스러운

dissent *n* pandae ŭigyŏn 반대
의견

dissident *n* pandaeja 반대자

dissolve 1 *v/t substance* nogida
녹이다 **2** *v/i (of substance)*
nokta 녹다

dissuade mallida 말리다

distance *n* kŏri 거리

distant mŏn 먼; *fig (aloof)*
sowŏnhan 소원한

distasteful shirŭn 싫은

distinct *(clear)* tturyŏt'an 뚜렷한; *(different)* tarŭn 다른

distinctive t'ŭgyuŭi 특유의

distinctly tturyŏt'age 뚜렷하게; *(decidedly)* hwaksshirhi 확실히

distinguish: ~ *between* shikppyŏrhada 식별하다

distinguished *(famous)* chŏmyŏnghan 저명한; *(dignified)* kip'um innŭn 기품 있는

distort waegok'ada 왜곡하다

distract *person* shimnanhage hada 심란하게 하다; *attention* ttan tero tollige hada 딴 데로 돌리게 하다

distraught mich'il tŭt'an 미칠 듯한

distress *n* komin 고민; *(physical)* kot'ong 고통

distribute nanuda 나누다

distribution nanuŏ chum 나누어 줌; COMM yut'ong 유통

distributor COMM paegŭbŏptcha 배급업자

district chiyŏk 지역; *(of city)* ku 구

district attorney chibang kŏmsa 지방 검사

distrust 1 *n* pulsshin 불신 2 *v/t* pulsshinhada 불신하다

disturb *(interrupt)* panghaehada 방해하다; *(upset)*

…ŭi maŭmŭl ŏjirŏp'ida …의 마음을 어지럽히다

disturbance *(interruption)* panghae 방해; ~s soyo 소요

disturbed *(worried)* maŭmi ŏjirŏun 마음이 어지러운

disturbing maŭmŭl ŏjirŏp'inŭn 마음을 어지럽히는

ditch *n* torang 도랑

dive 1 *n* ttwiŏdŭlgi 뛰어들기; *(underwater)* chamsu 잠수 2 *v/i* ttwiŏdŭlda 뛰어들다; *(underwater)* chamsuhada 잠수하다; *(of plane)* kŭpkkanghahada 급강하하다

diver *(off board)* taibŏ 다이버; *(underwater)* chamsubu 잠수부

diverge kallajida 갈라지다

diversify *v/i* comm saŏbŭl tagak'washik'ida 사업을 다각화시키다

diversion AUTO uhoe 우회; *(to distract)* chuŭirŭl ttan tero tollim 주의를 딴 데로 돌림

divert *traffic* uhoeshik'ida 우회시키다; *attention* ttan tero tollida 딴 데로 돌리다

divide nanuda 나누다

dividend FIN paedanggŭm 배당금

divine REL shinsŏnghan 신성한

diving taibing 다이빙

division MATH nanutssem 나눗셈; *(splitting into parts)* pulli 분리; *(of company)*

divorce

pusŏ 부서

divorce 1 *n* ihon 이혼 **2** *v/i* ihonhada 이혼하다

divorced ihonhan 이혼한

dizzy: *feel ~* hyŏn-gitchŭng-i nada 현기증이 나다

do 1 *v/t* hada 하다; *what are you ~ing tonight?* onŭl chŏnyŏk mwŏ halkkŏyeyo? 오늘 저녁에 뭐 할꺼에요?; *I don't know what to ~* ŏttŏk-kke haeya haltchi morŭgessŏyo 어떻게 해야 할지 모르겠어요 **2** *v/i well done!* chal haessŏyo! 잘 했어요!; *how ~ you ~?* chŏŭm poepkkessŭmnida? 처음 뵙겠습니다?

dock¹ 1 *n* NAUT pudu 부두 **2** *v/i (of ship)* pudue taeda 부두에 대다

dock² JUR p'igosŏk 피고석

doctor *n* MED ŭisa 의사

document *n* sŏryu 서류

documentary *(program)* tak'yument'ŏri 다큐멘터리

documentation sŏryu 서류

dodge *v/t blow* p'ihada 피하다; *question* tullŏdaeda 둘러대다

dog *n* kae 개

dogma kyori 교리

do-it-yourself sonsu mandŭlgi 손수 만들기

doll *(toy)* inhyŏng 인형

dollar tallŏ 달러

dolphin tolkkorae 돌고래

domestic *adj chore* kasaŭi 가사의; *news, policy* kungnaeŭi 국내의

domestic flight kungnaesŏn pihaenggi 국내선 비행기

dominant chuyohan 주요한; *(influential)* yuryŏk'an 유력한

dominate chibaehada 지배하다; *landscape* apttohada 압도하다

donate *money* kibuhada 기부하다

donkey tangnagwi 당나귀

donor *(of money)* kibuja 기부자

donut tonŏt 도넛

door mun 문

doorbell ch'oinjong 초인종

doorman toŏ maen 도어 맨

dormitory kisuksa 기숙사

dose *n* irhoe pogyongnyang 일회 복용량

dot *n* chŏm 점

dotted line chŏmsŏn 점선

double 1 *n* tu pae 두 배; *(person)* kkok talmŭn saram 꼭 닮은 사람 **2** *adj (twice as much)* tu paeŭi 두 배의; *whiskey* tŏbŭl 더블 **3** *adv* tu paero tu paero 두 배로 **4** *v/t* tu paero hada 두 배로 하다 **5** *v/i* tu paega toeda 두 배가 되다

double bed tŏbŭlbedŭ 더블베드

doublecheck tashi

hwaginhada 다시 확인하다

double click *n* tŏbŭl k'ŭllik
더블클릭

doublecross paebanhada
배반하다

double room iinyong pang
이인용 방

doubles (*tennis*) poksshik 복식

doubt 1 *n* ŭishim 의심;
(*uncertainty*) ŭigushim 의구심
2 *v/t* ŭishimhada 의심하다

doubtful *look* ŭishimtchŏgŭm
의심쩍은; *be* ~ (*of person*)
ŭishimsŭrŏpta 의심스럽다

doubtless hwaksshirhi 확실히

dough milkkaru panjuk
밀가루 반죽

dove pidulgi 비둘기

down 1 *adv* najŭn tchogŭro
낮은 쪽으로; ~ *there* chŏgi
araetchoge 저기 아래쪽에;
$200 ~ (*as deposit*) kyeyak-
kkŭm 200tallŏ 계약금
200달러; *be* ~ (*of price*)
naerida 내리다; (*not working*)
kojangna it-tta 고장나 있다
2 *prep* …ŭi araetchŏgŭro …의
아래쪽으로; (*along*) …ŭl / rŭl
ttara …을 / 를 따라

downfall *n* mollak 몰락;
(*cause of ruin*) shilp'aeŭi wŏnin
실패의 원인

download *v/t* taunrodinghada
다운로딩하다

down payment kyeyak-kkŭm
계약금

downpour p'ogu 폭우

downscale *adj* taejungtchŏgin
대중적인

downstairs 1 *adj*
araech'ŭng-ŭi 아래층의
2 *adv* araech'ung-e(sŏ)
아래층에 (서)

down-town 1 *adj* toshim-
ŭi 도심의 **2** *adv* toshimŭi
chungshimbue(sŏ) 도시의
중심부에 (서)

downturn (*economic*) kyŏnggi
ch'imch'e 경기 침체

doze 1 *n* sŏnjam 선잠 **2** *v/i*
cholda 졸다

dozen yŏldu kae 열두 개

draft 1 (*of air*) t'ongp'ung
통풍; (*of document*) ch'ogo
초고; MIL chingbyŏng 징병; ~
(*beer*) saengmaekstchu 생맥주

drafty t'ongp'ung-i chal toenŭn
통풍이 잘 되는

drag 1 *v/t* (*pull*) kkŭro tanggida
끌어 당기다 **2** *v/i* (*of show,
movie*) chiruhada 지루하다

dragon yong 용

drain 1 *n* (*pipe*) paesuro
배수로; (*under street*) hasugu
하수구 **2** *v/t water* ppaenaeda
빼내다; *glass, tank* piuda
비우다

drama (*art form*) hŭigok
희곡; (*excitement*) kŭktchŏgin
sanghwang 극적인 상황;
(*play: on TV*) tŭrama 드라마

dramatic yŏn-gŭgŭi 연극의;

(exciting) kŭkchŏgin 극적인

drapes k'ŏt'ŭn 커튼

drastic chinach'in 지나친; *measure* kwaganhan 과감한; *change* kyŏngnyŏrhan 격렬한

draw 1 *n (in lottery)* chebi ppopkki 제비 뽑기; *(attraction)* inkkiinnŭn kŏt 인기있는 것 2 *v/t picture* kŭrida 그리다; *cart* kkŭro tanggida 끌어 당기다; *curtain* ch'ida 치다; *knife* ppaeda 빼다; *(attract)* ...ŭi chuŭirŭl kkŭlda …의 주의를 끌다

drawback kyŏltchŏm 결점

drawer *(of desk)* sŏrap 서랍

drawing kŭrim 그림

dread 1 *n* turyŏwŏhada 두려워하다

dreadful mushimushihan 무시무시한; *weather* chidok'an 지독한

dream 1 *n* kkum 꿈 2 *v/t & v/i* kkumŭl kkuda 꿈을 꾸다; *(day~)* mongsanghada 몽상하다

dreary chiruhan 지루한

dress 1 *n (for woman)* tŭresŭ 드레스; *(clothing)* ot 옷 2 *v/t person* osŭl ip'ida 옷을 입히다 (*put ~ed)* ot ipta 옷 입다; *~ well* osŭl chal ipta 옷을 잘 입다

dresser *(dressing table)* hwajangdae 화장대; *(in kitchen)* ch'antchang 찬장

dressing *(for salad)* sosŭ 소스; MED pungdae 붕대

dress rehearsal ŭisang lihŏsŏl 의상 리허설

dried *fruit etc* mallin 말린

drier kŏnjogi 건조기

drift *v/i (of ship)* p'yoryuhada 표류하다; *(go off course)* hangnoesŏ pŏsŏnada 항로에서 벗어나다; *(of person)* chŏngch'ŏŏpsshi pangnanghada 정처없이 방랑하다

drill 1 *n (tool)* ch'ŏn-gonggi 천공기 2 *v/t hole* ttult'a 뚫다 3 *v/i (for oil)* kumŏng naeda 구멍 내다

drink 1 *n* mashil kŏt 마실 것 2 *v/t & v/i* mashida 마시다; *(consume alcohol)* surŭl mashida 술을 마시다

drinkable mashil su innŭn 마실 수 있는

drinking water mashinŭn mul 마시는 물

drip *v/i* ttokttok ttŏrŏjida 똑똑 떨어지다

drive 1 *n* unjŏn 운전; *(outing)* tŭraibŭ 드라이브; *(energy)* hwallyŏk 활력; COMPUT tŭraibŭ 드라이브 2 *v/t vehicle* molda 몰다; *(take in car)* ch'aro teryŏda chuda 차로 데려다 주다; *(power)* chakttongshik'ida 작동시키다 3 *v/i* unjŏnhada 운전하다

driver unjŏnja 운전자

driver's license unjŏn myŏnhŏtchŭng 운전 면허증

driveway ch'ado 차도

driving n unjŏn 운전

driving lesson unjŏn kyoyuk 운전 교육

driving test unjŏn myŏnhŏ shihŏm 운전 면허 시험

drizzle n isŭlbi 이슬비

droop v/i ch'uk nŭrŏjida 축 늘어지다; (of plant) shidŭlda 시들다

drop 1 n (of rain) pang-ul 방울; (small amount) yakkan 약간; (in price, temperature) harak 하락; (in number) kamso 감소 **2** v/t object ttŏrŏttŭrida 떨어뜨리다; from car naeryŏjuda 내려주다; from team chemyŏngshik'ida 제명시키다; charges, demand ch'wisohada 취소하다 **3** v/i ttŏrŏjida 떨어지다; (decline) harak'ada 하락하다; (of wind) chada 자다

dropout (school) chungt'oeja 중퇴자; (society) nagoja 낙오자

drought kamum 가뭄

drown v/i ikssahada 익사하다

drowsy narŭnhan 나른한

drug n MED yak 약; (illegal) mayak 마약

drug addict mayak sang-yongja 마약 상용자

drug dealer mayak p'anmaeja 마약 판매자

druggist yakssa 약사

drugstore yak-kkugi ttallin chap'wajŏm 약국이 딸린 잡화점

drug trafficking mayak kŏrae 마약 거래

drum n MUS puk 북; (in western music) tŭrŏm 드럼; (container) tŭrŏmt'ong 드럼통

drunk 1 n sulkkun 술꾼 **2** adj sul ch'wihan 술 취한

drunk driving ŭmju unjŏn 음주 운전

dry 1 adj clothes marŭn 마른; mouth, ground kŏnjohan 건조한 **2** v/t mallida 말리다 **3** v/i marŭda 마르다

dry-cleaner set'akso 세탁소

dry-cleaning (clothes) tŭraik'ŭllining 드라이클리닝

dryer (machine) kŏnjogi 건조기

due (owed) chiburhagiro toen innŭn 지불하기로 되어 있는; (proper) mattanghan 마땅한; be ~ (of train, baby etc) ... hal yejŏng-ida ··· 할 예정이다; ~ to (because of) ... ttaemune ··· 때문에

dull weather hŭrin 흐린; pain tunhan 둔한; (boring) chiruhan 지루한

duly (as expected) yejŏngdaero 예정대로; (properly) ch'ungbunhi 충분히

dump 1 *n (for garbage)* ssŭregi p'ŏrinŭn kot 쓰레기 버리는 곳; *(unpleasant place)* chijŏbunhan changso 지저분한 장소 **2** *v/t (throw away)* naebŏrida 내버리다; *(dispose of)* p'ŏrida 버리다; *waste* p'yegihada 폐기하다

dumpling tŏmp'ŭlling 덤플링

dune ondŏk 모래 언덕

dung ttong 똥

duplex (apartment) chungch'ŭnghyŏng-ŭi ap'at'ŭ 중층형의 아파트

duration chisok kigan 지속 기간

during ... tong-an ··· 동안

dusk haejil muryŏp 해질 무렵

dust *n* mŏnji 먼지

duty ŭimu 의무; *(task)* immu 임무; *(on goods)* kwanse 관세; *be on* ~ tangjigida 당직이다; *be off* ~ pibŏnida 비번이다

duty-free *adj* myŏnseŭi 면세의

DVD tibŭidi 디브이디

dye *v/t* yŏmsaek'ada 염색하다

dying chugŏganŭn 죽어가는; *tradition* soet'oehanŭn 쇠퇴하는

dynamic *person* hwalttongjŏgin 활동적인

dynamite *n* tainŏmait'ŭ 다이너마이트

dynasty wangjo 왕조

dyslexia toksŏ chang-ae 독서 장애

E

each 1 *adj* kak-kkagŭi 각각의 **2** *adv & pron* kak-kkak 각각; ~ *other* sŏro 서로

eager kanjŏrhan 간절한

eagle toksuri 독수리

ear kwi 귀

earache kwiari 귀앓이

early 1 *adj (not late)* iltchigin 일찍인; *(ahead of time)* irŭn 이른; *(farther back in time)* ch'ogŭin 초기의; *(in the near future)* pparŭn 빠른 **2** *adv (not late)* iltchik 일찍; *(ahead of time)* irŭge 이르게

earn pŏlda 벌다; *respect* pat-tta 받다

earnings sodŭk 소득

earphones iŏp'on 이어폰

earring kwigori 귀고리

earth *(soil)* hŭk 흙; *(world, planet)* chigu 지구

earthquake chijin 지진

east 1 *n* tongtchok 동쪽 **2** *adj* tongtchogŭi 동쪽의 **3** *adv travel* tongtchogŭro 동쪽으로

Easter Puhwaltchŏl 부활절

eastern tongbuŭi 동부의;
(East Asian) tongnyang-ŭi
동양의

East Sea Tonghae 동해

eastward tongtchoguro
동쪽으로

easy shwiun 쉬운; *(relaxed)*
p'yŏnanhan 편안한

eat *v/t & v/i* mŏktta 먹다

eccentric *adj* pyŏllan 별난

echo 1 *n* meari 메아리 **2** *v/i*
ullyŏ p'ŏjida 울려 퍼지다

eclipse *n (sun)* ilsshik 일식;
(moon) wŏlsshik 월식

ecofriendly ch'inhwan-
gyŏngjŏgin 친환경적인

ecological saengt'aehaktchŏgin
생태학적인

ecology saengt'aehak 생태학

economic kyŏngjeŭi 경제의

economical *(cheap)*
kyŏngjejŏgin 경제적인;
(thrifty) chŏryak'anŭn
절약하는

economics kyŏngjehak
경제학; *(financial aspects)*
kyŏngjejŏk ch'ŭngmyŏn
경제적 측면

economist kyŏngjehaktcha
경제학자

♦ **economize on** …ŭl / rŭl
chŏryak'ada …을 / 를
절약하다

economy kyŏngje 경제;
(saving) chŏryak 절약

economy class pot'ongsŏk
보통석

ecosystem saengt'aegye
생태계

ecstasy hwanghol 황홀

eczema sŭptchin 습진

edge *n (of knife)* nal 날; *(of
table)* mosŏri 모서리; *(of
road)* kajang chari 가장 자리;
(of cliff) kkŭt 끝

edible mŏgŭl su innŭn 먹을
수 있는

edit p'yŏnjip'ada 편집하다

edition p'an 판

editor p'yŏnjiptcha 편집자

educate kyoyuk'ada
교육하다

education kyoyuk 교육

eel chang-ŏ 장어

effect *n* yŏnghyang 영향;
come into ~ *(of law)*
shilsshidoeda 실시되다

effective *(efficient)*
hyokkwajŏgin 효과적인

efficiency nŭngnyul 능률; *(of
tool, method)* hyoyul 효율

efficient nŭngnyultchŏgin
능률적인; *machine, method*
hyoyultchŏgin 효율적인

effort *(struggle)* sugo 수고;
(attempt) noryŏk 노력

egg al 알; *(of chicken)* kyeran
계란

eggcup salmŭn talgyarŭl
nonnŭn k'ŏp 삶은 달걀를
놓는 컵

eggplant kaji 가지

ego

ego PSYCH chaa 자아; *(self-esteem)* chabushim 자부심

egocentric chagi chungshimūi 자기 중심의

eiderdown *(quilt)* orit'ŏl ibul 오리털 이불

either 1 *adj* ŏnū han tchogūi 어느 한 쪽의; *(both)* yangtchogūi 양쪽의 **2** *pron* ŏnū tchogina 어느 쪽이나 **3** *adv*: *I won't go* ~ na ttohan kaji ank'essŏyo 나 또한 가지 않겠어요 **4** *conj*: *~ X or Y* Xna Y xLⴏ Y

eject *v/t* ppaenaeda 빼내다

elaborate *adj* kongdūrin 공들인

elastic *n* komujul 고무줄

elbow *n* p'alkkumch'i 팔꿈치

elder *adj* yŏnsang-ūi 연상의

elderly nai chigūt'an 나이 지긋한

eldest 1 *adj* naiga kajang manūn 나이가 가장 많은 **2** *n*: *the ~* maji malt'i 맏이

elect *v/t* sŏn-gŏhada 선거하다

election sŏn-gŏ 선거

election campaign sŏn-gŏ undong 선거 운동

electric chŏn-giūi 전기의

electric chair chŏn-gi ūija 전기 의자

electrician chŏn-gi kisa 전기 기사

electricity chŏn-gi 전기

electrocute kamjŏnsashik'ida 감전사시키다

electronic chŏnjaūi 전자의

electronics chŏnja konghak 전자 공학

elegant kosanghan 고상한

elementary *(rudimentary)* kibonūi 기본의

elementary school ch'odūnghak-kkyo 초등학교

elephant k'okkiri 코끼리

elevator ellibeit'ŏ 엘리베이터

eligible chagyŏgi innūn 자격이 있는

eliminate *(get rid of)* chegŏhada 제거하다; *(rule out)* cheoehada 제외하다; *be ~d (from competition)* t'allak'ada 탈락하다

elite 1 *n* chŏng-ye 정예 **2** *adj* chŏng-yeūi 정예의

elk elk'ŭ 엘크

elm nūrūmnamu 느릅나무

eloquent ungbyŏnūi 웅변의

else: *anything* ~ kūbakkūi tarūn kŏsun? 그밖의 다른 것은?; *no one* — *came* tarūn nugudo oji anat-tta 다른 누구도 오지 않았다; *something* ~ tarūn ŏttŏn kŏt 다른 어떤 것; *or* ~ kūrŏch'i anūmyŏn 그렇지 않으면

elsewhere *(position)* ŏttŏn tarūn kosesŏ 어떤 다른 곳에서; *(motion toward)* ŏttŏn tarūn kosūro 어떤 다른 곳으로

e-mail n imeil 이메일

e-mail address imeil chuso 이메일 주소

emancipation haebang 해방

embargo n ch'urip'ang kŭmji 출입항 금지

embark v/i (by boat) paerŭl tada 배를 타다; (by plane) pihaenggie t'apsŭnghada 비행에 탑승하다

♦ **embark on** shijak'ada 시작하다

embarrass tanghwanghage hada 당황하게 하다

embarrassed tanghwanghan 당황한

embarrassing tanghwanghage hanŭn 당황하게 하는

embarrassment tanghwangham 당황함

embassy taesagwan 대사관

embezzlement hoengnyŏng 횡령

embodiment hwashin 화신

embrace n 1 po-ong 포옹 2 v/t (hug) p'o-onghada 포옹하다

embryo pae 배; (human) t'aea 태아

emerald emeraldŭ 에메랄드

emerge (appear) nat'anada 나타나다

emergency pisang 비상

emergency exit pisanggu 비상구

emergency landing pisang

ch'angnyuk 비상 착륙

emigrate iminhada 이민하다

eminent chŏmyŏnghan 저명한

emission (of gases) palssan 발산

emotion kamjŏng 감정

emotional kamjŏngjŏgin 감정적인; (full of emotion) kamdongjŏgin 감동적인

emperor hwangje 황제

emphasis kangjo 강조

emphasize kangjohada 강조하다

empire cheguk 제국

employ koyonghada 고용하다; (use) sayonghada 사용하다

employee koyong-in 고용인

employer koyongju 고용주

employment chigŏp 직업

empty 1 adj pin 빈 2 v/t glass piuda 비우다

enable kanŭnghage hada 가능하게 하다

enchanting maehoktchŏgin 매혹적인

enclose (in letter) tongbonghada 동봉하다; area turŭda 두르다

enclosure (with letter) tongbongmul 동봉물

encore n angk'orŭ 앙코르

encounter v/t problem mattakttŭrida 맞닥뜨리다

encourage kyŏngnyŏhada 격려하다

encouragement kyŏngnyŏ
격려

encyclopedia paek-kkwa
sajŏn 백과 사전

end 1 n (extremity) kkŭt 끝;
(of year) mal 말; in the ~
mach'imnae 마침내; at the ~
of July ch'irwŏl mal 칠월 말
2 v/t kkŭnnaeda 끝내다 **3** v/i
kkŭnnada 끝나다

endangered species
myŏltchong wigiŭi p'umjong
멸종 위기의 품종

endearing sarangsŭrŏun
사랑스러운

ending kyŏlmal 결말; GRAM
ŏmi 어미

endless kkŭdŏmnŭn 끝없는

endorse check isŏhada
이서하다; candidacy
chijihada 지지하다; product
ch'uch'ŏnhada 추천하다

end product wanjep'um
완제품

endurance chiguryŏk 지구력

endure 1 v/t kyŏndida
견디다 **2** v/i (last) chisok'ada
지속하다

end-user ch'oejong sayongja
최종 사용자

enemy chŏk 적

energetic hwalttongjŏgin
활동적인

energy (electricity etc) enŏji
에너지; (of person) him 힘

enforce kangnyŏk shilsshihada

강력 실시하다

engaged (to be married)
yak'onhan 약혼한

engagement (appointment)
yakssok 약속; (to be married)
yak'on 약혼

engagement ring yak'on
panji 약혼 반지

engine enjin 엔진

engineer n kisa 기사; NAUT
kigwansa 기관사

engineering konghak 공학

England Yŏngguk 영국

English 1 adj Yŏnggugŭi
영국의 **2** n (language) Yŏng-
ŏ 영어

engrave saegida 새기다

enigma susukkekki 수수께끼

enjoy chŭlgida 즐기다; ~
oneself chŭlgŏpkke chinaeda
즐겁게 지내다; ~! (eating)
mashitkke tŭseyo! 맛있게
드세요!

enjoyable chŭlgŏun 즐거운

enjoyment chŭlgŏum 즐거움

enlarge k'ŭge hada 크게 하다

enlist v/i MIL chawŏn ipttaehada
자원 입대하다

enormous kŏdaehan 거대한;
satisfaction etc taedanhan
대단한

enough 1 adj ch'ungbunhan
충분한 **2** pron ch'ungbunhan
yang 충분한 양; is
$50 ~? 50tallŏmyŏn
ch'ungbunhamnikka?

50달러면 충분합니까?; *I've
had ~!* 이제 kŭmanhae! 이제
그만해!
enroll v/i tŭngnok'ada
등록하다
ensure hwaksshirhage hada
확실하게 하다
enter 1 v/t (go into) …e
tŭrŏgada …에 들어가다;
(come into) …(ŭ)ro tŭrŏoda
…(으)로 들어오다;
competition …e ch'amgahada
…에 참가하다; COMPUT
imnyŏkshik'ida 입력시키다
2 v/i (go in) tŭrŏgada
들어가다; (come in) tŭrŏoda
들어오다 3 n COMPUT imnyŏk
입력
enterprise chinch'wijŏk kisang
진취적 기상; (venture)
saŏp 사업
entertain 1 v/t (amuse)
chŭlgŏpkke hada 즐겁게
하다 2 v/i (have guests)
taejŏp'ada 대접하다
entertainer yŏnyein 연예인
entertaining adj chaemiinnŭn
재미있는
entertainment orak 오락
enthusiasm yŏltchŏng 열정
enthusiast: …kwang …광;
jazz ~ chaejŭgwang 재즈광
enthusiastic yŏllyŏrhan
열렬한
entire chŏnch'eŭi 전체의
entirely wanjŏnhi 완전히

entitle chagyŏgŭl chuda
자격을 주다
entitled …(i)ranŭn chemogŭi
…(이)라는 제목의
entrance n ipkku 입구;
(entering) iptchang 입장
entrance fee iptchangnyo
입장료
entrust: ~ with matkkida
맡기다
entry (way in) ipkku 입구; (act
of entering) iptchang 입장; (to
country) ipkkuk 입국; (for
competition: person) ch'amgaja
참가자; (in diary) tŭngnok
등록
entry form ŭngmo sŏryu
응모 서류
envelope pongt'u 봉투
envious purŏwŏhanŭn
부러워하는; *be ~ of sb*
nugurŭl purŏwŏhada 누구를
부러워하다
environment hwan-gyŏng 환경
environmental hwan-gyŏng-ŭi
환경의
environmentalist
hwan-gyŏngbohoronja
환경보호론자
environmentally friendly
ch'inhwan-gyŏngjŏgin
친환경적인
envision sangsanghada
상상하다
envy 1 n saem 샘 2 v/t
purŏwŏhada 부러워하다

epidemic yuhaengppyŏng 유행병

epilepsy kanjilppyŏng 간질병

episode sap'wa 삽화; *(event)*
ep'isodŭ 에피소드

epoch shidae 시대

equal 1 *adj* kat'ŭn 같은 **2** *n*
tongtŭnghan chonjae 동등한
존재

equality p'yŏngdŭng 평등

equally kyundŭnghage
균등하게

equate: ~ *with* kat-ttago
saenggak'ada 같다고
생각하다

equator chŏkto 적도

equip katch'uŏ chuda 갖추어
주다

equipment changbi 장비

equivalent tongdŭnghan
동등한; *be* ~ *to* ...wa / kwa
tongdŭnghan kach'iga it-tta
…와 / 과 동등한 가치가
있다

era shidae 시대

eradicate pangmyŏrhada
박멸하다

erase chiuda 지우다

eraser chiugae 지우개

erosion ch'imshik 침식; *fig*
chŏmmŏkgŭm 좀먹음

erotic kwannŭngjŏgin
관능적인

errand shimburŭm 심부름

erratic *behavior* iltchŏnghaji
anŭn 일정하지 않은

error chalmot 잘못

erupt *(of volcano)*
punch'urhada 분출하다; *(of
riots)* palbarhada 발발하다

escalate hwaktttaehada
확대하다

escalator esŭk'ŏlleit'ŏ
에스컬레이터

escape 1 *n* tomang 도망;
(of gas) nuch'ul 누출 **2** *v/i*
tomanggada 도망가다; *(of
gas)* nuch'uldoeda 누출된다

escort *n* tongbanja 동반자;
(guard) kyŏnghowŏn 경호원

especially t'ŭkpyŏrhi 특별히

espionage sŭp'ai haeng-wi
스파이 행위

essential *adj* p'ilssujŏgin
필수적인

establish *(create)* mandŭlda
만들다; *(determine)*
iptchŭnghada 입증하다
company sŏllip'ada 설립하다

establishment *(firm, store etc)*
shisŏl 시설

estate ttang 땅; *(of dead
person)* yusan 유산

esthetic shimmijŏgin
심미적인

estimate 1 *n* kyŏnjŏk 견적
2 *v/t* p'yŏngkkahada 평가하다

estuary nŏlbun kang-ŏgwi
넓은 강어귀

eternal yŏngwŏnhan 영원한

ethical yullijŏgin 윤리적인

ethnic minjogŭi 민족의

ethnic group minjokchipttan 민족집단

ethnic minority sosu minjok 소수 민족

European 1 adj Yurŏbŭi 유럽의 **2** n Yurŏbin 유럽인

Europe Yurŏp 유럽

evacuate (clear people from) taep'ishik'ida 대피시키다; (leave) taep'ihada 대피하다

evade kyomyohi hoep'ihada 교묘히 회피하다

evaluate p'yŏngkkahada 평가하다

evangelist pogŭm chŏndosa 복음 전도사

evasive aemaehan 애매한

even 1 adj (regular) korŭn 고른; (level) p'yŏngp'yŏnghan 평평한; number tchakssuŭi 짝수의 **2** adv choch'ado 조차도; ~ my father naŭi abŏji choch'ado 나의 아버지 조차도; ~ better tŏuk tŏ naŭn 더욱 더 나은; not ~ choch'a ant'a 조차 않다; ~ so kŭrŏt'a hadŏrado 그렇다 하더라도; ~ if ... pirok ...1/ŭltchirado 비록 …1/을지라도

evening chŏnyŏk 저녁; this ~ onŭl chŏnyŏk 오늘 저녁; good ~ annyŏnghaseyo 안녕하세요

evening classes yagan suŏp 야간 수업

evening paper sŏk-kkan

shinmun 석간 신문

evenly (regularly) korŭge 고르게

event haengsa 행사; SPORTS shihap 시합

eventually kunggŭktchŏgŭro 궁극적으로

ever adv (with if, in future) ŏnjen-ga 언젠가; (with past tense) chigŭmkkaji 지금까지; for ~ ŏnjena 언제나; ~ since kŭ hu chulgot 그 후 줄곧

every modŭn 모든

everybody nuguna 누구나

everyday ilsangjŏgin 일상적인

everyone nuguna 누구나

everything modŭn kŏt 모든 것

everywhere modŭn kot 모든 곳; (wherever) ŏdidŭnji 어디든지

evict tchoch'anaeda 쫓아내다

evidence chŭnggŏ 증거; JUR chŭng-ŏn 증언

evidently punmyŏnghi 분명히

evil 1 adj ak'an 악한 **2** n ak sŏ 악

evoke image hwan-gishik'ida 환기시키다

evolution chinhwa 진화

evolve v/i (develop) paltchŏnhada 발전하다

ewe amnyang 암양

ex- ijŏnŭi 이전의

exact adj chŏnghwak'an 정확한

exactly chŏnghwak'i 정확히

exaggerate v/t & v/i kwajanghada 과장하다

exam shihŏm 시험

examine chosahada 조사하다;
MED chinch'arhada 진찰하다;
SCHOOL shihŏmhada 시험하다

example ye 예; *for ~* yerŭl tŭrŏsŏ 예를 들어서

exceed (*be more than*)
ch'ogwahada 초과하다; (*go beyond*) nŏmŏsŏda 넘어서다

exceedingly taedanhi 대단히

excellence ttwiŏnam 뛰어남

excellent ttwiŏnan 뛰어난

except ...ŭl / rŭl cheoehago
...을 / 를 제외하고

exception yeoe 예외

exceptional (*very good*)
iryejŏguro ttwiŏnan
이례적으로 뛰어난;
(*special*) t'ŭkppyŏrhan yeoeŭi
특별한 예외의

excerpt palch'we 발췌

excess 1 n kwado 과도 **2** adj
kwadahan 과다한

excess baggage ch'ogwa
suhamul 초과 수하물

exchange 1 n (*of views,
between schools*) kyohwan
교환; *in ~* kyohwanŭro
교환으로; *in ~ for*
...wa / kwa kyohwanŭro
...와 / 과 교환으로
2 v/t addresses matpakkuda
맞바꾸다; *~ for* kyohwanhada

교환하다

exchange rate FIN hwannyul
환율

excited hŭngbundoen 흥분된

exciting hŭngbunshik'inŭn
흥분시키는

exclamation point
nŭkkimp'yo 느낌표

exclude cheoehada 제외하다

exclusive hotel paet'ajŏgin
배타적인; *rights*
toktchŏmjŏgin 독점적인

excruciating pain komun
고문 받는 듯한
pannŭn tŭt'an

excursion tchalbŭn yŏhaeng
짧은 여행

excuse 1 n pyŏnmyŏng
변명 **2** v/t (*forgive*)
yongsŏhada 용서하다; *~ me*
shillyehamnida 실례합니다;
(*apology*) choesonghamnida
죄송합니다; *~ me? (pardon me?)* mwŏragoyo? 뭐라고요?

execute criminal sahyŏng
chip'aenghada 사형
집행하다; *plan* shirhaenghada
실행하다

execution (*of criminal*)
sahyŏng chip'aeng 사형
집행; (*of plan*) shirhaeng 실행

executive n kanbu 간부

exemplary mobŏmjŏgin
모범적인

exempt: *be ~ from* ...(ŭ)ro
put'ŏ myŏnjedoeda ...(으)로
부터 면제되다

exercise 1 *n (physical)*
undong 운동; SCHOOL yŏnsŭp
연습; MIL hullyŏn 훈련 2 *v/i*
undonghada 운동하다

exert *authority* parhwihada
발휘하다; ~ *oneself*
noryŏk'ada 노력하다

exertion noryŏk 노력

exhale naeshwida 내쉬다

exhaust 1 *n (fumes)* paech'ul
배출; *(pipe)* paegigwan
배기관 2 *v/t (use up)* ta ssŏ
pŏrida 다 써 버리다

exhausted *(tired)* nokch'oga
toen 녹초가 된

exhausting nokch'oga toege
hanŭn 녹초가 되게 하는

exhaustion nokch'oga p'iro
극도의 피로

exhibition chŏnshi 전시

exile *n* ch'ubang 추방; *(person)*
ch'ubangja 추방자

exist chonjaehada 존재하다

existence chonjae 존재; *(life)*
saenghwal 생활

existing hyŏnjonhanŭn
현존하는

exit *n* ch'ulgu 출구

exorbitant sangsang-ŭl
ch'owŏrhanŭn 상상을
초월하는

exotic iguktchŏgin 이국적인

expand 1 *v/t* nŏlp'ida 넓히다
2 *v/i* nŭlda 늘다; *(of metal)*
p'aengch'anghada 팽창하다

expect 1 *v/t* kidaehada

기대하다; *baby* imshinhada
임신하다; *(suppose)*
ch'uch'ŭk'ada 추측하다;
(demand) yoguhada 요구하다
2 *v/i* I ~ so kŭrŏl kŏyeyo
그럴 거예요

expectation kidae 기대;
~s *(demands)* changnaeŭi
hŭimang 장래의 희망

expedition t'amhŏm 탐험

expel *person* tchoch'anaeda
쫓아내다

expenditure chich'ul 지출

expense piyong 비용

expenses kyŏngbi 경비

expensive pissan 비싼

experience 1 *n (event)*
ch'ŏhŏm 체험; *(in life)*
kyŏnghŏm 경험; *(in particular
field)* kyŏngnyŏk 경력
2 *v/t pain, pleasure* nŭkkida
느끼다; *difficulty* kyŏkta 겪다

experienced kyŏnghŏminnŭn
경험있는

experiment 1 *n* shirhŏm 실험
2 *v/i* shirhŏmhada 실험하다

expert 1 *adj* sungnyŏndoen
숙련된 2 *n* chŏnmun-ga
전문가

expertise chŏnmun chishik /
kisul 전문 지식 / 기술

expiration kihan mallyo 기한
만료

expiration date kihan mallyo
mallyoil 유효 만료일

expire man-gidoeda 만기되다

explain *wt & v/i* sŏlmyŏnghada
설명하다

explanation sŏlmyŏng 설명

explode *v/i (of bomb)*
p'okpparhada 폭발하다

exploit *wt person*
ch'akch'wihada 착취하다;
resources kaebarhayŏ
iyonghada 개발하여
이용하다

exploration t'amhŏm 탐험

explore *country* tappsahada
답사하다; *possibility*
t'amsaek'ada 탐색하다

explosion p'okppal 폭발; *(in
population)* küptchüng 급증

export 1 *n (action)* such'ul
수출; *(item)* such'ulp'um
수출품 **2** *v/t goods*
such'urhada 수출하다

exporter such'urŏptcha
수출업자; *(country)*
such'ulguk 수출국

expose *scandal* p'ongnohada
폭로하다; *person* poyŏjuda
보여주다

express 1 *adj (fast)* küp'aeng-
üi 급행의; *(explicit)*
myŏngbaek'an 명백한
2 *n*: ~ *train / bus* küp'aeng
yŏlch'a / pŏssŭ 급행
열차 / 버스 *v/t feelings*
p'yohyŏnhada 표현하다

expression *(voicing, phrase)*
p'yohyŏn 표현; *(on face)*
p'yojŏng 표정

expressway kosokttoro
고속도로

expulsion *(from school)*
t'oehak 퇴학; *(of diplomat)*
ch'ubang 추방

extend nŏlp'ida 넓히다;
runway nŭrida 늘리다; *visa*
yŏnjanghada 연장하다

extension *(of visa)* yŏnjang
연장; TEL naesŏn 내선

extension cable yŏnjang
k'eibŭl 연장 케이블

extensive kwangbŏmwihan
광범위한

extent pŏmwi 범위

exterior 1 *adj* oegwansang-üi
외관상의 **2** *n (of building)*
oegwan 외관; *(of person)*
kŏnmosŭp 겉모습

external oebuüi 외부의

extinct *species* myŏltchongdoen
멸종된

extinguish *fire* kküda 끄다

extinguisher sohwagi 소화기

extortion kangt'al 강탈

extra 1 *n* ch'ugaüi kŏt 추가의
것 **2** *adj* ch'ugaüi 추가의;
be ~ (cost more) ch'ugaida
추가이다

extract 1 *n* inyong 인용 **2** *v/t*
kkŏnaeda 꺼내다; *oil* p'anaeda
파내다; *tooth* ppŏpta
뽑다; *information* ŏryŏpkke
ŏdŏnaeda 어렵게 얻어내다

extradition pŏmjoein indo
범죄인 인도

fall

extraordinary ŏmch'ŏngnan 엄청난

extravagant *(with money)* sach'isŭrŏun 사치스러운

extreme 1 *n* kŭkttan 극단 2 *adj* kŭksshimhan 극심한; *views* kŭktanjŏgin 극단적인

extremely taedanhi 대단히

extremist *n* kwagyŏngnonja 과격론자

extrovert *n* oehyangtchŏgin saram 외향적인 사람

eye nun 눈

eyebrow nunssŏp 눈썹

eyelash songnunssŏp 속눈썹

eyelid nunkkŏp'ul 눈꺼풀

eyeliner airainŏ 아이라이너

eyeshadow aishyaedou 아이섀도우

eyesight shiryŏk 시력

eyesore pogi hyunghan kŏt 보기 흉한 것

eyewitness mok-kkyŏktcha 목격자

F

fabric chingmul 직물

fabulous koengjanghan 굉장한

façade *(of building)* chŏngmyŏn 정면; *(of person)* kŏnmosŭp 겉모습

face *n* ŏlgul 얼굴; *lose ~* ch'emyŏnŭl ilt'a 체면을 잃다 2 *v/t person, the sea* majuboda 마주보다

facilitate shwipkke hada 쉽게 하다

facilities shisŏl 시설

fact sashil 사실; *in ~* sashirŭn 사실은

factor yoin 요인

factory kongjang 공장

fade *v/i (of colors)* paraeda 바래다

Fahrenheit Hwasshi 화씨

fail *v/i* shilp'aehada 실패하다

failure shilp'ae 실패

faint 1 *adj* hŭimihan 희미한 2 *v/i* kijŏrhada 기절하다

fair [1] *n (trade show)* muyŏk pangnamhoe 무역 박람회

fair [2] *adj hair* kŭmbarŭi 금발의; *(just)* kongjŏnghan 공정한

fairly *treat* kongjŏnghage 공정하게; *(quite)* kkwae 꽤

fairy tale tonghwa 동화

faith shilloe 신뢰; REL shinang 신앙

faithful ch'ungshirhan 충실한

fake 1 *n* katcha 가짜 2 *adj* katchaŭi 가짜의

fall [1] *v/i (of person, price etc)* ttŏrŏjida 떨어지다; *(of government)* munŏjida 무너지다; *(of tree)* ssŭrŏjida

fall out

; (of night) oda 오다
2 n (from high place) ch'urak
추락; (of government) punggoe
붕괴, (in temperature) harang
하강; (in price) harak 하락
♦ **fall out** (of hair) ppajida
빠지다; (argue) saiga t'ŭrŏjida
사이가 틀어지다

fall² n (autumn) kaŭl 가을
false kŏrŭttoen 그릇된
false teeth t'ŭlli 틀니
fame myŏngsŏng 명성
familiar adj (intimate) ch'in-
gŭnhan 친근한
family kajok 가족
family name sŏng 성
family planning kajok kyehoek
가족 계획
famine kigŭn 기근
famous yumyŏnghan 유명한
fan¹ n (supporter) p'aen 팬
fan² n sŏnp'unggi 선풍기;
(handheld) puch'ae 부채
fanatic n kwangshinja 광신자
fanatical kwangshinjŏgin
광신적인
fancy adj design mŏtchin 멋진
fancy dress kajang mudobok
가장 무도복
fang ŏmni 엄니
fantastic (very good)
hwansangjŏgin 환상적인;
(big) ŏmch'ŏngnan 엄청난
fantasy hwansang 환상
far adv mŏlli 멀리; ~ away
mŏlli ttŏrŏjin 멀리 떨어진;

how ~ is it to …? …kkaji
ŏlmana mŏn-gayo? …까지
얼마나 먼가요?; **as ~ as I
know** naega anŭn han 내가
아는 한

fare n (travel) yogŭm 요금
Far East Kŭktong 극동
farewell party songbyŏrhoe
송별회
farm n nongjang 농장
farmer nongbu 농부
farsighted shin-gyŏnjimyŏng-i
innŭn 선견지명이 있는;
(optically) wŏnshiŭi 원시의
farther adv tŏ mŏlli 더 멀리
farthest travel etc kajang mŏlli
가장 멀리
fascinate v/t maehoksshik'ida
매혹시키다
fascinating maehoktchŏgin
매혹적인
fascination (with subject)
yŏlgwang 열광
fascism p'asshijŭm 파시즘
fashion n yuhaeng 유행; (in
clothes) p'asshyŏn 패션
fashionable clothes yuhaeng-
ŭl ttarŭnŭn 유행을 따르는;
person yuhaeng-ŭl chal naenŭn
멋을 잘 내는
fashion designer p'aesshyŏn
tijainŏ 패션 디자이너
fast 1 adj pparŭn 빠른 **2** adv
pparŭge ppalli 빠르게 빨리; ~ **asleep**
kip'i chamdŭn 깊이 잠든
fasten v/t (fix) kojŏnghada

고정하다; *belt* ch'aeuda
채우다; *bag* chamgŭda
잠그다

fast food p'aesŭt'ŭp'udŭ
패스트푸드

fat 1 *adj* ttungttunghan 뚱뚱한
2 *n* chibang 지방

fatal *illness, error*
ch'imyŏngjŏgin 치명적인

fatality samangja 사망자

fate unmyŏng 운명

father *n* abŏji 아버지

father-in-law *(woman's)*
shiabŏji 시아버지; *(man's)*
chang-in 장인

fatigue *n* p'iro 피로

faucet mulkkoktchi 물꼭지

fault *n (defect)* kyŏltchŏm 결점;
it's your / my ~ nŏŭi / naŭi
chalmoshida 너의 / 나의
잘못이다

faulty kyŏltchŏm innŭn 결점
있는

favor hoŭi 호의; *be in* ~ *of*
…e ch'ansŏnghada …에
찬성하다

favorable *reply etc* hoŭijŏgin
호의적인

favorite *adj* cheil choahanŭn
제일 좋아하는

fax 1 *n* p'aeksŭ 팩스 **2** *v/t*
p'aeksŭro ponaeda 팩스로
보내다

FBI Yŏnbang Susaguk 연방
수사국

fear 1 *n* turyŏum 두려움 **2** *v/t*

turyŏwŏhada 두려워하다

feasible shirhaeng kanŭnghan
실행 가능한

feather kit'ŏl 깃털

feature *n* t'ŭktching 특징;
(in paper) kisa 기사; *(movie)*
changp'yŏn yŏnghwa 장편
영화

February iwŏl 이월

federal yŏnbang chŏngbuŭi
연방 정부의

fed up: be ~ *with* …e(ge)
chillida …에(게) 질리다

fee *(of doctor)* chillyobi
진료비; *(for entrance)*
iptchangnyo 입장료; *(for
school)* ip'akkŭm 입학금

feed *v/t* mŏgida 먹이다;
animal mŏgirŭl chuda 먹이를
주다

feedback p'idŭbaek 피드백

feel 1 *v/t (touch)* manjida
만지다; *pain, pleasure*
nŭkkida 느끼다; *(think)*
saenggak'ada 생각하다 **2** *v/i
(of cloth etc)* nŭkkimi it-tta
느낌이 있다

feeling *(of happiness)* nŭkkim
느낌; *(emotion)* kamjŏng
감정; *(sensation)* kamgak
감각

felony chungjoe 중죄

felt tip p'elt'ŭp'en 펠트펜

female 1 *adj* amk'ŏsŭi 암컷의;
person yŏsŏng-ŭi 여성의
2 *n (animal)* amk'ŏt 암컷

(person) yŏsŏng 여성
feminine *adj qualities*
yŏsŏngjŏgin 여성적인
feminism p'eminijŭm
페미니즘
feminist *n* p'eminisŭt'ŭ
페미니스트
fence ult'ari울타리
fender AUTO p'endŏ 펜더
fern yangch'iryu 양치류
ferocious hyungp'ohan
흉포한; *attack* chaninhan
잔인한
ferry *n* narutppae 나룻배
fertile *soil* piok'an 비옥한;
woman tasanŭi 다산의
fertility *(of soil)* piok 비옥; *(of
woman, animal)* tasan 다산
fertilizer *(for soil)* piryo 비료
fervent *admirer* yŏllyŏrhan
열렬한
festival ch'uktche 축제
festivities ch'uk'a haengsa
축하 행사
fetch *person* terigo oda 데리고
오다; *thing* kajyŏ oda 가져
오다; *price* ...e p'allida ...에
팔리다
fetus t'aea 태아
feud *n* purhwa 불화
fever yŏl 열
few 1 *adj (not many)* manch'i
anŭn 많지 않은; *a ~ (things)*
chogŭmŭi 조금의; *quite a ~*
myŏnmyŏt몇몇; ... **2** *pron*
kkwae manŭn 꽤 많은

(not many people) chŏgŭn suŭi
saram 적은 수의 사람; *(not
many things)* chŏgŭn suŭi kŏt
적은 수의 것; *a ~ (people)*
myŏnmyŏt saram 몇몇 사람;
(things) myŏnmyŏch'ŭi kŏt
몇몇것의
fewer *adj* tŏ chŏgŭn 더 적은
fiancé yak'onja 약혼자
fiancée yak'onnyŏ 약혼녀
fiasco taeshilp'ae 대실패
fiber *n* sŏmnyu 섬유
fiber optics kwangsŏmnyu
광섬유
fiction *(novels)* sosŏl 소설
fictitious hŏguŭi 허구의
fidget *v/i* anjŏlbujŏl mot'ada
안절부절 못하다
field *n* tŭlp'an 들판; *(for crops)*
pat 밭; *(for animals)* mokch'oji
목초지; *(for rice)* non 논; *(for
sport)* kyŏnggijang 경기장; *(of
knowledge etc)* punya 분야
fierce sanaun 사나운
fifty-fifty *adv* oship tae oshibŭro
오십 대 오십으로
fig muhwagwa 무화과
fight 1 *n* ssaum 싸움; *fig (for
survival, championship etc)*
t'ujaeng 투쟁; *(in boxing)*
kyŏnggi 경기 **2** *v/t person,
disease* ...wa / kwa ssauda
...와 / 과 싸우다 **3** *v/i* ssauda
싸우다
♦ **fight for** ...ŭl / rŭl wihae
ssauda ...을 / 를 위해

싸우다
figure n (digit) sutcha 숫자;
(of person) mommae 몸매;
(shape) hyŏngsang 형상
♦ **figure out** (understand)
ihaehada 이해하다; sum
kyesanhada 계산하다
file¹ n (of documents) sŏryuch'ŏl
서류철; COMPUT hwail 화일
file² n (tool) chul 줄
fill v/t ch'aeuda 채우다
♦ **fill in** hole maeuda 매우다
♦ **fill out** v/t form kiip'ada
기입하다
filling 1 n (in sandwich) sok
속; (in tooth) p'illing 필링
2 adj food paeburŭge hanŭn
배부르게 하는
film 1 n (for camera) p'illŭm
필름; (movie) yŏnghwa
영화 2 v/t person, event
ch'waryŏnghada 촬영하다
film star yŏnghwa sŭt'a 영화
스타
filter n p'ilt'ŏ 필터
filthy pulgyŏrhan 불결한
fin (of fish) chinŭrŏmi
지느러미
final 1 adj (last) majimagŭi
마지막의; decision ch'oejong-
ŭi 최종의 2 n SPORTS
kyŏlsŭng 결승
finalist kyŏlsŭngjŏn ch'ulchŏn
sŏnsu 결승전 출전 선수
finalize mamurihada

마무리하다
finally majimagŭro
마지막으로; (at last)
mach'imnae 마침내
finance 1 n chaejŏng 재정
2 v/t …e chagŭm chiwŏnŭl
hada …에 자금 지원을
하다
financial chaejŏng-ŭi 재정의
financial year hoegye yŏndo
회계 연도
find v/t ch'at-tta 찾다
♦ **find out** 1 v/t aranaeda
알아내다 2 v/i (inquire)
palk'yŏnaeda 밝혀내다;
(discover) aranaeda 알아내다
fine¹ adj weather malgŭn 맑은;
wine, performance hullyunghan
훌륭한; distinction misehan
미세한; that's ~ by me
nanŭn chohŭndeyo라는
좋은데요
fine² n (penalty) pŏlgŭm 벌금
finger n sonkkarak 손가락
fingernail sont'op 손톱
fingerprint n chimun 지문
finish 1 v/t kkŭnnaeda 끝내다
2 v/i kkŭnnada 끝나다 3 n (of
race) kyŏlsŭng 결승점
finish line kyŏlsŭngsŏn
결승선
fir chŏnnamu 전나무
fire 1 n pul 불; (electric, gas)
nanbang 난방; (blaze) hwajae
화재; be on ~ pul t'ago
it-tta 불 타고 있다 2 v/i

(shoot) ssoda 쏘다 **3** *v/t infml*
(dismiss) haegohada 해고하다

fire alarm hwajae kyŏngbogi
화재 경보기

fire department sobangsŏ
소방서

fire escape hwajae p'inan
changch'i 화재 피난 장치

fire extinguisher sohwagi
소화기

firefighter sobangsu 소방수

fireplace pyŏngnallo 벽난로

fireworks pulkkot 불꽃;
(display) pulkkonnori
불꽃놀이

firm¹ *adj grip* himinnŭn
힘있는; *muscles* tandanhan
단단한; *voice* hwakkohan
확고한

firm² *n COMM* hoesa 회사

first 1 *adj* ch'ŏŭmŭi 처음의
2 *adv arrive, finish* ch'ŏŭmŭro
처음으로; *(beforehand)* mŏnjŏ
먼저; *at ~* ch'ŏŭme 처음에

first aid ŭnggŭp ch'iryo 응급
치료

first-aid kit kugŭmnyak sangja
구급약 상자

first class *adj* iltŭngŭi
일등의; *(very good)*
ch'oegogŭbŭi 최고급의

first floor ilch'ŭng 일층

firsthand *adj* chiktchŏptchŏgin
직접적인

firstly usŏn 우선

first name irŭm 이름

fiscal year hoegye yŏndo
회계 연도

fish 1 *n* mulkkogi 물고기;
(to eat) saengsŏn 생선 **2** *v/i*
nakssihada 낚시하다

fisherman ŏbu 어부

fishing nakssi 낚시

fishing boat ŏsŏn 어선

fishing rod naksshit-ttae
낚싯대

fist chumŏk 주먹

fit¹ *n MED* paltchak 발작

fit² *adj (physically)* kŏn-ganghan
건강한; *(morally)* chŏk'ap'an
적합한

fit³ *v/i (of clothes)* mat-tta 맞다;
(of furniture etc) tŭrŏ mat-tta
들어 맞다

fitness kŏn-gangham 건강함

fitness center helssŭ k'ŭllŏp
헬스 클럽

fittings kŏnmul naebu
changch'i 건물 내부 장치

fix *v/t (attach)* kojŏnghada
고정하다; *(repair)* koch'ida
고치다; *meeting etc* ilsshirŭl
chŏnghada 일시를 정하다;
lunch chunbihada 준비하다;
(dishonestly) chojak'ada
조작하다

fixture *(in room)* sŏlbi 설비;
SPORTS chŏnggijŏn 정기전

flabby *muscles* nŭrŏjin 늘어진

flag¹ *n* kitppal 깃발

flake *n* yalbŭn chogak 얇은
조각

flow

flamboyant chashini nŏmch'yŏboinŭn 자신이 넘쳐보이는

flame (in airplane) pulkkil 불길; ~s pulkkil 불길

flammable kayŏnssŏng-ŭi 가연성의

flash 1 (of light) sŏmgwang 섬광; PHOT p'ŭllaeshwi 플래쉬 **2** v/i (of light) pich'ida 비치다

flashback kwagŏ hoesang changmyŏn 과거 회상 장면

flashlight hoejung chŏndŭng 회중 전등

flask pyŏng 병

flat adj p'yŏngp'yŏnghan 평평한; beer kim ppajin 김 빠진; battery, tire ta tarŭn 다 닳은; shoes najŭn kubŭi 낮은 굽의

flat rate iltchŏng-aek 일정액

flatter v/t ach'ŏmhada 아첨하다

flattery ach'ŏm 아첨

flavor n mat 맛

flawless hŭmŏmnŭn 흠없는

flea pyŏruk 벼룩

flee v/i tomangch'ida 도망치다

fleet n NAUT hamdae 함대

flesh sal 살

flexible kuburigi shwiun 구부리기 쉬운

flicker v/i kkamppagida 깜박이다

flies (on pants) paji ammun 바지 앞문

flight (in airplane) pihaeng 비행; (flying) nalgi 날기

flight number hanggongp'yŏn pŏnho 항공편 번호

flight path pihaeng kyŏngno 비행 경로

flimsy structure yak'an 약한; material tchijŏjigi shwiun 찢어지기 쉬운; excuse pinyak'an 빈약한

fling v/t naedŏnjida 내던지다

flipper (for swimmer) mulgalk'wi 물갈퀴

flirt v/i saeronggŏrida 새롱거리다

float v/i ttŭda 뜨다

flock (of sheep) tte 떼

flood 1 n hongsu 홍수 **2** v/t (of river) pŏmnamhada 범람하다

floodlight n t'ugwang chomyŏng 투광 조명

floor n (of room) marutppadak 마룻바닥; (story) ch'ŭng 층

floorboard padangnŏl 바닥널

floppy (disk) p'ŭllop'i tisŭk'ŭ 플로피 디스크

florist kkotchangsu 꽃장수

flour milkkaru 밀가루

flourish v/i (of plants) chal charada 잘 자라다; (of business) pŏnch'anghada 번창하다

flow v/i (of river) hŭrŭda 흐르다; (of traffic) sot'ongdoeda 소통되다 **2** n

(of river, information) hŭrŭm
흐름

flowchart chagŏp kongjŏngdo
작업 공정도

flower *n* kkot 꽃

flowerbed hwadan 화단

flowerpot hwabyŏng 화병

flu tok-kkam 독감

fluctuate *w/i* pyŏndonghada
변동하다

fluent *adj* yuch'anghan 유창한

fluid *n* aekch'e 액체

fluorescent hyŏnggwang-ŭi
형광의

flush *w/t toilet* …ŭi murŭl
naerida …의 물을 내리다

flute p'ŭllut'ŭ 플루트; *(large)*
taegŭm 대금; *(bamboo)* tanso
단소

fly[1] *n (insect)* p'ari 파리

fly[2] *n (on pants)* paji ammun
바지 앞문

fly[3] *w/i* nalda 날다; *(in plane)*
pihaenggiro yŏhaenghada
비행기로 여행하다

flying *n* pihaeng 비행

foam *n* kŏp'um 거품

focus *n (of attention)*, PHOT
ch'otchŏm 초점

fog an-gae 안개

foggy an-gae kkin 안개 낀

fold *w/t paper* chŏptta 접다;
cloth kaeda 개다; ~ *one's
arms* p'altchang-ŭl kkida
팔짱을 끼다

folder *also* COMPUT p'oldŏ 폴더

foliage ip 잎

folk *(people)* saram 사람

folk music minsok ŭmak
민속 음악

folk song minyo 민요

follow 1 *w/t* ttaragada
따라가다; *instructions*
ttarŭda 따르다; *TV series*
kyesok shich'ŏnghada 계속
시청하다 **2** *w/i (logically)*
sŏngnip'ada 성립하다

♦ **follow up** *inquiry* poganghada
보강하다

following *adj day* kŭ taŭmnŭi 그
다음의; *page* taŭmŭi 다음의

fond *(loving)* tajŏnghan
다정한; *be ~ of* …ŭl / rŭl
choahada …을 / 를 좋아하다

food ŭmshik 음식

food poisoning shiktchungdok
식중독

foolish ŏrisŏgŭn 어리석은

fool pabo 바보; *make a ~ of
oneself* usŭmkkŏriga toeda
웃음거리가 되다

foolproof *method* toel suga
ŏmnŭn 잘못 될 수가 없는

foot pal 발; *(length)* p'it'ŭ
피트; *on ~* kŏrŏsŏ 걸어서

football *(soccer)* ch'uk-kku
축구; *(American)* mishik
ch'uk-kku 미식 축구; *(ball)*
ch'uk-kkugong 축구공

footbridge yukkyo 육교

footnote kaktchu 각주

footpath indo 인도

footprint paltchaguk 발자국

for ◇ *(purpose, destination)* …
ŭl / rŭl wihan …을 / 를 위한;
a train ~ *Seoul* Sŏullo kanŭn
kich'a 서울로 가는 기차;
this is ~ *you* ikŏsŭn nŏrŭl
wihan kŏshida 이것은 너를
위한 것이다; *(time)* … tong-
an … 동안; ~ *three days*
sam il tong-an sam il 일 동안
◇ *(instead of, in behalf of)*:
let me do that ~ *you* chega
taeshin haedŭrigessŭmnida
제가 대신 해드리겠습니다

forbid kŭmjihada 금지하다

force 1 *n (violence)* p'ongnyŏk
폭력; *(of explosion, punch)*
him 힘; *the* ~*s* MIL chŏn-
gun 전군 2 *v/t someone*
kangyohada 강요하다

forecast *n* yesang 예상;
(weather) kisang yebo 기상
예보

foreground chŏn-gyŏng 전경

forehead ima 이마

foreign oegugŭi 외국의

foreign currency oehwa 외화

foreigner oegugin 외국인

foreign language oegugŏ
외국어

foreign policy oemu
chŏngch'aek 외무 정책

foresee yegyŏnhada 예견하다

forest sup 숲

foretell yŏnhada 예언하다

forever yŏng-wŏnhi 영원히

foreword sŏmun 서문

forfeit *v/t* sangshirhada
상실하다

forge *v/t (counterfeit)* mojohada
모조하다

forgery wijo 위조

forget it-tta 잊다

forgetful chal ijŏbŏrinŭn 잘
잊어버리는

forgive *v/t* & *v/i* yongsŏhada
용서하다

forgiveness yongsŏ 용서

fork *n* p'ok'ŭ 포크; *(in road)*
pun-gitchŏm 분기점

forklift chigech'a 지게차

form 1 *n* hyŏngt'ae 형태;
(document) yangshik 양식
2 *v/t clay* mandŭlda 만들다
3 *v/i (take shape)*
kuch'ehwadoeda 구체화되다

formal hyŏngshiktchŏgin
형식적인; *recognition*
kongtchŏgin 공적인

format 1 *v/t disk* p'omaet'ada
포맷하다; *document*
yangshik'wahada 양식화하다
2 *n (of paper etc)* k'ŭgi 크기;
(of program) hyŏngshik 형식

former chŏnŭi 전의; *the* ~
chŏnja 전자

formidable musŏun 무서운

formula kongshik 공식

forth: *back and* ~ apttwiro
앞뒤로; *and so* ~ kit'a
tŭngdŭng 기타 등등

fortnight *Br* tu chu 두 주

fortunate un choŭn 운 좋은

fortune un 운; *(money)* k'ŭn ton 큰 돈

fortune-teller chŏmjaeng-i 점쟁이

forward 1 *adv* ap'ŭro 앞으로
2 *n* SPORTS p'owŏdŭ 포워드
3 *v/t* mail hoesonghada 회송하다

fossil hwasŏk 화석

foster child ibyang-a 입양아

foster parents yangbumo 양부모

foul 1 *n* SPORTS panch'ik 반칙
2 *adj* smell yŏkkyŏun 역겨운; *weather* chidok'an 지독한

found *v/t* sŏllip'ada 설립하다

foundation *(of theory etc)* kŭn-gŏ 근거; *(organization)* chaedan 재단

foundations kich'o 기초

founder *n* sŏlliptcha 설립자

fountain punsu 분수

fox *n* yŏu 여우

fracture 1 *n* kŭm 금 **2** *v/t* …e kŭmgage hada …에 금가게 하다

fragile kkaejigi shwiun 깨지기 쉬운

fragment *n (of vase etc)* chogak 조각; *(of story)* tanp'yŏn 단편

fragrance hyanggi 향기

frail yak'an 약한

framework kusang 구상

France P'ŭrangssŭ 프랑스

frank soltchik'an 솔직한

frantic mich'in tŭt'an 미친 듯한

fraud sagi 사기; *(person)* sagikkun 사기꾼

freak 1 *n (event)* pyŏndŏk 변덕; *infml (person)* pyŏltchong 별종 **2** *adj* storm toryŏnhan 돌연한

freckle chugŭkkae 주근깨

free 1 *adj (at liberty)* chayuŭi 자유의; *(no cost)* muryoŭi 무료의; *room, table* pin 빈 **2** *v/t prisoners* sŏkppanghada 석방하다

freedom chayu 자유

freelance *adj* chayu kyeyagŭi 자유 계약의

free speech ŏllonŭi chayu 언론의 자유

freeway kosoktoro 고속도로

freeze 1 *v/t* ŏllida 얼리다; *bank account* tonggyŏrhada 동결하다; *video* sun-gan chŏngjishik'ida 순간 정지시키다 **2** *v/i (of water)* ŏlda 얼다

freezer naengdongshil 냉동실

freight *n* hwamul 화물

French 1 *adj* P'ŭrangssŭŭi 프랑스의 **2** *n (language)* P'ŭrangssŭŏ 프랑스어

French fries kamja t'wigim 감자 튀김; *(fast food)* hurench'ihurai 후렌치후라이

frequency pinbŏnham 빈번함; RADIO chup'asu 주파수

frequent adj chajün 잦은

frequently chaju 자주

fresh air, food shinsönhan 신선한; (cold) ssalssarhan 쌀쌀한; start saeroun 새로운; (impertinent) könbanjin 건방진

freshman shinipssaeng 신입생

friction mach'al 마찰

Friday kümnyoil 금요일

fridge naengjanggo 냉장고

fried egg kyeran hurai 계란 후라이

friend ch'in-gu 친구

friendly adj ch'inhan 친한; atmosphere tajönghan 다정한

friendship ujöng 우정

fries hurench'ihurai 후렌치후라이

fright kkamtchak nollam 깜짝 놀람

frighten v/t köptchuda 겁주다; be ~ed kömnada 겁나다

frill (on dress) p'üril 프릴; (extra) pugamul 부가물

frog kaeguri 개구리

from (in space, time) ...(esö)but'ö ...(에서) 부터 (origin: of people) ...(에서) 부터; (origin: of things) ...(으)로부터; a letter ~ Jo Chorobut'ö on p'yönji 조로부터 온 편지; I am ~ New Jersey chönün Nyujöji ch'ulsshinimnida 저는 뉴저지 출신입니다

front 1 n ap 앞; MIL, (weather) chönsön 전선; in ~ ap'e(sö) 앞에(서); (in a race) söndue(sö) 선두에(서); in ~ of ...üi aptchoge(sö) ...의 앞쪽에(서) **2** adj wheel, seat aptchogüi 앞쪽의

front door ammun 앞문

frontier kuk-kkyöng 국경; fig ch'oech'ömdan 최첨단

front page ilmyön 일면

front row aptchul 앞줄

frost söri 서리

frostbite tongsang 동상

frosting sölt'ang-ül ip'im 설탕을 입힘

frosty söriga naerinün 서리가 내리는

frown v/i tchip'urida 찌푸리다

frozen örün 어른

fruit kwail 과일

fruit juice kwail chusü 과일 주스

frustrated chwajöldoen 좌절된

frustrating tchajüngnanün 짜증나는

fry v/t (stir~) pokta 볶다; (deep~) t'wigida 튀기다

fuel n yöllyo 연료

fugitive n tomangja 도망자

fulfill shirhaenghada 실행하다

full glass kadük ch'an 가득 찬; hotel, bus kkwak ch'an 꽉 찬

full moon porümtal 보름달

full-time adv chönshiganjero 전시간제로

fully wanjŏnhi 완전히
fumes maeyŏn 매연
fun chaemi 재미; *have ~!*
chaemiittke chinaeseyo!
재미있게 지내세요!*;
*make ~ of ...*ŭl / rŭl nollida
…을/를 놀리다
function 1 *n (job)* chingnŭng
직능; *(of machine)* kŭnŭng
기능; *(reception etc)* haengsa
행사 2 *v/i* chaktonghada
작동하다
fund *n* chagŭm 자금
fundamental kibonjŏgin
기본적인
funeral changnyeshik 장례식
funeral home yŏng-anso
영안소
funny usŭun 우스운; *(odd)*
isanghan 이상한
fur t'ŏl 털

furious *(angry)* kyŏngnohanŭn
격노하는
furniture kagu 가구
further 1 *adj (additional)* tto
tarŭn 또 다른, *(more distant)*
tŏ mŏn 더 먼 2 *adv walk* tŏ
더; *2 miles ~* 2mailboda tŏ
mŏn 2마일보다 더 먼
furthest 1 *adj* kajang mŏn
가장 먼 2 *adv* kajang mŏlli
가장 멀리
fury *(anger)* kyŏngno 격노
fuse ELEC 1 *n* p'yujŭ 퓨즈 2 *v/i*
p'yujŭga kkŭnk'ida 퓨즈가
끊기다
fuss *n* nallibŏpsŏk 난리법석
fussy *person* kkadarou
까다로운
futile ssŭltte ŏmnŭn 쓸데 없는
future *n* mirae 미래; *in ~*
miraeenŭn 미래에는

G

gadget kanttanhan togu
간단한 도구
gain *v/t (acquire)* ŏt-tta 얻다
gale kangp'ung 강풍
gallery *(art)* hwarang 화랑
gallon kaellŏn 갤런
gamble tobak'ada 도박하다
gambler tobak-kkun 도박꾼
gambling tobak 도박
game *n* shihap 시합; *(sport)*
kyŏnggi 경기; *(kid's)* nori

놀이; *(tennis)* keim 게임
gang kaeng 갱
gangster nappŭn muri 나쁜
무리
gangway t'ongno 통로
gap *(in wall)* t'ŭm 틈; *(in time)*
kongbaek 공백
gape *v/i (of person)* ibŭl ttak
pŏlligo paraboda 입을 딱
벌리고 바라보다
garage *(parking)* ch'ago 차고;

(repairs) chadongch'a suriso
자동차 수리소

garbage ssŭregi 쓰레기;
(nonsense) maldo an toenŭn
sori 말도 안 되는 소리

garbage can ssŭregi t'ong
쓰레기 통

garden chŏng-wŏn 정원

garland n hwahwan 화환

garlic manŭl 마늘

gas n kasŭ 가스; *(gasoline)*
hwibaryu 휘발유

gasp v/i hŏltttŏk-kkŏrida
헐떡거리다

gas station chuyuso 주유소

gate taemun 대문; *(at airport)*
t'apssŭnggu 탑승구

gather v/t facts moŭda 모으다

gay 1 n tongsŏngaeja
동성애자 2 adj tongsŏngaeŭi
동성애의

♦ **gaze at** ...ŭl / rŭl ŭngsihada
…을 / 를 응시하다

gear n *(equipment)* yonggu
용구; AUTO kiŏ 기어

gear shift AUTO kiŏ
changch'i 기어 전환 장치

gel *(hair)* chel 젤; *(shower)*
mulbinu 물비누

gender sŏng 성

gene yujŏnja 유전자

general 1 n MIL changgun 장군
2 adj ilbanjŏgin 일반적인;
(overall) chŏnch'ejŏgin
전체적인

generalize ilbanhwahada

일반화하다

generally ilbanjŏguro
일반적으로

generate nat-tta 낳다; ELEC
palssaengshik'ida 발생시키다

generation sedae 세대

generator paltchŏn-gi 발전기

generosity nŏgŭrŏum
너그러움

generous inshim choŭn
인심 좋은; *(not critical)*
kwandaehan 관대한

genetic yujŏnjŏgin 유전적인

genetic fingerprint yujŏnja
chimun 유전자 지문

genetics yujŏnhak 유전학

genitals saengshikki 생식기

genius ch'ŏnjae 천재

gentle pudŭrŏun 부드러운;
person onhwahan 온화한

gentleman shinsa 신사

gents Br *(toilet)* namja
hwajangshil 남자 화장실

genuine chintchaŭi 진짜의;
person chinshirhan 진실한

geographical chirijŏk 지리적

geography chiri 지리

geological chijirŭi 지질의

geology chijil 지질; *(subject)*
chijirhak 지질학

geometry kihahak 기하학

germ segyun 세균

German adj Togirŭi 독일의

Germany Togil 독일

gesture n sontchit 손짓; fig
ŭisa p'yoshi 의사 표시

get *(obtain)* ŏt-tta 얻다; *(fetch)* kajyŏoda 가져오다; *(receive)* pat-tta 받다; *bus, train etc* t'ada 타다; *(understand)* alda 알다 ◊ *(become)*
…haejida …해지다; **~ tired** p'igonhaejida 피곤해지다 ◊ *(causative):* **~ sth done** muŏsŭl hage hada 무엇을 하게 하다; **~ sb to do** nuguege harago hada 누구에게 하라고 하다; **~ one's hair cut** mŏrirŭl charŭda 머리를 자르다 ◊ *(have opportunity):* **~ to do** muŏsŭl hae poda 무엇을 해보다 ◊ *have got* kajida 가지다 ◊ *have got to* …haeya hada …해야 하다

♦ **get on** *(to bike, train)* t'ada 타다; *(be friendly)* saiga chot'a 사이가 좋다; *(progress)* chinch'ŏkttoeda 진척되다

♦ **get out 1** *vi (of car etc)* naerida 내리다; **~!** nagayo! 나가요! **2** *v/t nail etc* ppaenaeda 빼내다

♦ **get up** *v/i (from bed, chair)* irŏnada 일어나다

gherkin chagŭn oi 작은 오이
ghetto pinmin-ga 빈민가
ghost kwishin 귀신
giant *n* kŏin 거인
gift sŏnmul 선물
giftwrap *v/t* p'ojanghada 포장하다
gigantic pangdaehan 방대한

giggle *v/i* kkilkkil ut-tta 낄낄 웃다
gin chin 진
ginger *n (spice)* saenggang 생강
ginseng insam 인삼
giraffe kirin 기린
girl sonyŏ 소녀
girl friend yŏja ch'in-gu 여자 친구; *(lover)* aein 애인
gist yotchŏm 요점
give chuda 주다; *(hand over)* drida 드리다; **~ sth to sb** muŏsŭl nuguege chuda 무엇을 누구에게 주다

♦ **give away** *(as present)* chuda 주다; *(betray)* paebanhada 배반하다

♦ **give in 1** *v/i (surrender)* kulbok'ada 굴복하다 **2** *v/t (hand in)* chech'urhada 제출하다

♦ **give up 1** *v/t smoking etc* kkŭnt'a 끊다 **2** *v/i (stop trying)* p'ogihada 포기하다

glacier pingha 빙하
glad kippŭn 기쁜
gladly kikkŏi 기꺼이
glamor maeryŏk 매력
glamorous maeryŏgi nŏmch'inŭn 매력이 넘치는
glance 1 *n* hŭlgŭt pom 흘긋 봄 **2** *v/i:* **~ at** …ŭl / rŭl hŭlgŭt poda …을 / 를 흘긋 보다
glare *v/i (of light)* nunbushige pinnada 눈부시게 빛나다

◆ **glare** at noryŏboda 노려보다

glass (material) yuri 유리; (for drink) k'ŏp 컵

glasses an-gyŏng 안경

glide (of bird) hwalgonghada 활공하다

glimpse v/t hŭlkkŭt poda 흘끗 보다

glitter v/i pantchakpantchak pinnada 반짝반짝 빛나다

gloat v/i kosohaehada 고소해하다

global chŏnsegyeŭi 전세계의; (no exception) t'onggwaljŏgin 통괄적인

globalization segyehwa 세계화

global warming segye onnanhwa 세계 온난화

globe (the earth) chigu 지구; (model) chigubon 지구본

gloomy mood uuhan 우울한; room ŏduk'ŏmk'ŏmhan 어두컴컴한

glorious climate malgŭn 맑은

glossary yong-ŏ p'uri 용어 풀이

glossy 1 adj paper kwangt'aek nanŭn 광택 나는 2 n (magazine) kogŭp chaptchi 고급 잡지

glove changgap 장갑

glow v/i (light) pich'ŭl naeda 빛을 내다; (fire) t'ada 타다

glue n p'ul 풀

glutinous rice ch'apssal 찹쌀

Go (game) Paduk 바둑

go v/i kada 가다; (leave: of train etc) ch'ulbarhada 출발하다; (leave: of people) ttŏnada 떠나다; (work) chakttonghada 작동하다; (become) ...haejida ...해지다; (match: of colors etc) ŏullida 어울리다; I must be ~ing ije kayaman hamnida 이제 가야만 합니다; let's ~! kapsshida! 갑시다!; hamburger to ~ haembŏgŏ p'ojanghaejuseyo 햄버거 포장해주세요; it's all gone ta ŏpssŏjyŏt-tta 다 없어졌다; be ~ing to do sth muŏsŭl hal kŏshida 무엇을 할 것이다

◆ **go back** toragada 돌아가다; (date back) kŏsŭllŏ ollagada 거슬러 올라가다

◆ **go down 1** v/t stairs naeryŏgada 내려가다 **2** v/i (of sun) chida 지다; (of ship, swelling) karaanjta 가라앉다

◆ **go in** (to room, of sun) tŭrŏgada 들어가다; (fit: of part etc) mat-tta 맞다

◆ **go off** v/i (leave) kabŏrida 가버리다; (of bomb) p'okpparhada 폭발하다; (of alarm) ullida 울리다

◆ **go on** (continue) kyesok'ada 계속하다; (happen) irŏnada 일어나다

go out

go out *(of person)* nagada 나가다; *(of light, fire)* kkŏjida 꺼지다

goal SPORTS kol 골; *(points)* tŭktchŏm 득점; *(objective)* mokp'yo 목표

goalkeeper kolk'ip'ŏ 골키퍼

goat yŏmso 염소

go-between chunggaeja 중개자

god shin 신

goddess yŏshin 여신

godfather taebu 대부

gold 1 *n* kŭm 금 2 *adj* kŭmŭi 금의

golden wedding kŭmhonshik 금혼식

goldfish kŭmbung-ŏ 금붕어

goldsmith kŭmsegongsa 금세공사

golf kolp'ŭ 골프

golf club kolp'ŭ k'ŭllŏp 골프 클럽

golf course kolp'ŭjang 골프장

gong *(iron)* ching 징; *(brass)* kkwaenggwari 꽹과리

good choŭn 좋은; *be ~ at* ...ŭl / rŭl charhada ...을 / 를 잘하다; *be ~ for sb* nuguege chot'a 누구게 좋다

goodbye annyŏng 안녕; *(polite: to person leaving)* annyŏnghi kaseyo 안녕히 가세요; *(polite: to person staying)* annyŏnghi kyeseyo

안녕히 계세요

Good Friday Sŏnggŭmnyoil 성금요일

good-looking chal saenggin 잘 생긴

good-natured sŏnggyŏgi choŭn 성격이 좋은

goods COMM sangp'um 상품

goose kŏwi 거위

gorgeous *day* hwach'anghan 화창한; *dress, woman* kŭnsahan 근사한

gorilla korilla 고릴라

Gospel Pogŭmsŏ 복음서

gossip 1 *n* chapttam 잡담; *(person)* sudajaengi 수다쟁이 2 *v/i* chapttamhada 잡담하다

government chŏngbu 정부

governor *(of province)* chisa 지사

grab *v/t* puyŏjapta 부여잡다

graceful uahan 우아한

grade *n (quality)* tŭnggŭp 등급; SCHOOL *year* hangnyŏn 학년; *(in exam)* sŏngjŏk 성적

gradual chŏmch'ajŏgin 점차적인

graduate 1 *n* chŏropssaeng 졸업생 2 *v/i* chŏrŏp'ada 졸업하다

graduation chŏrŏp 졸업

graffiti nakssŏ 낙서

grain nadal 낟알; *(in wood)* namutkkyŏl 나뭇결

gram kŭraem 그램

grammar munppŏp 문법

grand adj ungjanghan 웅장한
granddaughter sonnyŏ 손녀
grandfather harabŏji
할아버지
grandmother halmŏni
할머니
grandparents chobumo
조부모
grandson sonja 손자
granite hwagang-am 화강암
화강암
grant n (money) pojogŭm
보조금; (for university)
changhak-kkŭm 장학금
grape p'odo 포도
grapefruit kŭrep'ŭp'ŭrut'ŭ
그레이프프루트
graph top'yo 도표
graphics COMPUT kŭraep'ikssŭ
그래픽스
grasp 1 n (physical)
umk'yŏjapkki 움켜잡기;
(mental) ihaeryŏk 이해력
2 v/t (physically) umk'yŏjapta
움켜잡다
grass p'ul 풀
grasshopper mettugi 메뚜기
grate n (metal) soesalttae
쇠살대
grateful komapkke yŏginŭn
고맙게 여기는
gratitude kamsa 감사
grave n mudŏm 무덤
gravestone chagal 자갈
graveyard myoji 묘지
gravy yuktchŭp 육즙
gray adj hoesaegŭi 회색의

graze v/t arm etc kabyŏpkke
sŭch'ida 가볍게 스치다
greasy kirŭmkki manŭn
기름기 많은
great koengjanghi k'ŭn 굉장히
큰; (quantity) koengjanghi
manŭn 굉장히 많은; artist,
writer tae... 대...; infml (very
good) koengjanghi chŏun
굉장히 좋은
Great Britain Yŏngguk 영국
greatly koengjanghi 굉장히
greed yoksshim 욕심
greedy yoksshim manŭn 욕심
많은
green nokssaegŭi 녹색의
greenhouse gas
isanhwat'anso 이산화탄소
greet insahada 인사하다
greeting insa 인사
gridlock (traffic) kyot'ongmang
chŏngch'e 교통망 정체
grief pit'ong 비통
grieve pit'onghaehada
비통해하다
grim look ŏmhan 엄한;
prospect naenghok'an 냉혹한
grin 1 n shinggŭt usŭm 싱긋
웃음 **2** v/i shinggŭt ut-tta
싱긋 웃다
grind v/t meat etc kalda 갈다
grip 1 n (on rope etc) kkwak
chabŭm 꽉 잡음 **2** v/t kkwak
chapta 꽉 잡다
groan v/i shinŭmhada
신음하다

grocery store shingnyo chap'wajŏm 식료 잡화점

gross adj (coarse) sangsŭrŏun 상스러운; FIN ch'onggye 총계

ground 1 n ttang 땅; (reason) kŭn-gŏ 근거; ELEC chŏptchi 접지 **2** v/t ELEC chŏptchihada 접지하다

ground meat kan kogi 간 고기

groundwork kich'o chagŏp 기초 작업

group n muri 무리

grow 1 v/i charada 자라다; (of amount) k'ŏjida 커지다; (of business) sŏngjanghada 성장하다; ~ tired p'igonhaejida 피곤해지다 **2** v/t flowers kirŭda 기르다

♦ **grow up** charanada 자라나다

growl v/i ŭrŭrŏnggŏrida 으르렁거리다

grown-up n ŏrŭn 어른

growth sŏngjang 성장; (increase) chŭngga 증가; MED chongyang 종양

grubby tŏrŏun 더러운

grumble v/i t'udŏlgŏrida 투덜거리다

grunt v/i (of pig) kkulkkulgŏrida 꿀꿀거리다; (of person) kŏch'ilge shinŭmhada 거칠게 신음하다

guarantee 1 n pojŭng 보증 **2** v/t pojŭnghada 보증하다

guarantor pojŭng-in 보증인

guard 1 n (security ~) kyŏngbiwŏn 경비원; MIL poch'o 보초; (in prison) kyodogwan 교도관 **2** v/t chik'ida 지키다

guardian JUR hugyŏnin 후견인

guerrilla kerilla 게릴라

guess 1 n ch'uch'ŭk 추측 **2** v/t & v/i ch'uch'ŭk'ada 추측하다

guesswork ŏrimjimjak 어림짐작

guest sonnim 손님

guidance annae 안내

guide 1 n annaeja 안내자; (book) annaesŏ 안내서 **2** v/t annaehada 안내하다

guided tour kaidŭ t'uŏ 가이드 투어

guidelines chich'im 지침

guilt JUR yujoe 유죄; (feeling) choech'aek-kkam 죄책감

guilty JUR yujoeŭi 유죄의; (responsible) choe chiŭn 죄 지은

guinea pig morŭmot'ŭ 모르모트; fig shirhŏm chaeryo 실험 재료

guitar kit'a 기타

gulf man 만

gum (in mouth) inmom 잇몸; (glue) chŏmsŏng komu 점성 고무; (to chew) kkŏm 껌

gun ch'ong 총

gunman ch'onggi hyudaeja
총기 휴대자; *(robber)*
mujang kangdo 무장 강도

gust *n* tolp'ung 돌풍

gutter *(in street)* torang 도랑;

(on roof) homt'ong 홈통

guy *infml* namja 남자

gym ch'eyuk-kkwan 체육관

gynecologist sanbuinkkwa
ŭisa 산부인과 의사

H

habit sŭpkkwan 습관

habitat sŏshiktchi 서식지

hacker COMPUT haek'ŏ 해커

haddock haedŏk 해덕

haggle kkaktta 깎다

hair t'ŏl 털; *(on head)* mŏri
머리; *(single human ~)*
mŏrak'arak 머리카락

hairbrush mŏri sol 머리 솔

haircut: *have a ~* mŏrirŭl
charŭda 머리를 자르다

hairdresser miyongsa 미용사

hairdrier, hairdryer hedŭdŭraiŏ
헤어드라이어

hair remover chemoyong'um
제모용품

hairstyle mŏrihyŏng 머리형

half *n* pan 반; *~ (past) ten*
yŏlshi pan 열시 반; *~ an
hour* pan shigan 반 시간

half time *n* SPORTS chunggan
hyushik 중간 휴식

halfway *adv* chunggane
중간에

hall hol 홀; *(hallway in house)*
pokto 복도

halo wŏn-gwang 원광

halt 1 *v/i* mŏmch'uda 멈추다
2 *v/t* mŏmch'ugehada
멈추게하다

halve *v/t* panŭro hada 반으로
하다

ham haem 햄

hamburger haembŏgŏ 햄버거

hammer *n* mangch'i 망치

hamper *v/t (obstruct)*
panghaehada 방해하다

hamster haemsŭt'ŏ 햄스터

hand *n* son 손; *(of clock)*
shigye panŭl 시계 바늘; *on
the one ~ ..., on the other
~* hanp'yŏnŭronŭn ..., tarŭn
hanp'yŏnŭronŭn 한편으로는
..., 다른 한편으로는

♦ **hand over** kŏnnejuda
건네주다; *(to authorities)*
nŏmgyŏjuda 넘겨주다

hand baggage suhwamul
수화물

handcuffs sugap 수갑

handicap *n* shinch'e chang-ae
신체 장애

handicapped *(physically)*
shinch'e chang-aeja innŭn

신체 장애가 있는
handkerchief sonsugŏn
손수건
handle 1 *n* sonjabi 손잡이
2 *v/t* taruda 다루다
handmade sugong-ŭi 수공의
handshake akssu 악수
handsome chal saenggin
잘 생긴
handwriting yukp'il 육필
handwritten sonŭro ssŭn
손으로 쓴
handy *device* p'yŏllihan
편리한
hang 1 *v/t picture* kŏlda 걸다;
person mok maedalda 목
매달다 **2** *v/i* (*of dress, hair*)
nŭrŏjida 늘어지다
♦ **hang up** *v/i* TEL chŏnhwarŭl
kkŭnt'a 전화를 끊다
hanger (*for clothes*) otkkŏri
옷걸이
hangover sukch'wi 숙취
haphazard magujabiŭi
마구잡이의
happen irŏnada 일어나다
happily haengbok'age
행복하게; (*luckily*) un chok'e
운 좋게
happiness haengbok 행복
happy haengbok'an 행복한
harass koerop'ida 괴롭히다
harassment koerop'im
괴롭힘; *sexual* ~ sŏnghŭirong
성희롱
harbor *n* hanggu 항구

hard tandanhan 단단한;
(*difficult*) ŏryŏun 어려운; *facts*
hwak-kkohan 확고한
hardback changbŏmbon
장정본
hard-boiled *egg* talgyal
wansuk 달걀 완숙
hard currency kyohwan
kanŭng t'onghwa 교환 가능
통화
hardliner kanggyŏngnonja
강경론자
hardly kŏŭi ...haji ant'a 거의
...하지 않다
hardship kollan 곤란
hardware ch'ŏlmul 철물;
COMPUT hadŭweŏ 하드웨어
hard-working yŏlsshimhi
irhanŭn 열심히 일하는
harm 1 *n* hae 해 **2** *v/t* haech'ida
해치다
harmful haeroun 해로운
harmless muhaehan 무해한
harmony hwasŏng 화성;
(*relationship etc*) chohwa 조화
harp hap'ŭ 하프
harsh *word* kahok'an 가혹한;
light kŏsŭllinŭn 거슬리는
harvest *n* ch'usu 추수
hash browns kamja t'wigim
감자 튀김
hasty kŭp'an 급한
hat moja 모자
hatchback haech'ibaek
해치백
hate 1 *n* mium 미움 **2** *v/t*

heartburn

miwŏhada 미워하다

haunting tune noerirŭl ttonaji
annŭn 뇌리를 떠나지 않는

have ◊ kajida 가지다; can
I ~ ...? (give me) ...ŭl / rŭl
chushigessŭmnikka? ...을 / 를
주시겠습니까?; do you
~ ...? ...i / ka issŭmnikka?
◊ breakfast, lunch mŏkta 먹다
◊: ~ to (must) ...haeya hada
...해야 하다 (causative):
~ sth done muŏsŭl hage hada
무엇을 하게 하다; I had
my hair cut nanŭn mŏrirŭl
challat-tta 나는 머리를
잘랐다

♦ **have on** (wear) iptta 입다;
(have planned) kyehoek'aet-tta
계획했다

hawk mae 매

hay fever kŏnch'oyŏl 건초열

hazard lights AUTO pisangdŭng
비상등

hazel (tree) kaeamnamu
개암나무

hazelnut kaeam 개암

hazy view, memory hŭrin 흐린

he kŭ 그; ~'s American kŭnŭn
Miguk saramiyeyo 그는 미국
사람이에요 ◊ (omission):
who is ~? nuguyeyo?
누구예요?

head 1 n mŏri 머리; (boss,
leader) udumŏri 우두머리; (of
line) sŏndu 선두 **2** v/t (lead)
ikkŭlda 이끌다

headache tut'ong 두통

headhunter COMM injae
sŭk'aut'ŭ tamdangja 인재
스카우트 담당자

heading (in list) p'yoje 표제

headlight hedŭrait'ŭ
헤드라이트

headline mŏritkkisa 머릿기사

head office ponsa 본사

headphones hedŭp'on
헤드폰

headquarters ponbu 본부

heal 1 v/t natkke hada 낫게
하다 **2** v/i nat-tta 낫다

health kŏn-gang 건강

health food store kŏn-gang
shikp'umjŏm 건강 식품점

health insurance kŏn-gang
pohŏm 건강 보험

health resort poyangji 보양지

healthy kŏn-ganghan 건강한;
lifestyle kŏn-gang-e chohŭn
건강에 좋은

heap n ssaa ollin tŏmi 쌓아
올린 더미

hear tŭt-tta 듣다

hearing ch'ŏngnyŏk 청력

hearing aid poch'ŏnggi
보청기

heart shimjang 심장; (of city)
haeksshimbu 핵심부; know
sth by ~ muŏsŭl oeugo it-tta
무엇을 외우고 있다

heart attack shimjang mabi
심장 마비

heartburn kasŭmari 가슴앓이

hearts (in cards) hat'ŭ 하트

heat n yŏl 열

heated debate kyŏk'an 격한;
~ pool onsu suyŏngjang 온수
수영장

heater hit'ŏ 히터

heating nanbang changch'i
난방 장치

heatwave yŏlp'a 열파

heaven ch'ŏnguk 천국

heavy mugŏun 무거운; rain
manŭn 많은; traffic shimhan
심한; food sohwaga chal
andoenŭn 소화가 잘 안되는;
loss shimgak'an 심각한

hectic mopssi pappŭn 몹시
바쁜

hedgehog kosŭmdoch'i
고슴도치

heel twikkumch'i 뒤꿈치; (of
shoe) twich'uk 뒤축

height nop'i 높이; (of person)
k'i 키; (of plane) kodo 고도;
(of season) chŏltchŏng 절정

heir sangsogin 상속인

heiress yŏja sangsogin 여자
상속인

helicopter hellik'opt'ŏ
헬리콥터

hell chiok 지옥

hello (polite, to older people)
annyŏnghashimnikka
안녕하십니까; (to friend,
younger people) annyŏng
안녕; TEL yŏboseyo
여보세요

helmet helmet 헬멧

help 1 n toum 도움 2 v/t
toptta 돕다; ~ oneself (to
food) maŭmkkŏt tŭlda 마음껏
들다; I can't ~ it ŏtchŏl su
ŏpssŏyo 어쩔 수 없어요

helpful toumi toenŭn 도움이
되는

helpless (unable to cope)
honjasŏ ŏtchŏl su ŏmnŭn
혼자서 어쩔 수 없는

hemisphere pan-gu 반구

hemorrhage n ch'urhyŏl 출혈

hepatitis kannyŏm 간염

her 1 adj kŭnyŏŭi 그녀의
2 pron kŭnyŏrŭl 그녀를

herb hŏbŭ 허브

herb tea hŏbŭ ch'a 허브 차

here yŏgie(sŏ) 여기에(서);
~ you are (giving) yŏgi
issŭmnida 여기 있습니다; ~
we are! (finding) yŏgi itkkuna!
여기 있구나!

hereditary yujŏndoenŭn
유전되는

heritage yusan 유산

hermit ŭndunja 은둔자

hero yŏng-ung 영웅

heroin heroin 헤로인

heroine yŏjangbu 여장부

herpes MED p'ojin 포진

herring ch'ŏng-ŏ 청어

hers kŭnyŏŭi kŏt 그녀의 것

herself kŭnyŏ chashin 그녀
자신

hesitate mangsŏrida 망설이다

hitman

hesitation mangsŏrim 망설임

heterosexual *adj* isŏng-aeŭi 이성애의

hi annyŏng 안녕

hiccup *n* ttalkkukttchil 딸꾹질

hide 1 *v/t* sumgida 숨기다 2 *v/i* sumtta 숨다

hideaway ŭnshinch'ŏ 은신처

hiding place sumnŭn kot 숨는 곳

hierarchy kyegŭp chojik 계급 조직

high 1 *adj* nop'ŭn 높은 2 *n* AUTO koso kiŏ 고속 기어

high jump nop'i ttwigi 높이 뛰기

high-level kowi kogwanŭi 고위 고관의

highlight 1 *n* hailait'ŭ 하이라이트 2 *v/t* (with pen) kangjohada 강조하다; COMPUT pŭllogŭl ssŭiuda 블록을 씌우다

highlighter *(pen)* hyŏnggwangp'en 형광펜

highly *likely* k'ŭge 크게; *be ~ paid* nop'ŭn ponggŭbŭl pat-tta 높은 봉급을 받다

high point chŏltchŏng 절정

high school kodŭnghak-kkyo 고등학교

high society sangnyu sahoe 상류 사회

high-speed train kosok yŏlch'a 고속 열차

high tech *adj* ch'ŏmdan kisurŭi

첨단 기술의

highway kosokttoro 고속도로

hijack *v/t plane* kongjung napch'ihada 공중 납치하다

hijacker *(of plane)* kongjung napch'ibŏm 공중 납치범

hike *n* toboyŏhaeng 도보여행

hilarious usŭmŭl chaanaenŭn 웃음을 자아내는

hill ŏndŏk 언덕; *(slope)* samyŏn 사면

hilly kurŭngjidaeŭi 구릉지대의

him kŭrŭl 그를

himself kŭ chashin 그 자신

hinder panghaehada 방해하다

hint *n* hint'ŭ 힌트

hip kungdungi 궁둥이

hippopotamus hama 하마

his 1 *adj* kŭŭi 그의 2 *pron* kŭŭi kŏt 그의 것

historian sahaktcha 사학자

historic yŏkssasang-ŭro chungyohan 역사상으로 중요한

historical yŏkssajŏgin 역사적인

history yŏkssa 역사

hit 1 *v/t* ch'ida 치다; *(collide with)* ch'ungdorhada 충돌하다 2 *n (blow)* t'agyŏk 타격; MUS hit'ŭ 히트; *(success)* sŏnggong 성공

hitchhike p'yŏnsŭnghada 편승하다

hitman ch'ŏngbu sarinja 청부 살인자

HIV Inch'e Myŏnyŏk Kyŏlp'ip Pairŏsŭ 인체 면역 결핍 바이러스

HIV-positive Eijŭ yangsŏng panŭng 에이즈 양성 반응

hoarse mŏksshwin 목쉰

hoax *n* sogimsu 속임수

hobby ch'wimi 취미

hog *n* (*pig*) twaeji 돼지

hold 1 *v/t* (*in hands*) chaptta 잡다; (*support, in place*) chit'aenghada 지탱하다; (*passport, job*) kajida 가지다; (*prisoner*) puttchaptta 붙잡다; (*contain*) tamtta 담다; *the line* TEL kkŭntchimalgo kidariseyo 끊지말고 기다리세요 **2** *n* (*in plane etc*) hwamulsshil 화물실; *catch ~ of sth* muŏsŭl chaptta 무엇을 잡다

holdup (*robbery*) kangdo 강도; (*delay*) chich'e 지체

hole kumŏng 구멍

holiday (*single day*) hyuil 휴일; *Br* (*period*) hyuga 휴가

hollow sogi pin 속이 빈

holy sŏngsŭrŏun 성스러운

home 1 *n* kajŏng 가정; (*native country*) koguk 고국; (*town, region*) kohyang 고향; (*for old people*) yangnowŏn 양로원; *at ~* (*in my house*) nae chibe 내 집에; (*in my country*) nae koguge 내 고국에 **2** *adv* chibe 집에; (*in own country*)

koguge 고국에; (*in own town, part of country*) kohyang-e 고향에; *go ~* chibe kada 집에 가다; (*to own country*) koguge kada 고국에 가다; (*to town, region*) kohyang-e kada 고향에 가다

homeless *adj* chibŏmnŭn 집없는

homemade chibesŏ mandŭn 집에서 만든

homeopathy tongjongnyoppŏp 동종요법

home page homp'eiji 홈페이지

homesick *be ~* hyangsuppyŏng-ŭl alt'a 향수병을 앓다

home town kohyang 고향

homework SCHOOL suktche 숙제

homicide sarin 살인

homosexual *n* tongsŏng-aeja 동성애자

honest chŏngjik'an 정직한

honesty chŏngjik 정직

honeymoon *n* shinhon yŏhaeng 신혼 여행

honor 1 *n* myŏng-ye 명예 **2** *v/t* yeuhada 예우하다

honorable *person* torirŭl anŭn 도리를 아는

hood (*on head*) ose tallin moja 옷에 달린 모자

hook kalgori 갈고리; (*clothes*) kori 고리; (*fishing*)

naksshippanŭl 낚시바늘
hooky: *play ~* mudan
kyŏlssŏk'ada 무단 결석하다
hooligan pullyangbae 불량배
hope 1 *n* hŭimang 희망
2 *v/i* parada 바라다 3 *v/t:*
~ you like it maŭme tŭlmyŏn
chok'essŏyo 마음에 들면
좋겠어요
hopeful hŭimang-e ch'an
희망에 찬; *(promising)*
kamang-innŭn 가망있는
hopefully *say* kidaehamyŏ
기대하며; *(I / we hope)*
paraginde 바라건데
hopeless *position* hŭimang-ŭl
irŭn 희망을 잃은; *(useless:*
person) kamang ŏmnŭn 가망
없는
horizon chip'yŏngsŏn 지평선;
(at sea) sup'yŏngsŏn 수평선
horizontal sup'yŏng-ŭi 수평의
hormone horŭmon 호르몬
horoscope chŏmsŏngsul
점성술
horrible chidok'an 지독한
horrify: *I was horrified*
ch'unggyŏktch'ŏgiŏssŏyo
충격적이었어요
horrifying *experience*
kkŭmtchik'an 끔찍한
horror kongp'o 공포
horse mal 말
horsepower maryŏk 마력
horse race kyŏngma 경마
horticulture wŏnye 원예

hose hosŭ 호스
hospice yoyangso 요양소
hospitable hwandaehanŭn
환대하는
hospital pyŏng-wŏn 병원
hospitality hwandae 환대
host *n (at party)* chuin 주인;
(of TV show) sahoeja 사회자
hostage injil 인질
hostel *(youth ~)* yusŭhosŭt'el
유스호스텔
hostess *(at party)* antchuin
안주인; *(air ~)* sŭt'yuŏdisŭ
스튜어디스
hostility chŏkttaeshim
적대심
hot *water* ttŭgŏun 뜨거운;
weather tŏun 더운; *(spicy)*
maeun 매운
hot dog hattogŭ 핫도그
hotel hot'el 호텔
hour shigan 시간
house *n* chip 집; *at your ~*
nŏŭi chibesŏ 너의 집에서
housekeeper kajŏngbu
가정부
House of Representatives
Hawŏn 하원
housewife chubu 주부
housework chiban il 집안 일
how ŏttŏk'e 어떻게; *~*
are you? annyŏnghaseyo?
안녕하세요?; *~ about*
...? ...hanŭn kŏshi
ŏttŏgessŭmnikka? ...하는
것이 어떻겠습니까?; *~*

much? ŏlmank'ŭm? 얼만큼?;
~ many? ŏlmana mani? 얼마나 많이?; **~ often?** ŏlmana chaju? 얼마나 자주?

however kŭrŏna 그러나; **~ big they are** amuri k'ŭda hadŏrado 아무리 크다 하더라도

howl v/i ulbujit-tta 울부짖다

hug v/t antta 안다

huge kŏdaehan 거대한

human 1 n in-gan 인간 **2** adj in-ganjŏgin 인간적인

human being in-gan 인간

humane injŏng-innŭn 인정있는

humanitarian indojuŭiŭi 인도주의의

human resources insakkwa 인사과

humble kyŏmsonhan 겸손한; **origin** ch'ŏnhan 천한; **home** ch'orahan 초라한

humid sŭp'an 습한

humidity sŭpkki 습기

humiliate kuryogŭl chuda 굴욕을 주다

humor haehak 해학; (mood) kibun 기분

hunch (idea) yegam 예감

hundred paek 백

hunger paego'ŭm 배고픔

hungry paego'ŭn 배고픈; **I'm ~** paega kop'ayo 배가 고파요

hunt 1 n sanyang 사냥; (for criminal, missing child) susaek 수색 **2** v/t animal sanyanghada 사냥하다

hurricane t'aep'ung 태풍

hurry 1 n sŏdurŭm 서두름; **be in a ~** sŏdullŏ hada 서둘러 하다 **2** v/i sŏdurŭda 서두르다

♦ **hurry up** sŏdurŭda 서두르다; **~!** sŏdurŭseyo! 서두르세요!

hurt 1 v/i ap'ŭda 아프다 **2** v/t tach'ige hada 다치게 하다

husband namp'yŏn 남편

♦ **hush up** shwishwihaebŏrida 쉬쉬해버리다

hut odumak 오두막

hydraulic (water) suabŭi 수압의; (oil) yuabŭi 유압의

hydroelectric suryŏk chŏn-giŭi 수력 전기의

hygiene wisaeng 위생

hygienic wisaengsang-ŭi 위생상의

hymn sŏngga 성가

hyphen iŭmp'yo 이음표

hypochondriac n uultchŭng hwanja 우울증 환자

hypocrite wisŏnja 위선자

hypothermia chŏch'eontchŭng 저체온증

hysterical hisŭt'erisŏng-ŭi 히스테리성의; (very funny) ŏmch'ŏngnage usŭun 엄청나게 우스운

I

I ◊ na 나; H chŏ 저
◊ (omission): ~ **can't see** pol
su ŏpssŏyo 볼 수 없어요
ice ŏrŭm 얼음
icebox aisŭ pakssŭ 아이스
박스
ice cream aisŭ k'ŭrim 아이스
크림
icon (cultural) sang 상; COMPUT
aik'on 아이콘
icy road ŏrŭmi ŏrŭn 얼음이
얼은
idea saenggak 생각
ideal isangjŏgin 이상적인
identical tong-irhan 동일한
identification hwagin 확인;
(papers) chŭngmyŏngsŏ
증명서
identify hwaginhada 확인하다
identity card shinbun
chŭngmyŏngsŏ 신분 증명서
ideology ideollogi 이데올로기
idiot pabo 바보
idle adj person nat'aehan
나태한
idolize sungbaehada 숭배하다
if manyak ...myŏn 만약 ···면;
~ **you catch a cold** manyak
kamgie kŏllimyŏn 만약
감기에 걸리면
ignition AUTO chŏmhwa
changch'i 점화 장치; ~ **key**

igŭnishyŏn k'i 이그니션 키
ignorance muji 무지
ignore mushihada 무시하다
ill ap'ŭn 아픈; **be taken** ~
pyŏngdŭlda 병들다
illegal pulppŏbŭi 불법의
illegible ilkki ŏryŏun 읽기
어려운
illiterate munmaeng-ŭi 문맹의
illness pyŏng 병
illogical pinollijŏgin
비논리적인
illusion hwanyŏng 환영
illustration kŭrim 그림
image (of politician, company)
insang 인상
imaginary kasang-ŭi 가상의
imagination sangsang 상상
imaginative sangsangnyŏgi
p'ungbuhan 상상력이
풍부한
imagine sangsanghada
상상하다
imitate mobanghada 모방하다
imitation mobang 모방;
(something copied) mojop'um
모조품
immature misŏngsugŭi
미성숙의
immediate chŭksshiŭi 즉시의
immediately chŭkssiro
즉시로

immigrant *n* ijuja 이주자

immigration iju 이주

immoral pudodŏk'an 부도덕한

immortal pulmyŏrŭi 불멸의

immunity myŏnyŏk 면역; *diplomatic ~* oegyomyŏnch'aek 외교면책

impact *n (of vehicle)* ch'ungdol 충돌; *(effect)* yŏnghyang 영향

impartial kongjŏnghan 공정한

impassable t'onghaenghal su ŏmnŭn 통행할 수 없는

impatient sŏnggŭp'an 성급한

impediment *(in speech)* tŏdŭmgŏrim 더듬거림

imperial chegugŭi 제국의

impersonal piin-ganjŏgin 비인간적인

impetuous ch'ungdongjŏgin 충동적인

implement 1 *n* togu 도구 2 *v/t* shirhaenghada 실행하다

implicate: *~ sb in sth* nugurŭl muŏse yŏllu shik'ida 누구를 무엇에 연루 시키다

implication hamch'uk 함축

imply amshihada 암시하다

import 1 *n* suip 수입 2 *v/t* suip'ada 수입하다

importance chungnyosŏng 중요성

important chungnyohan 중요한

impossible pulganŭnghan 불가능한

impoverished pin-gone 빈곤에 tchidŭn 빈곤에 찌든

impression nŭkkim 느낌; *(impersonation)* hyungnaenaegi 흉내내기

impressive insangjŏgin 인상적인

imprison t'uok'ada 투옥하다

improve 1 *v/t* hyangsangshik'ida 향상시키다 2 *v/i* hyangsanghada 향상하다

improvement hyangsang 향상

impudent ppŏnppŏnsŭrŏun 뻔뻔스러운

impulsive ch'ungdongjŏgin 충동적인

in 1 *prep* …e(sŏ) …에 (서) ◊: *~ 1999* 1999nyŏne 1999년에; *~ two hours (from now)* tu shigan ane 두 시간 안에; *~ August* p'arwŏre 팔월에 ◊ ~ *English* Yŏng-ŏro 영어로; *one ~ ten* yŏl kae chung han kae 열 개 중 한 개 2 *adv*: *be ~ (at home, in building etc)* ane it-tta 안에 있다 3 *adj (fashionable)* yuhaenghanŭn 유행하는

inability munŭng 무능

inaccessible chŏpkŭnhagi ŏryŏun 접근하기 어려운

inadequate pujŏktanghan 부적당한

inappropriate pujŏktanghan 부적당한

indiscriminate

inaugural ch'wiimŭi 취임의
incentive tonggi 동기
incessant kkŭnimŏmnŭn 끊임없는
inch n inch'i 인치
incident sakkŏn 사건
incidentally mari nan-gime 말이 난김에
incite kyŏngnyŏhada 격려하다
incline: *be ~d to do sth* muŏsŭl hanŭn kyŏnghyang-i it-tta 무엇을 하는 경향이 있다
include p'ohamhada 포함하다
including prep …ŭl / rŭl p'ohamhayŏ …을 / 를 포함하여
inclusive 1 adj price p'ohamhan 포함한 2 prep p'ohamhayŏ 포함하여
incoherent tusŏŏmnŭn 두서없는
income sodŭk 소득
income tax sodŭkse 소득세
incoming flight toch'ak'anŭn 도착하는; president huiimŭi 후임의
incompatible people yangnip'al su ŏmnŭn 양립할 수 없는; systems hohwandoeji annŭn 호환되지 않는
incompetent munŭngnyŏk'an 무능력한
incomprehensible ihaehal su ŏmnŭn 이해할 수 없는

inconsiderate saryŏmnŭn 사려없는
inconsistent mosundoenŭn 모순되는
inconvenient pulp'yŏnhan 불편한
incorrect t'ŭllin 틀린
increase 1 v/t chŭnggasik'ida 증가시키다 2 v/i chŭnggahada 증가하다
incredible (good) midŏjiji annŭn 믿어지지 않는
incurable pulch'iŭi 불치의
indecisive kyŏlttanssŏng-i ŏmnŭn 결단성이 없는
indeed (in fact) chinsillo 진실로
indefinitely mugihanŭro 무기한으로
independence tongnip 독립
Independence Day Tongnip Kinyŏmil 독립 기념일
independent tongniptchŏgin 독립적인
India Indo 인도
indicate v/t karik'ida 가리키다
indifferent mugwanshimhan 무관심한
indigestion sohwa pullyang 소화 불량
indignant pun-gaehan 분개한
indirect kanjŏptchŏgin 간접적인
indiscriminate much'abyŏrŭi 무차별의

indispensable p'ilssuùi
필수의

indistinct tturyŏt'aji anûn
뚜렷하지 않은

individual 1 *n* kaein 개인 **2** *adj*
kaegaeûi 개개의; *(personal)*
kaeinûi 개인의

individually kaebyŏltchŏguro
개별적으로

indoor shillaeûi 실내의

indoors shillaee(sŏ)
실내에(서)

industrial sanŏbûi 산업의

industrial action nodong
chaeng-ûi haeng-wi 노동
쟁의 행위

industrial waste
sanŏpp'yegimul 산업폐기물

industry sanŏp 산업

inefficient pinûngnyultchŏgin
비능률적인

inequality pulp'yŏngdûng
불평등

inevitable p'ihal su ŏmnûn
피할 수 없는

inexpensive kapsshi ssan
값이 싼

inexperienced kyŏnghŏmi
ŏmnûn 경험이 없는

infamous angmyŏng nop'ûn
악명 높은

infant yua 유아

infantry pobyŏngdae 보병대

infatuated: *be ~ with sb*
nuguege holttak panhada
누구에게 홀딱 반하다

infected kamyŏmdoen 감염된

infection kamyŏm 감염

infectious chŏnyŏmssŏng-ûi
전염성의; *laugh* omgyŏjigi
shwiun 옮겨지기 쉬운

inferior *quality* iryuûi 이류의

inferiority complex yŏlttûng
ûishik 열등 의식

infidelity pujŏng 부정

infiltrate *v/t* ch'imip'ada
침입하다

infinite muhanhan 무한한

infinity muhan 무한

inflammable inhwassŏng-ûi
인화성의

inflammation MED yŏmtchûng
염증

inflation inp'ûlle(ishyŏn)
인플레(이션)

inflexible kup'il su ŏmnûn
굽힐 수 없는

influence 1 *n* yŏnghyang 영향
2 *v/t* yŏnghyang kkich'ida
영향 끼치다; *decision*
yŏnghyang chuda 영향 주다

influential yŏnghyangnyŏk
innûn 영향력 있는

influenza tok-kkam 독감

inform *v/t* allida 알리다

informal *meeting* pigongshigûi
비공식의; *dress*
p'yŏngsangbok ch'arimûi
평상복 차림의

information chŏngbo 정보

informer milgoja 밀고자

infuriating kyŏngnok'e hanŭn
격노케 하는

ingenious tokch'angjŏgin
독창적인

ingredient chaeryo 재료; *fig*
yoso 요소

inhabit kŏjuhada 거주하다

inhabitant kŏjuja 거주자

inhale 1 *v/t* pparadŭrida
빨아들이다 **2** *v/i (smoking)*
hŭbip'ada 흡입하다

inhaler hŭbipkki 흡입기

inherit sangsok'ada 상속하다

inhibition ŏktche 억제

in-house *adv work* sanaee(sŏ)
사내에(서)

inhuman injŏng ŏmnŭn 인정
없는

initial 1 *adj* ch'oech'oŭi
최초의 **2** *n* inishyŏl 이니셜

initiate kaeshihada 개시하다

initiative chudo 주도

inject MED chusahada
주사하다; *capital* t'uip'ada
투입하다

injured 1 *adj leg, feelings*
sangch'ŏ ibŭn 상처 입은
2 *n: the ~* pusangja 부상자

injury pusang 부상

ink ingk'ŭ 잉크

in-laws inch'ŏk 인척

inmate (*prison*) sugamja
수감자

inn yŏgwan 여관

inner naebuŭi 내부의

innocence (*of child*) sunjinham
순진함; JUR kyŏlbaek 결백

innocent sunjinhan 순진한;
JUR kyŏlbaek'an 결백한

innovative hyŏksshinjŏgin
혁신적인

in-patient ibwŏnhwanja
입원환자

input 1 *n (to project)* t'uip
투입; COMPUT imnyŏk 입력
2 *v/t* t'uip'ada 투입하다;
COMPUT imnyŏk'ada 입력하다

inquest wŏnin kyumyŏng
원인 규명

inquire munŭihada 문의하다

inquiry munŭi 문의

inquisitive t'amgujŏgin
탐구적인

insane mich'in 미친

insanity chŏngshin isang 정신
이상

inscription (*in book*) chemyŏng
제명

insect konch'ung 곤충

insecticide salch'ungje
살충제

insect repellent pangch'ungje
방충제

insecure puranhan 불안한

insensitive mugamgak'an
무감각한

insert *v/t* kkiwŏ nŏt'a 끼워
넣다

inside 1 *n* naebu 내부; **~ out**
twijibŏsŏ 뒤집어서 **2** *prep*
ane(sŏ) 안에(서); **~ of 2**

hours tushigan inae 두시간 이내 3 *adv stay* naebue(sŏ) 내부에 (서); *go, carry* anŭro 안으로 4 *adj* naebue innŭn 내부에 있는; ~ *information* naebu chŏngbo 내부 정보

insider naebuin 내부인

insides wijang 위장

insight t'ongch'al 통찰

insist chujanghada 주장하다

insistent chibyohan 집요한

insomnia pulmyŏntchŭng 불면증

inspect *work, baggage* chŏmgŏmhada 점검하다; *factory, school* shich'arhada 시찰하다

inspiration yŏnggam 영감

inspire *respect* pullŏ irŭk'ida 불러 일으키다; *be ~d by sb / sth* nuguege / muŏse yŏnggamŭl pat-tta 누구에게 / 무엇에 영감을 받다

instability puranjŏng 불안정

install sŏlch'ihada 설치하다

installment *(of story)* (yŏnjaeŭi) il hoebun (연재의) 일 회분; FIN punhal purip 분할 불입

instant 1 *adj* chŭk-kkaktchŏgin 즉각적인 2 *n* sun-gan 순간

instantaneous sunshik-kkanŭi 순식간의

instant coffee insŭt'ŏnt'ŭ k'ŏp'i 인스턴트 커피

instantly chŭksshi 즉시

instead taeshine 대신에; ~ *of* … taeshine … 대신에

instinct ponnŭng 본능

instinctive ponnŭngjŏgin 본능적인

institute *n* yŏn-guso 연구소; *(special home)* konggong kigwan 공공 기관

institution *(governmental)* kigwan 기관; *(sth traditional)* kwansŭp 관습

instruct *(order)* chishihada 지시하다; *(teach)* karŭch'ida 가르치다

instruction chishi sahang 지시 사항

instrument MUS ak-kki 악기; *(tool)* togu 도구

insulation ELEC chŏryŏn 절연; *(against cold)* panghan 방한

insulin inshyullin 인슐린

insult 1 *n* moyok 모욕 2 *v/t* moyok'ada 모욕하다

insurance pohŏm 보험

insurance company pohŏm hoesa 보험 회사

insurance policy pohŏm chŭngsŏ 보험 증서

insure pohŏme tŭlda 보험에 들다

intact *(whole)* sonsangdoeji anŭn 손상되지 않은

integrity *(of person)* chŏngjik 정직

intellectual 1 *adj* chitchŏgin

지적인 2 *n* chisŏng-in 지성인

intelligence chinŭng 지능;
(news) chŏngbo 정보

intelligent ttokttok'an 똑똑한

intend *(plan)* ...hal
chaktchŏng-ida …할
작정이다; ~ to do sth (do
on purpose) muŏsŭl ŭidohada
무엇을 의도하다

intense *pleasure* kangnyŏrhan
강렬한; *heat* kangnyŏk'an
강력한; *concentration*
kanghan 강한

intensive chiptchungjŏgin
집중적인

intensive care
chunghwanjashil 중환자실

intention ŭido 의도

intentional ŭidojŏgin
의도적인

interactive sangho
chagyonghanŭn 상호
작용하는

intercept *ball* karoch'aeda
가로채다; *message* yŏt-tŭt-tta
엿듣다; *missile* yogyŏk'ada
요격하다

intercom int'ŏk'ŏm 인터컴

intercourse sŏnggyo 성교

interest 1 *n* kwanshim 관심;
FIN ija 이자 2 *v/t* hŭngmirŭl
irŭk'ige hada 흥미를
일으키게 하다

interesting chaemiinnŭn
재미있는

interfere kansŏp'ada 간섭하다

♦ interfere with *plans*
panghaehada 방해하다

interference kansŏp 간섭;
RADIO honsŏn 혼선

interior 1 *adj* shillaeŭi 실내의
2 *n (of house)* shillae 실내

intermediary *n* chungjaeja
중재자

intermediate *adj* chungganŭi
중간의

internal naebuŭi 내부의

international *adj* kuktchejŏgin
국제적인

Internet Int'ŏnet 인터넷

interpret 1 *v/t* t'ongyŏk'ada
통역하다; *comment etc*
haesŏk'ada 해석하다 2 *v/i*
t'ongyŏk'ada 통역하다

interpretation t'ongyŏk 통역;
(of meaning) haesŏk 해석

interpreter t'ongyŏk-kka
통역가

interrogate shimmunhada
심문하다

interrupt 1 *v/t*
chungdanshik'ida 중단시키다
2 *v/i* chungdanhada 중단하다

interruption chungdan 중단

intersection kyoch'a 교차

interstate *n* chugan kosok toro
주간 고속 도로

interval shigan kan-gyŏk 시간
간격; *(in theater)* hyuge shigan
휴게 시간

intervene *(of police etc)*
chungjaehada 중재하다

interview 1 *n (on TV)*
int'ŏbyu 인터뷰; *(for job)*
myŏnjŏp 면접 2 *n (on TV)*
int'ŏbyuhada 인터뷰하다;
(for job) myŏnjŏp'ada
면접하다

intimacy ch'insuk'am 친숙함;
(sexual) kip'ŭn sai 깊은 사이

intimidate hyŏp-ppak'ada
협박하다

into anŭro 안으로; *translate ~
English* Yŏng-ŏro pŏnyŏk'ada
영어로 번역하다; *be ~ sth
infml (like)* muŏsŭl choahada
무엇을 좋아하다; *(be
interested in)* muŏse kwanshimi
it-tta 무엇에 관심이 있다

intolerable ch'amŭl su ŏmnŭn
참을 수 없는

intolerant ch'amŭlssŏng
ŏmnŭn 참을성 없는

intricate twiŏlk'in 뒤얽힌

intriguing hogishimŭl
chagŭk'anŭn 호기심을
자극하는

introduce sogaehada
소개하다

introduction *(to person, new
food, sport etc)* sogae 소개;
(in book) sŏron 서론; *(of new
techniques)* toip 도입

intruder ch'imiptcha 침입자

invade ch'imnyak'ada
침략하다

invalid *n* MED pyŏngjamuhyoŭi
병자무효의

invaluable *help* kapssŭl hearil
su ŏmnŭn 값을 헤아릴
수 없는

invasion ch'imnyak 침략

invent palmyŏnghada
발명하다

inventor palmyŏngga 발명가

invest 1 *v/t* t'ujadoeda
투자되다 2 *v/i* t'ujahada
투자하다

investigate chosahada
조사하다

investigation chosa 조사

investment t'uja 투자

invisible nune poiji annŭn 눈에
보이지 않는

invitation ch'odae 초대

invite ch'odaehada 초대하다

invoice *n* inboisŭ 인보이스

involve *work etc* subanhada
수반하다; *(concern)* kwan-
gyehada 관계하다

inwardly maŭmsogŭro
마음속으로

IQ aik'yu 아이큐

iron 1 *n* soe 쇠; *(for clothes)*
tarimi 다리미 2 *v/t*
tarimjirhada 다림질하다

ironic panŏjŏgin 반어적인

irony airŏni 아이러니

irrational purhamnihan
불합리한

irrelevant kwallyŏni ŏmnŭn
관련이 없는

irrespective: *~ of* …e kwan-
gyeŏpsshi …에 관계없이

irrigation kwan-gae 관개
irritable tchajŭng-ŭl chal
naenŭn 짜증을 잘 내는
irritate tchajŭngnage hada
짜증나게 하다
irritation ch'ajŭngnanŭn kŏt
짜증나는 것
Islam Isŭllamgyo 이슬람교
island sŏm 섬
isolate (socially) koripshik'ida
고립시키다; (separate)
pullihada 분리시키다
isolated house oettan 외딴;
occurrence ttaro 따로
issue 1 n (matter) chaengtchŏm
쟁점; (of magazine) ho 호
2 v/t passport palgŭp'ada
발급하다; supplies chigŭp'ada

지급하다
it ◊ (as subject) kŭgŏsŭn
그것은; (as object) kŭgŏsŭl
그것을 ◊ (not translated): ~'s
me chŏyeyo 저예요; that's ~!
(that's right) majayo! 맞아요!;
(I've finished) twaessŏyo!
됐어요!
italic it'aellikch'eŭi
이탤릭체의
Italy It'allia 이탈리아
itch 1 n karyŏum 가려움 **2** v/i
karyŏpta 가렵다
item hangmok 항목
itemize myŏngserŭl palk'ida
명세를 밝히다
its kŭgŏsŭi 그것의
itself kŭgŏt chach'e 그것 자체

J

jacket chaek'it 재킷
jade n pich'wi 비취
jail kyodoso 교도소
jam (on bread) chaem 잼
January irwŏl 일월
Japan Ilbon 일본
Japanese 1 adj Ilbonŭi
일본의 **2** n (person) Ilbon
saram 일본 사람; (language)
Ilbonŏ 일본어
jar n (container) tanji 단지
jaundice hwangdal 황달
jaw n t'ŏk 턱
jazz chaejŭ 재즈

jealous chilt'uhanŭn 질투하는
jeans ch'ŏngbaji 청바지
jellyfish haep'ari 해파리
jeopardize wit'aeropke hada
위태롭게 하다
jerk n (movement) kaptchagi
umjigim 갑자기 움직임
jet n chet'ŭgi 제트기; (of
water) punch'ul 분출
jetlag shich'aro inhan p'iro
시차로 인한 피로
Jew Yut'aein 유태인
jeweler posŏkssang 보석상
jewelry posŏngnyu 보석류

job chigŏp 직업; *(task)* il 일

jog v/i *(as exercise)* choginghada 조깅하다

join 1 v/i *(of roads etc)* hapch'yŏjida 합쳐지다; *(as member)* kaip'ada 가입하다 2 v/t *(connect)* yŏn-gyŏrhada 연결하다; *person* hamnyuhada 합류하다; *club* ip'oehada 입회하다

joint n ANAT kwanjŏl 관절; *(in woodwork)* chŏp'ap pubun 접합 부분

joint account kongdong yegŭm kyejwa 공동 예금 계좌

joint venture haptchak t'uja 합작 투자

joke n nongdam 농담; *(practical)* chittkkujŭn changnan 짓궂은 장난

jolt 1 n *(jerk)* tŏlk'ŏk-kkŏrim 덜컥거림 2 v/t *(push)* sege ch'ida 세게 치다

jostle v/t nanp'ok'age milda 난폭하게 밀다

journalism ŏllon 언론; *(profession)* ŏllon-gye 언론계

journalist kija 기자

journey n yŏhaeng 여행

joy kippŭm 기쁨

judge 1 n JUR p'ansa 판사; *(in competition)* simsa wiwŏn 심사 위원 2 v/t p'andanhada 판단하다

judgment JUR chaep'an 재판;

(opinion) p'andan 판단; *(good sense)* p'andannyŏk 판단력

judo yudo 유도

juice chusŭ 주스

July ch'irwŏl 칠월

jumble n twibŏmbŏk 뒤범벅

jump 1 n ttwiŏ orŭm 뛰어 오름; *(increase)* kŭpsangsŭng 급상승 2 v/i ttwiŏ orŭda 뛰어 오르다; *(in surprise)* p'ŏltchŏk ttwida 펄쩍 뛰다

jumpy shin-gyŏng kwaminŭi 신경 과민의

June yuwŏl 유월

junior adj ŏrin 어린; *(in rank)* sonaraeŭi 손아래의

junk *(garbage)* komul 고물

junk food chŏngk'ŭ p'udŭ 정크 푸드

junkie chungdoktcha 중독자

junk mail ssŭregi up'yŏnmul 쓰레기 우편물

juror paeshimwŏn 배심원

jury paeshimwŏndan 배심원단

just adv *(barely)* kyŏu 겨우; *(exactly)* mach'im 마침; *(only)* tanji 단지; ~ *about* mak kŭnyŏrŭl poassŏyo 막 그녀를 보았어요; *I've ~ seen her* mak kŭnyŏrŭl poassŏyo 막 그녀를 보았어요; ~ *about (almost)* kŏŭi 거의; ~ *now (a few moments ago)* panggŭm 방금; *(at the moment)* paro chigŭm 바로 지금

justice chŏng-ŭi 정의; *(of cause)* t'adang 타당

justify chōngdanghwahada 정당화하다

juvenile delinquent sonyōn pōmjoeja 소년 범죄자

K

karate k'arat'e 카라테

keep 1 v/t pogwanhada 보관하다; (not give back) chagi kōsūro hada 자기 것으로 하다; (store) kansuhada 간수하다; family puyanghada 부양하다; ~ a promise yakssogūl chik'ida 약속을 지키다; ~ trying kyesok noryōk'ada 계속 노력하다 ◊ (remain) ... itta ... 있다; (of food) ssōktchi ank'o kyōndida 썩지 않고 견디다

◆ **keep down** voice natch'uda 낮추다; cost chinjōngshik'ida 진정시키다; food padadūlida 받아들이다

◆ **keep up 1** v/i (when running etc) twijiji ank'o ttaragada 뒤지지 않고 따라가다 **2** v/t pace yujihada 유지하다; pants chit'aenghada 지탱하다

ketchup k'ech'ōp 케첩

kettle chujōnja 주전자

key 1 n yōlsoe 열쇠 키 키; COMPUT, (on piano) k'i 키; MUS cho 조 **2** adj (vital) maeu chunghyohan 매우 중요한 **3** v/t COMPUT k'irūl ch'ida

kick 1 n ch'agi 차기 **2** v/t & v/i ch'ada 차다

kid infml **1** n (child) ai 아이 **2** v/t nollida 놀리다 **3** v/i nongdamhada 농담하다

kidnap v/t napch'ihada 납치하다; child yugoehada 유괴하다

kidney shinjang 신장; (to eat) k'ongp'at 콩팥

kill v/t also time chugida 죽이다

kilogram k'illogūraem 킬로그램

kilometer k'illomit'ō 킬로미터

kind¹ adj ch'injōrhan 친절한

kind² n chongnyu 종류; what ~ of ...? ōttōn chongnyuūi ...? 어떤 종류의 ...?; ~ of sad infml ōnū chōngdo sūlp'ūda 어느 정도 슬프다

kindness ch'injōl 친절

king wang 왕

kiss 1 n k'isū 키스 **2** v/t & v/i

kit k'isŭhada 키스하다

kit changbi 장비; *(for assembly)* chorimnyongp'um 조립용품

kitchen puŏk 부억

kitten saekki koyang-i 새끼 고양이

knack yoryŏng 요령

knee n murŭp 무릎

kneel murŭp kkult'a 무릎 꿇다

knife n k'al 칼

knock 1 n *(at door)* mun tudŭrinŭn sori 문 두드리는 소리; *(blow)* t'agyŏk 타격 **2** v/t *(hit)* ch'ida 치다 **3** v/i *(at door)* nok'ŭhada 노크하다

♦ **knock down** *(of car)* ch'iŏ nŏmŏttŭrida 치어 넘어뜨리다; *building etc* hŏrŏ nŏmŏttŭrida 헐어 넘어뜨리다

♦ **knock out** *boxer etc* naga ttŏrŏjige hada 나가 떨어지게 하다

knot n maedŭp 매듭

know 1 v/t alda 알다; *language* ...e chŏngt'onghada ...에 정통하다; *(recognize)* araboda 알아보다 **2** v/i algo it-tta 알고 있다; *I don't ~* mollayo 몰라요

knowhow nohau 노하우

knowledge chishik 지식

Korea *(South)* Han-guk 한국; *(North)* Puk'an 북한

Korean 1 adj *(South)* Han-gugŭi 한국의; *(North)* Puk'anŭi 북한의 **2** n *(South)* Han-guk saram 한국 사람; *(North)* Puk'an saram 북한 사람; *(language)* Han-gugŏ 한국어

L

lab shirhŏmshil 실험실

label n kkorip'yo 꼬리표

labor n nodong 노동; *(giving birth)* punman 분만

lace n leisŭ 레이스; *(of shoe)* kkŭn 끈

lack 1 n pujok 부족 **2** v/t ...i / ga ŏptta ...이/가 없다 **3** v/i: *be ~ing* pujok'ada 부족하다

lacquerware ch'ilgi 칠기

ladder sadari 사다리

ladies' room yŏja hwajangshil 여자 화장실

lady sungnyŏ 숙녀

♦ **lag behind** twittŏrŏjida 뒤떨어지다

lake hosu 호수

lamb saekkiyang 새끼양; *(meat)* yanggogi 양고기

lame *person* chŏllŭmbariŭi 절름발이의

lamp tŭngppul 등불

land 1 n ttang ttŏ; *(shore)* yuktchi 육지; *(country)* nara 나라 2 v/i *(of plane)* ch'angnyuk'ada 착륙하다; *(of ball)* ttorŏjida 떨어지다

landing *(top of staircase)* ch'ŭnggyech'am 층계참

landlady *(of hostel)* yŏjuin 여주인

landlord *(of hostel)* chuin 주인

landmark yumyŏnghan kŏnch'ungmul 유명한 건축물

landscape n kyŏngch'i 경치

lane *(in country)* shigolkkil 시골길; *(alley)* chobŭn kil 좁은 길; AUTO ch'asŏn 차선

language ŏnŏ 언어

Laos Laosŭ 라오스

lap[1] *(of track)* han pak'wi 한 바퀴

lap[2] *(of person)* murŭp 무릎

laptop COMPUT laept'ap 랩탑

large k'ŭn 큰

largely *(mainly)* churo 주로

laryngitis huduyŏm 후두염

laser leijŏ 레이저

last[1] *adj (in series)* majimak 마지막; *(preceding)* chŏnbŏnŭi 전번의; **~ but one** majimagesŏ tu pŏntchae 마지막에서 두 번째; **~ night** ŏjetppam 어젯밤; **at ~** mach'imnae 마침내

last[2] v/i chisokttoeda 지속되다

lastly majimagŭro 마지막으로

late *(behind time)* nŭjŭn 늦은; *(at night)* pam nŭjŭn 밤 늦은

lately ch'oegŭne 최근에

later adv najung-e 나중에

latest *news* ch'oeshinŭi 최신의

Latin America Nammi 남미

latter hujaŭi 후자의

laugh 1 n usŭm 웃음 2 v/i ut-tta 웃다

♦ **laugh at** *(mock)* ...ŭl / rŭl piut-tta ...을 / 를 비웃다

laughter usŭm 웃음

launch 1 n *(boat)* chinsusŏn 진수선 n *(of rocket)* palsa 발사; *(of ship)* chinsu 진수; *(of product)* palmae 발매 2 v/t *rocket* palsahada 발사하다; *ship* chinsuhada 진수하다; *product* palmaehada 발매하다

launch pad palssadae 발사대

laundromat selp'ŭ set'akso 셀프 세탁소

laundry set'akso 세탁소; *(clothes)* set'angmul 세탁물

lavatory hwajangshil 화장실

law pŏp 법; *(subject)* pŏp'ak 법학

lawn chandi 잔디

lawsuit sosong 소송

lawyer pyŏnhosa 변호사

lay v/t *(put down)* not'a 놓다; *eggs* nat'a 낳다

layer n ch'ŭng 층

layout paech'i 배치

lazy *person* keŭrŭn 게으른; *day*

lead

hariŏmnŭn 하릴없는

lead¹ 1 *n race etc* sŏndue sŏda
선두에 서다; *team ikkŭlda*
이끌다; *(guide)* indohada
인도하다 2 *v/i (in race)*
sŏndue sŏda 선두에 서다;
(give leadership) t'ongsŏrhada
통솔하다

lead² *n (dog's)* kae chul 개 줄

lead³ *n (metal)* nap 납

leader chidoja 지도자

leadership chido 지도; ~
skills chidoryŏk 지도력

leading-edge *adj technology*
ch'ŏmdanŭi 첨단의

leaf ip 잎

leaflet chŏndan 전단

leak 1 *n saeŏ naom* 새어
나옴; *(of news)* nuch'ul 누출
2 *v/i* saeda 새다

lean¹ *v/i (at angle)* kidaeda
기대다; ~ *against*... ...
kidaeda ...에 기대다

lean² *adj meat* salk'ogiŭi
살코기의

leap 1 *n toyak* 도약 2 *v/i*
hultchŏk ttwida 훌쩍 뛰다

learn paeuda 배우다

learning *n (knowledge)* chishik
지식

lease 1 *n imdae* 임대 2 *v/t*
imdaehada 임대하다

least 1 *adv* kajang an 가장 안
2 *n: at* ~ chŏgodo 적어도

leather 1 *n kajuk* 가죽 2 *adj*
kajugŭi 가죽의

leave 1 *n (vacation)* hyuga
휴가; *on* ~ hyugarŭl ŏdŏ
휴가를 얻어 2 *v/t* ttŏnada
떠나다; *husband, wife* pŏrida
버리다; *(forget)* ijŏbŏrigo
잊어버리고 두고 kada 두고 가다; ~ *alone* (*not
touch*) kŭnyang kŭdaero tuda
그냥 그대로 두다; *(not
interfere with)* kansŏp'aji ant'a
간섭하지 않다; *be left*
namtta 남다 3 *v/i (of person)*
ttŏnada 떠나다; *(of plane, bus)*
ch'ulbarhada 출발하다

lecture *n kang-ŭi* 강의

lecturer kangsa 강사

ledge t'ŏk 턱

left 1 *adj* oentchogŭi 왼쪽의
2 *n* oentchok 왼쪽; POL chwaik
좌익; *on the* ~ oentchoge(sŏ)
왼쪽에(서) 3 *adv turn*
oentchogŭro 왼쪽으로

left-handed oensonjabi
왼손잡이

left-wing POL chwaik 좌익

leg tari 다리

legacy yusan 유산

legal hap-ppŏptchŏgin
합법적인; *(relating to the law)*
pŏptchŏgin 법적인

legality hap-ppŏp 합법

legalize hap-ppŏp'wahada
합법화하다

legend chŏnsŏl 전설

legible ilkki shwiun 읽기
쉬운

legislature ip-ppŏp-ppu 입법부

legitimate chŏkppŏbŭi 적법의

leisure yŏga 여가

lemon lemon 레몬

lemonade lemoneidŭ 레모네이드

lemon juice lemon chyussŭ 레몬 쥬스

lend: ~ sb sth nuguege muŏsŭl pillyŏjuda 누구에게 무엇을 빌려주다

length kiri 길이; at ~ explain kilge 길게; (eventually) mach'imnae 마침내

lengthen nŭllida 늘리다

lenient kwandaehan 관대한

lens lenjŭ 렌즈

leopard p'yobŏm 표범

less tŏl 덜; ~ interesting tŏl hŭngmiroun 덜 흥미로운; ~ than $200 200tallŏ miman 200달러 미만

lesson suŏp 수업

let v/t: ~ sb do sth nuga muŏt'age haejuda 누가 무엇을 해주다; ~ me go! noajwŏ! 놓아줘!; ~'s go kaja 가자; ~ go of sth muŏsŭl noa pŏrida 무엇을 놓아 버리다

lethal ch'imyŏngjŏgin 치명적인

letter (of alphabet) kŭltcha 글자; (in mail) p'yŏnji 편지

lettuce sangch'u 상추

leukemia paek'yŏlppyŏng 백혈병

level 1 adj surface p'yŏngp'yŏnghan 평평한; (in score) kat'ŭn sujunŭi 같은 수준의 2 n (on scale) sujun 수준; (quantity) yang 양

lever n chire 지레

liability insurance ch'aegim pohŏm 책임 보험

liable ch'aegimjyŏya hanŭn 책임져야 하는; be ~ to (likely) ...hanŭn kyŏnghyang-i it-tta …하는 경향이 있다

♦ liaise with yŏllagŭl ch'wihada 연락을 취하다

liar kŏjitmaljaeng-i 거짓말쟁이

liberal adj (broad-minded) maŭmi nŏlbŭn 마음이 넓은; POL chayujuŭiŭi 자유주의의

liberate haebangshik'ida 해방시키다

liberty chayu 자유

library tosŏgwan 도서관

license 1 n (for car) myŏnhŏtchŭng 면허증; (for export, TV, gun) hŏgatchŭng 허가증 2 v/t: be ~d (of car) myŏnhŏ pat-tta 면허 받다

license number tŭngnok pŏnho 등록 번호

license plate pŏnhop'an 번호판

lick v/t haltta 핥다

lid ttukkŏng 뚜껑

lie¹ 1 *n (untruth)* kŏjinmal 거짓말 **2** *v/i* kŏjinmarhada 거짓말하다

lie² *v/i (of person)* nuptta 눕다; *(of object)* it-tta 있다; *(be situated)* wich'ihada 위치하다

♦ **lie down** nuptta 눕다

life saengmyŏng 생명

life insurance saengmyŏng pohŏm 생명 보험

life jacket kumyŏng chokki 구명 조끼

life-threatening saengmyŏng-ŭl wihyŏp'anŭn 생명을 위협하는

lift 1 *v/t* tŭrŏ ollida 들어 올리다 **2** *v/i (of fog)* kŏch'ida 걷히다 **3** *n (in car)* t'aeugi 태우기

light¹ 1 *n* pit 빛; *(lamp)* tŭng 등 **2** *v/t fire, cigarette* pul puch'ida 불 붙이다; *(illuminate)* chomyŏnghada 조명하다 **3** *adj (not dark)* palgŭn 밝은 불 붙이다

light² *adj (not heavy)* kabyŏun 가벼운

light bulb paegyŏl chŏn-gu 백열 전구

lighter *(for cigarette)* lait'ŏ 라이터

lighting chomyŏng 조명

lightning pŏn-gae 번개

like¹ *prep* kat'ŭn 같은

like² *v/t* choahada 좋아하다; *I ~ her* nanŭn kŭnyŏrŭl choahamnida 나는 그녀를 좋아합니다; *I would ...* nanŭn ...ŭl / rŭl wŏnhamnida 나는 ...을 / 를 원합니다; *I would ~ to ...* nanŭn ...hago shipssŭmida 나는 ...하고 싶습니다; *would you ~ ...?* ...ŭl / rŭl wŏnhamnikka? ...을 / 를 원합니까?; *~ to do sth* muŏsŭl hago shipta 무엇을 하고 싶다; *if you ~* tangshini chot'amyŏn 당신이 좋다면

likeable hogami kanŭn 호감이 가는

likelihood kanŭngssŏng 가능성

likely *(probable)* amado 아마도

lily paek'ap 백합

limit 1 *n* han-gye 한계 **2** *v/t* hanjŏnghada 한정하다

limp *n* chŏlttuk-kkŏrim 절뚝거림

line¹ *n (on paper, phone)* sŏn 선; *(of people, trees)* chul 줄; *(of business)* saŏp 사업

line² *v/t coat etc ...(ŭ)ro anŭl taeda* ...(으)로 안을 대다

♦ **line up** *v/i* chul sŏda 줄 서다

linger nama it-tta 남아 있다

lining *(of clothes)* ankkam 안감; *(of pipe, brakes)* laining 라이닝

link 1 *n* yŏn-gwan 연관; *(in chain)* kori 고리 **2** *v/t* yŏn-gyŏrhada 연결하다

lion saja 사자
lip ipssul 입술
lipstick lipssŭt'ik 립스틱
liqueur lik'yurŭ 리큐르
liquid n aekch'e 액체
liquor sul 술
liquor store churyu p'anmaejŏm 주류 판매점
list n mongnok 목록
listen tŭt-tta 듣다
♦ **listen to ...** ŭl / rŭl tŭt-tta ...을 / 를 듣다
literature munhak 문학
litter ssŭregi 쓰레기
little adj chagŭn 작은 2 n: a ~ chogŭm 조금; a ~ wine p'odoju chogŭm 포도주 조금 3 adv chogŭm 조금: by ~ chogŭmsshik 조금씩; a ~ better chogŭm tŏ chŏŭn 조금 더 좋은
live[1] v/i salda 살다
live[2] adj broadcast saengbangsong 생방송
livelihood saenggye 생계
lively hwalgi ch'an 활기 찬
liver ANAT kanjang 간장; (food) kan 간
livestock kach'uk 가축
living 1 adj sara innŭn 살아 있는 2 n saenghwal 생활
living room kŏshil 거실
lizard tomabaem 도마뱀
load 1 n chim 짐 2 v/t chimŭl shilt'a 짐을 싣다
loaf: a ~ of bread ppang han

tŏng-ŏri 빵 한 덩어리
loan n taebu 대부; on ~ pillin 빌린 2 v/t: ~ sb sth nuguege muŏsŭl pillyŏjuda 누구에게 무엇을 빌려주다
lobby (hotel) lobi 로비; (theater) hyugeshil 휴게실; POL amnyŏk tanch'e 압력 단체
local 1 adj chibang-ŭi 지방의 2 n (person) chibang saram 지방 사람
locally kakkaie 가까이에
local time hyŏnji shigan 현지 시간
locate factory etc wich'irŭl chŏnghada 위치를 정하다
lock 1 n chamulssoe 자물쇠 2 v/t door chamgŭda 잠그다
locker lok'ŏ 로커
log (wood) t'ongnamu 통나무; (written) iltchi 일지
logic nolli 논리
logical nollijŏgin 논리적인
logo logo 로고
London Lŏndŏn 런던
lonely person oeroun 외로운; place koripptoen 고립된
long[1] adj kin 긴; it's a ~ way mŏryŏyo 멀어요; for a ~ time oraettong-an 오랫동안 2 adv orae 오래; don't be ~ kkumulgŏriji mara 꾸물거리지 마라; before then hwŏlsshin kŭ chŏne 훨씬 그 전에; before ~ kot 곧; so

~ as *(provided)* ...hanŭn han
...하는 한; **so ~!** annyŏng!
안녕!

long² *v/i:* **~ for** aet'age parada
애타게 바라다; **be ~ing
to do sth** muŏt hanŭn kŏsŭl
aet'age parada 무엇 하는
것을 애타게 바라다

long-distance *adj* changgŏriŭi
장거리의

long jump nŏlbi ttwigi 넓이
뛰기

long-range *missile* wŏn-
gŏriŭi 원거리의; *forecast*
changgijŏgin 장기적인

long-term *adj* changgiŭi
장기의

look 1 *n* (*appearance*) moyang
모양; (*glance*) pom 봄; **have
a ~ at** salp'yŏboda 살펴보다;
can I have a ~? pwado
toelkkayo? 봐도 될까요
2 *v/i* poda 보다; (*search*)
ch'ajaboda 찾아보다; (*seem*)
poida 보이다

♦ **look after** ...ŭl / rŭl
posalp'ida ...을 / 를
보살피다

♦ **look at** ...ŭl / rŭl poda
...을 / 를 보다; (*examine*)
...ŭl / rŭl salp'yŏboda
...을 / 를 살펴보다

♦ **look for** ...ŭl / rŭl ch'at-tta
...을 / 를 찾다

♦ **look out** *v/i* (*of window*)
pakkach'ŭl naedaboda 바깥을

naedaboda; **~!** choshimhae!
조심해라

♦ **look up to** (*respect*) chon-
gyŏnghada 존경하다

loose *wire* nŭsŭnhan 느슨한;
clothes hŏlgŏun 헐거운;
morals pangjonghan 방종한

loosen nŭsŭnhage hada
느슨하게 하다

lorry *Br* t'ŭrŏk 트럭

lose 1 *v/t* ilt'a 잃다; *game*
chida 지다 2 *v/i* SPORTS chida
지다; (*of clock*) nŭjŏjida
늦어지다; **I'm lost** nanŭn
kirŭl irŏbŏryŏssŏyo 나는
길을 잃어버렸어요

loser SPORTS p'aeja 패자

loss (*of object*) sonshil 손실;
(*of loved one*) sangshil 상실;
(*in business*) sonhae 손해

lost irŭn 잃은

lot: **a ~ of, ~s of** manŭn 많은;
a ~, ~s eat, talk etc mani
많이; **a ~ better** hwŏlsshin tŏ
choŭn 훨씬 더 좋은

lotion loshyŏn 로션

loud shikkŭrŏun 시끄러운

loudspeaker hwaksssŏnggi
확성기

lousy *infml* hyŏngp'yŏnŏmnŭn
형편없는

love 1 *n* sarang 사랑; (*in
tennis*) mudŭktchŏm 무득점;
be in ~ saranghago it-tta
사랑하고 있다; **fall in ~**
sarang-e ppajida 사랑에

빠지다 2 v/t saranghada 사랑하다

love affair yŏnae sakkŏn 연애 사건

lovely *face, color* arŭmdaun 아름다운; *person* sarangsŭrŏun 사랑스러운; *weather, meal* mŏtchin 멋진

lover aein 애인

low *adj wall, voice, quality* najŭn 낮은; *price* ssan 싼

loyal ch'ungsŏngsŭrŏun 충성스러운

luck un 운; *bad ~* purun 불운; *good ~* haeng-un 행운; *good ~!* haeng-unŭl pimnida! 행운을 빕니다!

luckily un chok'e 운 좋게

lucky *person* un choŭn 운

좋은; *number* haeng-unŭl kajyŏonŭn 행운을 가져오는

luggage suhwamul 수화물

lukewarm mijigŭnhan 미지근한

lull *n* chinjŏng 진정

lullaby chajangga 자장가

lump *(of sugar)* chogak 조각; *(swelling)* hok 혹

lump sum ilsshibul 일시불

lunar tarŭi 달의

lunatic *n* mich'igwang-i 미치광이

lunch chŏmshim 점심

lung p'ye 폐

lung cancer p'yeam 폐암

lust *n* yongmang 욕망

luxury 1 *n* sach'i 사치 **2** *adj* sach'isŭrŏun 사치스러운

M

machine kigye 기계

macho namjadaumŭl kangjohan 남자다움을 강조한

mad mich'in 미친

made-to-measure match'umŭi 맞춤의

madness kwanggi 광기

magazine chaptchi 잡지

magic 1 *n* masul 마술; *(tricks)* yosul 요술 **2** *adj* masurŭi 마술의

magician masulssa 마술사

magnet chasŏk 자석

magnetic chagiŭi 자기의

magnificent changnyŏhan 장려한

magnify hwakttaehada 확대하다

magnifying glass totppogi 돋보기

mah-jong majak 마작

maid *(in hotel)* hot'el chong-ŏbwŏn 호텔 종업원

mail 1 *n* up'yŏn 우편 **2** *v/t letter* p'yŏnjihada 편지하다

mailbox uch'et'ong 우체통; *(of house)* up'yŏnham 우편함; COMPUT meilbakssŭ 메일박스

mailman uch'ebu 우체부

main *adj* chudoen 주된

mainland pont'o 본토

mainly churo 주로

main street chungshimga 중심가

maintain *machine* yujihada 유지하다; *innocence* chujanghada 주장하다

major 1 *adj* chuyohan 주요한 **2** *n* MIL soryŏng 소령

majority taedasu 대다수; POL kwabansu 과반수

make 1 *n (brand)* sangp'yo 상표 **2** *v/t* mandŭlda 만들다; *made in Korea* Han-guksan 한국산 ◊ ~ *sb do sth (force)* nuguege muŏsŭl shik'ida 누구에게 무엇을 시키다; *(cause)* nuguege muŏt'age hada 누구를 무엇하게 하다 ◊ ~ *sb happy* nugurŭl haengbok'age hada 누구를 행복하게 하다

♦ **make out** *check* ssŭda 쓰다; *(see)* poda 보다; *(imply)* nŏnjishi pich'uda 넌지시 비추다

♦ **make up 1** *v/i (after quarrel)* hwahaehada 화해하다 **2** *v/t story* kkumida 꾸미다; *face* hwajanghada 화장하다;

(constitute) kusŏnghada 구성하다; ~ *one's mind* maŭmŭl chŏnghada 마음을 정하다

♦ **make up for** pŏlch'unghada 벌충하다

maker saengsanja 생산자

make-up *(cosmetics)* hwajangp'um 화장품

Malaysia Malleishia 말레이시아

Malaysian Malleishiain 말레이시아인

male 1 *adj* namsŏng-ŭi 남성의; *animal* suk'ŏsŭi 수컷의 **2** *n (man)* namja 남자; *(animal)* suk'ŏt 수컷

male chauvinist namsŏng uwŏltchuŭija 남성 우월주의자

malfunction *n* chakttong pullyang 작동 불량

malignant *tumor* akssŏng-ŭi 악성의

mall *(shopping)* sangga 상가

malnutrition yŏngnyang shiltcho 영양 실조

maltreatment hakttae 학대

mammal p'oyu tongmul 포유 동물

man *n* namja 남자; *(human being)* saram 사람; *(humanity)* illyu 인류

manage *v/t business* kwallihada 관리하다; *company* kyŏngnyŏnghada

경영하다; *bags* taruda
다루다; ~ *to …* iröktchörök
… haenaeda 이력저력 …
해나다 2 *v/i (cope)* kyŏndida
견디다

manageable taruki shwiun
다루기 쉬운

management kwalli 관리; *(of company)* kyŏngnyŏng 경영; *(managers)* kyŏngnyŏngjin
경영진

manager *(of department)*
kwalliin 관리인; *(of factory, people)* kwallija 관리자; *(of company)* kyŏngnyŏngja
경영자

managing director pujang
부장

mandatory ŭimujŏgin
의무적인

maneuver 1 *n* umjigim
움직임 2 *v/t* kyomyohi
umjigida 교묘히 움직이다

maniac mich'in saram 미친
사람

manipulate *person*
chojonghada 조종하다

man-made in-gong 인공

manner *(way)* pangshik 방식;
(attitude) t'aedo 태도

manners: *good / bad* ~
yeŭi parŭm / ŏpssŭm 예의
바름 / 없음; *have no* ~
yeŭia ŏptta 예의가 없다

manpower illyŏk 인력

mansion chŏt'aek 저택

manual 1 *adj* sonŭro hanŭn
손으로 하는 2 *n* sŏlmyŏngsŏ
설명서

manufacture *v/t* chejohada
제조하다

manufacturer chejoŏptcha
제조업자

many 1 *adj* manŭn 많은
2 *pron* manŭn kŏt 많은 것;
(people) manŭn saram 많은
사람; *a good* ~ taedanhi
manŭn 대단히 많은

map *n* chido 지도

marathon marat'on 마라톤

March samwŏl 삼월

march 1 *n* haengjin 행진;
(demo) temo haengjin 데모
행진 2 *v/i* haengjinhada
행진하다

margin *(of page)* yŏbaek 여백;
(profit ~) imun 이문

marine 1 *adj* padaŭi 바다의
2 *n* MIL haegun 해군

maritime haeyangŭi 해양의

mark 1 *n (stain)* ŏlluk 얼룩;
(sign, token) p'yoshi 표시;
SCHOOL sŏngjŏk 성적 2 *v/t
(stain)* chagugŭl naeda 자국을
내다; SCHOOL ch'aejŏmhada
채점하다; *(indicate)*
p'yoshihada 표시하다

market 1 *n* shijang 시장 2 *v/t*
p'anmaehada 판매하다

marketing maemae shijang

market research shijang
chosa 시장 조사

mark-up kagyŏk insang 가격 인상

marriage kyŏrhonshik 결혼식; *(institution)* kyŏrhon 결혼; *(being married)* kyŏrhon saenghwal 결혼 생활

marriage certificate kyŏrhon chŭngmyŏngsŏ 결혼 증명서

married kyŏrhonhan 결혼한

marry kyŏrhonhada 결혼하다; *get married* kyŏrhonhada 결혼하다

martial arts musul 무술

marvelous koengjanghi chõun 굉장히 좋은

Marxism Marŭk'ŭsŭjuŭi 마르크스주의

mascara masŭk'ara 마스카라

masculine namsŏngjŏgin 남성적인

mass n *(great amount)* taryang 다량

massacre n taeryang haksal 대량 학살

massage n anma 안마

massive kõdaehan 거대한

mass media taejung maech'e 대중 매체

master 1 n *(of dog)* chuin 주인 **2** v/t skill chŏngt'onghada 정통하다

masterpiece myŏngjak 명작

mastery chŏngbok 정복

match[1] *(for light)* sŏngnyang 성냥

match[2] **1** n *(competition)*

matching adj ŏullinŭn 어울리는

mate 1 n *(of animal)* tchak 짝 **2** v/i tchakthchit-tta 짝짓다

material n chaeryo 재료; *(fabric)* otkkam 옷감

materials charyo 자료

maternal ŏmŏniŭi 어머니의

maternity mosŏng 모성

math suhak 수학

mathematical suhagŭi 수학의

matter 1 n *(affair)* sakkŏn 사건; *(physical)* multchil 물질; *what's the ~?* musŭn iri issŭmnikka? 무슨 일이 있습니까? **2** v/i chungyohada 중요하다; *it doesn't ~* kŭgŏsŭn sanggwanŏptta 그것은 상관없다

mattress maet'ŭrisŭ 매트리스

mature adj sŏngsuk'an 성숙한

maturity sŏngsuk-kki 성숙기

maximum 1 adj ch'oedaeŭi 최대의 **2** n ch'oedae 최대

May owŏl 오월

may ◊ *(possibility)* …iltchido morŭnda …일지도 모른다; *it ~ rain* piga olthchido morŭnda 비가 올지도 모른다 ◊ *(permission)* …haedo chot'a 해도 좋다

maybe amado 아마도

May Day Nodongjŏl 노동절

memory stick

mayonnaise mayonejŭ
마요네즈
me na 나; H chŏ 저; *it's ~* nada
nida; H chŏimnida 저입니다;
he knows ~ kŭnŭn narŭl anda
그는 나를 안다
meal shiksa 식사
mean¹ (*with money*) insaek'an
인색한; (*nasty*) mot-ttoen
못된
mean² *v/t* ŭimihada 의미하다;
(*intend*) ŭidohada 의도하다
meaning ŭimi 의미
means (*financial*) chaesan
재산; (*way*) sudan 수단
meantime: *in the ~* kŭ saie
그 사이에
measure 1 *n* (*step*) pangch'aek
방책 2 *v/t* ch'issurŭl chaeda
치수를 재다
measurement (*action*)
ch'ŭktchŏng 측정; *~s*
(*dimensions*) ch'issu 치수
meat kogi 고기
mechanic kigyegong 기계공
mechanism kigye changch'i
기계 장치
medal medal 메달
media: *the ~* maesŭk'ŏm
매스컴
median strip chung-ang
pullidae 중앙 분리대
mediator chungjaein 중재인
medical 1 *adj* ŭihagŭi 의학의
2 *n* shinch'e kŏmsa 신체
검사

medicine (*science*) ŭihak 의학;
(*medication*) yak 약
mediocre chilla jŭn 질낮은
meditate myŏngsanghada
명상하다; (*Christianity*)
mukssanghada 묵상하다;
(*Buddhism*) ch'amsŏnhada
참선하다
medium 1 *adj* chunggan ŭi
중간의 2 *n* (*in size*) chunggan
k'ŭgi 중간 크기
meet 1 *v/t* mannada 만나다;
(*collect*) majunginagada
마중나가다; (*satisfy*)
ch'ungjokshik'ida
충족시키다 2 *v/i* mannada
만나다; (*in competition*)
taejŏnhada 대전하다; (*of
committee etc*) moida 모이다
3 *n* SPORTS kyŏnggi 경기
meeting hoeŭi 회의
melon melon 멜론
melt 1 *v/i* nokta 녹다 2 *v/t*
nogida 녹이다
member irwŏn 일원
memo memo 메모
memoirs hoegorok 회고록
memorable kiŏk'al manhan
기억할 만한
memorial *n* kinyŏmbi 기념비
memorize amgihada
암기하다
memory kiŏk 기억; (*faculty*)
kiŏngnyŏk 기억력
memory stick memori sŭt'ik
메모리 스틱

men's room namja
hwajangshil 남자 화장실
mend v/t koch'ida 고치다;
clothes susŏnhada 수선하다
meningitis noemangnyŏm
뇌막염
mental chŏngshinŭi 정신의
mentality chŏngshin sangt'ae
정신 상태
mention v/t ŏn-gŭp'ada
언급하다; *don't ~ it*
ch'ŏnmaneyo 천만에요
menu *also* COMPUT menyu 메뉴
merchandise sangp'um 상품
mercy chabi 자비
merger COMM hap-ppyŏng 합병
merit n *(worth)* kach'i 가치;
(advantage) changtchŏm 장점
merry yuk'waehan 유쾌한
merry-go-round hoejŏn
mongma 회전 목마
mess n ŏngmang-in kŏt
엉망인 것; *(trouble)* kon-
gyŏng 곤경
message mesiji 메시지
messy *room* ŏjiŏun 어지러운;
person hollanhage hanŭn
혼란하게 하는
metabolism shinjindaesa
신진대사
metal n kŭmsok 금속 2 adj
kŭmsogŭi 금속의
meteor yusŏng 유성
meteorology kisanghak
기상학
meter[1] *(for gas etc)* kyeryanggi

계량기; *(parking, in cab)*
yogŭm kyesan-gi 요금
계산기
meter[2] *(unit)* mit'ŏ 미터
method pangbŏp 방법
methodical iltchŏnghan
pangshige ttarŭn 일정한
방식에 따른
meticulous seshimhan 세심한
metropolitan adj taedoshiŭi
대도시의
Mexico Mekshik'o 멕시코
microphone maik'ŭ 마이크
microwave *(oven)* chŏnjarenji
전자렌지
midday chŏng-o 정오
middle 1 adj chungganŭi
중간의 2 n kaunde 가운데
middle-aged chungnyŏnŭi
중년의
middle-class adj
chungsanch'ŭng-ŭi 중산층의
Middle East Chungdong 중동
midnight chajŏng 자정
Midwest Chungsŏbu 중서부
midwife chosanwŏn 조산원
might ...iltchido morŭnda
...일지도 모른다; *I ~ be
late* chŏnŭn ama nŭjŭltchido
morŭgessŭmnida 저는 아마
늦을지도 모르겠습니다
migraine p'yŏndut'ong 편두통
migration iju 이주
mild onhwahan 온화한
mile mail 마일
militant n t'usa 투사

military 1 adj kunŭi 군의 2 n:
the ~ kun 군

milk n uyu 우유

millionaire paengman changja
백만 장자

mimic v/t hyungnaenaeda
흉내내다

mind 1 n chŏngshin 정신;
change one's ~ maŭmŭl
pakkuda 마음을 바꾸다 2 v/t
(look after) tolboda 돌보다;
(object to) ŏntchanahada
언짢아하다; *(heed)* maŭme
tuda 마음에 두다 3 v/i:
~! (careful) choshimhaseyo!
조심하세요!; *never*
~! shin-gyŏng ssŭl kŏt
ŏpssŭmnida! 신경 쓸 것
없습니다!; *I don't ~* chŏnŭn
sanggwanŏpssŭmnida 저는
상관없습니다

mine¹ pron naŭi kŏt 나의 것;
н chŏŭi kŏt 저의 것

mine² n (for coal etc) kwangsan
광산

mine³ n MIL chiroe 지뢰

mineral n kwangmul 광물

mineral water saengsu 생수

miniature adj sohyŏng-ŭi
소형의

minimal ch'oesoŭi 최소의

minimum 1 adj ch'oesohanŭi
최소한의 2 n ch'oeso 최소

minister POL changgwan 장관;
REL moksa 목사

ministry POL pu 부

---

miss

minor 1 adj poda chagŭn 보다
작은 2 n JUR misŏngnyŏnja
미성년자

minority sosup'a 소수파

minute¹ n (of time) pun 분

minute² adj (tiny) aju
chogŭman 아주 조그만;
(detailed) sangsehan 상세한

minutes (of meeting) ŭisarok
의사록

miracle kijŏk 기적

mirror n kŏul 거울; AUTO
paengmirŏ 백미러

miscarriage MED yusan 유산

miserable purhaenghan
불행한; weather koyak'an
고약한

misfortune purhaeng 불행

misjudge chalmot p'andanhada
잘못 판단하다

misleading odohanŭn
오도하는

mismanagement chalmott-
ttoen unyŏng 잘못된 운영

misprint n chalmot-ttoen
inswae 잘못된 인쇄

mispronounce t'ŭllin
parŭmŭl hada 틀린 발음을
하다

miss¹: *Miss Smith* Sŭmisŭ
yang 스미스 양

miss² v/t (not hit) noch'ida
놓치다; (not meet) ŏtkkallida
엇갈리다; (emotionally)
kŭriwŏhada 그리워하다; bus
noch'ida 놓치다; (not notice)

arach'aeji mot'ada 알아채지
못하다; *(not be present at)* ...e
ppajida ...에 빠지다

missile MIL misail 미사일

missing irŏborin 잃어버린;
be ~ ŏpssŏjida 없어지다

missionary sŏn-gyosa 선교사

mist an-gae 안개

mistake n shilssu 실수; *make
a ~* shilssuhada 실수하다

mistress *(lover)* chŏngbu
정부; *(of dog)* chuin 주인

mistrust 1 n pulshin 불신
2 v/t pulshinhada 불신하다

misty an-gae kkin 안개 낀

misunderstand ohaehada
오해하다

misunderstanding ohae 오해

mitt *(in baseball)* mit'ŭ 미트

mix 1 v/t *(mixture)* sŏkkŭn
kŏt 섞은 것; *(in cooking)*
honhammul 혼합물 **2** v/t
sŏkkta 섞다 **3** v/i *(socially)*
ŏullida 어울리다

mixed *feelings* hollanhan
혼란한

mixture honhap 혼합;
(medicine) mulyak 물약

moan v/i *(in pain)* shinŭmhada
신음하다

mob n p'oktto 폭도

mobile adj *person* umjigil su
innŭn 움직일 수 있는

mobile phone Br haendŭp'on
핸드폰

mock v/t hyungnaenaemyŏ

choronghada 흉내내며
조롱하다

mockery *(derision)* chorong
조롱

model 1 adj *boat etc* mohyŏng-
ŭi 모형의 **2** n *(miniature)*
mohyŏng 모형; *(pattern)*
ponbogi 본보기; *(fashion)*
model 모델

modem modem 모뎀

moderate adj chŏktttanghan
적당한; POL on-gŏnhan
온건한

modern hyŏndaeŭi 현대의

modernize v/t hyŏndaejŏgŭro
pakkuda 현대적으로 바꾸다

modest *home* susuhan 수수한;
(not conceited) kyŏmsonhan
겸손한

modify sujŏnghada 수정하다

moist ch'ukch'uk'an 축축한

moisturizer moisch'yŏraijŏ
모이스처라이저

mold¹ n *(on food)* komp'ang-i
곰팡이

mold² **1** n t'ŭl 틀 **2** v/t *clay
etc* t'ŭre nŏŏ mandŭlda 틀에
넣어 만들다

mom infml ŏmma 엄마

moment sun-gan 순간; *at the
~* chigŭmŭn 지금은; *for the
~* tangbun-gan 당분간

monarch kunju 군주

monastery sudowŏn 수도원

Monday wŏryoil 월요일

monetary kŭmnyung-ŭi
금융의

금융의
money ton 돈
Mongolia Monggo 몽고
monitor 1 n COMPUT monit'ŏ
모니터 2 v/t chik'yŏboda
지켜보다
monk sudosa 수도사
monkey wŏnsung-i 원숭이
monolog tokppaek 독백
monopolize toktchŏmhada
독점하다
monopoly toktchŏm 독점
monotonous tanjoroun
단조로운
monster n koemul 괴물
month tal 달, wŏl 월
monthly adj maedarŭi 매달의
monument kinyŏmbi 기념비
mood kibun 기분; be in
a good / bad ~ kibuni
chot'a / nappŭda 기분이
좋다 / 나쁘다
moon n tal 달
moral 1 adj todŏktchŏgin
도덕적인 2 n (of story)
kyohun 교훈; ~s todŏk
도덕; kwannyŏm 도덕 관념
morale sagi 사기
morality todŏksŏng 도덕성
more 1 adj tŏ manŭn 더 많은;
some ~ tea? ch'arŭl chom tŏ
tŭshigessŭmnikka? 차를 좀
더 드시겠습니까? 2 adv
tŏuk 더욱; ~ important tŏ
chung-yohan 더 중요한;
once ~ hanbŏn tŏ 한번 더; ~

than …poda tŏ mani …보다
더 많이; I don't live there
any ~ nanŭn tŏ isang kŏgi salji
ansŭmnida 나는 더 이상
거기 살지 않습니다 3 pron
tŏ 더; do you want some
~? tŏ wŏnhashimnikka? 더
원하십니까?
moreover kŏgidaga 거기다가
morning ach'im 아침; good ~
annyŏnghaseyo 안녕하세요;
(on waking up) annyŏnghi
chumusyŏssŏyo 안녕히
주무셨어요
morphine morŭp'in 모르핀
mosquito mogi 모기
most 1 adj taebubun의
대부분의 2 adv kajang
가장, (very) maeu 매우;
the ~ beautiful kajang
arŭmdaun 가장 아름다운;
~ of all muŏtppodado
무엇보다도 3 pron taebubun
대부분; at ~ manaya 많아야
mostly taebubunŭn 대부분은
mother n ŏmŏni 어머니
mother-in-law (woman's)
shiŏmŏni 시어머니; (man's)
changmo 장모
mother tongue mogugŏ
모국어
motivation tonggi puyŏ 동기
부여
motive tonggi 동기
motor mot'ŏ 모터
motorcycle ot'obai 오토바이

motorcyclist ot'obairŭl t'anŭn saram 오토바이를 타는 사람

mountain san 산

mountain bike sanak chajŏn-gŏ 산악 자전거

mountaineering tŭngsan 등산

mourn v/t ch'udohada 추도하다

mouse chwi 쥐; COMPUT mausŭ 마우스

mouth n ip 입; (of river) hagu 하구

move 1 n (in chess) su 수; (step, action) umjigim 움직임; (change of house) isa 이사 2 v/t object umjigida 움직이다; (transfer) omgida 옮기다; (emotionally) kamdongshik'ida 감동시키다 3 v/i umjigida 움직이다; (transfer) omgida 옮기다

movement umjigim 움직임; (organization) undong 운동

movie yŏnghwa 영화

movie theater yŏnghwagwan 영화관

moving (emotionally) kamdongjŏgin 감동적인

mph: at 50 ~ shisok 50maillo 시속 50마일로

Mr: ~ Kevin Brown K'ebin P'ŭraunsshi 케빈 브라운씨

Mrs: ~ Margo MacDonald Mago Maekttonaldŭ yŏsa 마고 맥도날드 여사

Ms: ~ Sunmi Lee Yi Sunmisshi 이 순미씨

much 1 adj manŭn 많은; there's not ~ difference pyŏllo tarŭji anayo 별로 다르지 않아요 2 adv mani 많이; very ~ aju mani 아주 많이; do you like it? – not ~ kŭgŏsŭl choahaeyo? – pyŏlloyo 그것을 좋아해요? – 별로요 3 pron manŭn kŏt 많은 것; nothing ~ pyŏllo 별로

mud chinhŭk 진흙

mug¹ n (for drink) mŏgŏjan 머그잔

mug² v/t (attack) nosang kangdojirŭl hada 노상 강도질을 하다

multinational n taguktchŏk kiŏp 다국적 기업

multiple adj tayanghan 다양한

multiply v/t kop'ada 곱하다

murder 1 n sarin 살인 2 v/t person sarinhada 살인하다

murderer sarinja 살인자

muscle kŭnyuk 근육

museum pangmulgwan 박물관

mushroom n pŏsŏt 버섯

music ŭmak 음악; (written) akppo 악보

musician ŭmak-kka 음악가

must ...haeya hada ···해야 하다; I ~ be late nanŭn nŭjŏsŏnŭn andoenda 나는 늦어서는 안된다

mustache k'otssuyŏm 콧수염

mustard kyŏja 겨자

mutter v/t & v/i chung-ŏlgŏrida 중얼거리다

mutual sanghoganŭi 상호간의

my naŭi 나의; H chŏŭi 저의
◊ *(for family, groups etc Korean usually uses 'our')* uriŭi 우리의

myself na chashin 나 자신

mysterious shinbihan 신비한

mystery shinbi 신비

myth shinhwa 신화

N

nag v/t & v/i chansorihada 잔소리하다

nail *(for wood)* mot 못; *(on finger, toe)* sont'op 손톱

nail file sont'optchul 손톱줄

nail polish maenik'yuŏ 매니큐어

nail scissors sont'op kkangnŭn kawi 손톱 깎는 가위

naive sunjinhan 순진한

naked pŏlgŏbŏsŭn 벌거벗은

name n irŭm 이름; *(on document)* sŏngmyŏng 성명; what's your ~? irŭmi muŏsshimnikka? 이름이 무엇입니까?; *(polite)* sŏnghami ŏttŏk'e toeshimnikka? 성함이 어떻게 되십니까?

nametag irŭmp'yo 이름표

nanny n yumo 유모

nap n nattcham 낮잠

napkin *(table)* naepk'in 냅킨; *(sanitary)* saengnidae 생리대

narrator iyagihanŭn saram 이야기하는 사람

narrow chobŭn 좁은; win kkakkasŭro ŏdŭn 가까스로 얻은

narrow-minded maŭmi chobŭn 마음이 좁은

nasty mot-ttoen 못된; smell, weather pulk'waehan 불쾌한; cut shimhan 심한

nation kuk-kka 국가

national 1 adj kuk-kkaŭi 국가의 2 n kungmin 국민

national anthem kuk-kka 국가; *(South Korean)* Aeguk-kka 애국가

nationality kuktchŏk 국적

nationalize kugyŏnghwahada 국영화하다

native adj ch'ulssaeng-ŭi 출생의; ~ language mogugŏ 모국어

native speaker wŏnŏmin 원어민

natural resources chayŏnŭi

자연의; *flavor* sunsuhan 순수한

natural gas ch'ŏnyŏn kassŭ 천연 가스

naturally *(of course)* tangnyŏnhi 당연히; *behave* chayŏnsŭrŏpkke 자연스럽게; *(by nature)* pollae 본래

nature chayŏn 자연; *(of person)* ch'ŏnsŏng 천성; *(of problem)* sŏngkkyŏk 성격

naughty chittkkujŭn 짓궂은

nausea mesŭkkŏum 메스꺼움

nauseous: *feel ~* t'ohal kŏt kat-tta 토할 것 같다

nautical hanghaeŭi 항해의

naval haegunŭi 해군의

navigate *v/i* hanghaehada 항해하다

navigator *(in ship, plane)* hanghaesa 항해사

navy haegun 해군

navy blue *adj* namsaegŭi 남색의

near 1 *adv* kakkai 가까이 **2** *prep* kakkaie 가까이에; *~ the bank* ŭnhaeng kakkaie 은행 가까이에 **3** *adj* kakkaun 가까운

nearby *adv* kakkapkke 가깝게

nearly kŏŭi 거의

neat kkaekkŭt'an 깨끗한; *person* tanjŏnghan 단정한; *whiskey* sunsuhan 순수한; *solution* hyŏnmyŏnghan 현명한; *infml (terrific)* kūnsahan 근사한

necessary p'iryohan 필요한; *it is ~ to ...* ...hal p'iryoga it-tta ...할 필요가 있다

necessity p'iryosŏng 필요성; *(sth necessary)* p'ilsup'um 필수품

neck mok 목

necklace mok-kkŏri 목걸이

necktie nekt'ai 넥타이

need 1 *n* p'iryo 필요; *in ~* toumi p'iryohan 도움이 필요한 **2** *v/t* p'iryohada 필요하다; *you don't ~ to wait* kidaril p'iryoga ŏptta 기다릴 필요가 없다

needle panŭl 바늘; MED chusa panŭl 주사 바늘

negative *adj* GRAM pujŏng-ŭi 부정의; *person* pujŏngjŏgin 부정적인; ELEC ŭmgŭgŭi 음극의

neglect 1 *n* pangch'i 방치 **2** *v/t* tolboji ant'a 돌보지 않다

negligence t'aeman 태만

negotiate *v/t & v/i* hyŏpssanghada 협상하다

neighbor iut saram 이웃 사람

neighborhood iut ŏut 이웃

neither 1 *adj* ŏnŭ ...to anin 어느 ...도 아닌 *(+ negative verb)* **2** *pron* ŏnŭ tchoktto ... 어느 쪽도 ... *(+ negative verb)* **3** *conj:* ~ *X nor Y* Xto Yto ... X도 Y도 ... *(+ negative verb)* **4** *adv:* ~ *do I*

nadoyo 나도요
Nepal Nep'al 네팔
nephew chok'a 조카
nerve shin-gyŏng 신경
nervous *person* shin-gyŏng-i
kwaminhan 신경이 과민한
net[1] *(for fishing)* kŭmul 그물;
(for tennis) net'ŭ 네트
net[2] *adj price* chŏngkka 정가
net profit suniik 순이익
network kŭmulmang 그물망;
COMPUT net'ŭwŏk'ŭ
네트워크
neurologist shin-gyŏngkwa
ŭisa 신경과 의사
neurotic *adj* shin-gyŏng
kwaminŭi 신경 과민의
neutral 1 *adj country*
chungnibŭi 중립의; *color*
chunggansaegŭi 중간색의
2 *n (gear)* chungnip wich'i
중립 위치
neutrality chungnipssŏng
중립성
never chŏltae 절대 (+ negative verb)
절대; *(past)* han bŏndo (+
negative verb) 한 번도
nevertheless kŭrŏmedo
pulguhago 그럼에도
불구하고
new saeroun 새로운
newborn *adj* kannan 갓난
news soshik 소식; *(TV, radio)*
nyusŭ 뉴스
newspaper shinmun 신문
newsreader nyusŭ

pangsonghanŭn saram 뉴스
방송하는 사람
news report nyusŭ podo
뉴스 보도
New Year Saehae 새해;
(public holiday) Shinjŏng
신정; *Happy ~!* Saehae pok
mani padŭseyo! 새해 복
많이 받으세요!
New Year's Day Saehae
Ch'ŏnnal 새해 첫날; *(lunar)*
Sŏllal 설날
New Year's Eve Sŏttal
Kŭmŭmnal 섣달 그믐날
New York Nyuyok 뉴욕
next 1 *adj* taŭmŭi 다음의
2 *adv* taŭme 다음에; *~ to*
(beside) …ŭi yŏp'e …의
옆에; *(in comparison with)* …e
iŏsŏ …에 이어서
next-door 1 *adj* yŏptchibŭi
옆집의 **2** *adv live* yŏptchibe
옆집에
next of kin kŭnch'in 근친
nice mŏtchin 멋진
nickname *n* pyŏlmyŏng 별명
niece yŏja chok'a 여자 조카
night *n* pam 밤; *11 o'clock at ~*
pam yŏrhanshi 밤 11시; *good
~* annyŏnghi chumushipsshiyo
안녕히 주무십시요, *infml*
chal cha 잘 자
nightclub nait'ŭ k'ŭllŏp
나이트클럽
nightdress chamot 잠옷
nightmare angmong 악몽; *fig*

angmonggat'ŭn kŏt 악몽같은
것
night school yagan hak-kkyo
야간 학교
no 1 adv aniyo 아니오
◊ (using 'yes', ie yes, that is
right): you don't know the
answer, do you? - ~, I don't
tabŭl morŭjiyo? - ye, mollayo
답을 모르죠? - 예,
몰라요 2 adj: there's ~
coffee left namŭn k'ŏp'iga
ŏptta 남은 커피가 없다; ~
smoking kŭmyŏn금연
nobody amudo (+ negative
verb) 아무도; ~ knows amudo
morŭnda 아무도 모른다
nod n kkŭdŏgim 끄덕임
noise sori 소리; (loud,
unpleasant) soŭm 소음
noisy shikkŭrŏun 시끄러운
nominate (appoint)
immyŏnghada 임명하다;
~ sb for a post (propose)
nugurŭl kongch'ŏnhada
누구를 공천하다
nonalcoholic alk'oori ŏmnŭn
알코올이 없는
noncommittal aemaemohohan
애매모호한
none amu kŏtto (+ negative
verb) 아무 것도; (person)
amudo (+ negative verb)
아무도
nonetheless kŭrŏmedo
그럼에도 불구하고

불구하고
non-iron tarimjiri p'iryoŏmnŭn
다림질이 필요없는
nonpayment mibul 미불
nonreturnable hwanbul
pulgaŭi 환불 불가의
nonsense maldo andoenŭn kŏt
말도 안되는 것
nonsmoker pihŭbyŏnja
비흡연자
nonstop 1 adj chik'aengŭi
직행의 2 adv chik'aeng-ŭro
직행으로
noodles kukssu 국수; (instant)
ramyŏn 라면; (chilled)
naengmyŏn 냉면
noon chŏng-o 정오
nor …to ttohan (+ negative
verb) …도 또한; ~ do I nado
anida 나도 아니다
normal chŏngsang-ŭi 정상의
normally pot'ong-ŭro
보통으로; (in normal way)
chŏngsang-ŭro 정상으로
north 1 n puk 북 2 adj
puktchogŭi 북쪽의 3 adv
travel puktchogŭro 북쪽으로
North America Pungmi 북미
North American 1 adj
Pungmiŭi 북미의 2 n
Pungmiin 북미인
northern pukppuŭi 북부의
North Korea Puk'an 북한
North Korean 1 adj Puk'anŭi
북한의 2 n Puk'an saram
북한 사람

nose k'o 코

nosebleed k'op'i 코피

nostalgia hyangsu 향수

nosy ch'amgyŏnhagi
choahanŭn 참견하기
좋아하는

not: ~ this one, that one
igŏshi anira chŏgŏt 이것이
아니라 저것; ~ there kŭgot
malgo 그곳 말고; ~ a lot
pyŏllo 별로 ◊ (with verbs): it's
~ ready igŏsŭn chunbitoeji
anat-tta 그것은 준비되어
않았고; I don't know nanŭn
morŭnda 나는 모른다; I am
~ American nanŭn Migugini
animnida 나는 미국인이
아닙니다; he didn't help
kŭnŭn toptchi anat-tta 그는
돕지 않았다

note n (short letter) tchalbŭn
p'yŏnji 짧은 편지; MUS
ŭmp'yo 음표; (to self) memo
메모; (comment on text) chu
주; take ~s chŏktta 적다

notebook kongch'aek 공책

notepaper p'yŏnjiji 편지지

nothing amu kŏt-tto 아무 것도 (+
negative verb); there's ~ left
amu kŏt-tto namtchi anat-tta 아무 것도
남지 않았다; for ~
thanks chŏnŭn kwaench'anayo
저는 괜찮아요

notice 1 n (on board, in street)
keshi 게시; (advance warning)

chuŭi 주의; (in paper) konggo
공고; (to leave job / house)
t'ongji 통지; at short ~
tchalbŭn shihane namgin
ch'ae 짧은 시한을 남긴
채; take no ~ of …e amurŏn
chuŭirŭl haji ant'a …에
아무런 주의를 하지 않다
2 v/t arach'aeda 알아채다

notify konggohada 공고하다

notorious angmyŏng nop'ŭn
악명 높은

nourishing yŏngnyang-innŭn
영양있는

novel n sosŏl 소설

novelist sosŏlga 소설가

November shibirwŏl 십일월

novice ch'oshimja 초심자

now chigŭm 지금; ~ and
again ttaettaero 때때로; by ~
chigŭmtchŭm 지금쯤; from ~
on chigŭmbut'ŏ 지금부터

nowadays yojŭm 요즈음

nowhere amu kosedo 아무
곳에도

nuclear haek 핵

nuclear energy haek enŏji
핵 에너지

nuclear power station
wŏnjaryŏk paltchŏnso 원자력
발전소

nuclear waste haek p'yegimul
핵 폐기물

nuclear weapons haek mugi
핵 무기

nude adj almomŭi 알몸의

nuisance kwich'anŭn kŏt
귀찮은 것
number n su 수; *(of room, house, phone)* pŏnho 번호
numerous manŭn 많은
nurse kanhosa 간호사
nursery yugashil 육아실; *(for*

plants) onshil 온실
nursing home *(old people)* yangnowŏn 양로원
nut kyŏn-gwa 견과; *(for bolt)* nŏt'ŭ 너트
nutritious yŏngnyang-i innŭn 영양이있는

O

oak *(tree)* ok'ŭnamu 오크나무; *(wood)* ok'ŭ 오크
oath JUR sŏnsŏ 선서
obedience sunjong 순종
obedient sunjonghanŭn 순종하는
obey ...e sunjonghada ...에 순종하다
obituary n pugo 부고
object[1] n *(thing)* mulch'e 물체; *(aim)* moktchŏk 목적; GRAM moktchŏgŏ 목적어
object[2] v/i pandaehada 반대하다
objection pandae 반대
objective 1 adj kaekkwanjŏgin 객관적인 **2** n mokp'yo 목표
obligation ŭimu 의무
obliterate city wanjŏnhi p'agoehada 완전히 파괴하다
obnoxious aju pulk'waehan 아주 불쾌한
obscene ŭmnanhan 음란한
observant kwanch'allyŏgi

yerihan 관찰력이 예리한
observation *(of nature)* kwanch'al 관찰; *(comment)* kwanch'al kyŏlgwa 관찰 결과
observe *(notice)* nunch'ich'aeda 눈치채다; *natural phenomena* kwanch'arhada 관찰하다
obsession kangbak kwannyŏm 강박 관념
obsolete p'yemuri toen 폐물이 된
obstacle chang-ae 장애
obstinate kojibi sen 고집이 센
obstruct road maktta 막다; *investigation* panghaehada 방해하다
obtain hoekttŭk'ada 획득하다
obvious myŏngbaek'an 명백한
occasion ttae 때
occasional kakkŭmŭi 가끔의
occasionally ttaettaero 때때로

occupant *(of car)* sŭnggaek 승객; *(of house)* chugŏja 주거자

occupation *(job)* chigŏp 직업; *(of country)* chŏmnyŏng 점령

occupy ch'ajihada 차지하다; *country* chŏmnyŏnghada 점령하다

occur *(happen)* irŏnada 일어나다

ocean pada 바다

o'clock: *at five / six* tasŏt / yŏsŏt shie 다섯 / 여섯 시에

October shiwŏl 시월

odd isanghan 이상한; *(not even)* holssu 홀수

odor naemsae 냄새

of *(possession)* …ŭi …의; *the color ~ the car* kŭ ch'aŭi saek 그 차의 색; *5 minutes ~ 12* yŏldushi obun jŏn 열두시 오분 전; *die ~ cancer* amŭro chuktta 암으로 죽다

off 1 *adv:* **be ~** *(of light, TV)* kkŏjyŏ it-tta 꺼져 있다; *(of lid)* yŏllyŏ it-tta 열려 있다; *(canceled)* ch'wisodoeda 취소되다; *walk ~* kŏrŏsŏ ka pŏrida 걸어서 가 버리다 **2** *adj:* *the ~ switch* chŏngji pŏt'ŭn 정지 버튼

offend *v/t* kibun sanghage hada 기분 상하게 하다

offense JUR wibŏp 위법

offensive 1 *adj* pulk'waehan 불쾌한 **2** *n* MIL konggyŏk

공격; *go onto the ~* konggyŏk'ada 공격하다

offer 1 *n* chegong 제공 **2** *v/t* chegonghada 제공하다; *~ sb sth* nuguege musŏul kwŏnhada 누구에게 무엇을 권하다

office samushil 사무실; *(building)* samushillyong kŏnmul 사무실용 건물

office block samushillyong koch'ŭng pilttŭing 사무실용 고층 빌딩

office hours ŏmmu shigan 업무 시간

officer MIL changgyo 장교; *(in police)* kyŏnggwan 경관

official 1 *adj* kongshigŭi 공식의; *(confirmed)* kongshik'wadoen 공식화된 **2** *n* kongmuwŏn 공무원

off-line chŏpssogŭl anhan sangt'aeŭi 접속을 안한 상태의

often chaju 자주

oil *n* kirŭm 기름; *(for machine)* sŏgyu 석유

oil company sŏgyu hoesa 석유 회사

oil tanker yujosŏn 유조선

oil well yujŏng 유정

ointment yŏn-go 연고

ok: *that's ~ by me* nanŭn kwaench'anayo 나는 괜찮아요; *are you ~?* *(well, not hurt)* kwaench'anŭseyo? 괜찮으세요?

old

old *person* nŭlgŭn 늙은;
building, car oraedoen 오래된;
(previous) yejŏnŭi 예전의;
(worn out) nalgŭn 낡은;
how ~ are you? tangshinŭn
myŏtssarimnikka? 당신은
몇살입니까?

old age nonyŏn 노년

old-fashioned kushigŭi
구식의

olive oil ollibŭ kirŭm 올리브
기름

Olympic Games Ollimp'ik
Keim 올림픽 게임

omit ppaeda 빼다

on 1 *prep: ~ the table*
t'eibŭl wie 테이블 위에;
~ the wall pyŏge 벽에;
the train kich'a-e 기차에;
~ TV t'ibŭiro TV로 **2** *adv:*
be ~ (of light, TV, computer
etc) k'yŏjyŏ it-tta 켜져
있다; *(of lid, top)* tach'yŏ
it-tta 닫혀 있다; *what's ~*
tonight? (on TV etc) onŭrŭn
muŏsŭl hamnikka? 오늘은
무엇을 합니까?; *(what's*
planned?) onŭrŭn muŏsŭl hal
kŏsimnikka? 오늘은 무엇을
할 것입니까? **3** *adj: the ~*
switch shijak pŏt'ŭn 시작
버튼

once *(one time)* han pŏn 한 번;
(formerly) hanttaee 한때에;
at ~ (immediately) chŭksshi
즉시; *all at ~ (suddenly)*

kaptchagi 갑자기; *(together)*
hankkŏbŏne 한꺼번에

one 1 *(number)* hana 하나, il
일 **2** *adj* hanaŭi 하나의; *~*
day ŏnŭ nal 어느 날 **3** *pron*
hana 하나; *which ~? (person)*
ŏnŭ saram? 어느 사람?;
(thing) ŏnŭ kŏt? 어느 것?

one-way street ilbang
t'onghaengno 일방 통행로

one-way ticket p'yŏndo
sŭngch'akkwŏn 편도 승차권

onion yangp'a 양파

on-line *adj* ollainŭi 온라인의

only 1 *adv* tanji 단지; *~ just*
kanshinhi 간신히 **2** *adj*
yuirhan 유일한; *~ son*
oeadŭl 외아들; *~ daughter*
oedongttal 외동딸

onto: *put X ~ Y (on top of)*
Xŭl / rŭl Ywie not'a X을 /
Y위에 놓다

open 1 *adj* yŏllyŏ innŭn 열려
있는; *(frank)* sumgimŏmnŭn
숨김없는 **2** *v/t* yŏlda 열다;
book p'ida 피다; *account*
t'ŭda 트다 **3** *v/i* yŏllida 열리다

opera op'era 오페라

operate 1 *v/i* MED susurŭl hada
수술을 하다 **2** *v/t machine*
chojonghada 조종하다

operation MED susul 수술

opinion ŭigyŏn 의견

opponent *(in game)* sangdae
상대; *(of reforms etc)* pandaeja
반대자

opportunity kihoe 기회
oppose pandaehada 반대하다
opposite 1 *adj direction,*
meaning pandaeŭi 반대의;
views sangbandoen 상반된
2 *n* pandae 반대
oppressive *rule* kahokhan
가혹한; *day* uurhagehanŭn
우울하게하는
optical illusion ch'akshi 착시
optimist nakch'ŏnjuŭija
낙천주의자
optimistic nakch'ŏnjŏgin
낙천적인
option sŏnt'aek-kkwŏn 선택권
optional sŏnt'aegŭi 선택의
or hogŭn 혹은, ttonŭn 또는
orange *n (fruit)* orenji 오렌지;
(color) chuhwangsaek 주황색
orange juice orenji chusŭ
오렌지 주스
orchestra ok'esŭt'ŭra
오케스트라
orchid nanch'o 난초
order 1 *n (command)*
myŏngnyŏng 명령; *(sequence)*
sunsŏ 순서; *(being well*
arranged) paeyŏl 배열;
(for goods, in restaurant)
chumun 주문; *out of ~*
(not functioning) kojangnan
고장난; *(not in sequence)*
sunsŏga pakkwin 순서가
바뀐 **2** *v/t goods, meal*
chumunhada 주문하다; *~ sb*
to do sth nuguege muŏsŭl

harago myŏngnyŏnghada
누구에게 무엇을 하라고
명령하다
ordinary pot'ong-ŭi 보통의
organic *food* yugi nongppŏbŭi
유기 농법의
organization kigu 기구
organize chojik'ada 조직하다
Orient Tongnyang 동양
origin kiwŏn 기원
original *adj (not copied)*
chintchaŭi 진짜의; *(first)*
ch'oech'oŭi 최초의
originally wŏllaenŭn 원래는
orphanage koawŏn 고아원
orthopedic chŏnghyŏng
oekkwaŭi 정형 외과의
other 1 *adj* tarŭn 다른 **2** *n*
the ~s (objects) namŏji kŏt
나머지 것; *(people)* namŏji
saram 나머지 사람
otherwise kŭroch'i anŭmyŏn
그렇지 않으면; *(differently)*
tarŭge 다르게
ounce onsŭ 온스
our uriŭi 우리의
ours uriŭi kŏt 우리의 것
ourselves uri chashin 우리
자신
out: *be ~ (of light, fire)* kkŏjyŏ
it-tta 꺼져 있다; *(of flower,*
sun) chyŏ it-tta 져 있다; *(not*
at home, in building) ŏptta
없다; *(not in competition)*
t'allak'ada 탈락하다; *(get)* ~!
nagaseyo! 나가세요

outbreak *(of violence, war)* tolbal 돌발

outcome kyŏlkkwa 결과

outdoors *adv* yaoeesŏ 야외에서

outer *wall etc* oebuŭi 외부의

outgoing *flight* ttŏnaganŭn 떠나가는; *personality* oehyangtchŏgin 외향적인

outlet *(of pipe)* paech'ulgu 배출구; *(for sales)* maejang 매장; ELEC sok'et 소켓

outlook chibesŏ pakkŭro 전망

out of ◊ *(motion)*: **run ~ the house** tallyŏnaoda 집에서 밖으로 달려나오다 ◊ *(position)*: **20 miles ~ Pusan** Pusan'ŭro put'ŏ 20mail ttŏrŏjin 디트로이트로 부터 20마일 떨어진 ◊ *(cause)* … ttaemune … 때문에 ◊ *(without)*: **we're ~ gas** urinŭn hwibalyuga ta ttŏrŏjyŏt-tta 우리는 휘발유가 다 떨어졌다 ◊: **5 ~ 10** yŏl chung tasŏt 10중 5

out-of-date kushigŭi 구식의

output 1 *n* saengsan 생산 **2** *v* *(produce)* saengsanhada 생산하

outrage 1 *n (feeling)* pun·gae 분개; *(act)* p'ongnyŏk 폭력

outrageous p'ongnyŏktchŏgin 폭력적인; *price* t'ŏmuniŏmnŭn 터무니없는

outside 1 *adj* surface, wall

pakkach'ŭi 바깥의 **2** *adv* sit pakkat'e 바깥에; *go* pakkŭro 밖으로 **3** *prep* …ŭi pakke …의 밖에

outsider oebusaram 외부사람

outskirts pyŏnduri 변두리

outstanding t'ŭktch'urhan 특출한; FIN miburŭi 미불의

oval *adj* talgyarhyŏng-ŭi 달걀형의

oven obŭn 오븐

over 1 *prep (above)* …ŭi witchoge …의 윗쪽에; *(across)* …ŭi chŏtchok p'yŏne …의 저쪽에; *(more than)* poda tŏ 보다 더 **2** *adv*: **be ~** *(finished)* kkŭnnada 끝나다; *(left)* namtta 남다; **~ here / there** yŏgie / chŏgie 여기에 / 저기에; **do sth ~** *(again)* muŏsŭl tashi toep'urihada 무엇을 다시 되풀이하다

overcoat oet'u 외투

overcome *difficulty* kŭkppok'ada 극복하다

overdo chinach'ige hada 지나치게 하다; *(cooking)* nŏmu ik'ida 너무 익히다

overdone *meat* chinach'ige ik'in 지나치게 익힌

overdose *n* kwaing pogyong 과잉 복용

overdraft chanaegŭl ch'ogwahanŭn inch'ul 잔액을 초과하는 인출

painkiller

overestimate kwadae
p'yŏngkkahada 과대
평가하다
overhead n FIN kanjŏppi
간접비
overhear uyŏnhi tŭt-tta
우연히 듣다
overlook (of building etc)
naeryŏdaboda 내려다보다;
(not see) motppoda 못보다
overnight adv travel pamsae
밤새
overpriced nŏmu pissan 너무
비싼
overrated kwadae
p'yŏngkkadoen 과대 평가된
overseas adv haeoero 해외로
overseas Koreans haeoe

kyop'o 해외 교포
oversight kan-gwaro inhan
shillsu 간과로 인한 실수
overtake ttarajaptta 따라잡다;
Br AUTO ch'uwŏrhada
추월하다
overtime adv work ch'ogwa
kŭnmu 초과 근무
owe v/t pitchida 빚지다
owing to ... ttaemune
... 때문에
own¹ v/t soyuhada 소유하다
own² 1 adj soyuŭi 소유의
2 pron: on his ~ honja 혼자
owner chuin 주인; (of hotel,
company etc) soyuja 소유자
ozone layer ojonch'ŭng
오존층

P

pace n (step) kŏrŭm 걸음;
(speed) soktto 속도
Pacific: the ~ (Ocean)
T'aep'yŏng-yang 태평양
Pacific Rim: the ~
T'aep'yŏng-yang yŏnan
태평양 연안
pack¹ n (back~) paenang
배낭; (of cereal, food) t'ong
통; (of cigarettes, cards) kap
갑 2 v/t bag, groceries etc
ssada 싸다; (of cigarettes,
cards) p'ojanghada
포장하다 3 v/i chim kkurida
짐 꾸리다

package n sop'o 소포; (of
offers etc) ilgwal 일괄
package deal ilgwal kŏrae
일괄 거래
packet pongji 봉지
padlock n chamulsoe 자물쇠
page¹ n (of book) p'eiji 페이지
page² v/t (call) hoch'urhada
호출하다
pagoda t'ap 탑
pail yangdong-i 양동이
pain ap'ŭm 아픔
painful ap'ŭn 아픈
painkiller chint'ongje 진통제

paint 1 *n* p'eint'ŭ 페인트; *(for artist)* mulkkam 물감 2 *v/t wall etc* ch'irhada 칠하다; *picture* kŭrida 그리다 3 *v/i* kŭrida 그리다

painter *(artist)* hwaga 화가

painting *(activity)* kŭrigi 그림 그리기; *(picture)* hoehwa chakp'um 회화 작품

pair ssang 쌍; *a ~ of shoes* shinbal han k'yŏlle 신발 한 켤레

pajamas chamot 잠옷

pale *person* ch'angbaek'an 창백한

palm *(of hand)* sonppadak 손바닥

pamphlet p'amp'ŭllet 팜플렛

pan *n* naembi 냄비

panic 1 *n* tanghwang 당황 2 *v/i* tanghwanghada 당황하다

pant *v/i* sumi ch'ada 숨이 차다

panties p'aent'i 팬티

pants paji 바지

pantyhose p'aent'i sŭt'ak'ing 팬티 스타킹

paper *n* chong-i 종이; *(news~)* shinmun 신문; *~s (identity)* shinbuntchŭng 신분증

paperback chong-ip'yojiŭi yŏmkkap'an ch'aek 종이표지의 염가판 책

parade *n (procession)* p'ŏreidŭ 퍼레이드

paradise nagwŏn 낙원

paragraph mundan 문단

parallel *n* p'yŏnghaeng 평행; *fig* yusattchŏm 유사점

paralyze mabishik'ida 마비시키다; *fig* muryŏkk'ehada 무력케하다

paramedic chun ŭiryo hwalttong chongsaja 준 의료 활동 종사자

paranoia p'ihae mangsang 피해 망상

paranoid *adj* p'ihae mangsang-ŭi 피해 망상의

paraplegic *n* habanshin mabihwanja 하반신 마비환자

parcel *n* sop'o 소포

pardon *v/t* yongsŏhada 용서하다; JUR samyŏnhada 사면하다; *~ me? mwŏraguyo?* 뭐라구요?

parent pumo 부모

parental pumo-ŭi 부모의

park[1] *(area)* kong-wŏn 공원

park[2] *v/i & v/t* AUTO chuch'ahada 주차하다

parking AUTO chuch'a 주차

parking garage chuch'ago 주차고

parking lot chuch'ajang 주차장

parking meter chuch'a yogŭmgi 주차 요금기

parking ticket chuch'a wiban ttaktchi 주차 위반 딱지

parliament ŭihoe 의회; *(in*

Korea) Kuk'oe 국회
parrot aengmusae 앵무새
part n *(portion)* pubun 부분;
(section) p'yŏn 편; *(area)*
chiyŏk 지역; *(of machine)*
pup'um 부품; *(in play)* yŏk 역;
(in hair) karŭma 가르마; **take
~ in** ch'amyŏhada 참여하다
participate ch'amgahada
참가하다
particular *(specific)*
t'ŭktchŏnghan 특정한;
(special) t'ŭkppyŏrhan
특별한; *(fussy)* kkadaroun
까다로운
particularly t'ŭkppyŏrhage
특별하게
partition n *(screen)* k'anmagi
칸막이
partly pubuntchŏgŭro
부분적으로
partner COMM tong-ŏptcha
동업자; *(personal)* paeuja
배우자; *(in activity)* tchak 짝
partnership COMM tong-ŏp
동업; *(in activity)* hyŏmnyŏk
협력 관계 kwan-gye
party n p'at'i 파티; POL
chŏngdang 정당; *(group)*
muri 무리
pass 1 n *(permit)*, SPORTS
p'aesŭ 패스; *(in mountains)*
sankkil 산길 **2** v/t *(hand)*
chŏnhaejuda 전해주다; *(go
past)* chinagada 지나가다;
AUTO ch'uwŏrhada 추월하다;

(go beyond) nŏmŏsŏda
넘어서다; *(approve)* sŭng-in
pat-tta 승인 받다; SPORTS
p'aesŭhada 패스하다; **~ an
exam** shihŏm'e hapkkyŏk'ada
시험에 합격하다 **3** v/i *(of
time)* ponaeda 보내다
passage pokto 복도; *(from
book)* tallak 단락
passenger sŭnggaek 승객
passer-by t'onghaengin
통행인
passion yŏltchŏng 열정;
(sexual) yoktchŏng 욕정
passive *adj* sudongjŏgin
수동적인
passport yŏkkwŏn 여권
password amho 암호
past 1 *adj (former)*
mŏnjŏtppŏnŭi 먼젓번의; **the
~ few days** chinan myŏch'il
지난 며칠 **2** n kwagŏ 과거;
in the ~ kwagŏe 과거에
3 *prep (in time)* nŏmŏ 넘어;
(in position) chinasŏ 지나서;
it's half ~ two tushi paniyeyo
두시 반이에요
pastime ch'wimi 취미
pastry *(for pie)* milkkaru
밀가루 *panjuk* 밀가루 반죽
paternal pugyeŭi 부계의;
pride, love pusŏngŭi 부성의
paternity pusŏng 부성
path kil 길
pathetic aech'ŏroun
애처로운; *infml (very bad)*

hyŏngp'yŏnŏmnŭn 형편없는

patience ch'amŭlsŏng
참을성

patient n hwanja 환자 2 adj
ch'amŭlsŏng innŭn 참을성
있는

patriotic aegukchŏgin
애국적인

patrol 1 n sunch'al 순찰 2 v/t
sunch'arhada 순찰하다

patrolman sunch'algwan
순찰관

patronizing sŏnshimŭl ssŭnŭn
tŭt'an 선심을 쓰는 듯한

pattern n (fabric) munŭi 무늬;
(model) ponbogi 본보기; (in
events) yangshik 양식

pause 1 n chungdan 중단 2 v/i
chungdanhada 중단하다

pavement (roadway) p'ojang
toro 포장 도로

paw n pal 발

pay 1 n posu 보수 2 v/t person
posurŭl chuda 보수를 주다;
sum chiburhada 지불하다; bill
nap-ppuhada 납부하다 3 v/i
chiburhada 지불하다

pay check ponggŭp 봉급

payday ponggŭmnal 봉급날

payment (of bill) nabip 납입;
(money) chibul 지불

pay phone kongjung chŏnhwa
공중 전화

PC (= personal computer)
p'isshi 피시; (= politically
correct) p'yŏn-gyŏng omnŭn

편견이 없는

peace p'yŏnghwa 평화; (quiet)
koyo 고요

peaceful p'yŏnghwaroun
평화로운

peach pokssung-a 복숭아

peak n (of mountain) chŏngsang
정상

peak hours p'ik'ŭ shigan
피크 시간

peanut butter ttangk'ong
pŏt'ŏ 땅콩 버터

pear pae 배

pearl chinju 진주

peck v/t (bite) tchoda 쪼다

peculiar (odd) kimyohan
기묘한

pedal n p'edal 페달

pedestrian n pohaengja
보행자

pediatrician soakkwa ŭisa
소아과 의사

pedicab samnyun t'aekssi
삼륜 택시

peel 1 n kkŏptchil 껍질
2 v/t fruit kkŏptchirŭl pŏtkkida
껍질을 벗기다 3 v/i (of skin)
p'ibuga pŏtkkyŏjida 피부가
벗겨지다

peer v/i chasehi poda 자세히
보다; ~ at ttturŏjige poda
뚫어지게 보다

pen n (ballpoint) polp'en 볼펜

penalize ch'ŏbŏrhada
처벌하다

penalty ch'ŏbŏl 처벌; SPORTS

p'aenŏlt'i 패널티

penalty clause (kyeyakŭi) wiyak pŏlch'ik chohang (계약의) 위약 벌칙 조항

pencil yŏnp'il 연필

pendant (necklace) mok-kkŏri 목걸이

penetrate kwant'onghada 관통하다; market chinch'urhada 진출하다

penicillin p'enishillin 페니실린

peninsula pando 반도

penitentiary kyodoso 교도소

pension yŏn-gŭm 연금

Pentagon: the ~ Miguk kukppangssŏng 미국 국방성

penthouse p'aent'ŭhausŭ 팬트하우스

people saram 사람; (race, tribe) minjok 민족

pepper huch'u 후추; (chili) koch'u 고추; (pimiento) p'imang 피망

percent p'ŏsent'ŭ 퍼센트

perception (by senses) kamji 감지; (of situation) inji 인지

perfect 1 adj wanbyŏk'an 완벽한 2 v/t wanjŏnhage hada 완전하게 하다

perfection wanbyŏk 완벽

perfectly wanbyŏk'age 완벽하게; (totally) wanjŏnhage 완전하게

perform (carry out) tahada 다하다; (of actor etc) kong-

yŏnhada 공연하다

performance (by actor) kong-yŏn 공연; (of employee, company) ŏmmu suhaeng 업무 수행; (of machine) sŏngnŭng 성능

perfume hyangsu 향수; (of flower) hyanggi 향기

perhaps amado 아마도

peril wihŏm 위험

perimeter chubyŏn 주변

period kigan 기간; (woman's) saengni 생리; (punctuation) mach'imp'yo 마침표

perjury wijŭng 위증

perm n p'ama 파마

permanent yŏnggujŏgin 영구적인

permanently yŏngguhi 영구히

permission hŏrak 허락

permit 1 n hŏgasŏ 허가서 2 v/t hŏrak'ada 허락하다

perpetual kkŭnimŏmnŭn 끊임없는

persecute pak'aehada 박해하다

persecution pak'ae 박해

persist chisok'ada 지속하다; ~ in kkŭndŏktchige toep'urihada 끈덕지게 되풀이하다

persistent person, questions kkŭndŏktchige toep'urihanŭn 끈덕지게 되풀이하는; rain etc chisoktchŏgin 지속적인

person saram 사람; *in ~ ponini* chiktchŏp 본인이 직접

personal *(private)* kaeintchŏgin 개인적인; *(individual)* kaeinŭi 개인의

personal computer kaeinnyong k'ŏmp'yut'ŏ 개인용 컴퓨터

personality sŏngkkyŏk 성격; *(celeb)* yumyŏng-in 유명인

personally *(for my part)* narossŏnŭn 나로서는; *(in person)* chiktchŏp 직접

personnel chigwŏn 직원; *(section)* insakkwa 인사과

perspiration ttam 땀

persuade sŏlttŭk'ada 설득하다

persuasion sŏlttŭk 설득

pessimist pigwanjuŭija 비관주의자

pessimistic pigwanjŏgin 비관적인

pest yuhaehan kŏt 유해한 것; *infml (person)* koltchitkkŏri 골칫거리

pester kwich'ank'e kulda 귀찮게 굴다

pesticide salch'ungje 살충제

pet *n* aewandongmul 애완동물

petition *n* ch'ŏng-wŏnsŏ 청원서

petrochemical sŏgyu hwahak chep'um 석유 화학 제품

petroleum sŏgyu 석유

petty *person* piyŏrhan 비열한; *detail* sishihan 시시한

pharmaceuticals cheyak 제약

pharmacist yakssa 약사

pharmacy *(store)* yak-kkuk 약국

phase shigi 시기

phenomenal koengjanghan 굉장한

philosopher ch'ŏrhaktcha 철학자

philosophical ch'ŏrhaktchŏgin 철학적인

philosophy ch'ŏrhak 철학

phobia kongp'otchŭng 공포증

phone 1 *n* chŏnhwa 전화 **2** *v/t* chŏnhwa kŏlda 전화 걸다 **3** *v/i* chŏnhwahada 전화하다

phone book chŏnhwabŏnhobu 전화번호부

phone booth kongjung chŏnhwa pakssŭ 공중 전화 박스

phonecall chŏnhwa 전화

phone number chŏnhwa pŏnho 전화 번호

phon(e)y *adj* katchaŭi 가짜의

photo *n* sajin 사진

photocopier pokssagi 복사기

photocopy 1 *n* pokssa 복사 **2** *v/t* pokssahada 복사하다

photographer sajinsa 사진사

photography sajin ch'waryŏng 사진 촬영

phrase *n* munkku 문구

physical adj (of the body) yukch'eŭi 육체의

physician naekkwa ŭisa 내과 의사

physicist mullihaktcha 물리학자

physics mullihak 물리학

physiotherapy mulli ch'iryo 물리 치료

piano p'iano 피아노

pick v/t (choose) sŏnt'aek'ada 선택하다; (flower) ttada 따다

◆ **pick up** v/t chibŏ tŭlda 집어 들다; (from ground) chuwŏ ollida 주워 올리다; person teryŏooda 데려오다; dry cleaning etc kajyŏooda 가져오다; (from airport etc) majung nagoda 마중 나오다; (in car) ch'a-e t'aeuda 차에 태우다; (sexual sense) ch'inhaejida 친해지다; skill paeuda 배우다

pickpocket somaech'igi 소매치기

pick-up (truck) t'ŭrŏk 트럭

picnic n sop'ung 소풍

picture n (photo) sajin 사진; (painting) hoehwa 회화; (illustration) kŭrim 그림

picturesque kŭrimgwa kat'ŭn 그림과 같은

pie p'ai 파이

piece chogak 조각; (component) pup'um 부품; a ~ of pie p'ai han chogak 파이

pierce kwant'onghada 관통하다; ears ttult'a 뚫다

pig twaeji 돼지; (person) twaejigat'ŭn nom 돼지같은 놈

pigeon pidulgi 비둘기

pile tŏmi 더미

pilgrimage sullye 순례

pill aryak 알약; the ~ kyŏnggu p'iimyak 경구 피임약

pillar kidung 기둥

pillow n pegae 베개

pilot n chojongsa 조종사

pilot plant shihŏm kongjang 시험 공장

PIN kaein hwagin pŏnho 개인 확인 번호

pin n p'in 핀; (in bowling) pollinggu'in 볼링핀; (badge) paetchi 배지

pinch n kkojipkki 꼬집기

pine n (tree) sonamu 소나무

pineapple p'ainaep'ŭl 파인애플

pink punhongsaegŭi 분홍색의

pioneering adj sŏn-gujŏgin 선구적인

pipe n kwan 관; (for smoking) p'aip'ŭ 파이프

pipeline p'aip'ŭrain 파이프라인

pirate v/t software p'yojŏrhada 표절하다

pistol kwŏnch'ong 권총

pitch 1 v/i (baseball) t'uguhada 투구하다

투구하다 2 *v/t* tent ch'ida
치다

pitcher[1] *n (baseball)* t'usu 투수
전자구

pitcher[2] *n (container)* chujŏnja
주전자

pitiful yŏnminŭl cha-anaenŭn
연민을 자아내는; *excuse*
hanshimhan 한심한

pity *n* tongjŏng 동정; *it's
a ~ that ...* ...hadani
aesŏk'agunyo ...하다니
애석하군요

pizza p'ija 피자

place 1 *n* changso 장소;
(home) chip 집; *(seat)* chari
자리; *at my ~* naŭi chibesŏ
나의 집에서 2 *v/t (put)*
not'a 놓다

plain *adj (clear)* myŏngbaek'an
명백한; *(not patterned)* mujiŭi
무지의

plan 1 *n* kyehoek 계획;
(drawing) sŏlgyedo 설계도
2 *v/t (prepare)* chunbihada
준비하다; *(design)* tijainhada
디자인하다; *~ to do ...* ...hal
kŏsŭl kyehoek'ada ...할 것을
계획하다

plane 1 *n (air~)* pihaenggi 비행기

planet haengsŏng 행성

plank nŏlppanji 널빤지

planning chunbi 준비

plant[1] *n* shingmul 식물 2 *v/t*
shimtta 심다

plant[2] *n (factory)* kongjang
공장; *(equipment)* changbi

장비

plaque *(on wall)* kinyŏm
aektcha 기념 액자

plaster *n (on wall)* hoebanjuk
회반죽

plastic 1 *n* p'ullasŭt'ik
플라스틱 2 *adj* p'ullasŭt'igŭi
플라스틱의

plastic bag pinil pongji 비닐
봉지

plastic surgery sŏnghyŏng
susul 성형 수술

plate *n (for food)* chŏpssi 접시

platform tansang 단상; RAIL
p'ŭllaetp'om 플랫폼

platinum *n* paek-kkŭm 백금

play 1 *n* THEAT yŏn-gŭk
연극; *(of children)* nori
놀이 2 *v/i (of children)*
nolda 놀다; *(of musician)*
yŏnjuhada 연주하다;
(SPORTS): *perform)* undonghada
운동하다; (SPORTS: *take part)*
ch'amgahada 참가하다 3 *v/t
music* yŏnjuhada 연주하다;
game hada 하다; *role* yŏn-
gihada 연기하다

player SPORTS kyŏnggija
경기자; MUS yŏnjuja 연주자

playing card k'adŭ 카드

playwright kŭktchak-kka
극작가

plea *n* kanch'ŏng 간청

plead *v/i*: *~ for* kanch'ŏnghada
간청하다; *~ guilty / not
guilty* yujoe / mujoerŭl

hangbyŏnhada 유죄 / 무죄를
항변하다
pleasant yuk'waehan 유쾌한
please 1 *adv* chebal 제발;
more tea? – *yes*, ch'a
tŏ hashigessŏyo? – ne, tŏ
chuseyo 차 더 하시겠어요?
– 네, 더 주세요; *do
mullonimnida 물론입니다
2 *vli* kippŭge hada 기쁘게
하다
pleased kippŭn 기쁜; ~
to meet you mannasŏ
pan-gapssŭmnida 만나서
반갑습니다
pleasure manjok 만족; *(not
business)* orak 오락
plenty p'ung-yo 풍요; ~ *of*
manŭn 많은
plot 1 *n* kyeryak 계략; *(of
novel)* kusŏng 구성 **2** *v/t
hoekch'aek'ada 획책하다
3 *v/i* ŭmmohada 음모하다
plow *n* chaenggi 쟁기
plug *n* (*for bath*) magae 마개;
ELEC p'ŭllŏgŭ 플러그; (*for
new book etc*) sŏnjŏnyong
ch'uch'ŏnsa 선전용 추천사
plum *n* chadu 자두
plumber paegwandong 배관공
plumbing (*pipes*) paegwan
배관
plump *adj* p'odongp'odonghan
포동포동한
plunge *v/i* torip'ada 돌입하다;
(*of prices*) harak'ada 하락하다

plus *prep* tŏhayŏ 더하여
pneumonia p'yeryŏm 폐렴
poach *v/t* (*cook*) ttŭgŏun mure
samtta 뜨거운 물에 삶다
poached egg suran 수란
P.O. Box sasŏham 사서함
pocket *n* hojumŏni 호주머니
pocketbook (*woman's*)
chagŭn sonkkabang 작은
손가방; (*wallet*) chigap 지갑;
(*book*) p'ok'etyong ch'aek
포켓용 책
pocketknife chumŏnik'al
주머니칼
poem shi 시
poet shiin 시인
poetry shi 시
point 1 *n* (*of knife*) kkŭt 끝;
(*in contest*) chŏmsu 점수;
(*purpose*) moktchŏk 목적; (*in
discussion*) yŏtchŏm 요점; (*in
decimals*) sosutchŏm 소수점
2 *v/i* sonkkaraguro karik'ida
손가락으로 가리키다
♦ **point at** karik'ida 가리키다
♦ **point out** chijŏk'ada
지적하다
pointless soyongŏmnŭn
소용없는
point of view kwantchŏm
관점
poison *n* tok 독
poke *v/t* ssushida 쑤시다;
(*stick*) k'uk tchirŭda 쿡
찌르다
poker (*cards*) p'ok'ŏ 포커

pole *(post)* kidung 기둥

police *n* kyŏngch'al 경찰

policeman kyŏngch'algwan
경찰관

police station kyŏngch'alsŏ
경찰서

policy¹ chŏngch'aek 정책

policy² *(insurance)* yak-kkwan
약관

polish 1 *n* kwangt'aekche
광택제 **2** *v/t* kwangnaeda
광내다

polite kongsonhan 공손한

politeness kongsonham
공손함

political chŏngch'ijŏgin
정치적인

politician chŏngch'iga 정치가

politics chŏngch'i 정치

poll *n (survey)* yŏron chosa
여론 조사

pollute oyŏmshik'ida
오염시키다

pollution oyŏm 오염

pond yŏnmot 연못

ponytail twiro mungnun mŏri
뒤로 묶는 머리

pool¹ *(swimming)* suyŏngjang
수영장; *(of water, blood)*
ungdŏng-i 웅덩이

pool² *(game)* Miguksshik
tanggu 미국식 당구

poor *adj* kananhan 가난한;
(not good) sŏt'urŭn 서투른;
(unfortunate) purhaengan
불행한

pop¹ *v/i (of balloon)* p'ŏng
hanŭn soriga nada 펑 하는
소리가 나다

pop² *n* MUS taejunggayo
대중가요

pop³ *infml (father)* appa 아빠

popcorn p'apk'on 팝콘

pope kyohwang 교황

poppy yanggwibi 양귀비

Popsicle® aisŭ k'eik'ŭ
아이스 케이크

popular inkki innŭn 인기
있는; *belief, support*
taejungchŏgin 대중적인

popularity inkki 인기

population in-gu 인구

porcelain *n* tojagi 도자기

pork twaejigogi 돼지고기

pornographic oesŏltchŏgin
외설적인

pornography p'orŭno 포르노

port *n (town)* hanggu 항구;
(area) pudu 부두; COMPUT
p'ot'ŭ 포트

portable 1 *adj* hyudaeyong-ŭi
휴대용의 **2** *n* TV p'ot'ŏbŭl
포터블

porter unbanin 운반인;
(doorman) munjigi 문지기

portion *n (food)* inbun 인분

portrait *n* ch'osanghwa 초상화

pose *v/i (for artist)* p'ojŭ
ch'wihada 포즈 취하다

position 1 *n* wich'i 위치;
(stance) chase 자세; *(in
race)* wi 위; *(point of*

view) kwantchŏm 관점; *(situation)* iptchang 입장 **2** v/t paech'ihada 배치하다

positive *attitude* chŏk-kkŭktchŏgin 적극적인; *response* kŭngjŏngjŏgin 긍정적인; *results* yangsŏng-ŭi 양성의; GRAM wŏnkkŭbŭi 원급의; ELEC yanggŭgŭi 양극의

possession soyu 소유; *(thing owned)* soyumul 소유물; ~**s** chaesan 재산

possibility kanŭngssŏng 가능성

possible kanŭnghan 가능한; *the best ~* ... kanŭnghan ch'oesŏnŭi ... 가능한 최선의 ...

possibly amado 아마도

post¹ *n (of wood etc)* kidung 기둥 **2** v/t *notice* keshihada 게시하다

post² v/t *guards* paech'ihada 배치하다

postage up'yŏn yogŭm 우편 요금

postcard yŏpssŏ 엽서

poster p'osŭt'ŏ 포스터

posting *(assignment)* immyŏng 임명

postmark soin 소인

post office uch'eguk 우체국

postpone yŏn-gihada 연기하다

posture chase 자세

pot *(cooking)* naembi 냄비; *(coffee, tea)* chujŏnja 주전자; *(for plant)* hwabun 화분

potato kamja 감자

potato chips kamja ch'ip 감자 칩

potential 1 *adj* chamjaejŏgin 잠재적인 **2** *n* chamjaeryŏk 잠재력

pothole *(in road)* p'aein kumŏng 패인 구멍

poultry *(birds)* kagŭm 가금; *(meat)* kagŭm kogi 가금 고기

pound¹ *n (weight)* p'aundŭ 파운드

pound² v/i *(of heart)* ttwida 뛰다

pound sterling p'aundŭ ton 파운드 돈

pour v/t *liquid* ssoda put-tta 쏟아 붓다

poverty kanan 가난

powder *n* karu 가루; *(for face)* pun 분

powder room hwajangshil 화장실

power *(strength)* him 힘; *(authority)* kwŏllyŏk 권력; *(energy)* enŏji 에너지; *(electricity)* chŏn-gi 전기

power cut chŏngjŏn 정전

powerful kangnyŏk'an 강력한

powerless muryŏk'an 무력한

power station paltchŏnso 발전소

PR hongbo 홍보

practical *experience*
shiltchejŏgin 실제적인;
person shillijŏgin 실리적인
practice 1 *n* shiltche 실제;
(training) yŏnssŭp 연습;
(rehearsal) lihŏsŏl 리허설;
(custom) sŭpkkwan 습관 **2** *v/i*
hullyŏnhada 훈련하다 **3** *v/t*
yŏnssŭp'ada 연습하다; *law*
etc chongsahada 종사하다
praise 1 *n* ch'ingch'an
칭찬 **2** *v/t* ch'ingch'anhada
칭찬하다
pray kidohada 기도하다
prayer kido 기도
precaution yebang 예방
precede *v/t (in time)* miri
haenghaejida 미리 행해지다
precious kwijunghan 귀중한
precise chŏnghwak'an 정확한
precisely chŏnghwak'age
정확하게
predecessor *(in job)* chŏnimja
전임자
predict yegyŏnhada 예견하다
predominant chuyohan
주요한
predominantly churo 주로
preface *n* sŏmun 서문
prefer sŏnhohada 선호하다
오히려 나은
preferable ohiryŏ naŭn
preference sŏnho 선호
preferential udaehanŭn
우대하는
pregnancy imshin 임신

pregnant imshinhan 임신한
prejudice *n* sŏnipkkyŏn
선입견
preliminary *adj* yebiŭi 예비의
premature birth chosan 조산
première *n* ch'oyŏn 초연
premises kunae 구내
premium *n (insurance)*
p'ŭrimiŏm 프리미엄
prepare *v/t* chunbihada
준비하다
prescription MED ch'ŏbangjŏn
처방전
presence issŭm 있음
present[1] **1** *adj (current)*
hyŏnjaeŭi 현재의; *be* ~
ch'amsŏk'ada 참석하다 **2** *n:*
the ~ hyŏnjae 현재; GRAM
hyŏnjaehyŏng 현재형; *at* ~
chigŭm 지금
present[2] **1** *n (gift)* sŏnmul
선물 **2** *v/t award* suyŏhada
수여하다; *program* sogaehada
소개하다
presentation palp'yo 발표
presently hyŏnjaeronŭn
현재로는; *(soon)* kot 곧
preserve *v/t peace etc* pojon
hada 보존하다; *wood etc*
pohohada 보호하다
presidency *(term)*
taet'ongnyŏng imgi 대통령
임기; *(office)* taet'ongnyŏngjik
대통령직
president POL taet'ongnyŏng
대통령; *(of company)* sajang

사장

presidential taet'ongnyŏngŭi 대통령의

press 1 n: *the* ~ ŏllon 언론 **2** v/t *button* nurŭda 누르다; *clothes* tarimjirhada 다림질하다

pressure 1 n amnyŏk 압력 **2** v/t amnyŏgŭl kahada 압력을 가하다

prestige myŏngsŏng 명성

presumably amado 아마도

pretend v/i ch'ŏk'ada 척하다

pretense kŏjit 거짓

pretext p'inggye 핑계

pretty 1 adj yeppŭn 예쁜 **2** adv (*quite*) sangdanghi 상당히

prevent maktta 막다

preview n (*of movie*) shisa 시사

previous ijŏnŭi 이전의

prey n mŏgi 먹이

price n kagyŏk 가격

priceless kapssŭl maegil su ŏmnŭn 값을 매길 수 없는

pride n charang 자랑; (*self-respect*) chajonshim 자존심

priest sŏngjiktcha 성직자

primary 1 adj chuyohan 주요한 **2** n POL yebisŏn-gŏ 예비선거

prime minister kungmuch'ongni 국무총리

primitive wŏnshiŭi 원시의; *conditions* wŏnshijŏgin 원시적인

prince wangja 왕자

princess kongju 공주

principal 1 adj chuyohan 주요한 **2** n SCHOOL kyojang 교장

principle (*moral*) toŭi 도의; (*rule*) wŏnch'ik 원칙

print 1 n (*in book*) inswae 인쇄 **2** v/t parhaenghada 발행하다; COMPUT inswaehada 인쇄하다

printer p'ŭrint'ŏ 프린터; (*person*) inswaeŏptcha 인쇄업자

prior adj ijŏnŭi 이전의

prioritize (*order*) usŏn sunwirŭl maegida 우선 순위를 매기다; (*put first*) usŏnkkwŏnŭl chuda 우선권을 주다

priority ch'oeusŏn sahang 최우선 사항

prison kamok 감옥

prisoner choesu 죄수

privacy sasaenghwal 사생활

private adj satchŏgin 사적인

privately naemirhage 내밀하게; *owned* min-gane 민간에 ŭihae 의해

privilege (*special treatment*) t'ŭktchŏn 특전; (*honor*) yŏnggwang 영광

prize n sang 상

prizewinner susangja 수상자

probability kamangsŏng 가망성

probable kŭrŏlttŭt'an 그럴듯한

probably ama 아마

probation *(in job)* kyŏnsŭp 견습; JUR chip'aeng yuye 집행 유예

probe n *(investigation)* ch'ŏltchŏhan chosa 철저한 조사

problem munje 문제

procedure chŏlch'a 절차

process 1 n kwajŏng 과정 2 v/t kagonghada 가공하다; *data* ch'ŏrihada 처리하다

proclaim sŏnŏnhada 선언하다

produce 1 n *(agricultural)* nongsanmul 농산물 2 v/t saengsanhada 생산하다; *(bring about)* yagihada 야기하다; *(bring out)* kkonaeda 꺼내다; *play, movie* chejak'ada 제작하다

producer saengsanja 생산자; *(of play, movie)* chejaktcha 제작자

product saengsanmul 생산물

production saengsan 생산; *(of play, movie)* chejak 제작

productive saengsanjŏgin 생산적인

productivity saengsanssŏng 생산성

profession chigŏp 직업

professional 1 adj p'ŭroŭi 프로의; *work* chŏnmunjŏgin 전문적인 2 n chŏnmunjik 전문직

chongsaja 전문직 종사자; *(not amateur)* p'ŭro 프로

professor kyosu 교수

profit n iik 이익

profitable suigi choŭn 수익이 좋은

profit margin sunsuik 순수익

program 1 n kyehoek 계획; RADIO, TV, COMPUT p'ŭrogŭraem 프로그램 2 v/t COMPUT p'ŭrogŭraem tchada 프로그램 짜다

programmer COMPUT p'ŭrogŭraemŏ 프로그래머

progress 1 n chinhaeng 진행 2 v/i *(in time)* chinhaengdoeda 진행되다; *(make ~)* chindoga nagada 진도가 나가다

prohibit kŭmjihada 금지하다

project[1] n *(plan)* kyehoek 계획; *(undertaking)* saŏp 사업; SCHOOL kwaje 과제; *(housing area)* chut'aek tanji 주택 단지

project[2] 1 v/t figures yesanhada 예산하다 2 v/i *(stick out)* t'wiŏnaoda 튀어나오다

projection *(forecast)* yesan 예산

projector yŏngsagi 영사기

prolific writer tajagŭi 다작의

prolong yŏnjanghada 연장하다

prom *(dance)* hak-kkyo ch'uktche 학교 축제

promise 1 n yaksok 약속 2 v/t yaksok'ada 약속하다

promote *employee* sŭngjinhada
승진하다; COMM sŏnjŏnhada
선전하다

promotion *(of employee)*
sŭngjin 승진; COMM p'anmae
ch'oktchin 판매 촉진

prompt *adj (on time)* shiganŭl
chik'inŭn 시간을 지키는;
(speedy) chŭk-kkaktchŏgin
즉각적인

pronounce parŭmhada
발음하다

proof *n* chŭnggŏ 증거

propaganda sŏnjŏn hwalttong
선전 활동

proper *(real)* chŏngshigŭi
정식의; *(correct)* parŭn 바른;
(fitting) almajŭn 알맞은

properly chedaero 제대로

property soyumul 소유물;
(land) ttang 땅

proportions yongjŏk 용적

proposal chean 제안; *(of
marriage)* ch'ŏnghon 청혼

propose 1 *v/t (suggest)*
cheanhada 제안하다; *(plan)*
kyehoek'ada 계획하다
2 *v/i (to marry)* ch'ŏnghonhada
청혼하다

prosecute *v/t* JUR kisohada
기소하다

prosecutor kŏmsa 검사

prosperous sŏnggonghan
성공한

prostitute *n* maech'unbu
매춘부

protect *v/t* pohohada 보호하다

protection poho 보호

protein tanbaektchil 단백질

protest 1 *n* hang-ŭi 항의;
(demo) temo 데모 2 *v/i*
panbak'ada 반박하다;
(demonstrate) temohada
데모하다

protester temoja 데모자

proud charangsŭrŏun
자랑스러운; *be ~ of*
charangsŭrŏpkke yŏgida
자랑스럽게 여기다

prove chŭngmyŏnghada
증명하다

provide chegonghada
제공하다; *~d (that)* …
…ranŭn chokkŏnŭro …라는
조건으로

province chibang 지방

provisional imshijŏgin
임시적인

provoke *(annoy)* sŏngggashige
hada 성가시게 하다

proximity kŭnjŏp 근접

psychiatric chŏngshinkkwaŭi
정신과의

psychiatrist chŏngshinkkwa
ŭisa 정신과 의사

psychiatry chŏngshinŭihak
정신의학

psychoanalysis chŏngshin
punsŏk 정신 분석

psychoanalyst chŏngshin
punsŏk haktcha 정신 분석
학자

psychological shimnijŏgin
심리적인

psychological shimnihaktcha
심리학자

psychology shimnihak 심리학

public 1 *adj* konggaejŏgin
공개적인 **2** *n: the ~* taejung
대중

publication *(of book)* ch'ulp'an
출판; *(by newspaper)* parhaeng
발행

publicity sŏnjŏn 선전

publicly konggaejŏguro
공개적으로

public relations hongbo 홍보

publish ch'ulp'anhada
출판하다

publisher ch'ulp'ansa 출판사

pull 1 *v/t* kkŭlda 끌다; *tooth*
ppopta 뽑다; *muscle* murihage
ssŭda 무리하게 쓰다 **2** *v/i*
tanggida 당기다

♦ **pull out** *v/i (of agreement)*
ch'ŏrhoehada 철회하다; *(of
competition)* ppajida 빠지다

pulse maekppak 맥박

pump n p'ŏmp'ŭ 펌프

punch 1 *n (blow)* chumŏktchil
주먹질 **2** *v/t (with fist)*
huryŏch'ida 후려치다

punctual shiganŭl ŏmsuhanŭn
시간을 엄수하는

punish ch'ŏbŏrhada 처벌하다

punishment ch'ŏbŏl 처벌

pupil *(of eye)* nunttongja 눈동자

purchase 1 *n* kumae 구매

2 *v/t* kumaehada 구매하다

purchaser maeipcha 매입자

pure *silk* sunsuhan 순수한; *air,
water* kkaekkŭt'an 깨끗한;
(morally) kyŏlbaek'an 결백한

purely wanjŏnhi 완전히

purify *water* chŏnghwahada
정화하다

purple chajuppich'ŭi 자주빛의

purpose moktchŏk 목적; *on ~*
kouijŏguro 고의적으로

purse *n (pocketbook)*
haendŭbaek 핸드백

pursue *v/t person* ch'ujŏk'ada
추적하다

pursuer ch'ujŏktcha 추적자

push *v/t (shove)* milda 밀다;
button nurŭda 누르다

put not'a 놓다

♦ **put down** not'a 놓다;
deposit sŏnburhada 선불하다;
rebellion chinap'ada 진압하다

♦ **put off** *light, TV* kkŭda 끄다;
(deter) tannyŏmshik'ida
단념시키다

♦ **put on** *light, TV* k'yŏda 켜다;
music t'ŭlda 틀다; *coat* iptta
입다; *shoes* shintta 신다;
make-up hada 하다

♦ **put out** *hand* naemilda
내밀다; *fire* sohwahada
소화하다

♦ **put up** *v/t hand* tŭlda 들다;
person chaewŏjuda 재워주다;
(erect) seuda 세우다; *price*
ollida 올리다; *poster* puch'ida

붙이다

♦ put up with ch'amtta 참다

puzzle n susukkekki
수수께끼; (game) p'ŏjŭl 퍼즐

Q

qualification chagyŏk 자격
qualified doctor etc
chagyŏktchŭng-i innŭn
자격증이 있는
qualify v/i SCHOOL chagyŏgŭl
ŏt-tta 자격을 얻다; (in
contest) yesŏnŭl t'onggwahada
예선을 통과하다
quality p'umjil 품질;
(characteristic) sŏngjil 성질
quantity yang 양
quarrel 1 n tat'um 다툼 2 v/i
tat'uda 다투다
quarter n sabunŭi il 사분의
일; a ~ of an hour shibobun
십오분; a ~ of 5 tasŏtsshi
shibobun chŏn 다섯시
십오분 전; ~ after 5
tasŏtsshi shibobun 다섯시
십오분
quarterfinal chunjun-
gyŏlssŭng 준준결승
quarterly 1 adj kyeganŭi
계간의 2 adv kyeganŭro
계간으로
queen yŏwang 여왕
query 1 n ŭimun 의문 2 v/t
(doubt) ŭimunŭl chegihada
의문을 제기하다
question 1 n chilmun 질문

2 v/t person chilmunhada
질문하다; (doubt) ŭishimhada
의심하다
question mark murŭmp'yo
물음표
questionnaire chilmunsŏ
질문서
quick pparŭn 빠른
quickly pparŭge 빠르게
quiet choyonghan 조용한; life,
town koyohan 고요한
quit n kŭmanduda
그만두다 2 v/i chiktchang-
ŭl kŭmanduda 직장을
그만두다
quite (fairly) kkwae 꽤;
(completely) wanjŏnhi 완전히;
I didn't ~ understand ta
ihaehal su ŏpssŏssŏyo 다
이해할 수 없었어요; ~ !
chŏngmal! 정말!; ~ a lot
kkwae manŭn 꽤 많은
quiz n k'wijŭ 퀴즈
quota mok 몫
quote 1 n (from author)
inyongmun 인용문; (price)
kyŏnjŏk 견적; (~ mark) inyong
puho 부호 2 v/t text
inyonghada 인용하다; price
kyŏnjŏk'ada 견적하다

R

rabbit t'okki 토끼
race 1 n SPORTS kyŏngju 경주
2 v/i chiltchuhada 질주하다
racial injong-ŭi 인종의
racism injong ch'abyŏltchuŭi
인종 차별주의
racist n injong ch'abyŏltchuŭija
인종 차별주의자
rack n (for bikes) chuch'adae
주차대; (for bags on train)
sŏnban 선반; (for CDs) kkoji
꽂이
racket¹ SPORTS lak'et 라켓
racket² (noise) soŭm 소음;
(criminal) pujŏnghan tonppŏri
부정한 돈벌이
radar leida 레이다
radiator nanbanggi 난방기; (in
car) ladiet'ŏ 라디에이터
radical adj kŭnbonjŏgin
근본적인; POL kŭptchinjŏgin
급진적인
radio ladio 라디오
radioactive pangsanŭng-i
innŭn 방사능이 있는
rag (for cleaning)
hŏnggŏptchogak 헝겊조각
rage n kyŏngno 격노
raid n (MIL, police) kŭpsŭp
급습; (robbers) ch'imip 침입
rail (on track) ch'ŏltto 철도;
(hand-) nan-gan 난간

railings ult'ari 울타리
railroad ch'ŏltto 철도
railroad station kich'ayŏk
기차역
rain 1 n pi 비; the ~s changma
장마 2 v/i piga oda 비가
오다; it's ~ing piga onda
비가 온다
raincoat ubi 우비
rainy piga onŭn 비가 오는
raise 1 n (in pay) insang 인상
2 v/t kid k'iuda 키우다
rally n (meeting) taehoe 대회
ranch moktchang 목장
rancher moktchangju 목장주
random 1 adj mujagwiŭi
무작위의 2 n: at ~ mujagwiro
무작위로
range n (of goods) pŏmwi
범위; (of airplane) hangsok
kŏri 항속 거리; (of
mountains) sanmaek 산맥
rank n MIL kyegŭp 계급
ransack satssach'i twijida
샅샅이 뒤지다
ransom momkkap 몸값
rape 1 n kanggan 강간 2 v/t
kangganhada 강간하다
rapid shinssok'an 신속한
rapids kŭmnyu 급류
rare tŭmun 드문
rarely tŭmulge 드물게

rash¹ MED paltchin 발진

rash² adj sŏnggŭp'an 성급한

raspberry namuttalgi 나무딸기

rat n chwi 쥐

rate n chindo 진도; (of exchange) hwannyul 환율

rather (fairly) taso 다소

rational hamnijŏgin 합리적인

rationalize v/t production hyoyurhwahada 효율화하다

rattlesnake pang-ulbaem 방울뱀

raw food nalkkŏsŭi 날것의; sugar, iron kagonghaji anŭn 가공하지 않은

raw materials wŏllyo 원료

ray pit 빛

razor myŏndok'al 면도칼

razor blade myŏndonal 면도날

reach v/t city etc toch'ak'ada 도착하다; (go as far as) ...e tat'a ...에 닿다; decision ...e irŭda ...에 이르다

react panjagyonghada 반작용하다

reaction panjagyong 반작용

reactionary adj pandong-ŭi 반동의

reactor (nuclear) wŏnjaro 원자로

read v/t & v/i iltta 읽다

reader (person) tokssŏga 독서가

readily admit sŏnttŭt 선뜻

reading tokssŏ 독서; (from meter etc) ch'ŭktchŏng 측정

ready (prepared) chunbidoen 준비된; (willing) kikkŏi ...handa 기꺼이 ...한다

real chintcha-ŭi 진짜의

realistic hyŏnshiltchŏgin 현실적인

reality hyŏnshil 현실

realize v/t kkaedat-tta 깨닫다

really chŏngmallo 정말로; (very) taedanhi 대단히; ~? chŏngmariyeyo? 정말이에요?

realtor pudongsan chunggaein 부동산 중개인

rear adj twiŭi 뒤의; lights twittchogŭi 뒷쪽의

reason n (faculty) isŏng 이성; (cause) iyu 이유

reasonable person punbyŏl innŭn 분별 있는; price chŏkttanghan 적당한

reassuring anshimhage hanŭn 안심하게 하는

rebel n panyŏktcha 반역자

rebellion pallan 반란

recall v/t ambassador sohwanhada 소환하다; (remember) sanggihada 상기하다

receipt yŏngsujŭng 영수증; acknowledge ~ of ...ŭl / rŭl padassŭmŭl injŏnghada ...을 / 를 받았음을 인정하다

receive pat-tta 받다

recent ch'oegŭnŭi 최근의

recently ch'oegŭne 최근에
reception (in hotel, office) p'ŭront'ŭ 프론트; (party) lisepsshyŏn p'at'i 리셉션 파티; (welcome) hwanyŏng 환영; RADIO sushin 수신
reception desk annae tesŭk'ŭ 안내 데스크
receptionist chŏpssuwŏn 접수원
recession pulgyŏnggi 불경기
recipe choribŏp 조리법
recipient (of parcel etc) such'wiin 수취인; (of money) suryŏng-in 수령인
reciprocal sanghoganŭi 상호간의
recite poem nangsonghada 낭송하다
reckless mumohan 무모한
reckon ...rago saenggak'ada …라고 생각하다
recognition (of state, achievements) injŏng 인정
recognize araboda 알아보다; (distinguish) pun-ganhada 분간하다; POL state sŭng-inhada 승인하다
recommend ch'uch'ŏnhada 추천하다
recommendation ch'uch'ŏn 추천
reconciliation (of people) hwahae 화해
recondition ...ŭl / rŭl surihada …을 / 를 수리하다

reconnaissance MIL chŏngch'al 정찰
reconsider v/t & v/i chaegohada 재고하다
record 1 n MUS lek'ŏdŭ 레코드; SPORTS etc kyŏnggi kirok 경기 기록; (in database) hanbŏrŭi teit'ŏ 한벌의 데이터; (in archives) kirok munsŏ 기록 문서
2 v/t (tape etc) nogŭmhada 녹음하다
record-breaking kirogŭl kkaenŭn 기록을 깨는
record holder kirok poyuja 기록 보유자
recording nogŭm 녹음
recover 1 v/t (get back) toech'at-tta 되찾다 **2** v/i MED hoebok'ada 회복하다
recovery MED hoebok 회복
recreation orak 오락
recruit 1 n MIL shinbyŏng 신병; (to company) shinip sawŏn 신입 사원 **2** v/t new staff mojip'ada 모집하다
recruitment shin-gyu mojip 신규 모집
rectangle chikssagak'yŏng 직사각형
recurrent chaebarhanŭn 재발하는
recycle chaesaeng iyonghada 재생 이용하다
recycling chaesaeng iyong 재생 이용

red ppalgan 빨간
Red Cross Chŏksshiptcha 적십자

redevelop *part of town*
chaegaebarhada 재개발하다

red-handed: *catch ~*
hyŏnhaengbŏmŭro chaptta
현행범으로 잡다

redhead mŏri'aragi pulgŭn
saram 머리카락이 붉은
사람

red light ppalgan pul 빨간 불

red tape kwallyojŏk
hyŏngshiktchuŭi 관료적
형식주의

reduce churida 줄이다

reduction kamso 감소

reel *n* (*of film*) til 릴; (*of thread*)
shilp'ae 실패

♦ **refer to** …ŭl / rŭl ŏn-gŭp'ada
…을 / 를 언급하다

referee SPORTS shimp'an 심판

reference ŏn-gŭp 언급; (*for
job*) ch'uch'ŏnsŏ 추천서; (*~
number*) chohoe 조회

referendum kungmin t'up'yo
국민 투표

refinery chŏngjeso 정제소

reflect 1 *v/t light* pansahada
반사하다 2 *v/i* (*think*)
komgomhi saenggak'ada
곰곰이 생각하다

reflection pansadoen kŭrimja
반사된 그림자; (*thought*)
shimsasuk-kko 심사숙고

reflex pansa shin-gyŏng 반사

신경

reform 1 *n* kaehyŏk 개혁 2 *v/t*
kaehyŏk'ada 개혁하다

refreshing *experience*
ch'amshinhan 참신한; ~
drink ch'ŏngnyang ŭmnyo
청량 음료

refrigerate naengjanghada
냉장하다

refrigerator naengjanggo
냉장고

refuel *v/i* yŏllyorŭl pogŭp pat-
tta 연료를 보급 받다

refugee nanmin 난민

refund 1 *n* hwanbul 환불 2 *v/t*
hwanburhada 환불하다

refusal kŏjŏl 거절

refuse kŏjŏrhada 거절하다

regard 1 *n*: (*kind*) ~s anbu
안부 2 *v/t*: *~ as* kanjuhada
간주하다

regardless: ~ *of* …e kaeŭich'i
ank'o …에 개의치 않고

regime POL chŏngkkwŏn 정권

regiment *n* yŏndae 연대

region chibang 지방

regional chiyŏgŭi 지역의

register 1 *n* tŭngnok 등록
2 *v/t birth, death* shin-gohada
신고하다; *car* tŭngnok'ada
등록하다; *letter* tŭngkkiro
puch'ida 등기로 부치다 3 *v/i*
(*for course*) tŭngnogŭl hada
등록을 하다; (*with police*)
shin-gohada 신고하다

regret 1 *v/t* huhoehada

후회하다 2 *n* yugam 유감

regular 1 *adj* kyuch'iktchŏgin
규칙적인; *pattern* iltchŏnghan
일정한; *(normal)* pot'ong-ŭi
보통의 2 *n (at bar etc)* tan-
gol 단골

regulate kyujehada 규제하다

regulation *(rule)* kyuch'ik
규칙

rehearsal lihŏsŏl 리허설

rehearse *v/t & v/i* lihŏsŏrhada
리허설하다

reimburse …ŭi piyong-ŭl
kaptta …의 비용을 갚다

reinforce poganghada
보강하다; *beliefs*
kanghwahada 강화하다

reject *v/t* kŏjŏrhada 거절하다

relapse MED chaebal 재발

related ch'inch'ŏgi toenŭn
친척이 되는; *event, ideas*
kwallyŏni innŭn 관련이 있는

relation *(family)* ch'inch'ŏk
친척; *(link)* kwan-gye 관계

relationship kwan-gye 관계

relative 1 *n* ch'inch'ŏk 친척
2 *adj* sangdaejŏgin 상대적인

relatively sandaejŏguro
상대적으로

relax *v/i* p'yŏnhi shwida 편히
쉬다

relaxation kinjang wanhwa
긴장 완화

relay *n*: ~ *(race)* kyeju kyŏnggi
계주 경기

release 1 *n (from prison)*

sŏkppang 석방; *(of CD etc)*
palmae 발매 2 *v/t prisoner*
sŏkppanghada 석방하다;
brake p'ulda 풀다

relent maŭmi nugŭrŏjida
마음이 누그러지다

relentless tanhohan 단호한;
rain sajŏng-ŏmnŭn 사정없는

relevant kwallyŏdoen 관련된

reliable shilloehal su innŭn
신뢰할 수 있는

relief anshim 안심

relieve *pressure, pain* churida
줄이다; *be ~d (at news etc)*
anshimi toeda 안심이 되다

religion chonggyo 종교

relocate *v/i* ijŏnhada 이전하다

reluctance naek'iji anŭm
내키지 않음

reluctant: *be ~ to do sth*
muŏsŭl hanŭn kŏshi naek'iji
ant'a 무엇을 하는 것이
내키지 않다

♦ **rely on** ŭijihada 의지하다

remain *(be left)* namgyŏjida
남겨지다; *(stay)* kyesok …
it-tta 계속 … 있다

remark *n* ŏn-gŭp 언급

remarkable chumok'al
manhan 주목할 만한

remedy *n* MED ch'iryo 치료; *fig*
kujech'aek 구제책

remember kiŏk'ada 기억하다

remind *v/t*: ~ *sb of sth*
nuguege muŏsŭl kiŏng nage
hada 누구에게 무엇을

기억 나게 하다; *(bring to attention)* nuguege muǒsǔl ilkkaewǒjuda 누구에게 무엇을 일깨워주다

reminder saegangnage hanǔn kǒt 생각나게 하는 것; COMM tǒkch'oktchang 독촉장

reminisce hoesang 회상

remnant yumul 유물

remorse chach'aek 자책

remote *village* oettan 외딴; *ancestor* mǒn 먼

remote control wǒnkkyǒk chojong 원격 조종

removal chegǒ 제거

remove ch'iuda 치우다; *lid* pǒtkkida 벗기다; *coat* pǒt-tta 벗다; *doubt* ǒpssaeda 없애다

renew *contract etc* kaengshinhada 갱신하다; *talks* jaegaehada 재개하다

renounce p'ogihada 포기하다

renowned yumyǒnghan 유명한

rent 1 *n* imdaeryo 임대료; *for ~* imdaeyong 임대용 **2** *v/t* imdaehada 임대하다

rental imdae kǔmaek 임대 금액

rental car imdae chadongch'a 임대 자동차

reopen *n store* chaegaejanghada 재개장하다

rep COMM seiljŭ maen 세일즈 맨

repair *v/t* koch'ida 고치다

repay kaptta 갚다

repeal *v/t law* p'yejihada 폐지하다

repeat 1 *v/t* panbok'ada 반복하다 **2** *n (TV program)* chaebangsong 재방송

repeated panboktoenǔn 반복되는

repel *v/t attack* kyǒkt'oehada 격퇴하다; *insects* moranaeda 몰아내다

repercussions p'agǔp hyǒkkwa 파급 효과

repetitive toep'uridoenǔn 되풀이되는

replace toedollyǒnot'a 되돌려놓다; *(take place of)* taeshinhada 대신하다

replacement huimja 후임자; *(thing)* taech'ep'um 대체품

replica poktchep'um 복제품

reply 1 *n* taedap 대답 **2** *v/t & v/i* taedap'ada 대답하다

report 1 *n (account)* pogosǒ 보고서; *(by journalist)* podo 보도 **2** *v/t (to authorities)* pogohada 보고하다

reporter kija 기자

represent *(act for)* taerihada 대리하다; *(stand for)* taep'yohada 대표하다

representative *n* taeriin 대리인; COMM taep'yoja 대표자; POL taebyǒnja 대변자

repress *revolt* ǒgap'ada 억압하다; *feeling* ǒngnurǔda

reprieve 억누르다; *laugh* ch'amtta 참다

reprieve 1 *n* chip'aeng yuye 집행 유예 **2** *v/t prisoner* chip'aeng-ŭl yuyehada 집행을 유예하다

reprimand *v/t* chilch'aek'ada 질책하다

reprisal poksu 복수

reproach *n* pinan 비난

reproduce 1 *v/t* chaehyŏnhada 재현하다 **2** *v/i* BIOL chaesaengshik'ada 재생식하다

republic konghwaguk 공화국

republican 1 *n* konghwadangjuŭija 공화당주의자; *Republican* POL Konghwadang-wŏn 공화당원 **2** *adj* Konghwadang-ŭl chijihanŭn 공화당을 지지하는

Republic of Korea Taehanmin-guk 대한민국

repulsive mesŭkkŏun 메스꺼운

reputable p'yŏngp'ani choŭn 평판이 좋은

reputation p'yŏngp'an 평판

request 1 *n* yoch'ŏng 요청 **2** *v/t* ch'ŏnghada 청하다

require p'iryohada 필요하다

requirement (need) yogu 요구; (condition) chokkŏn 조건

rescue 1 *n* kujo 구조 **2** *v/t* kujohada 구조하다

research *n* yŏn-gu 연구

research and development yŏn-gu kaebal 연구 개발

resemble tamtta 닮다

resent ...e pun-gaehada ...에 분개하다

reservation (of room, table) yeyak 예약

reserve 1 *n* (store) pich'uk 비축; SPORTS hubo sŏnsu 후보 선수 **2** *v/t seat, table* yeyak'ada 예약하다

residence (stay) ch'eryu 체류

residence permit kŏju hŏga 거주 허가

resident *n* kŏjuja 거주자

resign *v/i* sajik'ada 사직하다

resignation sajik 사직

resist *v/t* chŏhanghada 저항하다

resistance chŏhang 저항

resolution (decision) kyŏlshim 결심; (determination) kyŏryŏnham 결연함

resort *n* (place) hyuyangji 휴양지

resource chawŏn 자원

resourceful p'ungbuhan kiryagŭl 기략이 풍부한

respect 1 *n* chon-gyŏng 존경; (consideration) paeryŏ 배려 **2** *v/t person* chon-gyŏnghada 존경하다; *law* chonjunghada 존중하다

respectable hullyunghan

훌륭한

respond taedap'ada 대답하다;
(react) panŭnghada 반응하다

response taedap 대답;
(reaction) panŭng 반응

responsibility ch'aegim 책임

responsible chaegimi innŭn
책임이 있는

rest¹ 1 *n* hyushik 휴식 **2** *v/i*
shwida 쉬다 *3 v/t (lean etc)*
kidaeda 기대다

rest²: *the ~* namŏji 나머지

restaurant shikttang 식당

restore *building* pok-kkuhada
복구하다

restrain cheap'ada 제압하다;
~ oneself chajehada
자제하다

restraint *(moderation)* ŏktche
억제

restrict chehanhada 제한하다

restricted area MIL chehan-
guyŏk 제한구역

restriction chehan 제한

rest room hwajangshil 화장실

result *n* kyŏlgwa 결과

resume *v/t* chaegaehada
재개하다

résumé iryŏkssŏ 이력서

retail *adv* somaero 소매로

retaliate pokssuhada 복수하다

retire *v/i (from work)*
ŭnt'oehada 은퇴하다

retirement ŭnt'oe 은퇴

retract *v/t statement*
ch'ŏlhoehada 철회하다

retreat *v/i* MIL hut'oehada
후퇴하다

retrieve toech'at-tta 되찾다

retrospective *(of movies)*
hoegojŏn 회고전

return 1 *n* kwihwan 귀환;
(giving back) panhwan 반환;
COMPUT shirhaeng 실행;
(in tennis) pan-gyŏk 반격
2 *v/t (give back)* tollyŏjuda
돌려주다; *(put back)*
tollyŏnot'a 돌려놓다; *favor*
podap'ada 보답하다 **3** *v/i*
toedoragada 되돌아가다; *(of
times, doubts)* chaehyŏnhada
재현하다

return flight wangbok
pihaenggi 왕복 비행기

reunion chaehoe 재회

reunite *v/t* chaegyŏrhap'ada
재결합하다

reveal *(show)* tŭrŏnaeda
드러내다; *secret* palk'ida
밝히다

revealing *remark* palk'yŏjunŭn
밝혀주는

revenge *n* pobok 보복

revenue seip 세입

reverse 1 *n (opposite)* pandae
반대; *(back)* twittchang 뒷장
AUTO hujin 후진 **2** *v/i* AUTO
hujinhada 후진하다

review 1 *n (of book)*
pip'yŏng 비평 **2** *v/t book*
nonp'yŏnghada 논평하다;
SCHOOL pokssŭp'ada 복습하다

reviewer p'yŏngnon-ga 평론가

revise v/t opinion, text sujŏnghada 수정하다

revision sujŏng 수정

revisionism POL sujŏngjuŭi 수정주의

revive 1 v/t custom puhwarhada 부활하다 2 v/i (of business) hoeboktoeda 회복되다

revolt 1 n pallan 반란 2 v/i pallanhada 반란하다

revolting (awful) hyŏmogamŭl nŭkkige hanŭn 혐오감을 느끼게 하는

revolution POL hyŏngmyŏng 혁명; (turn) hoejŏn 회전

revolutionary 1 n POL hyŏngmyŏngga 혁명가 2 adj idea hyŏngmyŏngjŏgin 혁명적인

revolutionize hyŏngmyŏng-ŭl irŭk'ida 혁명을 일으키다

revolver kwŏnch'ong 권총

revulsion kyŏkppyŏn 격변

reward n posang 보상; (financial) posu 보수

rewarding porami innŭn 보람이 있는

rewrite v/t tashi ssŭda 다시 쓰다

rheumatism lyumat'ijŭm 류마티즘

rhyme n un 운

rhythm lidŭm 리듬

rib n kalbippyŏ 갈비뼈

ribbon libon 리본

rice ssal 쌀; (cooked) pap 밥

rice bowl pap kŭrŭt 밥 그릇

rich 1 adj puyuhan 부유한; food mashi chinhan 맛이 진한 2 n: the ~ puja 부자

rid: get ~ of ŏpssaeda 없애다

ride 1 n t'am 탐; (journey) yŏhaeng 여행 2 v/t horse, bike t'ada 타다 3 v/i (on horse) sŭngmahada 승마하다; (on bike, in vehicle) t'ada 타다

ridicule 1 n choso 조소 2 v/t choronghada 조롱하다

ridiculous t'ŏmuniŏmnŭn 터무니없는

rifle n soch'ong 소총

right 1 adj (correct) mannŭn 맞는; (proper, just) olbarŭn 올바른; (suitable) chŏktchŏrhan 적절한; (not left) orŭntchogŭi 오른쪽의; be ~ (of person) mat-tta 맞다; that's ~! paro kŭgŏya! 바로 그거야! 2 adv (directly) paro 바로; (correctly) olbarŭge 올바르게; (not left) orŭntchogŭro 오른쪽으로; ~ now (immediately) tangjang 당장; (at the moment) chigŭm 지금 3 n (civil etc) kwŏlli 권리; (not left) orŭntchok 오른쪽, POL uik 우익; on the ~ orŭntchoge(sŏ) 오른쪽에(서)

rightful owner etc hap-ppŏptchŏgin 합법적인

right-handed orŭnsonjabiŭi 오른손잡이의

right wing n POL uik 우익; SPORTS uch'ŭk konggyŏkssu 우측 공격수

rigid tandanhan 단단한; attitude wangohan 완고한

rigorous discipline ŏmkkyŏk'an 엄격한; tests myŏnmirhan 면밀한

rim (of wheel) t'eduri 테두리

ring¹ wŏnhyŏng 원형; (on finger) panji 반지; (boxing) ling 링

ring² 1 n (of bell) ullim 울림 2 v/t bell ullida 울리다 3 v/i (of bell) ullida 울리다

ringleader chumoja 주모자

rinse 1 n (for hair) linssŭ 린스 2 v/t clothes hengguda 헹구다; hair linssŭhada 린스하다

riot 1 n p'okttong 폭동 2 v/i p'okttongŭl irŭk'ida 폭동을 일으키다

rip 1 n tchijŏjin kot 찢어진 곳 2 v/t cloth tchit-tta 찢다

ripe fruit igŭn 익은

rip-off n infml sagi 사기

rise v/i (of sun) ttŏorŭda 떠오르다; (of price, level) orŭda 오르다

risk n wihŏm 위험

rival n kyŏngjaengja 경쟁자

rivalry kyŏngjaeng 경쟁

river kang 강

road kil 길

roadblock parik'eidŭ 바리케이드

road map toro chido 도로 지도

roadsign toro p'yojip'an 도로 표지판

roam toradanida 돌아다니다

roar v/i (of lion) p'ohyohada 포효하다; (of person) kohamch'ida 고함치다

roast 1 v/t kupta 굽다 2 v/i (of food) kuwŏjida 구워지다

rob kangt'arhada 강탈하다

robber kangdo 강도

robbery kangdojil 강도질

robot lobot 로봇

robust t'ŭnt'ŭnhan 튼튼한

rock 1 n tol 돌 2 v/i (of boat) chindonghada 진동하다

rocket n lok'et 로켓

rock 'n' roll lakk'ŏllol 락큰롤

role yŏk'al 역할

role model ponbogiga toenŭn saram 본보기가 되는

roll 1 n (bread) lolppang 롤빵; (of film) tong 통 2 v/i (of ball etc) kurŭda 구르다

roller blade n lollŏ pŭlleidŭ 롤러 블레이드

roller skate n lollŏ sŭk'eit'ŭ 롤러 스케이트

romantic lomaent'ik'an 로맨틱한

roof chibung 지붕

room

room pang 방; *(space)* changso 장소

roommate lum meit'ŭ 룸 메이트

room service lum ssŏbissŭ 룸 서비스

root ppuri 뿌리

rope pattchul 밧줄

rose BOT changmi 장미

rot 1 *n* ssŏgŭm 썩음 2 *v/i* ssŏktta 썩다

rotate *v/i* hoejŏnhada 회전하다

rotten ssŏgŭn 썩은

rough *adj* surface ult'ungbult'unghan 울퉁불퉁한; *(violent)* nanp'ok'an 난폭한; sea sananun 사나운; *(approximate)* taegang-ŭi 대강의

roughly *(approx)* taeryak 대략

round 1 *adj* tunggŭn 둥근 2 *n (of competition)* hoe 회

round trip wangbok yŏhaeng 왕복 여행

rouse *(from sleep)* kkaeda 깨다; *interest* chaguk'ada 자극하다

route kil 길

routine 1 *adj* ilssangjŏgin 일상적인 2 *n* ilgwa 일과

row *(line)* yŏl 열

rowboat chŏnnún pae 젓는 배

royal *adj* wang-ŭi 왕의

rub *vt* munjirŭda 문지르다

rubber 1 *n* komu 고무 2 *adj* komuŭi 고무의

rude muryehan 무례한

rudeness murye 무례

rudimentary kich'oŭi 기초의

rug kkalgae 깔개; *(blanket)* tamnyo 담요

rugged *scenery* pawi t'usŏng-iŭi 바위 투성이의

ruin 1 *n*: ~s yujŏk 유적 2 *v/t party* mangch'ida 망치다; *plan* manggattúrida 망가뜨리다; be ~ed *(financially)* p'asanhada 파산하다

rule 1 *n* kyuch'ik 규칙; as a ~ taech'ero 대체로 2 *v/t country* tasŭrida 다스리다 3 *v/i (king)* t'ongch'ihada 통치하다

ruler *(for measuring)* cha 자; *(of state)* t'ongch'ija 통치자

ruling *adj* POL chibaehanŭn 지배하는

rumor *n* somun 소문

run 1 *n (on foot)* talligi 달리기; *(in pantyhose)* orŭi p'ullim 올의 풀림 2 *v/i tallida* 달리다; *(of river)* hŭrŭda 흐르다; *(of trains)* unhaengdoeda 운행되다; *(of faucet)* hŭrŭda 흐르다; *(of play)* yŏnsok kong-yŏndoeda 연속 공연되다; *(of engine)* umjigida 움직이다; *(of software)* shirhaengtoeji ant'a 실행되지 않다; ~ for President taet'ongnyŏnge ch'ulmahada 대통령에

출마하다 3 *v/t* race
kyŏngjuhada 경주하다 3
miles tallida 달리다; *business*
unyŏnghada 운영하다
run-down *person* chich'in
지친; *area* hŏrŭmhan 허름한
runner kyŏngjuja 경주자
runner-up ch'atchŏmja 차점자
running water yusu 유수
runway hwalchuro 활주로
rural shigorŭi 시골의

rush 1 *n* mopssi sŏdurŭm
몹시 서두름 **2** *v/i* sŏdurŭda
서두르다
rush hour ch'ult'oegŭn shigan
출퇴근 시간
Russia Lŏshia 러시아
rust *n* nok 녹
rusty nogi sŭn 녹이 슨;
French etc sŏt'un 서툰
ruthless kach'aŏmnŭn
가차없는

S

sack *n* p'odae 포대
sad sŭlp'ŭn 슬픈
sadist sadisŭt'ŭ 사디스트
sadly sŭlp'ŭge 슬프게;
(regrettably) huhoesŭrŏpkkedo
후회스럽게도
sadness sŭlp'ŭm 슬픔
safe 1 *adj* anjŏnhan 안전한
2 *n* kŭmgo 금고
safely *arrive* musahi 무사히;
drive anjŏnhage 안전하게
safety anjŏn 안전
safety pin anjŏnp'in 안전핀
sail 1 *n* tot 돛; *(trip)* hanghae
항해 **2** *v/i* hanghaehada
항해하다; *(depart)*
ch'urhanghada 출항하다
sailboat yot'ŭ 요트
sailing SPORTS yot'ŭ kyŏnggi
요트 경기
sailor subyŏng 수병; SPORTS

yot'ŭ kyŏnggija 요트 경기자
saint sŏng-in 성인
sake: *for my / your ~*
narŭl / nŏrŭl wihaesŏ
나를 / 너를 위해서
salad saellŏdŭ 샐러드
salary wŏlgŭp 월급
sale p'anmae 판매; *(reduced prices)* harin p'anmae 할인
판매; *for ~* maemae 매매
sales clerk p'anmae chŏmwŏn
판매 점원
salesman seiljŭmaen
세일즈맨
salmon yŏnŏ 연어
salt sogŭm 소금
salty tchan 짠
salute 1 *n* MIL kyŏngnye 경례
2 *v/t & v/i* MIL kyŏngnyehada
경례하다
same 1 *adj* kat'ŭn 같은

2 pron: the ~ kat'ŭn kŏt 같은 것 **3** adv: sound the ~ soriga ttok-kkat'ayo 소리가 똑같아요

sample n kyŏnbon 견본

sanction n (penalty) chejae 제재

sand n morae 모래

sandal saendŭl 샌들

sandwich n saendŭwich'i 샌드위치

sane chejŏngshinŭi 제정신의

sanitarium yoyangso 요양소

sanitary conditions wisaeng-ŭi 위생의

sanitary napkin saengnidae 생리대

sanitation (installations) wisaengsŏlbi 위생설비; (waste removal) wisaengch'ŏri 위생처리

sanity chejŏngshin 제정신

sarcasm p'ungja 풍자

sarcastic pinjŏngdaenŭn 빈정대는

satellite in-gong-wisŏng 인공위성

satire p'ungja 풍자

satirical p'ungjajŏgin 풍자적인

satisfaction manjok 만족

satisfactory manjok'an 만족한; (just ok) kŭjŏ kŭrŏn 그저 그런

satisfy manjoksshik'ida 만족시키다; thirst,

conditions ch'ungjokshik'ida 충족시키다

Saturday t'oyoil 토요일

sauce sossŭ 소스

saucer pach'im chŏpsshi 받침 접시

sauna sauna 사우나

sausage soshiji 소시지

savage adj animal yasaeng-ŭi 야생의; attack chaninhan 잔인한; criticism hokttok'an 혹독한

save 1 v/t (rescue) kuhada 구하다; time, money chŏryak'ada 절약하다; COMPUT chŏjanghada 저장하다 **2** v/i (put money aside) chŏgŭmhada 저금하다 **3** n SPORTS tŭktchŏm maganaegi 득점 막아내기

saving (amount) chŏryakpun 절약분; (act) chŏryak 절약

savings yegŭm 예금

savory adj (not sweet) tchaptcharhan 짭짤한

saw n (tool) t'op 톱

say v/t marhada 말하다

saying sokttam 속담

scaffolding pal'an 발판

scale n (size) kyumo 규모; (of map) ch'ukch'ŏk 축척; MUS ŭmgye 음계

scales (to weigh) chŏul 저울

scan v/t page chasehi salp'yŏboda 자세히 살펴보다; MED chŏngmil

chosahada 정밀 조사하다;
COMPUT sŭk'aenhada
스캔하다

scandal sŭk'aendŭl 스캔들

scanner MED, COMPUT sŭk'aenŏ
스캐너

scar n hyungt'ŏ 흉터

scarce mojaranŭn 모자라는

scarcely: ~ any kŏŭi ŏptta
거의 없다

scare 1 v/t kŏptchuda 겁주다;
be ~d of musŏwŏhada
무서워하다 2 n puran 불안

scarf (neck) mokttori 목도리;
(over head) sŭk'ap'ŭ 스카프

scary mushimushihan
무시무시한

scatter 1 v/t leaflets, seeds
ppurida 뿌리다 2 v/i (of
crowd) hŭt'ŏjida 흩어지다

scenario shinario 시나리오

scene THEAT chang 장; (view)
changmyŏn 장면; (of crash)
hyŏnjang 현장; (argument)
soran 소란

scenery p'unggyŏng 풍경;
THEAT mudae paegyŏng 무대
배경

scent n hyanggi 향기

schedule n (of events) yejŏng
예정; (of work) iltchŏng 일정;
(for trains) shiganp'yo 시간표;
be on ~ yejŏngdaeroida
예정대로이다; be behind ~
yejŏngboda nŭt-tta 예정보다
늦다

scheduled flight chŏnggi
hanggongp'yŏn 정기 항공편

scheme n (plan) kyehoek
계획; (plot) moŭi 모의

schizophrenia chŏngshin
punyŏltchŭng 정신 분열증

scholarship hangmun 학문;
(financial award) changhak-
kkŭm 장학금

school hak-kkyo 학교;
(university) taehak 대학

schoolchildren hakttong 학동

schoolteacher hak-kkyo
sŏnsaengnim 학교 선생님

sciatica chwagol shin-
gyŏngt'ong 좌골 신경통

science kwahak 과학

scientific kwahaktchŏgin
과학적인

scientist kwahaktcha 과학자

sci-fi kongsang kwahak sosŏl
공상 과학 소설

scissors kawi 가위

scoff v/i nollida 놀리다

scold v/t kkujitta 꾸짖다

scooter AUTO sŭk'ut'ŏ 스쿠터

scope pŏmwi 범위;
(opportunity) kihoe 기회

scorch v/t kŭsŭllida 그슬리다

score SPORTS 1 n tŭktchŏm
득점 2 v/t chŏmsurŭl
kirok'ada 기록하다 3 v/i
tŭktchŏmhada 득점하다

scorn n kyŏngmyŏl 경멸

scornful kyŏngmyŏrhanŭn
경멸하는

scowl n tchinggŭrin ŏlgul
찡그린 얼굴

scrap 1 n (metal) p'yech'ŏl
폐철; (little bit) chogŭm 조금
2 v/t project etc p'yegishik'ida
폐기시키다

scrape v/t kŭktta 긁다

scratch 1 n (on paint) kŭlk'in
chaguk 긁힌 자국 **2** v/t
itch kŭktta 긁다; (by cat etc)
halk'wida 할퀴다

scream 1 n oech'imsori
외침소리 **2** v/i sorich'ida
소리치다

screen 1 n (in room) k'anmagi
칸막이; (protective) magi
막이; (for movie) sŭk'ŭrin
스크린; COMPUT hwamyŏn
화면 **2** v/t (protect, hide)
kamch'uda 감추다; (for
security) sŏnbyŏrhada
선별하다

screw n nasamot 나사못

screwdriver tŭraibŏ 드라이버

scribble v/t kalgyŏ ssŭgi 갈겨
쓰기

script (for play) taebon 대본;
(writing) kŭltchach'e 글자체

scriptwriter chak-kka 작가

scroll n (manuscript) turumari
두루마리

scrub v/t munjirŭda 문지르다

scruples todŏk kwannyŏm
도덕 관념

scrutinize chasehi chosahada
자세히 조사하다

scuba diving sŭk'ubŏ taibing
스쿠버 다이빙

sculpture n chogak 조각;
(object) chogakp'um 조각품

sea pada 바다; by the ~ pada
yŏp'e 바다 옆에

seafood haesanmul 해산물

seafront padatkka 바닷가

seal 1 n (on document)
pong-in 봉인 **2** v/t container
milbonghada 밀봉하다

sea level: above / below ~
haesumyŏn wie / araee 해수면
위에 / 아래에

seam n (on dress) solgi 솔기

search 1 n susaek 수색 **2** v/t
ch'at-tta 찾다

♦ **search for** ch'at-tta 찾다;
person susaek'ada 수색하다

searchlight t'amjodŭng
탐조등

search party susaekttae
수색대

seasick paemŏlmiga nan
배멀미가 난

season n (of year) kyejŏl 계절;
(for tourism) ch'ŏl 철

seasoning chomiryo 조미료

season ticket (for train etc)
chŏnggi sŭngch'akkwŏn 정기
승차권; (for stadium, opera)
chŏnggi iptchangkkwŏn 정기
입장권

seat n chari 자리, (of pants)
kungdung-i 궁둥이

seat belt chwasŏk pelt'ŭ

좌석 벨트
seaweed haech'o 해초;
edible ~ kim 김
secluded mölli ttŏrŏjyŏ
hanjŏk'an 멀리 떨어져
한적한
second 1 *n (of time)* ch'o
초 2 *adj* tu pŏntchaeŭi
두 번째의 3 *adv* come tu
pŏntchaero 두 번째로
secondary education
chungdŭng kyoyuk 중등
교육
second-best *adj* tu pŏntchaero
chal hanŭn 두 번째로
잘하는
second class *adj* ticket
idŭngsŏgŭi 이등석의
secondhand *adj* chunggoŭi
중고의
secondly tultchaero 둘째로
second-rate iryuŭi 이류의
secrecy kimil 기밀
secret *n* pimil 비밀
secretary pisŏ 비서; POL
changgwan 장관
Secretary of State Kungmu
Changgwan 국무부 장관
secretive t'ŏ noch'i annŭn 터
놓지 않는
sect punp'a 분파
section *(of book, text)* kwa 과;
(of company) pusŏ 부서
sector chŏngnyŏk 영역
secure *adj* shelf, job anjŏnhan
안전한; *feeling* anshimhanŭn

안심하는
security *(in job)* anjŏnsŏng
안전성; *(for investment)*
pojang 보장; *(at airport)*
poan 보안
security guard kyŏngbiwŏn
경비원
sedan AUTO ssallongch'a
쌀롱차
sedative *n* chinjŏngje 진정제
seduce yuhok'ada 유혹하다
see boda 보다; *(understand)*
alda 알다; *can I ~ the
manager?* ch'aegimjarŭl
mannal su issŭlkkayo?
책임자를 만날 수
있을까요?; *~ you!* tto
mannayo! 또 만나요!
◆ see off *(at airport etc)*
paeunghada 배웅하다
seed sshi 씨
seeing (that) …(i)gi ttaemune
…(이)기 때문에
seek *v/t* job ch'at-tta 찾다
seem …kŏt kat-tta …것 같다
seemingly pogienŭn 보기에는
segment pubun 부분
segregate pullihada 분리하다
seize chaptta 잡다; *(of
customs, police)* amnyuhada
압류하다
seldom tŭmulge 드물게
select 1 *v/t* sŏnt'aek'ada
선택하다 2 *adj (exclusive)*
chŏngsŏnhan 정선한

selection sŏnt'aek 선택; *(that chosen)* sŏnt'aekttoen kŏt 선택된 것

selective anmogi nop'ŭn 안목이 높은

self-confidence chashin 자신

self-conscious chaŭishigi kanghan 자의식이 강한

self-defense chagi pang-ŏ 자기 방어

self-employed chayŏng-ŭi 자영업

selfish igijŏgin 이기적인

self-respect chajonshim 자존심

self-service selp'ŭssŏbisŭŭi 셀프서비스의

sell 1 *v/t* p'alda 팔다 2 *v/i (of product)* p'anmaedoeda 판매되다

semester hak-kki 학기

semi *(truck)* t'ŭrŏk 트럭

semicircle panwŏn 반원

semifinal chun-gyŏlssŭng 준결승

seminar semina 세미나

senate sang-wŏn 상원

senator sang-wŏnŭiwŏn 상원의원

send *v/t* ponaeda 보내다

senile nosoehan 노쇠한

senior sonwiŭi 손위의; *(in rank)* sanggŭbŭi 상급의

senior citizen ŏrŭshin 어르신

sensation kamgak 감각; *(surprising event)* sensseisyŏn 센세이션

sensational sesangŭl ttŏdŭlssŏk'age hanŭn 세상을 떠들썩하게 하는; *(very good)* nunbushin 눈부신

sense *n (meaning)* ttŭt 뜻; *(purpose, point)* ŭimi 의미; *(common ~)* sangshik 상식; *(of sight, smell etc)* kamgak 감각; *(feeling)* nŭkkim 느낌

sensible punbyŏri innŭn 분별이 있는; *advice* hyŏnmyŏnghan 현명한

sensitive *skin* min-gamhan 민감한; *person* yeminhan 예민한

sensuality kwangnŭng 관능

sentence *n* GRAM munjang 문장; JUR p'an-gyŏl 판결

sentimental kamsangtchŏgin 감상적인

Seoul Sŏul 서울

separate 1 *adj* pyŏlgaeŭi 별개의 2 *v/t* pullihada 분리하다 3 *v/i (of couple)* pyŏlgŏhada 별거하다

separated *couple* pyŏlgŏhan 별거한

separation pulli 분리; *(of couple)* pyŏlgŏ 별거

September kuwŏl 구월

sequel sokp'yŏn 속편

sequence *n* sunsŏ 순서

sergeant chungsa 중사

serial *n* yŏnsongmul 연속물

serial number illyŏnbŏnho

일련번호
series yŏnsok 연속
serious shimgak'an 심각한;
(earnest) chinjian 진지한
seriously shimhage 심하게
serve 1 *n (in tennis)* sŏbŭ
서브 2 *v/t food* naeda 내다;
customer moshida 모시다
3 *v/i (in post, job)* kŭnmuhada
근무하다; *(in tennis)*
sŏbŭhada 서브하다
service 1 *n* sŏbissŭ 서비스
2 *v/t vehicle, machine*
sŏbissŭhada 서비스하다
service charge sŏbissŭryo
서비스료
service industry sŏbissŭ sanŏp
서비스 산업
service station chuyuso
주유소
session *(of Congress etc)*
kaejŏng chungim 개정 중임
set 1 *n (of tools, books, scenery,
in tennis)* set'ŭ 세트; *(for
movie)* ch'waryŏngjangso
촬영장소 2 *v/t (place)* not'a
놓다; *date* chŏnghada 정하다;
alarm clock match'uŏ not'a
맞추어 놓다; ~ *the table*
sang-ŭl ch'arida 상을 차리다
3 *v/i (of sun)* chida 지다; *(of
glue)* ŭnggohada 응고하다
4 *adj ideas* hwak-kkohan
확고한; ~ *meal* chŏngshik
정식
setback hut'oe 후퇴

settle 1 *v/i (of dust)* karaantta
가라앉다; *(to live)*
chŏngch'ak'ada 정착하다
2 *v/t dispute* hwahaeshik'ida
화해시키다; *debts*
ch'ŏngsanhada 청산하다
settlement *(of claim, debt)*
ch'ŏngsan 청산; *(of dispute)*
hwahae 화해
sever *v/t arm, cable*
chŏlttanhada 절단하다
several *adj* myŏngmyŏch'ŭi
몇몇의 2 *pron* myŏt kae
몇 개
severe *illness* shimhan 심한;
teacher, face ŏmkkyŏk'an
엄격한; *weather* mojin 모진
sew *v/t* kkwemaeda 꿰매다
sewer hasugwan 하수관
sewing panŭjil 바느질
sex *(act)* sŏnggyo 성교;
(gender) sŏng 성
sexual sŏngtchŏgin 성적인
sexy ssekssihan 섹시한
shabby nalgŭn 낡은
shade *n ŭngdal 응달; *(for
lamp)* karigae 가리개; *(of
color)* saektcho 색조; *(on
window)* pŭllaindŭ 블라인드
shadow *n* kŭrimja 그림자
shady kŭnŭljin 그늘진;
dealings ŭishimsŭrŏun
의심스러운
shake 1 *v/t hŭndŭlda 흔들다;
~ *hands* akssuhada 악수하다;
2 *v/i ttŏlda 떨다; *(of building)*

shallow

hŭndŭllida 흔들리다

shallow yat'ŭn 얕은; *person* ch'ŏnbak'an 천박한

shame 1 *n* such'ishim 수치심; *what a ~!* chŏngmal andwaessŏyo! 정말 안됐어요! 2 *v/t* mangshinshik'ida 망신시키다

shampoo *n* shyamp'u 샴푸

shape *n* moyang 모양

share 1 *n* mok 몫; FIN chushik 주식 2 *v/t* punbaehada 분배하다; *opinion* hamkke hada 함께 하다

shareholder chuju 주주

shark sangŏ 상어

sharp *adj* knife nalk'aroun 날카로운; *mind* myŏngminhan 명민한; *pain* sarŭl enŭn tŭt'an 살을 에는 듯한; *taste* chagŭktchŏgin 자극적인

shatter *v/t* pusuda 부수다; *illusions* kkaejida 깨지다

shattering *news, experience* ch'imyŏngjŏgin 치명적인

shave *v/t & v/i* myŏndohada 면도하다

shaver myŏndogi 면도기

shawl shyol 숄

she kŭnyŏ 그녀 ◊ *(omission): who is ~?* nuguyeyo? 누구예요?

shed¹ *v/t blood, tears* hŭllida 흘리다

shed² *n* ch'anggo 창고

sheep yang 양

sheer *adj madness, luxury* wanjŏnhan 완전한; *cliffs* kap'arŭn 가파른

sheet *(for bed)* shit'ŭ 시트; *(of paper)* chang 장

shelf sŏnban 선반

shell *n* kkŏptchil 껍질; MIL yut'an 유탄

shellfish kapkkangnyu 갑각류

shelter 1 *n (refuge)* p'inanch'ŏ 피난처; *(against air raids)* taep'iho 대피호; *(at bus stop)* chŏngnyujang 정류장 2 *v/i* p'ihada 피하다 3 *v/t* pohohada 보호하다

shift 1 *n (in views)* pyŏnhwa 변화; *(in work)* kyodae 교대 2 *v/t* omgida 옮기다 3 *v/i* omgida 옮기다; *(of opinion)* pyŏnhada 변하다

shift work kyodae kŭnmu 교대 근무

shine 1 *v/i* pinnada 빛나다 2 *v/t light* pich'uda 비추다

shingles MED taesangp'ojin 대상포진

ship 1 *n* pae 배 2 *v/t (send)* ponaeda 보내다; *(by sea)* sŏnjŏk'ada 선적하다

shipment hwamul 화물

shirk kŭllihada 게을리하다

shirt shyŏch'ŭ 셔츠

shiver *v/i* ttŏlda 떨다

shock 1 *n* ch'unggyŏk 충격; ELEC shyok'ŭ 쇼크 2 *v/t*

nollage hada 놀라게 하다

shocking ch'unggyŏktchŏgin 충격적인; *infml (very bad)* chidok'an choch'i anŭn 지독하지 좋지 않은

shoe shinbal 신발

shoot *v/t* ssoda 쏘다; *(kill)* ch'ongsarhada 총살하다; *movie* ch'waryŏnghada 촬영하다

shop 1 *n* sangjŏm 상점 **2** *v/i* shijangboda 시장보다

shopkeeper somaesang-in 소매상인

shopper shyop'inghanŭn saram 쇼핑하는 사람

shopping shyop'ing 쇼핑; *(items)* chang bon mulgŏn 장 본 물건

shore mulkka 물가

short *adj (in height)* k'iga chagŭn 키가 작은; *distance* tchalbŭn 짧은; *time* oraedoeji anŭn 오래되지 않은; *be ~ of* mojarada 모자라다

shortage pujok 부족

shortcoming kyŏltchŏm 결점

shortcut chirŭmkkil 지름길

shorten *v/t* churida 줄이다; *hair* tchalkke hada 짧게 하다

shortfall pujok 부족

short-lived tanmyŏnghan 단명한

shortly *(soon)* kot 곧

shorts panbaji 반바지; *(underwear)* sogot 속옷

shortsighted kŭnshiŭi 근시의

short-term tan-gigan 단기간

shot ch'ongsŏri 총소리; *(photo)* sajin 사진

shotgun yŏpch'ong 엽총

should haeya hada 해야 하다; *what ~ I do?* nanŭn musŭn irŭl haeya hamnikka? 나는 무슨 일을 해야 합니까?; *you ~n't do that* tangshinŭn kŭrŏk'e hamyŏn andoemnida 당신은 그렇게 하면 안됩니다

shoulder *n* ŏkkae 어깨

shout 1 *n* pimyŏngsori 비명소리 **2** *v/i* sorich'ida 소리치다 **3** *v/t order* myŏngnyŏnghada 명령하다

shove 1 *n* ttemiligi 떼밀기 **2** *v/t* mirŏnaeda 밀어내다 **3** *v/i* milda 밀다

show 1 *n* THEAT, TV shyo 쇼; *(display)* p'yohyŏn 표현 **2** *v/t passport* poyŏjuda 보여주다; *interest, emotion* nat'anaeda 나타내다 **3** *v/i (be seen)* poida 보이다; *(of movie)* sangyŏngdoeda 상영되다

shower 1 *n (rain)* sonagi 소나기; *(to wash)* shyawŏ 샤워 **2** *v/i* shyawŏhada 샤워하다

show-off hŏp'ungjang-i 허풍장이

shred *v/t paper* kalgari tchijŏbŏrida 갈가리

찢어버리다: *food* chogak naeda 조각 내다

shrewd pint'ŭm ŏmnŭn 빈틈 없는

shrimp saeu 새우

shrink *v/i* churŏdŭlda 줄어들다

shrug: ~ *one's shoulders* ŏkkaerŭl ŭssŭk-kkŏrida 어깨를 으쓱거리다

shudder *v/i* (*of person*) momsŏrich'ida 몸서리치다; (*of building*) ttŏllida 떨리다

shun p'ihada 피하다

shut 1 *v/t* tat-tta 닫다 **2** *v/i* tatch'ida 닫히다

♦ **shut up** *v/i* choyonghi hada 조용히 하다; ~! choyonghi hae! 조용히 해!

shuttle service shyŏt'ŭl sŏbissŭ 셔틀 서비스

shy sujubŏhanŭn 수줍어하는

sick a'ŭn 아픈; *I'm going to be* ~ (*vomit*) t'ohallaeyo 토할래요; *be* ~ *of* chigyŏpta 지겹다

sick leave pyŏngga 병가

side *n* (*of box, house*) yŏmmyŏn 옆면; (*of room, field*) ch'ungmyŏn 측면; (*of mountain*) kyŏngsa-myŏn 경사면; (*of person*) yŏpkkuri 옆구리, SPORTS t'im 팀; *I'm on your* ~ tangshin p'yŏniyeyo 당신 편이에요; ~ *by* ~ naranhi 나란히

sideboard ch'antchang 찬장

sideburns saltchŏk 살쩍

side effect pujagyong 부작용

side street kolmok-kkil 골목길

sidewalk indo 인도

sigh 1 *n* hansum 한숨 **2** *v/i* hansum chit-tta 한숨 짓다

sight *n* kwanggyŏng 광경; (*sense*) shiryŏk 시력; ~*s* (*of city*) kyŏnggwan 경관

sightseeing kwan-gwang 관광

sign *n* (*indication*) kimi 기미; (*road* ~) p'yojip'an 표지판; (*outside store*) kanp'an 간판

signal 1 *n* shinho 신호 **2** *v/i* AUTO shinhohada 신호하다

signature sŏmyŏng 서명

significance chungnyosŏng 중요성

significant chungdaehan 중대한; (*large*) sangdanghan 상당한

sign language suhwa 수화

silence 1 *n* koyo 고요; (*of person*) ch'immuk 침묵 **2** *v/t* ch'immukshik'ida 침묵시키다

silent choyonghan 조용한

silk 1 *n* pidan 비단 **2** *adj shirt etc* pidanŭi 비단의

silly ŏrisŏgŭn 어리석은

silver 1 *n* ŭn 은 **2** *adj* ŭnŭi 은의; *hair* ŭnppich'ŭi 은빛의

similar pisŭt'an 비슷한

similarity yusa 유사

simple shwiun 쉬운; *person*
tansunhan 단순한
simplicity kanttanham 간단함
simplify tansunhwahada
단순화하다
simply kanttanhage 간단하게;
(absolutely) chŏngmal 정말
simultaneous tongshiŭi
동시의
sin *n* choe 죄
since 1 *prep* ihuro 이후로; ~
last week chinan chu ihuro
지난 주 이후로 **2** *adv*
iraero 이래로 **3** *conj* ...han
hue ...한 후에; *(because)*
...hagi ttaemune ...하기
때문에
sincere sŏngshirhan 성실한
sincerity sŏngshil 성실
sing noraehada 노래하다
Singapore Shinggap'orŭ
싱가포르
singer kasu 가수
single *adj* *(sole)* hana 하나;
(not double) han kyŏp 한 겹;
(not married) toksshinja
독신자
single room irinshil 일인실
sinister saak'an 사악한
sink 1 *n* shingk'ŭ 싱크 **2** *v/i*
karaantta 가라앉다; *(of sun)*
chida 지다
sip *v/t* holtchak-kkŏrida
홀짝거리다
sir sŏnsaengnim 선생님
siren sairen 사이렌

sister yŏja hyŏngje 여자 형제
sister-in-law *(man's elder
brother's wife)* hyŏngsu 형수;
(wife's younger sister) ch'ŏje
처제; *(husband's younger /
elder sister)* shinui 시누이;
*(woman's younger / elder
brother's wife)* olk'e 올케
sit *v/i* antta 앉다
♦ **sit down** antta 앉다
sitcom shit'ŭk'om 시트콤
site *n* changso 장소
sitting room kŏshil 거실
situated: be ~ wich'ihada
위치하다
situation sanghwang 상황
size k'ŭgi 크기; *(of jacket,
shoes)* ch'issu 치수
skate *v/i* sŭk'eit'ŭ t'ada
스케이트 타다
skateboard *n* sŭk'eit'ŭbodŭ
스케이트보드
skeptic hoeŭironja 회의론자
skeptical hoeŭijŏgin
회의적인
skepticism hoeŭiron 회의론
sketch 1 *n* sŭk'ech'i 스케치;
THEAT ch'ongŭk 촌극 **2** *v/t*
sŭk'ech'ihada 스케치하다
ski 1 *n* sŭk'i 스키 **2** *v/i* sŭk'i
t'ada 스키 타다
skid *n* mikkŭrŏm 미끄럼
2 *n* mikkŭrŏjida 미끄러지다
skiing sŭk'i t'agi 스키 타기
ski lift sŭk'i lip'ŭt'ŭ 스키
리프트

skill kisul 기술
skilled sungnyŏndoen 숙련된
skillful nŭngsuk'an 능숙한
skin n p'ibu 피부; *(of animal)* kajuk 가죽
skinny kkangmarŭn 깡마른
skip 1 n *(little jump)* ttwiŏ orŭm 뛰어 오름 2 *v/t (omit)* ppattŭrida 빠뜨리다
skipper NAUT sŏnjang 선장; *(of team)* chujang 주장
skirt n ch'ima 치마
skull tugaegol 두개골
sky hanŭl 하늘
skyscraper mach'ŏllu 마천루
slack *discipline, rope* nŭsŭnhan 느슨한; *person* pujuŭihan 부주의한; *period* pulgyŏngggiŭi 불경기의
slacken *v/t rope* nŭsŭnhage hada 느슨하게 하다; *pace* nŭtch'uda 늦추다
slam *v/t door* k'wang tat-tta 쾅 닫다
slander n chungsang 중상
slang sogŏ 속어
slant *v/i* kiulda 기울다
slap 1 n ch'igi 치기 2 *v/t* ch'alssak ttaerida 찰싹 때리다
slash 1 n *(cut)* pegi 베기; *(punctuation)* sŭllaeshwi 슬래쉬 2 *v/t costs* sak-kkamhada 삭감하다
slaughter n tosal 도살; *(of people)* hakssal 학살

slave n noye 노예
sleazy t'arak'an 타락한
sleep 1 n cham 잠; *go to ~* chami tŭlda 잠이 들다 2 *v/i* chada 자다
sleeping bag sŭllip'ing paek 슬리핑 백
sleeping pill sumyŏnje 수면제
sleepless *night* cham mot irunŭn 잠 못 이루는
sleepy *town* choyonghan 조용한; *I'm ~* chollyŏyo 졸려요
sleeve somae 소매
slender *figure* kanyalp'ŭn 가냘픈; *margin* ŏlma andoenŭn 얼마 안되는
slice 1 n *(of bread)* chogak 조각 2 *v/t loaf etc* yalkke charŭda 얇게 자르다
slide 1 n *(for kids)* mikkŭrŏmt'ŭl 미끄럼틀; PHOT sŭllaidŭ 슬라이드 2 *v/i* mikkŭrojida 미끄러지다
slight *adj person* kanyalp'ŭn 가냘픈; *(small)* yakkanŭi 약간의
slightly yakkan 약간
slim 1 *adj* nalsshinhan 날씬한; *chance* hŭibak'an 희박한 2 *v/i* sal ppaeda 살 빼다
slip *v/i (on ice)* mikkŭrŏjida 미끄러지다; *(of quality etc)* chŏhadoeda 저하되다
slipper sŭllip'ŏ 슬리퍼
slippery mikkŭrŏun 미끄러운

slit 1 *n* (*tear*) tchijŏjin kot
찢어진 곳; (*in skirt*) kilge
t'ŭn kot 길게 튼 곳 2 *v/t*
tchijŏ yŏlda 찢어 열다

slogan *n* sŭllogŏn 슬로건

slope 1 *n* kyŏngsa 경사; (*of
mountain*) kisŭk 기슭 2 *v/i*
kyŏngsajida 경사지다

sloppy *adj* pujuŭihan
부주의한

slot *n* t'ŭmsae 틈새

slouch *v/i* momŭl kuburida
몸을 구부리다

slow nŭrin 느린

slowly ch'ŏnch'ŏnhi 천천히

slum *n* pinmin-ga 빈민가

slump *n* COMM pulgyŏnggi
불경기

slurred *speech* parŭmi
punmyŏngch'i anŭn 발음이
분명치 않은

slush nok-kki shijak'an nun
녹기 시작한 눈

sly kyohwarhan 교활한

small *adj* chagŭn 작은; (*in
amount*) chŏgŭn 적은

small hours shimnya 심야

small talk chattam 잡담

smart *adj* mŏtchin 멋진;
(*intelligent*) ttokttok'an 똑똑한

smash 1 *n* AUTO ch'ungdol
충돌 2 *v/t* (*break*) pusuda
부수다; (*hit hard*) kangt'ahada
강타하다 3 *v/i* (*break*)
pusŏjida 부서지다

smear *n* (*of ink*) ŏlluk 얼룩;

(*on character*) otchŏm 오점

smell 1 *n* naemsae 냄새 2 *v/t*
...ŭi naemsaerŭl mat-tta ...의
냄새를 맡다 3 *v/i* (*bad*)
naemsaega nada 냄새가 나다

smile 1 *n* miso 미소 2 *v/i*
misojit-tta 미소짓다

smirk *n* nŭnggŭlmajŭn usŭm
능글맞은 웃음

smoke 1 *n* yŏn-gi 연기 2 *v/t*
cigarette p'iuda 피우다 3 *v/i*
yŏn-giga nada 연기가 나다

smoker hŭbyŏnja 흡연자

smoking hŭbyŏn 흡연; *no ~*
kŭmyŏn 금연

smolder (*of fire*) yŏn-giman
p'iuda 연기만 피우다

smooth *adj* maekkŭrŏun
매끄러운; *ride* pudŭrŏun
부드러운; *transition*
sunjoroun 순조로운

smother *flames* tŏp'ŏ kkŭda
덮어 끄다; *person* chilsshik
shik'ida 질식 시키다

smug chal nan ch'ehanŭn 잘
난 체하는

smuggle *v/t* milssuhada
밀수하다

smuggler milssuŏptcha
밀수업자

smuggling milssu 밀수

snack *n* kanshik 간식

snake *n* paem 뱀

snap 1 *v/t* (*break*) purŏttŭrida
부러뜨리다; (*say sharply*)
ttakttak-kkŏrida 딱딱거리다

snarl 2 v/i (break) purŏjida
부러지다

snarl v/i ŭrŭrŏnggŏrida
으르렁거리다

snatch v/t chabach'aeda
잡아채다; (steal) humch'ida
훔치다

sneakers undonghwa 운동화

sneer v/i piut-tta 비웃다

sneeze v/i chaech'aegihada
재채기하다

sniff v/t (smell) k'oro tŭrishwida
코로 들이쉬다

sniper chŏgyŏkppyŏng
저격병

snob songmul 속물

snooty kŏmanhan 거만한

snore v/i k'o kolda 코 골다

snow 1 adv: ~ hot nŏmu
tŏun 너무 더운; not ~ much
nŏmu manch'i ank'e 너무
많지 않게; ~ much better
hwŏlsshin tŏ chŏun 훨씬 더
좋은; ~ am I / do I nado
kŭraeyo / kŭrŏk'e haeyo 나도
그래요 / 그렇게 해요;
and ~ on kit'a tŭngdŭng
기타 등등; ~ what? kŭraesŏ
ŏtchaet-ttanŭn kŏya? 그래서
어쨌다는 거야? **2** pron:

I hope ~ kŭrŏk'e toegil
paramnida 그렇게 되길
바랍니다 **3** conj (for that
reason) kŭgŏsŭro inhaesŏ
그것으로 인해서; (in order
that) kŭraesŏ 그래서

soak v/t (steep) tamgŭda
담그다; (of rain) chŏksshida
적시다

soaked hŭmppŏk chŏjŭn
흠뻑 젖은

soap n pinu 비누; ~ (opera)
yŏnsok tŭrama 연속 드라마

soar (of rocket etc) sosa orŭda
솟아 오르다; (of prices)
ch'isot-tta 치솟다

sob v/i hŭnŭkkyŏ ulda 흐느껴
울다

sober ch'wihaji anŭn 취하지
않은

soccer ch'uk-kku 축구

sociable sagyojŏgin 사교적인

social adj sahoeŭi 사회의

socialism sahoejuŭi 사회주의

socialist adj sahoejuŭijŏgin
사회주의적인 **2** n
sahoejuŭija 사회주의자

socialize saramgwa sagwida
사람과 사귀다

social worker sahoe saŏpkka
사회 사업가

society sahoe 사회;
(organization) tanch'e 단체

sock yangmal 양말

socket ELEC sok'et 소켓; (of
arm) kwanjŏl 관절

soda (~ *water*) t'ansansu
탄산수; (*ice-cream*)
k'ŭrimsoda 크림소다; (*soft
drink*) ch'ŏngnyang ŭmnyo
청량 음료

sofa sop'a 소파

soft *pillow* p'ukssinhan
푹신한; *voice, music, skin*
pudŭrŏun 부드러운; *light*
onhwahan 온화한; (*lenient*)
kwandaehan 관대한

soft drink ch'ŏngnyang ŭmnyo
청량 음료

software sop'ŭt'ŭweŏ
소프트웨어

soil n (*earth*) hŭk 흙

solar energy t'aeyang enŏji
태양 에너지

soldier kunin 군인

sole n (*foot, shoe*) padak 바닥

solemn (*serious*) ŏmssuk'an
엄숙한

solid *adj* (*hard*) tandanhan
단단한; *gold sun* 순; (*sturdy*)
t'ŭnt'ŭnhan 튼튼한; *support*
kangnyŏk'an 강력한

solidarity tan-gyŏl 단결

solitaire (*game*) sollit'erŭ
솔리테어

solitary *life* kodok'an 고독한;
(*single*) tan hanaŭi 단 하나의

solitude kodok 고독

solo n (*of singer*) tokch'ang
독창; (*of player*) toktchu 독주
2 *adj* honjaŭi 혼자의

solution haedap 해답;

solve p'ulda 풀다

somber kŏmusŭrŭmhan
거무스름한; (*serious*)
ch'imurhan 침울한

some 1 *adj* ŏttŏn 어떤 **2** *pron*
(*people*) ŏttŏn saramdŭl 어떤
사람들; (*things*) ŏttŏn kŏt
어떤 것; *would you like
~?* chom hashigessŏyo? 좀
하시겠어요?

somebody nugun-ga 누군가

someday ŏnjen-ga 언젠가

somehow ŏttŏk'edŭnji
어떻게든지; (*for unknown
reason*) ŏtchŏnji 어쩐지

someone → somebody

someplace → somewhere

something muŏshin-
ga 무엇인가; *is ~
wrong?* muŏshi chalmot
toeŏssŭmnikka? 무엇이 잘못
되었습니까?

sometimes ttaettaero 때때로

somewhere 1 *adv* ŏdin-gae
어딘가에 **2** *pron*: *let's go ~
quiet* ŏdi choyonghan kosŭro
kapsshida 어디 조용한
곳으로 갑시다

son adŭl 아들

song norae 노래

son-in-law sawi 사위

soon kot 곧; *as ~ as ~* …haja
maja …하자 마자; *as ~ as
possible* kanŭnghan han ppalli
가능한 한 빨리

soothe chinjŏngshik'ida
진정시키다
sophisticated seryŏndoen
세련된; *machine* chŏnggyohan
정교한
sordid tŏrŏun 더러운
sore *adj* (*painful*) ap'ŭn 아픈
sorrow *n* sulp'ŭm 슬픔
sorry (*sad*) sŭlp'ŭn 슬픈;
sight pulssanghan 불쌍한;
(*I'm*) ~ (*apology*) mianhae
미안해; (*polite*) mianhamnida
미안합니다; *I'll be ~ to
leave* ttŏnani yugamimnida
떠나니 유감입니다;
I'm ~ for her kŭ yŏjaga
andwaetkunyo 그 여자가
안됐군요
sort 1 *n* chongnyu 종류 2 *v/t*
pullyuhada 분류하다; sort out
kubunhada 구분하다; COMPUT
sound 1 *n* sori 소리 2 *v/i:
that ~s interesting*
chaemiissŭl kŏt kat'ayo
재미있을 것 같아요
soundproof *adj* pang-ŭmŭi
방음의
soup (*western*) sup'ŭ 수프;
(*Korean*) kuk 국
sour *adj* shin 신; *milk* sanghan
상한
source *n* wŏnch'ŏn 원천; (*of
river*) suwŏnji 수원지

South Africa Namap'ŭrik'a
남아프리카
South America Nammi 남미
Southeast Asia Tongnam
Ashia 동남 아시아
southern nambuŭi 남부의
South Korea Namhan 남한
South Korean 1 *adj* Namhanŭi
남한의 2 *n* (*person*)
Namhanin 남한인
souvenir kinyŏmp'um 기념품
sovereignty tongnipkuk
독립국
sow *v/t seeds* ppurida 뿌리다
soy sauce kanjang 간장
spa onch'ŏn 온천
space *n* (*beyond earth*) uju
우주; (*area*) pin k'an 빈 칸;
(*room*) konggan 공간
spacecraft ujusŏn 우주선
space shuttle uju
wangbokssŏn 우주 왕복선
spacious tŭnŏlbŭn 드넓은
spade sap 삽
Spain Sŭp'ein 스페인
Spanish *adj* Sŭp'einŭi
스페인의
spare 1 *adj* yebiŭi 예비의 2 *n*
(*part*) yebip'um 예비품
spare ribs kalbi 갈비
spare room yebi pang
예비 방
spare time namnŭn shigan
남는 시간
spark *n* pulkkot 불꽃
spark plug chŏmhwajŏn

점화전

sparse *vegetation* sanjaehanŭn 산재하는

speak marhada 말하다; *~ing* TEL chŏndeyo 전데요

speaker (at conference) yŏnsŏltcha 연설자; (for audio) sŭp'ik'ŏ 스피커

special t'ŭkpyŏrhan 특별한; (particular) t'ŭktchŏnghan 특정한

specialist chŏnmun-ga 전문가

specialize (of company) chŏnmunŭro hada 전문으로 하다; (of student) chŏngonghada 전공하다

specially → *especially*

specialty chŏnmun 전문

species chong 종

specific t'ŭktchŏnghan 특정한

specify myŏnggihada 명기하다

specimen kyŏnbon 견본; MED p'yobon 표본

spectacle (impressive sight) changgwan 장관

spectator kwan-gaek 관객

speculate v/i ch'uk'ŭk'ada 추측하다; FIN t'ugihada 투기하다

speech (address) yŏnsŏl 연설

speed 1 n soktto 속도 **2** v/i ppalli kada 빨리 가다; AUTO kwasok'ada 과속하다

speeding n AUTO kwasok 과속

speed limit soktto chehan

spell¹ v/t & v/i ch'ŏltchahada 철자하다

spell² n (period) kigan 기간

spelling ch'ŏltcha 철자

spend *money* ssŭda 쓰다; *time* ponaeda 보내다

spice n yangnyŏm 양념

spider kŏmi 거미

spill 1 v/t ŏptchirŭda 엎지르다 **2** v/i ŏptchillŏjida 엎질러지다

spin 1 v/t hoejŏnshik'ida 회전시키다 **2** v/i (of wheel) hoejŏnhada 회전하다

spinach shigŭmch'i 시금치

spinal ch'ŏkch'uŭi 척추의

spine ch'ŏkch'u 척추; (of book) tŭng 등

spin-off pusanmul 부산물

spiral n nasŏnhyŏng-ŭi 나선형의

spirit n chŏngshin 정신; (soul) yŏnghon 영혼; (energy) hwalgi 활기

spirits¹ (alcohol) chŭngnyuhayŏ mandŭn sul 증류하여 만든 술

spirits² (morale) sagi 사기

spiritual adj chŏngshinchŏgin 정신적인

spit v/i (of person) ch'imŭl paett-tta 침을 뱉다

spite n agŭi 악의

spiteful agŭi innŭn 악의 있는

splash v/t t'wigida 튀기다

splendid mŏtchin 멋진

splendor hwaryŏham 화려함

splinter n kashi 가시

split 1 n (in wood) tchogaejim 쪼개짐; (disagreement) purhwa 불화; (division, share) mok 몫 **2** v/t log tchogaeda 쪼개다; party etc punyŏlshik'ida 분열시키다

spoil v/t mangch'ida 망치다; child pŏrŭdŏpsshi mandŭlda 버릇없이 만들다

spoilsport infml punwigi kkaenŭn saram 분위기 깨는 사람

spoilt adj child pŏrŭtŏmnŭn 버릇없는

spokesperson taebyŏnin 대변인

sponsor n (for visa) pojŭngin 보증인; (for sport) huwŏnja 후원자

sponsorship huwŏn 후원

spontaneous chabaltchŏgin 자발적인

spoon n sutkkarak 숟가락

sporadic sanbaltchŏgin 산발적인

sport n sŭp'och'ŭ 스포츠

sportscar sŭp'och'ŭ k'a 스포츠 카;

sportsman namja undongga 남자 운동가

sportswoman yŏja undongga 여자 운동가

spot¹ (pimple) yŏdŭrŭm 여드름; (from measles etc)

panjŏm 반점; (in pattern) mulppang-ul munŭi 물방울 무늬

spot² (place) changso 장소

spot³ v/t (notice) arach'aeda 알아채다; (identify) shikppyŏrhada 식별하다

spot check mujagwi ch'uch'ul kŏmsa 무작위 추출 검사

spotlight n sŭp'otŭrait'ŭ 스포트라이트

sprain 1 n ppim 삠 **2** v/t ppida 삐다

sprawl v/i k'ŭn taetcharo ppŏt-tta 큰 대자로 뻗다; (of city) sabang-ŭro ppŏt-tta 사방으로 뻗다

spray 1 n (of sea) mulbora 물보라; (paint, for hair) sŭp'ŭrei 스프레이 **2** v/t ppurida 뿌리다

spread 1 n (of disease) manyŏn 만연; (of religion) pogŭp 보급 **2** v/t (lay) p'yŏlch'ida 펼치다; jam parŭda 바르다; news, disease p'ŏttŭrida 퍼뜨리다 **3** v/i p'ŏjida 퍼지다

spring¹ n (season) pom 봄

spring² n (device) yongsuch'ŏl 용수철

springboard taibing tae 다이빙 대

sprinkle v/t ppurida 뿌리다

sprint n SPORTS tan-gŏri yukssang kyŏnggi 단거리 육상 경기 **2** v/i chiltchuhada

질주하다
spurt 1 n (in race) punbal 분발
2 v/i (of liquid) ppumŏjyŏ
naoda 뿜어져 나오다
spy n kanch'ŏp 간첩
♦ **spy on** kamshihada
감시하다
squalid chijŏbunhan 지저분한
squander nangbihada
낭비하다
square 1 adj sagak'yŏng-ŭi
사각형의; ~ mile p'yŏngbang
mail 평방 마일 2 n
sagak'yŏng 사각형; (in town)
kwangjang 광장
squash¹ n (to eat) hobak 호박
squash² n (game) sŭk'wŏshi
스쿼시
squash³ v/t nullŏ
tchigŭrŏttŭrida 눌러
찌그러뜨리다
squat v/i ungk'urigo antta
웅크리고 앉다; (illegally)
mudan kŏjuhada 무단
거주하다
squeak v/i (of mouse)
tchiktchik-kkŏrida
찍찍거리다; (of hinge etc)
ppigŏk-kkŏrida 삐걱거리다
squeeze v/t kkwak chwida 꽉
쥐다; orange tchada 짜다
squint n sap'alnun 사팔눈
stab v/t tchirŭda 찌르다
stability anjŏngssŏng 안정성
stable adj anjŏngdoen 안정된
stadium kyŏnggijang 경기장

staff n (employees) chigwŏn
직원; (teachers) kyosa 교사
stage¹ (in project) tan-gye
단계; (of journey) yŏjŏng 여정
stage² n THEAT mudae 무대
stagger v/i hwich'ŏnggŏrida
휘청거리다
stain 1 n (mark) ŏlluk 얼룩;
(for wood) ch'aksaek
착색 2 v/t (dirty)
tŏrŏp'ida 더럽히다; wood
ch'aksaek'ada 착색하다
stainless steel n sŭt'einresŭ
스테인레스
stair kyedan 계단; the ~s
ch'ŭnggye 층계
stake n (of wood) malttuk
말뚝; (gambling) p'antton
판돈; (investment) t'uja 투자
stale bread shinsŏnhaji anŭn
신선하지 않은
stall v/i (of car) mŏmch'uda
멈추다; (for time)
kyomyohage shiganŭl kkŭlda
교묘하게 시간을 끌다
stamina ch'eryŏk 체력
stammer 1 n maldŏdŭm
말더듬 2 v/i marŭl tŏdŭmtta
말을 더듬다
stamp¹ n (for letter) up'yo
우표 2 v/t passport tojang
tchikta 도장 찍다
stance (position) iptchang
입장
stand 1 n (at exhibition)
kwallamsŏk 관람석 2 v/i (not

stand by *sit*) sŏda 서다; *(rise)* irŏsŏda 일어서다 3 *v/t (tolerate)* ch'amtta 참다

♦ **stand by 1** *v/i (be ready)* taegihada 대기하다 2 *v/t person* chijihada 지지하다; *decision* kojip'ada 고집하다

♦ **stand for** *(represent)* p'yoshihada 표시하다

♦ **stand up** *v/i* irŏsŏda 일어서다

standard 1 *adj (usual)* pot'ong-ŭi 보통의 2 *n (level)* kijun 기준; *(norm)* p'yojun 표준

standardize *v/t* kyugyŏk'wahada 규격화한다

standard of living saenghwal sujun 생활 수준

standby *(for flight)* taegihago innŭn 대기하고 있는

standpoint kwantchŏm 관점

standstill: be at a ~ mŏmch'un 멈춘

staple diet chuyoshikttan 주요식단

stapler hoch'ik'isŭ 호치키스

star 1 *n* pyŏl 별; *fig* sŭt'a 스타; **four-~** mugunghwa nesŭl 무궁화 넷의 2 *v/i (in movie)* chuyŏnhada 주연하다

stare *v/i*: **~ (at)** (…ŭl / rŭl) ppani ch'yŏdaboda (…을 / 를) 빤히 쳐다보다

Stars and Stripes sŏngjogi 성조기

start 1 *n* shijak 시작 2 *v/i* shijakdoeda 시작되다; *(of car)* shidongdoeda 시동되다 3 *v/t* shijak'ada 시작하다; *engine* shidongshik'ida 시동시키다; *business* seuda 세우다

starter *(food)* ep'it'aijyŏ 에피타이저; AUTO shidongjangch'i 시동장치

starvation kia 기아

starve *v/i* kumjurida 굶주리다

state¹ *n (condition)* sangt'ae 상태; *(part of country)* chu 주; *(country)* kuk-kka 국가; *the States* Miguk 미국 2 *adj capital etc* chu(rib)ŭi 주 (립) 의

state² *v/t* kongshiktchŏguro parŏnhada 공식적으로 발언하다

State Department (Mi)Kungmusŏng (미) 국무성

statement *(police)* chinsul 진술; *(announcement)* palp'yo 발표; *(bank)* (ŭnhaeng) t'ongjang 통장

state-of-the-art *adj* ch'oech'ŏmdanŭi 최첨단의

statesman chŏngch'iga 정치가

station *n* RAIL yŏk 역; RADIO, TV pangsongguk 방송국

stationary chŏngjihan 정지한

stationery munbanggu 문방구

statistics (science) t'onggyehak 통계학; (figures) t'onggye 통계

statue sang 상

status chiwi 지위

status symbol shinbunŭi sangjing 신분의 상징

stay 1 n ch'eryu 체류 2 v/i mŏmurŭda 머무르다; (in a condition) yujihada 유지하다; ~ in a hotel hot'ere mukda 호텔에 묵다; ~ right there! kŏgisŏ kkomtchakchi hajima! 거기서 꼼짝도 하지마

steady adj (not shaking) ttŏlliji annŭn 떨리지 않는; (regular) iltchŏnghan 일정한

steak sŭt'eik'ŭ 스테이크

steal v/t humch'ida 훔치다

steam n kim 김

steamer (for cooking) tchimt'ong 찜통

steel 1 n kangch'ŏl 강철 2 adj kangch'ŏllo mandŭn 강철로 만든

steep adj hill kap'arŭn 가파른

steer v/t chojonghada 조종하다

steering wheel haendŭl 핸들

stem n (of plant) chulgi 줄기

step n (pace) kŏrŭm 걸음; (stair) kyedan 계단; (measure) choch'i 조치

♦ step down (from post etc) mullŏnada 물러나다

stereo n sŭt'ereo 스테레오

stereotype n chŏnhyŏng 전형

sterilize purimk'ehada 불임케 하다; equipment sodok'ada 소독하다

stern adj ŏmkkyŏk'an 엄격한

steroids sŭt'eroidŭ 스테로이드

stew n sŭt'yu 스튜

steward (on plane, ship) samujang 사무장

stewardess sŭt'yuŏdisŭ 스튜어디스

stick¹ n makttaegi 막대기; (of policeman) konbong 곤봉

stick² 1 v/t (glue) puch'ida 붙이다 2 v/i put-tta 붙다; (jam) tallabut-tta 달라붙다

sticky kkŭnjŏk-kkŏrinŭn 끈적거리는

stiff adj leather ppŏtppŏt'an 뻣뻣한; muscle ppŏgŭnhan 뻐근한; manner ttakttak'an 딱딱한; competition shimhan 심한

stifle v/t yawn kkuk ch'amtta 꾹 참다; debate ŏktchehada 억제하다

stifling tapttap'an 답답한

stigma omyŏng 오명

still¹ 1 adj koyohan 고요한 2 adv: keep ~! kamanhi issŏ! 가만히 있어!

still² adv (yet) ajikkto 아직도; (nevertheless) kŭraedo 그래도; ~ more tŏ-uk tŏ 더욱 더

stillborn: be ~ sasandoeda 사산되다

stimulant chakŭktche 자극제
stimulate chagŭk'ada
자극하다
stimulation hŭngbun 흥분
stimulus chagŭk 자극
sting 1 v/t (of bee, jellyfish)
ssoda 쏘다 2 v/i (hurt)
ttakkŭmgŏrida 따끔거리다
stipulate kyujŏnghada
규정하다
stir v/t hwijŏt-tta 휘젓다
stir-fry v/t poktta 볶다
stitch 1 (sewing) panŭlttam
바늘땀; (in knitting) k'o 코;
~es MED panŭl panŭt ba 바늘 2 v/t
(sew) kkwemaeda 꿰매다
stock 1 n (reserves) chŏjang
저장; (of store) sangp'um
상품; FIN chushik 주식; in
~ maejang-e innŭn 매장에
있는; out of **~** maejindoen
매진된 2 v/t COMM katch'uda
갖추다
stockbroker chushik
chungmae-in 주식 중매인
stock exchange chŭngkkwŏn
kŏraeso 증권 거래소
stockholder chuju 주주
stock market chŭngkkwŏn
shijang 증권 시장
stockpile n pich'uk 비축
stomach n (organ) wi 위;
(abdomen) pae 배
stomach-ache pokt'ong 복통
stone n (material) sŏktcho
석조; (pebble) tol 돌

stony ground tori manŭn 돌이
많은
stoop v/i (bend) ungk'ŭrida
웅크리다; (have bent back)
tŭng-i kuptta 등이 굽다
stop 1 n (for train) yŏk 역;
(for bus) chŏngnyujang
정류장 2 v/t (put an end
to) mŏmch'uda 멈추다;
(prevent) mot'age hada 못하게
하다; (cease) kŭmanduda
그만두다; car etc mŏmch'uge
hada 멈추게 하다 3 v/i
mŏmch'uda 멈추다; (of rain)
kŭch'ida 그치다; (of bus)
sŏda 서다
stopover chamshi mŏmum
잠시 머뭄
stop sign mŏmch'um shinho
멈춤 신호
storage pogwan 보관
store 1 n kage 가게; (stock)
chŏjang 저장; (storehouse)
ch'anggo 창고 2 v/t
chŏjanghada 저장하다
storm n p'okp'ung 폭풍
stormy p'okp'ung-u-ga ch'inŭn
폭풍우가 치는; relationship
kyŏngnyŏrhan 격렬한
story¹ iyagi 이야기; (in
newspaper) kisa 기사
story² (of building) ch'ŭng 층
stove (for cooking) yoriyong
konno 요리용 곤로; (for
heating) sŭt'obŭ 스토브
straight 1 adj kodŭn

string

곧은; *(honest)* soltchik'an 솔직한; *whiskey* sŭt'ŭreit'ŭ 스트레이트 2 *adv (in a straight line)* ttokpparo 똑바로; *(directly)* kot-tchang 곧장; ~ *ahead* be paro ap'e 바로 앞에; *go* ttokpparo 똑바로;~*away* chŭksshi 즉시

straighten *v/t* ttokpparŭge hada 똑바르게 하다

straightforward soltchik'an 솔직한; *(simple)* kanttanhan 간단한

strain *n (on rope)* p'aengp'aengham 팽팽함; *(on engine)* muri 무리; *(on person)* kinjang 긴장

strand *v/t: be ~ed* odogado mot'ada 오도가도 못하다

strange isanghan 이상한; *(unknown)* morŭnŭn 모르는

stranger natssŏn saram 낯선 사람

strap *n (of bag)* kajuk-kkŭn 가죽끈; *(of dress)* kkŭn 끈; *(of watch)* chul 줄

strategy *(plan)* kyehoek 계획

straw *(for drink)* sŭt'ŭro 스트로

strawberry ttalgi 딸기

stray *n (animal)* ttŏdori chimsŭng 떠돌이 짐승

stream *n (of water, of people)* mulkkyŏl 물결

street kŏri 거리

streetcar chŏnch'a 전차

strength him 힘; *(strong point)* changtchŏm 장점; *(of wind)* kangdo 강도; *(of friendship)* kangham 강함; *(of currency)* kangse 강세

strengthen *v/t* kanghage hada 강하게 하다

stress 1 *n (emphasis)* akssent'ŭ 악센트; *(tension)* sŭt'ŭresŭ 스트레스 2 *v/t urgency* kangjohada 강조하다

stressful sŭt'ŭresŭga shimhan 스트레스가 심한

stretch *n (of land, water)* p'yŏlch'yŏjim 펼쳐짐 2 *v/t material* nŭrida 늘이다; *income* akkyŏ ssŭda 아껴 쓰다 3 *v/i (to relax)* tchuk ppŏt-tta 쭉 뻗다; *(to reach)* naemilda 내밀다

strict ŏmhan 엄한; *orders* ŏmkkyŏon an ŏmgyŏn

stride *n* k'ŭn kŏrŭm 큰 걸음

strike 1 *n (of workers)* p'aŏp 파업; *(in baseball)* sŭt'ŭraik'ŭ 스트라이크; *be on* ~ tongmaeng p'aŏp chung-ida 동맹 파업 중이다 2 *v/i (attack)* konggyŏk'ada 공격하다; *(of disaster)* ttŏrŏjida 떨어지다 3 *v/t person* ttaerida 때리다; *object* pudich'ida 부딪히다; *oil* palgyŏnhada 발견하다

string *n* kkŭn 끈; *(of violin, tennis racket etc)* chul 줄

strip 1 v/t (remove) pŏtkkida
벗기다; (undress) osŭl
pŏtkkida 옷을 벗기다 **2** v/i
(undress) osŭl pŏt-tta 옷을
벗다

stripe chulmunŭi 줄무늬

strive v/i: ~ **for** …ŭl / rŭl
ŏdŭryŏgo noryŏk'ada …
을 / 를 얻으려고
노력하다

stroke 1 n MED noejol 뇌졸; (in
writing) hoek 획; (swimming)
suyŏngpŏp 수영법 **2** v/t
ssŭdadŭmtta 쓰다듬다

stroll n sanch'aek 산책

stroller (for baby) yumoch'a
유모차

strong person himsen
힘센; feeling kanghan 강한;
structure kyŏn-gohan 견고한;
candidate yuryŏk'an 유력한;
wind ssen 센; coffee chinhan
진한; drink tok'an 독한;
taste kangnyŏlhan 강렬한;
smell chidok'an 지독한;
views kanggyŏnghan 강경한;
currency kangseŭi 강세의

structural kujosang-ŭi
구조상의

structure n kujo 구조; (sth
built) kŏnch'ungmul 건축물

struggle 1 n (fight) ssa-um
싸움; (hard time) akchŏn
kot'u 악전 고투 **2** v/i (have a
hard time) akchŏn kot'uhada
악전 고투하다

stub n (of cigarette) kkongch'o
꽁초

stubborn kojibi ssen 고집이
센; defense wan-ganghan
완강한

stuck-up infml kŏmanhan
거만한

student hakssaeng 학생

studio (of artist) chagŏpsshil
작업실; (recording) nogŭmshil
녹음실; (film) yŏnghwa
ch'waryŏngso 영화 촬영소;
(TV) pangsongshil 방송실

study 1 n (room) sŏjae 서재;
(learning) kongbu 공부;
(research) yŏn-gu 연구
2 v/t (at school) kongbuhada
공부하다; (examine) chal
salp'yŏboda 잘 살펴보다
3 v/i kongbuhada 공부하다

stuff n mulgŏn 물건;
(belongings) chim 짐

stuffing (for food) sok 속

stuffy room t'ongp'ung-i
chal andoenŭn 통풍이 잘
안되는; person ttakttak'an
딱딱한

stumble hŏt-ttidida 헛디디다

stumbling block chang-aemul
장애물

stun kijŏlsshik'ida
기절시키다; (of news)
ŏribŏngbŏnghage hada
어리벙벙하게 하다

stupid ŏrisŏgŭn 어리석은

stupidity ŏrisŏgŭm 어리석음

stutter *v/i* marŭl tŏdŭmtta 말을 더듬다

style *n* pangbŏp 방법; *(of writing)* munch'e 문체; *(fashion)* yuhaeng 유행; *(elegance)* p'umkkyŏk 품격

subconscious: *the ~* mu-ŭishik 무의식

subcontract *v/t* hach'ŏnghada 하청하다

subcontractor hach'ŏng-ŏptcha 하청업자

subdued kara-anjŭn 가라앉은; *light* natch'un 낮춘

subject *n (topic)* chuje 주제; *(of learning)* kwamok 과목; GRAM chuŏ 주어

subjective chugwanjŏgin 주관적인

submarine chamsuham 잠수함

submissive sunjongjŏgin 순종적인

submit *v/t plan* chech'urhada 제출하다

subordinate *n* araet saram 아랫 사람

♦ **subscribe to** *magazine* chŏnggi kudok'ada 정기 구독하다

subscription chŏnggi kudok 정기 구독

subside *(of flood)* ppajida 빠지다; *(of storm)* karaantta 가라앉다; *(of building)* naeryŏantta 내려앉다

subsidiary *n* chahoesa 자회사

subsidy pojogŭm 보조금

substance *(matter)* multchil 물질

substantial sangdanghan 상당한

substitute *n* taeriin 대리인; *(for commodity)* taeyongp'um 대용품; SPORTS pogyŏl sŏnsu 보결 선수

subtitle *n* chamak 자막

subtle mimyohan 미묘한

subtract *v/t* ppaeda 빼다

suburb kyo-oe 교외; *the ~s* kŭn-gyo 근교

subway chihach'ŏl 지하철

succeed *v/i* sŏnggonghada 성공하다

success sŏnggong 성공

successful sŏnggongjŏgin 성공적인

successive it-ttarŭn 잇따른

successor huimja 후임자

succulent chŭbi manŭn 즙이 많은

such 1 *adj (of that kind)* kŭrŏn 그런; *~ a (so much of a)* kŭ chŏngdo-ŭi 그 정도의 **2** *adv* kŭrŏk'e 그렇게; *it was ~ a hot day* kŭrŏk'e tŏun nariŏssŏyo 그렇게 더운 날이었어요

suck ppara mŏktta 빨아 먹다

suction huimja 흡입

sudden kaptchaksŭrŏn 갑작스런

suddenly 384

suddenly kaptchagi 갑자기
sue v/t kosohada 고소하다
suffer v/i kosaenghada 고생하다
sufficient ch'ungbunhan 충분한
suffocate v/i chilsshiksshahada 질식사하다
sugar n sŏlt'ang 설탕
suggest cheanhada 제안하다
suggestion chean 제안
suicide chasal 자살; *commit ~* charsarhada 자살하다
suit 1 n yangbok han pŏl 양복 한 벌 **2** v/t (of clothes, color) ŏullida 어울리다
suitable chŏkttanghan 적당한
suitcase yŏhaeng kabang 여행 가방
suite (of rooms) sŭwit'ŭ 스위트; (furniture) sop'a sett'ŭ 소파 셋트
sulk v/i purut'unghaejida 부루퉁해지다
sum (total) ch'onggye 총계; (amount) kŭmaek 금액; (in arithmetic) kyesan 계산
summarize v/t yoyak'ada 요약하다
summary n yoyak 요약
summer yŏrŭm 여름
summit chŏngsang 정상; POL sunoe hoedam 수뇌 회담
summon sojip'ada 소집하다
sun t'aeyang 태양; *in the ~* haetppyŏch'e(sŏ) 햇볕에(서)

sunbathe ilgwangnyogŭl hada 일광욕을 하다
sunblock haetppyŏt ch'adannyong k'ŭrim 햇볕 차단용 크림
sunburn haetppyŏch'e t'am 햇볕에 탐
Sunday iryoil 일요일
sunglasses saegan-gyŏng 색안경
sunrise ilch'ul 일출
sunset ilmol 일몰
sunshine haetppit 햇빛
suntan haetppyŏch'e t'am 햇볕에 탐
superb koengjanghi ttwiŏnan 굉장히 뛰어난
superficial p'yomyŏnjŏgin 표면적인; person ch'ŏnbak'an 천박한
superfluous pulp'iryohan 불필요한
superintendent (of apartments) kwalliin 관리인
superior 1 adj poda ttwiŏnan 보다 뛰어난 **2** n (in hierarchy) wittsaram 윗사람
supermarket sup'ŏmak'et 수퍼마켓
superpower POL ch'ogangdaeguk 초강대국
superstitious mishinŭl minnŭn 미신을 믿는
supervise kamdok'ada 감독하다
supervisor (at work)

kamdoktcha 감독자

supper chŏnyŏk shikssa 저녁 식사

supplier COMM konggŭbwŏn 공급원

supply 1 n konggŭp 공급 **2** v/t konggŭp'ada 공급하다

support 1 n t'odae 토대; *(backing)* chiji 지지 **2** v/t *structure* chit'aenghada 지탱하다; *(financially)* puyanghada 부양하다; *(back)* chijihada 지지하다

supporter chijija 지지자; SPORTS huwŏnja 후원자

supportive chal towajunŭn 잘 도와주는

suppose *(imagine)* kajŏnghada 가정하다; *be ~d to ...* *(be meant to)* ...hagiro toeŏit-tta ...하기로 되어있다; *(be said to be)* ...(ŭ)ro allyŏjyŏ it-tta ...(으)로 알려져 있다; *you are not ~d to ...* *(not allowed)* ...haji ank'iro toeŏit-tta ...하지 않기로 되어있다

suppress *rebellion etc* chinap'ada 진압하다

Supreme Court Kodŭng Pŏbwŏn 고등 법원

sure 1 *adj: I'm ~* hwaksshinhamnida 확신합니다 **2** *adv: ~!* mullon! 물론!

surely pandŭshi 반드시; *(gladly)* kikkŏi 기꺼이

surf 1 n *(on sea)* millyŏdŭnŭn p'ado 밀려드는 파도 **2** v/t: *~ the Net* int'ŏnesŭl tullŏboda 인터넷을 둘러보다

surface n p'yomyŏn 표면; *(of water)* sumyŏn 수면

surfing sŏp'ing 서핑

surge n *(growth)* kŭpssangsŭng 급상승

surgeon oekkwa ŭisa 외과 의사

surgery susul 수술

surname sŏng 성

surplus 1 n ing-yŏ 잉여 **2** adj namŏjiŭi 나머지의

surprise 1 n nollaum 놀라움 **2** v/t nollage hada 놀라게 하다; *be ~d* nollada 놀라다

surprising nollaun 놀라운

surrender v/i MIL hangbok'ada 항복하다

surround v/t tullŏ ssada 둘러 싸다

surroundings hwan-gyŏng 환경

survival saranamŭm 살아남음

survive saranamtta 살아남다

survivor saengjonja 생존자

suspect 1 n hyŏmŭija 혐의자 **2** v/t *person* ŭishimhada 의심하다; *(suppose)* chimjak'ada 짐작하다

suspend *(from duties)* chŏngjishik'ida 정지시키다

suspense sŏsŭp'ensŭ 서스펜스

suspicion ŭishim 의심

suspicious (causing suspicion) susanghan 수상한; (feeling it) ŭishimsŭrŏun 의심스러운

swallow v/t & v/i samk'ida 삼키다

swan paektcho 백조

sway v/i hŭndŭlgŏrida 흔들리다

swear v/i yogŭl hada 욕을 하다; JUR sŏnsŏhada 선서하다

swearword yok 욕

sweat 1 n ttam 땀 2 v/i ttamŭl hŭllida 땀을 흘리다

sweater sŭwet'ŏ 스웨터

sweatshirt sŭwet'ŭ shyŏch'ŭ 스웨트 셔츠

sweep v/t floor ssŭlda 쓸다

sweet adj taste tan 단

sweet and sour adj saek'omdalk'omhan 새콤달콤한

sweetcorn oksusu 옥수수

sweetener kammiryo 감미료

swell v/i put-tta 붓다

swelling n MED pugi 부기

swerve v/i pinnagada 빗나가다

swim 1 v/i suyŏnghada 수영하다 2 n suyŏng 수영

swimming pool suyŏngjang 수영장

swimsuit suyŏngbok 수영복

swindle n sagi 사기

swing 1 n (child's) kŭne 그네

2 v/t hŭndŭlda 흔들다 3 v/i hŭndŭlgŏrida 흔들거리다; (turn) hoejŏnshik'ida 회전시키다; (of opinion) kiulda 기울다

switch 1 n (for light) sŭwich'i 스위치 2 v/t (change) pakkuda 바꾸다 3 v/i (change) pakkwida 바뀌다

♦ **switch off** v/t kkŭda 끄다

♦ **switch on** v/t k'yŏda 켜다

swollen puŭn 부은

sword kŏm 검

syllabus kaeyo 개요

symbol (character) kiho 기호; (poetic) sangjing 상징

symbolic sangjingjŏgin 상징적인

symmetric(al) taech'ingjŏgin 대칭적인

sympathetic (showing pity) tongjŏnghanŭn 동정하는; (understanding) chal arajunŭn 잘 알아주는

sympathizer POL tongjoja 동조자

sympathy tongjŏngshim 동정심; (understanding) ihae 이해

symphony kyohyanggok 교향곡

symptom chŭnghu 증후

synthetic happssŏng-ŭi 합성의

syringe chusagi 주사기

system ch'egye 체계; (method) pangshik 방식

T

table n sang 상; *(of figures)* p'yo 표

tablespoon k'ŭn sutkkarak 큰 숟가락

tablet MED allyak 알약

table tennis t'ak-kku 탁구

taboo adj kŭmgiŭi 금기의

tact chaech'i 재치

tactful chaech'i innŭn 재치 있는

tactics chŏnsul 전술

tactless chaech'i ŏmnŭn 재치 없는

tag *(label)* kkorip'yo 꼬리표

tail light midŭng 미등

tailor chaebongsa 재봉사

tailor-made match'umŭi 맞춤의; *solution* ansŏng match'umŭi 안성 맞춤의

Taiwan Taeman 대만

Taiwanese 1 adj Taemanŭi 대만의 2 n Taemanin 대만인

take v/t *(remove)* kajigo kada 가지고 가다; *(transport)* t'aewŏ chuda 태워 주다; *(accompany)* terigo kada 데리고 가다; *(accept: credit cards)* pat-tta 받다; *exam* ch'ida 치다; *degree* ch'widŭk'ada 취득하다; *sb's temperature* chaeda 재다; *(endure)* ch'amtta 참다;

(require) p'iryoro hada 필요로 하다; *how long does it ~?* ŏlmana kŏllimnikka? 얼마나 걸립니까?; *I'll ~ it (shopping)* igŏsŭro hagessŭmnida 이것으로 하겠습니다

◆ **take out** *(from pocket)* kkŏnaeda 꺼내다; *appendix etc* ppoptta 뽑다; *(to dinner etc)* terigo nagada 데리고 나가다; *insurance* ...e tŭlda …에 들다

◆ **take over** 1 v/t *company* insuhada 인수하다 2 v/i *(of new management etc)* chang-ak'ada 장악하다

◆ **take up** *carpet* tŭrŏ ollida 들어 올리다; *(carry up)* wiro unbanhada 위로 운반하다; *judo etc* paegui shijak'ada 배우기 시작하다; *space, time* ch'ajihada 차지하다

takeoff *(of plane)* iryuk 이륙

takeover COMM insu 인수

tale iyagi 이야기

talented chaenŭng-i innŭn 재능이 있는

talk 1 v/i & v/t marhada 말하다 2 n *(conversation)* taehwa 대화; *(lecture)* kangnyŏn 강연

talk show chwadamhoe 좌담회

tall k'iga k'ŭn 키가 큰

tame

tame *adj* kildŭryŏjin 길들여진
tampon t'amp'on 탐폰
tangerine milgam 밀감,
kyul 귤
tank AUTO, MIL t'aengk'ŭ 탱크
tanker *(ship)* yujosŏn 유조선;
(truck) yujoch'a 유조차
tanned haetppyŏch'e t'an
햇볕에 탄
Taoism Togyo 도교
tap 1 *n* kkoktchi 꼭지 **2** *v/t*
(knock) kabyŏpkke tudŭrida
가볍게 두드리다; *phone*
toch'ŏnghada 도청하다
tape 1 *n* t'eip'ŭ 테이프
2 *v/t (record)* nogŭmhada
녹음하다; *(stick)* t'eip'ŭro
puch'ida 테이프로 붙이다
tape measure chulja 줄자
tape recorder nogŭmgi 녹음기
target 1 *n* kwanyŏk 과녁
(for sales) mokp'yo 목표
2 *v/t market* mokp'yoro hada
목표로 하다
tarmac *(at airport)* hwaltchuro
활주로
tart *n* kwail p'ai 과일 파이
task immu 임무
taste 1 *n (sense)* migak 미각;
(of food etc) mat 맛; *(in clothes
etc)* ch'wihyang 취향 **2** *v/t*
matppoda 맛보다
tattoo munshin 문신
taunt *n* chorong 조롱
taut p'aengp'aenghan 팽팽한
tax *n* segŭm 세금

tax-free myŏnseŭi 면세의
taxi t'aeksshi 택시
tax payer napseja 납세자
tax return *(form)* napsse shin-
gosŏ 납세 신고서
tea ch'a 차; *green ~* nokch'a
녹차; *black ~* hongch'a 홍차
teabag ch'a pongji 차 봉지
teach karŭch'ida 가르치다
teacher sŏnsaeng 선생
teacup ch'atchan 찻잔
team t'im 팀
teamwork hyŏpttong chagŏp
협동 작업
teapot chattchujŏnja 찻주전자
tear¹ 1 *n (in cloth etc)* tchijŏjin
t'ŭm 찢어진 틈 **2** *v/t*
tchit-tta 찢다 **3** *v/i (go fast)*
chiltchuhada 질주하다
tear² *(in eye)* nunmul 눈물
tearful nunmul ŏrin 눈물 어린
tear gas ch'oerugasŭ 최루가스
tease *v/t* nollida 놀리다
teaspoon ch'atssutkkarak
찻숟가락
technical kisultchŏgin
기술적인
technician kisultcha 기술자
technique kisul 기술
technological kwahak
kisulsang-ŭi 과학 기술상의
technology kwahak kisul
과학 기술
teenager t'ineijŏ 틴에이저
telecommunications
t'ongshin 통신

telephone 1 *n* chŏnhwa 전화
2 *v/t person …* ege chŏnhwarŭl kŏlda …에게 전화를 걸다
3 *v/i* chŏnhwahada 전화하다
telephone call chŏnhwa 전화
telephone number chŏnhwa pŏnho 전화 번호
telephoto lens mang-wŏn lenjŭ 망원 렌즈
television t'ellebijŏn 텔레비전; (set) t'ellebijŏn susanggi 텔레비전 수상기
television program t'ellebijŏn p'ŭrogŭraem 텔레비전 프로그램
tell *v/t story* marhada 말하다; *difference* kubyŏrhada 구별하다; **~ sb sth** nuguege muŏsŭl marhada 누구에게 무엇을 말하다; **~ sb to do sth** nuguege muŏsŭl harago marhada 누구에게 무엇을 하라고 말하다
teller ŭnhaeng ch'ullabwŏn 은행 출납원
temp 1 *n (employee)* imshi chigwŏn 임시 직원
temper *(bad)* sŏngjil 성질; **keep one's ~** hwarŭl ch'amtta 화를 참다; **lose one's ~** hwarŭl naeda 화를 내다
temperamental *(moody)* pyŏndŏkssŭrŏun 변덕스러운
temperature ondo 온도; *(fever)* yŏl 열
temple REL sawŏn 사원

temporary ilsshijŏgin 일시적인
tempting yuhoktchŏgin 유혹적인
tenant ch'ayongja 차용자
tendency kyŏnghyang 경향
tender¹ *(sore)* manjimyŏn ap'ŭn 만지면 아픈; *(affectionate)* tajŏnghan 다정한; *steak* yŏnhan 연한
tender² *n* COMM ipch'al 입찰
tennis t'enissŭ 테니스
tennis court t'enissŭ chang 테니스 장
tense *adj muscle* kinjangdoen 긴장된; *moment* kinjangdoenŭn 긴장되는
tension *(of rope)* p'aengp'aengham 팽팽함; *(emotional)* kinjang 긴장; *(in movie)* kinbak-kkam 긴박감
tent ch'ŏnmak 천막
tentative chujŏhanŭn 주저하는
tepid mijigŭnhan 미지근한
term *(time)* kigan 기간; SCHOOL hakki 학기; *(condition)* kiil 기일; **in the long / short ~** changgijŏgŭro / tan-gijŏgŭro 장기적으로 / 단기적으로
terminal 1 *n (at airport, for buses)* t'ŏminŏl 터미널 2 *adj* MED pulch'iŭi 불치의
terminate *v/t contract* wanjŏnhi kkŭnnaeda 완전히 끝내다; *pregnancy* nakt'aeshik'ida 낙태시키다

terminus chongchŏm 종점

terrain chihyŏng 지형

terrible kkŭmtchik'an 끔찍한

terrific koengjangan 굉장한

terrify kŏmnage hada 겁나게
하다

terrifying kŏmnage hanŭn
겁나게 하는

territorial waters yŏnghae
영해

territory yŏngt'o 영토

terrorism t'erŏrijŭm 테러리즘

terrorist t'erŏbŏm 테러범

terrorize wihyŏp'ada
위협하다

test 1 *n* shihŏm 시험 2 *v/t*
shihŏmhada 시험하다;
product shirhŏmhada
실험하다

testify *v/i* JUR chŭng-ŏnhada
증언하다

tetanus p'asangp'ung 파상풍

text 1 *n* ponmun 본문; (~
message) munja meshiji 문자
메시지 2 *v/t* munja meshijirŭl
ponaeda 문자 메시지를
보내다

textbook kyokkwasŏ 교과서

textile chingmul 직물

texture kyŏl 결

Thailand T'aeguk 태국

than ...poda …보다; *bigger*
~ *me* naboda tŏ k'ŭn 나보다
더 큰

thank *v/t* kamsahada
감사하다; ~ *you* (polite)

kamsahamnida 감사합니다

thankful kamsahanŭn
감사하는

thanks kamsa 감사; ~!
komapssŭmnida!
고맙습니다!; (to friend or
younger person) komawŏ!
고마워!; *no* ~ animnida,
kwaench'anssŭmnida.
아닙니다, 괜찮습니다

Thanksgiving (Day) Ch'usu
Kamsajŏl 추수 감사절

that 1 *adj* chŏ 저; ~ *one*
(thing) chŏgŏt 저것;
(person) chŏ saram 저
사람 2 *pron*: *what's* ~?
chŏgŏsŭn muŏshimnikka?
저것은 무엇입니까?;
who's ~? chŏ saramŭn
nuguimnikka? 저 사람은
누구입니까? ◊ (relative)
...hanŭn …하는; *the
person* ~ *you see* tangshini
pogo innŭn saram 당신이
보고 있는 사람 3 *conj*: *I
think* ~ ...chŏnŭn …rago
saenggak'amnida 저는
…라고 생각합니다

thaw *v/i* noktta 녹다

the no translation

theater kŭktchang 극장

theft toduktchil 도둑질

their kŭdŭrŭi 그들의

theirs kŭdŭrŭi kŏt 그들의 것

them kŭdŭl 그들

theme t'ema 테마

themselves kŭdŭl chashin 그들 자신

then kŭ ttae 그 때; *(after)* kŭrigo nasŏ 그리고 나서; *(deducing)* kŭrŏt'amyŏn 그렇다면

theory iron 이론

therapist ch'iryo chŏnmun-ga 치료 전문가

therapy ch'iryo 치료

there kŭ kose 그 곳에; ~ *is / are* …i / tŭri it-tta … 이/가 있어; ~ *is / are not* … …i / tŭri ŏptta …이/들이 없는; ~ *you are* (giving) yŏgi issŭmnida 여기 있습니다; ~ *he is!* kŭga chŏgi ittkkunyo 그가 저기 있군요

therefore ttarasŏ 따라서

thermometer ondogye 온도계

thermos flask poonbyŏng 보온병

these 1 *adj* igŏttŭrŭi 이것들의 **2** *pron* igŏttŭl 이것들

they *(persons)* kŭdŭl 그들; *(things)* kŭgŏttŭl 그것들 ◊ *(omission): who are ~?* nuguyeyo? 누구예요?

thick tukkŏun 두꺼운; *fog* chit'ŭn 짙은; *soup* kŏltchuk'an 걸쭉한; *hair* such'i manŭn 숱이 많은

thief totuk 도둑

thigh nŏptchökttari 넓적다리

thin *material* yalbŭn 얇은; *hair, line* kanŭn 가는; *person* marŭn 마른; *soup* mulgŭn 묽은

thing kŏt 것, ~s *(belongings)* soyumul 소유물

think saenggak'ada 생각하다; *I ~ so* kŭrŏn kŏt kat'ayo 그런 것 같아요

Third World Chesam Segye 제3 세계

thirst kaltchüng 갈증

thirsty: *be ~* mongmarŭda 목마르다

this 1 *adj* i 이; ~ *one* igŏt 이것 **2** *pron* igŏt 이것; ~ *is (introducing)* i saramŭn …imnida 이 사람은 … 입니다; TEL chŏnŭn …imnida 저는 …입니다

thorough *search, person* ch'ŏltchŏhan 철저한

those 1 *adj people* kŭdŭrŭi 그들의; *things, animals* kŭgŏttŭrŭi 그것들의 **2** *pron (people)* kŭdŭl 그들; *(things, animals)* kŭgŏttŭl 그것들

though 1 *conj (although)* …ijiman …이지만; *as ~* mach'i …ch'ŏrŏm 마치 …처럼 **2** *adv (however)* kŭrŏt'ŏrado 그럴지라도

thought saenggak 생각; *(collective)* sasang 사상

thoughtful saenggagi kip'ŭn 생각이 깊은; *(considerate)* saryŏ kip'ŭn 사려 깊은

thoughtless namŭl koryŏhaji annŭn 남을 고려하지 않는

thousand ch'ŏn 천; **~s of**
su ch'ŏnŭi su 천의; **ten ~**
man 만
thread n shil 실
threat wihyŏp 위협
threaten wihyŏp'ada
위협하다
thrill 1 n chŏnyul 전율
2 v/t: **be ~ed** kamgyŏk'ada
감격하다
thriller sŭrillŏmul 스릴러물
thrilling kamgyŏk'age hanŭn
감격하게 하는
thrive (of plant) ulch'anghage
charada 울창하게 자라다;
(of economy) pŏnch'anghada
번창하다
throat mokkumŏng 목구멍
throb v/i (of heart) ttwida 뛰다;
(of music) tŏllida 떨리다
throne wangjwa 왕좌
through 1 prep ◊ (across)
...ŭl t'onghayŏ ...을 통하여
◊ (during) ...ŭi tong-an naenae
...의 동안 내내; **Monday ~
Friday** wŏryoilbut'ŏ kŭmnyoil
tong-an naenae 월요일부터
금요일 동안 내내 **2** adv:
wet ~ mongttang chŏjŏt-tta
몽땅 젖었다 **3** adj: **be ~** (of
couple) kwan-gyega kkŭnnada
관계가 끝나다
throw 1 v/t tŏnjida 던지다 **2** n
tŏnjigi 던지기
♦ **throw out** naebŏrida
내버리다; person naetchot-tta

내쫓다
thumb n ŏmji sonkkarak 엄지
손가락
thumbtack app'in 압핀
thump n (blow) chumŏktchil
주먹질; (noise) k'unghanŭn
sori 쿵하는 소리
thunder n ch'ŏndung 천둥
thunderstorm noeu 뇌우
Thursday mogyoil 목요일
thwart panghaehada 방해하다
Tibet T'ibet'ŭ 티베트
ticket p'yo 표
ticket machine p'yo chadong
p'anmaegi 표 자동 판매기
ticket office maep'yoso
매표소
tickle v/t kanjirŏp'ida
간지럽히다
tidy person tanjŏnghan 단정한;
room chŏngdondoen 정돈된
♦ **tidy up** chŏngdonhada
정돈하다
tie 1 n (necktie) nekt'ai 넥타이;
(SPORTS: even result) tongtchŏm
동점 **2** v/t knot choida
조이다; hands muktta 묶다
tiger horang-i 호랑이
tight adj clothes kkok kkinŭn
꼭 끼는; security tandanhan
단단한; (hard to move) kkok
kkiin 꼭 끼인; (not leaving
time) ch'okppak'an 촉박한
tighten screw tandanhi choida
단단히 조이다; security
kanghwahada 강화하다

time shigan 시간; *(occasion)* pŏn 번; *have a good ~!* choŭn shiganŭl ponaeseyo! 좋은 시간을 보내세요!; *what's the ~?* myŏt shiimnikka? 몇 시입니까?; *on ~* chŏnggage chŏngak'e; *in no ~* kot 곧

time out SPORTS t'aim aut 타임 아웃

timetable shiganp'yo 시간표

time zone p'yojun shiganttae 표준 시간대

timid kŏmmanŭn 겁많은

timing shigirŭl match'ugi 시기를 맞추기; *(of actor, dancer)* t'aiming 타이밍

tinfoil ŭnjong-i 은종이

tinted *glasses* saek-kkal innŭn 색깔 있는

tiny chogŭmahan 조그마한

tip¹ *n (of stick)* kkŭt 끝; *(of cigarette)* p'ilt'ŏ 필터

tip² *n (advice)* pigyŏl 비결; *(money)* t'ip 팁

tippy-toe: *on ~* palkkŭt'ŭro 발끝으로

tire¹ t'aiŏ 타이어

tire² *v/i* chich'ida 지치다

tired p'igonhan 피곤한; *be ~ of ...* ... shiltchŭng nada ··· 싫증 나다

tissue ANAT chojik 조직; *(paper)* hwajangji 화장지

title chemok 제목

to 1 *prep* ...(ŭ)ro ··· (으) 로; ~

Korea Han-gugŭro 한국으로; *Monday ~ Wednesday* wŏryoilbut'ŏ suyoilkkaji 월요일부터 수요일까지 2 *(with verbs): learn ~ drive* unjŏnhanŭn kŏsŭl paeuda 운전하는 것을 배우다; *nice ~ eat* mŏk-kkie choŭn 먹기에 좋은 3 *adv: ~ and fro* apttwiro 앞뒤로

toast 1 *n* t'osŭt'ŭ 토스트; *(drinking)* kŏnbae 건배 2 *v/t (drinking)* kŏnbaehada 건배하다

tobacco tambae 담배

today onŭl 오늘

toe *n* palkkarak 발가락

together hamkke 함께; *(at same time)* tongshie 동시에

toilet hwajangshil 화장실

toilet paper hwajangji 화장지

toiletries semyŏn yongp'um 세면 용품

token *(sign)* p'yoshi 표시

tolerant kwanyong innŭn 관용 있는

tolerate ch'amtta 참다

toll *(for bridge, road)* t'onghaengnyo 통행료; TEL t'onghwaryo 통화료

toll-free TEL muryo t'onghwa 무료 통화

tomato t'omat'o 토마토

tomato ketchup t'omat'o k'ech'ap 토마토 케찹

tombstone pisŏk 비석

tomorrow naeil 내일; *the day after* ~ more 모레
ton (*of color*) saektcho 색조;
tone (*of color*) saektcho 색조; MUS ŭmsaek 음색; ~ *of voice* mokssori 목소리
tongue *n* hyŏ 혀
tonic (water) t'onik wŏt'ŏ 토닉 워터
tonight onŭl pam 오늘 밤
tonsillitis p'yŏndosŏnnyŏm 편도선염
too (*also*) to 도; (*excessively*) nŏmu 너무; *me* ~ chŏdoyo 저도요
tool togu 도구
tooth i 이
toothache ch'it'ong 치통
toothbrush ch'itssol 칫솔
toothpaste ch'iyak 치약
top 1 *n* witppubun 윗부분; (*of hill, tree*) kkokttaegi 꼭대기; (*lid*) ttukkŏng 뚜껑; (*of class*) sangnyu 상류; (*clothing*) sang-ŭi 상의; (AUTO: *gear*) t'opkkŏ 톱기어; *on* ~ *of* ...ŭi wie ...의 위에; *at the* ~ *of* ...ŭi witchoge ...의 위쪽에 **2** *adj floor* maenwiŭi 맨위의; *managers* sangbuŭi 상부의; *speed* ch'oegoŭi 최고의
topic hwaje 화제
top secret kŭkppi 극비
torment 1 *n* kot'ong 고통 **2** *v/t* koerop'ida 괴롭히다
torture 1 *n* komun 고문 **2** *v/t*
komunhada 고문하다
toss *v/t ball* kabyŏppke tŏnjida 가볍게 던지다; ~ *a coin* tongjŏnŭl tŏnjyŏ chŏnghada 동전을 던져 정하다
total 1 *n* hapkkye 합계 **2** *adj amount* chŏnch'eŭi 전체의; *disaster, stranger* wanjŏnhan 완전한 **3** *v/t infml car* wanjŏnhi pusuda 완전히 부수다
totally wanjŏnhi 완전히
touch 1 *n* chŏpch'ok 접촉; (*sense*) ch'ok-kkam 촉감; SPORTS t'ŏch'i 터치; *keep in* ~ *with sb* nuguwa kyesok yŏllak'ada 누구와 계속 연락하다 **2** *v/t* manjida 만지다; (*emotionally*) kamdongshik'ida 감동시키다 **3** *v/i* manjida 만지다
touching *adj* kamdongshik'inŭn 감동시키는
touchy *person* chinach'ige yeminhan 지나치게 예민한
tough *person* ŏkssen 억센; *meat* chilgin 질긴; *question* ŏryŏun 어려운; *material* kŏch'in 거친; *punishment* ŏmhan 엄한
tour 1 *n* kwan-gwang 관광 **2** *v/t* kwan-gwanghada 관광하다
tourism kwan-gwang-ŏp 관광업
tourist kwan-gwanggaek 관광객

tourist (information) office
kwan-gwang annaeso 관광
안내소

tour operator kwan-gwang-
ŏptcha 관광업자

tow v/t kkŭlda 끌다

toward prep ...ŭl / rŭl
hyanghayŏ …을 / 를 향하여

towel sugŏn 수건

tower n t'ap 탑

town toshi 도시

town hall shich'ŏng 시청

toxic toksssŏng-ŭi 독성의

toy changnankkam 장난감

trace v/t (find) susaek'ada
수색하다

track n (path) kil 길; (race)
t'ŭraek 트랙; RAIL ch'ŏltto 철도

tractor t'ŭraekt'ŏ 트랙터

trade 1 n muyŏk 무역;
(profession) chigŏp 직업
2 v/i (do business) changsahada
장사하다

trade fair muyŏk chŏnshihoe
무역 전시회

trademark tŭngnok sangp'yo
등록 상표

tradition chŏnt'ong 전통

traditional chŏnt'ongjŏgin
전통적인

traffic n kyot'ong 교통

traffic circle lot'ŏri 로터리

traffic cop infml kyot'ong sun-
gyŏng 교통 순경

traffic jam kyot'ong ch'ejŭng
교통 체증

traffic light shinhodŭng 신호등

tragedy pigŭk 비극

tragic pigŭktchŏgin 비극적인

trail 1 n (path) kil 길 2 v/t
(follow) ttaragada 따라가다;
(tow) kkŭlda 끌다

trailer t'ŭreillŏ 트레일러;
(mobile home) idong chut'aek
이동 주택; (of movie)
yegop'yŏn 예고편

train n kich'a 기차

train 2 1 v/t hullyŏnshik'ida
훈련시키다; employee
kyoyukshik'ida 교육시키다
2 v/i yŏnssŭp'ada 연습하다;
(of teacher etc) kyoyukpat-tta
교육받다

trainee kyŏnsŭpssaeng 견습생

trainer SPORTS k'och'i 코치

training SPORTS hullyŏn 훈련;
(of staff) kyoyuk 교육

train station kich'ayŏk 기차역

traitor paebanja 배반자

tranquilizer chinjŏngje 진정제

transaction kŏrae 거래

transfer 1 v/t omgida
옮기다; money songgŭmhada
송금하다 2 v/i (traveling)
omgyŏt'ada 옮겨타다 3 n
idong 이동; (of money)
songgŭmhwan 송금환

transform v/t
pyŏnhyŏngshik'ida
변형시키다

transformer ELEC pyŏnapkki
변압기

transfusion chuip 주입

transition pyŏnhwa 변화

transitional kwadojŏgin 과도적인

translate pŏnyŏk'ada 번역하다

translation pŏnyŏk 번역

translator pŏnyŏkka 번역가

transmission (of program) pangsong 방송; (of disease) chŏnyŏm 전염; AUTO pyŏnsokki 변속기

transmit TV pangsonghada 방송하다; MED chŏnyŏmshik'ida 전염시키다

transpacific T'aep'yŏngyang hoengdanŭi 태평양 횡단의

transparent t'umyŏnghan 투명한

transplant v/t MED ishik'ada 이식하다

transport 1 v/t susonghada 수송하다 **2** n susong 수송

trap 1 n (for animal) tŏt 덫; (question) hamjŏng 함정 **2** v/t: *be ~ped* hamjŏng-e ppajida 함정에 빠지다

trash (garbage) ssŭregi 쓰레기; (poor product) pullyangp'um 불량품

trashcan ssŭregi t'ong 쓰레기 통

trashy ssŭlmoŏmnŭn 쓸모없는

traumatic chŏngshinjŏk shyok'ŭrŭl chunŭn 정신적 쇼크를 주는

travel 1 n yŏhaeng 여행 **2** v/i yŏhaenghada 여행하다

travel agency yŏhaengsa 여행사

traveler yŏhaenggaek 여행객

traveler's check yŏhaengja sup'yo 여행자 수표

travel expenses yŏhaeng piyong 여행 비용

travel insurance yŏhaeng pohŏm 여행 보험

tray chaengban 쟁반

treacherous paebanhanŭn 배반하는

tread 1 n palkkŏrŭm 발걸음; (of tire) t'ŭredŭ 트레드 **2** v/i paltta 밟다

treason panyŏk 반역

treasure n pomul 보물

Treasury Department Chaemusŏng 재무성

treat 1 n k'ŭn kippŭm 큰 기쁨 **2** v/t material taruda 다루다; illness ch'iryohada 치료하다; person taeuhada 대우하다

treaty choyak 조약

tree namu 나무

tremble ttŏlda 떨다; (of hand, voice) ttŏllida 떨리다

tremendously (very) koengjanghi 굉장히; (a lot) maeu 매우

tremor (earth) yaktchin 약진

trend kyŏnghyang 경향

trendy ch'oeshin yuhaeng-ŭi 최신 유행의

trial JUR kongp'an 공판; *(of equipment)* shihŏm 시험; **on ~** JUR kongp'an chung 공판 중

triangle samgak'yŏng 삼각형

tribe pujok 부족

trick 1 *n* sogimsu 속임수 2 *v/t* sogida 속이다

trigger *n* pang-asoe 방아쇠
♦ trigger off yubarhada 유발하다

trim *v/t* sonjirhada 손질하다; *cost* sak-kkamhada 삭감하다

trip 1 *n (journey)* yŏhaeng 여행 2 *v/i* kŏllyŏ nŏmŏjida 걸려 넘어지다 3 *v/t person* kŏrŏ nŏmŏttŭrida 걸어 넘어뜨리다

triumph *n* sŭngni 승리

trivial sasohan 사소한

troops kundae 군대

trophy usŭngk'ŏp 우승컵

tropical yŏlttaeŭi 열대의

trouble 1 *n (difficulty)* munje 문제; *(inconvenience)* pulp'yŏn 불편; *(disturbance)* malssŏng 말썽; **no ~** munje ŏpssŭmnida 문제 없습니다 2 *v/t (worry)* kŏktchŏngshik'ida 걱정시키다; *(bother, disturb)* kwich'ank'e hada 귀찮게 하다

troublemaker malssŏngkkun 말썽꾼

trousers *Br* paji 바지

trout song-ŏ 송어

truce hyujŏn 휴전

truck hwamulch'a 화물차

truck driver t'ŭrŏk unjŏnsa 트럭 운전사

true chŏngmarŭi 정말의; *friend* chintchaŭi 진짜의; **come ~** shirhyŏndoeda 실현된다

truly chŏngmallo 정말로; **Yours ~** ...ollim …올림

trunk *(of tree)* chulgi 줄기; *(of body)* momttung-i 몸뚱이; *(of elephant)* k'o 코; *(of car)* t'ŭrŏngk'ŭ 트렁크

trust 1 *n* shilloe 신뢰; *(in organization)* shinyong 신용 2 *v/t* shilloehada 신뢰하다

trustworthy shilloehal su innŭn 신뢰할 수 있는

truth chinshil 진실; *(fact)* sashil 사실

truthful chinshirhan 진실한

try 1 *v/t* noryŏk'ada 노력하다; *food* mŏgŏboda 먹어보다; JUR chaep'anhada 재판하다 2 *v/i* haeboda 해보다

T-shirt t'ishyŏch'ŭ 티셔츠

tub *(bath)* yoktcho 욕조; *(for yoghurt etc)* kwak 곽

tube *(pipe)* kwan 관; *(of toothpaste etc)* t'yubŭ 튜브

Tuesday hwayoil 화요일

tug *n* NAUT yeinsŏn 예인선

tuition suŏp 수업

tulip t'yullip 튤립

tummy pae 배

tumor chongnyang 종양

tuna ch'amch'i 참치

tune *n* koktcho 곡조

tunnel *n* t'ŏnŏl 터널

turbulence *(in air travel)* nangiryu 난기류

turkey ch'ilmyŏnjo 칠면조

turn 1 *n (rotation)* hoejŏn 회전; *(in road)* mot'ung-i 모퉁이; *it's my ~* che ch'aryeimnida 제 차례입니다 **2** *v/t key etc* tollida 돌리다; *wheel* hoejŏnshik'ida 회전시키다; *corner* tolda 돌다 **3** *v/i (of driver, car)* tolda 돌다; *(of wheel)* hoejŏnhada 회전하다

♦ **turn down** *v/t offer* kŏjŏrhada 거절하다; *volume, heat* churida 줄이다

♦ **turn off 1** *v/t TV, engine* kkŭda 끄다; *(of driver)* tarŭn killo tŭrŏsŏda 다른 길로 들어서다

♦ **turn on** *v/t TV etc* k'yŏda 켜다; *infml (sexually)* sŏngjŏkchŏgŭro hŭngbunshik'ida 성적으로 흥분시키다

♦ **turn up 1** *v/t collar* seuda 세우다; *volume, heat* nop'ida 높이다 **2** *v/i (arrive)* nat'anada 나타나다

turnover FIN maesanggo 매상고

turnpike yuryo kosokttoro 유료 고속도로

turnstile shiptchahyŏng hoejŏnshik mun 십자형 회전식 문

turtle kŏbuk 거북

tuxedo t'ŏksshido 턱시도

TV t'ibi 티비

tweezers choktchippke 족집게

twice tu pŏn 두 번; *(amount)* tu pae 두 배

twin beds t'ŭwin pedŭ 트윈 베드

twinge *(pain)* ssushinŭn tŭt'an ap'ŭm 쑤시는 듯한 아픔

twins ssangdung-i 쌍둥이

twist 1 *v/t* kkoda 꼬다; *~ one's ankle* palmogŭl ppida 발목을 삐다 **2** *v/i (of road)* kuburŏjida 구부러지다

two tul 둘, i 이

tycoon kŏmul 거물

type 1 *n (sort)* yuhyŏng 유형 **2** *v/i (use keyboard)* t'aja ch'ida 타자 치다

typical chŏnhyŏngjŏgin 전형적인

tyrant p'ok-kkun 폭군

U

ugly hyunghan 흉한

UK Yŏngguk 영국

ulcer kweyang 궤양

ultimate kunggŭktchŏgin 궁극적인; *(best)* ch'oesang-ŭi 최상의

ultimatum ch'oehu t'ongch'ŏp 최후 통첩

umbrella usan 우산

umpire *n* shimp'an 심판

UN Kuktche Yŏnhap 국제 연합

unanimous manjang-ilch'iŭi 만장일치의

unassuming kyŏmsonhan 겸손한

unauthorized muhŏgaŭi 무허가의

unavoidable p'ihal su ŏmnŭn 피할 수 없는

unaware: *be ~ of* …ŭl / rŭl kkaedatchi mot'ada …을 / 를 깨닫지 못하다

unbalanced PSYCH puranjŏnghan 불안정한

unbearable kyŏndil su ŏmnŭn 견딜 수 없는

unbelievable midŭl su ŏmnŭn 믿을 수 없는; *infml* ŏmch'ŏngnan 엄청난

uncertain *future* purhwaksshirhan 불확실한

uncle *(father's brother, single)* samch'on 삼촌; *(mother's brother, single)* oesamch'on 외삼촌; *(father's sister's husband)* komobu 고모부; *(mother's sister's husband)* imobu 이모부

uncomfortable pulp'yŏnhan 불편한

unconditional mujokkŏnŭi 무조건의

unconscious MED muŭishik sangt'aeŭi 무의식 상태의; PSYCH muŭishiktchŏgin 무의식적인

uncontrollable chajehal su ŏmnŭn 자제할 수 없는

uncover tŏpk'aerŭl pŏtkkida 덮개를 벗기다; *plot* palk'yŏnaeda 밝혀내다

undamaged sonsangdoeji anŭn 손상되지 않은

undeniable pujŏnghal su ŏmnŭn 부정할 수 없는

under *prep* …ŭi arae …의 아래에; *(less than)* … miman … 미만

underage: *be ~* misŏngnyŏnjaida 미성년자이다

undercarriage ch'angnyuk changch'i 착륙 장치

undercut *v/t* COMM poda tŏ kkakka chegonghada 보다 더 깎아 제공하다

underdog yaktcha 약자

underdone tŏl ik'in 덜 익힌

underestimate *v/t* kwasop'yŏngkkahada 과소평가하다

undergo *treatment* pat-tta 받다; *experience* kyŏktta 겪다

underground *adj also* POL chiha(ŭi) 지하 (의)

undergrowth tŏmbul 덤불

underline *v/t text* mitchul kŭt-tta 밑줄 긋다

underlying *problems* kŭnwŏnjŏgin 근원적인

underneath 1 *prep* …ŭi mit'e …의 밑에 **2** *adv* mit'e 밑에

underpants p'aench'ŭ 팬츠

underskirt sokch'ima 속치마

understaffed inwŏni pujok'an인원이 부족한

understand ihaehada 이해하다

understandably ihaehal su itkke 이해할 수 있게

understanding 1 *adj person* ihaeshiminnŭn 이해심있는 **2** *n (of situation)* ihae 이해; *(agreement)* tong-ŭi 동의

understatement ŏktchedoen p'yohyŏn 억제된 표현

undertaking saŏp 사업; *(promise)* yakssok 약속

underwear sogot 속옷

underworld *(criminal)* amhŭkkka 암흑가

undisputed amudo nŏmboji mot'al 아무도 넘보지 못할

undoubtedly ŭishimhal yŏji ŏpsshi 의심할 여지 없이

undress *wi* ot pŏtkkida 옷 벗기다

unearth *remains* palgurhada 발굴하다

unemployed 1 *adj* shiltchik'an 실직한 **2** *n: the ~* shiropptcha 실업자

unemployment shirŏp 실업

uneven *quality* kyunirhaji anŭn 균일하지 않은; *surface* korŭji anŭn 고르지 않은

unexpected yesanghaji mot'an 예상하지 못한

unfair pulgongjŏnghan 불공정한

unfaithful pujŏnghan 부정한

unfavorable *conditions* hogami an-ganŭn 호감이 안가는; *report* hoŭijŏgi anin 호의적이 아닌

unfit undong pujogin 운동 부족인; *(morally)* pujŏkkkyŏgin 부적격인

unforeseen yesanghaji mot'an 예상하지 못한

unforgettable ijŭl su ŏmnŭn 잊을 수 없는

unforgivable yongsŏhal su ŏmnŭn 용서할 수 없는

unfortunately purhaenghi 불행히

unfriendly pulch'injŏrhan 불친절한

ungrateful kamsahal chul morŭnŭn 감사할 줄 모르는

unhappiness purhaeng 불행

unhappy purhaenghan 불행한; *customers* pulmansŭrŏun 불만스러운

unharmed musahan 무사한

uniform *n* MIL chebok 제복; *(school)* kyobok 교복

unify t'ong-irhada 통일하다

uninhabited sarami salji annŭn

사람이 살지 않는

unintentional koŭiga anin
고의가 아닌

union POL yŏnhap 연합; *(labor ~)* nojo 노조

unique tokt'ŭk'an 독특한

unite 1 *v/t* kyŏrhap'ada 결합하다 2 *v/i* hanaga toeda 하나가 되다

United Nations Kuktche Yŏnhap 국제 연합

United States (of America) Miguk 미국

unity t'ong-il 통일

universal pop'yŏnjŏgin 보편적인

university taehak-kkyo 대학교

unkind pulch'injŏrhan 불친절한

unleaded (gasoline) muyŏn hwibaryu 무연 휘발유

unless ...haji anŭmyŏn …하지 않으면

unlikely: *be ~* ...l/ŭl kŏt kach'i ant'a …ㄹ/을 것 같지 않다

unload naerida 내리다

unlucky unmnŭn 운없는

unmistakable t'ŭllimŏmnŭn 틀림없는

unnatural pujayŏnsŭrŏun 부자연스러운

unnecessary pulp'iryohan 불필요한

unofficial pigongshiktchŏgin 비공식적인

unpack p'ulda 풀다

unpaid *job* mugŭbŭi 무급의

unpleasant pulk'waehan 불쾌한

unpopular inkkiŏmnŭn 인기없는; *step* chijipat-tchi mot'anŭn 지지받지 못하는

unpredictable yech'ŭk'al su ŏmnŭn 예측할 수 없는

unproductive pisaengsanjŏgin 비생산적인

unprofessional chŏnmunindaptchi anŭn 전문인답지 않은; *job* pip'ŭrojŏgin 비프로적인

unprofitable iigi ŏmnŭn 이익이 없는

unqualified *worker* chagyŏgi ŏmnŭn 자격이 없는

unrealistic pihyŏnsshiltchŏgin 비현실적인

unreasonable pihamnijŏgin 비합리적인

unrelated kwan-gyeŏmnŭn 관계없는

unreliable midŭl su ŏmnŭn 믿을 수 없는

unrest puran 불안

unruly tarugi himdŭn 다루기 힘든

unsatisfactory manjokssŭrŏptchi mot'an 만족스럽지 못한

unscrew nasarŭl p'ulda 나사를 풀다; *top* magaerŭl yŏlda 마개를 열다

unsettled

unsettled *weather, market* pyŏnhagi shwiun 변하기 쉬운; *lifestyle* iltchŏngch'i anŭn 일정치 않은

unskilled misuk'an 미숙한

unsuccessful sŏnggonghaji mot'an 성공하지 못한; *candidate* nakssŏndoen 낙선된

unsuitable pujŏkttanghan 부적당한

untidy chijŏbunhan 지저분한

until *prep* kkaji 까지; *from Monday ~ Friday* wŏryoilbut'ŏ kŭmnyoilkkaji 월요일부터 금요일까지

untiring *efforts* chich'iji annŭn 지치지 않는

untrue sashiri anin 사실이 아닌

unusual tŭmun 드문

unusually tŭmulge 드물게

unwell momi choch'i anŭn 몸이 좋지 않은

unwilling *be ~ to do sth* muŏsŭl hanŭn kŏsŭl naek'yŏhaji ant'a 무엇을 하는 것을 내켜하지 않다

up *adv* wie 위에; *~ on the roof* chibung wie 지붕 위에; *be ~ (out of bed)* irŏna it-tta 일어나 있다; *(of sun)* ttŏolla it-tta 떠올라 있다; *(of price)* olla it-tta 올라 있다; *what's ~?* musŭn il issŭmnikka? 무슨 일 있습니까

upbringing kajŏng kyoyuk 가정 교육

update *v/t file* ch'oeshinŭi kŏsŭro pakkuda 최신의 것으로 바꾸다

upheaval k'ŭn pyŏnhwa 큰 변화; *(social)* kyŏkppyŏn 격변

uphold *rights* yujihada 유지하다

upkeep *n* yuji 유지

upper *part* wi tchogŭi 위 쪽의; *~ deck* sanggapp'an 상갑판

uprising p'okttong 폭동

uproar *(loud noise)* soran 소란; *(protest)* hang-ŭi 항의

upscale *adj hotel etc* kop'umkkkyŏgŭi 고품격의

upset 1 *v/t glass* twijiptta 뒤집다; *person* kibun sanghagehada 기분 상하게하다 **2** *adj person* kibun sanghan 기분 상한; *have an ~ stomach* paet'alloda 배탈나다

upstairs *adv* wich'ŭng-e 위층에

up-to-date ch'oeshinŭi 최신의

upturn *(economy)* hojŏn 호전

uranium uranyum 우라늄

urban toshiŭi 도시의

urge *n* ch'ungdong 충동

urgency kin-gŭp 긴급

urgent kŭp'an 급한

us uri 우리

US(A) Miguk 미국

use 1 *v/t* ssŭda 쓰다 2 *n*
sayong 사용; *be of no ~
to sb* nuguege ssŭlmo ŏpta
누구에게 쓸모 없다

used¹ *car etc* ch'unggo 중고

used²: *be ~ to sth* muŏse
iksŭk'aejyŏ it-tta무엇에
익숙해져 있다; *get ~ to sth*
muŏse iksŭk'aejida무엇에
익숙해지다

useful ssŭlmoinnŭn 쓸모있는

useless ssŭlmoŏmnŭn
쓸모없는; *infml person*
mojaran 모자란

user sayongja 사용자

user-friendly sayonghagi
shwiun 사용하기 쉬운

usual pot'ong-ŭi 보통의; *as
~ pot'ong ttaech'ŏrŏm* 보통
때처럼

usually pot'ong 보통

utterly wanjŏnhi 완전히

U-turn yut'ŏn U턴; *fig*
wanjŏnhan t'albakkum 완전한
탈바꿈

V

vacant piŏ innŭn 비어 있는;
look mŏnghan 멍한

vacate piuda 비우다

vacation *n* hyuga 휴가; *be
on ~* hyuga chung-ida 휴가
중이다

vacationer hyuga yŏhaenggaek
휴가 여행객

vaccinate yebang
chŏptchonghada 예방
접종하다

vaccine paekshin 백신

vacuum *n* chin-gong 진공

vacuum cleaner chin-gong
ch'ŏngsogi 진공 청소기

vague mohohan 모호한;
feeling ŏryŏmp'ut'an 어렴풋한

vain 1 *adj person* hŏyŏngshimi
manŭn 허영심이 많은 2 *n:*

in ~ hŏt-ttoege 헛되게

valid *visa* yuhyohan 유효한;
reason t'adanghan 타당한

valley koltchagi 골짜기

valuable 1 *adj* kwijunghan
귀중한 2 *n: ~s* kwijungp'um
귀중품

value 1 *n* kach'i 가치 2 *v/t*
sojunghi yŏgida 소중히
여기다

van ponggoch'a 봉고차

vanilla *n* panilla 바닐라

vanish sarajida 사라지다

vapor chŭnggi 증기

variable *adj* kabyŏnŭi 가변의;
moods pyŏndŏksŭrŏun
변덕스러운

variation pyŏndong 변동

varied tayanghan 다양한

variety

variety pyŏnhwa 변화; *(type)* tayangsŏng 다양성

various *(several)* yŏrŏ 여러; *(different)* kaji kakssagŭi가 가지 각색의

varnish n nisŭ 니스

vary *v/i* pakkwida 바뀌다; *it varies* ch'ŏnch'amanbyŏrijiyo 천차만별이지요

vase kkotpyŏng 꽃병

vast kwanghwarhan 광활한; *knowledge* pangdaehan 방대한

VCR pŭi ssi al 브이 시이 알

veal songaji kogi 송아지 고기

vegetable yach'ae 야채

vegetarian n ch'aeshiktchuŭija 채식주의자

vehicle unban sudan 운반 수단

velvet pelbet 벨벳

vending machine chadong p'anmaegi 자동 판매기

venereal disease sŏngppyŏng 성병

ventilation t'onggi 통기

venture n *(undertaking)* mohŏm 모험; COMM t'ugijŏk saŏp 투기적 사업

venue changso 장소

verb tongsa 동사

verdict JUR p'yŏnggyŏl 평결; *fig* p'andan 판단

♦ **verge on** kŏŭi kat-tta 거의 같다

verify *(check)* chŭngmyŏnghada 증명하다; *(confirm)* hwaginhada 확인하다

vermin haech'ung 해충

versatile *person* tajaedanŭnghan 다재다능한; *gadget* mannŭng-ŭi 만능의

verse chŏl 절; *(poetry)* shi 시

versus SPORTS, JUR tae 대

very *adv* taedanhi 대단히; *was it cold? – not ~* ch'uwŏssŏyo? – maninŭn aniŏssŏyo 추웠어요? – 많이는 아니었어요; *the ~ best* kajang choŭn 가장 좋은

vessel NAUT pae 배

veteran 1 n pet'erang 베테랑 **2** *adj* *(old)* orae sayonghan 오래 사용한; *(experienced)* pet'erang-ŭi 베테랑의

veterinarian suŭisa 수의사

via kyŏngnyuhayŏ 경유하여

viable *plan* hyoryŏgi innŭn 효력이 있는

vibrate *v/i* hŭndŭllida 흔들리다

vice ak 악

vice president *(of company)* pusajang 부사장; *(of state)* put'ongnyŏng 부통령

vice versa pandaero 반대로

vicinity kŭnch'ŏ 근처

vicious *dog* sŏngjiri koyak'an 성질이 고약한; *attack, temper* chidok'an 지독한

victim hŭisaengja 희생자

victory sŭngni 승리

video 1 n pidio 비디오 **2** *v/t* pidioro ch'waryŏnghada 비디오로 촬영하다

video camera pidio k'amera 비디오 카메라

video cassette pidio k'aset'ŭ 비디오 카세트

video recorder pidio nok'wagi 비디오 녹화기

Vietnam Pet'ŭnam 베트남

view *n* kyŏngch'i 경치; *(of situation)* kyŏnhae 견해; **in ~ of** ...ŭl / rŭl salp'yŏbomyŏn …을 / 를 살펴보면

viewer TV shich'ŏngja 시청자

viewpoint kwantchŏm 관점

vigor hwalgi 활기

village maŭl 마을

villager maŭl saram 마을 사람

vindictive poboktchŏgin 보복적인

vine p'odonamu 포도나무

vinegar shikch'o 식초

vintage *n (of wine)* ch'oegogŭp p'odoju 최고급 포도주

violate *rules* wibanhada 위반하다

violation: *traffic ~* kyot'ong wiban 교통 위반

violence p'ongnyŏk 폭력

violent nanp'okhan 난폭한; *storm* kyŏngnyŏrhan 격렬한

violin paiollin 바이올린

VIP yoin 요인

viral *infection* pairŏsŭŭi 바이러스의

virtual sashilsang-ŭi 사실상의

virtually kŏŭi 거의

virus pairŏsŭ 바이러스

visa pija 비자

visibility nune poim 눈에 보임

visible poinŭn 보이는

vision shiryŏk 시력; REL *etc* hwanyŏng 환영

visit 1 *n* pangmun 방문 2 *v/t* pangmunhada 방문하다

visitor sonnim 손님; *(to museum etc)* kwallamgaek 관람객; *(to sight-seeing place)* kwan-gwanggaek 관광객

visual shigaktchŏgin 시각적인

visualize maŭm soge ttŏollida 마음 속에 떠올리다; *(foresee)* yegyŏnhada 예견하다

vital p'ilssujŏgin 필수적인

vitamin pit'amin 비타민

vitamin pill pit'amin chŏngje 비타민 정제

vivid *color* kangnyŏrhan 강렬한; *imagination* saengsaenghan 생생한

vocabulary ŏhwi 어휘

voice *n* mokssori 목소리

voicemail ŭmsŏng up'yŏn 음성 우편

volcano hwasan 화산

voltage chŏnap 전압

volume *(of container)* ip-ppang yongjŏk 입방 용적; *(of business)* yang 양; *(of book)* han kwŏn 한 권; *(of radio etc)* ŭmnyang 음량

voluntary *adj* chabaltchŏgin 자발적인

volunteer 1 *n* chawŏnja
자원자 **2** *v/i* chajinhaesŏ hada
자진해서 하다

vomit *v/t* t'ohada 토하다

voracious *appetite*
wangsŏnghan 왕성한

vote 1 *n* t'up'yo 투표
2 *v/i* POL t'up'yohada
투표하다; ~ *for / against*

...e ch'ansŏng / pandae
t'up'yohada ···에 찬성/반대
투표하다

voyage hanghae 항해

vulgar chŏsok'an 저속한

vulnerable *(to attack)*
konggyŏk tanghagi
shwiun 공격 당하기
쉬운

W

wad *n (of bills)* tabal 다발; *(of cotton)* mungch'i 뭉치

wade kŏrŏsŏ kŏnnŏda 걸어서
건너다

wag *v/t* hŭndŭlda 흔들다

wage *n* wŏlgŭp 월급

wagon: be on the ~ *infml*
surŭl kkŭnt'a 술을 끊다

wail *v/i* ulbujit-tta 울부짖다

waist hŏri 허리

waistline hŏrisŏn 허리선

wait 1 *n* kidarim 기다림 **2** *v/i*
kidarida 기다리다

waiter weit'ŏ 웨이터

waiting list taegija myŏngdan
대기자 명단

waiting room taegishil 대기실

waitress weit'ŭrisŭ
웨이트리스

wake 1 *v/i: ~ (up)* chami
kkaeda 잠이 깨다 **2** *v/t*
kkaeuda 깨우다

wake-up call moning k'ol

모닝 콜

walk 1 *n* kŏtkki 걷기; *go for
a* ~ sanch'aek'hada 산책하다
2 *v/i* kŏt-tta 걷다; *(not take
car etc)* kŏrŏsŏ kada 걸어서
가다; *(hike)* tobo yŏhaenghada
도보 여행하다

wall pyŏk 벽

wallet chigap 지갑

wallpaper *n* pyŏktchi 벽지

Wall Street Wŏl Sŭt'ŭrit'ŭ월
스트리트

walnut hodu 호두

wander *v/i* ttŏdoradanida
떠돌아다니다; *(of attention)*
sanmanhaejida 산만해지다

want *v/t* wŏnhada 원하다;
(need) p'iryohada 필요하다; ~
to do sth muŏsŭl hago shipta
무엇을 하고 싶다

want ad saenghwal kwanggo
생활 광고

wanted *adj (by police)* chimyŏng

subaedoen 지명 수배된

war n chŏnjaeng 전쟁

warden (of prison)
kyodosojang 교도소장

warehouse ch'anggo 창고

warfare chŏnjaeng 전쟁

warhead t'anbu 탄두

warm adj tŭun 더운; welcome
etc ttattŭt'an 다뜻한

warmhearted ch'injŏrhan
친절한

warmth on-gi 온기; (of
welcome) onjŏng 온정

warn kyŏnggohada 경고하다

warning n kyŏnggo 경고

warped fig pitturŏjin 비뚤어진

warrant n yŏngtchang 영장

warranty pojŭng 보증

warship kunham 군함

wartime chŏnshi 전시

wary: be ~ of ...ŭi / rŭl
ŭishimhada …의 / 를
의심하다

wash 1 v/t clothes ppalda 빨다;
dishes taktta 닦다; hands sshit-
tta 씻다 2 v/i sshit-tta 씻다
♦ wash up (hands and face)
sshit-tta 씻다

washbasin semyŏn-gi 세면기

washer (for faucet) washyŏ
와셔

washing machine set'ak-kki
세탁기

washroom hwajangshil
화장실

waste 1 n nangbi 낭비;

(industrial) p'yegimul 폐기물
2 v/t nangbihada 낭비하다

waste basket hyujit'ong
휴지통

watch 1 n (timepiece) shigye
시계 2 v/t TV poda 보다; (spy
on) kamshihada 감시하다;
(look after) tolbwajuda
돌봐주다 3 v/i chik'yŏboda
지켜보다

water 1 n mul 물 2 v/t plant
murŭl chuda 물을 주다

waterfall p'okp'o 폭포

water level suwi 수위

watermelon subak 수박

waterproof adj pangsudoenŭn
방수되는

wave¹ n (in sea) p'ado 파도

wave² 1 v/i (with hand) sonŭl
hŭndŭlda 손을 흔들다 2 v/t
flag hŭndŭlda 흔들다

way 1 n (method) pangbŏp
방법; (~ of doing sth) pangshik
방식; (route) kil 길; this
~ (like this) irŏk'e 이렇게;
(in this direction) itchogŭro
이쪽으로; by the ~ kŭrŏnde
그런데; lose one's ~ kirŭl
ilt'a 길을 잃다; be in the
~ panghaega toeda 방해가
되다; no ~! ŏrimdo ŏpssŏ!
어림도 없어! 2 adv infml
(much) nŏmu 너무

way in ippku 입구

way of life saenghwal pangshik
생활 방식

way out

way out ch'ulgu 출구; *fig* haegyŏlch'aek 해결책

we uri 우리 ◊ *(omission)*; *where are ~ going?* ŏdiro kayo? 어디로 가요?

weak yak'an 약한; *coffee* yŏnhan 연한

weaken 1 *v/t* yak'agehada 약하게 하다

wealth pu 부

wealthy puyuhan 부유한

weapon mugi 무기

wear 1 *n: ~ (and tear)* tarŭm 닳음 2 *v/t (have on)* ipta 입다

♦ **wear out** *v/t* chich'ige hada 지치게 하다; *shoes* tara ttŏrŏjige hada 닳아 떨어지게 하다

weary chich'in 지친

weather *n* nalsshi 날씨

weather forecast ilgi yebo 일기 예보

web: *spider's ~* kŏmijip 거미집; *COMPUT* Wep 웹

website wep sa-it'ŭ 웹 사이트

wedding kyŏrhonshik 결혼식

wedding ring kyŏrhon panji 결혼 반지

Wednesday suyoil 수요일

weed *n* chapch'o 잡초

week chu 주; *a ~ tomorrow* p'aril twie 팔일 뒤에

weekday p'yŏng-il 평일

weekend chumal 주말; *on the ~* chumare 주말에

weekly *adj* maeju-ŭi 매주의

weep ulda 울다

weigh 1 *v/t* mugerŭl talda 무게를 달다 2 *v/i* mugega nagada 무게가 나가다

weight muge 무게

weird isanghan 이상한

welcome 1 *v/t* hwanyŏng pannŭn 환영 받는; *you're ~* ch'ŏnmaneyo 천만에요 2 *n (for guests)* hwanyŏng 환영 3 *v/t guests* hwanyŏnghada 환영하다; *decision* kikkŏi padadŭrida 기꺼이 받아들이다

welfare poktchi 복지; *(financial assistance)* saenghwal pojo 생활 보조

well[1] *n (for water)* umul 우물

well[2] 1 *adv* chal 잘; *as ~ (too)* ...do ...도; *as ~ as (in addition)* ...ppunmanira ...do ...뿐만아니라 ...도; *~!* irŏn, irŏn! 이런, 이런!; *...* kŭlsse ... 글쎄 *...* 2 *adj: be ~* chal it-tta 잘 있다

well-behaved p'umhaeng-i tanjŏnghan 품행이 단정한

well-dressed chŏun osŭl ibŭn 좋은 옷을 입은

well-known chal allyŏjin 잘 알려진

well-off puyuhan 부유한

west 1 *n* sŏtchok 서쪽; *the West* Sŏyang 서양 2 *adj* sŏ 서 3 *adv* sŏtchogŭro 서쪽으로

West Coast *(US)* (Migugŭi)

T'aep'yŏng-yang Yŏnan
(미국의) 태평양 연안
western 1 *adj* sŏtchogŭi
서쪽의; *Western* Sŏyang-ŭi
서양의 2 *n (movie)* sŏbugŭk
서부극

Westerner Sŏyang saram
서양 사람

wet *adj* chŏjŭn 젖은; *(rainy)*
piga onŭn 비가 오는

whale korae 고래

what 1 *pron* muŏt 무엇; ~
is it? wae? 왜?; ~ *about heading
home?* chibŭro kanŭn kŏshi
ŏttŏk'esssŏyo? 집으로 가는
것이 어떻겠어요?; *so* ~?
kŭraesŏ? 그래서? 2 *adj (what
kind of)* ŏttŏn 어떤 ◊ *(which)*
ŏnŭ 어느

whatever 1 *pron* …hanŭn
kŏsŭn muŏshidŭnji …하는
것은 무엇이든지;
(regardless of) …i / ga
…hal chirado …이 / 가 …할
지라도 2 *adj* ŏttŏn …(i)rado
어떤 …(이)라도

wheat mil 밀

wheel n pak'wi 바퀴

wheelchair hwilch'ŏ 휠체어

when 1 *adv* ŏnje 언제 2 *conj*
…hal ttae …할 때; ~ *I was a
child* naega ŏryŏssŭl ttae 내가
어렸을 때

whenever …l / ŭl ttaemada
…ㄹ / 을 때마다

where 1 *adv* ŏdi 어디; ~ *to?*
ŏdiro kamnikka? 어디로
갑니까? 2 *conj: this is* ~
I used to live yŏgiga naega
sarat-ttŏn koshimnida 여기가
내가 살았던 곳입니다

wherever 1 *conj* …hanŭn
kosŭn ŏdidŭnji …하는 곳은
어디든지 2 *adv* taech'e ŏdi-e
대체 어디에

whether …inji …인지; ~ …
or … …inji …inji …인지 …
인지

which 1 *adj* ŏnŭ 어느 2 *pron*
(interrogative) ŏnŭ kŏt 어느
것; *(relative)* …hanŭn …하는

whichever 1 *adj* …irado
어느 …이라도 2 *pron*
…hanŭn kŏsŭn ŏnŭ kŏshidŭn
…하는 것은 어느 것이든

while *conj: ~* … …hanŭn tong-
an …하는 동안

whip 1 *n* ch'aetchiktchil
채찍질 2 *v/t (hit)*
ch'aetchiktchirhada
채찍질하다

whirlpool *(for relaxation)*
chak'uji 자쿠지

whiskey wisŭk'i 위스키

whisper 1 *n* sokssagim
속삭임 2 *v/t & v/i* sokssagida
속삭이다

whistle 1 *n (sound)* hwip'aram
휘파람; *(device)* hogak 호각
2 *v/i* hwip'aramŭl pulda
휘파람을 불다

white 1 n hayan saek 하얀 색;
(person) paegin 백인 **2** adj
hayan 하얀; *person* paegin
백인

white-collar worker samjik
sawŏn 사무직 사원

White House Paegak-kkwan
백악관

white wine paekp'odoju
백포도주

who *(interrogative)* nugu 누구
◊ *(relative)* ...hanŭn ...하는

whoever ...hanŭn nugudŭnji
...하는 누구든지

whole adj modŭn 모든

wholesale adv tomaekkapssŭro
도매값으로

wholesome kŏn-gang-e chohŭn
건강에 좋은

whose 1 pron *(interrogative)*
nuguŭi kŏt 누구의 것;
(relative) ...hanŭn ...하는
2 adj nuguŭi 누구의

why wae 왜

wicked saak'an 사악한

wicket *(in bank etc)* ch'anggu
창구

wide adj nŏlbŭn 넓은; *range*
kwangbŏmwihan 광범위한

widely used, known nŏlke 넓게

wide-open nŏlke yŏllin
넓게 열린

widespread manyŏndoen
만연된

widow kwabu 과부

widower horabi 홀아비

width p'ok 폭

wife anae 아내

wild adj animal, flower
yasaeng 야생; *applause*
yŏlgwangtchŏgin 열광적인

wildlife yasaeng tongmul
야생 동물

will¹ n JUR yusŏ 유서

will² n *(willpower)* ŭiji 의지

will³ *(future)*: I ~ let you
know tomorrow naeil
allyŏdŭrigessŭmnida 내일
알려드리겠습니다; ~ you
be there? kŏgi issŭl kkŏyeyo?
거기 있을 꺼예요?; ~
you have some more tea?
ch'arŭl tŏ tŭshigessŏyo? 차를
더 드시겠어요?

willing: be ~ to do ... kikkŏi
...hada 기꺼이 ...하다

willingly kikkŏi 기꺼이

willpower ŭijiryŏk 의지력

win 1 n sŭng-ni 승리 **2** v/t &
v/i igida 이기다

wind¹ n param 바람

wind² v/i *(of path etc)* kubijida
굽이지다

wind instrument kwanak-kki
관악기

window ch'angmun 창문;
COMPUT windou 윈도우

windowsill ch'angt'ŏk 창턱

windshield *(chadongch'a)*
amnyuri *(자동차)* 앞유리

wine p'odoju 포도주

wing n nalgae 날개;

right ~ / left ~ SPORTS, POL uik / chwaik 우익 / 좌익

wink 1 *n* wingk'ŭ 윙크
2 *v/i (of person)* wingk'ŭhada 윙크하다

winner usŭngja 우승자

winnings sanggŭm 상금

winter *n* kyŏul 겨울

winter sports kyŏul sŭp'och'ŭ 겨울 스포츠

wipe *v/t* taktta 닦다; *tape* chiuda 지우다

wire ch'ŏlssa 철사; ELEC chŏngit-tchul 전깃줄

wiring ELEC paesŏn 배선

wisdom chihye 지혜

wise hyŏnmyŏng-han 현명한

wish 1 *n* sowŏn 소원; *best ~es* modŭn iri chal toegirŭl paramnida 모든 일이 잘 되기를 바랍니다 **2** *v/t*: *I ~ that ...* nanŭn ...hagirŭl paramnida 나는 ...하기를 바랍니다

wit *(humor)* chaech'i 재치

witch manyŏ 마녀

with ◊ *(accompanied by, proximity)* ...wa / kwa hamkke ...와 / 과 함께; *I live ~ my aunt* nanŭn nae imowa hamkke samnida 나는 내 이모와 함께 삽니다; *~ no money* ton ŏpssi 돈 없이 ◊ *(agency)* ...(ŭ)ro ...(으) 로; *stabbed ~ a knife* k'allo tchillin 칼로 찔린 ◊ *(cause)*

...(ŭ)ro ... (으) 로; *shivering ~ fear* turyŏumŭro ttŏnŭn 두려움으로 떠는 ◊ *(possession)* ...i / ga innŭn ...이 / 가 있는; *the house ~ the red door* ppalgan muni innŭn kŭ chip 빨간 문이 있는 그 집

withdraw *v/t complaint* ch'wisohada 취소하다; *money* ppaenaeda 빼내다; *troops* ch'ŏlssushik'ida 철수시키다

withdrawn *adj person* naesŏngjŏgin 내성적인

wither shidŭlda 시들다

withhold poryuhada 보류하다

within *prep (inside)* ...ane(sŏ) ...안에(서); *(time)* ...inae-e ...이내에; *(distance)* ...ane ...안에

without ...ŏpsshi ...없이; *looking* poji ank'o 보지 않고

withstand kyŏndiŏnaeda 견디어내다

witness *n* JUR chŭng-in 증인; *(of accident)* mok-kkyŏktcha 목격자

witty chaech'i-innŭn 재치있는

wolf *n* nŭkttae 늑대

woman yŏja 여자

women's lib yŏsŏng haebang undong 여성 해방 운동

won FIN wŏn 원

wonder 1 *n (amazement)* nollaum 놀라움 **2** *v/i* ŭi-ahage yŏgida 의아하게 여기다

wonderful nollaun 놀라운

wood namu 나무; *(forest)* sup 숲

wooden namuro toen 나무로 된

wool yangmo 양모

woolen *adj* mojik 모직

word *n* tanŏ 단어

wording p'yohyŏn 표현

word processing wŏdŭ p'ŭrosesŭrŭl sayong 워드 프로세스를 사용

work 1 *n* il 일 **2** *v/i* irhada 일하다; *(of student)* kongbuhada 공부하다; *(of machine)* umjigida 움직이다

♦ **work out 1** *v/t solution* haegyŏrhada 해결하다 **2** *v/i (at gym)* undonghada 운동하다; *(of relationship)* chal toeda 잘 되다

workaholic *n* ilppŏlle 일벌레

workday *(hours of work)* kŭnmu shigan 근무 시간; *(not holiday)* p'yŏng-il 평일

worker nodongja 노동자

workmanship somsshi 솜씨

work of art yesulp'um 예술품

work permit nodong hŏga 노동 허가

workshop chagŏptchang 작업장; wŏk'ŭshyop 워크숍

world segye 세계

world war segye taejŏn 세계 대전

worldwide *adj* segyejŏgin 세계적인

worn-out tarhappajin 닳아빠진; *person* chich'in 지친

worried kŏktchŏngsŭrŏn 걱정스런

worry 1 *n* kŏktchŏng 걱정 **2** *v/t* kŏktchŏngshik'ida 걱정시키다; *(upset)* puranhage hada 불안하게 하다 **3** *v/i* kŏktchŏnghada 걱정하다

worse 1 *adj* tŏ nappŭn 더 나쁜 **2** *adv* tŏ nappŭge 더 나쁘게

worsen *v/i* tŏ nappajida 더 나빠지다

worst 1 *adj* kajang nappŭn 가장 나쁜 **2** *adv* kajang nappŭge 가장 나쁘게

worth *adj:* be ~ FIN ...ŭi kach'iga it-tta ...의 가치가 있다; be ~ seeing 볼 만하다

worthless kach'iga ŏmnŭn 가치가 없는

worthwhile *cause* porami innŭn 보람이 있는

would: ~ you like to go to the movies? yŏnghwa porŏ kalkkayo? 영화 보러 갈까요?; ~ you tell her that ...? kŭnyŏege ...rago marhaejushigessŭmnikka? 그녀에게 ...라고 말해주시겠습니까?

wound *n* pusang 부상

wrap *v/t gift* ssada 싸다; *(wind)* kamtta 감다

wrapping paper p'ojangji 포장지

wreck *n* chanhae 잔해

2 *v/t* ŏngmang-ŭro p'agoehada 엉망으로 파괴하다

wreckage chanhae 잔해

wrecker kujoch'a 구조차

wrench *n (tool)* lench'i 렌치

wriggle *v/i* momburimch'ida 몸부림치다

wrinkle *n* churŭm 주름

wrist sonmok 손목

wristwatch sonmok shigye 손목 시계

write ssŭda 쓰다

writer chak-kka 작가

writing *(as career)* kŭl ssŭgi 글 쓰기; *(hand–)* kŭlsshi 글씨; *(words)* ssŭgi 쓰기; *(script)*

kirok 기록

writing paper p'ilgi yongji 필기 용지

wrong 1 *adj* t'ŭllin 틀린; *decision* chalmot-ttoen 잘못된; *be ~ (of person)* t'ŭllida 틀리다; *(morally)* nappŭda 나쁘다; *what's ~?* musŭn iriyeyo? 무슨 일이에요?; *there is something ~ with the car* ch'a-e muŏshin-ga isang-i it-tta 차에 무엇인가 이상이 있다 2 *adv* chalmot 잘못; *go ~ (of person)* t'arak'ada 타락하다; *(of plan etc)* chalmot-ttoeda 잘못되다 3 *n* chalmot 잘못

wrong number chalmot kŏllin chŏnhwa 잘못 걸린 전화

X

X-ray *n* Xsŏn X선

Y

yacht yot'ŭ 요트

yard[1] *(of house)* twinmadang 뒷마당; *(storage)* mulgŏn tunŭn kot chang-so 물건 두는 곳

yard[2] *(measure)* yadŭ 야드

yawn 1 *n* hap'um 하품 2 *v/i* hap'umhada 하품하다

year nyŏn 년

yearly *adj* maenyŏnŭi 매년의

yell 1 *n* koham 고함 2 *v/i* koham chirŭda 고함 지르다

yellow *adj* noran 노란

yes ye 예 ◊ *(using 'no', ie no, that is not right): you don't know the answer, do you? – oh –, I do* tabŭl morŭjyo? – aniyo, arayo 답을 모르죠? – 아니요, 알아요
yesterday ŏje 어제; *the day before –* kŭjŏkke 그저께
yet: as – ajik-kkaji 아직까지; *is he here? – not –* kŭnŭn yŏgi wassŏyo? – ajik anwassŏyo 그는 여기 왔어요? – 아직 안왔어요
yield 1 *n (interest)* iik 이익
2 *v/i (to enemy)* kulbok'ada 굴복하다; *(of traffic)* yangbohada 양보하다
yoghurt yogurŭt'ŭ 요구르트
you nŏ 너; *(polite)* tangshin 당신; *(plural)* nŏhŭidŭl 너희들 *(polite plural)* yŏrŏbundŭl 여러분들 ◊ *(omission): when do – come back?* ŏnje toraol kŏmnikka? 언제 돌아올 겁니까?

young chŏlmŭn 젊은
your nŏŭi 너의; *(polite)* tangshinŭi 당신의; *(plural)* nŏhŭidŭrŭi 너희들의; *(polite plural)* yŏrŏbundŭrŭi 여러분들의
yours nŏŭi kŏt 너의 것; *(polite)* tangshinŭi kŏt 당신의 것; *(plural)* nŏhŭidŭrŭi kŏt 너희들의 것; *(polite plural)* yŏrŏbundŭrŭi kŏt 여러분들의 것
yourself ne chashin 네 자신; *(polite)* tangshin chashin 당신 자신
yourselves nŏhŭidŭl chashin 너희들 자신; *(polite)* tangshindŭl chashin 당신들 자신
youth ch'ŏngch'un-gi 청춘기; *(young man)* chŏlmŭni 젊은이; *(young people)* chŏlmŭn saram 젊은 사람
youth hostel yusŭ hosŭt'el 유스 호스텔

Z

zap *v/t* COMPUT saktchehada 삭제하다
zebra ŏllungmal 얼룩말
Zen Buddhism sŏnbulgyo 선불교

zero kong 공
zip code up'yŏn pŏnho 우편 번호
zipper chip'ŏ 지퍼
zone chidae 지대
zoo tongmurwŏn 동물원

Numbers

Korean			Sino-Korean	
0	kong	공	yŏng	영
1	hana	하나	il	일
2	tul	둘	i	이
3	set	셋	sam	삼
4	net	넷	sa	사
5	tasŏt	다섯	o	오
6	yŏsŏt	여섯	yuk	육
7	ilgop	일곱	ch'il	칠
8	yŏdŏl	여덟	p'al	팔
9	ahop	아홉	ku	구
10	yŏl	열	ship	십
11	yŏrhana	열 하나	shibil	십일
12	yŏldul	열 둘	shibi	십이
13	yŏlsset	열 셋	shipssam	십삼
14	yŏllet	열 넷	shipssa	십사
15	yŏldasŏt	열 다섯	shibo	십오
16	yŏlyŏsŏt	열 여섯	shimyuk	십육
17	yŏrilgop	열 일곱	shipch'il	십칠
18	yŏlyŏdŏl	열 여덟	shipp'al	십팔
19	yŏrahop	열 아홉	shipkku	십구
20	sŭmul	스물	iship	이십
21	sŭmul hana	스물 하나	ishibil	이십일
30	sŏrŭn	서른	samship	삼십
35	sŏrŭn tasŏt	서른 다섯	samshibo	삼십오
40	mahŭn	마흔	saship	사십
50	shwin	쉰	oship	오십
60	yesun	예순	yukssip	육십
70	irhŭn	일흔	ch'ilssip	칠십
80	yŏdŭn	여든	p'alssip	팔십
90	ahŭn	아흔	kuship	구십

100	*no native Korean*	paek	백
101	*numbers above 99*	paegil	백일
200		ibaek	이백
1,000		ch'ŏn	천
2,000		ich'ŏn	이천
10,000		man	만
20,000		iman	이만
100,000		shimman	십만
1,000,000		paengman	백만
2,000,000		ibaengman	이백만
10,000,000		ch'ŏnman	천만
100,000,000		ŏk	억
1,000,000,000		ship ŏk	십억
8,655		p'alch'ŏnyuk-paegoshibo	팔천육백오십오

Korean numbers are usually used with countwords such as **chan** 잔 (cup), **myŏng** 명 (person), **k'yŏlle** 켤레 (pair), **pŏn** 번 (time). When used in this way **hana, tul, set**, and **net** contract to **han, tu, se, ne**:

k'ŏp'i han chan
커피 한 잔
a cup of coffee

kyosu se myŏng
교수 세 명
three professors

Sino-Korean numbers are used with (amongst other things) dates, money and foreign loanwords. To tell the time, Korean numbers are used for hours and Sino-Korean for minutes and seconds:

ich'ŏn-gu-nyŏn irwŏl iril
이천구년 일월 일일
1st January 2009

samship k'illomit'ŏ
삼십 킬로미터
30 kilometres

ohu seshi samship-ppun
오후 세시 삼십분
3.30pm

han shigan shippun och'o
한 시간 십분 오초
1 hour, 10 minutes and 5 seconds